ROUTLEDGE LIBRARY EDITIONS:
CINEMA

Volume 9

MOTION PICTURE SERIES AND SEQUELS

MOTION PICTURE SERIES AND SEQUELS
A Reference Guide

BERNARD A. DREW

LONDON AND NEW YORK

First published in 1990

This edition first published in 2014
by Routledge
2 Park Square, Milton Park, Abingdon, Oxfordshire OX14 4RN

Simultaneously published in the USA and Canada
by Routledge
711 Third Avenue, New York, NY 10017

Routledge is an imprint of the Taylor and Francis Group, an informa business

First issued in paperback 2015

© 1990 Bernard A. Drew

All rights reserved. No part of this book may be reprinted or reproduced or utilised in any form or by any electronic, mechanical, or other means, now known or hereafter invented, including photocopying and recording, or in any information storage or retrieval system, without permission in writing from the publishers.

Trademark notice: Product or corporate names may be trademarks or registered trademarks, and are used only for identification and explanation without intent to infringe.

British Library Cataloguing in Publication Data
A catalogue record for this book is available from the British Library

ISBN 978-0-415-83865-8 (Set)
eISBN 978-1-315-85201-0 (Set)
ISBN 978-0-415-72665-8 (hbk) (Volume 9)
ISBN 978-1-138-97650-4 (pbk) (Volume 9)
ISBN 978-1-315-85585-1 (ebk) (Volume 9)

Publisher's Note
The publisher has gone to great lengths to ensure the quality of this book but points out that some imperfections from the original may be apparent.

Disclaimer
The publisher has made every effort to trace copyright holders and would welcome correspondence from those they have been unable to trace.

MOTION PICTURE SERIES AND SEQUELS
A Reference Guide

Bernard A. Drew

GARLAND PUBLISHING, INC. • NEW YORK & LONDON
1990

© 1990 Bernard A. Drew
All rights reserved

Library of Congress Cataloging-in-Publication Data

Drew, Bernard A. (Bernard Alger), 1950–
  Motion picture series and sequels: a reference guide / Bernard A. Drew.
    p.   cm. — (Garland reference library of the humanities; vol. 1186) (Garland bibliographies on series and sequels)
  Includes bibliographical references.
  ISBN 0-8240-4248-4 (alk. paper)
  I. Title. II. Series. III. Series: Garland bibliographies on series and sequels.
PN1995.9.S29D66   1990
016.79143'75—dc20   90-3321
                                                                  CIP

Printed on acid-free, 250-year-life paper
Manufactured in the United States of America

Contents

Introduction by Bernard A. Drew......................7

Motion Picture Series & Sequels.....................13

References...366

Title Index..371

Addenda..407

Hopalong Cassidy (William Boyd) wears black and rides a white horse in some sixty-six oat-operas.

The New Return of Son of Sequel Rides Again IV: The Introduction

Film companies in the last decade have milked formulas for all they're worth. For 1989 alone, there were some forty-five major motion pictures which were sequels or part of a series, from *American Ninja 3: Blood Hunt* to *Zapped Again*, and including what have become near annual offerings of *Friday the 13th*, *Police Academy* and *Star Trek*. The $250 million box office success of *Batman* assures sequels for years to come.

Nineteen eighty-nine is not an isolated year; there were some forty sequel or series films distributed in 1988, twenty or more in each of the two years before that (including *Dirty Harry*, *Superman* and *Delta Force* entries). And at this writing nearly twenty-five are already in production for 1990, among them *Godfather III*, *Gremlins 2*, *48 HRS. II*, *Class of Nuke 'Em High II*, *Ernest Goes to Jail* and *Rocky V*.

It's gotten so blatant that in *Back to the Future 2*, a good chuckle is provided by a visual gag in which a movie marquee -- without great exaggeration -- advertises *Jaws 19*. (*Back to the Future 3*, by the way, is being released in 1990.)

8 MOTION PICTURE SERIES & SEQUELS

One might attribute this creative laziness to a generally moribund decade artistically; to a generation of viewers raised on television and accustomed to repeat, episodic entertainment (as Vincent Canby does in a recent essay in *The New York Times*); to the demise of the studio system and the assumption of power by accountants and deal makers; to a relatively thriving economy and conservative political era; or whatever.

Except that motion picture "sequel-itis" has been around as long as movies themselves.

The fact is, where there has been popular success -- whatever the medium -- there has been a sequel or a series. (The Bible's Old Testament, after all, was followed by a New Testament; after World War I there naturally came World War II.)

In the silent film era, slapstick *Mabel* comedies featuring nimble Mabel Normand, frequently teamed with chubby Roscoe "Fatty" Arbuckle, and *Ambrose* shorts starring walrus-mustached Mack Swain were hits of the day. They begat feuding *Cohens and Kellys* and raucous *Bowery Boys,* inquisitive *Torchy Blanes* and vine-swinging *Tarzans* mid-century, and sexy *Emmanuelles,* haunting *Halloweens* and thrilling *James Bonds* today.

Given this history of motion picture series, maybe what's most conspicuous today is that studios are numbering rather than re-titling films in sequence. Many who attended motion picture shows in the 1940s have fond memories of the movie series then popular: from *Roy Rogers and Gabby Hayes* oaters and *Frankenstein Monster* scarers to *Charlie Chan* puzzlers and *Andy Hardy* romancers. But then, at least, they had the decency to call their pictures *Son of (Kong)* or *Return of (The Whistler)* or *(The Lone Ranger) Rides Again.*

Motion picture series cross all genres: Westerns (*Red Ryder*), mystery and suspense (*Miss Marple*), fantasy (*Conan the Barbarian*) and horror (*Count Yorga*), adventure (*Romancing the Stone*), monsters (*King Kong*), martial arts (*Enter the Dragon*), juvenile (*Pippi Longstocking*), musical (*Kay Kyser*), comedy (*Laurel and

Hardy), science fiction (*Flash Gordon*), adult (*Candy*), romance (*Tammy*), family (*Blondie*) and animal (*The Black Stallion*).

Motion picture series know no geographic bounds. There have been British series (*Carry On...*); French series (Francois Truffaut's *Antoine Doinels*); Canadian series (*Meatballs*); and Australian series (*Mad Max*). *Tora-San Goes to Vienna* in 1989 became the first of forty-one Japanese titles to cross the ocean for general circulation here. As if we hadn't had enough with the dozens of *Godzilla* pictures from that country!

Movie series aren't to be laughed at monetarily. The *Abbott and Costello* comedies are credited with having kept Universal Studio's head above the water in particularly poor times. And many a schlock series keeps a dubious production company at work these days. Of 1989's top 14 films, as reported by *Variety*, four were big-budget sequels (*Indiana Jones and the Last Crusade, Lethal Weapon 2, Ghostbusters II* and *Back to the Future, Part II*) and two are already spawning sequels (*Batman* and *Honey, I Shrunk the Kids*); they jointly grossed $933 million.

Admittedly income figures for series pictures are slightly ballooned due to merchandising tie-ins. But as an aside, for those aghast at the proliferation of *Pee Wee, Freddy, Police Academy* and *Batman* souvenirs available these days, consider this: one of the earliest merchandising tie-ins with a film series was in 1913 with the marketing of *Alkali Ike* dolls in the image of comic actor Augustus Carney, astride a hobby horse. *Alkali Ike* pictures were set in the fictitious town of Snakeville and featured a motley crew of performers including Mustang Pete, Coyote Simpson and Sophia Clutts. Hot stuff for the time.

From the beginning, filmmakers have relied on print sources for stories and series characters. *Raffles,* the gentleman thief of E.W. Hornung's stories, typically, was first brought to the screen in 1905. *Happy Hooligan* and *Foxy Grandpa* (both filmed beginning in 1901-02) were swiped from the newspaper comic strips. The longest accumulations of films based on the same literary characters -- but without studio or performer continuity -- are Arthur Conan Doyle's *Sherlock Holmes* (which the *1990 Guinness Book of World Records* estimates has inspired some 150 pictures) and Bram Stoker's *Dracula* (with more than 100 entries).

What was the longest running film series <u>with one actor in the same character role?</u> Here's a hint: It was a Western. Buster Crabbe as *Billy the Kid?* No, only forty-two pictures. Charles Starrett as the *Durango Kid?* Nope, only sixty-five films. How about William Boyd as *Hopalong Cassidy?* Again no, only sixty-six entries.

The longest series is also one of the earliest series: *Bronco Billy*. Actor G.M. Anderson had a minor role in director Edwin S. Porter's *The Great Train Robbery* (1903), widely considered to be the first true narrative film. Anderson directed a few pictures on his own, then formed a production partnership with George K. Spoor, called Essanay (standing for S and A). He set up shop in Colorado in 1907 and played his *Bronco Billy* cowboy role (and a few others) in one-reelers, turning out one a week -- for 376 consecutive weeks.

That's a lot of popcorn and movie tickets!

* * *

This reference guide lists some 906 English-language (or sub-titled or dubbed) motion pictures beginning in the silent picture era which had one or more sequels. The earliest-filmed entry in the book is *Willie's First Smoke* (Edison, 1899); the latest are announced sequels to *Honey, I Shrunk the Kids* and *Major League* (likely to appear in 1990-91).

Given for each series is a brief plot description including book, play or other source; individual titles, studio distributor, year, director (d) and major performers (s). Alternate titles (aka) are given where known. Other works listed in the bibliography may be consulted for full casts or plot details and critical evaluations and historical perspectives.

Remakes are not included unless the original source also had filmed sequels. For example, several versions of the same *Sherlock Holmes* and *Dracula* tales are listed as there were also sequels. *Ruggles of Red Gap,* thrice filmed, is not listed as all were based on a single book and did not deviate appreciably from the plot. For information on remakes see particularly Nowlan and Nowlan.

Penny Singleton brought Chic Young's newspaper comic strip character BLONDIE to life on the silver screen. Her co-star was Arthur Lake as Dagwood.

Animated pictures (such as *Droopy* or *Peanuts*) are not included; see Lenberg among other sources for listings of cartoon series. Television mini-series (for example *Roots*) are not included, but tele-movies are (not many spawned sequels, though a number of theatrical films prompted tele-movie followups). Marrill is a good source of information on TV movies.

Documentaries (such as *Pumping Iron*) and concert films (*U2* or *Richard Pryor Live*, for example) are not included, nor are compilations of excerpts from earlier feature films (such as *That's Entertainment*) or short comedy or animated subjects (such as *Bugs Bunny* cartoons or *Laurel and Hardy* two-reelers) re-edited for feature release or television broadcast.

Film sequels which were released directly to the videocassette market (*CHUD II* or *The Chinese Connection II*, for example) are included. Short subjects are included. A large (but not exhaustive) listing of recent adult or X-rated films is included; the plots for obvious reasons are not given in any great detail, if at all. Their inclusion is to demonstrate the pervasion of sequel-itis in <u>all</u> genres.

Series which derived from continuing appearances by the same actor or combination of actors, such as Abbott and Costello, the Marx Brothers or Gene Autry and Smiley Burnette provided an interesting dilemma for the compiler. They are generally included here (with italicized headings) if there is any sense of continuity to the storylines or characterizations. *The Three Stooges* essentially played the same roles in each of their pictures, even if their character names or situations changed. Likewise *Whip Wilson and Fuzzy Knight* essayed virtually the same parts in each of their oat-operas.

Variant films based on the same historical incidents or characters -- such as Abraham Lincoln or Napoleon, the Civil War or baseball -- are included only if a studio did make an attempt at a series based on those particular historical characters or situations.

The text was prepared utilizing a Macintosh-based desktop publishing system. Because of timing requirements in order to facilitate compilation of the index, a number of entries (indicated by an A, B or C number suffix) were included (and indexed) at the last minute. These entries come at both ends of the spectrum: they are largely announcements of pending 1990 productions and listings of turn-of-the-century silent films. Their inclusion (plus another very-last-minute thirty in the Addenda) brings the total number of entries in the volume to 936 even though the proper numbering ends at 845.

-- Bernard A. Drew
Great Barrington, Massachusetts
1 February 1990

Taking command of the situation is THE SAINT, played in five films 1939-40 by George Sanders.

MOTION PICTURE SERIES & SEQUELS

1. *ABBOTT AND COSTELLO*
The vaudeville comedy team successfully made a transition to motion pictures. Bud Abbott is the pompous, domineering partner, Lou Costello the chubby, naive, easily intimidated mate. (Listed under BUCK PRIVATES are two other films.)
ONE NIGHT IN THE TROPICS (Universal, 1940) d A. Edward Sutherland, s Bud Abbott, Lou Costello, Allan Jones, Nancy Kelly.
IN THE NAVY (Universal, 1941) d Arthur Lubin, s Bud Abbott, Lou Costello, Dick Powell, Andrews Sisters.
HOLD THAT GHOST (Universal, 1941) d Arthur Lubin, s Bud Abbott, Lou Costello, Richard Carlson, Joan Davis.
KEEP 'EM FLYING (Universal, 1941) d Arthur Lubin, s Bud Abbott, Lou Costello, Martha Raye.
RIDE 'EM COWBOY (Universal, 1942) d Arthur Lubin, s Bud Abbott, Lou Costello, Dick Foran, Anne Gwynne.
RIO RITA (MGM, 1942) d S. Sylvan Simon, s Bud Abbott, Lou Costello, Kathryn Grayson.
PARDON MY SARONG (Universal, 1942) d Erle C. Kenton, s Bud Abbott, Lou Costello, Virginia Bruce.
WHO DONE IT? (Universal, 1942) d Erle C. Kenton, s Bud Abbott, Lou Costello, Patric Knowles.
IT AIN'T HAY (Univeral, 1943) d Erle C. Kenton, s Bud Abbott, Lou Costello, Patsy O'Connor.
HIT THE ICE (Universal, 1943) d Charles Lamont, s Bud Abbott, Lou Costello, Ginny Simms.
IN SOCIETY (Universal, 1944) d Jean Yarbrough, s Bud Abbott, Lou Costello, Marion Hutton, Kirby Grant.
LOST IN A HAREM (MGM, 1944) d Charles Riesner, s Bud Abbott, Lou Costello, Marilyn Maxwell.
THE NAUGHTY NINETIES (Universal, 1945) d Jean Yarbrough, s Bud Abbott, Lou Costello, Alan Curtis.
ABBOTT AND COSTELLO IN HOLLYWOOD (MGM, 1945) d S. Sylvan Simon, s Bud Abbott, Lou Costello.
HERE COME THE CO-EDS (Universal, 1945) d Jean Yarbrough, s Bud Abbott, Lou Costello, Peggy Ryan.

14 MOTION PICTURE SERIES & SEQUELS

LITTLE GIANT (Universal, 1946) d William A. Seiter, s Bud Abbott, Lou Costello, Brenda Joyce.
THE TIME OF THEIR LIVES (Universal, 1946) d Charles Barton, s Bud Abbott, Lou Costello, Marjorie Reynolds.
THE WISTFUL WIDOW OF WAGON GAP (Universal-International, 1947) d Charles T. Barton, s Bud Abbott, Lou Costello, Marjorie Main, George Cleveland.
THE NOOSE HANGS HIGH (Eagle-Lion, 1948) d Charles Barton, s Bud Abbott, Lou Costello.
ABBOTT AND COSTELLO MEET FRANKENSTEIN (Universal-International, 1948) d Charles T. Barton, s Bud Abbott, Lou Costello, Lon Chaney, Bela Lugosi.
MEXICAN HAYRIDE (Universal-International, 1948) d Charles T. Barton, s Bud Abbott, Lou Costello.
ABBOTT AND COSTELLO MEET THE KILLER, BORIS KARLOFF (Universal-International, 1949) d Charles T. Barton, s Bud Abbott, Lou Costello, Boris Karloff.
ABBOTT AND COSTELLO IN THE FOREIGN LEGION (Universal-International, 1950) d Charles Lamont, s Bud Abbott, Lou Costello.
ABBOTT AND COSTELLO MEET THE INVISIBLE MAN (Universal-International, 1951) d Charles Lamont, s Bud Abbott, Lou Costello, Nancy Guild.
COMIN' ROUND THE MOUNTAIN (Universal-International, 1951) d Charles Lamont, s Bud Abbott, Lou Costello, Dorothy Shay.
JACK AND THE BEANSTALK (Warner Brothers, 1952) d Jean Yarbrough, s Bud Abbott, Lou Costello.
LOST IN ALASKA (Universal-International, 1952) d Jean Yarbrough, s Bud Abbott, Lou Costello.
ABBOTT AND COSTELLO MEET CAPTAIN KIDD (Warner Brothers, 1952) d Charles Lamont, s Bud Abbott, Lou Costello, Charles Laughton, Hilary Brooke.
ABBOTT AND COSTELLO GO TO MARS (Universal, 1953) d Charles Lamont, s Bud Abbott, Lou Costello.
ABBOTT AND COSTELLO MEET DR. JEKYLL AND MR. HYDE (Universal, 1953) d Charles Lamont, s Bud Abbott, Lou Costello.
ABBOTT AND COSTELLO MEET THE KEYSTONE KOPS (Universal, 1955) d Charles Lamont, s Bud Abbott, Lou Costello, Fred Clark, Lynn Bari.
ABBOTT AND COSTELLO MEET THE MUMMY (Universal, 1955) d Charles Lamont, s Bud Abbott, Lou Costello, Marie Windsor.
DANCE WITH ME, HENRY (United Artists, 1956) d Charles Barton, s Bud Abbott, Lou Costello.
THE WORLD OF ABBOTT AND COSTELLO (Universal, 1956) s Bud Abbott, Lou Costello.

2. ABSENT-MINDED PROFESSOR, THE

Professor Ned Brainard invents a remarkable bouncy substance, Flubber, and a series of misadventures follow. The character was revived in 1989 on the Walt Disney television program.
THE ABSENT-MINDED PROFESSOR (Disney, 1961) d Robert Stevenson, s
 Fred MacMurray, Nancy Olson.
SON OF FLUBBER (Disney, 1963) d Robert Stevenson, s Fred MacMurray,
 Nancy Olson, Keenan Wynn.

3. AFTER THIRTY
Mr. and Mrs. Sidney Drew appeared together in a series of silent comedies. After his death in 1919, she (Lucille McVey Drew) teamed with John Cumberland for AFTER THIRTY stories for Pathe.

4. AIRPLANE
The pictures are spoofs of extravagant aviation films such as AIRPORT.
AIRPLANE (Paramount, 1980) d Jim Abrahams, David Zucker, Jerry Zucker, s
 Robert Hays, Julie Hagerty, Lloyd Bridges.
AIRPLANE II: THE SEQUEL (Paramount, 1982) d Ken Finkelman, s Robert
 Hays, Julie Hagerty, Lloyd Bridges.

5. AIRPORT
The dramatic pictures are based on the Arthur Hailey bestselling novel and take place at a major metropolitan airport.
AIRPORT (Universal, 1970) d George Seaton, s Burt Lancaster, Dean Martin,
 George Kennedy, Helen Hayes, Jean Seberg, Jacqueline Bisset.
AIRPORT 1975 (Universal, 1974) d Jack Smight, s Charlton Heston, Karen
 Black, George Kennedy, Efrem Zimbalist Jr.
AIRPORT '77 (Universal, 1977) d Jerry Jameson, s Jack Lemmon, Lee Grant,
 Brenda Vaccaro, George Kennedy, James Stewart.
THE CONCORDE-AIRPORT '79 (Universal, 1979) d David Lowell Rich, s
 Alain Delon, Susan Blakely, Robert Wagner.

6. ALFIE
The rather amoral leading character can't settle into a permanent relationship with any of his various women friends.
ALFIE (EMI/Signal, 1966) d Lewis Gilbert, s Michael Caine, Vivien Merchant,
 Shirley Ann Field.
ALFIE DARLING (EMI/Signal, 1975) d Ken Hughes, s Alan Price, Jill
 Townsend.

7. ALIAS JIMMY VALENTINE
The master safecracker is featured in tales based on a story by O. Henry and a derivative play by Paul Armstrong. The leading character also appeared in television and radio series.
ALIAS JIMMY VALENTINE (World Pictures, 1915) s Robert Warwick.
ALIAS JIMMY VALENTINE (Metro, 1920) d Edmund Mortimer, s Bert
 Lytell, Vola Vale.

ALIAS JIMMY VALENTINE (MGM, 1929) d Jack Conway, s William
    Haines, Lelia Hyams.
THE RETURN OF JIMMY VALENTINE (Republic, 1936) d Lewis D. Collins,
    s Roger Pryor, Charlotte Henry.
THE AFFAIRS OF JIMMY VALENTINE (Republic, 1942) d Bernard
    Vorhaus, s Dennis O'Keefe, Ruth Terry.

8. ALIAS SMITH & JONES
Cowboys on the run from the law, Hannibal Heyes (Peter Deuel and, later, Roger Davis), alias Joshua Smith, and Kid Curry (Ben Murphy), alias Thaddeus Jones, are promised clemency if they go straight. The first entry below is a two-hour television pilot, the second is a pasted together pair of television (CBS 1971-73) episodes.
ALIAS SMITH AND JONES (Universal, 1971) d William A. Seiter, s Peter
    Deuel, Ben Murphy, Forrest Tucker, Susan Saint James.
THE LONG CHASE (Universal, 1972) d Alexander Singer, s Roger Davis,
    Ben Murphy, Rod Cameron, Sally Field.

9. ALIEN
A merciless being penetrates the bodies of crew members on a spacecraft. Actress Sigourney Weaver, the only survivor of the first picture, in the second returns to the slimy leech monster's planet-of-origin.
ALIEN (20th Century-Fox, 1979) d Ridley Scott, s Tom Skeritt, Sigourney
    Weaver, John Hurt.
ALIENS (20th Century-Fox, 1986) d James Cameron, s Sigourney Weaver,
    Carrie Henn, Michael Biehn.

10. ALKALI IKE
This is a silent comedy series set in the made-up town of Snakeville and featuring Augustus Carney as the title character with William Todd as Mustang Pete. Many entries were directed by E. Mason Hopper. The list is incomplete.
ALKALI IKE'S AUTOMOBILE (Essanay, 1911) s Augustus Carney, William
    Todd, Betty Brown.
MUSTANG PETE'S LOVE AFFAIR (Essanay, 1911) s Augustus Carney,
    William Todd.
ALKALI IKE'S LOVE AFFAIR (Essanay, 1912) s Augustus Carney.
ALKALI IKE'S BOARDING HOUSE (Essanay, 1912) s Augustus Carney,
    G.M. Anderson.
ALKALI IKE'S CLOSE SHAVE (Essanay, 1912) s Augustus Carney, G.M.
    Anderson.
ALKALI IKE'S MOTORCYCLE (Essanay, 1912) s Augustus Carney, G.M.
    Anderson.
ALKALI IKE'S PANTS (Essanay, 1912) s Augustus Carney, G.M. Anderson.
A WESTERN KIMONO (Essanay, 1912) s Augustus Carney.
ALKALI BEATS BRONCO BILLY (Essanay, 1912) s Augustus Carney,
    G.M. Anderson.

ALKALI IKE PLAYS THE DEVIL (Essanay, 1912) s Augustus Carney, G.M. Anderson.
ALKALI IKE STUNG! (Essanay, 1912) s Augustus Carney, G.M. Anderson.
ALKALI IKE'S MOTHER-IN-LAW (Essanay, 1913) s Augustus Carney.
ALKALI IKE IN JOYVILLE (Essanay, 1913) s Augustus Carney.
ALKALI IKE'S GAL (Essanay, 1913) s Augustus Carney.
ALKALI IKE'S HOMECOMING (Essanay, 1913) s Augustus Carney.
ALKALI IKE'S MISFORTUNES (Essanay, 1913) s Augustus Carney.
ALKALI IKE AND THE HYPNOTIST (Essanay, 1913) s Augustus Carney.

11. ALLAN QUATERMAIN
The hero of a series of adventure novels by Henry Rider Haggard, Quatermain and guide Umbopa and other companions explore Africa and other exotic worlds.
KING SOLOMON'S MINES (Gaumont, 1937) d Robert Stevenson, s Cedric Hardwicke, Paul Robeson.
KING SOLOMON'S MINES (MGM, 1950) d Compton Bennett and Andrew Morton, s Stewart Granger, Richard Carlson.
WATUSI (MGM, 1959) d Kurt Neumann, s George Montgomery, Taina Elg, Rex Ingram.
KING SOLOMON'S MINES (Cannon, 1985) d J. Lee Thompson, s Richard Chamberlain, Sharon Stone..
ALLAN QUATERMAIN AND THE LOST CITY OF GOLD (Cannon, 1986) d Gary Nelson, s Richard Chamberlain, Sharon Stone.

12. *ALLAN "ROCKY" LANE AND EDDY WALLER*
The B Westerns feature staunch gunslinger Lane with Waller playing pard Nugget Clark.
THE WILD FRONTIER (Republic, 1947) d Phillip Ford, s Allan "Rocky" Lane, Eddy Waller.
BANDITS OF DARK CANYON (Republic, 1947) d Phillip Ford, s Allan "Rocky" Lane, Eddy Waller, Linda Johnson.
OKLAHOMA BADLANDS (Republic, 1948) d Yakima Canutt, s Allan "Rocky" Lane, Eddy Waller, Mildred Coles.
THE BOLD FRONTIERSMAN (Republic, 1948) d Phillip Ford, s Allan "Rocky" Lane, Eddy Waller.
CARSON CITY RAIDERS (Republic, 1948) d Yakima Canutt, s Allan "Rocky" Lane, Eddy Waller.
MARSHAL OF AMARILLO (Republic, 1948) d Phillip Ford, s Allan "Rocky" Lane, Eddy Waller.
DESPERADOES OF DODGE CITY (Republic, 1948) d Phillip Ford, s Allan "Rocky" Lane, Eddy Waller.
THE DENVER KID (Republic, 1948) d Phillip Ford, s Allan "Rocky" Lane, Eddy Waller.
SUNDOWN IN SANTA FE (Republic, 1948) d R.G. Springsteen, s Allan "Rocky" Lane, Eddy Waller.

18 MOTION PICTURE SERIES & SEQUELS

RENEGADES OF SONORA (Republic, 1948) d R.G. Springsteen, s Allan "Rocky" Lane, Eddy Waller.
SHERIFF OF WICHITA (Republic, 1949) d R.G. Springsteen, s Allan "Rocky" Lane, Eddy Waller.
DEATH VALLEY GUNFIGHTER (Republic, 1949) d R.G. Springsteen, s Allan "Rocky" Lane, Eddy Waller, Gail Davis.
FRONTIER MARSHAL (Republic, 1949) d Fred C. Brannon, s Allan "Rocky" Lane, Eddy Waller, Gail Davis.
WYOMING BANDIT (Republic, 1949) d Philip Ford, s Allan "Rocky" Lane, Eddy Waller.
BANDIT KING OF TEXAS (Republic, 1949) d Fred C. Brannon, s Allan "Rocky" Lane, Eddy Waller, Helen Stanley.
NAVAJO TRAIL RAIDERS (Republic, 1949) d R.G. Springsteen, s Allan "Rocky" Lane, Eddy Waller, Barbara Bestar.
POWDER RIVER RUSTLERS (Republic, 1949) d Philp Ford, s Allan "Rocky" Lane, Eddy Waller, Gerry Ganzer.
GUNMEN OF ABILENE (Republic, 1950) d Fred C. Brannon, s Allan "Rocky" Lane, Eddy Waller.
CODE OF THE SILVER SAGE (Republic, 1950) d Fred C. Brannon, s Allan "Rocky" Lane, Eddy Waller, Kay Christopher.
SALT LAKE RAIDERS (Republic, 1950) d Fred C. Brannon, s Allan "Rocky" Lane, Eddy Waller, Martha Hyer.
COVERED WAGON RAID (Republic, 1950) d R.G. Springsteen, s Allan "Rocky" Lane, Eddy Waller, Lyn Thomas.
VIGILANTE HIDEOUT (Republic, 1950) d Fred C. Brannon, s Allan "Rocky" Lane, Eddy Waller, Virginia Herrick.
FRISCO TORNADO (Republic, 1950) d R.G. Springsteen, s Allan "Rocky" Lane, Eddy Waller, Martha Hyer.
RUSTLERS ON HORSEBACK (Republic, 1950) d Fred C. Brannon, s Allan "Rocky" Lane, Eddy Waller, Claudia Barrett.
LEADVILLE GUNSLINGER (Republic, 1952) d Harry Kellar, s Allan "Rocky" Lane, Eddy Waller, Elaine Riley.
BLACK HILLS AMBUSH (Republic, 1952) d Harry Kellar, s Allan "Rocky" Lane, Eddy Waller, Lesley Banning.
THUNDERING CARAVANS (Republic, 1952) d Harry Kellar, s Allan "Rocky" Lane, Eddy Waller, Mona Knox.
DESPERADOES OUTPOST (Republic, 1952) d Philip Ford, s Allan "Rocky" Lane, Eddy Waller.
MARSHAL OF CEDAR ROCK (Republic, 1953) d Harry Kellar, s Allan "Rocky" Lane, Eddy Waller, Phyllis Coates.
SAVAGE FRONTIER (Republic, 1953) d Harry Kellar, s Allan "Rocky" Lane, Eddy Waller, Dorothy Patrick.
BANDITS OF THE WEST (Republic, 1953) d Harry Kellar, s Allan "Rocky" Lane, Eddy Waller, Cathy Downs.
EL PASO STAMPEDE (Republic, 1953) d Harry Kellar, s Allan "Rocky" Lane, Eddy Waller, Phyllis Coates.

13. ALL CREATURES GREAT AND SMALL
James Herriot's Yorkshire veterinary reminiscences are the basis for these films. There was also a British TV series, aired in the United States over public television, featuring the cast of the third feature listed.
ALL CREATURES GREAT AND SMALL (Talent Associates/EMI, 1974) d Claude Whatham, s Simon Ward, Anthony Hopkins.
ALL THINGS BRIGHT AND BEAUTIFUL (1979) [aka IT SHOULDN'T HAPPEN TO A VET] d Eric Till, s John Alderton, Lisa Harrow.
ALL CREATURES GREAT AND SMALL (1986 TV movie) d Terence Dudley, s Christopher Timothy, Robert Hardy, Peter Davison, Carol Drinkwater.

14. ALLIGATOR
The not-to-be-taken-seriously pictures are about a reptile terrorizing America.
ALLIGATOR (Group I Films, 1980) d Lewis Teague, s Robert Forster, Robin Riker.
ALLIGATOR II (Group I Films, 1988)

15. ALL QUIET ON THE WESTERN FRONT
Erich Maria Remarque's World War I novel of the same title provides the plot for these films.
ALL QUIET ON THE WESTERN FRONT (Universal, 1930) d Lewis Milestone, s Lew Ayres, Louis Wolheim.
THE ROAD BACK (Universal, 1937) d James Whale, s John King, Richard Cromwell.

15A. ALPHONSE AND GASTON
These are silent comedies greatly resembling vaudeville routines. The characters -- ever so polite -- were created in 1902 by newspaper cartoonist Fred Opper.
ALPHONSE AND GASTON HELPING IRISHMEN (American Mutoscope & Biograph, 1902)
ALPHONSE AND GASTON NO. 1 (American Mutoscope & Biograph, 1902)
ALPHONSE AND GASTON NO. 2 (American Mutoscope & Biograph, 1902)
ALPHONSE AND GASTON NO. 3 (American Mutoscope & Biograph, 1902)

16. ALVIN PURPLE
The Australian sex films sport a hero who has women falling all over him.
ALVIN PURPLE (New World Video, 1973/1985) d Tom Burstall, s Graeme Blundell, Christine Amor, Valerie Blake.
ALVIN PURPLE RIDES AGAIN (New World Video, 1985) d Tom Burstall, s Graeme Blundell, Jacki Weaver, Penny Hackforth.

17. AMAZING TAILS
These are X-rated pictures.
AMAZING TAILS I (Caballero, 1985) s Buffy Davis, Marc Wallice.
AMAZING TAILS II (Caballero, 1987) s Buffy Davis, Tom Byron.

AMAZING TAILS III (Caballero, 1987) s Trinity Loren, Buffy Davis.

18. AMBROSE AND WALRUS
Silent slapstick characters played by Mack Swain (Ambrose) and Chester Conklin (Walrus) for Mack Sennett's Keystone Studio are featured in these pictures. Ambrose is a hulking lecher, Walrus a comic villain. The list is likely incomplete.
AMBROSE'S FIRST FALSEHOOD (Keystone, 1914) d Mack Sennett, s
    Mack Swain, Minta Durfee, Slim Summerville.
LEADING LIZZIE ASTRAY (Keystone, 1914)
A BUSY DAY (Keystone, 1914) d Charles Chaplin, s Mack Swain, Charles
    Chaplin.
AMBROSE'S SOUR GRAPES (Keystone, 1915) s Mack Swain, Chester
    Conklin
WILFUL AMBROSE (Keystone, 1915) s Mack Swain.
AMBROSE'S FURY (1915) s Mack Swain, Minta Durfee, Louise Fazenda.
AMBROSE'S LOFTY PERCH (Keystone, 1915) d Dell Henderson, s Mack
    Swain, Louise Fazenda.
AMBROSE'S NASTY TEMPER (Keystone, 1915) s Mack Swain.
AMBROSE'S LITTLE HATCHET (Keystone, 1915) s Mack Swain, Minta
    Durfee, Louise Fazenda.
THE BATTLE OF AMBROSE AND WALRUS (Keystone, 1915) s Mack
    Swain, Chester Conklin, Dora Rodgers.
WHEN AMBROSE DARED WALRUS (Keystone, 1915) s Mack Swain,
    Chester Conklin.
AMBROSE'S CUP OF WOE (Keystone-Triangle, 1916) d Fred Fishback and
    Herman Raymaker, s Mack Swain, May Emory.
VAMPIRE AMBROSE (Keystone-Triangle, 1916) d Fred Fishback, s Mack
    Swain, Polly Moran.
AMBROSE'S RAPID RISE (Keystone-Triangle, 1916) d Fred Fishback, s
    Mack Swain, Louella Maxam.
SAFETY FIRST AMBROSE (Keystone-Triangle, 1916) d Fred Fishback, s
    Mack Swain, Polly Moran.

19. AMERICAN GRAFFITI
The first picture is about three young men on the eve of going off to college. The second revisits them a few years later.
AMERICAN GRAFFITI (Univeral/Lucasfilm, Coppola, 1973) d George Lucas,
    s Richard Dreyfuss, Ronny Howard, Paul Le Mat.
MORE AMERICAN GRAFFITI (Universal/Lucasfilm, 1979) d B.W.L. Norton,
    s Ron Howard, Paul Le Mat, Candy Clark.

20. AMERICAN NINJA
Martial arts is the theme of these films, set in the Caribbean. The hero is Joe Armstrong, his partner is Curtis Jackson. The production of a fourth entry was announced in late 1989.

AMERICAN NINJA (Cannon, 1986) d Sam Firstenberg, s Michael Dudikoff, Steve James, Judie Aronson.
AMERICAN NINJA 2: THE CONFRONTATION (Cannon, 1987) d Sam Firstenberg, s Michael Dudikoff, Steve James.
AMERICAN NINJA 3: BLOOD HUNT (Cannon, 1989) d Cedric Sundstrom, s David Bradley, Steve James.

20A. AMERICAN SOLDIER IN LOVE AND WAR, THE
These are early silent film dramas.
THE AMERICAN SOLDIER IN LOVE AND WAR NO. 1 (American Mutoscope & Biograph, 1903)
THE AMERICAN SOLDIER IN LOVE AND WAR NO. 2 (American Mutoscope & Biograph, 1903)
THE AMERICAN SOLDIER IN LOVE AND WAR NO. 3 (American Mutoscope & Biograph, 1903)

21. AMITYVILLE HORROR, THE
Jay Anson's purported non-fiction bestseller about a surburban house inhabited by a terrifying entity is the basis for the first of these pictures. The second was developed from Hans Holzer's *Murder in Amityville*.
THE AMITYVILLE HORROR (American-International, 1979) d Stuart Rosenberg, s James Brolin, Margot Kidder, Rod Steiger.
AMITYVILLE II: THE POSSESSION (Orion, 1982) d Damiano Damiani, s Burt Young, Rutanya Alda.
AMITYVILLE 3-D (Orion, 1983) [aka AMITYVILLE III: THE DEMON] d Richard Fleischer, s Tony Roberts, Tess Harper.

21A. ANDY
Andy Clark and William Wadsworth are among the players in this Edison silent film series issued circa 1914.

22. *ANDY CLYDE*
These talkie comedy shorts frequently have Clyde playing the role of Ed "Pop" Martin.
THE BRIDE's RELATIONS (Mack Sennett/Educational, 1929) d Mack Sennett, s Andy Clude, Johnny Burke, Harry Gribbon.
THE OLD BARN (Mack Sennett/Educational, 1929) d Mack Sennett, s Andy Clyde, Johnny Burke.
WHIRLS AND GIRLS (Mack Sennett/Educational, 1929) d Mack Sennett, s Andy Clude, Harry Gribbon.
THE BEE'S BUZZ (Mack Sennett/Educational, 1929) d Mack Sennett, s Andy Clyde, Thelma Hill.
THE BIG PALOOKA (Mack Sennett/Educational, 1929) d Mack Sennett, s Andy Clyde, Harry Gribbon.
GIRL CRAZY (Mack Sennett/Educational, 1929) d Mack Sennett, s Andy Clyde, Vernon Dent.

THE BARBER'S DAUGHTER (Mack Sennett/Educational, 1929) d Mack Sennett, Thelma Hill.
THE CONSTABLE (Mack Sennett/Educational, 1929) d Mack Sennett, s Andy Clyde, Thelma Hill.
THE LUNKHEAD (Mack Sennett/Educational, 1929) d Mack Sennett, s Andy Clyde, Harry Gribbon.
THE GOLFERS (Mack Sennett/Educational, 1929) d Mack Sennett, s Andy Clyde, Harry Gribbon.
A HOLLYWOOD STAR (Mack Sennett/Educational, 1929) d Mack Sennett, s Andy Clude, Harry Gribbon, Marjorie Beebe.
CLANCY AT THE BAT (Mack Sennett/Educational, 1929) d Earle Rodney, s Andy Clyde, Harry Gribbon.
THE NEW HALFBACK (Mack Sennett/Educational, 1929) d Mack Sennett, s Andy Clyde.
UPPERCUT O'BRIEN (Mack Sennett/Educational, 1929) d Earle Rodney, s Andy Clyde, Harry Gribbon.
SCOTCH (Mack Sennett/Educational, 1930) d Mack Sennett, s Andy Clyde, Billy Bevan.
SUGAR PLUM PAPA (Mack Sennett/Educational, 1930) d Mack Sennett, s Andy Clyde, Harry Gribbon.
BULLS AND BEARS (Mack Sennett/Educational, 1930) d Mack Sennett, s Andy Clyde, Marjorie Beebe.
MATCH PLAY (Mack Sennett/Educational, 1930) d Mack Sennett, s Andy Clyde.
RADIO KISSES (Mack Sennett/Educational, 1930) d Leslie Pearce, s Andy Clyde, Marjorie Beebe.
FAT WIVES FOR THIN (Mack Sennett/Educational, 1930) d Mack Sennett, s Andy Clyde, Marjorie Beebe.
CAMPUS CRUSHES (Mack Sennett/Educational, 1930) d Mack Sennett, s Andy Clyde, Marjorie Beebe.
THE CHUMPS (Mack Sennett/Educational, 1930) d Mack Sennett, Andy Clyde.
GOODBYE LEGS (Mack Sennett/Educational, 1930) d Mack Sennett, s Andy Clyde, Marjorie Beebe.
HELLO, TELEVISION (Mack Sennett/Educational, 1930) d Leslie Pearce, s Andy Clyde, Ann Christy.
AVERAGE HUSBAND (Mack Sennett/Educational, 1930) d Mack Sennett, s Andy Clyde, Natalie Moorehead.
VACATION LOVES (Mack Sennett/Educational, 1930) d Mack Sennett, s Andy Clyde, Betty Boyd.
THE BLUFFER (Mack Sennett/Educational, 1930) s Andy Clyde, Patsy O'Leary.
GRANDMA'S GIRL (Mack Sennett/Educational, 1930) d Mack Sennett, s Andy Clyde.
TAKE YOUR MEDICINE (Mack Sennett/Educational, 1930) d Edward Cline, s Andy Clyde, Patsy O'Leary.

DON'T BITE YOUR DENTIST (Mack Sennett/Educational, 1930) d Edward Cline, s Andy Clyde, Daphne Pollard.
RACKET CHEERS (Mack Sennett/Educational, 1930) d Mack Sennett, s Andy Clyde, Daphne Pollard.
NO, NO, LADY (Mack Sennett/Educational, 1931) d Edward Cline, s Andy Clyde, Dorothy Christy.
THE COLLEGE VAMP (Mack Sennett/Educational, 1931) d William Beaudine, s Andy Clyde, Yola D'Arvil.
THE DOG DOCTOR (Mack Sennett/Educational, 1931) d Phil Whitman, s Andy Clyde, Patsy O'Leary.
JUST A BEAR (Mack Sennett/Educational, 1931) d Babe Stafford, s Andy Clyde, Harry Gribbon.
IN CONFERENCE (Mack Sennett/Educational, 1931) d Edward Cline, s Andy Clyde, Harry Gribbon.
THE COW-CATCHER'S DAUGHTER (Mack Sennett/Educational, 1931) d Babe Stafford, s Andy Clyde, Harry Gribbon.
GHOST PARADE (Mack Sennett/Educational, 1931) d Mack Sennett, s Andy Clyde.
MONKEY BUSINESS IN AFRICA (Mack Sennett/Educational, 1931) d Mack Sennett, s Andy Clyde, Marjorie Beebe.
FAINTING LOVER (Mack Sennett/Educational, 1931) d Mack Sennett, s Andy Clyde, Vernon Dent.
TOO MANY HUSBANDS (Mack Sennett/Educational, 1931) d Leslie Pearce, s Andy Clyde, Irene Thompson.
THE CANNONBALL (Mack Sennett/Educational, 1931) d Del Lord, s Andy Clyde, Ann Hernandez.
SPEED (Mack Sennett/Educational, 1931) d Mack Sennett, s Andy Clyde, Marjorie Beebe.
TAXI TROUBLES (Mack Sennett/Educational, 1931) d Del Lord, s Andy Clyde.
ALL-AMERICAN KICKBACK (Mack Sennett/Educational, 1931) d Del Lord, s Andy Clyde, Harry Gribbon.
HALF HOLIDAY (Mack Sennett/Educational, 1931) d Babe Stafford, s Andy Clyde, Alice Ward.
SHOPPING WITH WIFIE (Mack Sennett/Educational, 1932) d Babe Stafford, s Andy Clyde, Dorothy Granger.
HEAVENS! MY HUSBAND (Mack Sennett/Educational, 1932) d Babe Stafford, s Andy Clyde, Dorothy Granger.
SPEED IN THE GAY '90s (Mack Sennett/Educational, 1932) d Del Lord, s Andy Clyde, Barney Oldfield.
THE BOUDOIR BUTLER (Mack Sennett/Educational, 1932) d Leslie Pearce, s Andy Clyde, Irene Thompson.
ALASKA LOVE (Mack Sennett/Educational, 1932) d Babe Stafford, s Andy Clyde, Matt McHugh.
FOR THE LOVE OF LUDWIG (Mack Sennett/Educational, 1932) d Emil Harberger, s Andy Clyde.

24 MOTION PICTURE SERIES & SEQUELS

HIS ROYAL SHYNESS (Mack Sennett/Educational, 1932) d Leslie Pearce, s Andy Clyde, Dorothy Granger.
THE GIDDY AGE (Mack Sennett/Educational, 1932) d Babe Stafford, s Andy Clyde, Dorothy Granger.
SUNKISSED SWEETIES (Educational, 1932) d Harry Edwards, s Andy Clyde, Vernon Dent.
A FOOL ABOUT WOMEN (Educational, 1932) d Harry Edwards, s Andy Clyde, Faye Pierre.
BOY, OH, BOY (Educational, 1932) d Harry Edwards, s Andy Clyde, Gwen Lee.
ARTISTS MUDDLES (Educational, 1933) d Harry Edwards, s Andy Clyde, Vernon Dent.
FEELING ROSY (Educational, 1933) d Harry Edwards, s Andy Clyde, Lita Chevret.
LOOSE RELATIONS (Educational, 1933) d Harry Edwards, s Andy Clyde, Lita Chevret.
BIG SQUEAL (Educational, 1933) d Charles Lamont, s Andy Clyde, Billy Bevan.
DORA'S DUNKIN' DONUTS (Educational, 1933) d Harry Edwards, s Andy Clyde, Shirley Temple.
HIS WEAK MOMENT (Educational, 1933) d Harry Edwards, s Andy Clyde, Cecilia Parker.
FROZEN ASSETS (Educational, 1933) d Harry Edwards, s Andy Clyde, Eddie Phillips.
AN OLD GYPSY CUSTOM (Educational, 1934) d Harry Edwards, s Andy Clyde.
SUPER SNOOPER (Educational, 1934) d Harry Edwards, s Andy Clyde, Jason Robards.
HELLO, PROSPERITY (Educational, 1934) d Charles Lamont, s Andy Clyde, Ethel Sykes.
HALF-BAKED RELATIONS (Educational, 1934) d Charles Lamont, s Andy Clyde, Jack Shutta.
IT'S THE CAT'S (Columbia, 1934) d Al Ray, s Andy Clyde, Dorothy Granger.
IN THE DOG HOUSE (Columbia, 1934) d Arthur Ripley, s Andy Clyde, Vivian Oakland.
I'M A FATHER (Columbia, 1935) d James Horne, s Andy Clyde, Lillian Elliott.
OLD SAWBONES (Columbia, 1935) d Del Lord, s Andy Clyde, Lucille Ward.
TRAMP TRAMP TRAMP (Columbia, 1935) d Charles Lamont, s Andy Clyde, Dot Farley.
ALIMONY ACHES (Columbia, 1935) d Charles Lamont, s Andy Clyde, Jan Duggan.
IT ALWAYS HAPPENS (Columbia, 1935) d Del Lord, s Andy Clyde, Geneva Mitchell.
HOT PATRIKA (Columbia, 1935) d Preston Black, s Andy Clyde.
CAUGHT IN THE ACT (Columbia, 1935) d Del Lord, s Andy Clyde, Anne O'Neal.

MOTION PICTURE SERIES & SEQUELS 25

SHARE THE WEALTH (Columbia, 1936) d Del Lord, s Andy Clyde, Mary Gordon.
PEPPERY SALT (Columbia, 1936) d Del Lord, s Andy Clyde, Mary Lou Dix.
MISTER SMARTY (Columbia, 1936) d Preston Black, s Andy Clyde.
AM I HAVING FUN (Columbia, 1936) d Preston Black, Andy Clyde, Arthur Housman.
LOVE COMES TO NOONEYVILLE (Columbia, 1936) d Preston Black, s Andy Clyde, Esther Howard.
KNEE ACTION (Columbia, 1937) d Charles Lamont, s Andy Clyde, Vivien Oakland.
STUCK IN THE STICKS (Columbia, 1937) d Preston Black, s Andy Clyde, Esther Howard.
MY LITTLE FELLER (Columbia, 1937) d Charles Lamont, s Andy Clyde.
LODGE NIGHT (Columbia, 1937) d Preston Black, s Andy Clyde.
GRACIE AT THE BAT (Columbia, 1937) d Del Lord, s Andy Clyde, Louise Stanley.
HE DONE HIS DUTY (Columbia, 1937) d Charles Lamont, s Andy Clyde, Bob McKenzie.
THE OLD RAID MULE (Columbia, 1937) d Charley Chase, s Andy Clyde, Olin Howland.
JUMP, CHUMP, JUMP (Columbia, 1938) d Del Lord, s Andy Clyde.
ANKLES AWAY (Columbia, 1938) d Charley Chase, s Andy Clyde, Ann Doran.
SOUL OF A HEEL (Columbia, 1938) d Del Lord, s Andy Clyde, Gertrude Sutton.
NOT GUILTY ENOUGH (Columbia, 1938) d Del Lord, s Andy Clyde.
HOME ON THE RAGE (Columbia, 1938) d Del Lord, s Andy Clyde, Shemp Howard.
SWING, YOU SWINGERS (Columbia, 1939) d Jules White, s Andy Clyde.
BOOM GOES THE GROOM (Columbia, 1939) d Charley Chase, s Andy Clyde, Vivien Oakland.
NOW IT CAN BE SOLD (Columbia, 1939) d Del Lord, s Andy Clyde, Anita Garvin.
TROUBLE FINDS ANDY CLYDE (Columbia, 1939) d Jules White, s Andy Clyde, Dick Curtis.
ALL-AMERICAN BLONDES (Columbia, 1939) d Del Lord, s Andy Clyde, Dick Curtis.
ANDY CLYDE GETS SPRING CHICKEN (Columbia, 1939) d Jules White, s Andy Clyde, Richard Fiske.
MR. CLYDE GOES TO BROADWAY (Columbia, 1940) d Del Lord, s Andy Clyde, Vivien Oakland.
MONEY SQUAWKS (Columbia, 1940) d Jules White, s Andy Clyde, Shemp Howard.
BOOBS IN THE WOODS (Columbia, 1940) d Del Lord, s Andy Clyde, Esther Howard.
FIREMAN, SAVE MY CHOO CHOO (Columbia, 1940) d Del Lord, s Andy Clyde.

A BUNDLE OF BLISS (Columbia, 1940) d Jules White, s Andy Clyde, Esther Howard.
THE WATCHMAN TAKES A WIFE (Columbia, 1941) d Del Lord, s Andy Clyde.
RING AND THE BELLE (Columbia, 1941) d Del Lord, s Andy Clyde.
YANKEE DOODLE ANDY (Columbia, 1941) d Jules White, s Andy CLyde, Dorothy Appleby.
HOST TO A GHOST (Columbia, 1941) d Del Lord, s Andy Clyde.
LOVABLE TROUBLE (Columbia, 1941) d Del Lord, s Andy Clyde, Esther Howard.
SAPPY BIRTHDAY (Columbia, 1942) d Harry Edwards, s Andy Clyde.
HOW SPRY I AM (Columbia, 1942) d Jules White, s Andy Clyde, Mary Dawn.
ALL WORK AND NO PAY (Columbia, 1942) d Del Lord, s Andy Clyde, Frank Lackteen.
SAPPY PAPPY (Columbia, 1942) d Harry Edwards, s Andy Clyde, Barbara Pepper.
WOLF IN THIEF'S CLOTHING (Columbia, 1943) d Jules White, s Andy Clyde.
A MAID MADE MAD (Columbia, 1943) d Del Lord, s Andy Clyde, Barbara Pepper.
FARMER FOR A DAY (Columbia, 1943) d Jules White, s Andy Clyde.
HE WAS ONLY FEUDIN' (Columbia, 1943) d Harry Edwards, s Andy Clyde.
HIS TALE IS TOLD (Columbia, 1944) d Harry Edwards, s Andy Clyde, Christine McIntyre.
YOU WERE NEVER UGLIER (Columbia, 1944) d Jule White, s Andy Clyde.
GOLD IS WHERE YOU LOSE IT (Columbia, 1944) d Jules White, s Andy Clyde, Emmet Lynn.
HEATHER AND YON (Columbia, 1944) d Harry Edwards, s Andy Clyde.
TWO LOCAL YOKELS (Columbia, 1945) d Jules White, s Andy Clyde.
A MINER AFFAIR (Columbia, 1945) d Jules White, s Andy Clyde, Charles Rogers.
THE BLONDE STAYED ON (Columbia, 1946) d Harry Edwards, s Andy Clyde, Christine McIntyre.
SPOOK TO ME (Columbia, 1945) d Jules White, s Andy Clyde.
ANDY PLAYS HOOKY (Columbia, 1946) d Edward Bernds, s Andy Clyde.
TWO JILLS AND A JACK (Columbia, 1947) d Jules White, s Andy Clyde, Dorothy Granger.
WIFE TO SPARE (Columbia, 1947) d Edward Bernds, s Andy Clyde, Christine McIntyre.
EIGHT-BALL ANDY (Columbia, 1948) d Edward Bernds, s Andy Clyde, Dick Wessel.
GO CHASE YOURSELF (Columbia, 1948) d Jules White, s Andy Clyde.
SUNK IN THE SINK (Columbia, 1949) d Jules White, s Andy Clyde.
MARINATED MARINER (Columbia, 1950) d Hugh McCollum, s Andy Clyde, Jean Willes.

A BLUNDERFUL TIME (Columbia, 1950) d Jules White, s Andy Clyde, Margie Liszt.
BLONDE ATOM BOMB (Columbia, 1951) d Jules White, s Andy Clyde.
A BLISSFUL BLUNDER (Columbia, 1952) d Jules White, s Andy Clyde, Ruth Godfrey.
HOOKED AND ROOKED (Columbia, 1952) d Jules White, s Andy CLyde, Emmett Lynn.
FRESH PAINTER (RKO, 1953) d Hal Yates, s Andy Clyde, Gil Lamb.
PARDON MY WRENCH (RKO, 1953) d Hal Yates, s Andy Clyde, Gil Lamb.
LOVE'S A-POPPIN (Columbia, 1953) d Jules White, s Andy Clyde, Phil Van Zandt.
OH, SAY, CAN YOU SUE (Columbia, 1953) d Jules White, s Andy Clyde.
TWO APRIL FOOLS (Columbia, 1954) d Jules White, s Andy Clyde.
SCRATCH SCRATCH SCRATCH (Columbia, 1955) d Jules White, s Andy Clyde, Dorothy Granger.
ONE SPOOKY NIGHT (Columbia, 1955) d Jules White, s Andy Clyde.
ANDY GOES WILD (Columbia, 1956) d Jules White, s Andy CLyde, Dick Wessel.
PARDON MY NIGHTSHIRT (Columbia, 1956) d Jules White, s Andy Clyde.

23. ANDY HARDY
Small-town America is celebrated in the series of pictures about Judge James Hardy, his wife Marian, their son Andy and daughter Joan. The stories were derived from Aurania Rouverol's play *Skidding*.
A FAMILY AFFAIR (MGM, 1937) d George B. Seitz, s Lionel Barrymore, Cecilia Parker, Mickey Rooney
YOU'RE ONLY YOUNG ONCE (MGM, 1938) d George B. Seitz, s Lewis Stone, Cecilia Parker, Mickey Rooney, Fay Holden, Ann Rutherford.
JUDGE HARDY'S CHILDREN (MGM, 1938) d George B. Seitz, s Lewis Stone, Mickey Rooney.
LOVE FINDS ANDY HARDY (MGM, 1938) d George B. Seitz, s Lewis Stone, Mickey Rooney, Judy Garland.
OUT WEST WITH THE HARDYS (MGM, 1938) d George B. Seitz, s Lewis Stone, Mickey Rooney, Cecilia Parker.
THE HARDYS RIDE HIGH (MGM, 1939) d George B. Seitz, s Mickey Rooney, Lewis Stone.
ANDY HARDY GETS SPRING FEVER (MGM, 1939) d W.S. Van Dyke II, s Lewis Stone, Mickey Rooney, Fay Holden.
JUDGE HARDY AND SON (MGM, 1940) d George B. Seitz, s Lewis Stone, Mickey Rooney, Cecilia Parker, Fay Holden.
ANDY HARDY MEETS DEBUTANTE (MGM, 1940) d George B. Seitz, s Lewis Stone, Mickey Rooney, Cecilia Parker, Fay Holden.
ANDY HARDY'S PRIVATE SECRETARY (MGM, 1941) d George B. Seitz, s Lewis Stone, Mickey Rooney, Fay Holden.
LIFE BEGINS FOR ANDY HARDY (MGM, 1941) d George B. Seitz, s Lewis Stone, Mickey Rooney, Judy Garland, Fay Holden.

THE COURTSHIP OF ANDY HARDY (MGM, 1942) d George B. Seitz, s Lewis Stone, Mickey Rooney, Cecilia Parker, Fay Holden.
ANDY HARDY'S DOUBLE LIFE (MGM, 1942) d George B. Seitz, s Lewis Stone, Mickey Rooney, Cecilia Parker, Fay Holden.
ANDY HARDY'S BLONDE TROUBLE (MGM, 1944) d Willis Goldbeck, s Lewis Stone, Mickey Rooney, Sara Haden, Fay Holden.
LOVE LAUGHS AT ANDY HARDY (MGM, 1946) d Willis Goldbeck, s Mickey Rooney, Lewis Stone, Sara Haden.
ANDY HARDY COMES HOME (MGM, 1958) d Howard Koch, s Mickey Rooney, Patricia Breslin, Fay Holden, Cecilia Parker.

24. ANGEL
By day she's a high-school honors student, by night she's a Hollywood hooker and vigilante.
ANGEL (New World, 1984) d Robert Vincent O'Neil, s Donna Wilkes, Cliff Gorman, Susan Tyrrell.
AVENGING ANGEL (New World, 1985) d Robert Vincent O'Neil, s Betsy Russell, Rory Calhoun, Susan Tyrrell
ANGEL III: THE FINAL CHAPTER (New World, 1988) d Tom DeSimone, s Mitzi Kapture, Mark Blankfield.

25. *ANGEL*
These are X-rated films.
ANGEL OF THE NIGHT (Intropics, 1985) s Angel, Paul Thomas.
ANGEL OF THE ISLAND (Intropics, 1989) s Angel, John Leslie.
ANGEL'S BACK (Intropics, 1988) s Angel, Joey Silvera.

26. ANGELIQUE
Angelique is a seventeenth century heroine from a series of bawdy novels by Serge and Anne Golon. The list is incomplete.
ANGELIQUE (1964) d Bernard Borderie, s Michele Mercier, Robert Hossein.

27. ANNABEL
A press agent hopes to get wild publicity for his client through various schemes.
THE AFFAIRS OF ANNABEL (RKO, 1938) d Ben Stoloff, s Jack Oakie, Lucille Ball.
ANNABEL TAKES A TOUR (RKO, 1938) d Lew Landers, s Jack Oakie, Lucille Ball.

28. ANNE OF THE GREEN GABLES
Lucy Maud Montgomery's books set in rural Canada and about an orphaned girl named Anne Shirley inspired these films. The last two aired episodically over American public television.
ANNE OF THE GREEN GABLES (Realart, 1919) s Mary Miles Minter, Paul Kelly.

ANNE OF THE GREEN GABLES (RKO, 1934) d George Nichols, s Anne
    Shirley, Tom Brown, O.P. Heggie.
ANNE OF WINDY POPLARS (RKO, 1940) d Jack Hively, s Anne Shirley,
    James Ellison.
ANNE OF GREEN GABLES (1985 Canadian TV movie) d Kevin Sullivan, s
    Megan Follows, Richard Farnsworth, Colleen Dewhurst.
ANNE OF AVONLEA (1987 TV movie) d Kevin Sullivan, s Megan Follows,
    Colleen Dewhurst, Frank Converse.

29. ANTHONY GETHRYN
Philip MacDonald's literary sleuth is the son of an English squire and a
Spanish artist. He appeared in books published 1924-59.
THE RASP (Fox, 1931) d Michael Powell, s Claude Horton, Phyllis Loring.
THE NURSEMAID WHO DISAPPEARED (Warner Brothers, 1939) d Arthur
    Woods, s Arthur Margetson, Peter Coke.
23 PACES TO BAKER STREET (20th Century-Fox, 1956) d Henry
    Hathaway, s Van Johnson, Vera Miles.
THE LIST OF ADRIAN MESSENGER (Universal, 1963) d John Huston, s
    George C. Scott, Dana Wynter.

30. ANTOINE DOINEL
Director Francois Truffaut's autobiographical series features this hero. In the
first film a neglected Parisian youth takes up small-time crime. The second
entry contains an "Antoine and Colette" episode.
THE 400 BLOWS (Zenith Film, 1959) d Francois Truffaut, s Jean-Pierre
    Leaud, Patric Auffay, Claire Maurier.
LOVE AT TWENTY (Embassy, 1962) d Francois Truffaut, s Renzo Rossellini,
    Shintaro Ishihara.
STOLEN KISSES (Lopert, 1968) d Francois Truffaut, s Jean-Pierre Leaud,
    Delphine Seyrig.
BED AND BOARD (Columbia, 1970) d Francois Truffaut, s Jean-Pierre Leaud,
    Claude Jade, Hiroko Berghauer, Jacques Tati.
LOVE ON THE RUN (AMLF, 1979) d Francois Truffaut, s Jean-Pierre Leaud,
    Marie-France Pisier.

31. APPLE DUMPLING GANG, THE
Don Knotts and Tim Conway are bumbling Western bad guys.
THE APPLE DUMPLING GANG (Buena Vista, 1975) d Norman Tokar, s Bill
    Bixby, Susan Clark, Don Knotts, Tim Conway.
THE APPLE DUMPLING GANG RIDES AGAIN (Buena Vista, 1979) d
    Vincent McEveety, s Tim Conway, Don Knotts.

32. ARSENE LUPIN
The classic criminal hero was created by Maurice LeBlanc in a series of books
beginning in 1907.
ARSENE LUPIN (Greater Film, 1917) s Earle Williams
THE TEETH OF THE TIGER (Paramount, 1919) s David Powell

30 MOTION PICTURE SERIES & SEQUELS

813 (Robertson-Cole, 1920) s Wedgewood Newell
ARSENE LUPIN (MGM, 1932) d Jack Conway, s Lionel Barrymore, Karen Morley.
ARSENE LUPIN RETURNS (MGM, 1938) d George Fitzpaurice, s Melvyn Douglas, Warren William, Virginia Bruce.
ENTER ARSENE LUPIN (Universal, 1944) d Ford Beebe, s Charles Korvin, Ella Raines.
THE ADVENTURES OF ARSENE LUPIN (1957) s Robert Lamoureaux.

33. ARTHUR
The spoiled and generally intoxicated millionaire hero of these pictures stumbles into romance, guided by his valet.
ARTHUR (Orion/Warner Brothers, 1981) d Steve Gordon, s Dudley Moore, Liza Minnelli, John Gielgud.
ARTHUR 2 ON THE ROCKS (Orion/Warner Brothers, 1988) d Bud Yorkin, s Dudley Moore, Liza Minnelli, John Gielgud.

34. ARTISTS AND MODELS
These daffy pix feature a troupe of dancers and comics.
ARTISTS AND MODELS (Paramount, 1937) d Raoul Walsh, s Jack Benny, Ida Lupino, Judy Canova.
ARTISTS AND MODELS ABROAD (Paramount, 1938) d Mitchell Leisen, s Jack Benny, Joan Bennett, Mary Boland.

35. AUNT PEG
These adult films are about a movie producer and her many lovers.
AUNT PEG (Cal Vista, 1980) d Wes Brown, s Juliet Anderson, John Holmes.
AUNT PEG'S FULFILLMENT (Cal Vista, 1982) d Wes Brown, s Juliet Anderson, John Leslie, Suzy Reynolds, John C. Holmes.
AUNT PEG GOES HOLLYWOOD (Caballero, 1983) d Paul G. Vatelli, s Judith Anderson, Rhonda Jo Petty.

The Three Stooges -- Jerry "Curly" Howard, Larry Fine and Moe Howard -- are about to pull a fast one on Vernon Dent (driving auto) in one of their two-reel comedies for Columbia.

36. BAB
These are silent motion pictures based on Mary Roberts Rinehart's story series in *The Saturday Evening Post*. Bab Archibald is a boarding school girl.
BAB'S DIARY (Famous Players, 1917) s Marguerite Clark.
BAB'S BURGLAR (Famous Players, 1917) s Marguerite Clark.
BAB'S MATINEE IDOL (Famous Players, 1917) s Marguerite Clark.
BAB'S CANDIDATE (Famous Players-Lasky, 1920) s Marguerite Clark.
FINDER'S KEEPERS (Universal, 1928)

37. BABES IN ARMS
Youths put on a show in the first picture, and head for Broadway in the second.
BABES IN ARMS (MGM, 1939) d Arthur Freed, s Judy Garland, Mickey Rooney.
BABES ON BROADWAY (MGM, 1941) d Arthur Freed, s Judy Garland, Mickey Rooney.

38. BABY BURLESKS
Produced by a Poverty Row studio, Educational Films, these movies feature Shirley Temple.
THE RUNT PAGE (Educational Films, 1931) d Roy La Verne, s Shirley Temple.
WAR BABIES (Educational Films, 1932) [aka WHAT PRICE GLORIA] d Charles Lamont, s Shirley Temple.
THE PIE COVERED WAGON (Educational Films, 1932) d Charles Lamont, s Shirley Temple.
GLAD RAGS TO RICHES (Educational Films, 1932) d Charles Lamont, s Shirley Temple.
THE KID'S LAST FIGHT (Educational Films, 1932) d Charles Lamont, s Shirley Temple.
KID IN HOLLYWOOD (Educational Films, 1932) d Charles Lamont, s Shirley Temple.
POLLYTIX IN WASHINGTON (Educational Films, 1932) d Charles Lamont, s Shirley Temple.
KID IN AFRICA (Educational Films, 1932) d Charles Lamont, s Shirley Temple.

39. BABYFACE
These are adult films.
BABYFACE (VCA, 1977) s Cubbles Malone, Amber Hunt.
BABYFACE 2 (VCA, 1987) s Candie Evans, Tom Byron.

40. BABYLON BLUE
The pictures are rated X.
BABYLON BLUE (Video-X-Pix, 1984) s Sharon Kane, Joey Silvera.
BABYLON PINK II (Command, 1988) s Nikki Knights, Robert Bullock.
BABYLON PINK III (Command, 1988) s Ona Zee, Shanna McCullough.

41. BABY PEGGY
These shorts feature child actress Peggy Montgomery.

42. BABY SANDY
Sandra Lee "Baby Sandy" Henville is featured here as a precocious child.
SANDY (Universal, 1939) [aka UNEXPECTED FATHER] s Baby Sandy.
SANDY IS A LADY (Universal, 1940) d Charles Lamont, s Nan Grey, Baby Sandy, Eugene Pallette.
SANDY GETS HER MAN (Universal, 1940) d Otis Garrett, s Paul Smith, Stuart Erwin, Una Merkel, Baby Sandy.
SANDY STEPS OUT (Universal, 1940) s Baby Sandy.

43. BACKSIDE TO THE FUTURE
These films carry an X rating; the titles are a takeoff on the next entry.
BACKSIDE TO THE FUTURE (Zane, 1986) s Erica Boyer, Paul Thomas.
BACKSIDE TO THE FUTURE II (Zane, 1988) s Samantha Strong, Tom Byron.

44. BACK TO THE FUTURE
Marty McFly soars into the immediate past, in the first of these comedies, and into the future in the second, tinkering with events along the way.
BACK TO THE FUTURE (Universal, 1985) d Robert Zemeckis, s Michael J. Fox, Christopher Lloyd, Crispin Glover, Lea Thompson.
BACK TO THE FUTURE II (Universal, 1989) d Robert Zemeckis, s Michael J. Fox, Lea Thompson, Christopher Lloyd.
BACK TO THE FUTURE III (Universal, announced 1990) d Robert Zemeckis, s Michael J. Fox, Lea Thompson, Christopher Lloyd.

45. BAD GIRLS
A photographer and his model provide the sparse plotline for these X-raters.
BAD GIRLS (Collectors Video, 1981) d Svetlana, s Pia Snow, Jasmine DuBay.
BAD GIRLS II (Collector's Video, 1983) d Svetlana and David I. Fraser, s Blair Castle, Ron Jeremy.
BAD GIRLS III (Gourmet, 1984) s Crystal Breeze.
BAD GIRLS IV (Gourmet, 1986) d David I. Frazer and Svetlana, s Shauna Grant, Tina Ross, Jamie Gillis.

46. BAD NEWS BEARS, THE
A losing Little League team is brought out of its doldrums by a girl pitcher.
THE BAD NEWS BEARS (Paramount, 1976) d Michael Ritchie, s Walter Matthau, Tatum O'Neal.
THE BAD NEWS BEARS IN BREAKING TRAINING (Paramount, 1977) d Michael Pressman, s William Devane, Clifton James, Jackie Earle Haley.
THE BAD NEWS BEARS GO TO JAPAN (Paramount, 1978) d John Berry, s Tony Curtis, Jackie Earle Haley.

47. BARBARA DARE
These are X-rated pictures.
BARBARA DARE'S SURF, SAND AND SEX (Essex, 1987) s Barbara Dare, Tom Byron.
BARBARA DARE'S ROMAN HOLIDAY (Essex, 1988) s Barbara Dare, John Leslie.

48. BARBARIAN QUEEN
Women band together to fight off raiders in this swords-and-sorcery cheesecake series.
BARBARIAN QUEEN (Concorde, 1985) d Hector Olivers, s Lana Clarkson, Latka Shea.
BARBARIAN QUEEN II (Concorde, 1988) d Joe Finley, s Lana Clarkson, Greg Wrangler.

48A. BARBER, THE
These are silent comedies.
THE BARBER'S QUEER COSTUME (American Mutoscope & Biograph, 1902)
THE BARBER'S DEE-LIGHT (American Mutoscope & Biograph, 1905)
THE BARBER'S PRETTY PATIENT (American Mutoscope & Biograph, 1905)

49. BARNEY GOOGLE AND SNUFFY SMITH
The hillbilly characters are based on W. DeBeck's newspaper comic strip.
HILLBILLY BLITZKRIEG (Monogram, 1942) d Ray Mack, s Bud Duncan, Cliff Nazarro.
PRIVATE SNUFFY SMITH (Monogram, 1942) [aka SNUFFY SMITH: YARDBIRD] d Edward F. Cline, s Bud Duncan, Edgar Kennedy.

49A. BASEBALL BILL
These silent pictures were issued 1916-17. There may be other titles.
BASEBALL BILL s Smilin' Billy Mason
THE BLACK NINE s Smilin' Billy Mason
FLIRTING WITH MARRIAGE s Smilin' Billy Mason
STRIKE ONE! s Smilin' Billy Mason

50. BASKET CASE
A telepathic dwarf twin seeks revenge on doctors.
BASKET CASE (Analysis, 1982) d Frank Henenlotter, s Kevin VanHentryck, Terri Susan Smith.
BASKET CASE 2 (SGE Productions, announced 1990)

51. BATAAN
The first of these pictures tells the story of soldiers holding off advancing Japanese during World War II.
BATAAN (MGM, 1943) d Tay Garnett, s Robert Taylor, George Murphy.

34 MOTION PICTURE SERIES & SEQUELS

BACK TO BATAAN (RKO, 1945) d Edward Dmytryk, s John Wayne, Anthony Quinn.

52. BATMAN
The DC comics character who wears a bat-like costume while fighting crime was created in 1939 by artist Bob Kane and writer Bill Finger. The first two films are serials; the third utilizes the performers from the campy TV series which ran on ABC 1966-68.
BATMAN (Columbia, 1943) (15-chapter serial) d Lambert Hillyer, s Lewis Willson, Douglas Croft, J. Carrol Naish.
BATMAN AND ROBIN (Columbia, 1950) (15-episode serial) d Spencer Bennet, s Robert Lowery, John Duncan, Jane Adams.
BATMAN (20th Century-Fox, 1966) d Leslie H. Martinson, s Adam West, Burt Ward, Alan Napier, Neil Hamilton.
BATMAN (Warner Brothers, 1989) d Tim Burton, s Michael Keaton, Jack Nicholson, Kim Basinger.
BATMAN II, III, IV, V, VI, VII... (Anticipated, considering previous listing's $250 million box office take in 1989)

53. BEACH MOVIES
Bikini-clad teenaged girls, surfboarding teenaged boys, dopey scientists and dopier motorcyclists and rock-and-roll music: a sure formula.
BEACH PARTY (American International, 1963) d William Asher, s Frankie Avalon, Annette Funicello, Bob Cummings, Harvey Lembeck.
MUSCLE BEACH PARTY (American International, 1964) d William Asher, s Frankie Avalon, Annette Funicello, Buddy Hackett, Don Rickles.
BIKINI BEACH (American International, 1964) d William Asher, s Frankie Avalon, Annette Funicello, Keenan Wynn, Harvey Lembeck, Don Rickles.
PAJAMA PARTY (American International, 1964) d Don Weis, s Tommy Kirk, Annette Funicello, Dorothy Lamour, Elsa Lanchester, Buster Keaton.
BEACH BLANKET BINGO (American International, 1965) d William Asher, s Frankie Avalon, Annette Funicello, Paul Lynde, Linda Evans, Buster Keaton.
HOW TO STUFF A WILD BIKINI (American International 1965) d William Asher, s Annette Funicello, Dwayne Hickman, Brian Donlevy, Buster Keaton, Mickey Rooney.
GHOST IN THE INVISIBLE BIKINI (American International 1966) d Don Weis, s Tommy Kirk, Dwayne Hickman, Aron Kincaid, Nancy Sinatra.
BACK TO THE BEACH (Paramount, 1987) d Lyndall Hobbs, s Frankie Avalon, Annette Funicello.

54. BEAU GESTE
Sir Percival Christopher Wren's novel of the French Foreign Legion inspired these movies.
BEAU GESTE (Famous Players/Lasky, 1926) d Herbert Brenon, s Ronald Colman, Neil Hamilton.

BEAU SABREUR (Paramount, 1928) d John Waters, s Gary Cooper, Evelyn Brent, Noah Beery.
BEAU IDEAL (RKO, 1931), d Herbert Brenon, s Lester Vail, Ralph Forbes.
BEAU GESTE (Paramount, 1939) d William A. Wellman, s Gary Cooper, Robert Preston.
BEAU GESTE (Universal, 1966) d Douglas Heyes, s Telly Savalas, Guy Stockwell.
LAST REMAKE OF BEAU GESTE (Universal, 1977) d Marty Feldman, s Marty Feldman, Michael York, Ann-Margaret.

55. BEDROOM EYES
A voyeuristic stockbroker has to prove himself innocent of murder.
BEDROOM EYES (1986) d William Fruet, s Kenneth Gilman, Dayle Haddon.
BEDROOM EYES II (Announced by Distant Horizon, 1990) d Chuck Vincent, s Wings Hauser, Kathy Shower.

56. BEHIND BLUE EYES
These films are rated X.
BEHIND BLUE EYES (Moonlight, 1986) s Krista Lane, Jamie Gillis.
BEHIND BLUE EYES II (Moonlight, 1988) s Shanna McCullough, Robert Bullock.

57. BEHIND THE GREEN DOOR
The first of these X-rated films featured the woman whose face for a time appeared on Ivory Snow packaging.
BEHIND THE GREEN DOOR (Mitchell Brothers, 1975) d Mitchell Brothers, s Marilyn Chambers
BEHIND THE GREEN DOOR: THE SEQUEL (Mitchell Brothers, 1986) d Mitchell Brothers, s Missy Manners, James Martin.

58. BELLES OF ST. TRINIAN'S
Students from a British school for girls disrupt a horse stealing plot, as well as their school, in the first of these movies based on Ronald Searle cartoons.
BELLES OF ST. TRINIAN'S (British Lion/London Fils, 1954) d Frank Launder, s Alastair Sim, Joyce Grenfell.
BLUE MURDER AT ST. TRINIAN'S (British Lion, 1958) d Frank Launder, s Terry-Thomas, George Cole, Joyce Grenfell.
PURE HELL AT ST. TRINIAN'S (Continental, 1961) d Frank Launder, s Cecil Parker, Joyce Grenfell.
THE GREAT ST. TRINIAN'S TRAIN ROBBERY (British Lion, 1966) d Frank Launder and Sidney Gilliat, s Frankie Howard, Reg Varney.

59. BELLE STARR
The real-life Western outlaw turns up in a number of motion pictures.
BELLE STARR (20th Century-Fox, 1941) d Irving Cummings, s Randolph Scott, Gene Tierney.

BELLE STARR'S DAUGHTER (20th Century-Fox, 1948) d Lesley Selander, s George Montgomery, Ruth Roman, Rod Cameron.
MONTANA BELLE (RKO, 1952) d Allan Dwan, s Jane Russell, George Brent.
SON OF BELLE STARR (Allied Artists, 1953) d Frank McDonald, s Keith Larsen, Dona Drake.
BELLE STARR (Entheos Productions/Hanna-Barbera, 1980) (CBS-TV movie) d John A. Alonzo, s Elizabeth Montgomery.

60. BENJI
The movies offer the adventures of a little dog.
BENJI (Mulberry Square, 1974) d Joe Camp, s Higgins, Peter Breck, Deborah Walley.
FOR THE LOVE OF BENJI (Mulberry Square, 1977) d Joe Camp, s Benji, Patsy Garrett, Cynthia Smith.
OH, HEAVENLY DOG (20th Century Fox, 1980) d Joe Camp, s Chevy Chase, Higgins, Jane Seymour.
BENJI THE HUNTED (Buena Vista, 1987) d Joe Camp, s Benji, Red Steagall, Frank Inn.

61. *BEN TURPIN*
The cross-eyed slapstick comedian of silent films played backup in numerous Essanay pictures before undertaking his own Vogue series.
NATIONAL NUTS (Vogue, 1916) d Jack Dillon, s Ben Turpin.
WHEN PAPA DIED (Vogue, 1916) d Jack Dillon, s Ben Turpin.
HIS BLOWOUT (Vogue, 1916) [aka THE PLUMBER] d Jack Dillon, s Ben Turpin.
THE DELINQUENT BRIDEGROOM (Vogue, 1916) d Jack Dillon, s Ben Turpin.
THE IRON MITT (Vogue, 1916) d Jack Dillon, s Ben Turpin.
JUST FOR A KID (Vogue, 1916) d Jack Dillon, s Ben Turpin.
HIRED AND FIRED (Vogue, 1916) [aka THE LEADING MAN] d Jack Dillon, s Ben Turpin.
A DEEP SEA LIAR (Vogue, 1916) [aka THE LANDLUBBER] d Jack Dillon, s Ben Turpin.
FOR TEN THOUSAND BUCKS (Vogue, 1916) d Rube Miller, s Ben Turpin.
LOST AND FOUND (Vogue, 1916) d Rube Miller, s Ben Turpin.
SOME LIARS (Vogue, 1916) d Rube Miller, s Ben Turpin.
THE STOLEN BOOKING (Vogue, 1916) d Rube Miller, s Ben Turpin.
DOCTORING A LEAK (Vogue, 1916) [aka A TOTAL LOSS] d Rube Miller, s Ben Turpin.
POULTRY A LA MODE (Vogue, 1916) [aka THE HAREM] d Rube Miller, s Ben Turpin.
DUCKING A DISCORD (Vogue, 1916) d Rube Miller, s Ben Turpin.
HE DID AND HE DIDN'T (Vogue, 1916) d Rube Miller, s Ben Turpin.
PICTURE PIRATES (Vogue, 1916) d Rube Miller, s Ben Turpin.
SHOT IN THE FRACAS (Vogue, 1916) d Rube Miller, s Ben Turpin.

MOTION PICTURE SERIES & SEQUELS 37

JEALOUS JOLTS (Vogue, 1916) d Rube Miller, s Ben Turpin.
THE WICKED CITY (Vogue, 1916) d Rube Miller, s Ben Turpin.
A CIRCUS CYCLONE (Vogue, 1917) d Rube Miller, s Ben Turpin.
THE MUSICAL MARVELS (Vogue, 1917) d Robin Williamson, s Ben Turpin.
THE BUTCHER'S NIGHTMARE (Vogue, 1917) d Robin Williamson, s Ben Turpin.
HIS BOGUS BOAST (Vogue, 1917) [aka A CHEERFUL LIAR] d Robin Williamson, s Ben Turpin.
A STUDIO STAMPEDE (Vogue, 1917) d Robin Williamson, s Ben Turpin.
FRIGHTENED FLIRTS (Vogue, 1917) d Robin Williamson, s Ben Turpin.
WHY BEN BOLTED (Vogue, 1917) [aka HE LOOKED CROOKED] d Robin Williamson, s Ben Turpin.
MASKED MIRTH (Vogue, 1917) d Robin Williamson, s Ben Turpin.
BUCKING THE TIGER (Vogue, 1917) d Robin Williamson, s Ben Turpin.
CAUGHT IN THE END (Vogue, 1917) d Robin Williamson, s Ben Turpin.
A CLEVER DUMMY (Mack Sennett, 1917) s Ben Turpin.
LOST -- A COOK (Mack Sennett, 1917) s Ben Turpin.
A PAWNBROKER'S HEART (Mack Sennett, 1917) d Edward Cline, s Ben Turpin.
ROPING HER ROMEO (Mack Sennett, 1917) d Fred Fishback and Hampton Del Ruth, s Ben Turpin.
ARE WAITRESSES SAFE? (Mack Sennett, 1917) d Victor Heerman, s Ben Turpin.
TAMING TARGET CENTER (Mack Sennett, 1917) s Ben Turpin.
SHERIFF NELL'S TUSSLE (Mack Sennett, 1918) d William Campbell, s Ben Turpin.
SAUCY MADELINE (Mack Sennett, 1918) d F. Richard Jones, s Ben Turpin.
THE BATTLE ROYAL (Mack Sennett, 1918) d F. Richard Jones, s Ben Turpin.
TWO TOUGH TENDERFEET (Mack Sennett, 1918) d F. Richard Jones, s Ben Turpin.
SHE LOVED HIM PLENTY (Mack Sennett, 1918) d F. Richard Jones, s Ben Turpin.
SLEUTHS (Mack Sennett, 1918) d F. Richard Jones, s Ben Turpin.
WHOSE LITTLE WIFE ARE YOU? (Mack Sennett, 1918) d Edward Cline, s Ben Turpin.
HIDE AND SEEK, DETECTIVES (Mack Sennett, 1918) d Edward Cline, s Ben Turpin.
CUPID'S DAY OFF (Mack Sennett, 1919) d Edward Cline, s Ben Turpin.
EAST LYNNE WITH VARIATIONS (Mack Sennett, 1919) d Edward Cline, s Ben Turpin.
WHEN LOVE IS BLIND (Mack Sennett, 1919) d Edward Cline, s Ben Turpin.
NO MOTHER TO GUIDE HIM (Mack Sennett, 1919) d Mal St. Clair and Erle Kenton, s Ben Turpin.
YANKEE DOODLE IN BERLIN (Mack Sennett, 1919) s Ben Turpin.
UNCLE TOM WITHOUT THE CABIN (Mack Sennett, 1919) d Ray Hunt,

38 MOTION PICTURE SERIES & SEQUELS

SALOME VS. SHENENDOAH (Mack Sennett, 1919) d Erle Kenton and Ray Hunt, s Ben Turpin.
THE STAR BOARDER (Mack Sennett, 1920) d James Davis, s Ben Turpin.
DOWN ON THE FARM (Mack Sennett, 1920) d Erle Kenton and Ray Grey, s Ben Turpin.
MARRIED LIFE (Mack Sennett, 1920) d Erle Kenton, s Ben Turpin.
A SMALL TOWN IDOL (Mack Sennett, 1921) d Erle Kenton, s Ben Turpin.
LOVE'S OUTCAST (Mack Sennett, 1921) d J.A. Waldron, s Ben Turpin.
LOVE AND DOUGHNUTS (Mack Sennett, 1921) d Roy Del Ruth, s Ben Turpin.
BRIGHT EYES (Mack Sennett, 1922) d Roy Del Ruth, s Ben Turpin.
STEP FORWARD (Mack Sennett, 1922) d F. Richard Jones, s Ben Turpin.
HOME MADE MOVIES (Mack Sennett, 1922) d Ray Grey and Gus Meins, s Ben Turpin.
THE SHRIEK OF ARABY (Mack Sennett, 1923) d F. Richard Jones, s Ben Turpin.
WHERE'S MY WANDERING BOY TONIGHT? (Mack Sennett, 1923) d J.A. Waldron, s Ben Turpin.
PITFALLS OF A BIG CITY (Mack Sennett, 1923) d J.A. Waldron, s Ben Turpin.
ASLEEP AT THE SWITCH (Mack Sennett, 1923) d Roy Del Ruth, s Ben Turpin.
THE DAREDEVIL (Mack Sennett, 1923) d Del Lord, s Ben Turpin.
TEN DOLLARS OR TEN DAYS (Mack Sennett, 1924) d Del Lord, s Ben Turpin.
THE HOLLYWOOD KID (Mack Sennett, 1924) d Del Lord, s Ben Turpin.
YUKON JAKE (Mack Sennett, 1924) d Del Lord, s Ben Turpin.
ROMEO AND JULIET (Mack Sennett, 1924) d Reggie Morris and Harry Sweet, s Ben Turpin.
THREE FOOLISH WEEKS (Mack Sennett, 1924) d Reggie Morris and Ed Kennedy, s Ben Turpin.
THE REEL VIRGINIAN (Mack Sennett, 1924) d Reggie Morris and Ed Kennedy, s Ben Turpin.
WILD GOOSE CHASER (Mack Sennett, 1925) d Lloyd Bacon, s Ben Turpin.
RASPBERRY ROMANCE (Mack Sennett, 1925) d Lloyd Bacon, s Ben Turpin.
THE MARRIAGE CIRCUS (Mack Sennett, 1925) d Reggie Morris and Ed Kennedy, s Ben Turpin.
WHEN A MAN'S A PRINCE (Mack Sennett, 1926) d Edward Cline, s Ben Turpin.
A PRODIGAL BRIDEGROOM (Mack Sennett, 1926) d Lloyd Bacon, s Ben Turpin.
A HAREM KNIGHT (Mack Sennett, 1926) d Gil Pratt, s Ben Turpin.
A BLONDE'S REVENGE (Mack Sennett, 1926) d Del Lord, s Ben Turpin.
A HOLLYWOOD HERO (Mack Sennett, 1927) d Harry Edwards, s Ben Turpin.
THE JOLLY JILTER (Mack Sennett, 1927) d Edward Cline, s Ben Turpin.

BROKE IN CHINA (Mack Sennett, 1927) s Ben Turpin.
PRIDE OF PIKEVILLE (Mack Sennett, 1927) s Ben Turpin.
LOVE'S LANGUID LURE (Mack Sennett, 1927) s Ben Turpin.
DADDY BOY (Mack Sennett, 1927) d Harry Edwards, s Ben Turpin.

61A. BETTY
These are silent comedies.
BETTY SETS THE PACE (1919) s Muriel Ostriche.
BETTY TAKES A HAND (1919) s Muriel Ostriche.
BETTY'S GREEN-EYED MONSTER (1919) s Muriel Ostriche.

62. BEVERLY HILLS COP
A street-wise Detroit detective tracks down killers in Los Angeles.
BEVERLY HILLS COP (Paramount, 1984) d Martin Brest, s Eddie Murphy, Judge Reinhold, Ronny Cox, Lisa Eilbacher.
BEVERLY HILLS COP II (Paramount, 1987) d Tony Scott, s Eddie Murphy, Judge Reinhold, Brigitte Nielsen.

63. BEYOND THE DOOR
The films are tales of possession by hellish-beings.
BEYOND THE DOOR (Film Ventures International, 1975) d Oliver Hellman, s Juliet Mills, Richard Johnson.
BEYOND THE DOOR 2 (Film Ventures International, 1979) [aka SHOCK] d Mario Bava, s Darla Nicolodi, John Steiner.

64. BIG BAD MAMA
A bank robbing moll and her daughters are on the run from the law.
BIG BAD MAMA (New World, 1974) d Steve Carver, s Angie Dickinson, William Shatner.
BIG BAD MAMA II (Concorde, 1987) d Jim Wynorski, s Angie Dickinson, Robert Culp.

65. BIG BROADCAST, THE
These variety show pictures, set at a radio station, include a number of top entertainers of the day.
THE BIG BROADCAST (Paramount Publix, 1932) d Frank Tuttle, s Bing Crosby, Kate Smith, Cab Calloway.
THE BIG BROADCAST OF 1936 (Paramount, 1935) d Norman Taurog, s Jack Oakie, George Burns, Gracie Allen, Ethel Merman, Bill "Bojangles" Robinson.
THE BIG BROADCAST OF 1937 (Paramount, 1936) d Mitchell Leisen, s Jack Benny, Martha Raye.
THE BIG BROADCAST OF 1938 (Paramount, 1938) d Mitchell Leisen, s W.C. Fields, Dorothy Lamour, Bob Hope.

66. BILL
A retarded adult goes out on his own after being in an institution for 46 years.

40 MOTION PICTURE SERIES & SEQUELS

BILL (1981 TV movie) d Anthony Page, s Mickey Rooney, Dennis Quaid.
BILL: ON HIS OWN (1983 TV movie) d Anthony Page, s Mickey Rooney, Helen Hunt.

67. BILL AND BOB
Two-reeler silent Westerns, also called THE ADVENTURES OF BILL AND BOB, feature twins Robert and William Steele.

68. BILL AND SALLY REARDON
These screwball comedies have a mystery twist.
THERE'S ALWAYS A WOMAN (Columbia, 1938) d Alexander Hall, s Melvyn Douglas, Joan Blondell.
THERE'S THAT WOMAN AGAIN (Columbia, 1939) d Alexander Hall, s Melvyn Douglas, Virgina Bruce.

69. *BILL CODY AND ANDY SHUFORD*
The B Westerns team actors Cody and Shuford.
DUGAN OF THE BADLANDS (Monogram, 1931) d R.N. Bradbury, s Bill Cody, Andy Shuford, Blanche Mehaffey.
THE MONTANA KID (Monogram, 1931) d Harry Fraser, s Bill Cody, Andy Shuford, Doris Hill.
OKLAHOMA JIM (Monogram, 1931) d Harry Fraser, s Bill Cody, Andy Shuford, Marion Burns.
GHOST CITY (Monogram, 1932) d Harry Fraser, s Bill Cody, Andy Shuford, Helen Forrest.
MASON OF THE MOUNTED (Monogram, 1932) d Harry Fraser, s Bill Cody, Andy Shuford, Nancy Drexel.
LAW OF THE NORTH (Monogram, 1932) d Harry Fraser, s Bill Cody, Andy Shuford, Nadine Dore.
TEXAS PIONEERS (Monogram, 1932) d Harry Fraser, s Bill Cody, Andy Shuford, Sheila Mannors.
LAND OF WANTED MEN (Monogram, 1932) d Harry Fraser, s Bill Cody, Andy Shuford, Ada Ince.

71. BILL CRANE
The crime movies derive from books by Jonathan Latimer. A liquor-loving detective takes on sleazy clients. The pictures were issued in the studio's CRIME CLUB series.
THE WESTLAND CASE (Universal, 1937) d Christy Cabanne, s Preston Foster, Frank Jenks, Carol Hughes.
LADY IN THE MORGUE (Universal, 1938) d Otis Garrett, s Preston Foster, Patricia Ellis.
THE LAST WARNING (Universal, 1939) d Al Rogell, s Preston Foster, Frank Jenks, France Robinson.

72. BILLY
The silent pix feature Billy Quirk.

BILLY FOOS DAD (1913) s Billy Quirk.
BILLY'S TROUBLES (1913) s Billy Quirk.
BILLY'S WAGER (1915) s Billy Quirk.

73. BILLY BEVAN
The silent film comedian with the brush mustache, playing supporting roles in silent comedies from 1917, starred in his own two-reelers for Mack Sennett.
LET' ER GO (Mack Sennett, 1920) d James Davis, s Billy Bevan.
THE QUACK DOCTOR (Mack Sennett, 1920) d George Gray and Billy
    Bevan, s Billy Bevan.
IT'S A BOY (Mack Sennett, 1920) d Noel Smith, s Billy Bevan.
MY GOODNESS (Mack Sennett, 1920) d Noel Smith, s Billy Bevan.
LOVE, HONOR AND BEHAVE (1920) d F. Richard Jones and Erle Kenton, s
    Billy Bevan.
A FIRESIDE BREWER (Mack Sennett, 1920) d Noel Smith, s Billy Bevan.
A SMALL TOWN IDOL (1921) d Erle Kenton, s Billy Bevan.
BE REASONABLE (Mack Sennett, 1921) d Roy Del Ruth, s Billy Bevan.
BY HECK (Mack Sennett, 1921) d Roy Del Ruth, s Billy Bevan.
ASTRAY FROM THE STEERAGE (Mack Sennett, 1921) d Frank Powell, s
    Billy Bevan.
THE DUCK HUNTER (Mack Sennett, 1922) d Roy Del Ruth, s Billy Bevan.
ON PATROL (Mack Sennett, 1922) d F. Richard Jones, s Billy Bevan.
OH DADDY (Mack Sennett, 1922) d Roy Del Ruth, s Billy Bevan.
GYMNASIUM JIM (Mack Sennett, 1922) d F. Richard Jones, s Billy Bevan.
MA AND PA (Mack Sennett, 1922) d Roy Del Ruth, s Billy Bevan.
WHEN SUMMER COMES (Mack Sennett, 1922) d Roy Del Ruth, s Billy
    Bevan.
NIP AND TUCK (Mack Sennett, 1923) d Roy Del Ruth, s Billy Bevan.
INBAD THE SAILOR (Mack Sennett, 1923) d Erle Kenton, s Billy Bevan.
ONE SPOOKY NIGHT (Mack Sennett, 1924) s Billy Bevan.
WALL STREET BLUES (Mack Sennett, 1924) s Billy Bevan.
LIZZIES OF THE FIELD (Mack Sennett, 1924) d Del Lord, s Billy Bevan.
WANDERING WAISTLINES (Mack Sennett, 1924) s Billy Bevan.
THE CANNON BALL EXPRESS (Mack Sennett, 1924) d Del Lord, s Billy
    Bevan.
HONEYMOON HARDSHIPS (Mack Sennett, 1925) d Tom Garnett and
    Jefferson Moffitt, s Billy Bevan.
GIDDAP (Mack Sennett, 1925) d Del Lord, s Billy Bevan.
THE LION'S WHISKERS (Mack Sennett, 1925) d Del Lord, s Billy Bevan.
SKINNERS IN SILK (Mack Sennett, 1925) d Del Lord, s Billy Bevan.
SUPER-HOOPER-DYNE LIZZIES (Mack Sennett, 1925) d Del Lord, s Billy
    Bevan.
SNEEZING BEEZERS (Mack Sennett, 1925) d Del Lord, s Billy Bevan.
THE IRON NAG (Mack Sennett, 1925) d Del Lord, s Billy Bevan.
BUTTER FINGERS (Mack Sennett, 1925) d Del Lord, s Billy Bevan.
OVER THERE-ABOUTS (Mack Sennett, 1925) s Billy Bevan.
FROM RAGS TO BRITCHES (Mack Sennett, 1925) s Billy Bevan.

42 MOTION PICTURE SERIES & SEQUELS

WHISPERING WHISKERS (Mack Sennett, 1926) d Del Lord, s Billy Bevan.
TRIMMED IN GOLD (Mack Sennett, 1926) s Billy Bevan.
CIRCUS TODAY (Mack Sennett, 1926) d Lloyd Bacon, s Billy Bevan.
WANDERING WILLIES (Mack Sennett, 1926) d Del Lord, s Billy Bevan.
HAYFOOT, STRAWFOOT (Mack Sennett, 1926) d Gil Pratt and Jefferson Moffitt, s Billy Bevan.
FIGHT NIGHT (Mack Sennett, 1926) d Gil Pratt, s Billy Bevan.
MUSCLE BOUND MUSIC (Mack Sennett, 1926) d Alf Goulding, s Billy Bevan.
ICE COLD COCOS (Mack Sennett, 1926) d Del Lord, s Billy Bevan.
A SEA DOG'S TALE (Mack Sennett, 1926) d Del Lord, s Billy Bevan.
HUBBY'S QUIET LITTLE GAME (Mack Sennett, 1926) d Del Lord, s Billy Bevan.
HOBOKEN TO HOLLYWOOD (Mack Sennett, 1926) d Del Lord, s Billy Bevan.
MASKED MAMAS (Mack Sennett, 1926) s Billy Bevan.
THE DIVORCE DODGER (Mack Sennett, 1926) d Del Lord, s Billy Bevan.
FLIRTY FOUR-FLUSHERS (Mack Sennett, 1926) d Eddie Cline, s Billy Bevan.
SHOULD SLEEPWALKERS MARRY? (Mack Sennett, 1927) s Billy Bevan.
PEACHES AND PLUMBERS (Mack Sennett, 1927) s Billy Bevan.
A SMALL TOWN PRINCESS (Mack Sennett, 1927) s Billy Bevan.
THE BULL FIGHTER (Mack Sennett, 1927) d Earle Rodney, s Billy Bevan.
CURED IN THE EXCITEMENT (Mack Sennett, 1927) d Earle Rodney, s Billy Bevan.
THE GOLF NUT (Mack Sennett, 1927) d Harry Edwards, s Billy Bevan.
GOLD DIGGER OF WEEPAH (Mack Sennett, 1927) d Harry Edwards, s Billy Bevan.
THE BEACH CLUB (Mack Sennett, 1928) d Harry Edwards, s Billy Bevan.
THE BEST MAN (Mack Sennett, 1928) d Harry Edwards, s Billy Bevan.
THE BICYCLE FLIRT (Mack Sennett, 1928) d Harry Edwards, s Billy Bevan.
HIS UNLUCKY NIGHT (Mack Sennett, 1928) d Harry Edwards, s Billy Bevan.
MOTORBOAT MAMAS (Mack Sennett, 1928) d Harry Andrews, s Billy Bevan.
MOTORING MAMAS (Mack Sennett, 1928) d Phil Whitman, s Billy Bevan.
HUBBY'S LATEST ALIBI (Mack Sennett, 1928) d Phil Whitman, s Billy Bevan.
HUBBY'S WEEKEND TRIP (Mack Sennett, 1928) d Harry Edwards, s Billy Bevan.
THE LION'S ROAR (Educational, 1928) s Billy Bevan.
HIS NEW STENO (Mack Sennett, 1928) d Phil Whitman, s Billy Bevan.
CALLING HUBBY'S BLUFF (Mack Sennett, 1929) d Harry Edwards, s Billy Bevan.
BUTTON MY BACK (Mack Sennett, 1929) d Phil Whitman, s Billy Bevan.
FOOLISH HUSBANDS (Mack Sennett, 1929) d Phil Whitman, s Billy Bevan.
PINK PAJAMAS (Mack Sennett, 1929) d Phil Whitman, s Billy Bevan.

DON'T GET JEALOUS (Mack Sennett, 1929) s Billy Bevan.

74. BILLY CARSON
Billy Carson, alias Billy the Kid, is featured in this Western series. His sidekick is Fuzzy Q. Jones.
BILLY THE KID OUTLAWED (PRC, 1940) d Peter Stewart (Sam Newfield), s Bob Steele, Louise Currie, Al St. John.
BILLY THE KID IN TEXAS (PRC, 1940) d Sam Newfield, s Bob Steele, Terry Walker, Al St. John.
BILLLY THE KID'S GUN JUSTICE (PRC, 1940) d Peter Stewart (Sam Newfield), s Bob Steele, Louise Currie, Al St. John.
BILLY THE KID'S RANGE WAR (PRC, 1941) d Peter Stewart (Sam Newfield), s Bob Steele, Al St. John, Joan Barclay, Rex Lease.
BILLY THE KID'S FIGHTING PALS (PRC, 1941) d Sherman Scott (Sam Newfield), s Bob Steele, Al St. John, Phyllis Adair.
BILLY THE KID IN SANTE FE (PRC, 1941) d Peter Stewart (Sam Newfield), s Bob Steele, Al St. John, Rex Lease, Dennis Moore.
BILLY THE KID WANTED (PRC, 1941) d Sherman Scott (Sam Newfield), s Buster Crabbe, Al St. John.
BILLY THE KID'S ROUNDUP (PRC, 1941) d Sherman Scott (Sam Newfield), s Buster Crabbe, Al St. John.
BILLY THE KID TRAPPED (PRC, 1942) d Sherman Scott (Sam Newfield), s Buster Crabbe, Al St. John, Anne Jeffreys.
BILLY THE KID'S SMOKING GUNS (PRC, 1942) d Sherman Scott (Sam Newfield), s Buster Crabbe, Al St. John, Joan Barclay.
LAW AND ORDER (PRC, 1942) d Sherman Scott (Sam Newfield), s Buster Crabbe, Al St. John.
SHERIFF OF SAGE VALLEY (PRC, 1942) d Sherman Scott (Sam Newfield), s Buster Crabbe, Al St. John.
THE MYSTERIOUS RIDER (PRC, 1942) d Sam Newfield, s Buster Crabbe, Al St. John.
THE KID RIDES AGAIN (PRC, 1943) d Sherman Scott (Sam Newfield), s Buster Crabbe, Al St. John.
FUGITIVE OF THE PLAINS (PRC, 1943) d Sam Newfield, s Buster Crabbe, Al St. John.
WESTERN CYCLONE (PRC, 1943) d Sam Newfield, s Buster Crabbe, Al St. John, Marjorie Manners.
CATTLE STAMPEDE (PRC, 1943) d Sam Newfield, s Buster Crabbe, Al St. John, Frances Gladwin.
THE RENEGADE (PRC, 1943) d Sam Newfield, s Buster Crabbe, Al St. John, Lois Ransom.
DEVIL RIDERS (PRC, 1943) d Sam Newfield, s Buster Crabbe, Al St. John, Patti McCarthy.
FRONTIER OUTLAWS (PRC, 1944) d Sam Newfield, s Buster Crabbe, Al St. John, Frances Gladwin.
THUNDERING GUN SLINGERS (PRC, 1944) d Sam Newfield, s Buster Crabbe, Al St. John, Frances Gladwin.

VALLEY OF VENGEANCE (PRC, 1944) d Sam Newfield, s Buster Crabbe, Al St. John, Evelyn Finley.
THE DRIFTER (PRC, 1944) d Sam Newfield, s Buster Crabbe, Al St. John, Carol Parker.
FUZZY SETTLES DOWN (PRC, 1944) d Sam Newfield, s Buster Crabbe, Al St. John, Patti McCarthy, Charles King.
BLAZING FRONTIER (PRC, 1944) d Sam Newfield, s Buster Crabbe, Al St. John.
RUSTLER'S HIDEOUT (PRC, 1944) d Sam Newfield, s Buster Crabbe, Al St. John, Patti McCarthy.
WILD HORSE PHANTOM (PRC, 1944) d Sam Newfield, s Buster Crabbe, Al St. John.
OATH OF VENGEANCE (PRC, 1944) d Sam Newfield, s Buster Crabbe, Al St. John.
LIGHTNING RAIDERS (PRC, 1945) d Sam Newfield, s Buster Crabbe, Al St. John.
HIS BROTHER'S GHOST (PRC, 1945) d Sam Newfield, s Buster Crabbe, Al St. John.
SHADOWS OF DEATH (PRC, 1945) d Sam Newfield, s Buster Crabbe, Al St. John, Donna Dax.
GANGSTER'S DEN (PRC, 1945) d Sam Newfield, s Buster Crabbe, Al St. John.
STAGECOACH OUTLAWS (PRC, 1945) d Sam Newfield, s Buster Crabbe, Al St. John, Frances Gladwin.
BORDER BADMEN (PRC, 1945) d Sam Newfield, s Buster Crabbe, Al St. John.
FIGHTING BILL CARSON (PRC, 1945) d Sam Newfield, s Buster Crabbe, Al St. John.
PRAIRIE RUSTLERS (PTC, 1945) d Sam Newfield, s Buster Crabbe, Al St. John, Evelyn Finley.
GENTLEMEN WITH GUNS (PRC, 1946) d Sam Newfield, s Buster Crabbe, Al St. John, Patricia Knox, Steve Darrell.
TERRORS ON HORSEBACK (PRC, 1946) d Sam Newfield, s Buster Crabbe, Al St. John, Patti McCarthy.
GHOST OF HIDDEN VALLEY (PRC, 1946) d Sam Newfield, s Buster Crabbe, Al St. John.
PRAIRIE BADMEN (PRC, 1946) d Sam Newfield, s Buster Crabbe, Al St. John, Patricia Knox.
OVERLAND RIDERS (PRC, 1946) d Sam Newfield, s Buster Crabbe, Al St. John.
OUTLAW OF THE PLAINS (PRC, 1946) d Sam Newfield, s Buster Crabbe, Al St. John.

74A. BILLY FORTUNE
These silent films feature Victor Potel. They were issued by Universal circa 1919.

75. BILLY JACK
A peace-loving half-breed karate expert protects a free school challenged by townspeople, in the first entry; in the third, he ventures to Washington, D.C., in the same vein as MR. SMITH GOES TO WASHINGTON.
BILLY JACK (Warner Brothers, 1971) d T.C. Frank (Tom Laughlin), s Tom Laughlin, Delores Taylor.
THE TRIAL OF BILLY JACK (Taylor-Laughlin, 1974) d Frank Laughlin, s Tom Laughlin, Delores Taylor
BILLY JACK GOES TO WASHINGTON (Taylor-Laughlin, 1978) d Tom Laughlin, s Tom Laughlin, Delores Taylor.

BILLY THE KID
See **BILLY CARSON**

76. BITCH, THE
These pictures are rated X.
THE BITCH (Fantasy, 1987) s Angela Baron, Mike Horner.
THE BITCH IS BACK (Fantasy, 1988) s Angela Baron, Randy West.

77. BLACK CAESAR
A black gangster works his way to the top of the Harlem rackets.
BLACK CAESAR (American International, 1973) d Larry Cohen, s Fred Williamson, D'Urville Martin, Julius Harris.
HELL UP IN HARLEM (American International, 1973) d Larry Cohen, s Fred Williamson, Julius W. Harris.

78. BLACK STALLION, THE
Walter Farley's *Black Stallion* novels inspired these films. Alec Ramsey befriends a wild stallion, The Black. A second sequel is said to be in the works in 1990.
THE BLACK STALLION (United Artists/Omni Zoetrope, 1979) d Carroll Ballard, s Kelly Reno, Mickey Rooney, Teri Garr.
THE BLACK STALLION RETURNS (MGM-UA/Coppola/Zoetrope, 1983) d Robert Dalva, s Kelly Reno, Teri Garr.

79. BLACULA
The horror films are derived from Bram Stoker's classic tale *Dracula,* but with a Black cast.
BLACULA (American International, 1972) d William Crain, s William Marshall, Denise Nicholas.
SCREAM, BLACULA, SCREAM (American International, 1973) d Bob Kelljan, s William Marshall, Pam Grier.

80. BLAKE OF SCOTLAND YARD
Angus/James Blake, one of Scotland Yard's finest, appears in three serials. The second entry was publicized as the first talking serial.
BLAKE OF SCOTLAND YARD (1927) (serial) s Hayden Stevenson

ACE OF SCOTLAND YARD (Universal, 1929) (10-chapter serial) d Ray Taylor, s Crawford Kent, Florence Allen.
BLAKE OF SCOTLAND YARD (1936) (15 episodes) d Bob Hill, s Ralph Byrd, Joan Barclay, Dickie Jones, Herbert Rawlinson.

81. BLOB, THE
These are horror films featuring a slimy space invader.
THE BLOB (Tonylyn, 1958) d Irwin S. Yeaworth Jr., s Steve McQueen.
SON OF BLOB (1972) [aka BEWARE! THE BLOB] d Larry Hagman, s Robert Walker, Richard Stahl, Carol Lynley, Godfrey Cambridge.

82. BLONDES AND REDHEADS, THE
This listing of the comedy shorts in this series is incomplete.
FLIRTING IN THE PARK (RKO, 1933) d George Stevens, s Carol Tevis, June Brewster, Grady Sutton.
HUNGER PAINS (1935)
PICKLED PEPPERS (1935) s Carol Tevis, Dorothy Granger, Grady Sutton

83. BLONDIE
Featured in Chic Young's syndicated newspaper comic strip and its derivative movie series are the Bumsteads: Dagwood and Blondie, their children, pets and neighbors.
BLONDIE (Columbia, 1938) d Frank R. Strayer, s Penny Singleton, Arthur Lake, Larry Simms.
BLONDIE MEETS THE BOSS (Columbia, 1939) d Frank R. Strayer, s Penny Singleton, Arthur Lake
BLONDIE TAKES A VACATION (Columbia, 1939) d Frank R. Strayer, s Penny Singleton, Arthur Lake, Larry Simms.
BLONDIE BRINGS UP BABY (Columbia, 1939) d Frank R. Strayer, s Penny Singleton, Arthur Lake, Larry Simms.
BLONDIE ON A BUDGET (Columbia, 1940) d Frank R. Strayer, s Penny Singleton, Arthur Lake, Larry Simms.
BLONDIE HAS SERVANT TROUBLE (Columbia, 1940) d Frank R. Strayer, s Penny Singleton, Arthur Lake, Larry Simms.
BLONDIE PLAYS CUPID (Columbia, 1940) d Frank R. Strayer, s Penny Singleton, Arthur Lake, Larry Simms.
BLONDIE GOES LATIN (Columbia, 1941) d Frank R. Strayer, s Penny Singleton, Arthur Lake, Larry Simms.
BLONDIE IN SOCIETY (Columbia, 1941) d Frank R. Strayer, s Penny Singleton, Arthur Lake, Larry Simms.
BLONDIE GOES TO COLLEGE (Columbia, 1942) d Frank R. Strayer, s Penny Singleton, Arthur Lake, Larry Simms.
BLONDIE'S BLESSED EVENT (Columbia, 1942) d Frank R. Strayer, s Penny Singleton, Arthur Lake, Larry Simms.
BLONDIE FOR VICTORY (Columbia, 1942) d Frank R. Strayer, s Penny Singleton, Arthur Lake, Larry Simms.

IT'S A GREAT LIFE (Columbia, 1943) d Frank R. Strayer, s Penny Singleton, Arthur Lake, Larry Simms.
FOOTLIGHT GLAMOUR (Columbia, 1943) d Frank R. Strayer, s Penny Singleton, Arthur Lake, Larry Simms.
LEAVE IT TO BLONDIE (Columbia, 1945) d Abby Berlin, s Penny Singleton, Arthur Lake, Larry Simms.
BLONDIE KNOWS BEST (Columbia, 1946) d Abby Berlin, s Penny Singleton, Arthur Lake, Larry Simms.
LIFE WITH BLONDIE (Columbia, 1946) d Abby Berlin, s Penny Singleton, Arthur Lake, Larry Simms.
BLONDIE'S LUCKY DAY (Columbia, 1946) d Abby Berlin, s Penny Singleton, Arthur Lake, Larry Simms.
BLONDIE'S BIG MOMENT (Columbia, 1947) d Abby Berlin, s Penny Singleton, Arthur Lake, Larry Simms.
BLONDIE'S HOLIDAY (Columbia, 1947) d Abby Berlin, s Penny Singleton, Arthur Lake, Larry Simms.
BLONDIE IN THE DOUGH (Columbia, 1947) d Abby Berlin, s Penny Singleton, Arthur Lake, Larry Simms.
BLONDIE'S ANNIVERSARY (Columbia, 1947) d Abby Berlin, s Penny Singleton, Arthur Lake, Larry Simms.
BLONDIE'S REWARD (Columbia, 1948) d Abby Berlin, s Penny Singleton, Arthur Lake, Larry Simms.
BLONDIE'S SECRET (Columbia, 1949) d Edward Bernds, s Penny Singleton, Arthur Lake, Larry Simms.
BLONDIE'S BIG DEAL (Columbia, 1949) d Edward Bernds, s Penny Singleton, Arthur Lake, Larry Simms.
BLONDIE HITS THE JACKPOT (Columbia, 1949) d Edward Bernds, s Penny Singleton, Arthur Lake, Larry Simms.
BLONDIE'S HERO (Columbia, 1950) d Edward Bernds, s Penny Singleton, Arthur Lake, Larry Simms.
BEWARE OF BLONDIE (Columbia, 1950) d Edward Bernds, s Penny Singleton, Arthur Lake, Larry Simms.

84. BODIES IN HEAT
The pictures are for adults only.
BODIES IN HEAT (Caballero, 1984) d Paul Vatelli, s Annette Haven, Herschel Savage.
BODIES IN HEAT: THE SEQUEL (Dreamland, 1989) s Annette Haven, Mike Horner.

85. BOGGY CREEK
Anthropologist and others seek the creature of Boggy Creek.
THE LEGEND OF BOGGY CREEK (Howco International, 1972) d Charles B. Pierce, s Willie E. Smith, John P. Nixon.
RETURN TO BOGGY CREEK (777 Distributors, 1977) d Tom Moore, s Dawn Welles, Dana Plato.

THE BARBARIC BEAST OF BOGGY CREEK, PART II (Howco International, 1985) [aka BOGGY CREEK II] d Charles B. Pierce, s Charles B. Pierce, Cindy Butler.

86. BOMBA THE JUNGLE BOY
The Roy Rockwood-created Bomba boys' books (twenty volumes published 1926-38) provided the impetus for this movie series.
BOMBA THE JUNGLE BOY (Monogram, 1949) d Ford Beebe, s Johnny Sheffield, Peggy Ann Garner.
BOMBA ON PANTHER ISLAND (Monogram, 1949) d Ford Beebe, s Johnny Sheffield, Allene Roberts.
BOMBA AND THE LOST VOLCANO (Monogram, 1950) d Ford Beebe, s Johnny Sheffield, Donald Woods, Marjorie Lord.
BOMBA AND THE HIDDEN CITY (Monogram, 1950) d Ford Beebe, s Johnny Sheffield, Sue England.
BOMBA AND THE ELEPHANT STAMPEDE (Monogram, 1951) d Ford Beebe, s Johnny Sheffield, Donna Martell, Edith Evanson.
BOMBA AND THE LION HUNTERS (Monogram, 1951) d Ford Beebe, s Johnny Sheffield, Ann B. Todd.
BOMBA AND THE AFRICAN TREAURE (Monogram, 1952) d Ford Beebe, s Johnny Sheffield, Laurette Luex.
BOMBA AND THE JUNGLE GIRL (Monogram, 1952) d Ford Beebe, s Johnny Sheffield, Karen Sharpe.
SAFARI DRUMS (Monogram, 1953) d Ford Beebe, s Johnny Sheffield, Barbara Bestar, Emory Parnell.
THE GOLDEN IDOL (Monogram, 1953) d Ford Beebe, s Johnny Sheffield, Anne Kimball.
KILLER LEOPARD (Monogram, 1954) d Ford Beebe, s Johnny Sheffield, Russ Conway.
LORD OF THE JUNGLE (Monogram, 1955) d Ford Beebe, s Johnny Sheffield, Wayne Morris, Nancy Hale.

87. BONZO
An overly intelligent chimpanzee stars in these films.
BEDTIME FOR BONZO (Univesal, 1951) d Frederick de Cordova, s Ronald Reagan, Diana Lynn.
BONZO GOES TO COLLEGE (Universal, 1952) d Frederick de Cordova, s Maureen O'Sullivan, Charles Drake.

88. BOOGEYMAN
These horror films involve a haunted broken mirror.
THE BOOGEYMAN (Interbest American Enterprises, 1980) [aka THE BOGEY MAN] d Ulli Lommel, s Suzanna Love; Michael Love, John Carradine.
THE BOOGEYMAN II (New West, 1983) [aka REVENGE OF THE BOOGEYMAN] d Bruce Starr, s Suzanna Love, Shana Hall, Ulli Lomell.

89. BOSTON BLACKIE
A former jewel thief and con artist turns good guy in the pictures based on Jack Boyle's book. There was also a Boston Blackie radio show in 1944-45 with Chester Morris and later Harlow Wilcox and a 1951 television program with Kent Taylor.
BOSTON BLACKIE'S LITTLE PAL (1918)
BLACKIE'S REDEMPTION (1919)
MISSING MILLIONS (1922)
THE FACE IN THE FOG (1922)
BOSTON BLACKIE (1923)
CROOKED ALLEY (1923)
THROUGH THE DARK (1924)
THE RETURN OF BOSTON BLACKIE (1927)
MEET BOSTON BLACKIE (Columbia, 1941)
CONFESSIONS OF BOSTON BLACKIE (Columbia, 1941)
ALIAS BOSTON BLACKIE (Columbia, 1942) d Robert Florey, s Chester Morris, Rochelle Hudson.
BOSTON BLACKIE GOES HOLLYWOOD (Columbia, 1942) d Lew Landers, s Chester Morris, Adele Mara.
AFTER MIDNIGHT WITH BOSTON BLACKIE (Columbia, 1943) d Lew Landers, s Chester Morris, George E. Stone.
ONE MYSTERIOUS NIGHT (Columbia, 1944) d Oscar Boetticher Jr., s Chester Morris, Richard Lane.
BOSTON BLACKIE BOOKED ON SUSPICION (Columbia, 1945) d Arthur Dreifuss, s Chester Morris, Lynn Merrick.
BOSTON BLACKIE'S RENDEZVOUS (Columbia, 1945) d Arthur Dreifuss, s Chester Morris, Nina Foch.
A CLOSE CALL FOR BOSTON BLACKIE (Columbia, 1946) d Lew Landers, s Chester Morris, Lynn Merrick.
THE PHANTOM THIEF (Columbia, 1946) d D. Ross Lederman, s Chester Morris, Jeff Donnell, Richard Lane.
BOSTON BLACKIE AND THE LAW (Columbia, 1946) D. Ross Lederman, s Chester Morris, Trudy Marshall.
TRAPPED BY BOSTON BLACKIE (Columbia, 1948) d Seymour Friedman, s Chester Morris, June Vincent, Richard Lane.
BOSTON BLACKIE'S CHINESE VENTURE (Columbia, 1949) d Seymour Friedman, s Chester Morris, Maylia, Richard Lane.

90. BOWERY BOYS
Slip Mahoney, Sach Debussy Jones, Gabe Moreno, Butch, Chuck and Whitey are members of a neighborhood gang who hang out at Louie Dombrowsky's sweet shop. (See also DEAD END KIDS, EAST SIDE KIDS and LITTLE TOUGH GUYS.)
IN FAST COMPANY (Monogram, 1946) d Del Lord, s Leo Gorcey, Huntz Hall, Bobby Jordan, Billy Benedict, David Gorcey.

50 MOTION PICTURE SERIES & SEQUELS

BOWERY BOMBSHELL (Monogram, 1946) d Phil Karlson, s Leo Gorcey, Huntz Hall, Bobby Jordan, Billy Benedict, David Gorcey.
LIVE WIRES (Monogram, 1946) d Phil Karlson, s Leo Gorcey, Huntz Hall, Bobby Jordan, Billy Benedict.
SPOOK BUSTERS (Monogram, 1946) d William Beaudine, s Leo Gorcey, Huntz Hall, Bobby Jordan, Billy Benedict, Gabriel Dell.
MR. HEX (Monogram, 1946) d William Beaudine, s Leo Gorcey, Huntz Hall, Bobby Jordan, David Gorcey, Gabriel Dell.
BOWERY BUCKAROOS (Monogram, 1947) d William Beaudine, s Leo Gorcey, Huntz Hall, Bobby Jordan, Billy Benedict, David Gorcey.
HARD BOILED MAHONEY (Monogram, 1947) d William Beaudine, s Leo Gorcey, Huntz Hall, Bobby Jordan, Billy Benedict, David Gorcey.
NEWS HOUNDS (Monogram, 1947) d William Beaudine, s Leo Gorcey, Huntz Hall, Bobby Jordan, Gabriel Dell, Billy Benedict.
ANGELS' ALLEY (Monogram, 1947) d William Beaudine, s Leo Gorcey, Huntz Hall, Bobby Jordan, Gabriel Dell, Billy Benedict.
JINX MONEY (Monogram, 1948) d William Beaudine, s Leo Gorcey, Huntz Hall, Bobby Jordan, Billy Benedict, David Gorcey.
SMUGGLERS COVE (Monogram, 1948) d William Beaudine, s Leo Gorcey, Huntz Hall, Bobby Jordan, Billy Benedict, David Gorcey.
TROUBLE MAKERS (Monogram, 1948) d Reginald Le Borg, s Leo Gorcey, Huntz Hall, Bobby Jordan, Billy Benedict, David Gorcey.
ANGELS IN DISGUISE (Monogram, 1949) d Jean Yarbrough, s Leo Gorcey, Huntz Hall, Gabriel Dell, Billy Benedict, David Gorcey, Bernard Gorcey.
BLONDE DYNAMITE (Monogram, 1950) d William Beaudine, s Leo Gorcey, Huntz Hall, Gabriel Dell, Billy Benedict, David Gorcey, Bernard Gorcey.
FIGHTING FOOLS (Monogram, 1949) d Reginald Le Borg, s Leo Gorcey, Huntz Hall, Gabriel Dell, Billy Benedict, David Gorcey, Bernard Gorcey.
HOLD THAT BABY (Monogram, 1949) d Reginald Le Borg, s Leo Gorcey, Huntz Hall, Gabriel Dell, Billy Benedict, David Gorcey, Bernard Gorcey.
MASTER MINDS (Monogram, 1949) d Jean Yarbrough, s Leo Gorcey, Huntz Hall, Gabriel Dell, Billy Benedict, David Gorcey, Bernard Gorcey.
BLUES BUSTERS (Monogram, 1950) d William Beaudine, s Leo Gorcey, Huntz Hall, Gabriel Dell, Billy Benedict, David Gorcey, Bernard Gorcey.
LUCKY LOSERS (Monogram, 1950) d William Beaudine, s Leo Gorcey, Huntz Hall, Gabriel Dell, Billy Benedict, David Gorcey, Bernard Gorcey.
TRIPLE TROUBLE (Monogram, 1950) d Jean Yarbrough, s Leo Gorcey, Huntz Hall, Gabriel Dell, Billy Benedict, David Gorcey, Bernard Gorcey.
BOWERY BATTALION (Monogram, 1951) d William Beaudine, s Leo Gorcey, Huntz Hall, Billy Benedict, David Gorcey, Bernard Gorcey.

CRAZY OVER HORSES (Monogram, 1951) d William Beaudine, s Leo Gorcey, Huntz Hall, Billy Benedict, David Gorcey, Bernard Gorcey.
GHOST CHASERS (Monogram, 1951) d William Beaudine, s Leo Gorcey, Huntz Hall, Billy Benedict, David Gorcey, Bernard Gorcey.
LET'S GO NAVY (Monogram, 1951) d William Beaudine, s Leo Gorcey, Huntz Hall, Billy Benedict, David Gorcey, Bernard Gorcey.
FEUDIN' FOOLS (Monogram, 1952) d William Beaudine, s Leo Gorcey, Huntz Hall, Billy Benedict, David Gorcey, Bernard Gorcey, Bennie Bartlett.
HERE COME THE MARINES (Monogram, 1952) d William Beaudine, s Leo Gorcey, Huntz Hall, Billy Benedict, David Gorcey, Bernard Gorcey, Bennie Bartlett.
HOLD THAT LINE (Monogram, 1952) d William Beaudine, s Leo Gorcey, Huntz Hall, David Gorcey, Bernard Gorcey.
NO HOLDS BARRED (Monogram, 1952) d William Beaudine, s Leo Gorcey, Huntz Hall, David Gorcey, Bernard Gorcey, Bennie Bartlett.
CLIPPED WINGS (Allied Artists, 1952) d Edward Bernds, s Leo Gorcey, Huntz Hall, David Gorcey, Bernard Gorcey, Bennie Bartlett.
JALOPY (Allied Artists, 1953) d William Beaudine, s Leo Gorcey, Huntz Hall, David Gorcey, Bernard Gorcey, Bennie Bartlett.
LOOSE IN LONDON (Allied Artists, 1953) d Edward Bernds, s Leo Gorcey, Huntz Hall, David Gorcey, Bernard Gorcey.
PRIVATE EYES (Allied Artists, 1953) d Edward Bernds, s Leo Gorcey, Huntz Hall, Bernard Gorcey, Bennie Bartlett.
BOWERY BOYS MEET THE MONSTERS (Allied Artists, 1954) d Edward Bernds, s Leo Gorcey, Huntz Hall, Bernard Gorcey, Bennie Bartlett, David Gorcey.
JUNGLE GENTS (Allied Artists, 1954) d Edward Bernds, s Leo Gorcey, Huntz Hall, Bernard Gorcey, Bennie Bartlett, David Gorcey.
PARIS PLAYBOYS (Allied Artists, 1954) d William Beaudine, s Leo Gorcey, Huntz Hall, Bernard Gorcey.
BOWERY TO BAGDAD (Allied Artists, 1955) d Edward Bernds, s Leo Gorcey, Huntz Hall, Bernard Gorcey, Bennie Bartlett, David Gorcey.
HIGH SOCIETY (Allied Artists, 1955) d William Beaudine, s Leo Gorcey, Huntz Hall, Bernard Gorcey, Bennie Bartlett.
JAIL BUSTERS (Allied Artists, 1955) d William Beaudine, s Leo Gorcey, Huntz Hall, Bernard Gorcey.
SPY CHASERS (Allied Artists, 1955) d Edward Bernds, s Leo Gorcey, Huntz Hall, David Gorcey, Bernard Gorcey.
DIG THAT URANIUM (Allied Artists, 1956) d Edward Bernds, s Leo Gorcey, Huntz Hall, Bernard Gorcey, David Gorcey, Bennie Bartlett.
CRASHING LAS VEGAS (Allied Artists, 1956) d Jean Yarbrough, s Leo Gorcey, Huntz Hall, David Gorcey.
FIGHTING TROUBLE (Allied Artists, 1956) d George Blair, s Huntz Hall, Stanley Clements, David Gorcey.
HOT SHOTS (Allied Artists, 1956) d Jean Yarbrough, s Huntz Hall, Stanley Clements, David Gorcey.

52 MOTION PICTURE SERIES & SEQUELS

SPOOK CHASERS (Allied Artists, 1957) d George Blair, s Huntz Hall, Stanley Clements, David Gorcey.
HOLD THAT HYPNOTIST (Allied Artists, 1957) d Austen Jewell, s Huntz Hall, Stanley Clements.
LOOKING FOR DANGER (Allied Artists, 1957) d Austen Jewell, s Huntz Hall, Stanley Clements.
UP IN SMOKE (Allied Artists, 1958) d William Beaudine, s Huntz Hall, Stanley Clements.
IN THE MONEY (Allied Artists, 1958) d William Beaudine, s Huntz Hall, Stanley Clements.

91. BOY FRIENDS, THE
These are buddy pictures.
DOCTOR'S ORDERS (MGM, 1930) d Arch Heath, s Mickey Daniels, Grady Sutton, David Sharpe, Mary Kornman.
BIGGER AND BETTER (MGM, 1930) d Edgar Kennedy, s Mickey Daniels, Grady Sutton, David Sharpe, Mary Kornman.
LADIES LAST (MGM, 1930) d George Stevens, s Mickey Daniels, Grady Sutton, David Sharpe, Mary Kornman.
BLOOD AND THUNDER (MGM, 1931) d George Stevens, s Mickey Daniels, Grady Sutton, David Sharpe, Mary Kornman.
HIGH GEAR (MGM, 1931) d George Stevens, s Mickey Daniels, Grady Sutton, David Sharpe, Mary Kornman.
LOVE FEVER (MGM, 1931) d Robert McGowan, s Mickey Daniels, Grady Sutton, David Sharpe, Mary Kornman, Thelma Todd.
AIR TIGHT (MGM, 1931) d George Stevens, s Mickey Daniels, Grady Sutton, David Sharpe, Mary Kornman.
CALL A COP (MGM, 1931) d George Stevens, s Mickey Daniels, Grady Sutton, David Sharpe, Mary Kornman.
MAMA LOVES PAPA (MGM, 1931) d George Stevens, s Mickey Daniels, Grady Sutton, David Sharpe, Mary Kornman.
THE KICKOFF (MGM, 1931) d George Stevens, s Mickey Daniels, Grady Sutton, David Sharpe, Mary Kornman.
LOVE PAINS (MGM, 1932) d James Horne, s Mickey Daniels, Grady Sutton, David Sharpe, Mary Kornman.
THE KNOCKOUT (MGM, 1932) d Anthony Mack, s Mickey Daniels, Grady Sutton, David Sharpe, Mary Kornman.
YOU'RE TELLING ME (MGM, 1932) d Anthony Mack and Lloyd French, s Mickey Daniels, Grady Sutton, David Sharpe, Mary Kornman.
TOO MANY WOMEN (MGM, 1932) d Anthony Mack and Lloyd French, s Mickey Daniels, Grady Sutton, David Sharpe, Mary Kornman.
WILD BABIES (MGM, 1932) d Anthony Mack and Lloyd French, s Mickey Daniels, Grady Sutton, Mary Kornman, Charles Rogers.

92. BOYS TOWN
Father Flanagan works to establish a place for troubled boys.

BOYS TOWN (MGM, 1938) d Norman Taurog, s Spencer Tracy, Mickey Rooney.
MEN OF BOYS TOWN (MGM, 1941) d Norman Taurog, s Spencer Tracy, Mickey Rooney.

93. BREAKIN'
Breakdancing is the theme of these films. In the second entry, three young dancers try to save a youth center.
BREAKIN' (MGM/UA-Cannon Group, 1984) d Joel Silberg, s Lucinda Dickey, Adolfo Quinones.
BREAKIN' 2: ELECTRIC BOOGALOO (Tri-Star, 1984) d Sam Firstenberg, s Lucinda Dickey, Adolfo Quinones, Michael Chambers.

94. BRENDA STARR
These pictures are based on Dale Messick's newspaper comic strip featuring a redheaded journalist. The character first appeared in 1940, working for *The Flash*.
BRENDA STARR -- REPORTER (Columbia, 1945) (serial) d Wallace W. Fox, s Joan Woodbury, Kane Richmond.
BRENDA STARR (1989) d Robert Ellis Miller, s Brooke Shields, Tony Peck.

95. BRIDGE ON THE RIVER KWAI, THE
The prison camp dramas are based on a novel by Pierre Boulle.
THE BRIDGE ON THE RIVER KWAI (Columbia, 1957) d David Lean, s William Holden, Alec Guinness.
RETURN FROM THE RIVER KWAI (Tri-Star Pictures, 1989) d Andrew McLaglen, s Nick Tate, Denholm Elliott.

96. BROADWAY MELODY
The pictures are set in the backstage (and front) world of the musical theater.
BROADWAY MELODY OF 1936 (MGM, 1935) d Roy Del Ruth, s Jack Benny, Eleanor Powell, Robert Taylor.
BROADWAY MELODY OF 1938 (MGM, 1937) d Roy Del Ruth, s Robert Taylor, Eleanor Powell.
BROADWAY MELODY of 1940 (MGM, 1940) d Norman Taurog, s Fred Astaire, George Murphy, Eleanor Powell.

97. BRONCO BILLY
G. M. "Bronco Billy" Anderson (1882-1971) appeared in an Edwin S. Porter one-reeler, THE GREAT TRAIN ROBBERY (1903), and went on to act in, produce and direct films, mostly Westerns. In 1907-16, for his own (in partnership with George K. Spoor) Essanay company, he is said to have made a Bronco Billy two-reel Western a week for 376 weeks. Anderson's leading ladies included Evelyn Selbie. The listing here is incomplete. (See also RANCH GIRL and THE SHERIFF.)
BRONCO BILLY AND THE BABY (Essanay, 1907) s G.M. "Bronco Billy" Anderson.

BRONCO BILLY'S REDEMPTION (Essanay, 1910) s G.M. "Bronco Billy" Anderson.
BRONCO BILLY'S ADVENTURE (Essanay, 1911) s G.M. "Bronco Billy" Anderson.
BRONCO BILLY OUTWITTED (Essanay, 1912) s G.M. "Bronco Billy" Anderson.
ALKALI BESTS BRONCO BILLY (Essanay, 1912) s G.M. "Bronco Billy" Anderson.
BRONCO BILLY'S LOVE AFFAIR (Essanay, 1912) s G.M. "Bronco Billy" Anderson.
BRONCO BILLY'S MEXICAN WIFE (Essanay, 1912) s G.M. "Bronco Billy" Anderson.
BRONCO BILLY'S HEART (Essanay, 1912) s G.M. "Bronco Billy" Anderson.
BRONCO BILLY'S PROMISE (Essanay, 1912) s G.M. "Bronco Billy" Anderson.
THE REWARD OF BRONCO BILLY (Essanay, 1912) s G.M. "Bronco Billy" Anderson.
BRONCO BILLY'S OATH (Essanay, 1913) s G.M. "Bronco Billy" Anderson.
WHY BRONCO BILLY LEFT BEAR COUNTRY (Essanay, 1913) s G.M. "Bronco Billy" Anderson.
BRONCO BILLY AND THE MAID (Essanay, 1913) s G.M. "Bronco Billy" Anderson.
BRONCO BILLY AND THE OUTLAW'S MOTHER (Essanay, 1913) s G.M. "Bronco Billy" Anderson.
BRONCO BILLY'S BROTHER (Essanay, 1913) s G.M. "Bronco Billy" Anderson.
BRONCO BILLY'S GUNPLAY (Essanay, 1913) s G.M. "Bronco Billy" Anderson.
BRONCO BILLY'S LAST DEED (Essanay, 1913) s G.M. "Bronco Billy" Anderson.
BRONCO BILLY'S WARD (Essanay, 1913) s G.M. "Bronco Billy" Anderson.
BRONCO BILLY AND THE SHERIFF'S KID (Essanay, 1913) s G.M. "Bronco Billy" Anderson.
INFLUENCE ON BRONCO BILLY (Essanay, 1913) s G.M. "Bronco Billy" Anderson.
BRONCO BILLY AND THE SQUATTER'S DAUGHTER (Essanay, 1913) s G.M. "Bronco Billy" Anderson.
BRONCO BILLY AND THE STEP-SISTERS (Essanay, 1913) s G.M. "Bronco Billy" Anderson.
BRONCO BILLY'S SISTER (Essanay, 1913) s G.M. "Bronco Billy" Anderson.
BRONCO BILLY'S GRATEFULNESS (Essanay, 1913) s G.M. "Bronco Billy" Anderson.
BRONCO BILLY'S WAY (Essanay, 1913) s G.M. "Bronco Billy" Anderson.
BRONCO BILLY'S SECRET (Essanay, 1913) s G.M. "Bronco Billy" Anderson.
BRONCO BILLY'S FIRST ARREST (Essanay, 1913) s G.M. "Bronco Billy" Anderson.

BRONCO BILLY'S SQUARENESS (Essanay, 1913) s G.M. "Bronco Billy" Anderson.
BRONCO BILLY'S CHRISTMAS DEED (Essanay, 1913) s G.M. "Bronco Billy" Anderson.
BRONCO BILLY'S INDIAN ROMANCE (Essanay, 1914) s G.M. "Bronco Billy" Anderson.
TREACHERY OF BRONCO BILLY'S PAL (Essanay, 1914) s G.M. "Bronco Billy" Anderson.
BRONCO BILLY AND THE RATTLER (Essanay, 1914) s G.M. "Bronco Billy" Anderson.
BRONCO BILLY'S TRUE LOVE (Essanay, 1914) s G.M. "Bronco Billy" Anderson.
BRONCO BILLY -- GUN MAN (Essanay, 1914) s G.M. "Bronco Billy" Anderson.
BRONCO BILLY'S CLOSE CALL (Essanay, 1914) s G.M. "Bronco Billy" Anderson.
BRONCO BILLY'S SERMON (Essanay, 1914) s G.M. "Bronco Billy" Anderson.
BRONCO BILLY'S LEAP (Essanay, 1914) s G.M. "Bronco Billy" Anderson.
BRONCO BILLY'S CUNNING (Essanay, 1914) s G.M. "Bronco Billy" Anderson.
BRONCO BILLY'S DUTY (Essanay, 1914) s G.M. "Bronco Billy" Anderson.
BRONCO BILLY AND THE MINE SHARK (Essanay, 1914) s G.M. "Bronco Billy" Anderson.
BRONCO BILLY'S OUTLAW (Essanay, 1914) s G.M. "Bronco Billy" Anderson.
BRONCO BILLY'S JEALOUSY (Essanay, 1914) s G.M. "Bronco Billy" Anderson.
BRONCO BILLY'S PUNISHMENT (Essanay, 1914) s G.M. "Bronco Billy" Anderson.
BRONCO BILLY AND THE SHERIFF (Essanay, 1914) s G.M. "Bronco Billy" Anderson.
BRONCO BILLY GUARDIAN (Essanay, 1914) s G.M. "Bronco Billy" Anderson.
BRONCO BILLY AND THE BAD MAN (Essanay, 1914) s G.M. "Bronco Billy" Anderson.
BRONCO BILLY AND THE SETTLER'S DAUGHTER (Essanay, 1914) s G.M. "Bronco Billy" Anderson.
BRONCO BILLY AND THE RED HAND (Essanay, 1914) s G.M. "Bronco Billy" Anderson.
THE INTERFERENCE OF BRONCO BILLY (Essanay, 1914) s G.M. "Bronco Billy" Anderson.
BRONCO BILLY'S BIBLE (Essanay, 1914) s G.M. "Bronco Billy" Anderson.
BRONCO BILLY AND THE CLAIM JUMPERS (Essanay, 1914) s G.M. "Bronco Billy" Anderson.
BRONCO BILLY AND THE ESCAPED BANDIT (Essanay, 1914) s G.M. "Bronco Billy" Anderson.

BRONCO BILLY AND THE LAND GRABBER (Essanay, 1915) s G.M. "Bronco Billy" Anderson.
BRONCO BILLY AND THE LUMBER KING (Essanay, 1915) s G.M. "Bronco Billy" Anderson.
BRONCO BILLY AND THE POSSE (Essanay, 1915) s G.M. "Bronco Billy" Anderson.
BRONCO BILLY EVENS MATTERS (Essanay, 1915) s G.M. "Bronco Billy" Anderson.
BRONCO BILLY MISLED (Essanay, 1915) s G.M. "Bronco Billy" Anderson.
BRONCO BILLY WELL REPAID (Essanay, 1915) s G.M. "Bronco Billy" Anderson.
BRONCO BILLY'S MARRIAGE (Essanay, 1915) s G.M. "Bronco Billy" Anderson.
BRONCO BILLY AND THE FALSE NOTE (Essanay, 1915) s G.M. "Bronco Billy" Anderson.
BRONCO BILLY AND THE VIGILANTE (Essanay, 1915) s G.M. "Bronco Billy" Anderson.
BRONCO BILLY'S PARENTS (Essanay, 1915) s G.M. "Bronco Billy" Anderson.
BRONCO BILLY'S PROTEGE (Essanay, 1915) s G.M. "Bronco Billy" Anderson.
BRONCO BILLY AND THE BABY (Essanay, 1915) s G.M. "Bronco Billy" Anderson.
BRONCO BILLY'S SENTENCE (Essanay, 1915) s G.M. "Bronco Billy" Anderson.
BRONCO BILLY'S TEACHINGS (Essanay, 1915) s G.M. "Bronco Billy" Anderson.
BRONCO BILLY AND THE CARD SHARP (Essanay, 1915) s G.M. "Bronco Billy" Anderson.
BRONCO BILLY BEGINS LIFE ANEW (Essanay, 1915) s G.M. "Bronco Billy" Anderson.
BRONCO BILLY SHEEPMAN (Essanay, 1915) s G.M. "Bronco Billy" Anderson.
BRONCO BILLY'S GREASER DEPUTY (Essanay, 1915) s G.M. "Bronco Billy" Anderson.
BRONCO'S SURRENDER (Essanay, 1915) s G.M. "Bronco Billy" Anderson.
BRONCO BILLY'S WORD OF HONOR (Essanay, 1915) s G.M. "Bronco Billy" Anderson.
BRONCO BILLY'S COWARDLY BROTHER (Essanay, 1915) s G.M. "Bronco Billy" Anderson.
BRONCO BILLY STEPS IN (Essanay, 1915) s G.M. "Bronco Billy" Anderson.
BRONCO BILLY'S MARRIAGE (Essanay, 1915) s G.M. "Bronco Billy" Anderson.
BRONCO BILLY'S VENGEANCE (Essanay, 1915) s G.M. "Bronco Billy" Anderson.

MOTION PICTURE SERIES & SEQUELS 57

BRONCO BILLY AND THE REVENUE AGENT (Essanay, 1916) s G.M. "Bronco Billy" Anderson.

98. BROTHER RAT
Three military cadets have girl, money and school problems.
BROTHER RAT (Warner Brothers, 1938) d William Keighley, s Priscilla Lane, Wayne Morris, Jonnie Davis.
BROTHER RAT AND A BABY (Warner Brothers, 1940) d Ray Enright, s Priscilla Lane, Wayne Morris, Eddie Albert.

99. BUCK PRIVATES
Two sidewalk tie hustlers join the Army to avoid a confrontation with the police, and accidentally become heroes at boot camp. In the sequel, the boys are discharged.
BUCK PRIVATES (Universal, 1941) d Arthur Lubin, s Bud Abbott, Lou Costello, Andrews Sisters, Nat Pendleton.
BUCK PRIVATES COME HOME (Universal, 1947) d Charles T. Barton, s Bud Abbott, Lou Costello.

100. BUCK ROGERS
Buck Rogers was featured in the first American science fiction newspaper comic strip in 1929, adapted by Phil Nowlan from his novel *Armaggedon 2419* and drawn by Dick Calkins.
BUCK ROGERS (Universal, 1939) (twelve episodes) [aka DESTINATION SATURN, re-edited version] d Ford Beebe and Saul Goodkind, s Larry "Buster" Crabbe, Constance Moore.
BUCK ROGERS IN THE 25th CENTURY (Universal, 1979) d Daniel Haller, s Gil Gerard, Pamela Hensley, Erin Gray.

101. BUDDY MESSINGER COMEDIES
Broadway Distributing produced these short comedies with a cast of children.

102. BUD 'N' BEN WESTERNS
These are second-feature Westerns.
GIRL TROUBLE (Reliable, 1934) d Bernard B. Ray, s Jack Perrin, Ben Corbett, Lola Tate, Mary Draper.
ARIZONA NIGHTS (Reliable, 1934) d Bernard B. Ray, s Jack Perrin, Ben Corbett.
RAWHIDE MAIL (Reliable, 1934) d Bernard B. Ray, s Jack Perrin, Ben Corbett, Lillian Gilmore.
RAINBOW RIDERS (Reliable, 1934) d Bennett Cohen, s Jack Perrin, Ben Corbett, Virginia Browne Faire.
RIDIN' GENTS (Reliable, 1934) d Bennett Cohen, s Jack Perrin, Ben Corbett, Doris Hill.

103. BUDDY
The silent films feature a juvenile actor. The list may be incomplete.

58 MOTION PICTURE SERIES & SEQUELS

BUDDY'S FIRST CALL (Vitagraph, 1914) s Paul Kelly.
BUDDY'S DOWNFALL (Vitagraph, 1914) s Paul Kelly.
BUDDY'S FIRST CALL (Vitagraph, 1914) s Paul Kelly.

104. BULLDOG DRUMMOND
H.C. "Sapper" McNeile's fictional adventurer inspired these movies.
BULLDOG DRUMMOND (Astra National/Hollandia Film, 1922) s Carlyle Blackwell.
BULLDOG DRUMMOND'S THIRD ROUND (Astra National, 1925) [aka THE THIRD ROUND] d Jack Buchanan.
BULLDOG DRUMMOND (United Artists, 1929) d F. Richard Jones, s Ronald Colman, Joan Bennett.
TEMPLE TOWER (Fox, 1930) d Donald Gallagher, s Kenneth MacKenna, Marceline Day.
THE RETURN OF BULLDOG DRUMMOND (British International Pictures, 1934) d Walter Summers, s Ralph Richardson, Ann Todd.
BULLDOG DRUMMOND STRIKES BACK (United Artists, 1934) d Roy Del Ruth, s Ronald Colman, Loretta Young.
BULLDOG DRUMMOND ESCAPES (Paramount, 1936) s Ray Milland.
BULLDOG DRUMMOND AT BAY (Associated British Picture, 1937) d Norman Lee, s John Lodge, Dorothy Mackaill.
BULLDOG DRUMMOND ESCAPES (Paramount, 1937) d James Hogan, s Ray Milland, Heather Angel.
BULLDOG DRUMMOND COMES BACK (Paramount, 1937) d Louis King, s John Howard, John Barrymore.
BULLDOG DRUMMOND'S REVENGE (Paramount, 1937) d Louis King, s John Howard, John Barrymore.
BULLDOG DRUMMOND'S PERIL (Paramount, 1938) d James Hogan, s John Howard, John Barrymore, Louise Campbell.
BULLDOG DRUMMOND IN AFRICA (Paramount, 1938) d Louis King, s John Howard, Heather Angel.
ARREST BULLDOG DRUMMOND! (Paramount, 1938) d James Hogan, s John Howard, Heather Angel.
BULLDOG DRUMMOND'S SECRET POLICE (Paramount, 1939) d James Hogan, s John Howard, Heather Angel.
BULLDOG DRUMMOND'S BRIDE (Paramount, 1939) d James Hogan, s John Howard, Heather Angel.
BULLDOG DRUMMOND SEES IT THROUGH (1939) s Jack Buchanan.
BULLDOG DRUMMOND AT BAY (Columbia, 1947) d Sidney Salkow, s Ron Randell, Anita Louise.
BULLDOG DRUMMOND STRIKES BACK (Columbia, 1947) d Frank McDonald, s Ron Randell, Gloria Henry.
THE CHALLENGE (20th Century-Fox, 1948) d Jean Yarbrough, s Tom Conway, June Vincent.
THIRTEEN LEAD SOLDIERS (20th Century-Fox, 1948) d Frank McDonald, s Tom Conway, Helen Westcott.

CALLING BULLDOG DRUMMOND (MGM, 1951) d Victor Saville, s Walter Pidgeon, Margaret Leighton.
DEADLIER THAN THE MALE (Universal, 1967) d Ralph Thomas, s Richard Johnson, Elke Sommer.
SOME GIRLS DO (Universal, 1971) d Ralph Thomas, s Richard Johnson, Daliah Lavi.

104A. BUMPTIOUS
The films are silent comedies.
BUMPTIOUS TAKES UP AUTOMOBILING (Edison, 1910)
BUMPTIOUS PLAYS BASEBALL (Edison, 1910)
BUMPTIOUS AS AN AVIATOR (Edison, 1910)
HOW BUMPTIOUS PAPERED THE PARLOR (Edison, 1910)
THE JOKE THEY PLAYED ON BUMPTIOUS (Edison, 1910)
BUMPTIOUS AS A FIREMAN (Edison, 1910)
MR. BUMPTIOUS ON BIRDS (Edison, 1910
BUMPTIOUS AS ROMEO (Edison, 1911)
MR. BUMPTIOUS, DETECTIVE (Edison, 1911)

104B. BUNGLES
These are silent comedies.
BUNGLES' ELOPEMENT (1916)
BUNGLES ENFORCES THE LAW (1916)
BUNGLES LANDS A JOB (1916)
BUNGLES' RAINY DAYS (1916)

105. BUNNY
Silents featuring John Bunny and Flora Finch were also called BUNNYGRAPHS or BUNNYFINCHES. The list may be incomplete.
BUNNY's SUICIDE (Vitagraph, 1912) [aka BUNNY ATTEMPTS SUICIDE] s John Bunny, Flora Finch.
BUNNY ALL AT SEA (Vitagraph, 1912) s John Bunny, Flora Finch.
BUNNY AT THE DERBY (Vitagraph, 1912) s John Bunny, Flora Finch.
BUNNY AND THE DOGS (Vitagraph, 1912) s John Bunny, Flora Finch.
BUNNY AND THE TWINS (Vitagraph, 1912) s John Bunny, Flora Finch.
BUNNY BLARNEYED [aka THE BLARNEY STONE] (Vitagraph, 1913) s John Bunny, Flora Finch.
BUNNY AS A REPORTER (Vitagraph, 1913) s John Bunny, Flora Finch.
BUNNY FOR THE CAUSE (Vitagraph, 1913) s John Bunny, Flora Finch.
BUNNY'S MISTAKE (Vitagraph, 1913) s John Bunny, Flora Finch.
BUNNY'S DILEMMA (Vitagraph, 1913) s John Bunny, Flora Finch.
BUNNY VS. CUTEY (Vitagraph, 1913) s John Bunny, Flora Finch.
BUNNY AND THE BUNNY HUG (Vitaphone, 1913)
BUNNY'S HONEYMON (Vitagraph, 1913) s John Bunny, Flora Finch.
BUNNY BUYS A HAREM (Vitagraph, 1914) s John Bunny, Flora Finch.
BUNNY IN DISGUISE (Vitagraph, 1914) s John Bunny, Flora Finch.
BUNNY BACKSLIDES (Vitagraph, 1914) s John Bunny, Flora Finch.

BUNNY'S LITTLE BROTHER (Vitagraph, 1914) s John Bunny, Flora Finch.
BUNNY'S SCHEME (Vitagraph, 1914) s John Bunny, Flora Finch.
BUNNY'S SWELL AFFAIR (Vitagraph, 1914) s John Bunny, Flora Finch.
BUNNY'S BIRTHDAY (Vitagraph, 1914) s John Bunny, Flora Finch.
BUNNY'S MISTAKE (Vitagraph, 1914) s John Bunny, Flora Finch.
BUNNY IN BUNNYLAND (Vitagraph, 1915) s John Bunny, Flora Finch.

BUNNYFINCHES
See **BUNNY**

BUNNYGRAPHS
See **BUNNY**

106. *BURNS AND ALLEN*
George Burns and Gracie Allen team for these pictures. They also appeared on radio. (See also THE BIG BROADCAST.)
BURNS AND ALLEN IN LAMBCHOPS (Warner Brothers-Vitaphone, 1929) s George Burns, Gracie Allen.
FIT TO BE TIED (Paramount, 1930) d Ray Cozine, s George Burns, Gracie Allen.
PULLING A BONE (Paramount, 1930) d Howard Bretherton, s George Burns, Gracie Allen.
THE ANTIQUE SHOP (Paramount, 1931) d Ray Cozine, s George Burns, Gracie Allen, Chester Chute.
ONCE OVER, LIGHT (Paramount, 1931) d Howard Bretherton, s George Burns, Gracie Allen.
ONE HUNDRED PERCENT SERVICE (Paramount, 1932) d Ray Cozine, s George Burns, Gracie Allen.
OH MY OPERATION (Paramount, 1932) d Ray Cozine, s George Burns, Gracie Allen.
THE BABBLING BOOK (Paramount, 1932) d Aubrey Scotto, s George Burns, Gracie Allen, Donald Meek.
LET'S DANCE (Paramount, 1933) d Aubrey Scotto, s George Burns, Gracie Allen.
WALKING THE BABY (Paramount, 1933) d Aubrey Scotto, s George Burns, Gracie Allen.
INTERNATIONAL HOUSE (Paramount, 1933) d Edward Sutherland, s W.C. Fields, George Burns, Gracie Allen.
COLLEGE HUMOR (Paramount, 1933) d Wesley Ruggles, s George Burns, Gracie Allen, Bing Crosby, Jack Oakie.
SIX OF A KIND (Paramount, 1934) d Leo McCarey, s George Burns, Gracie Allen, W.C. Fields.
WE'RE NOT DRESSING (Paramount, 1934) d Norman Taurog, s George Burns, Gracie Allen, Bing Crosby, Carole Lombard, Ethel Merman.
MANY HAPPY RETURNS (Paramount, 1934) d Norman Z. McLeod, s George Burns, Gracie Allen, Guy Lombardo and his Orchestra.

MOTION PICTURE SERIES & SEQUELS 61

LOVE IN BLOOM (Paramount, 1935) d Elliott Nugent, s Joe Morrison, Dixie Lee, George Burns, Gracie Allen.
HERE COMES COOKIE (Paramount, 1935) d Norman Z. McLeod, s George Burns, Gracie Allen, George Barbier, Betty Furness.
COLLEGE HOLIDAY (Paramount, 1936) d Frank Tuttle, s Jack Benny, Martha Raye, George Burns, Gracie Allen.
A DAMSEL IN DISTRESS (RKO, 1937) d George Stevens, s George Burns, Gracie Allen, Fred Astaire, Joan Fontaine.
COLLEGE SWING (Paramount, 1938) d Raoul Walsh, s George Burns, Gracie Allen, Martha Raye, Bob Hope.
HONOLULU (MGM, 1939) d Eddie Buzzell, s Eleanor Powell, Robert Young, George Burns, Gracie Allen.

107. BUSTER BROWN
This comedy series derived from the comic strip created by R.F. Outcault in 1902. The films are alternatingly directed by Gus Meins and Francis Corby, for Stern Brothers, and feature Doreen Turner and Pete the Pup.
BUSTER'S JOKE ON PAPA (Edison, 1903)
BUSTER AND TIGE PUT A BALLOON VENDER OUT OF BUSINESS (Edison, 1904)
BUSTER BROWN AND THE DUDE (Edison, 1904)
BUSTER'S DOG TO THE RESCUE (Edison, 1904)
PRANKS OF BUSTER BROWN AND HIS DOG TIGE (Edison, 1904)
BUSTER MAKES ROOM FOR HIS MAMA AT THE BARGAIN COUNTER (Edison, 1904)
BUSTER AND HIS DOG: BE A GOOD BOY (American Mutoscope & Biograph, 1904)
BUSTER AND HIS DOG: BUSTER QUIET (American Mutoscope & Biograph, 1904)
BUSTER AND HIS DOG: GOOD DOG (American Mutoscope & Biograph, 1904)
BUSTER AND HIS DOG: THE INSTRUCTIONS (American Mutoscope & Biograph, 1904)

108. *BUSTER KEATON*
The silent and, later, talkie comedian was known as the "Great Stone Face." His films typically offer a sceptical man who must prove himself before a woman will consent to become his wife. He is indifferent to danger, and his inventiveness and athletic skills enable him to survive.
ONE WEEK (Metro, 1920) d Buster Keaton and Eddie Cline, s Buster Keaton.
CONVICT 13 (Metro, 1920) d Buster Keaton and Eddie Cline,s Buster Keaton.
THE SCARECROW (Metro, 1920) d Buster Keaton and Eddie Cline,s Buster Keaton.
NEIGHBORS (Metro, 1921) d Buster Keaton and Eddie Cline,s Buster Keaton

THE HAUNTED HOUSE (Metro, 1921) d Buster Keaton and Eddie Cline, s Buster Keaton.
HARD LUCK (Metro, 1921) d Buster Keaton and Eddie Cline, s Buster Keaton.
THE HIGH SIGN (Metro, 1921) d Buster Keaton and Eddie Cline, s Buster Keaton.
THE GOAT (Metro, 1921) d Buster Keaton and Mal St. Clair, s Buster Keaton.
THE PLAYHOUSE (First National, 1921) d Buster Keaton and Eddie Cline, s Buster Keaton.
THE BOAT (First National, 1921) d Buster Keaton and Eddie Cline, s Buster Keaton.
THE PALEFACE (First National, 1922) d Buster Keaton and Eddie Cline, s Buster Keaton.
COPS (First National, 1922) s Buster Keaton.
MY WIFE'S RELATIONS (First National, 1922) d Buster Keaton and Eddie Cline, s Buster Keaton.
THE BLACKSMITH (First National, 1922) d Buster Keaton and Mal St. Clair, s Buster Keaton.
THE FROZEN NORTH (First National, 1922) d Buster Keaton and Eddie Cline, s Buster Keaton.
DAY DREAMS (First National, 1922) d Buster Keaton and Eddie Cline, s Buster Keaton.
THE ELECTRIC HOUSE (First National, 1922) d Buster Keaton and Eddie Cline, s Buster Keaton.
THE BALLOONATIC (First National, 1923) d Buster Keaton and Eddie Cline, s Buster Keaton.
THE LOVE NEST (First National, 1923) d Buster Keaton, s Buster Keaton.
THE THREE AGES (MGM, 1923) d Buster Keaton and Eddie Cline, s Buster Keaton.
OUR HOSPITALITY (MGM, 1923) d Buster Keaton and John G. Blystone, s Buster Keaton.
SHERLOCK JR. (MGM, 1924) d Buster Keaton, s Buster Keaton.
THE NAVIGATOR (MGM, 1924) d Buster Keaton and Donald Crisp, s Buster Keaton.
SEVEN CHANCES (MGM, 1925) d Buster Keaton, s Buster Keaton.
GO WEST (MGM, 1925) d Buster Keaton, s Buster Keaton.
BATTLING BUTLER (MGM, 1926) d Buster Keaton, s Buster Keaton.
THE GENERAL (United Artists, 1927) d Buster Keaton and Clyde Bruckman, s Buster Keaton.
THE COLLEGE (United Artists, 1927) d James Horn, s Buster Keaton.
STEAMBOAT BILL JR. (United Artists, 1928) d Charles F. Reisner, s Buster Keaton.
THE CAMERAMAN (MGM, 1928) d Edward Sedgwick, s Buster Keaton.
SPITE MARRIAGE (MGM, 1929) d Edward Sedgwick, s Buster Keaton.
FREE AND EASY (MGM, 1930) [aka EASY GO] s Buster Keaton.
DOUGH BOYS (MGM, 1930) s Buster Keaton.

PARLOR BEDROOM AND BATH (MGM, 1930) s Buster Keaton.
SIDEWALKS OF NEW YORK (MGM, 1931) s Buster Keaton.
THE PASSIONATE PLUMBER (MGM, 1932) s Buster Keaton.
SPEAK EASILY (MGM, 1932) s Buster Keaton.
WHAT! NO BEER? (MGM, 1933) s Buster Keaton.
THE GOLD GHOST (Educational, 1933) d Charles Lamont, s Buster Keaton, Dorothy Dix.
ALLEZ OOP (Educational, 1934) d Charles Lamont, s Buster Keaton, Dorothy Sebastian.
PALOOKA FROM PADUCAH (Educational, 1935) d Charles Lamont, s Buster Keaton, Joe, Myra and Louise Keaton.
ONE-RUN ELMER (Educational, 1935) d Charles Lamont, s Buster Keaton, Lona Andre.
HAYSEED ROMANCE (Educational, 1935) d Charles Lamont, s Buster Keaton, Jane Jones.
AN OLD SPANISH CUSTOM (Educational, 1935) d Charles Lamont, s Buster Keaton, Vernon Dent.
TARS AND STRIPES (Educational, 1935) d Charles Lamont, s Buster Keaton, Vernon Dent.
THE E-FLAT MAN (Educational, 1935) d Charles Lamont, s Buster Keaton, Dorothea Kent.
THE TIMID YOUNG MAN (Educational, 1935) d Mack Sennett, s Buster Keaton, Lona Andre.
GRAND SLAM OPERA (Educational, 1936) d Charles Lamont, s Buster Keaton, Diana Lewis.
THREE ON A LIMB (Educational, 1936) d Charles Lamont, s Buster Keaton, Lona Andre.
BLUE BLAZES (Educational, 1936) d Raymond Kane, s Buster Keaton, Arthur Jarrett.
THE CHEMIST (Educational, 1936) d Al Christie, s Buster Keaton, Marlyn Stuart.
MIXED MAGIC (Educational, 1936) d Raymond Kane, s Buster Keaton, Eddie Lambert.
JAIL BAIT (Educational, 1937) d Charles Lamont, s Buster Keaton, Harold Goodwin.
DITTO (Educational, 1937) d Charles Lamont, s Buster Keaton, Gloria Brewster.
LOVE NEST ON WHEELS (Educational, 1937) d Charles Lamont, s Buster Keaton, Myra Keaton.
PEST FROM THE WEST (Columbia, 1939) d Del Lord, s Buster Keaton, Lorna Gray.
MOOCHING THROUGH GEORGIA (Columbia, 1939) d Jules White, s Buster Keaton, Monty Collins.
NOTHING BUT PLEASURE (Columbia, 1940) d Jules White, s Buster Keaton, Dorothy Appleby.
PARDON MY BERTH MARKS (Columbia, 1940) d Jules White, s Buster Keaton, Dorothy Appleby.

THE TAMING OF THE SNOOD (Columbia, 1940) d Jules White, s Buster Keaton, Dorothy Appleby.
THE SPOOK SPEAKS (Columbia, 1940) d Jules White, s Buster Keaton, Elsie Ames.
HIS EX MARKS THE SPOT (Columbia, 1940) d Jules White, s Buster Keaton, Elsie Ames.
SO YOU WON'T SQUAWK (Columbia, 1941) d Del Lord, s Buster Keaton,
SHE'S OIL MINE (Columbia, 1941) d Jules White, s Buster Keaton, Elsie Ames.
GENERAL NUISANCE (Columbia, 1941) d Jules White, s Buster Keaton, Elsie Ames.

109. BUTCH CASSIDY AND THE SUNDANCE KID
The Western movie about two outlaws prompted a prequel. (See also MRS. SUNDANCE.)
BUTCH CASSIDY AND THE SUNDANCE KID (20th Century-Fox, 1969) d George Roy Hill, s Paul Newman, Robert Redford, Katharine Ross.
BUTCH AND SUNDANCE: THE EARLY DAYS (20th Century-Fox, 1979) d Richard Lester, s William Katt, Tom Berenger.

110. BUZZY
The low-budget oaters feature a juvenile star, Robert "Buzz" Henry.
BUZZY RIDES THE RANGE (Ellkay 1940) d Richard C. Kahn, s Buzzy Henry, Dave O'Brien, Dorothy Short.
BUZZY AND THE PHANTOM PINTO (Ellkay 1941) [aka PHANTOM PINTO and WESTERN TERROR (Astor 1948)] d Richard C. Kahn, s Buzzy Henry, Dave O'Brien, Claire Rochelle.

Sgt. Callahan makes a point with recruits Martin and Mahoney in the action-comedy POLICE ACADEMY (1984).

111. CADDYSHACK
The Brushwood Country Club is the setting for these occasionally crude comedy pictures.
CADDYSHACK (Orion/Warner Brothers, 1980) d Harold Ramis, s Chevy Chase, Rodney Dangerfield, Bill Murray.
CADDYSHACK II (Warner Brothers, 1988) d Alan Arkush, s Jackie Mason, Chevy Chase.

112. CALAMITY ANNE
These silents were directed by Allan Dwan and starred Louise Lester. The list may not be complete.
CALAMITY ANNE'S WARD (1912) d Allan Dwan, s Louise Lester.
CALAMITY ANNE DETECTIVE (1913) d Allan Dwan, s Louise Lester.
CALAMITY ANNE'S INHERITANCE (1913) d Allan Dwan, s Louise Lester, J. Warren Kerrigan.

113. CANDY
These X-raters feature a naive heroine.
EROTIC ADVENTURES OF CANDY (Wonderful World of Video, 1978) d Gail Palmer, s Carol Connors, John C. Holmes.
CANDY GOES TO HOLLYWOOD (Wonderful World of Video, 1978) d Gail Palmer, s Carol Connors, John Leslie.

114. CANNON
Frank Cannon, the heavyweight private investigator, was featured on a CBS television series from 1971-76. The first picture below is a pilot, the second an out-of-retirement followup.
CANNON (Quin Martin Productions, 1971) (CBS-TV movie) d George McCowan, s William Conrad.
THE RETURN OF FRANK CANNON (QM Productions, 1980) (CBS-TV movie) d Corey Allen, s William Conrad.

115. CANNONBALL RUN, THE
A cross-country auto race is played for action and laughs in these pictures. Of like theme are non-series THE GUMBALL RALLY and CANNONBALL.
THE CANNONBALL RUN (Golden Harvest, 1981) d Hal Needham, s Burt Reynolds, Roger Moore, Farrah Fawcett.
CANNONBALL RUN II (Golden Harvest, 1984) d Hal Needham, s Burt Reynolds, Dom DeLuise, Shirley MacLaine.

116. CAPPY RICKS
Books by Peter B. Kyne featuring a West Coast lumberman and shipping magnate inspired these pictures.
CAPPY RICKS RETURNS (Republic, 1935) [aka CAPPY RICKS COMES BACK]
THE AFFAIRS OF CAPPY RICKS (Republic, 1937)
THE GO-GETTER (Warner Brothers, 1937)

117. CAPTAIN AMERICA
This comic book character created by Jack Kirby and Joe Simon first appeared in 1941, his garb an American flag motif, his mission eradicating the foreign enemy.
CAPTAIN AMERICA (Republic, 1944) (15 chapters) d John English and Elmer Clifton, s Dick Purcell, Lorna Gray, Lionel Atwill.
CAPTAIN AMERICA (Universal, 1979) (CBS-TV) d Rod Holcomb, s Reb Brown, Heather Menzies.
CAPTAIN AMERICA II (Universal, 1979) (CBS-TV movie) d Ivan Nagy, s Reb Brown, Connie Sellecca.
CAPTAIN AMERICA (21st Century Film, announced for 1990)

118. CAPTAIN BLOOD
Rafael Sabatini's trio of swashbuckling novels about Peter Blood (a British surgeon wrongly accused of crime) inspired these pictures.
CAPTAIN BLOOD (Vitagraph, 1924) d David Smith, s J. Warren Kerrigan, Jean Paige.
CAPTAIN BLOOD (Warner Brothers, 1935) d Michael Curtiz, s Errol Flynn, Olivia de Havilland.
CAPTAIN BLOOD (1947) d Frank Launder, s Stewart Granger, Kathleen Ryan.
FORTUNES OF CAPTAIN BLOOD (Columbia, 1950) d Gordon Douglas, s Louis Hayward, Patricia Medina.
CAPTAIN BLOOD, FUGITIVE (1952) s Louis Hayward.
CAPTAIN PIRATE (Columbia, 1952) d Ralph Murphy, s Louis Hayward, Patricia Medina.
CAPTAIN BLOOD (1960) d Andre Hunebelle, s Jean Marais, Elsa Martinelli.
SON OF CAPTAIN BLOOD (1962) d Tulio Demicheli, s Sean Flynn.

119. CAPTIVE WILD WOMAN
An orangutan is transformed by a scientist into a woman, and proceeds to run amuk.
CAPTIVE WILD WOMAN (Universal, 1943) d Edward Dmytryk, s John Carradine, Evelyn Ankers, Milburn Stone.
JUNGLE WOMAN (Universal, 1944) d Reginald LeBorg, s Acquanetta, Evelyn Ankers.
JUNGLE CAPTIVE (Universal, 1945) d Harold Young, s Otto Kruger, Amelita Ward.

119A. CAREER OF CRIME, A
These are early silent dramatic pictures.
A CAREER OF CRIME NO. 1 (American Mutoscope & Biograph, 1902)
A CAREER OF CRIME NO. 2 (American Mutoscope & Biograph, 1902)
A CAREER OF CRIME NO. 3 (American Mutoscope & Biograph, 1902)
A CAREER OF CRIME NO. 4 (American Mutoscope & Biograph, 1902)

120. CARMILLA TRILOGY
Sheridan LeFanu's vampire novel was the basis for several films.
VAMPYR (1931) d Carl Dryer, s Sybille Schmitz
BLOOD AND ROSES (1960) d Roger Vadim, s Elsa Martinelli.
THE VAMPIRE LOVERS (Hammer/AIP, 1970) d Roy Ward Baker, s Ingrid Pitt, Pippa Steele.
LUST FOR A VAMPIRE (Hammer, 1970) [aka TO LOVE A VAMPIRE] d Jimmy Sangster, s Yutte Stensgaard, Suzanna Leigh.
TWINS OF EVIL (Hammer, 1971) [aka THE GEMINI TWINS, VIRGIN VAMPIRES, TWINS OF DRACULA] d John Hough, s Peter Cushing, Madeleine Collinson, May Collinson.

121. CARPETBAGGERS, THE
Harold Robbins' novel of young man who inherits his father's fortune was the basis for the first picture. The followup is a prequel in which the hero tracks down his parents' killers.
THE CARPETBAGGERS (Paramount, 1964) d Edward Dmytryk, s George Peppard, Alan Ladd.
NEVADA SMITH (Paramount, 1966) d Henry Hathaway, s Steve McQueen, Karl Malden.

122. CARRY ON
These British farces feature a rotating cast of characters.
CARRY ON SERGEANT (Governor, 1959) d Gerald Thomas, s William Hartnell, Bob Monkhouse.
CARRY ON NURSE (Governor, 1960) d Gerald Thomas, s Kenneth Connor, Kenneth Williams.
CARRY ON TEACHER (Governor, 1962) d Gerald Thomas, s Ted Ray, Kenneth Connor.
CARRY ON CONSTABLE (Governor Films, 1961)
CARRY ON REGARDLESS (Anglo-Amalgamated, 1961) d Gerald Thomas, s Sidney James, Kenneth Connor.
CARRY ON CRUISING (Anglo-Amalgamated, 1962) d Gerald Thomas, s Sidney James, Kenneth Williams.
CARRY ON CABBIE (Warner Brothers-Pathe, 1963) [aka CALL ME A CAB] d Gerald Thomas, s Sidney James, Hattie Jacques, Kenneth Connor.
CARRY ON JACK (Warner Brothers-Pathe, 1963) [aka CARRY ON VENUS] d Gerald Thomas, s Bernard Cribbins, Juliet Mills.
CARRY ON CLEO (Warner Brothers-Pathe, 1965) d Gerald Thomas, s Amanda Barrie, Sidney James, Kenneth Williams, Joan Sims.
CARRY ON SPYING (Warner Brothers-Pathe, 1965) d Gerald Thomas, s Kenneth Williams, Barbara Windsor.
CARRY ON COWBOY (Warner Brothers-Pathe, 1966) d Gerald Thomas, s Sidney James, Kenneth Williams.
CARRY ON SCREAMING (Warner Brothers-Pathe, 1966) d Gerald Thomas, s Harry H. Corbett, Kenneth Williams, Fenella Fielding.

CARRY ON DOCTOR (Rank, 1968) d Gerald Thomas, s Frankie Howerd, Kenneth Williams.
CARRY ON UP THE KHYBER (Rank, 1968) d Gerald Thomas, s Sidney James, Kenneth Williams.
CARRY ON AGAIN DOCTOR (Rank, 1969) d Gerald Thomas, s Kenneth Williams, Sidney James.
CARRY ON CAMPING (Rank, 1969) d Gerald Thomas, s Sidney James, Kenneth Williams.
CARRY ON LOVING (Rank, 1970) d Gerald Thomas, s Sidney James, Kenneth Williams.
CARRY ON UP THE JUNGLE (Rank, 1970) d Gerald Thomas, s Frankie Howerd, Sidney James.
CARRY ON AT YOUR CONVENIENCE (1971) d Gerald Thomas, s Sidney James, Joan Simms.
CARRY ON HENRY VIII (Rank/American International, 1972) [aka CARRY ON HENRY] d Gerald Thomas, s Sidney James, Kenneth Williams, Joan Sims.
CARRY ON YOUR MATRON
CARRY ON ABROAD
CARRY ON GIRLS
CARRY ON DICK
CARRY ON BEHIND (1975) d Gerald Thomas, s Elke Sommer, Kenneth Williams.
CARRY ON ENGLAND (Fox/Rank, 1976) d Gerald Thomas, s Kenneth Connor, Windsor Davies.
CARRY ON EMMANUELLE (Hemdale International, 1978) d Gerald Thomas, s Suzanne Danielle, Kenneth Williams.

122A. CASEY
These pictures are early silent comedies.
CASEY AND HIS NEIGHBOR'S GOAT (Edison, 1903)
CASEY'S CHRISTENING (Edison, 1904)
CASEY'S FRIGHTFUL DREAM (Edison, 1905)

123. CAT PEOPLE
A woman has the ability to turn into a panther.
CAT PEOPLE (RKO 1942) d Jacques Tourneur, s Simone Simon, Kent Smith.
THE CURSE OF THE CAT PEOPLE (RKO, 1944) d Robert Wise, Gunther V. Fritsch, s Simone Simon, Kent Smith.
CAT PEOPLE (Universal/RKO, 1982) d Paul Schraeder, s Natassia Kinski, Malcolm McDowell.

124. CAUGHT FROM BEHIND
These are adult films.
CAUGHT FROM BEHIND (Hollywood, 1983) d Hal Freeman, s Ali Moore, Ron Jeremy.

CAUGHT FROM BEHIND II (Hollywood, 1984) d Hal Freeman, s Rose Marie.
CAUGHT FROM BEHIND III (Hollywood, 1985) d Hal Freeman, s Ali Moore.
CAUGHT FROM BEHIND IV (Hollywood, 1986) d Hal Freeman, s Keli Richards.
CAUGHT FROM BEHIND V (Hollywood, 1986) d Ron Jeremy, s Patti Petite, Billy Dee.
CAUGHT FROM BEHIND VI (Hollywood, 1986) d Hal Freeman, s Kari Foxx, Troy Tanier.

125. C. AUGUSTE DUPIN
Edgar Allan Poe wrote three stories about a consulting detective; these are the cinema versions.
THE MURDERS IN THE RUE MORGUE (Sol. A. Rosenberg Productions, 1914)
MURDERS IN THE RUE MORGUE (Universal, 1932) d Robert Florey, s Leon Waycoff, Bela Lugosi.
MYSTERY OF MARIE ROGET (Universal, 1942) d Phil Rosen, s Patric Knowles, Maria Montez.
PHANTOM OF THE RUE MORGUE (Warner Brothers, 1954) (in 3-D) d Roy Del Ruth, s Steve Forrest, Karl Malden.
MURDERS IN THE RUE MORGUE (American International, 1971) d Gordon Hessler, s Jason Robards, Christine Kaufmann.

126. CHANDU THE MAGICIAN
Spiritualist Chandu, Master of White Magic, battles thugs.
CHANDU THE MAGICIAN (Fox, 1932) d William Cameron Menzies and Marcel Varnel, s Edmund Lowe, Bela Lugosi, Irene Ware.
THE RETURN OF CHANDU (THE MAGICIAN) (1934) (twelve chapters) d Ray Taylor, s Bela Lugosi, Maria Alba.
CHANDU AND THE MAGIC ISLE

127. CHARLEY CHASE
Chase was a popular silent and sound film comedian. Listed here are talkie shorts only. His character frequently is a dapper and smart if naive young man caught in bizarre situations. In some he is married, in others he is single and has a sharp eye for the ladies.
AT FIRST SIGHT (Hal Roach/Pathe, 1924) s Charley Chase.
ONE OF THE FAMILY (Hal Roach/Pathe, 1924) s Charley Chase.
JUST A MINUTE (Hal Roach/Pathe, 1924) s Charley Chase.
POWDER AND SMOKE (Hal Roach/Pathe, 1924) s Charley Chase.
A PERFECT LADY (Hal Roach/Pathe, 1924) s Charley Chase.
HARD KNOCKS (Hal Roach/Pathe, 1924) s Charley Chase.
LOVE'S DETOUR (Hal Roach/Pathe, 1924) s Charley Chase.
DON'T FORGET (Hal Roach/Pathe, 1924) s Charley Chase.
THE FRAIDY CAT (Hal Roach/Pathe, 1924) s Charley Chase.

PUBLICITY PAYS (Hal Roach/Pathe, 1924) s Charley Chase.
APRIL FOOL (Hal Roach/Pathe, 1924) s Charley Chase.
POSITION WANTED (Hal Roach/Pathe, 1924) s Charley Chase.
YOUNG OLDFIELD (Hal Roach/Pathe, 1924) s Charley Chase.
STOLEN GOODS (Hal Roach/Pathe, 1924) s Charley Chase.
JEFFRIES, JR. (Hal Roach/Pathe, 1924) s Charley Chase.
WHY HUSBANDS GO MAD (Hal Roach/Pathe, 1924) s Charley Chase.
A TEN MINUTE EGG (Hal Roach/Pathe, 1924) s Charley Chase.
SEEING NELLIE HOME (Hal Roach/Pathe, 1924) s Charley Chase.
SWEET DADDY (Hal Roach/Pathe, 1924) s Charley Chase.
WHY MEN WORK (Hal Roach/Pathe, 1924) s Charley Chase.
OUTDOOR PAJAMAS (Hal Roach/Pathe, 1924) s Charley Chase.
SITTIN' PRETTY (Hal Roach/Pathe, 1924) s Charley Chase.
TOO MANY MAMAS (Hal Roach/Pathe, 1924) s Charley Chase.
BUNGALOW BOOBS (Hal Roach/Pathe, 1924) s Charley Chase.
ACCIDENTAL ACCIDENTS (Hal Roach/Pathe, 1924) s Charley Chase.
ALL WET (Hal Roach/Pathe, 1924) s Charley Chase.
THE POOR FISH (Hal Roach/Pathe, 1924) s Charley Chase.
THE ROYAL RAZZ (Hal Roach/Pathe, 1924) s Charley Chase.
HELLO BABY (Hal Roach/Pathe, 1924) s Charley Chase.
FIGHTING FLUID (Hal Roach/Pathe, 1924) s Charley Chase.
THE FAMILY ENTRANCE (Hal Roach/Pathe, 1925) s Charley Chase.
PLAIN AND FANCY GIRLS (Hal Roach/Pathe, 1925) s Charley Chase.
SHOULD HUSBANDS BE WATCHED (Hal Roach/Pathe, 1925) s Charley
    Chase.
HARD BOILED (Hal Roach/Pathe, 1925) s Charley Chase.
IS MARRIAGE THE BUNK? (Hal Roach/Pathe, 1925) s Charley Chase.
BAD BOY (Hal Roach/Pathe, 1925) s Charley Chase.
BIG RED RIDING HOOD (Hal Roach/Pathe, 1925) s Charley Chase.
LOOKING FOR SALLY (Hal Roach/Pathe, 1925) s Charley Chase.
WHAT PRICE GOOFY? (Hal Roach/Pathe, 1925) s Charley Chase.
ISN'T LIFE TERRIBLE? (Hal Roach/Pathe, 1925) s Charley Chase.
INNOCENT HUSBANDS (Hal Roach/Pathe, 1925) s Charley Chase.
NO FATHER TO GUIDE HIM (Hal Roach/Pathe, 1925) s Charley Chase.
THE CARETAKER'S DAUGHTER (Hal Roach/Pathe, 1925) s Charley Chase.
THE UNEASY THREE (Hal Roach/Pathe, 1925) s Charley Chase.
HIS WOODEN WEDDING (Hal Roach/Pathe, 1925) s Charley Chase.
CHARLEY, MY BOY (Hal Roach/Pathe, 1926) s Charley Chase.
MAMA BEHAVE (Hal Roach/Pathe, 1926) s Charley Chase.
DOG SHY (Hal Roach/Pathe, 1926) s Charley Chase.
MUM'S THE WORD (Hal Roach/Pathe, 1926) s Charley Chase.
LONG FLIV THE KING (Hal Roach/Pathe, 1926) s Charley Chase.
MIGHTY LIKE A MOOSE (Hal Roach/Pathe, 1926) s Charley Chase.
CRAZY LIKE A FOX (Hal Roach/Pathe, 1926) s Charley Chase.
BROMO AND JULIET (Hal Roach/Pathe, 1926) s Charley Chase.
TELL 'EM NOTHING (Hal Roach/Pathe, 1926) s Charley Chase.
BE YOUR AGE (Hal Roach/Pathe, 1926) s Charley Chase.

THERE AIN'T NO SANTA CLAUS (Hal Roach/Pathe, 1926) s Charley Chase.
MANY SCRAPPY RETURNS (Hal Roach-MGM, 1927) s Charley Chase.
ARE BRUNETTES SAFE? (Hal Roach-MGM, 1927) s Charley Chase.
A ONE MAMA MAN (Hal Roach-MGM, 1927) s Charley Chase.
FORGOTTEN SWEETIES (Hal Roach-MGM, 1927) s Charley Chase.
BIGGER AND BETTER BLONDES (Hal Roach-MGM, 1927) s Charley Chase.
FLUTTERING HEARTS (Hal Roach-MGM, 1927) s Charley Chase.
WHAT WOMEN DID FOR ME (Hal Roach-MGM, 1927) s Charley Chase.
NOW I'LL TELL YOU ONE (Hal Roach-MGM, 1927) s Charley Chase.
ASSISTANT WIVES (Hal Roach-MGM, 1927) s Charley Chase.
THE STING OF STINGS (Hal Roach-MGM, 1927) s Charley Chase.
THE LIGHTER THAT FAILED (Hal Roach-MGM, 1927) s Charley Chase.
THE WAY OF ALL PANTS (Hal Roach-MGM, 1927) s Charley Chase.
US (Hal Roach-MGM, 1927) s Charley Chase.
NEVER THE DAMES SHALL MEET (Hal Roach-MGM, 1927) s Charley Chase.
ALL FOR NOTHING (Hal Roach-MGM, 1928) s Charley Chase.
THE FAMILY GROUP (Hal Roach-MGM, 1928) s Charley Chase.
ACHING YOUTHS (Hal Roach-MGM, 1928) s Charley Chase.
LIMOUSINE LOVE (Hal Roach-MGM, 1928) s Charley Chase.
THE FIGHTING PEST (Hal Roach-MGM, 1928) s Charley Chase.
IMAGINE MY EMBARRASSMENT (Hal Roach-MGM, 1928) s Charley Chase.
IS EVERYBODY HAPPY? (Hal Roach-MGM, 1928) s Charley Chase.
ALL PARTS (Hal Roach-MGM, 1928) s Charley Chase.
THE BOOSTER (Hal Roach-MGM, 1928) s Charley Chase.
CHASING HUSBANDS (Hal Roach-MGM, 1928) s Charley Chase.
RUBY LOVE (Hal Roach-MGM, 1928) s Charley Chase.
OFF TO BUFFALO (Hal Roach-MGM, 1928) s Charley Chase.
THIN TWINS (Hal Roach-MGM, 1928) s Charley Chase.
MOVIE NIGHT (Hal Roach-MGM, 1928) s Charley Chase.
THE BIG SQUAWK (Roach-MGM, 1929) d Warren Doane, s Charley Chase, Nena Quartaro.
LEAPING LOVE (Roach-MGM, 1929) d Warren Doane, s Charley Chase, Isabelle Keith.
SNAPPY SNEEZER (Roach-MGM, 1929) d Warren Doane, s Charley Chase, Thelma Todd.
CRAZY FEET (Roach-MGM, 1929) d Warren Doane, s Charley Chase, Thelma Todd.
STEPPING OUT (Roach-MGM, 1929) d Warren Doane, s Charley Chase, Thelma Todd.
GREAT GOBS (Roach-MGM, 1929) d Warren Doane, s Charley Chase, Edgar Kennedy.
THE REAL McCOY (MGM-Roach, 1930) d Warren Doane, s Charley Chase, Thelma Todd.

WHISPERING WHOOPEE (MGM-Roach, 1930) d James W. Horne, s Charley Chase, Thelma Todd.
ALL TEED UP (MGM-Roach, 1930) d Edgar Kennedy, s Charley Chase, Thelma Todd.
FIFTY MILLION HUSBANDS (MGM-Roach, 1930) d Edgar Kennedy and James W. Horne, s Charley Chase, Ruth Hiatt.
FAST WORK (MGM-Roach, 1930) d James W. Horne, s Charley Chase, June Marlowe.
GIRL SHOCK (MGM-Roach, 1930) d James W. Horne, s Charley Chase, Carmen Guerrero.
DOLLAR DIZZY (MGM-Roach, 1930) d James W. Horne, s Charley Chase, Thelma Todd.
LOOSER THAN LOOSE (MGM-Roach, 1930) d James W. Horne, s Charley Chase, Thelma Todd.
HIGH C'S (MGM-Roach, 1930) d James W. Horne, s Charley Chase, Thelma Todd.
THUNDERING TENORS (MGM-Roach, 1931) d James W. Horne, s Charley Chase, Lillian Elliott.
THE PIP FROM PITTSBURGH (MGM-Roach, 1931) d James Parrott, s Charley Chase, Thelma Todd.
ROUGH SEAS (MGM-Roach, 1931) d James Parrott, s Charley Chase, Thelma Todd.
ONE OF THE SMITHS (MGM-Roach, 1931) d James Parrott, s Charley Chase, James Finlayson.
THE PANIC IS ON (MGM-Roach, 1931) d James Parrott, s Charley Chase, Virginia Whiting.
SKIP THE MALOO! (MGM-Roach, 1931) d James Parrott, s Charley Chase, Jacqueline Wells.
WHAT A BOZO! (MGM-Roach, 1931) d James Parrott, s Charley Chase, Gay Seabrook.
THE HASTY MARRIAGE (MGM-Roach, 1931) d Gil Pratt, s Charley Chase, Lillian Elliott.
THE TABASCO KID (MGM-Roach, 1932) d James W. Horne, s Charley Chase, Frances Lee.
THE NICKEL NURSER (MGM-Roach, 1932) d Warren Doane, s Charley Chase, Thelma Todd.
IN WALKED CHARLEY (MGM-Roach, 1932) d Warren Doane, s Charley Chase, Jacqueline Wells.
FIRST IN WAR (MGM-Roach, 1932) d Warren Doane, s Charley Chase, Luis Alberni.
YOUNG IRONSIDES (MGM-Roach, 1932) d James Parrott, s Charley Chase, Muriel Evans.
GIRL GRIEF (MGM-Roach, 1932) d James Parrott, s Charley Chase, Muriel Evans.
NOW WE'LL TELL ONE (MGM-Roach, 1932) d James Parrott, s Charley Chase, Muriel Evans.

MOTION PICTURE SERIES & SEQUELS 73

MR. BRIDE (MGM-Roach, 1932) d James Parrott, s Charley Chase, Muriel Evans.
FALLEN ARCHES (MGM-Roach, 1933) d Gus Meins, s Charley Chase, Muriel Evans.
NATURE IN THE WRONG (MGM-Roach, 1933) s Charley Chase, Muriel Evans.
HIS SILENT RACKET (MGM-Roach, 1933) s Charley Chase, Muriel Evans.
ARABIAN NIGHTS (MGM-Roach, 1933) s Charley Chase, Muriel Evans.
SHERMAN SAID IT (MGM-Roach, 1933) d Charles Parrott, s Charley Chase, Nita Pike.
MIDSUMMER MUSH (MGM-Roach, 1933) d Charles Parrott, s Charley Chase, Betty Mack.
LUNCHEON AT TWELVE (MGM-Roach, 1933) d Charles Parrott, s Charley Chase, Betty Mack.
THE CRACKED ICEMAN (MGM-Roach, 1934) d Charles Parrott and Eddie Dunn, s Charley Chase, Betty Mack.
FOUR PARTS (MGM-Roach, 1934) d Charles Parrott and Eddie Dunn, s Charley Chase, Betty Mack.
I'LL TAKE VANILLA (MGM-Roach, 1934) d Charles Parrott and Eddie Dunn, s Charley Chase, Betty Mack.
ANOTHER WILD IDEA (MGM-Roach, 1934) d Charles Parrott and Eddie Dunn, s Charley Chase, Betty Mack.
IT HAPPENED ONE DAY (MGM-Roach, 1934) d Charles Parrott and Eddie Dunn, s Charley Chase, Betty Mack.
SOMETHING SIMPLE (MGM-Roach, 1934) d Charles Parrott and Walter Weems, s Charley Chase, Betty Mack.
YOU SAID A HATFUL! (MGM-Roach, 1934) d Charles Parrott, s Charley Chase, Dorothy Appleby.
FATE'S FATHEAD (MGM-Roach, 1934) d Charles Parrott, s Charley Chase, Dorothy Appleby.
THE CHASES OF PIMPLE STREET (MGM-Roach, 1934) d Charles Parrott, s Charley Chase, Betty Mack.
OKAY TOOTS! (MGM-Roach, 1935) d Charles Parrott and William Terhune, s Charley Chase, Jeanie Roberts.
POKER AT EIGHT (MGM-Roach, 1935) d Charles Parrott, s Charley Chase, Constance Bergen.
SOUTHERN EXPOSURE (MGM-Roach, 1935) d Charles Parrott, s Charley Chase, Constance Bergen.
THE FOUR-STAR BOARDER (MGM-Roach, 1935) d Charles Parrott, s Charley Chase, Constance Bergen.
NURSE TO YOU (MGM-Roach, 1935) d Charles Parrott and Jefferson Moffitt, s Charley Chase, Muriel Evans.
MANHATTAN MONKEY BUSINESS (MGM-Roach, 1935) d Charles Parrott and Harold Law, s Charley Chase, Joyce Compton.
PUBLIC GHOST NO. 1 (MGM-Roach, 1935) d Charles Parrott and Harold Law, s Charley Chase, Joyce Compton.

LIFE HESITATES AT 40 (MGM-Roach, 1936) d Charles Parrott and Harold Law, s Charley Chase, Joyce Compton.
THE COUNT TAKES THE COUNT (MGM-Roach, 1936) d Charles Parrott and Harold Law, s Charley Chase, Antoinette Lees.
VAMP TILL READY (MGM-Roach, 1936) d Charles Parrott and Harold Law, s Charley Chase, Wilma Cox.
ON THE WRONG TREK (MGM-Roach, 1936) d Charles Parrott and Harold Law, s Charley Chase, Rosina Lawrence.
NEIGHBORHOOD HOUSE (MGM-Roach, 1936) d Charles Parrott and Harold Law, s Charley Chase, Rosina Lawrence.
THE GRAND HOOTER (Columbia, 1937) d Del Lord, s Charley Chase, Peggy Stratford.
FROM BAD TO WORSE (Columbia, 1937) d Del Lord, s Charley Chase, Peggy Stratford.
THE WRONG MISS WRIGHT (Columbia, 1937) d Charles Lamont, s Charley Chase, Peggy Stratford.
CALLING ALL DOCTORS (Columbia, 1937) d Charles Lamont, s Charley Chase.
THE BIG SQUIRT (Columbia, 1937) d Del Lord, s Charley Chase, Lucille Lund.
MAN BITES LOVE BUG (Columbia, 1937) d Del Lord, s Charley Chase, Mary Russell.
TIME OUT FOR TROUBLE (Columbia, 1938) d Del Lord, s Charley Chase, Louise Stanley.
THE MIND NEEDER (Columbia, 1938) d Del Lord, s Charley Chase, Ann Doran.
MANY SAPPY RETURNS (Columbia, 1938) d Del Lord, s Charley Chase, Ann Doran.
THE NIGHTSHIRT BANDIT (Columbia, 1938) d Jules White, s Charley Chase, Phyllis Barry.
PIE A LA MAID (Columbia, 1938) d Del Lord, s Charley Chase, Ann Doran.
THE SAP TAKES A WRAP (Columbia, 1939) d Del Lord, s Charley Chase, Gloria Blondell.
THE CHUMP TAKES A BUMP (Columbia, 1939) d Del Lord, s Charley Chase.
RATTLING ROMEO (Columbia, 1939) d Del Lord, s Charley Chase, Ann Doran.
SKINNY THE MOOCHER (Columbia, 1939) d Del Lord, s Charley Chase, Ann Doran.
TEACHER'S PEST (Columbia, 1939) d Del Lord, s Charley Chase, Richard Fiske.
THE AWFUL GOOF (Columbia, 1939) d Del Lord, s Charley Chase, Linda Winters.
THE HECKLER (Columbia, 1940) d Del Lord, s Charley Chase, Bruce Bennett.
SOUTH OF THE BOUDOIR (Columbia, 1940) d Del Lord, s Charley Chase, Helen Lynd.

HIS BRIDAL FRIGHT (Columbia, 1940) d Del Lord, s Charley Chase, Iris Meredith.

128. CHARLIE CHAN
The inscrutible police officer of Chinese ancestry originally appeared in Earl Derr Biggers' series of mystery novels published 1925-32. The TV series THE NEW ADVENTURES OF CHARLIE CHAN (ITC, 1957-78) featured J. Carroll Naish as Chan.
THE HOUSE WITHOUT A KEY (Pathe, 1926) (ten-part serial) d George B. Seitz, s George Kuwa, Allene Ray.
CHINESE PARROT (Universal, 1928) d Paul Leni, s Kamiyama Sojin, Marian Nixon.
BEHIND THAT CURTAIN (Fox, 1929) d Irving Cummings, s Warner Baxter, Lois Moran, E.L. Park.
CHARLIE CHAN CARRIES ON (Fox, 1931) d Hamilton MacFadden, s Warner Oland, John Garrick.
THE BLACK CAMEL (Fox, 1931) d Hamilton MacFadden, s Warner Oland, Sally Eilers, Bela Lugosi.
CHARLIE CHAN'S CHANCE (Fox, 1932) d John Blystone, s Warner Oland, Linda Watkins.
CHARLIE CHAN'S GREATEST CASE (Fox, 1933) d Hamilton MacFadden, s Warner Oland, Heather Angel.
CHARLIE CHAN'S COURAGE (Fox, 1934) d George Hadden, s Warner Oland, Donald Woods.
CHARLIE CHAN IN LONDON (Fox, 1934) d Eugene Forde, s Warner Oland, Drue Leyton.
CHARLIE CHAN IN PARIS (Fox, 1935) d Lewis Seiler, s Warner Oland, Mary Brian, Keye Luke.
CHARLIE CHAN IN EGYPT (Fox, 1935) d Louis King, s Warner Oland, Pat Paterson.
CHARLIE CHAN IN SHANGHAI (20th Century-Fox, 1935) d James Tinling, s Warner Oland, Irene Hervey.
CHARLIE CHAN'S SECRET (20th Century-Fox, 1936) d Gordon Wiles, s Warner Oland, Rosina Lawrence.
CHARLIE CHAN AT THE CIRCUS (20th Century-Fox, 1936) d Harry Lachman, s Warner Oland, Keye Luke.
CHARLIE CHAN AT THE RACE TRACK (20th Century-Fox, 1936) d H. Bruce Humberstone, s Warner Oland, Keye Luke.
CHARLIE CHAN AT THE OPERA (20th Century-Fox, 1936) d H. Bruce Humberstone, s Warner Oland, Boris Karloff.
CHARLIE CHAN AT THE OLYMPICS (20th Century-Fox, 1937) d H. Bruce Humberstone, s Warner Oland, Katherine DeMille.
CHARLIE CHAN ON BROADWAY (20th Century-Fox, 1937) d Eugene Forde, s Warner Oland, Keye Luke.
CHARLIE CHAN AT MONTE CARLO (20th Century-Fox, 1937) d Eugene Forde, s Warner Oland, Keye Luke, Virginia Field.

CHARLIE CHAN IN HONOLULU (20th Century-Fox, 1938) d H. Bruce Humberstone, s Sidney Toler, Phyllis Brooks, Sen Yung.
CHARLIE CHAN IN RENO (20th Century-Fox, 1939) d Norman Foster, s Sidney Toler, Ricardo Cortez.
CHARLIE CHAN AT TREASURE ISLAND (20th Century-Fox, 1939) d Norman Foster, s Sidney Toler, Cesar Romero.
CHARLIE CHAN IN CITY OF DARKNESS (20th Century-Fox, 1939) d Herbert I. Leeds, s Sidney Toler, Lynn Bari.
CHARLIE CHAN IN PANAMA (20th Century-Fox, 1940) d Norman Foster, s Sidney Toler, Jean Rogers.
CHARLIE CHAN'S MURDER CRUISE (20th Century-Fox, 1940) d Eugene Forde, s Sidney Toler, Marjorie Weaver.
CHARLIE CHAN AT THE WAX MUSEUM (20th Century-Fox, 1940) d Lynn Shores, s Sidney Toler, Sen Yung.
MURDER OVER NEW YORK (20th Century-Fox, 1940) d Harry Lachman, s Sidney Toler, Marjorie Weaver.
DEAD MEN TELL (20th Century-Fox, 1941) d Harry Lachman, s Sidney Toler, Sheila Ryan.
CHARLIE CHAN IN RIO (20th Century-Fox, 1941) d Harry Lachman, s Sidney Toler, Mary Beth Hughes.
CASTLE IN THE DESERT (20th Century-Fox, 1942) d Harry Lachman, s Sidney Toler, Arleen Whelan.
CHARLIE CHAN IN THE SECRET SERVICE (Monogram, 1944) d Phil Rosen, s Sidney Toler, Gwen Kenyon, Mantan Moreland, Benson Fong.
THE CHINESE CAT (Monogram, 1944) d Phil Rosen, s Sidney Toler, Benson Fong, Mantan Moreland.
BLACK MAGIC (Monogram, 1944) [aka CHARLIE CHAN IN BLACK MAGIC] d Phil Rosen, s Sidney Toler, Mantan Moreland, Frances Chan.
THE JADE MASK (Monogram, 1945) d Phil Rosen, s Sidney Toler, Edwin Luke, Mantan Moreland.
THE SCARLET CLUE (Monogram, 1945) d Phil Rosen, s Sidney Toler, Benson Fong, Mantan Moreland.
THE SHANGHAI COBRA (Monogram, 1945), d Phil Karlson, s Sidney Toler, Benson Fong, Mantan Moreland.
THE RED DRAGON (Monogram, 1945) d Phil Rosen, s Sidney Toler, Fortunio Bonanova, Benson Fong.
DARK ALIBI (Monogram, 1946) d Phil Karlson, s Sidney Toler, Mantan Moreland.
SHADOWS OVER CHINATOWN (Monogram, 1946) d Terry Morse, s Sidney Toler, Mantan Moreland, Victor Sen Yung.
DANGEROUS MONEY (Monogram, 1946) d Terry Morse, s Sidney Toler, Gloria Warren.
THE TRAP (Monogram, 1947) d Howard Bertherton, s Sidney Toler, Mantan Moreland.
THE CHINESE RING (Monogram, 1947) d William Beaudine, s Roland Winters, Warren Douglas.

DOCKS OF NEW ORLEANS (Monogram, 1948) d Derwin Abrahams, s Roland Winters, Victor Sen Yung, Mantan Moreland.
THE SHANGHAI CHEST (Monogram, 1948) d William Beaudine, s Roland Winters, Mantan Moreland.
THE GOLDEN EYE (Monogram, 1948) [aka MYSTERY OF THE GOLDEN EYE and CHARLIE CHAN AND THE GOLDEN EYE] d William Beaudine, s Roland Winters, Mantan Moreland.
THE FEATHERED SERPENT (Monogram ,1948) d William Beaudine, s Roland Winters, Keye Luke.
SKY DRAGON (Monogram, 1949) d Lesley Selander, s Roland Winters, Keye Luke, Mantan Moreland.
HAPPINESS IS A WARM CLUE (Universal, 1971) (NBC-TV movie 1979) [aka THE RETURN OF CHARLIE CHAN] dDaryl Duke, s Ross Martin, Richard Haydn, Louise Sorel.
CHARLIE CHAN AND THE CURSE OF THE DRAGON QUEEN (American Cinema, 1981) d Clive Donner, s Peter Ustinov, Lee Grant.

129. CHARLIE CHAPLIN
The silent and later sound film comedian developed the personna of the Little Tramp -- bowler hat, thumb-size mustache, cane and swaggering walk. He's the seedy vagabond, the "little guy" who loves and loses but refuses to give up. (In some cases, direction credits are given to Mack Sennett in the lack of information to the contrary.)
KID AUTO RACES AT VENICE (Keystone, 1914) d Henry Lehrman, s Charles Chaplin, Charlotte Fitzpatrick.
MABEL'S STRANGE PREDICAMENT (Keystone, 1914) d Mack Sennett and Henry Lehrman, s Mabel Normand, Charles Chaplin, Chester Conklin.
BETWEEN SHOWERS (Keystone, 1914) d Henry Lehrman, s Charles Chaplin, Chester Conklin, Ford Sterling.
A FILM JOHNNIE (Keystone, 1914) d Mack Sennett, s Charles Chaplin, Roscoe "Fatty" Arbuckle, Minta Durfee.
TANGO TANGLES (Keystone, 1914) d Mack Sennett, s Charles chaplin, Roscoe "Fatty" Arbuckle, Chester Conklin, Ford Sterling.
HIS FAVORITE PASTIME (Keystone, 1914) d George Nichols, s Charles Chaplin, Peggy Pearce, Roscoe "Fatty" Arbuckle.
THE STAR BOARDER (Keystone, 1914) d Mack Sennett, s Charles Chaplin, Alice Davenport, Edgar Kennedy.
TWENTY MINUTES OF LOVE (Keystone, 1914) d Mack Sennett, s Charles Chaplin, Minta Durfee.
CAUGHT IN A CABARET (Keystone, 1914) d Mabel Normand and Charles Chaplin, s Mabel Normand, Charles Chaplin.
CAUGHT IN THE RAIN (Keystone, 1914) d Charles Chaplin, s Charles Chaplin, Alice Davenport, Mack Swain.
THE FATAL MALLET (Keystone, 1914) d Charles Chaplin, Mabel Normand and Mack Sennett, s Charles Chaplin, Mabel Normand, Mack Swain.

78 MOTION PICTURE SERIES & SEQUELS

MABEL'S BUSY DAY (Keystone, 1914) d Charles Chaplin and Mabel Normand, s Charles Chaplin, Mabel Normand, Slim Summerville.
LAUGHING GAS (Keystone, 1914) d Charles Chaplin, s Charles Chaplin, Mack Swain, Alice Howell.
THE PROPERTY MAN (Keystone, 1914) d Charles Chaplin, s Charles Chaplin, Harry McCoy.
THE FACE ON THE BALLROOM FLOOR (Keystone, 1914) d Charles Chaplin, s Charles Chaplin, Chester Conklin, Vivian Edwards.
RECREATION (Keystone, 1914) d Charles Chaplin, s Charles Chaplin.
THE MASQUERADER (Keystone, 1914) d Charles Chaplin, s Charles Chaplin, Roscoe "Fatty" Arbuckle.
HIS NEW PROFESSION (Keystone, 1914) d Charles Chaplin, s Charles Chaplin, Minta Durfee.
THE ROUNDERS (Keystone, 1914) d Charles Chaplin, s Charles Chaplin, Roscoe "Fatty" Arbuckle, Minta Durfee.
THE NEW JANITOR (Keystone, 1914) d Charles Chaplin, s Charles Chaplin, Al. St. John, Minta Durfee.
THOSE LOVE PANGS (Keystone, 1914) d Charles Chaplin, s Charles Chaplin, Cecile Arnold.
DOUGH AND DYNAMITE (Keystone, 1914) d Charles Chaplin, s Charles Chaplin, Phyllis Allen.
GENTLEMAN OF NERVE (Keystone, 1914) d Charles Chaplin, s Charles Chaplin, Mabel Normand, Mack Swain.
HIS MUSICAL CAREER (Keystone, 1914) d Charles Chaplin, s Charles Chaplin, Charles Chase.
HIS TRYSTING PLACE (Keystone, 1914) d Charles Chaplin, s Charles Chaplin, Mabel Normand.
GETTING ACQUAINTED (Keystone, 1914) d Charles Chaplin, s Charles Chaplin, Phyllis Allen.
HIS PREHISTORIC PAST (Keystone, 1914) d Charles Chaplin, s Charles Chaplin, Mack Swain.
HIS NEW JOB (Essanay, 1915) d Charles Chaplin, s Charles Chaplin, Ben Turpin.
A NIGHT OUT (Essanay, 1915) d Charles Chaplin, s Charles Chaplin, Bud Jamison, Edna Purviance.
THE CHAMPION (Essanay, 1915) d Charles Chaplin, s Charles Chaplin, Edna Purviance.
IN THE PARK (Essanay, 1915) d Charles Chaplin, s Charles Chaplin, Edna Purviance.
A JITNEY ELOPEMENT (Essanay, 1915) d Charles Chaplin, s Charles Chaplin, Edna Purviance.
THE TRAMP (Essanay, 1915) d Charles Chaplin, s Charles Chaplin, Edna Purviance.
BY THE SEA (Essanay, 1915) d Charles Chaplin, s Charles Chaplin, Ben Turpin.
WORK (Essanay, 1915) d Charles Chaplin, s Charles Chaplin, Edna Purviance.

MOTION PICTURE SERIES & SEQUELS

A WOMAN (Essanay, 1915) d Charles Chaplin, s Charles Chaplin, Edna Purviance.
THE BANK (Essanay, 1915) d Charles Chaplin, s Charles Chaplin, Edna Purviance, Lloyd Bacon.
SHANGHAIED (Essanay, 1915) d Charles Chaplin, s Charles Chaplin, Edna Purviance.
A NIGHT IN THE SHOW (Essanay, 1915) d Charles Chaplin, s Charles Chaplin, Leo White.
POLICE (Essanay, 1916) d Charles Chaplin, s Charles Chaplin, Edna Purviance.
TRIPLE TROUBLE (Essanay, 1918) d Charles Chaplin, s Charles Chaplin, Edna Purviance.
THE FLOORWALKER (Mutual, 1916) d Charles Chaplin, s Charles Chaplin, Edna Purviance, Eric Campbell.
THE FIREMAN (Mutual, 1916) d Charles Chaplin, s Charles Chaplin, Edna Purviance.
THE VAGABOND (Mutual, 1916) d Charles Chaplin, s Charles Chaplin,, Leo White.
ONE A.M. (Mutual, 1916) d Charles Chaplin, s Charles Chaplin.
THE COUNT (Mutual, 1916) d Charles Chaplin, s Charles Chaplin, Eric Campbell.
THE PAWNSHOP (Mutual, 1916) d Charles Chaplin, s Charles Chaplin, Edna Purviance.
BEHIND THE SCREEN (Mutual, 1916) d Charles Chaplin, s Charles Chaplin,, Albert Austin, Eric Campbell.
THE RINK (Mutual, 1916) d Charles Chaplin, s Charles Chaplin,, Edna Purviance, Charlotte Mineau.
EASY STREET (Mutual, 1917) d Charles Chaplin, s Charles Chaplin, Edna Purviance.
THE CURE (Mutual, 1917) d Charles Chaplin, s Charles Chaplin,, Edna Purviance.
THE IMMIGRANT (Mutual, 1917) d Charles Chaplin, s Charles Chaplin, Eric Campbell, Edna Purviance.
THE ADVENTURER (Mutual, 1917) d Charles Chaplin, s Charles Chaplin, Eric Campbell.
A DOG'S LIFE (First National, 1918) d Charles Chaplin, s Charles Chaplin, Edna Purviance.
SUNNYSIDE (First National, 1919) d Charles Chaplin, s Charles Chaplin, Edna Purviance.
A DAY'S PLEASURE (First National, 1919) d Charles Chaplin, s Charles Chaplin, Jackie Coogan, Babe London.
THE KID (First National, 1921) d Charles Chaplin, s Charles Chaplin, Jackie Coogan.
THE IDLE CLASS (First National, 1921) d Charles Chaplin, s Charles Chaplin, Edna Purviance.
PAY DAY (First National, 1922) d Charles Chaplin, s Charles Chaplin, Mack Swain.

THE GOLD RUSH (United Artists, 1925) d Charles Chaplin, s Charles Chaplin, Mack Swain.
THE CIRCUS (United Artists, 1928) d Charles Chaplin, s Charles Chaplin, Merna Kennedy.
CITY LIGHTS (United Artists, 1931) d Charles Chaplin, s Charles Chaplin, Virginia Cherill.
MODERN TIMES (United Artists, 1936) d Charles Chaplin, s Charles Chaplin, Paulette Goddard.

130. CHARLIE McCARTHY
Edgar Bergen and his wooden puppet Charlie McCarthy also appear in a dozen film shorts for Vitaphone, 1933-35.
CHARLIE McCARTHY, DETECTIVE (Universal, 1939) d Frank Tuttle, s Edgar Bergen.
LOOK WHO'S LAUGHING (RKO, 1941) d Allan Dwan, s Edgar Bergen, Jim and Marion Jordan.

130A. CHIEF FLYNN, SECRET SERVICE
This circa 1919 silent film series features Herbert Rawlinson.

130B. CHILD'S PLAY
A child's Chucky doll is possessed by the evil soul of a killer.
CHILD'S PLAY (United Artists, 1988) d Tom Holland, s Catherine Hicks, Chris Sarandon, Alex Vincent.
CHILD'S PLAY II (Universal, announced 1990) d John Lafia, s Alex Vincent, Jenny Agutter.

130C. CHIMMIE FADDEN
These are silent, black-and-white pictures.
CHIMMIE FADDEN (Paramount, 1915) s Victor Moore, Tom Forman, Ernest Jay, Mrs. Lewis McCord.
CHIMMIE FADDEN OUT WEST (Paramount, 1915) s Victor Moore, Tom Forman, Ernest Jay, Mrs. Lewis McCord.

131. CHINESE CONNECTION, THE
These martial arts films offer Bruce Lee as Chen Chen, in the original, avenging the death of his mentor. Bruce Li as Chen Shan, in the followup, carries out his brother's wish to re-establish a martial arts school in Shanghai.
THE CHINESE CONNECTION (1979) d Lo Wei, s Bruce Lee, Miao Ker Hsio.
THE CHINESE CONNECTION II (Trans World International, 1987) s Bruce Li

132. CHIP OF THE FLYING U
B.M. Bower wrote a series of Western novels featuring the cowhands at the Flying U Ranch; these are the film versions.

CHIP OF THE FLYING U (Selig, 1914) d Colin Campbell, s Tom Mix, Kathlyn Williams.
THE GALLOPING DEVIL (Canyon, 1920) d Nate Watt
CHIP OF THE FLYING U (Universal, 1926) d Lynn Reynolds
FLYING U RANCH (Robertson-Cole, 1927) d Robert De Lacy
CHIP OF THE FLYING U (Universal, 1939) d Ralph Staub, s Johnny Mack Brown, Bob Baker, Fuzzy Knight.

133. CHEAPER BY THE DOZEN
These family tales are about a household with twelve children.
CHEAPER BY THE DOZEN (20th Century-Fox, 1950) d Walter Lang, s Clifton Webb, Myrna Loy, Jeanne Crain.
BELLES ON THEIR TOES (20th Century-Fox, 1952) d Henry Levin, s Myrna Loy, Jeanne Crain.

134. CHEECH & CHONG
The comedy team of Richard "Cheech" Marin and Thomas Chong play dopers ever on the look out for the weed.
UP IN SMOKE (Paramount, 1978) d Lou Adler, s Richard Marin, Thomas Chong, Stacy Keech.
CHEECH & CHONG'S NEXT MOVIE (Universal, 1980) d Thomas Chong, s Richard "Cheech" Marin, Thomas Chong, Evelyn Guerrero.
CHEECH & CHONG'S NICE DREAMS (Columbia, 1981) d Thomas Chong, s Richard "Cheech" Marin, Thomas Chong, Evelyn Guerrero.
CHEECH & CHONG's STILL SMOKIN' (Paramount, 1983) d Thomas Chong, s Richard "Cheech" Marin, Thomas Chong.
CHEECH & CHONG'S THE CORSICAN BROTHERS (United Artists, 1984) d Thomas Chong, s Richard "Cheech" Marin, Thomas Chong.

135. CHIMP COMEDIES
The Tiffany short subjects have casts of chimpanzees.

136. CHINATOWN
Seedy 1940s detective J.J. Gettes is featured in gritty whodunits involving land and water (first film) and oil (second).
CHINATOWN (Paramount, 1974) d Roman Polanski, s Jack Nicholson, Faye Dunaway, John Huston.
THE TWO JAKES (Paramount, announced 1990) d Jack Nicholson, s Jack Nicholson, Harvy Keitel, Meg Tilly.

137. C.H.U.D.
Cannibalistic Humanoid Underground Dwellers are featured in the original picture. In the sequel, one of the ghouls supposedly destroyed runs rampant, biting victims and turning them into zombies.
C.H.U.D. (1984) d Douglas Cheek, s John Heard, Daniel Stern.
C.H.U.D. II: BUD THE CHUD (Vestron, 1989) d David Irving, s Robert Vaughn, June Lockhart.

138. CIPHER BUREAU, THE
These are counterespionage pictures.
THE CIPHER BUREAU (Grand National, 1938) d Charles Lamont, s Leon Ames, Charlotte Wynters.
PANAMA PATROL (Grand National, 1939) d Charles Lamont, s Leon Ames, Charlotte Wynters.

139. CIRCLE OF CHILDREN, A
A teacher of disturbed children holds center stage in these movies.
A CIRCLE OF CHILDREN (Edgar J. Sherick Productions/20th Century Fox Television, 1977) d Don Taylor, s Jane Alexander.
LOVEY: A CIRCLE OF CHILDREN, PART II (Time-Life Television Productions, 1978) (CBS-TV movie) d Jud Taylor, s Jane Alexander.

140. CISCO KID, THE
O. Henry wrote a short story, *The Caballero's Way*, about a Robin Hood-like Mexican hero, the inspiration for these pictures. There was also a radio series 1942-46 (with Jackson Beck as Cisco, Louis Sorin as sidekick Pancho) and a syndicated television series 1950-56 (featuring Duncan Renaldo and Leo Carillo as Cisco and Pancho, respectively).
IN OLD ARIZONA (Fox Film, 1929) d Raoul Walsh and Irving Cummings, s Edmund Lowe, Warner Baxter.
THE CISCO KID (Fox Film, 1931), d Irving Cummings, s Warner Baxter, Edmund Lowe, Conchita Montenegro.
THE RETURN OF THE CISCO KID (20th Century-Fox, 1939) d Herbert I. Leeds, s Warner Baxter, Lynn Bari.
THE CISCO KID AND THE LADY (20th Century-Fox, 1939) d Herbert I. Leeds, s Cesar Romero, Marjorie Weaver, Chris-Pin Martin.
VIVA CISCO KID (20th Century-Fox, 1940) d Norman Foster, s Cesar Romero, Jean Rogers, Chris-Pin Martin.
LUCKY CISCO KID (20th Century-Fox, 1940) d H. Bruce Humberstone, s Cesar Romero, Mary Beth Hughes, Dana Andrews.
THE GAY CABALLERO (20th Century-Fox, 1940) d Otto Brower, s Cesar Romero, Sheila Ryan, Robert Sterling.
ROMANCE OF THE RIO GRANDE (20th Century-Fox, 1941), d Herbert I. Leeds, s Cesar Romero, Patricia Morison, Lynne Roberts.
RIDE ON, VAQUERO (20th Century-Fox, 1941) d Herbert I. Leeds, s Cesar Romero, Mary Beth Hughes, Lynne Roberts, Chris-Pin Martin.
THE CISCO KID RETURNS (Monogram, 1945) d John P. McCarthy, Duncan Renaldo, Martin Garralaga.
THE CISCO KID IN OLD NEW MEXICO (Monogram, 1945) d Phil Rosen, s Duncan Renaldo, Martin Garralaga, Gwen Kenyon.
SOUTH OF THE RIO GRANDE (Monogram, 1945) d Lambert Hillyer, s Duncan Renaldo, Martin Garralaga.
THE GAY CAVALIER (Monogram, 1946) d William Nigh, s Gilbert Roland, Martin Garralaga.

SOUTH OF MONTEREY (Monogram, 1946) d William Nigh, s Gilbert Roland, Martin Garralaga.
BEAUTY AND THE BANDIT (Monogram, 1946) d William Nigh, s Gilbert Roland, Ramsay Ames.
RIDING THE CALIFORNIA TRAIL (Monogram, 1947) d William Nigh, s Gilbert Roland, Frank Yaconelli, Teala Loring.
ROBIN HOOD OF MONTEREY (Monogram, 1947) d Christy Cabanne, s Gilbert Roland, Chris-Pin Martin, Evelyn Brent.
KING OF THE BANDITS (Monogram, 1947) d Christy Cabanne, s Gilbert Roland, Chris-Pin Martin.
THE VALIANT HOMBRE (United Artists, 1949) d Wallace Fox, s Duncan Renaldo, Leo Carillo.
THE GAY AMIGO (United Artists, 1949) d Wallace Fox, s Duncan Renaldo, Leo Carillo.
THE DARING CABALLERO (United Artists, 1949) d Wallace Fox, s Duncan Renaldo, Leo Carillo.
SATAN'S CRADLE (United Artists, 1949) d Ford Beebe, s Duncan Renaldo, Leo Carillo.
THE GIRL FROM SAN LORENZO (United Artists, 1950) d Derwin Abrahams, s Duncan Renaldo, Leo Carillo, Jane Adams.

140A. CLARENCE THE COP
These early, silent comedies feature a hero in blue.
CLARENCE, THE COP (American Mutoscope & Biograph, 1903)
CLARENCE, THE COP, ON THE FEED STORE BEAT (Edison, 1904)

141. CLARK AND McCULLOUGH
These films team comedians Bobby Clark and Paul McCullough.
CLARK AND McCULLOUGH IN THE INTERVIEW (Fox, 1928) s Bobby Clark, Paul McCullough.
CLARK AND McCULLOUGH IN THE HONOR SYSTEM (Fox, 1928) s Bobby Clark, Paul McCullough.
THE BATH BETWEEN (Fox, 1929) d Ben Stoloff, s Bobby Clark, Paul McCullough.
THE DIPLOMATS (Fox, 1929) d Norman Taurog, s Bobby Clark, Paul McCullough.
WALTZING AROUND (Fox, 1929) d Harry Sweet, s Bobby Clark, Paul McCullough.
IN HOLLAND (Fox, 1929) d Norman Taurog, s Bobby Clark, Paul McCullough.
BELLE OF SAMOA (Fox, 1929) d Marcel Silver, s Bobby Clark, Paul McCullough.
BENEATH THE LAW (Fox, 1929) d Harry Sweet, s Bobby Clark, Paul McCullough.
THE MEDICINE MEN (Fox, 1929) d Norman Taurog, s Bobby Clark, Paul McCullough.
MUSIC FIENDS (Fox, 1929) d Harry Sweet, s Bobby Clark, Paul McCullough.

KNIGHTS OUT (Fox, 1929) d Norman Taurog, s Bobby Clark, Paul McCullough, Clifford Dempsey.
ALL STEAMED UP (Fox, 1929) d Norman Taurog, s Bobby Clark, Paul McCullough.
HIRED AND FIRED (Fox, 1929) d Norman Taurog, s Bobby Clark, Paul McCullough, Helen Bolton.
DETECTIVES WANTED (Fox, 1929) d Norman Taurog, s Bobby Clark, Paul McCullough.
FALSE ROOMERS (RKO, 1931) d Mark Sandrich, s Bobby Clark, Paul McCullough, James Findlayson.
A MELON-DRAMA (RKO, 1931) d Mark Sandrich, s Bobby Clark, Paul McCullough.
SCRATCH AS CATCH CAN (RKO, 1931) d Mark Sandrich, s Bobby Clark, Paul McCullough.
THE ICEMAN'S BALL (RKO, 1932) d Mark Sandrich, s Bobby Clark, Paul McCullough, Vernon Dent.
THE MILLIONAIRE CAT (RKO, 1932) d Mark Sandrich, s Bobby Clark, Paul McCullough.
JITTERS THE BUTLER (RKO, 1932) d Mark Sandrich, s Bobby Clark, Paul McCullough.
HOKUS FOCUS (RKO, 1933) d Mark Sandrich, s Bobby Clark, Paul McCullough.
THE DRUGGIST'S DILEMMA (RKO, 1933) d Mark Sandrich, s Bobby Clark, Paul McCullough.
THE GAY NIGHTIES (RKO, 1933) d Mark Sandrich, s Bobby Clark, Paul McCullough.
KICKIN' THE CROWN AROUND (RKO, 1933) d Sam White, s Bobby Clark, Paul McCullough.
FITS IN A FIDDLE (RKO, 1933) d Sam White, s Bobby Clark, Paul McCullough.
SNUG IN THE JUG (RKO, 1933) d Ben Holmes, s Bobby Clark, Paul McCullough.
HEY NANNY NANNY (RKO, 1934) d Ben Holmes, s Bobby Clark, Paul McCullough.
IN THE DEVIL'S DOGHOUSE (RKO, 1934) d Ben Holmes, s Bobby Clark, Paul McCullough.
BEDLAM OF BEARDS (RKO, 1934) d Ben Holmes, s Bobby Clark, Paul McCullough.
LOVE AND HISSES (RKO, 1934) d Sam White, s Bobby Clark, Paul McCullough.
ODOR IN THE COURT (RKO, 1934) d Ben Holmes, s Bobby Clark, Paul McCullough.
EVERYTHING'S DUCKY (RKO, 1934) d Ben Holmes, s Bobby Clark, Paul McCullough.
IN A PIG'S EYE (RKO, 1934) d Ben Holmes, s Bobby Clark, Paul McCullough.

FLYING DOWN TO ZERO (RKO,1935) d Lee Marcus, s Bobby Clark, Paul McCullough.
ALIBI BYE BYE (RKO, 1935) d Ben Holmes, s Bobby Clark, Paul McCullough, Dorothy Granger, Tom Kennedy.

142. CLASS OF NUKE 'EM HIGH
Radiation from a nuclear power plant has odd effects on students at a nearby high school.
CLASS OF NUKE 'EM HIGH (Troma, 1987) d Richard W. Haines, s Janelle Brady, Gilbert Brenton.
SUBHUMANOID MELTDOWN: CLASS OF NUKE 'EM HIGH PART II (Troma, announced 1990)

143. CLAUDIA
Based on a Rose Franken play, the first picture is the story of immature woman married to architect.
CLAUDIA (20th Century-Fox, 1943) d Edmund Goulding, s Dorothy McGuire, Robert Young.
CLAUDIA AND DAVID (20th Century-Fox, 1946) d Walter Lang, s Dorothy McGuire, Robert Young.

144. CLEOPATRA JONES
A Black CIA agent battles drug dealers.
CLEOPATRA JONES (Warner Brothers, 1973) d Jack Starrett, s Tamara Dobson.
CLEOPATRA JONES AND THE CASINO OF GOLD (Warner Brothers, 1975) d Chuck Bail, s Tamara Dobson.

145. CLUB EXOTICA
The sex films are about women auditioning male erotic dancers for a new club.
CLUB EXOTICA (Western Visuals, 1986) d Jerome Tanner, s Taija Rae, Careena Collins.
CLUB EXOTICA II: THE NEXT DAY (Western Visuals) s Careea Collins, Mike Horner.

146. COCOON
Senior citizens in Florida find rejuvenation thanks to visiting aliens; the movies are based on David Saperstein's novel.
COCOON (20th Century Fox, 1985) d Ron Howard, s Don Ameche, Wilford Brimley, Hume Cronyn.
COCOON: THE RETURN (20th Century Fox, 1988) d Daniel Petrie, s Don Ameche, Wilford Brimley, Hume Cronyn.

147. COFFIN ED JOHNSON AND GRAVEDIGGER JONES
Chester Himes penned nine novels featuring the team of Black policemen, published 1957-83.

86 MOTION PICTURE SERIES & SEQUELS

COTTON COMES TO HARLEM (United Artists, 1970) d Ossie Davis, s Godfrey Cambridge, Raymond St. Jacques.
COME BACK, CHARLESTON BLUE (United Artist, 1972) d Mark Warren, s Raymond St. Jacques, Godfrey Cambridge.

148. COHEN
These short silent comedies were made by Mack Sennett.
COHEN COLLECTS A DEBT (Keystone, 1912) s Fred Mace, Ford Sterling.
COHEN AT CONEY ISLAND (Keystone, 1912) [aka COHEN AT CONEY ISLAND] s Mack Sennett, Mabel Normand, Ford Sterling.
COHEN'S OUTING (Keystone, 1913) d Wilfred Lucas, s Ford Sterling, Charles Avery, Alice Davenport.
COHEN'S FIRE SALE (Keystone, 1913)
COHEN'S ADVERTISING SCHEME (Keystone, 1913)
COHEN SAVES THE FLAG (Keystone, 1913) d Mack Sennett, s Ford Sterling, Mabel Normand.

149. COHENS AND KELLYS, THE
George Sidney and Charles Murray play bickering Jewish and Irish neighbors.
THE COHENS AND KELLYS IN NEW YORK (Universal, 1927) s George Sidney, Charles Murray.
THE COHENS AND KELLYS IN PARIS (Universal, 1928) s George Sidney, Charles Murray.
THE COHENS AND KELLYS IN ATLANTIC CITY (Universal, 1929) s George Sidney, Charles Murray.
THE COHENS AND KELLYS IN AFRICA (Universal, 1930) s George Sidney, Charles Murray.
THE COHENS AND KELLYS IN SCOTLAND (Universal, 1930) s George Sidney, Charles Murray.
THE COHENS AND KELLYS IN HOLLYWOOD (Universal, 1932) s George Sidney, Charles Murray.
THE COHENS AND KELLYS IN TROUBLE (Universal, 1933) s George Sidney, Charles Murray.

150. COLLEGE SCANDAL
Two students are murdered just before the annual campus show.
COLLEGE SCANDAL (Paramount, 1935) d Elliott Nugent, s Arline Judge, Kent Taylor.
SWEATER GIRL (Paramount, 1942) d William Clemens, s Eddie Bracken, June Preisser.

151. COLUMBO
The smarter-than-he-looks, rumpled Los Angeles police lieutenant was also featured in television series which aired 1971-78 and 1988- .
PRESCRIPTION: MURDER (Universal, 1968) (NBC-TV movie) d Richard Irving, s Peter Falk, Gene Barry.

RANSOM FOR A DEAD MAN (Universal, 1971) (NBC-TV movie) s Peter Falk, Lee Grant.

152. COMING OF ANGELS, A
These pictures are erotic take-offs on the television series CHARLIE'S ANGELS and feature an all-female detective team investigating crimes between sex scenes.
A COMING OF ANGELS (VCA Pictures, 1977) d Joel Scott, s Leslie Bovee.
A COMING OF ANGELS: THE SEQUEL (Caballero, 1985) d Joe and Guido Williams, s Annette Haven.

153. CONAN THE BARBARIAN
Robert E. Howard wrote a series of heroic fantasy tales for *Weird Tales* magazine in the 1930s. With renewed popularity since the 1960s, there have been several dozen new Conan novels penned by others. A Conan-like character is also portrayed by Schwarzenegger in RED SONJA, somewhat based on another Howard story.
CONAN THE BARBARIAN (Dino de Laurentiis/Pressman, 1981) d John Milius, s Arnold Schwarzenegger, James Earl Jones, Sandahl Bergman.
CONAN THE DESTROYER (Dino de Laurentiis/Pressman, 1984) d Richard Fleischer, s Arnold Schwarzenegger, Grace Jones.

154. CONFESSIONS OF...
These British sex farces feature Askwith as a window cleaner.
CONFESSIONS OF A WINDOW CLEANER (Columbia, 1974) d Val Guest, s Robin Askwith, Anthony Booth, Linda Hayden.
CONFESSIONS OF A POP PERFORMER (Columbia, 1975) d Norman Cohen, s Robin Askwith.
CONFESSIONS FROM A HOLIDAY CAMP (Columbia, 1977) d Norman Cohen, s Robin Askwith.

155. COP AU VIN
These thrillers find center stage a shrewd policeman.
COP AU VIN (1984) d Claude Chabrol, s Jean Poiret, Stephane Audran.
INSPECTOR LAVARDIN

156. CORLISS ARCHER
A sixteen year old, to help out a secretly married brother who is overseas, pretends to be pregnant.
KISS AND TELL (Columbia, 1945) d Richard Wallace, s Shirley Temple, Jerome Courtland.
A KISS FOR CORLISS (United Artists, 1949) d Richard Wallace, s Shirley Temple, David Niven.

157. COUNT OF MONTE CRISTO, THE
From Alexandre Dumas' book, the wrongly accused Count of Monte Cristo escapes from prison and seeks vengeance.

MONTE CRISTO (Selig Polyscope, 1912) d Colin Campbell, s Hobart Bosworth, William T. Santschi.
MONTE CRISTO (Fox, 1922) d Emmet J. Flynn, s John Gilbert, Estelle Taylor.
THE COUNT OF MONTE CRISTO (Reliance, 1934) d Rowland V. Lee, s Robert Donat, Elissa Landi.
SON OF MONTE CRISTO (United Artists, 1940) d Rowland V. Lee, s Louis Hayward, Joan Bennett.
THE RETURN OF MONTE CRISTO (Columbia, 1947) d Henry Levin, s Louis Hayward, Barbara Britton.
THE COUNT OF MONTE CRISTO (Sirius, 1954) d Robert Vernay, s Jean Marasi, Lia Amanda.
THE COUNT OF MONTE CRISTO (1961) d Claude Autant-Lra, s Louis Jourdan, Yvonne Furneaux.
THE COUNT OF MONTE CRISTO (ITC Entertainment, 1975) (NBC-TV movie) d David Greene, s Richard Chamberlain, Tony Curtis.

158. COUNT WALDEMAR DANINSKY
The main character is a werewolf, descended from Count Imre Wolfstein, in a series of Spanish (and later Japanese-Spanish) horror films.
FRANKENSTEIN'S BLOODY TERROR (Maxper, 1967) [aka HELL'S CREATURES and THE MARK OF THE WOLFMAN and THE VAMPIRE OF DR. DRACULA and THE WOLFMAN OF COUNT DRACULA] d Enrique L. Eguiluz, s Paul Naschy (Jacinto Molina), Diane Konopka.
NIGHTS OF THE WEREWOLF (Kin, 1968) d Rene Govar, s Paul Naschy (Jacinto Molina), Monique Brainville.
DRACULA VERSUS FRANKENSTEIN (International Jaguar, 1969) aka FRANKENSTEIN and ASSIGNMENT TERROR and THE MAN WHO CAME FROM UMMO] d Tulio Demichelli, s Michael Rennie, Karen Dor, Paul Naschy (Jacinto Molina).
SHADOW OF THE WEREWOLF (HiFi Stereo/Plata, 1970) [aka THE WEREWOLF'S SHADOW and THE WEREWOLF VERSUS THE VAMPIRE WOMEN and THE BLACK HARVEST OF COUNTESS DRACULA] d Leon Klimovsky, s Paul Naschy (Jacinto Molina), Paty Shepard.
THE FURY OF THE WOLFMAN (Maxper, 1971) d Jose Maria Zabalza, s Paul Naschy (Jacinoto Molina), Perla Cristal.
DOCTOR JEKYLL AND THE WEREWOLF (Arturo Gonzalez, 1971) [aka DR. JEKYLL AND THE WOLFMAN] d Leon Klimovsky, s Paul Naschy (Jacinto Molina), Shirley Corrigan.
CURSE OF THE DEVIL (Loyus/Producciones Escorpion, 1973) [aka THE RETURN OF WALPURGIS and THE BLACK HARVEST OF COUNTESS DRACULA] d Carlos Aured, s Paul Naschy (Jacinto Molina), Faye Falcon.

NIGHT OF THE HOWLING BEAST (Profilmes, 1975) [aka THE
   WEREWOLF AND THE YETI] d Miguel Iglesias Bonns, s Paul
   Naschy (Jacinto Molina), Grace Mills.
THE RETURN OF THE WOLFMAN (Dalmata, 1980) d Jacinto Molina, s
   Paul Naschy (Jacinto Molina), Silvia Aguilar.
THE BEAST AND THE MAGIC SWORD (Aconito/Amachi, 1983) d Jacinto
   Molina, s Paul Naschy (Jacinto Molina), Shigeru Amachi.

159. COUNT YORGA, VAMPIRE
The horror pictures feature a Dracula drink-alike.
COUNT YORGA, VAMPIRE (Erica/American International, 1970) d Bob Kelljan,
   s Robert Quarry, Roger Perry, Donna Anders.
THE RETURN OF COUNT YORGA (American International/Peppertree,
   1971) d Bob Kelljan, s Robert Quarry, Mariette Hartley.

160. CRAIG KENNEDY
Arthur B. Reeve's fictional creation Kennedy is an American "scientific
detective." He was played by Donald Woods in a 1952 TV series.
THE EXPLOITS OF ELAINE (1915) (serial) s Pearl White, Arnold Daly.
THE NEW EXPLOITS OF ELAINE (1915) s Pearl White, Arnold Daly.
THE ROMANCE OF ELAINE (1916) s Pearl White, Arnold Daly.
THE CARTER CASE: THE CRAIG KENNEDY SERIAL (1919) s Herbert
   Rawlinson
THE CLUTCHING HAND (Stage and Screen, 1936) (15 chapters) d Albert
   Herman, s Jack Mulhall, Marion Shilling, Yakima Canutt.
THE RADIO DETECTIVE (1926) (serial) s John Price
THE AMAZING EXPLOITS OF THE CLUTCHING HAND (1936)

161. CRAZY FAT ETHEL
An asylum escapee goes on the rampage.
DEATH NURSE (1987) d Nick Phillips, s Priscilla Alden, Michael Flood.
CRAZY FAT ETHEL II (1987) d Nick Phillips, s Priscilla Alden, Michael
   Flood.

162. CREATURE FROM THE BLACK LAGOON
A scaly water monster, found in the Amazon River, terrorizes his captors.
CREATURE FROM THE BLACK LAGOON (Universal, 1954) d Jack Arnold,
   s Richard Carlson, Julia Adams.
REVENGE OF THE CREATURE (Universal, 1955) d Jack Arnold
THE CREATURE WALKS AMONG US (Universal, 1956) d John Sherwood.

163. CREEPER, THE
Actor Rondo Hatton, who suffered from a glandular deformity, plays a killer
called Oxton Creeper in the Sherlock Holmes film THE PEARLS OF DEATH,
and reprises the character for other films.
THE PEARL OF DEATH (Universal, 1944) d Roy William Neill, s Basil
   Rathbone, Nigel Bruce, Rondo Hatton.

HOUSE OF HORRORS (Universal, 1946) [aka JOAN MEDFORD IS MISSING] d Jean Yarbrough, s Bill Goodwin, Robert Lowery, Virginia Grey, Rondo Hatton.
THE BRUTE MAN(Universal, 1946) d Jean Yarbrough, s Tom Neal, Rondo Hatton.

164. CREEPSHOW
The horror pictures, homages to the 1950s E.C. comic books, are penned by scaremaster Stephen King.
CREEPSHOW (United Film Distribution, 1982) d George Romero, s Hal Holbrook, Adrienne Barbeau.
CREEPSHOW II (New World, 1987) d Michael Gornick, s Lois Chiles, George Kennedy.

165. CRIME DOCTOR
Dr. Robert Ordway the psychologist/criminologist first appeared on a radio show which aired over CBS 1940-47.
CRIME DOCTOR (Columbia, 1943) d Michael Gordon, s Warner Baxter, Margaret Lindsay.
CRIME DOCTOR'S STRANGEST CASE (Columbia, 1943) d Eugene J. Forde, s Warner Baxter, Lynn Merrick.
SHADOWS IN THE NIGHT (Columbia, 1944) d Eugene J. Forde, s Warner Baxter, Nina Foch.
CRIME DOCTOR'S COURAGE (Columbia, 1945) d George Sherman, s Warner Baxter, Hillary Brooke.
CRIME DOCTOR'S WARNING (Columbia, 1945) d William Castle, s Warner Baxter, John Litel.
CRIME DOCTOR'S MAN HUNT (Columbia, 1946) d William Castle, s Warner Baxter, Ellen Drew.
JUST BEFORE DAWN (Columbia, 1946) d William Castle, s Warner Baxter, Adelle Roberts.
THE MILLERSON CASE (Columbia, 1947) d George Archainbaud, s Warner Baxter, Nancy Saunders.
CRIME DOCTOR'S GAMBLE (Columbia, 1947) d William Castle, s Warner Baxter, Micheline Cheirel.
CRIME DOCTOR'S DIARY (Columbia, 1949) d Seymour Friedman, s Warner Baxter, Stephen Dunne, Lois Maxwell.

166. CRIME DOES NOT PAY
The series of two-reel shorts offers terse re-enactments of crimes of the day.
BURIED LOOT (MGM, 1935) d George B. Seitz, s Robert Taylor, Robert Livingston.
ALIBI RACKET (MGM, 1935) d George B. Seitz.
DESERT DEATH (MGM, 1935) d George B. Seitz, s Raymond Hatton, Harvey Stephens.
A THRILL FOR THELMA (MGM, 1935) d Edward Cahn, s Irene Hervey, Robert Warwick.

HIT AND RUN DRIVER (MGM, 1935) d Edward Cahn, s Morgan Wallace, Jonathan Hale.
PERFECT SET-UP (MGM, 1936) d Edward Cahn.
FOOLPROOF (MGM, 1936) d Edward Cahn, s Niles Welch, Alonzo Price.
THE PUBLIC PAYS (MGM, 1936) d Erroll Taggart, s Paul Stanton, Cy Kendall.
TORTURE MONEY (MGM, 1936) d Harold S. Bucquet.
GIVE TILL IT HURTS (MGM, 1937) d Felix Feist, s Janet Beecher, Howard Hickman.
BEHIND THE CRIMINAL (MGM, 1937) d Harold S. Bucquet, s Edward Emerson, Walter Kingsford.
WHAT PRICE SAFETY (MGM, 1938) d Harold S. Bucquet, s John Wray, George Huston.
MIRACLE MONEY (MGM, 1938) d Leslie Fenton, s John Miljan, Claire DuBrey.
COME ACROSS (MGM, 1938) d Harold S. Bucquet, s Bernard Nedell, Donald Douglas.
A CRIMINAL IS BORN (MGM, 1938) d Leslie Fenton, s Beorge Breakston, David Durand.
THEY'RE ALWAYS CAUGHT (MGM, 1938) d Harold S. Bucquet, s Stanley Ridges, John Eldredge.
THINK IT OVER (MGM, 1938) d Jacques Tourneur, s Lester Matthews, Dwight Frye.
THE WRONG WAY OUT (MGM, 1938) d Gustav Machaty, s Linda Terry, Kenneth Howell.
MONEY TO LOAN (MGM, 1939) d Joe Newman, s Alan Dinehart, Paul Guilfoyle.
WHILE AMERICA SLEEPS (MGM, 1939) d Fred Zinnemann, s Dick Purcell, Roland Varno.
HELP WANTED (MGM, 1939) d Fred Zinnemann, s Tom Heal, Jo Ann Sayers.
THINK FIRST (MGM, 1939) d Roy Rowland, s Laraine Day, Marc Lawrence.
DRUNK DRIVING (MGM, 1939) d David Miller, s Dick Purcell, Jo Ann Sayers.
POUND FOOLISH (MGM, 1940) d Felix Feist, s Neil Hamilton, Lynne Carver.
KNOW YOUR MONEY (MGM, 1940) d Joe Newman, s Dennis Moore, Noel Madison.
JACKPOT (MGM, 1940) d Roy Rowland, s Tom Neal, Ann Morris.
WOMEN IN HIDING (MGM, 1940) d Joe Newman, s Marsha Hunt.
BUYER BEWARE (MGM, 1940) d Joe Newman, s Charles Arnt.
SOAK THE OLD (MGM, 1940) d Sammy Lee, s Ralph Morgan, Kenneth Christy.
YOU THE PEOPLE (MGM, 1940) d Roy Rowland, s C. Henry Gordon.
RESPECT THE LAW (MGM, 1941) d Joe Newman.
FORBIDDEN PASSAGE (MGM, 1941) d Fred Zinnemann, s Harry Woods.

COFFINS ON WHEELS (MGM, 1941) d Joe Newman, s Cy Kendall, Darryl Hickman.
SUCKER LIST (MGM, 1941) d Roy Rowland, s Lynne Carver, John Archer.
FOR THE COMMON DEFENSE (MGM, 1942) d Allen Kenward, s Van Johnson, Douglas Fowley.
KEEP 'EM SAILING (MGM, 1942) d Basil Wrangell, s Jim David, Lou Smith.
PLAN FOR DESTRUCTION (MGM, 1943) d Edward Cahn, s Lewis Stone.
PATROLLING THE ETHER (MGM, 1944) d Paul Burnford.
EASY LIFE (MGM, 1944) d Walter Hart, s Bernard Thomas.
DARK SHADOWS (MGM, 1944) d Paul Burnford, s Arthur Space.
FALL GUY (MGM, 1945) d Paul Burnford, s Leon Ames.
THE LAST INSTALLMENT (MGM, 1945) d Walter Hart, s Cameron Mitchell.
PHANTOMS INC. (MGM, 1945) d Harold Young, s Frank Reicher.
A GUN IN HIS HAND (MGM, 1945) d Joseph Losey, s Anthony Caruso.
PURITY SQUAD (MGM, 1945) d Harold Kress, s Byron Foulger, Dick Elliott.
LUCKIEST GUY IN THE WORLD (MGM, 1947) d Joe Newman, s Barry Nelson, Eloise Hardt.

167. CRITTERS
Tiny, hairy creatures invade Earth.
CRITTER (New Line, 1986) d Stephen Herek, s Dee Wallace Stone, M. Emmet Walsh.
CRITTERS 2: THE MAIN COURSE (New Line, 1988) d Mick Garris, s Scott Grimes, Lian Curtis.

168. CROCODILE DUNDEE
The boisterous Australian adventurer Crocodile Dundee is persuaded by a news reporter to visit New York, in the initial outing. In the followup, she is kidnapped and the scene moves back Down Under.
CROCODILE DUNDEE (Paramount, 1986) d Peter Faiman, s Paul Hogan, Linda Kozlowski.
CROCODILE DUNDEE II (Paramount, 1988) d John Cornell, s Paul Hogan, Linda Kozlowski.

169. CURSE, THE
A meteorite lands in Tennessee and begins to drive people crazy. The plot is loosely based on H.P. Lovecraft's *The Color Out of Space*, which was previously filmed as DIE, MONSTER, DIE!.
THE CURSE (Trans World, 1987) [aka THE FARM] d David Keith, s Wil Wheaton, Claude Akins.
CURSE II: THE BITE

170. D.A., THE
These television films served as pilots for a courtroom drama series which aired on NBC 1971-72. Robert Conrad plays Deputy D.A. Paul Ryan, with Harry Morgan his chief assistant and Julie Cobb a public defender.
THE D.A.: MURDER ONE (Mark VII/Universal, 1969) (NBC-TV movie) d Boris Sagal, s Howard Duff, Diane Baker.
THE D.A.: CONSPIRACY TO KILL (Mark VII/Universal, 1971) (NBC-TV movie) d Paul Krasny, s Robert Conrad, William Conrad.

171. DALLAS COWBOYS CHEERLEADERS, THE
A reporter works undercover on a cheering squad learning about the pressures as the young women ready for the Super Bowl, etc.
DALLAS COWBOY CHEERLEADERS (Aubrey/Hamner Productions, 1979) (ABC-TV movie) d Bruce Bilson, s Jane Seymour, Laraine Stephens, Bert Convy.
DALLAS COWBOYS CHEERLEADERS II (Aubrey/Hammer Productions, 1980) (ABC-TV movie) d Michael O'Herlihy, s John Davidson, Laraine Stephens, Bert Convy.

172. DANGER ZONE
The first picture's plot involves singers, dope dealers and a rampant psycho.
DANGER ZONE (1986) d Henry Vernon, s Michael Wayne, Jason Williams.
DANGER ZONE PART II: REAPER'S REVENGE (Skouras, 1988) d Dan Yarussi, s Jason Williams.

173. DAUGHTERS OF JOSHUA MCCABE
To hold onto his land, a fur trapper recruits a disreputable group of women to act as his daughters.
THE DAUGHTERS OF JOSHUA CABE (Spelling/Goldberg, 1972) (ABC-TV movie) d Philip Leacock, s Buddy Ebsen, Karen Valentine, Lesley Anne Warren, Sandra Dee.
THE DAUGHTERS OF JOSHUA CABE RETURN (Spelling/Goldberg, 1975) (ABC-TV movie) d David Lowell Rich, s Dan Dailey, Dub Taylor, Ronne Troup.
THE NEW DAUGHTERS OF JOSHUA CABE (Spelling/Goldberg, 1976) (ABC-TV movie) d Bruce Bilson, s John McIntire, Jack Elam, Liberty Williams.

174. DAVY CROCKETT
The frontiersman was a hero of the Texas Alamo.
SON OF DAVY CROCKETT (Columbia, 1941) d Lambert Hillyer, s Bill Elliott, Iris Meredith, Dub Taylor.
DAVY CROCKETT, INDIAN SCOUT (Reliance, 1950) d Lew Landers, s George Montgomery, Ellen Drew.
DAVY CROCKETT, KING OF THE WILD FRONTIER (Buena Vista, 1955) d Norman Foster, s Fess Parker, Buddy Ebsen.

94 MOTION PICTURE SERIES & SEQUELS

DAVY CROCKETT AND THE RIVER PIRATES (Buena Vista, 1956) d
  Norman Foster, s Fess Parker, Buddy Ebsen.

175. DAWN
A fifteen-year-old runaway meets up with a young hustler.
DAWN: PORTRAIT OF A TEENAGE RUNAWAY (Worldvision
  Enterprises, 1976) (NBC-TV movie) d Randal Kleiser, s Eve Plumb,
  Leigh McCloskey.
ALEXANDER: THE OTHER SIDE OF DAWN (Douglas S. Cramer
  Productions, 1977) (NBC-TV movie) d John Erman, s Leigh McClosley,
  Eve Plumb.

176. DEAD END KIDS
Juvenile delinquents from New York's East Side -- Spit, Dippy, Tommy, Angel, Milty, TB (the names changed over the years) -- were first featured in Sidney Kingsley's play *Dead End*. Their popularity in the movie version resulted in an ongoing series, and also prompted the BOWERY BOYS, LITTLE TOUGH GUYS and EAST SIDE KIDS series.
DEAD END (United Artists, 1937) d William Wyler, s Sylvia Siddney, s Joel
  McCrea, Humphrey Bogart, Billy Halop, Marjorie Main, Huntz Hall,
  Bobby Jordan, Leo B. Gorcey, Gabriel Dell, Bernard Punsley.
CRIME SCHOOL (Warner Brothers, 1938) d Lewis Seiler, s Billy Halop,
  Bobby Jordan, Huntz Hall, Leo Gorcey, Bernard Punsley, Gabriel Dell,
  Humphrey Bogart.
ANGELS WITH DIRTY FACES (Warner Brothers, 1938) d Michael Curtiz, s
  James Cagney, Pat O'Brien, Humphrey Bogart, Billy Halop, Leo Gorcey,
  Gabriel Dell, Huntz Hal.
THEY MADE ME A CRIMINAL (Warner Brothers, 1939) d Busby Berkeley,
  s John Garfield, s Huntz Hall, Gabriel Dell, Leo Gorcey, Bobby Jordan.
HELL'S KITCHEN (Warner Brothers, 1939) d Lewis Seiler and E.A. Dupont,
  s Billy Halop, Bobby Jordan, Leo Gorcey, Huntz Hall, Gabriel Dell,
  Bernard Punsley.
ANGELS WASH THEIR FACES (Warner Brothers, 1939) d Ray Enright, s
  Ann Sheridan, Ronald Reagan, Billy Halop, Bonita Granville, Bobby
  Jordan, Leo Gorcey, Huntz Hall.
THE DEAD END KIDS ON DRESS PARADE (Warner Brothers, 1939) [aka
  ON DRESS PARADE] d William Clemens, s Billy Halop, Bobby
  Jordan, Huntz Hall, Gabriel, Dell, Leo Gorcey, Bernard Punsley.

177. DEADLY SPAWN
Aliens from outer space raid New Jersey.
DEADLY SPAWN (Filmline/21st Century, 1983) d Douglas McKeown, s
  Charles George Hildebrandt.
DEADLY SPAWN II: METAMORPHOSIS (Filmline, 1988)

178. DEAR RUTH

Norman Krasna's play inspired these pictures about a soldier on leave, visiting his girlfriend only to find he has been fooled by her kid sister, who has written love letters under her name.
DEAR RUTH (Paramount, 1947) d William Russell, s Joan Caulfield, William Holden.
DEAR WIFE (Paramount, 1949) d Richard Haydn, s William Holden, Joan Caulfield.
DEAR BRAT (Paramount, 1951) d William A. Seiter, s Mona Freeman, Billy De Wolfe.

179. DEATHSTALKER
Swords and scorcery: a warrior teams with a princess to battle a magician.
DEATHSTALKER: THE LAST GREAT WARRIOR (New World, 1984) d John Watson, s Richard Hill, Barbi Benton.
DEATHSTALKER II: DUEL OF THE TITANS (1987) d Jim Wynorski, s John Terlesky, Monique Gabrielle.
DEATHSTALKER III: THE WARRIORS FROM HELL (Concorde, 1988) d Alfonso Corona, s John Allen Nelson.

180. DEATH WISH
Brian Garfield wrote the original vigilante books about an architect who blows away the scum who raped his wife.
DEATH WISH (Paramount, 1974) d Michael Winner, s Charles Bronson, Hope Lang.
DEATH WISH II (Warner Brothers, 1982) d Michael Willer, s Charles Bronson, Jill Ireland.
DEATH WISH 3 (Cannon, 1985) d Michael Winner, s Charles Bronson, Deborah Raffin.
DEATH WISH 4: THE CRACKDOWN (Cannon, 1987) d J. Lee Thompson, s Charles Bronson, Kay Lenz.

181. DEBBIE
A Dallas Cowgirls cheerleader has a number of escapades in these X-rated films.
DEBBIE DOES DALLAS (VCX 1978) d Jim Clark, s Bambi Woods.
DEBBIE DOES DALLAS PART 2 (Caballero, 1982) d Jim Clark, s Bambi Woods.
DEBBIE DOES 'EM ALL (Cal Vista, 1985) d Bob Vosse, s Angel, Shanna McCullough.
DEBBIE DOES DALLAS 4 (Video Exclusives, 1988) s Dana Lynn, Ron Jeremy.
DEBBIE 4 HIRE (Executive, 1988) s Nina Hartley, Jon Martin.
DEBBIE GOES TO HAWAII (Vidco, 1989) s Nina Hartley, Jon Martin.

182. DEEP THROAT
In these adult pictures, the heroine's sex organ is in other than its usual place.

DEEP THROAT (Arrow, 1972) d Gerard Damiano, s Linda Lovelace, Harry Reems.
DEEP THROAT II (Arrow, 1987) s Krista Lane, Sheena Horne.
DEEP THROAT III (Arrow, 1989) s Aja, Peter North.

DEERSLAYER
See **LEATHERSTOCKING**

183. DELTA FORCE
An anti-terrorist squad is called in when an airplane is hijacked.
DELTA FORCE (Cannon, 1986) d Menahem Golan, s Chuck Norris, Lee Marvin.
DELTA FORCE II: AMERICA'S RED ARMY (Cannon, 1989) d Aaron Norris, s Chuck Norris.

184. DEMONS
Monsters mangle innocent victims.
DEMONS (1986) d Lamberto Bava, s Urbano Barberini.
DEMONS 2 (1987) d Lamberto Bava, s David Knight, Nancy Brill.

185. DESPERADO
A roving cowboy finds adventure in the Old West.
DESPERADO (1987 TV movie) d Virgil W. Vogel, s Alex McArthur, David Warner.
THE RETURN OF DESPERADO (1988 TV movie) d E.W. Swackhamer, s Alex McArthur, Robert Foxworth, Billy Dee Williams.

186. DESPERATE DESMOND
Harry Hershfield's newspaper comic strip was turned into a brief series of silent comedies ca 1911-12.

187. DEVIL IN MISS JONES, THE
These are hardcore sex pictures.
THE DEVIL IN MISS JONES (VCX, 1972) d Gerard Damiano, s Georgina Spelvin, Harry Reems.
THE DEVIL IN MISS JONES II (VCA, 1983) d Henri Pachard, s Georgina Spelvin.
THE DEVIL IN MISS JONES III (VCA, 1986) s Lois Ayres, Amber Lynn.
THE DEVIL IN MISS JONES IV (VCA, 1987) s Lois Ayres, Paul Thomas.

187A. DIAMOND FROM THE SKY, THE
The first entry is a thirty-chapter silent action serial, the second its four-chapter follow-up.
THE DIAMOND FROM THE SKY (American Mutoscope & Biograph, 1915) s Irving Cummings, William Russell, Lottie Pickford.
THE SEQUEL TO THE DIAMOND FROM THE SKY (American Mutoscope, 1916)

188. DIAMOND JIM BRADY
The eccentric nineteenth century millionaire who was in love with showgirl Lillian Russell is portrayed by actor Edward Arnold in both pictures.
DIAMOND JIM (Universal, 1935) d A. Edward Sutherland, s Edward Arnold, Jean Arthur, Binnie Barnes.
LILLIAN RUSSELL (20th Century-Fox, 1940) d Irving Cummings, s Alice Faye, Don Ameche, Henry Fonda, Edward Arnold.

189. DICK BARTON
The British radio sleuth (1946-51) was transferred to film.
DICK BARTON SPECIAL AGENT (Exclusive Films, 1948)
DICK BARTON STRIKES BACK (Exclusive Films, 1949)
DICK BARTON AT BAY (Exclusive Films, 1950)

190. DICK FRANCIS MYSTERIES
Horse racing usually provides the background to these mysteries featuring investigator David Cleveland.
BLOOD SPORT (TV movie, 1989) s Ian McShane.
IN THE FRAME (TV movie, 1989) s Ian McShane, Lyman Ward.
TWICE SHY (TV movie, 1989) s Ian McShane, Geraldine Fitzgerald.

191. DICK TRACY
Chet Gould's comic strip cop (who debuted in 1931) was popular in the serials. Ralph Byrd also appeared in the television show, 1951-52.
DICK TRACY (Republic, 1937) (15-part serial) d Ray Taylor and Alan James, s Ralph Byrd, Kay Hughes, Smiley Burnette.
DICK TRACY RETURNS (Republic, 1938) (15-episode serial) d William Witney and John English, s Ralph Byrd, Lynn Roberts, Charles Middleton.
DICK TRACY'S G-MEN (Republic, 1939) (serial in 15 episodes) d William Witney and John English, s Ralph Byrd, Irving Pichel, Ted Pearson.
DICK TRACY VERSUS CRIME INC. (Republic, 1941) (15 chapters) d William Witney and John English, s Ralph Byrd, Michael Owen, Jan Wiley.
DICK TRACY, DETECTIVE (RKO, 1945) d William Berke, s Morgan Conway, Anne Jeffreys, Mike Mazurki.
DICK TRACY VERSUS CUEBALL (RKO, 1946) d Gordon Douglas, s Morgan Conway, Anne Jeffreys.
DICK TRACY MEETS GRUESOME (RKO, 1947) [aka DICK TRACY'S AMAZING ADVENTURE] d John Rawlins, s Boris Karloff, Ralph Byrd, Anne Gwynne.
DICK TRACY'S DILEMMA (RKO, 1947) [aka MARK OF THE CLAW] d John Rawlins, s Ralph Byrd, Lyle Latell.
DICK TRACY VERSUS THE PHANTOM EMPIRE (Republic, 1953) (serial) s Ralph Byrd.

DICK TRACY (Touchstone, announced 1990) d Warren Beatty, s Warren Beatty, Madonna, George C. Scott.

192. DIE HARD
Terrorists strike a Los Angeles high rise. The first picture is based on Walter Wager's novel *58 Minutes*. The second film is about terrorists at an airport.
DIE HARD (20th Century-Fox, 1988) d John McTiernan, s Bruce Willlis, Bonnie Bedelia.
DIE HARD 2 (20th Century-Fox, announced 1990) d Renny Harlin, s Bruce Willis.

193. DIRTY DOZEN, THE
These World War II actioners find a group of military misfits recruited for an impossible mission.
THE DIRTY DOZEN (MGM, 1967) d Robert Aldrich, s Lee Marvin, Ernest Borgnine, Charles Bronson, Donald Sutherland, Jim Brown.
THE DIRTY DOZEN: THE NEXT MISSION (1985 TV movie) d Andrew V. McLaglen, s Lee Marvin, Ernest Borgnine.
THE DIRTY DOZEN: THE DEADLY MISSION (1987 TV movie) d Lee H. Katzin, s Telly Savalas, Ernest Borgnine.
THE DIRTY DOZEN: THE FATAL MISSION (1988 TV movie) d Lee H. Katzin, s Telly Savalas, Ernest Borgnine.
THE DIRTY DOZEN: THE SERIES (1988 TV movie) d Kevin Connor, s Ben Murphy, John Bradley.

194. DIRTY HARRY
Clint Eastwood is tough cop Harry Callahan, best known for leveling a handgun and challenging a young hoodlum: "Go ahead, make my day."
DIRTY HARRY (Warner Brothers, 1971) d Don Siegel, s Clint Eastwood, Harry Guardino.
MAGNUM FORCE (Warner Brothers, 1973) d Ted Post, s Clint Eastwood, Hal Holbrook.
THE ENFORCER (Warner Brothers, 1976) d James Fargo, s Clint Eastwood, Tyne Daly, Harry Guardino.
SUDDEN IMPACT (Warner Brothers, 1983) d Clint Eastwood, s Clint Eastwood, Sondra Locke.
THE DEAD POOL (Warner Brothers, 1988) d Buddy Van Horn, s Clint Eastwood, Patricia Clarkson.

195. DJANGO
These Spaghetti Westerns find a bounty hunter mixing in a scuffle between Mexicans and American soldiers.
DJANGO (BRC/Tecisa, 1965) d Sergio Corbucci, s Franco Nero, Loredana Nusclak.
DJANGO SHOOTS FIRST (FICA, 1966) d Alberto De Martino, s Glenn Saxon, Fernando Sancho.

A FEW DOLLARS FOR DJANGO (1966) [aka A FEW DOLLARS FOR GYPSY] d Leon Klimovsky, s Antonio De Teffe, Gloria Osuna, Frank Wolff.

196. DOBIE GILLIS
A college student named Dobie Gillis, his beatnik friend Maynard G. Krebs, girlfriend Zelda Gilroy, rival Chatsworth Osborne Jr., etc, were also featured in a television series carried over CBS 1953-57 (cast members from which are featured in the second two listings).
THE AFFAIRS OF DOBIE GILLIS (MGM, 1953) d Don Weis, s Bobby Van.
WHATEVER HAPPENED TO DOBIE GILLIS? (1977 TV movie) s Dwayne Hickman, Bob Denver.
BRING ME THE HEAD OF DOBIE GILLIS (1988 TV movie) d Stanley Z. Cherry, s Dwayne Hickman, Bob Denver, Connie Stevens, Sheila James.

197. DOCTOR...
Richard Gordon's novel is the basis for this satiric series about Dr. Simon Sparrow.
DOCTOR IN THE HOUSE (Republic, J. Arthur Rank, 1954) d Ralph Thomas, s Dirk Bogarde, Muriel Pavlow.
DOCTOR AT SEA (Republic, J. Arthur Rank, 1956) d Ralph Thomas, s Dirk Bogarde, Brigitte Bardot.
DOCTOR AT LARGE (Universal, J. Arthur Rank, 1957) d Ralph Thomas, s Dirk Bogarde, Muriel Pavlow.
DOCTOR IN LOVE (Governor, J. Arthur Rank, 19562) d Ralph Thomas, s Michael Craig, Virginia Maskell.
DOCTOR IN DISTRESS (Governor, J. Arthur Rank, 1964) d Ralph Thomas, s Dirk Bogarde, Samantha Eggar.

198. DOCTOR WHO
The British science fiction hero has appeared on television since 1963; to date, seven actors have played the Time Lord role, with a variety of companions and returning villains. An eighth actor played the role in these motion pictures. The Doctor, who wanders through space in his TARDIS, has also appeared in a stage play. Most of the television scripts have been novelized.
DOCTOR WHO AND THE DALEKS (Regal Films/Lion International, 1965) d Gordon Flemyng, s Peter Cushing, Roy Castle, Jennie Linden.
THE DALEKS: INVASION EARTH 2150 AD (Lion International, 1966) d Gordon Flemyng; s Peter Cushing, Bernard Cribbins, Ray Brooks.

199. DON BARRY AND LYNN MERRICK
These are B Westerns.
TWO GUN SHERIFF (Republic, 1941) d George Sherman, s Don Barry, Lynn Merrick.
DESERT BANDIT (Republic, 1941) d George Sherman, s Don Barry, Lynn Merrick.

KANSAS CYCLONE (Republic, 1941) d George Sherman, s Don Barry, Lynn Merrick.
THE APACHE KID (Republic, 1941) d George Sherman, s Don Barry, Lynn Merrick.
DEATH VALLEY OUTLAWS (Republic, 1941) d George Sherman, s Don Barry, Lynn Merrick.
A MISSOURI OUTLAW (Republic, 1941) d George Sherman, s Don Barry, Lynn Merrick, Al St. John.
ARIZONA TERROR (Republic, 1942) d George Sherman, s Don Barry, Lynn Merrick, Al St. John.
STAGECOACH EXPRESS (Republic, 1942) d George Sherman, s Don Barry, Lynn Merrick, Al St. John.
JESSE JAMES JR. (Republic, 1942) d George Sherman, s Don Barry, Lynn Merrick, Al St. John.
CYCLONE KID (Republic, 1942) d George Sherman, s Don Barry, Lynn Merrick, Al St. John.
THE SOMBRERO KID (Republic, 1942) d George Sherman, s Don Barry, Lynn Merrick, Slim Andrews.
OUTLAWS OF PINERIDGE (Republic, 1942) d William Witney, s Don Barry, Lynn Merrick, Emmett Lynn.
DEAD MAN'S GULCH (Republic, 1943) d John English, s Don Barry, Lynn Merrick, Emmett Lynn.
CARSON CITY CYCLONE (Republic, 1943) d Howard Bretherton, s Don Barry, Lynn Merrick, Emmett Lynn.
DAYS OF OLD CHEYENNE (Republic, 1943) d Elmer Clifton, s Don Barry, Lynn Merrick, Emmett Lyn.
FUGITIVE FROM SONORA (Republic, 1943) d Howard Bretherton, s Don Barry, Lynn Merrick, Wally Vernon.

200. DON CAMILLO
The adventures of a smalltown Italian priest are based on books by Giovanni Guareschi, including *Don Camillo and The Prodigal Son*. There was also a 1980 BBC television series, DON CAMILLO, with Mario Adorf.
THE LITTLE WORLD OF DON CAMILLO (London Films, 1951) d Jules Duvivier, s Fernandel
DON CAMILLO MONSEIGNEUR (1961) s Fernaldel.
THE RETURN OF DON CAMILLO (1965) d Julien Duvivier, s Fernandel, Gino Cervi.

201. *DOROTHY PAGE*
"The world's only singing cowgirl" stars in these second-feature pictures.
RIDE 'EM COWGIRL (Grand National, 1939) s Dorothy Page, Milton Frome.
SINGING COWGIRL (Grand National, 1939) s Dorothy Page

202. DORTMUNDER AND GANG
Donald E. Westlake wrote a series of humorous crime/caper novels which inspired these pictures.

THE HOT ROCK (20th Century-Fox, 1972) d Peter Yates, s Robert Redford, George Segal.
BANK SHOT (United Artists, 1974) d Gower Champion, s George C. Scott, Joanna Cassidy.
JIMMY THE KID (New World, 1982) d Gary Nelson, s Gary Coleman, Paul LeMat.
WHY ME? (TWE, 1989) d Gene Quintano, s Christophe Lambert, Kim Greist, Christopher Lloyd.

203. DRACULA
Bram Stoker's vampire novel, set in part in exotic Transylvania, has been constantly translated to celluloid. See also NOSFERATU and BLACULA, COUNT YORGA, VAMPIRE and COUNT WALDEMAR DANINSKY and the CARMILLA TRILOGY entries. This listing does not include pictures made in other than the United States or British commonwealth countries. According to Robertson's *Guinness Film Facts & Feats*, Dracula has appeared in some 148 films as compared to the Frankenstein Monster's ninety-six.
DRACULA (Universal, 1931) d Tod Browning, s Bela Lugosi, Edward Van Sloan.
DRACULA'S DAUGHTER (Universal, 1936) d Lambert Hillyer, s Gloria Holden, Otto Kruger.
SON OF DRACULA (Universal, 1943) d Robert Siodmak, s Lon Chaney Jr., J. Edward Bromberg.
HOUSE OF FRANKENSTEIN (Universal, 1944) d Erle C. Kenton, s John Carradine, Lon Chaney Jr., Boris Karloff.
HOUSE OF DRACULA (Universal, 1945) d Erle C. Kenton, s John Carradine, Lon Chaney Jr., Onslow Stevens.
ABBOTT AND COSTELLO MEET FREANKENSTEIN (Universal, 1948) d Charles T. Barton, s Bela Lugosi, Bud Abbott, Lou Costello, Lon Chaney Jr.
BLOOD OF DRACULA (Carmel, 1957) [aka BLOOD IS MY HERITAGE and BLOOD OF THE DEMON] d Herbert L. Strock, s Jerry Blaine, Gail Ganley, Sandra Harrison.
FRANKENSTEIN MEETS DRACULA (1957) s Victor Fabian.
RETURN OF THE WOLFMAN (1957) s Victor Fabian
REVENGE OF DRACULA (1957) s Victor Fabian.
THE RETURN OF DRACULA (Gramercy, 1958) [aka THE FANTASTIC DISAPPEARING MAN and THE CURSE OF DRACULA] d Paul Landres, s Francis Lederer, Norma Eberhardt.
THE HORROR OF DRACULA (Hammer, 1958) [aka DRACULA] d Terence Fisher, s Peter Cushing, Christopher Lee.
BLACK INFERNO (1958)
THE TEENAGE FRANKENSTEIN (1959) s Gene Gronemeyer
SLAVE OF THE VAMPIRE (1959) s Gene Gronemeyer
I WAS A TEENAGE VAMPIRE (1959) s Don Glut.
PAWNS OF SATAN (1959) s Richard Christy

THE BRIDES OF DRACULA (Hammer, 1960) d Terence Fisher, s Davis Peel, Peter Cushing.
MONSTER RUMBLE (1961) s Donald Glut.
HOUSE ON BARE MOUNTAIN (Jeffrey Smithers, 1962)
KISS ME QUICK! (1964)
BATMAN DRACULA (1964) s Jack Smith
BILLY THE KID VERSUS DRACULA (Circle, 1965) d William Beaudine, s John Carradine.
DRACULA -- PRINCE OF DARKNESS (Hammer, 1965) [aka DISCIPLE OF DRACULA and REVENGE OF DRACULA and THE BLOODY SCREAM OF DRACULA] d Terence Fisher, s Christopher Lee.
HORROR OF DRACULA (1966) s Glenn Sherrard.
DR. TERROR'S GALLERY OF HORRORS (1966) s Mitch Evans.
THE WORST CRIME OF ALL! (1966) s Pluto Felix
CHAPPAQUA (1966)
DRACULA'S WEDDING DAY (1967)
VAMPIRE (1967) s Harrison Marks.
A TASTE OF BLOOD (1967) s Bill Rogers
DRACULA HAS RISEN FROM THE GRAVE (Hammer, 1968) [aka DRACULA'S REVENGE] d Freddie Francis, s Christopher Lee.
DRACULA MEETS THE OUTER SPACE CHICKS (1968)
DRACULA, THE DIRTY OLD MAN (1969) s Vince Kelly
ONE MORE TIME (1969) s Christopher Lee
THE BLOOD OF DRACULA'S CASTLE (A and E Film, 1969) d Al Adamson and Jean Hewitt, s John Carradine, Alex d'Arcy.
DRACULA Vs. FRANKENSTEIN (1969) [aka BLOOD OF FRANKENSTEIN]
TALES OF BLOOD AND TERROR (1969)
DOES DRACULA REALLY SUCK (1969)
MAD MONSTER PARTY (1969)
TASTE THE BLOOD OF DRACULA (Hammer, 1969) d Peter Sasdy, s Christopher Lee, Linda Hayden.
COUNTESS DRACULA (HAMMER, 1970) d Peter Sasdy, s Ingrid Pitt, Nigel Green.
EVERY HOME SHOULD HAVE ONE (1970) s Marty Feldman
GUESS WHAT HAPPENED TO COUNT DRACULA? (1970) s Des Roberts
THE SCARS OF DRACULA (Hammer/EMI, 1970) d Roy Ward Baker, s Christopher Lee, Jenny Hanley.
COUNT DRACULA (Feniz/Corona/Filmar/Towers of London, 1970) [aka BRAM STOKER'S COUNT DRACULA and DRACULA 71 and THE NIGHTS OF DRACULA] d Jesus Franco, s Christopher Lee, Herbert Lom, Klaus Kinski.
DRACULA (TV movie, 1971) s Denholm Elliott.
THE MAD LUST OF A HOT VAMPIRE (1971) s Jim Parker.
THE LUST OF DRACULA (1971)
ONCE UPON A PRIME TIME (1971)
DRACULA, A FAMILY ROMANCE (1972)

DRACULA A.D. 1972 (1972) s Christopher Lee
DRACULA'S GREAT LOVE (Janus/Eva, 1972) [aka CEMETERY GIRLS and DRACULA'S VIRGIN LOVERS] d Javier Aguirre, s Paul Naschy, Haydee Politoff.
SON OF DRACULA (1973) s Harry Nillson
THE HOUSE OF DRACULA'S DAUGHTER (1973)
SHADOW OF DRACULA (1973)
THE SATANIC RITES OF DRACULA (Hammer, 1973) [aka COUNT DRACULA AND HIS VAMPIRE BRIDE and DRACULA IS DEAD... AND WELL AND LIVING IN LONDON] d Alan Gibson, s Christopher Lee, Peter Cushing, Joanna Lumley.
DRACULA (Universal/Dan Curtis Productions, 1974) (CBS-TV movie) d Dan Curtis, s Jack Palance, Simon Ward, Nigel Davenport.
LEGEND OF THE SEVEN GOLDEN VAMPIRES (1974) s John Forbes-Robertson.
VAMPIRA (World Film Services, 1974) d Clive Donner, s David Niven, Peter Bayliss.
DRACULA'S BLOOD (1974) s Hope Stansbury.
DRACULA IS NOT DEAD (1975)
OLD DRACULA (American International, 1975) d Clive Donner.
DEAFULA (Signscope, 1975) d Peter Wechsberg, s Peter Wechsberg, James Randall.
DRACULA IN THE PROVINCES (Coralta Cinematografica, 1975) d Lucio Fulci, s Lando Buzzanca, Sylva Koscina.
TENDER DRACULA (Scotia American, 1975)
COUNT DRACULA (TV movie, 1977) Louis Jourdan.
LADY DRACULA (TV 13/IFV, 1977) d Franz-Joseph Gottlieb, s Evelyne Kraft, Christine Buchegger.
DRACULA'S DOG (Crown International, 1978) [aka ZONTAN -- HOUND OF DRACULA] d Albert Brand, s Michael Pataki, Jose Ferrer.
NOCTURNA (Compass International, 1978) d Harry Tampa (Harry Hurwitz), s John Carradine.
COUNT DRACULA AND HIS VAMPIRE BRIDE (Dynamite Entertainment, 1978) d Alan Gibson, s Christopher Lee.
LOVE AT FIRST BITE (American International, 1979) s George Hamilton.
THE SEVEN BROTHERS MEET DRACULA (Dynamite Entertainment, 1979) d Roy Ward Baker.
HALLOWEEN THAT ALMOST WASN'T (TV movie, 1979) s Judd Hirsch.
VAMPIRE (TV movie, 1979) s Richard Lynch.
MAMA DRACULA (Valisa/Radio Television Belge Francaise, 1979) d Boris Szulzinger, s Maria Schneider, Louise Fletcher.
DRACULA (Universal, 1979) d John Badham, s Frank Langella.
DRACULA AND SON (Gaumont, 1979) d Edouard Molinaro.
DRACULA BITES THE BIG APPLE (1979) s Peter Lowey.
DRACULA SUCKS (Kodiak, 1980) d Philip Marshak, s Jamie Gillis.
DRACULA'S LAST RITES (Cannon, 1980) d Dinibuc Oarusm, s Gerald Fielding.

104 MOTION PICTURE SERIES & SEQUELS

STAR VIRGIN (1980) s Johnny Harden.
DRACULA BLOWS HIS COOL (Martin, 1982) d Carlo Ombra.
DRACULA RISES FROM THE COFFIN (Tai Chang/ROK, 1982) d Lee Hyoung Pyo, s Kang Yong Suk, Park Yang Rae.
DRACULA, SOVEREIGN OF THE DAMNED (1983)
DRACULA: THE LOVE STORY (Skouras Pictures, 1989) d Deran Sarafian, s Brendan Hughes, Steve Bond.

204. DRAGNET
This realistic police drama had two NBC television runs with Jack Webb playing Sgt. Joe Friday, from 1955-59 and 1967-70. Yet another version began airing in syndication in 1989. Friday was also featured on a radio show 1949-56.
DRAGNET (Warner Brothers, 1954) d Jack Webb, s Jack Webb, Ben Alexander, Richard Boone.
DRAGNET (Mark VII, 1969) (NBC-TV movie) d Jack Webb, s Jack Webb, Harry Morgan.
DRAGNET (Universal, 1987) d Tom Mankiewicz, s Dan Aykroyd, Tom Hanks.

205. DR. CHRISTIAN
Country doctor Paul Christian is a physician who cares.
MEET DR. CHRISTIAN (RKO, 1939) d Bernard Vorhaus, s Jean Hershoolt, Dorothy Lovett.
THE COURAGEOUS DR. CHRISTIAN (RKO, 1940) d Bernard Vorhaus, s Jean Hersholt, Dorothy Lovett.
DR. CHRISTIAN MEETS THE WOMEN (RKO, 1940) d William McGann, s Jean Hersholt, Dorothy Lovett, Edgar Kennedy.
REMEDY FOR RICHES (RKO, 1940) d Erle C. Kenton, s Jean Hersholt, Dorothy Lovett.
MELODY FOR THREE (RKO, 1941) d Erle C. Kenton, s Jean Hersholt, Fay Wrap.
THEY MEET AGAIN (RKO, 1941) d Erle C. Kenton, s Jean Hersholt, Dorothy Lovett

206. DR. GOLDFOOT
Vincent Price plays a mad scientist in these teenage movies.
DR. GOLDFOOT AND THE BIKINI MACHINE (American-International, 1966) d Norman Taurog, s Vincent Price, Frankie Avalon, Dwayne Hickman, Susan Hart.
DR. GOLDFOOT AND THE GIRL BOMBS (American-International, 1966) d Mario Bava, s Vincent Price, Fabian, Franco Franchi, Laura Antonelli.

207. DR. JEKYLL AND MR. HYDE
Robert Louis Stevenson's novel of the ultimate schizophrenic was filmed many times.

THE STRANGE CASE OF DR. JEKYLL AND MR. HYDE (Selig Polyscope, 1908)
THE DUALITY OF MAN (1910)
DR. JEKYLL AND MR. HYDE (Thanhouser, 1912)
DR. JEKYLL AND MR. HYDE (Pioneer, 1913) s Sheldon Lewis.
DR. JEKYLL AND MR. HYDE (Paramount-Artcraft, 1920) d John Stewart Robertson, s John Barrymore, Martha Mansfield.
DR. JEKYLL AND MR. HYDE (Louis B. Mayer, 1920) d Louis B. Mayer, s Sheldon Lewis, Alexander Shannon.
DR. JEKYLL AND MR. HYDE (Paramount, 1931) d Rouben Mamoulian, s Frederic March, Rose Hobart.
DR. JEKYLL AND MR. HYDE (MGM, 1941) d Victor Fleming, s Spencer Tracy, Ingrid Bergman.
THE SON OF DR. JEKYLL (Columbia, 1951) d Seymour Friedman, s Louis Hayward, Jody Lawrence.
DR. JEKYLL (1951)
ABBOTT AND COSTELLO MEET DR. JEKYLL AND MR. HYDE (1953)
MY FRIEND JEKYLL (Cinematografica Marino Girolami/CEI Incom, 1960) [aka MY PAL DR. JEKYLL] d Marino Girolami, s Ugo Tognazzi.
THE TWO FACES OF DR. JEKYLL (Hammer, 1961) [aka HOUSE OF FRIGHT and JEKYLL'S INFERNO] d Terence Fisher, s Paul Massie, Dawn Addams.
DOCTOR JEKYLL AND SISTER HYDE (Hammer, 1971) d Roy Ward Baker, s Ralph Bates, Martine Beswick.
I, MONSTER (British Lions-Amicus, 1971) [aka THE MAN WITH TWO HEADS] d Stephen Weeks, s Christopher Lee, Peter Cushing, Susan Jameson.
DR. JEKYLL AND MR. BLOOD (Mishkin, 1972) [aka THE MAN WITH TWO HEADS] d Andy Milligan, s Denis de Marne, Julia Stratton.
DR. BLACK, MR. HYDE (1976) [aka THE WATTS MONSTER, DR. BLACK AND MR. WHITE] d William Crain, s Bernie Casey, Rosalind Cash.
DR. JEKYLL JR. (Medusa, 1979) [aka DR. AND MRS. JEKYLL and JEKYLL JR.] d Steno, s Paolo Villaggio.
DR. HECKYL AND MR. HYPE (1980) d Charles B. Griffith, s Oliver Reed, Sunny Johnson.
THE BLOOD OF DR. JEKYLL (Whodunit/Allegro, 1981) [aka DOCTOR JEKYLL AND MISS OSBOURNE) `d Walerian Borowczyk, s Udo Kier, Marina Pierro.
DR. JEKYLL'S DUNGEON OF DEATH (Hyde, 1982) d James Wood, s James Mathers, John Kearnery.
JEKYLL AND HYDE TOGETHER AGAIN (Paramount, 1982) d Jerry Belson, s Mark Blankfield, Bess Armstrong.
DR. JEKYLL AND MR. HYDE -- A JOURNEY INTO FEAR (Allied Entertainment 1988) d Gerard Kikoine, s Anthony Perkins, Glynis Barber.
JEKYLL & HYDE (ABC-TV movie, 1990) d David Wickes, s Michael Caine, Cheryl Ladd.

208. DR. KILDARE

James Kildare, M.D., was featured in novels by Max Brand (Frederick Faust). Kildare, Dr. Leonard Gillespie and the other characters also turned up in a television series aired by NBC 1961-66 and featuring Richard Chamberlain and Raymond Massey.

INTERNS CAN'T TAKE MONEY (Paramount, 1937) d Alfred Santell, s Joel McCrea, Barbara Stanwyck.
YOUNG DR. KILDARE (MGM, 1938) d Harold S. Bucquet, s Lew Ayres, Lionel Barrymore.
CALLING DR. KILDARE (MGM, 1939) d Harold S. Bucquet, s Lew Ayres, Lionel Barrymore.
THE SECRET OF DR. KILDARE (MGM, 1939) d Harold S. Bucquet, s Lew Ayres, Lionel Barrymore.
DR. KILDARE'S STRANGEST CASE (MGM, 1940) d Harold S. Bucquet, s Lew Ayres, Lionel Barrymore.
DR. KILDARE GOES HOME (MGM, 1940) d Harold S. Bucquet, s Lew Ayres, Lionel Barrymore.
DR. KILDARE'S CRISIS (MGM, 1940) d Harold S. Bucquet, s Lew Ayres, Lionel Barrymore.
THE PEOPLE VS. DR. KILDARE (MGM, 1941) d Harold S. Bucquet, s Lew Ayres, Lionel Barrymore.
DR. KILDARE'S WEDDING DAY (MGM, 1941) d Harold S. Bucquet, s Lew Ayres, Lionel Barrymore.
DR. KILDARE'S VICTORY (MGM, 1942) d W.S. Van Dyke II, s Lew Ayres, Lionel Barrymore.
CALLING DR. GILLESPIE (MGM, 1942) d Harold S. Bucquet, s Lionel Barrymore, Philip Dorn.
DR. GILLESPIE'S NEW ASSISTANT (MGM, 1943) d Wilis Goldbeck, s Lionel Barrymore, Van Johnson.
DR. GILLESPIE'S CRIMINAL CASE (MGM, 1943) d Wilis Goldbeck, s Lionel Barrymore, Van Johnson.
THREE MEN IN WHITE (MGM, 1944) d Wilis Goldbeck, s Lionel Barrymore, Van Johnson.
BETWEEN TWO WOMEN (MGM, 1944) d Wilis Golbeck, s Van Johnson, Lionel Barrymore.
DARK DELUSIONS (MGM, 1947) d Wilis Goldbeck, s Lionel Barrymore, James Craig.

209. DR. MABUSE

The main character of the films is a master criminal. The first two entries were originally one picture.

DR. MABUSE: DER SPIELER (THE GAMBLER) (1922) d Fritz Lang, s Rudolf Klein-Rogge, Aud Egede Nissen.
DR. MABUSE, KING OF CRIME (1922) d Fritz Lang, s Rudolf Klein-Rogge, Aud Egede Nissen.

THE TESTAMENT OF DR. MABUSE (1933) [aka THE CRIME OF DR. MABUSE and THE LAST WILL OF DR. MABUSE] d Fritz Lang, s Rudolf Klein-Rogge, Otto Wernicke.
THE THOUSAND EYES OF DR. MABUSE (1960) [aka THE SECRET OF DR. MABUSE and THE DIABOLICAL DR. MABUSE] d Fritz Lang, s Dawn Addams, Peter Van Eyck.

210. DR. PHIBES
A disfigured musical prodigy seeks revenge against the doctors who were unable to save his wife's life.
THE ABOMINABLE DR. PHIBES (American International, 1971) d Robert Fuest, s Vincent Price, Joseph Cotton.
DR. PHIBES RISES AGAIN (American International, 1972) d Robert Fuest, s Vincent Price.

211. DR. TERROR
These are horror-fantasy movies.
DR. TERROR'S HOUSE OF HORRORS (Amicus, 1965) d Freddie Francis, s Peter Cushing, Donald Sutherland.
DR. TERROR'S GALLERY OF HORRORS (American General, 1967) [aka RETURN FROM THE PAST and THE BLOOD SUCKERS] d David L. Hewitt, s Lon Chaney Jr., John Carradine.

211A. DUDE, THE
These are silent comedy pictures.
THE DUDE AND THE BATHING GIRLS (American Mutoscope & Biograph, 1903)
THE DUDE AND THE BURGLARS (American Mutoscope & Biograph, 1903)

212. DUNCAN MACLAIN
Captain Duncan Maclain is a blind detective who solves crimes with the help of a dog. The character appeared in thirteen books written by Baynard H. Kendrick from 1937-61.
THE LAST EXPRESS (Universal, 1938) d Otis Garrett, s Kent Taylor, Dorothea Kent.
EYES IN THE NIGHT (MGM, 1942) d Fred Zinnemann, s Ann Harding, Edward Arnold.
THE HIDDEN EYE (MGM, 1945) d Richard Whorf, s Edward Arnold, Frances Rafferty, Ray Collins.

213. DURANGO KID, THE
These are Charles Starrett Western vehicles.
THE DURANGO KID (Columbia, 1940) d Lambert Hillyer, s Charles Starrett, Luana Walters.
THE RETURN OF THE DURANGO KID (Columbia, 1945) d Derwin Abrahamas, s Tex Harding, Betty Roadman.

RUSTLERS OF THE BADLANDS (Columbia, 1945) d Derwin Abrahams, s Charles Starrett, Dub Taylor, Sally Bliss.
BLAZING THE WESTERN TRAIL (Columbia, 1945) d Vernon Keays, s Charles Starrett, Tex Harding, Dub Taylor, Carole Matthews.
OUTLAWS OF THE ROCKIES (Columbia, 1945) d Ray Nazarro, s Charles Starrett, Tex Harding, Dub Taylor.
LAWLESS EMPIRE (Columbia, 1945) d Vernon Keays, s Charles Starrett, Tex Harding, Dub Taylor, Mildred Law.
TEXAS PANHANDLE (Columbia, 1945) d Ray Nazarro, s Charles Starrett, Tex Harding, Dub Taylor, Nanette Parks.
BOTH BARRELS BLAZING (Columbia, 1945) d Derwin Abrahams, s Charles Starrett, Tex Harding, Dub Taylor, Pat Parrish.
FRONTIER GUNLAW (Columbia, 1946) d Derwin Abrahams, s Charles Starrett, Tex Harding, Dub Taylor, Jean Stevens.
ROARING RANGERS (Columbia, 1946) d Ray Nazarro, s Charles Starrett, Smiley Burnette, Adelle Roberts.
GUNNING FOR VENGEANCE (Columbia, 1946) d Ray Nazarro, s Charles Starrett, Smiley Burnette.
GALLOPING THUNDER (Columbia, 1946) d Ray Nazarro, s Charles Starret, Smiley Burnette.
TWO FISTED STRANGER (Columbia, 1945) d Ray Nazarro, s Charles Starrett, Smiley Burnett, Doris Houck.
THE DESERT HORSEMAN (Columbia, 1946) d Ray Nazarro, s Charles Starrett, Smiley Burnette, Adelle Roberts.
HEADING WEST (Columbia, 1946) d Ray Nazarro, s Charles Starrett, Smiley Burnette.
LANDRUSH (Columbia, 1946) d Vernon Keays, s Charles Starrett, Smiley Burnette, Doris Houck, Emmett Lynn.
TERROR TRAIL (Columbia, 1946) d Ray Nazarro, s Charles Starrett, Smiley Burnette, Barbara Pepper.
THE FIGHTING FRONTIERSMAN (Columbia, 1946) d Derwin Abrahams, s Charles Starrett, Smiley Burnette, Helen Mowery.
SOUTH OF THE CHISHOLM TRAIL (Columbia, 1947) d Derwin Abrahams, s Charles Starrett, Smiley Burnette, Nancy Saunders.
THE LONE HAND TEXAN (Columbia, 1947) d Ray Nazarro, s Charles Starrett, Smiley Burnette, Mary Newton.
WEST OF DODGE CITY (Columbia, 1947) d Ray Nazarro, s Charles Starrett, Smiley Burnette, Nancy Saunders.
LAW OF THE CANYON (Columbia, 1947) d Ray Nazarro, s Charles Starrett, Smiley Burnette, Nancy Saunders.
PRAIRIE RAIDERS (Columbia, 1947) d Derwin Abrahams, s Charles Starrett, Smiley Burnette, Nancy Saunders.
THE STRANGER FROM PONCA CITY (Columbia, 1947) d Derwin Abrahams, s Charles Starrett, Smiley Burnette, Virginia Hunter.
RIDERS OF THE LONE STAR (Columbia, 1947) d Derwin Abrahams, s Charles Starrett, Smiley Burnette, Virginia Hunter.

MOTION PICTURE SERIES & SEQUELS 109

BUCKAROO FROM POWDER RIVER (Columbia, 1947) d Ray Nazarro, s Charles Starrett, Smiley Burnette, Eve Miller, Forrest Taylor.
LAST DAYS OF BOOT HILL (Columbia, 1947) d Ray Nazarro, s Charles Starrett, Smiley Burnette, Virginia Hunter.
SIX-GUN LAW (Columbia, 1948) d Ray Nazarro, s Charles Starrett, Smiley Burnette, Nancy Saunders.
PHANTOM VALLEY (Columbia, 1948) d Ray Nazarro, s Charles Starrett, Smiley Burnette, Virginia Hunter.
WEST OF SONORA (Columbia, 1948) d Ray Nazarro, s Charles Starrett, Smiley Burnette, Steve Darrell.
WHIRLWIND RAIDERS (Columbia, 1948) d Vernon Keays, s Charles Starrett, Smiley Burnette, Nancy Saunders.
BLAZING ACROSS THE PECOS (Columbia, 1948) d Ray Nazarro, s Charles Starrett, Smiley Burnette, Patricia White, Chief Thundercloud.
TRAIL TO LAREDO (Columbia, 1948) d Ray Nazarro, s Charles Starrett, Smiley Burnette.
EL DORADO PASS (Columbia, 1948) d Ray Nazarro, s Charles Starrett, Smiley Burnette, Elena Verdugo.
QUICK ON THE TRIGGER (Columbia, 1948) d Ray Nazarro, s Charles Starrett, Smiley Burnette, Lyle Talbot.
CHALLENGE OF THE RANGE (Columbia, 1949) d Ray Nazarro, s Charles Starrett, Smiley Burnette, Paula Raymond.
SOUTH OF DEATH VALLEY (Columbia, 1949) d Ray Nazarro, s Charles Starrett, Smiley Burnette, Gail Davis.
BANDITS OF EL DORADO (Columbia, 1949) d Ray Nazarro, s Charles Starrett, Smiley Burnette, George J. Lewis.
LARAMIE (Columbia, 1949) d Ray Nazarro, s Charles Starrett, Smiley Burnette, Marjorie Stapp.
RENEGADES OF THE SAGE (Columbia, 1949) d Ray Nazarro, s Charles Starrett, Smiley Burnette, Leslie Banning.
THE BLAZING TRAIL (Columbia, 1949) d Ray Nazarro, s Charles Starrett, Smiley Burnette, Marjorie Stapp.
DESERT VIGILANTE (Columbia, 1949) d Fred F. Sears, s Charles Starrett, Smiley Burnette.
HORSEMEN OF THE SIERRAS (Columbia, 1949) d Fred F. Sears, s Charles Starrett, Smiley Burnette, Lois Hall.
OUTCASTS OF BLACK MESA (Columbia, 1950) d Ray Nazarro, s Charles Starrett, Smiley Burnette, Martha Hyer.
TRAIL OF THE RUSTLERS (Columbia, 1950) d Ray Nazarro, s Charles Starrett, Smiley Burnette, Gail Davis.
TEXAS DYNAMO (Columbia, 1950) d Ray Nazarro, s Charles Starrett, Smiley Burnette, Lois Hall.
STREETS OF GHOST TOWN (Columbia, 1950) d Ray Nazarro, s Charles Starrett, Smiley Burnette, Mary Ellen Kay.
ACROSS THE BADLANDS (Columbia, 1950) d Fred F. Sears, s Charles Starrett, Smiley Burnette, Helen Mowery.

110 MOTION PICTURE SERIES & SEQUELS

RAIDERS OF TOMAHAWK CREEK (Columbia, 1950) d Fred F. Sears, s Charles Starrett, Smiley Burnette, Kay Buckley.
LIGHTNING GUNS (Columbia, 1950) d Fred F. Sears, s Charles Starrett, Smiley Burnette, Gloria Henry.
FRONTIER OUTPOST (Columbia, 1950) d Ray Nazarro, s Charles Starrett, Smiley Burnette, Lois Hall.
PRAIRIE ROUNDUP (Columbia, 1951) d Fred F. Sears, s Charles Starrett, Smiley Burnette, Mary Castle.
RIDIN' THE OUTLAW TRAIL (Columbia, 1951) d Fred F. Sears, s Charles Starrett, Smiley Burnette, Sunny Vickers.
FORT SAVAGE RAIDERS (Columbia, 1951) d Ray Nazarro, s Charles Starrett, Smiley Burnette, John Dehner.
SNAKE RIVER DESPERADOES (Columbia, 1951) d Fred F. Sears, s Charles Starrett, Smiley Burnette, Monte Blue.
BONANZA TOWN (Columbia, 1951) d Fred F. Sears, s Charles Starrett, Smiley Burnette, Fred F. Sears.
CYCLONE FURY (Columbia, 1951) d Ray Nazarro, s Charles Starrett, Smiley Burnette, Clayton Moore.
THE KID FROM AMARILLO (Columbia, 1951) d Ray Nazarro, s Charles Starrett, Smiley Burnette, Harry Lauter.
PECOS RIVER (Columbia, 1951) d Fred F. Sears, s Charles Starrett, Smiley Burnette, Delores Sidener.
SMOKY CANYON (Columbia, 1951) d Fred F. Sears, s Charles Starrett, Smiley Burnette, Jack Mahoney.
THE HAWK OF WILD RIVER (Columbia, 1952) d Fred F. Sears, s Charles Starrett, Smiley Burnette, Jack Mahoney.
LARAMIE MOUNTAINS (Columbia, 1952) d Ray Nazarro, s Charles Starrett, Smiley Burnette, Jack Mahoney.
THE ROUGH, TOUGH WEST (Columbia, 1952) d Ray Nazarro, s Charles Starrett, Smiley Burnette, Carolina Cotton.
JUNCTION CITY (Columbia, 1952) d Ray Nazarro, s Charles Starrett, Smiley Burnette, Jack Mahoney.
THE KID FROM BROKEN GUN (Columbia, 1952) d Fred F. Sears, s Charles Starrett, Smiley Burnette, Jack Mahoney.

Eddie Murphy is about to go into action in BEVERLY HILLS COP *(1984).*

214. EAST SIDE KIDS, THE

Mugs, Glimpy, Danny, Scruno and other gang members are featured in these pictures, some made simultaneous with the LITTLE TOUGH GUYS series. The two series, which evolved from the DEAD END KIDS series, eventually became the BOWERY BOYS series.

EAST SIDE KIDS (Monogram, 1940) d Robert F. Hill, s Harris Berger, Hally Chester.
BOYS OF THE CITY (Monogram, 1940) d Joseph H. Lewis, s Leo Gorcey, Bobby Jordan, "Sunshine Sammy" Morrison, David Gorcey.
THAT GANG OF MINE (Monogram, 1940) d Joseph H. Lewis, s Leo Gorcey, Bobby Jordan, "Sunshine Sammy" Morrison, David Gorcey.
PRIDE OF THE BOWERY (Monogram, 1941) d Sam Katzman, s Leo Gorcey, Bobby Jordan, "Sunshine Sammy" Morrison, David Gorcey.
FLYING WILD (Monogram, 1941) d Sam Katzman, s Leo Gorcey, Bobby Jordan, "Sunshine Sammy" Morrison, David Gorcey.
BOWERY BLITZKRIEG (Monogram, 1941) s Leo Gorcey, Bobby Jordan, "Sunshine Sammy" Morrison, David Gorcey.
SPOOKS RUN WILD (Monogram, 1941) d Sam Katzman, s Leo Gorcey, Bobby Jordan, "Sunshine Sammy" Morrison, David Gorcey.
MR. WISE GUY (Monogram, 1942) d William Nigh, s Leo Gorcey, Bobby Jordan, "Sunshine Sammy" Morrison, David Gorcey, Huntz Hall.
LET'S GET TOUGH (Monogram, 1942) d Wallace Fox, s Leo Gorcey, Huntz Hall, Bobby Jordan, "Sunshine Sammy" Morrison, David Gorcey, Gabriel Dell.
SMART ALECKS (Monogram, 1941) d Wallace Fox, s Leo Gorcey, Huntz Hall, "Sunshine Sammy" Morrison, David Gorcey, Gabriel Dell.
'NEATH BROOKLYN BRIDGE (Monogram, 1942) d Wallace Fox, s Leo Gorcey, Huntz Hall, "Sunshine Sammy" Morrison, David Gorcey, Gabriel Dell, Bobby Jordan.
KID DYNAMITE (Monogram, 1943) d Wallace Fox, s Leo Gorcey, Huntz Hall, "Sunshine Sammy" Morrison.
CLANCY STREET BOYS (Monogram, 1943) d William Beaudine, s Leo Gorcey, Huntz Hall, "Sunshine Sammy" Morrison, Bobby Jordan, Bennie Bartlett.
GHOSTS ON THE LOOSE (Monogram, 1943) d William Beaudine, s Leo Gorcey, Huntz Hall, "Sunshine Sammy" Morrison, Bobby Jordan, Billy Benedict.
MR. MUGGS STEPS OUT (Monogram, 1943) d William Beaudine, s Leo Gorcey, Huntz Hall, "Sunshine Sammy" Morrison, Bobby Jordan, Bobby Stone.
MILLION DOLLAR KID (Monogram, 1944) d Wallace Fox, s Leo Gorcey, Huntz Hall, Billy Benedict.
FOLLOW THE LEADER (Monogram, 1944) d William Beaudine, s Leo Gorcey, Huntz Hall.
BLOCK BUSTERS (Monogram, 1944) d Wallace Fox, s Leo Gorcey, Huntz Hall, Gabriel Dell.

BOWERY CHAMPS (Monogram, 1944) d William Beaudine, s Leo Gorcey, Huntz Hall, Billy Benedict, Gabriel Dell.
DOCKS OF NEW YORK (Monogram, 1945) d Wallace Fox, s Leo Gorcey, Huntz Hall, Billy Benedict.
MR. MUGGS RIDES AGAIN (Monogram, 1945) d Wallace Fox, s Leo Gorcey, Huntz Hall, Billy Benedict.
COME OUT FIGHTING (Monogram, 1945) d William Beaudine, s Leo Gorcey, Huntz Hall, Gabriel Dell, Billy Benedict.

215. EASY ACES, THE
The husband-and-wife team from radio (1930-49), Goodman and Jane Ace, were known for their snappy repartee. The list of film shorts is incomplete.
TOPNOTCHERS
AN OLD-FASHIONED MOVIE

216. ECSTASY GIRLS, THE
These pictures are of the adult variety.
THE ECSTASY GIRLS (Caballero, 1979) d Robert McCallum, s Jamie Gillis, Serena.
THE ECSTASY GIRLS II (Caballero, 1986) s Heather Wayne, Jamie Gillis.

217. EDDIE AND THE CRUISERS
The hero of these pictures is a Bruce Springsteen/Elvis Presley musical hybrid from a working class background.
EDDIE AND THE CRUISERS (Embassy, 1983) d Martin Davidson, s Tom Berenger, Michael Pare, Joe Pantoliano.
EDDIE AND THE CRUISERS II: EDDIE LIVES! (Scotti Brothers Pictures, 1989) d Jean-Claude Lord, s Michael Pare, Marina Orsini, Bernie Coulson.

218. *EDDIE DEAN AND EMMETT LYNN*
These are B Westerns teaming Eddie Dean and Emmett Lynn.
SONG OF OLD WYOMING (PRC, 1945) d Robert Emmett Tansey, s Eddie Dean, Lash LaRue, Emmett Lynn, Jennifer Holt.
ROMANCE OF THE WEST (PRC, 1946) d Robert Emmett Tansey, s Eddie Dean, Emmett Lynn, Joan Barton.
THE CARAVAN TRAIL (PRC, 1946) d Robert Emmett Tansey, s Eddie Dean, Emmett Lynn, Lash LaRue, Jean Carlin.

219. *EDDIE DEAN AND ROSCOE ATES*
Roscoe Ates plays Soapy Jones, sidekick to Eddie Dean, in this series of B Westerns.
COLORADO SERENADE (PRC, 1946) d Emmett Tansey, s Eddie Dean, Roscoe Ates, Mary Kenyon.
DRIFTIN' RIVER (PRC, 1946) d Emmett Tansey, s Eddie Dean, Roscoe Ates, Shirley Patterson.

TUMBLEWEED TRAIL (PRC, 1946) d Emmett Tansey, s Eddie Dean, Roscoe Ates, Shirley Patterson.
STARS OVER TEXAS (PRC, 1946) d Emmett Tansey, s Eddie Dean, Roscoe Ates, Shirley Patterson.
WILD WEST (PRC, 1946) d Emmett Tansey, s Eddie Dean, Roscoe Ates.
WILD COUNTRY (PRC, 1947) d Ray Taylor, s Eddie Dean, Roscoe Ates.
RANGE BEYOND THE BLUE (PRC, 1947) d Ray Taylor, s Eddie Dean, Roscoe Ates, Helen Mowery.
WEST TO GLORY (PRC, 1947) d Ray Taylor, s Eddie Dean, Roscoe Ates, Delores Castle.
BLACK HILLS (PRC, 1947) d Ray Taylor, s Eddie Dean, Roscoe Ates, Shirley Patterson.
SHADOW VALLEY (PRC, 1947) d Ray Taylor, s Eddie Dean, Roscoe Ates, Jennifer Holt.
CHECK YOUR GUNS (PRC, 1948) d Ray Taylor, s Eddie Dean, Roscoe Ates, Nacy Gates.
TORNADO RANGE (PRC, 1948) d Ray Taylor, s Eddie Dean, Roscoe Ates, Jennifer Holt.
THE WESTWARD TRAIL (PRC, 1948) d Ray Taylor, s Eddie Dean, Roscoe Ates.
HAWK OF POWDER RIVER (PRC, 1948) d Ray Taylor, s Eddie Dean, Roscoe Ates,
THE TIOGA KID (PRC, 1948) d Ray Taylor, s Eddie Dean, Roscoe Ates, Jennifer Holt.

219A. EDGAR
Johnny Jones is featured in this circa 1918 silent film series.

EDGAR KENNEDY
See **MR. AVERAGE MAN**

220. EDGAR WALLACE
These second features are based on the fictional works of British writer Edgar Wallace and were issued 1960-63.
THE CLUE OF THE TWISTED CANDLE
A MARRIAGE OF CONVENIENCE
THE MALPAS MYSTERY
THE MAN WHO WAS NOBODY
THE CLUE OF THE NEW PIN
THE FOURTH SQUARE
PARTNERS IN CRIME
THE MAN AT THE CARLTON TOWER
THE CLUE OF THE SILVER KEY
ATTEMPT TO KILL
THE SINISTER MAN d Clive Donner
NEVER BACK LOSERS
MAN DETAINED

114 MOTION PICTURE SERIES & SEQUELS

RICOCHET
THE DOUBLE
THE RIVALS
TO HAVE AND TO HOLD
THE PARTNER
FIVE TO ONE
ACCIDENTAL DEATH
WE SHALL SEE
DOWNFALL
THE VERDICT
WHO WAS MADDOX? d Geoffrey Nethercott
ACT OF MURDER
FACE OF A STRANGER
NEVER MENTION MURDER d John Nelson
THE MAIN CHANCE
GAME FOR THREE LOSERS
DEAD MAN'S CHEST
CHANGE PARTNERS
STRANGLER'S WEB d John Moxey
BACKFIRE
CANDIDATE FOR MURDER
FLAT TWO
THE SHARE-OUT
NUMBER SIX
TIME TO REMEMBER
PLAYBACK d John Nelson Burton
SOLO FOR SPARROW
LOCKER 69
DEATH TRAP
THE SET-UP
ON THE RUN
THE £20,000 KISS
INCIDENT AT MIDNIGHT
RETURN TO SENDER

221. EIGHT IS ENOUGH
In the television comedy-drama series which aired over ABC 1977-81, Dick Van Patten and Diana Hyland (later Betty Buckley) supervise a family of eight. The series was based on Thomas Braden's book *Eight Is Enough*.
EIGHT IS ENOUGH: A FAMILY REUNION (TV Movie, 1987) d Harry Harris, s Dick Van Patten, Willie Aames, Brian Patrick Clarke.
AN EIGHT IS ENOUGH WEDDING (NBC TV movie, 1989) d Stan Latham, s Dick Van Patten, Sandy Faison, Grant Goodeve.

222. 87th PRECINCT, THE
Ed McBain's series of police procedural novels feature Detectives Steve Carella, Cotton Hawes, Meyer Meyer, Andy Parker, Bert Kling and others.

MOTION PICTURE SERIES & SEQUELS 115

There was also a television program 1961-62 featuring Robert Lansing as Carella and Gena Rowlands as his deaf-mute wife Teddy.
COP HATER (United Artists, 1958) d William Berke, s Robert Loggia, Gerald O'Loughlin.
THE MUGGER (United Artists, 1958) d William Berke, s Kent Smith, Nan Martin.
HIGH AND LOW (Continental, 1963) d Akira Kurosawa, s Toshiro Mifune.
WITHOUT APPARENT MOTIVE (20th Century-Fox, 1972) d Philippe Labro, s Jean-Louis Trintignant.
FUZZ (20th Century-Fox, 1972) d Richard A. Colla, s Burt Reynolds, Raquel Welch.

ELAINE
 See **CRAIG KENNEDY**

223. EL BRENDEL
El Brendel was a vaudevillian with a Swedish dialect. He appeared in a series of short comedies. This list is incomplete.
WHAT! NO MEN? (Vitaphone)
THE LONESOME TRAILER
READY WILLING BUT UNABLE
SWEET SPIRITS OF THE NIGHTER
THE BLITZ KISS

224. ELEANOR AND FRANKLIN ROOSEVELT
These films are about the American President and his wife.
ELEANOR AND FRANKLIN (Talent Associates, 1976) (ABC-TV movie) d Daniel Petrie, s Jane Alexander, Edward Herrmann.
ELEANOR AND FRANKLIN: THE WHITE HOUSE YEARS (Talent Associates, 1977) (ABC-TV movie) d Daniel Petrie, s Jane Alexander, Edward Herrmann.
F.D.R. -- THE LAST YEAR (Titus, 1980) (NBC-TV movie) d Anthony Page, s Jason Robards, Eileen Heckart.
ELEANOR, FIRST LADY OF THE WORLD (Embassy Television, 1982) (CBS-TV movie) d John Erman, s Jean Stapleton, E.G. Marshall.

225. ELLERY QUEEN
Frederic Dannay and Manfred Lee used the joint pseudonym Ellery Queen to write a series of mystery puzzle novels about a gentleman detective named Ellery Queen, the son of a police inspector. Queen also appeared in four television series, a radio show and these films.
THE SPANISH CAPE MYSTERY (Republic, 1935) d Lewis D. Collins, s Donald Cook, Helen Twelvetrees.
THE MANDARIN MYSTERY (Republic, 1937) d Ralph Staub, s Eddie Quillan, Charlotte Henry.
ELLERY QUEEN -- MASTER DETECTIVE (Columbia, 1940) d Kurt Neumann, s Ralph Bellamy, Margaret Lindsay.

ELLERY QUEEN'S PENTHOUSE MYSTERY (Columbia, 1941) d James
    Hogan, s Ralph Bellamy, Margaret Lindsay.
ELLERY QUEEN AND THE PERFECT CRIME (Columbia, 1941) d James
    Hogan, s Ralph Bellamy, Margaret Lindsay, Charley Grapewin.
ELLERY QUEEN AND THE MURDER RING (Columbia, 1941) d James
    Hogan, s Ralph Bellamy, Margaret Lindsay.
A CLOSE CALL FOR ELLERY QUEEN (Columbia, 1942) d James Hogan, s
    William Gargan, Margaret Lindsay.
A DESPERATE CHANCE FOR ELLERY QUEEN (Columbia, 1942) d James
    Hogan, s William Gargan, Margaret Lindsay.
ENEMY AGENTS MEET ELLERY QUEEN (Columbia, 1942) d James
    Hogan, s William Gargan.
ELLERY QUEEN: DON'T LOOK BEHIND YOU (Universal, 1971) (NBC-TV
    broadcast) d Barry Shear, s Peter Lawford, Harry Morgan, Stefanie
    Powers.
ELLERY QUEEN (Universal, 1975) (NBC-TV broadcast) [aka TOO MANY
    SUSPECTS] d David Greene, s Jim Hutton, David Wayne.

226. ELMO
These films feature Elmo Lincoln, who also played the role of TARZAN in another series.
ELMO THE MIGHTY (1919) (serial) s Elmo Lincoln.
ELMO THE FEARLESS (1920) (serial) s Elmo Lincoln.

227. ELSA MAXWELL
ELSA MAXWELL'S HOTEL FOR WOMEN (20th Century-Fox, 1939)
ELSA MAXWSELL'S PUBLIC DEB No. 1 (20th Century-Fox, 1940)

228. EMMANUELLE
Styish eroticism, R-rated, marks these pictures, from the book by Emmanuelle Arsan.
EMMANUELLE (Columbia, 1974) d Just Jaeckin, s Sylvia Kristel, Marika
    Green.
EMMANUELLE II (1975) s Sylvia Kristel
EMMANUELLE, THE JOYS OF A WOMAN (Paramount, 1976) d Francis
    Giacobetti, s Sylvia Kristel, Catherine Rivet.
TRAP THEM AND KILL THEM (Fulvia Cinematografica/Flora/Gico
    Cinematografica, 1977) d Joe d'Amato, s Laura Gemser, Gabriele Tinti.
EMMANUELLE IN AMERICA (1978) d Joe D'Amato, s Laura Gemser.
GOODBYE, EMMANUELLE (Miramax, 1979) d Francois Letterier, s Sylvia
    Kristel.
EMMANUELLE AROUND THE WORLD (Jerry Gross, 1980) d Joe D'Amato,
    s Laura Gemser.
EMMANUELLE, THE QUEEN OF SADOS (1982) d Evangelos Founistakis,
    Ilias Milonakos, s Laura Gemser.
EMMANUELLE IN BANGKOK (?) d Joe D'Amato, s Laura Gemser.
EMMANUELLE 4 (AAA/Sedpa, 1984) d Francis Leroy and Iris Letans.

EMMANUELLE 6 (ASP/EVEREST, 1988) d Otto Weiser, s Nathalie Uher.

229. EMPIRE OF ASH
EMPIRE OF ASH
EMPIRE OF ASH II
EMPIRE OF ASH III (North American Releasing, ca 1988) d Lloyd Simandl and Michael Mazo, s Melanie Kilgour, William Smith.

230. ENTER THE DRAGON
An Oriental hero uses his martial arts skills to defeat villains.
ENTER THE DRAGON (Warner Brothers/Concord, 1973) d Robert Clouse, s Bruce Lee.
RETURN OF THE DRAGON (Concorde, 1973) d Bruce Lee, s Bruce Lee, Chuck Norris.

231. ENTER THE NINJA
Mercenaries take on jungle fighters.
ENTER THE NINJA (Cannon, 1981) d Menahem Golan, s Franco Nero, Susan George.
REVENGE OF THE NINJA (Cannon, 1983) d Sam Firstenberg, s Sho Kosugi, Keith Vitali.
NINJA III -- THE DOMINATION (Cannon, 1984) d Sam Firstenberg, s Lucinda Dickey, Jordan Bennett, Sho Kosugi.

232. ERNEST
Dim-witted Ernest P. Worrell, popularized in television commercials, is featured in these movies.
ERNEST GOES TO CAMP (Touchstone, 1987) d John R. Cherry III, s Jim Varney, Iron Eyes Cody.
ERNEST SAVES CHRISTMAS (Touchstone, 1988) d John R. Cherry III, s Jim Varney.
ERNEST GOES TO JAIL (Touchstone, announced 1990) d John R. Cherry III, s Jim Varney, Gailian Sartain, Barbara Bush.

233. ESCAPE TO WITCH MOUNTAIN
These pictures are mystery-fantasies about a pair of orphans with psychic powers.
ESCAPE TO WITCH MOUNTAIN (Buena Vista, 1975) d John Hough, s Eddie Albert, Ray Milland, Kim Richards.
RETURN FROM WITCH MOUNTAIN (Buena Vista, 1978) d John Hough, s Bette Davis, Christopher Lee.

234. EVERY WHICH WAY BUT LOOSE
The Clint Eastwood comedies are about a good ol' boy's romantic entanglements, bare-fisted fights and naughty orangutan friend Clyde.
EVERY WHICH WAY BUT LOOSE (Warner Brothers, 1978) d James Fargo, s Clint Eastwood, Sondra Locke, Geoffrey Lewis, Ruth Gordon.

ANY WHICH WAY YOU CAN (Warner Brothers, 1980) d Buddy Van Horn, s Clint Eastwood, Sondra Locke, Geoffrey Lewis, Ruth Gordon, Clyde.

235. EVERY WOMAN HAS A FANTASY
And according to these filmmakers, it's X-rated.
EVERY WOMAN HAS A FANTASY (VCA, 1984) d Edward Brown, s Rachel Ashley, John Leslie.
EVERY WOMAN HAS A FANTASY II (VCA, 1986) s Lois Ayres, John Leslie.

236. EVIL DEAD, THE
Demons possess young people at a remote forest cabin and force them to kill each other.
THE EVIL DEAD (New Line, 1983) d Sam Raimi, s Bruce Campbell, Ellen Sandweiss.
EVIL DEAD 2: DEAD BY DAWN (New Line, 1987) d Sam Raimi, s Bruce Campbell, Sarah Berry.

237. EXORCIST, THE
William Peter Blatty's novel of a possessed girl inspired the movies.
THE EXORCIST (Warner Brothers, 1973) d William Friedkin, s Ellen Burstyn, Max Von Sydow, Linda Blair.
EXORCIST II: THE HERETIC (Warner Brothers, 1977) d John Boorman, s Richard Burton, Linda Blair, Louise Fletcher.
THE EXORCIST: 1990 (announced 1990) d William Peter Blatty, s George C. Scott, Sylvia Sidney.

237A. EXPLOITS OF TUBBY
Featured in this circa 1917 silent series from Hepworth are Violet Hopson and Chrissie White.

238. EXTERMINATOR, THE
A Vietnam vet played by Robert Ginty seeks revenge on a gang.
THE EXTERMINATOR (Interstar, 1980) d James Glickenhause, s Christopher George, Samantha Eggar, Robert Ginty.
EXTERMINATOR II (Cannon, 1984) d Mark Buntzman, s Robert Ginty, Mario Van Peebles, Deborah Geffner.

239. EYE OF THE EAGLE
This violent action series features jungle warfare.
EYE OF THE EAGLE (Concorde, 1987) d Cirio H. Santiago, s Brett Clark, Robert Patrick.
EYE OF THE EAGLE II (Concorde, 1988) d Carl Franklin, s Todd Field, Andy Wood.

240. FALCON, THE

This series of films about a gentleman Robin Hood is modeled after THE SAINT and was begun by the same studio after a rights dispute with Leslie Charteris, author of the Saint books.

THE GAY FALCON (RKO, 1941) d Irving Reis, s George Sanders, Wendy Barrie, Allen Jenkins.
A DATE WITH THE FALCON (RKO, 1941) d Irving Reis, s George Sanders, Wendy Barrie.
THE FALCON TAKES OVER (RKO, 1942) d Irving Reis, s George Sanders, Lynn Bari.
THE FALCON'S BROTHER (RKO, 1942) d Stanley Logan, s George Sanders, Tom Conway, Jane Randolph.
THE FALCON STRIKES BACK (RKO, 1943) d Edward Dmytryk, s Tom Conway, Harriet Hilliard.
THE FALCON AND THE CO-EDS (RKO, 1943) d William Clemens, s Tom Conway, Jean Brooks.
THE FALCON IN DANGER (RKO, 1943) d William Clemens, s Tom Conway, Jean Brooks.
THE FALCON IN HOLLYWOOD (RKO, 1944) d Gordon Douglas, s Tom Conway, Barbara Hale.
THE FALCON IN MEXICO (RKO, 1944) d William Berke, s Tom Conway, Mona Maris.
THE FALCON OUT WEST (RKO, 1944) d William Clemens, s Tom Conway, Carole Gallagher.
THE FALCON IN SAN FRANCISCO (RKO, 1945) d Joseph H. Lewis, s Tom Conway, Rita Corday.
THE FALCON'S ALIBI (RKO, 1946) d Ray McCarey, s Tom Conway, Rita Corday.
THE FALCON'S ADVENTURE (RKO, 1946) d William Berke, s Tom Conway, Madge Meredith.
THE DEVIL'S CARGO (Film Classics, 1948) d John F. Link, s John Calvert, Rochelle Hudson.
APPOINTMENT WITH MURDER (Film Classics, 1948) d Jack Bernhard, s John Calvert, Catherine Craig.
SEARCH FOR DANGER (Film Classics, 1949) d Don Martin, s John Calvert, Albert Dekker.

241. FANTASY ISLAND

At a remote island resort, visitors bring lifelong dreams true. The movies are pilots for the ABC series which aired 1978-84.

FANTASY ISLAND (Spelling/Goldberg Productions, 1977) (ABC-TV movie) d Richard Lang, s Ricardo Montalban, Bill Bixby.
RETURN TO FANTASY ISLAND (Spelling/Goldberg Productions, 1978) (ABC-TV movie) d George McCowan, s Ricardo Montalban, Adrienne Barbeau.

242. FATHER BROWN

G.K. Chesterton wrote fifty-one stories about the perceptive cleric-detective, Father Brown. There was also a 1974 TV series with Kenneth More, entitled FATHER BROWN, and a BBC radio series, FATHER BROWN STORIES (1984-85) with Andrew Sachs.
FATHER BROWN, DETECTIVE (Paramount, 1934) d Edward Sedgwick, s Walter Connolly, Paul Lukas, Gertrude Michael.
THE DETECTIVE (Columbia, 1954) [aka FATHER BROWN] d Robert Hammer, s Alec Guiness.
THE GIRL IN THE PARK (1980) d John Llewelyn Moxey, s Barnard Hughes.

243. FATHER OF THE BRIDE
From Edward Streeter's novel: Kay Banks announces her plans to marry Buckley Dunstan and her parents, Stanley and Ellie, make preparations for the wedding.
FATHER OF THE BRIDE (MGM, 1950) d Vincente Minnelli, s Spencer Tracy, Joan Bennett, Elizabeth Taylor, Don Taylor.
FATHER'S LITTLE DIVIDEND (MGM, 1951) d Vincente Minnelli, s Spencer Tracy, Joan Bennett, Elizabeth Taylor, Don Taylor.

244. FATTY
Roscoe Arbuckle starred in silent film comedies for Mack Sennett's Keystone Studio. He later teamed with Mabel Normand (see MABEL entry). This list is strictly of FATTY titles; the comedian also made other pictures.
FATTY'S DAY OFF (Keystone, 1913) d Wilfred Lucas, s Roscoe "Fatty" Arbuckle, Minta Durfee.
FATTY AT SAN DIEGO (Keystone, 1913) d George Nichols, s Roscoe "Fatty" Arbuckle, Minta Durfee.
FATTY JOINS THE FORCE (Keystone, 1914) d George Nichols, s Roscoe "Fatty" Arbuckle.
FATTY'S FLIRTATION (Keystone, 1913) d George Nichols, s Roscoe "Fatty" Arbuckle, Minta Durfee.
FATTY AND THE HEIRESS (Keystone, 1913) d Roscoe Arbuckle, s Roscoe "Fatty" Arbuckle, Minta Durfee.
FATTY'S FINISH (Keystone, 1913) d Roscoe Arbuckle, s Roscoe "Fatty" Arbuckle, Minta Durfee.
FATTY'S GIFT (Keystone, 1914) d Roscoe Arbuckle, s Roscoe "Fatty" Arbuckle.
FATTY'S DEBUT (Keystone, 1914) d Roscoe Arbuckle, s Roscoe "Fatty" Arbuckle, Minta Durfee.
FATTY'S WINE PARTY (Keystone, 1914) d Roscoe Arbuckle, s Roscoe "Fatty" Arbuckle, Minta Durfee.
FATTY AND MINNIE HE-HAW (Keystone, 1914) d Roscoe Arbuckle, s Roscoe "Fatty" Arbuckle, Minta Durfee.
FATTY AGAIN (Keystone, 1914) d Roscoe Arbuckle, s Roscoe "Fatty" Arbuckle.
FATTY'S JONAH DAY (Keystone, 1914) d Roscoe Arbuckle, s Roscoe "Fatty" Arbuckle.

FATTY'S MAGIC PANTS (Keystone, 1914) d Roscoe Arbuckle, s Roscoe "Fatty" Arbuckle.
FATTY'S CHANCE ACQUAINTANCE (Keystone, 1914) d Roscoe Arbuckle, s Roscoe "Fatty" Arbuckle.
FATTY AND MABEL'S SIMPLE LIFE (Keystone, 1915) d Roscoe Arbuckle, s Roscoe "Fatty" Arbuckle, Mabel Normand.
FATTY'S FAITHFUL FIDO (Keystone, 1915) d Roscoe Arbuckle, s Roscoe "Fatty" Arbuckle, Minta Durfee.
FATTY'S NEW ROLE (Keystone, 1915) d Roscoe Arbuckle, s Roscoe "Fatty" Arbuckle.
FICKLE FATTY'S FALL (Keystone, 1915) d Roscoe Arbuckle, s Roscoe "Fatty" Arbuckle, Minta Durfee.
FATTY AND MABEL'S MARRIED LIFE (Keystone, 1915) d Roscoe Arbuckle, s Roscoe "Fatty" Arbuckle, Mabel Normand.
FATTY'S RECKLESS FLING (Keystone, 1915) d Roscoe Arbuckle, s Roscoe "Fatty" Arbuckle, Minta Durfee.
FATTY AND THE BROADWAY STARS (Keystone, 1915) d Roscoe Arbuckle, s Roscoe "Fatty" Arbuckle.
FATTY AND MABEL AT THE SAN DIEGO EXPOSITION (Keystone, 1915) d Roscoe Arbuckle, s Roscoe "Fatty" Arbuckle, Mabel Normand.
MABEL, FATTY AND THE LAW (Keystone, 1915) d Roscoe Arbuckle, s Roscoe "Fatty" Arbuckle, Mabel Normand.
FATTY'S NEW ROLE (Keystone, 1915) d Roscoe Arbuckle, s Roscoe "Fatty" Arbuckle.
MABEL'S AND FATTY'S WASH DAY (Keystone, 1915) d Mabel Normand and Eddie Dillon, s Mabel Normand, Roscoe "Fatty" Arbuckle.
MABEL'S AND FATTY'S SIMPLE LIFE (Keystone, 1915) d Mabel Normand and Eddie Dillon, s Mabel Normand, Roscoe "Fatty" Arbuckle
FATTY AND MABEL VIEWING THE WORLD'S FAIR AT SAN FRANCISCO (Keystone, 1915) d Mabel Normand and Roscoe "Fatty" Arbuckle, s Mabel Normand, Roscoe "Fatty" Arbuckle.
FATTY'S PLUCKY PUP (Keystone, 1915) d Roscoe Arbuckle, s Roscoe "Fatty" Arbuckle.
FATTY'S TINTYPE TANGLE (Keystone, 1915) d Roscoe Arbuckle, s Roscoe "Fatty" Arbuckle.
FATTY AND MABEL ADRIFT (1916) d Roscoe Arbuckle, s Mabel Normand, Roscoe "Fatty" Arbuckle.
FATTY AT CONEY ISLAND (1917) d Roscoe Arbuckle, s Roscoe "Fatty" Arbuckle.

245. FEMME
These are erotic feature films.
FEMME (VCA, 1984) d Candida Royalle, s Tish Ambrose, Michael Knight.
FEMME II: URBAN HEAT (VCA, 1985) d Candida Royalle, s Marita Ekberg, Taija Rae, Scott Baker.
FEMME III: CHRISTINA'S SECRET d Candida Royalle

246. FIBBER McGEE AND MOLLY
Radio found a hit in the teller of tall tales and his patient wife. FIBBER McGEE AND MOLLY evolved from the show SMACKOUT, which ran on Chicago radio 1930-35. The adventures at 79 Wistful Vista, with such neighbors as Throckmorton P. Gildersleeve (see also THE GREAT GILDERSLEEVE entry), Doc Gamble, Beulah the maid, Wallace Wimple, Sis and others, continued to 1957.
LOOK WHO'S LAUGHING (RKO, 1941) d Allan Dwan, s Jim and Marion Jordan, Edgar Bergen.
HERE WE GO AGAIN (RKO, 1942) d Allan Dwan, s Jim and Marion Jordan.
HEAVENLY DAYS (RKO, 1944) d Howard Estabrook, s Jim and Marion Jordan.

246A. FINN AND HADDIE
See POKE AND JABBS entry for description.

247. FIRESTORM
These are adult pictures.
FIRESTORM (Command, 1984) s Joanna Storm, Kay Parker.
FIRESTORM II (Command, 1987) s Tish Ambrose, Ali Moore, John Leslie.

248. FISTS OF FURY
These are martial arts pictures.
FISTS OF FURY (National General, 1973) d Lo Wei, s Bruce Lee.
FISTS OF FURY PART 2 (21st Century, 1980) d Jimmy Shaw.

249. FIVE LITTLE PEPPERS, THE
These family films about a man raising five kids are based on the book *The Five Little Peppers and How They Grew* (1881) by Margaret Sidney.
THE FIVE LITTLE PEPPERS AND HOW THEY GREW (Columbia, 1939) d Charles Barton, s Edith Fellows, Clarence Kolb.
THE FIVE LITTLE PEPPERS AT HOME (Columbia, 1940) d Charle Barton, s Edith Fellows, Dorothy Ann Seese.
THE FIVE LITTLE PEPPERS IN TROUBLE (Columbia, 1940)
OUT WEST WITH THE PEPPERS (Columbia, 1940) d Charles Barton, s Edith Fellows, Dorothy Ann Seese.

250. FLAG LIEUTENANT, THE
Based on the W.P. Drury and Leo Tovar play, these movies are about a man branded a coward after saving a fort from Bashi Bazouks and letting his amnesiac friend take the credit.
THE FLAG LIEUTENANT (Barker/Jury, 1919) d Percy Nash, s Ivy Close, George Wynn, Dorothy Fane, Ernest Wallace.
THE FLAG LIEUTENANT (Astra-National, 1926) d Maurice Elvey, s Henry Edwards, Lillian Oldland, Fred Raynham, Dorothy Secombe.

FURTHER ADVENTURES OF THE FLAG LIEUTENANT (Neo-Art, 1927) d W.P. Kellino, s Henry Edwards, Isabel Jeans, Lillian Oldland, Lyn Harding.
THE FLAG LIEUTENANT (British & Dominion, 1932) d Henry Edwards, s Henry Edwards, Anna Neagle.

251. FLASH CASEY
George Harmon Coxe's Jack Casey, photographer for the *Boston Express*, was featured in prose beginning with stories in *Black Mask*, later in six novels (1942-64).
WOMEN ARE TROUBLE (MGM, 1936) d Errol Taggart, s Stuart Erwin, Paul Kelly, Florence Rice.
HERE'S FLASH CASEY (Grand National, 1937) d Lynn Shores, s Eric Linden, Boots Mallory.

252. FLASH GORDON
These space operas are based on the newspaper comic strip created by Alex Raymond in 1934. Gordon, his sidekicks Dr. Hans Zarkov and Dale Arden battle Ming the Merciless of the planet Mongo.
FLASH GORDON (Universal, 1936) [aka SPACESHIP TO THE UNKNOWN] d Frederick Stephani, s Larry "Buster" Crabbe, Jean Rogers, Charles Middleton, Priscilla Lawson, John Lipson.
FLASH GORDON CONQUERS THE UNIVERSE (Universal, 1940) (twelve chapters) [aka PURPLE DEATH FROM OUTER SPACE] d Ford Beebe and Ray Taylor, s Larry "Buster" Crabbe, Carol Hughes, Charles Middleton, Frank Shannon.
FLASH GORDON'S TRIP TO MARS (Universal, 1938) (fifteen chapters) [aka THE DEADLY RAY FROM MARS] d Ford Beebe and Robert Hill, s Larry "Buster" Crabbe, Jean Rogers, Charles Middleton.
FLASH GORDON (Universal, 1980) d Mike Hodges, s Sam J. Jones, Melody Anderson.

252A. FLESH GORDON
These sex films are elaborate spoofs of the previous, science fiction entry, and feature Flesh Gordon, Eve Ardor, Dr. Jerkoff and Emperor Wang the Merciless.
FLESH GORDON (Media, 1978) d Michael Benveniste, s Jason Williams, Suzanne Fields.
FLESH GORDON MEETS THE COSMIC CHEERLEADERS (Maurice Smith Productions, announced 1990) d Howard Zine, s Vince Merdocco, Robin Kaluski.

253. FLETCH
Gregory McDonald's humorous crime novels about an investigative journalist inspired these pictures.
FLETCH (Universal, 1985) d Michael Ritchie, s Chevy Chase, Dana Wheeler-Nicholson.

FLETCH LIVES (Universal, 1989) d Michael Ritchie, s Chevy Chase, Hal Holbrook, Julianne Phillips.

254. FLIPPER
Two youngsters live with their dad at the Coral Key Park in Florida, where their playmate is a dolphin, Flipper. A television program with the same characters aired on NBC from 1964-68.
FLIPPER (MGM, 1963) d James Clark, s Chuck Connors, Luke Halpin.
FLIPPER'S NEW ADVENTURE (MGM, 1964) d Leon Benson, s Luke Halpin, Pamela Franklin.

255. THE FLY
A scientist experimenting with a matter transfer machine exchanges part of his body with a housefly's. From a short story by George Langelaan.
THE FLY (20th Century-Fox, 1958) d Kurt Neumann, s Al Hedison, Patricia Owens, Vincent Price.
RETURN OF THE FLY (20th Century-Fox, 1959) d Edward L. Bernds, s Vincent Price, Brett Halsey.
CURSE OF THE FLY (20th Century-Fox, 1965) d Don Sharp, s Brian Donlevy, Carole Gray.
THE FLY (1986) d David Cronenberg, s Jeff Goldblum, Geena Davis.
THE FLY II (20th Century-Fox, 1989) d Chris Walas, s Eric Stoltz, Daphne Zuniga.

256. FOOD OF THE GODS
H.G. Wells' novel about common animals being transformed into monsters provided the framework for these pictures.
VILLAGE OF THE GIANTS (Embassy, 1965) d Bert I. Gordon, s Tomy Kirk, Johnny Crawford, Beau Bridges, Ronny Howard, Tisha Sterling.
FOOD OF THE GODS (American International, 1976) d Bert I. Gordon, s Marjoe Gortner, Pamela Franklin.
GNAW: FOOD OF THE GODS, PART 2 (Concorde, 1989) d Damian Lee, s Paul Coufos, Lisa Schrage.

256A. 48 HRS.
A jiving convict is released to the custody of a gruff, jaded cop in order to track down the former's deranged partner in the first of these violent action-comedies.
48HRS. (Paramount, 1982) d Walter Hill, s Nick Nolte, Eddie Murphy, Annette O'Toole.
48HRS. II (Paramount, announced 1990) d Walter Hill, s Eddie Murphy, Nick Nolte.

257. FOUR DAUGHTERS
Fannie Hurst's story *Sister Act* is about the loves of the Lemp sisters, daughters of a music professor; it formed the basis for these pictures.

FOUR DAUGHTERS (Warner Brothers, 1938) d Michael Curtiz, s Claude Rains, Priscilla Lane, Rosemary Lane, Lola Lane, Gale Page, John Garfield.
FOUR WIVES (Warner Brothers, 1939) d Michael Curtiz, s Claude Rains, Priscilla Lane, Rosemary Lane, Lola Lane, Gale Page.
FOUR MOTHERS (Warner Brothers, 1941) d William Keighley, s Claude Rains, Priscilla Lane, Rosemary Lane, Lola Lane, Gale Page.
YOUNG AT HEART (Warner Brothers, 1954) d Gordon Douglas, s Doris Day, Frank Sinatra, Gig Young.

257A. FOXY GRANDPA
These are early silent comedies. The first entry features scenes from William A. Brady's musical production. Charles E. Schultze created the newspaper comic strip featuring the main character in 1900 for the *New York Herald*.
THE CREATORS OF FOXY GRANDPA (American Mutoscope & Biograph, 1902) s Joseph Hart, Carrie DeMar, Charles E. Schultze.
THE BOYS TRY TO PUT ONE OVER ON FOXY GRANDPA (American Mutoscope & Biograph, 1902) s Joseph Hart.
THE BOYS, STILL DETERMINED, TRY IT AGAIN ON FOXY GRANDPA, WITH THE SAME RESULT (American Mutoscope & Biograph, 1902) s Joseph Hart.
THE BOYS HELP THEMSELVES TO FOXY GRANDPA'S CIGARS (American Mutoscope & Biograph, 1902) s Joseph Hart.
THE BOYS THINK THEY HAVE ONE ON FOXY GRANDPA, BUT HE FOOLS THEM (American Mutoscope & Biograph, 1902) s Joseph Hart.
FOXY GRANDPA AND POLLY IN A LITTLE HILARITY (American Mutoscope & Biograph, 1902) s Joseph Hart.
FOXY GRANDPA SHOWS THE BOYS A TRICK OR TWO WITH THE TRAMP (American Mutoscope & Biograph, 1902) s Joseph Hart.
FOXY GRANDPA TELLS THE BOYS A FUNNY STORY (American Mutoscope & Biograph, 1902) s Joseph Hart.
WHY FOXY GRANDPA ESCAPED A DUCKING (American Mutoscope & Biograph, 1903) s Joseph Hart.
FOXY GRANDPA'S THUMB BOOK (American Mutoscope & Biograph, 1903) s Joseph Hart.

258. FRANCIS THE TALKING MULE
Peter Stirling befriends a jackass with a sense of humor and an ability to talk (voice of Chill Wills for all but the last picture, for which Paul Frees spoke).
FRANCIS (Universal, 1949) d Arthur Lubin, s Donald O'Connor, Patricia Medina.
FRANCIS GOES TO THE RACES (Universal, 1951) d Arthur Lubin, s Donald O'Connor, Piper Laurie.
FRANCIS GOES TO WEST POINT (Universal, 1952) d Arthur Lubin, s Donald O'Connor, Lori Nelson.

126 MOTION PICTURE SERIES & SEQUELS

FRANCIS COVERS THE BIG TOWN (Universal, 1953) d Donald O'Connor, Nancy Guild.
FRANCIS JOINS THE WACS (Universal, 1954) d Arthur Lubin, s Donald O'Connor, Julia Adams.
FRANCIS IN THE NAVY (Universal, 1955) d Arthur Lubin, s Donald O'Connor, Martha Hyer.
FRANCIS IN THE HAUNTED HOUSE (Universal, 1956) d Charles Lamont, s Mickey Rooney, Virginia Welles.

259. FRANKENSTEIN'S MONSTER

Mary Shelley's tale of a scientist's misguided creation of a living monster inspired dozens of motion pictures. Listed are pictures released in the United States.

FRANKENSTEIN (Edison, 1910) d J. Searle Dawley, s Charles Ogle, Augustus Phillips.
LIFE WITHOUT SOUL (Ocean, 1915) d Joseph W. Smiley, s Percy Darrell Standing.
FRANKENSTEIN'S MONSTER (Albertini, 1920) [aka THE MONSTER OF FRANKENSTEIN] d Eugenio Testa, s Luciano Albertini, Umberto Guarracino.
FRANKENSTEIN (Universal, 1931) d James Whale, s Colin Clive, Mae Clark, Boris Karloff.
BRIDE OF FRANKENSTEIN (Universal, 1935) d James Whale, s Boris Karloff, Colin Clive, Valerie Hobson, Elsa Lanchester.
SON OF FRANKENSTEIN (Universal, 1939) d Rowland V. Lee, s Basil Rathbone, Boris Karloff, Bela Lugosi.
THE GHOST OF FRANKENSTEIN (Universal, 1942) d Erle C. Kenton, s Sir Cedric Hardwicke, Lon Chaney Jr.
FRANKENSTEIN MEETS THE WOLF MAN (Universal, 1943) d Roy William Neill, s Lon Chaney Jr., Bela Lugosi, Ilona Massey.
HOUSE OF FRANKENSTEIN (Universal, 1944) d Erle C. Kenton, s Boris Karloff, J. Carrol Naish, Lon Chaney Jr.
HOUSE OF DRACULA (Universal, 1945) d Erle C. Kenton, s Lon Chaney Jr., John Carradine, Martha O' Driscoll.
ABBOTT AND COSTELLO MEET FRANKENSTEIN (Universal, 1948) d Charles T. Barton, s Bud Abbott, Lou Costello, Lon Chaney Jr., Bela Lugosi, Glenn Strange.
THE CURSE OF FRANKENSTEIN (Hammer/Warner, 1957), d Terence Fisher, s Peter Cushing, Christopher Lee, Hazel Court.
I WAS A TEENAGE FRANKENSTEIN (American International, 1957), d Herbert L. Strock, s Whit Bissell, Phyllis Coates, Robert Burton, Gary Conway.
FRANKENSTEIN'S DAUGHTER (Layton/Astor, 1958) [aka SHE MONSTER OF THE NIGHT] d Richard E. Cunha, s John Ashley, Sandra Knight.
THE REVENGE OF FRANKENSTEIN (Hammer/Columbia, 1958), d Terence Fisher, s Peter Cushing, Francis Matthews, Eunice Gayson.

FRANKENSTEIN -- 1970 (Allied Artists, 1958), d Howard W. Koch, s Boris Karloff, Tom Duggan, Jana Lund.
ORLAK THE HELL OF FRANKENSTIN (Filmadora Independiente, 1960) [aka THE HELL OF FRANKENSTEIN] d Rafael Baledon, s Joaquin Cordero, Armando Calvo.
THE EVIL OF FRANKENSTEIN (Hammer/Universal, 1964), d Freddie Francis, s Peter Cushing, Peter Woodthorpe, Sandor Eles.
FRANKENSTEIN CREATED WOMAN (Hammer/Seven Arts, 1966) [aka FRANKENSTEIN MADE WOMAN] d Terence Fisher, s Peter Cushing, Susan Denberg.
FRANKENSTEIN MEETS THE SPACE MONSTER (Allied Artists, 1966) d Robert Gaffney, s Robert Reilly, James Karen.
JESSE JAMES MEETS FRANKENSTEIN'S DAUGHTER (Embassy, 1966) d William Beaudine, s John Lupton, Estelita Rodriguez, Cal Bolder.
FRANKENSTEIN CONQUERS THE WORLD (American-International, 1966) [aka FRANKENSETIN AND THE GIANT LIZARD] d Inoshiro Honda.
FRANKENSTEIN MUST BE DESTROYED (Hammer/Warner Brothers, 1969), d Terence Fisher, s Peter Cushing, Veronica Carlson.
THE HORROR OF FRANKENSTEIN (Hammer/American Continental Films, 1970), d Jimmy Sangster, s Ralph Bates, Graham James, Kate O'Mara.
DRACULA VS. FRANKENSTEIN (Independent-International Pictures, 1971) d Al Adamson, s J. Carrol Naish, Lon Chaney Jr.
FRANKENSTEIN'S BLOODY TERROR (Independent-International Pictures, 1971) d Henry L. Egan.
LADY FRANKENSTEIN (Condor, 1971) [aka MADAME FRANKENSTEIN] d Mel Welles, s Joseph Cotten, Sara Bay.
FRANKENSTEIN: THE TRUE STORY (Universal, 1973) (NBC-TV broadcast) d Jack Smight, s James Mason, Leonard Whiting, Jane Seymour.
FRANKENSTEIN (TV movie, 1973) d Glenn Jordan, s Robert Foxworth, Susan Strassberg, Bo Svenson.
BLACKENSTEIN (Firso, 1973) [aka BLACK FRANKENSTEIN] d William A. Levy, s John Hart, Joe DiSue, Ivory Stone.
FRANKENSTEIN (Dan Curtis Productions, 1973) (for ABC-TV broadcast) d Glenn Jordan, s Robert Foxworth, Susan Strasberg, Bo Svenson.
FRANKENSTEIN (Bryanston, 1974) d Paul Morrissey.
FRANKENSTEIN AND THE MONSTER FROM HELL (Paramount, 1974) d Terence Fisher, s Peter Cushing, Shane Briant.
YOUNG FRANKENSTEIN (20th Century-Fox, 1974) d Mel Brooks, s Gene Wilder, Peter Boyle, Teri Garr.
FRANKENSTEIN'S CASTLE OF FREAKS (Aquarius, 1975) d Robert Oliver.
FRANKENSTEIN'S ISLAND (1981) d Jerry Warren, s John Carradine, Robert Clarke.
THE VINDICATOR (Canadian, 1986) [aka FRANKENSTEIN '88] d Jean-Claud Lord, s Terri Austin, Richard Cox, Pam Grier.

FRANKENSTEIN '90 (Full Moon, 1989) d Frank Henenlotter, s James Lorinz, Patty Mullen, Louise Lasser.
FRANKENSTEIN UNBOUND (20th Century-Fox, 1989) d Roger Corman, s Raul Julia, John Hurt.

260. FRECKLES
Gene Stratton Porter's novel contained the original of this story about a disabled orphan who gets job at a lumber camp, holds off the crooks and woos a pretty girl.
FRECKLES (1912)
FRECKLES (1917)
FRECKLES (FBO, 1928) d Leo Meehan, s John Fox Jr., Gene Stratton Porter.
FRECKLES (RKO, 1935) d Edward Killy and William Hamilton, s Tom Brown, Virginia Weidler.
FRECKLES COMES HOME (Monogram, 1942) d Jean Yarbrough, s Johnny Downs, Gale Storm.
FRECKLES (20th Century-Fox, 1960) d Andrew V. McLaglen, s Martin West, Carol Christensen.

FREDDY KRUEGER
See **NIGHTMARE ON ELM STREET**

261. *FRED SCOTT AND FUZZY KNIGHT*
These are B Westerns starring a singing cowboy.
MELODY OF THE PLAINS (Spectrum, 1937) d Sam Newfield, s Fred Scott, Al "Fuzzy" St. John, Louise Small.
THE FIGHTING DEPUTY (Spectrum, 1937) d Sam Newfield, s Fred Scott, Al "Fuzzy" St. John, Marjorie Beebe.
MOONLIGHT ON THE RANGE (Spectrum, 1937) d Sam Newfield, s Fred Scott, Al "Fuzzy" St. John, Lois January.
THE ROAMING COWBOY (Spectrum, 1938) d Robert Hill, s Fred Scott, Al "Fuzzy" St. John, Lois January.
ROUNDUP (Spectrum, 1938) d Sam Newfield, s Fred Scott, Al "Fuzzy" St. John, Christine McIntyre.
KNIGHT OF THE PLAINS (Spectrum, 1938) d Sam Newfield, s Fred Scott, Al "Fuzzy" St. John, Marion Weldon.
SONGS AND BULLETS (Spectrum, 1938) d Sam Newfield, s Fred Scott, Al "Fuzzy" St. John, Alice Ardell.

262. FRENCH CONNECTION, THE
It's cops vs. drug dealers in these suspense-action pictures.
THE FRENCH CONNECTION (20th Century-Fox, 1971) d William Friedkin, s Gene Hackman, Roy Scheider.
THE FRENCH CONNECTION II (20th Century-Fox, 1975) d John Frankenheimer, s Gene Hackman, Fernando Rey.

263. FRESHMAN, THE

Harold Lamb, hearing a factory whistle, stops five yards short of the goal line in his college's big football game.
THE FRESHMAN (Harold Lloyd/Pathe Eschange, 1925) d Sam Taylor, s Harold Lloyd, Jobyna Ralston.
THE SIN OF HAROLD DIDDLEBOCK (United Artists, 1926) [aka MAD WEDNESDAY] d Preston Sturges, s Harold Lloyd, Frances Hamsden.

264. FRIDAY THE 13TH
Jason, the murderous character in the hockey mask, has also appeared beginning in 1989 in a syndicated television series of the same title.
FRIDAY THE 13TH (Paramount, 1980) d Sean S. Cunningham, s Betsy Palmer, Adrienne King.
FRIDAY THE 13TH, PART II (Paramount, 1981) d Steve Miner, s Betsy Palmer, Amy Steel, John Furey.
FRIDAY THE 13TH, PART III (Paramount, 1982) d Steve Miner, s Dana Kimmell, Paul Kratka.
FRIDAY THE 13TH, PART IV: THE FINAL CHAPTER (Paramount, 1984) d Joseph Zito, s Crispin Glover, Kimberly Beck.
FRIDAY THE 13TH, PART V (Paramount, 1985) d Danny Steinmann, s John Shepard, Melanie Kinnaman.
FRIDAY THE 13TH, PART VI: JASON LIVES (Paramount, 1986) d Tom McLoughlin, s Thom Mathews, Jennifer Cooke.
FRIDAY THE 13TH, PART VII: THE NEW BLOOD (Paramount, 1988) d John Carl Buchler, s Lar Park Lincoln, Terry Kiser.
FRIDAY THE 13TH, PART VIII: JASON TAKES MANHATTAN (Paramount, 1989) d Rob Hedden.

265. FRIDAY THE 13TH
These pictures bear little resemblance to the above horror entry; they're X-rated.
FRIDAY THE 13TH: A NUDE BEGINNING (Vidco, 1987) s Amber Lynn, Nina Hartley.
FRIDAY THE 13TH: PART II (Vidco, 1989) s Barbii, Joey Silvera.

266. FRIGHT NIGHT
"Do you have a taste for terror?" asks an advertisement for the second picture in this horror series. "Apparently, the suckers are back."
FRIGHT NIGHT (1985) d Tom Holland, s Chris Sarandon, William Ragsdale, Amanda Bears, Roddy McDowall.
FRIGHT NIGHT 2 (New Century/Vista, 1989) d Tommy Lee Wallace, s Roddy McDowall, William Ragsdale, Traci Lin, Julie Carmen.

267. FROG, THE
Based on Edgar Wallace book *The Fellowship of the Frog*, the pictures are about a powerful criminal organization and efforts of the CID to knock it down.
THE FROG (Wilcox/GFD, 1937) d Jack Raymond, s Gordon Harker, Carol Godner.

THE RETURN OF THE FROG (Imperator, 1938) d Maurice Elvey, s Gordon Harker, Una O'Connor.

FRONTIER MARSHAL
See **JOHNNY MACK BROWN**

268. FRONTIER MARSHALS
This is a series of second-feature Westerns.
TUMBLEWEED TRAIL (PRC, 1942) d Peter Stewart (Sam Newfield), s Art Davis, Bill "Cowboy Rambler" Boyd, Lee Powell.
TEXAS MANHUNT (PRC, 1942) d Peter Stewart (Sam Newfield), s Art Davis, Bill "Cowboy Rambler" Boyd, Lee Powell.
RAIDERS OF THE WEST (PRC, 1942) d Peter Stewart (Sam Newfield), s Art Davis, Bill "Cowboy Rambler" Boyd, Lee Powell.
ROLLING DOWN THE GREAT DIVIDE (PRC, 1942) d Peter Stewart (Sam Newfield), s Art Davis, Bill "Cowboy Rambler" Boyd, Lee Powell.
ALONG THE SUNDOWN TRAIL (PRC, 1942) d Peter Stewart (Sam Newfield), s Art Davis, Bill "Cowboy Rambler" Boyd, Lee Powell.
PRAIRIE PALS (PRC, 1942) d Peter Stewart (Sam Newfield), s Art Davis, Bill "Cowboy Rambler" Boyd, Lee Powell.

269. FU MANCHU
Sax Rohmer penned a series of novels featuring an Oriental menace, Dr. Fu Manchu, who is pursued by Nayland Smith and his associate Dr. Jack Petrie
THE MYSTERIOUS DR. FU MANCHU (Paramount, 1929) d Rowland V. Lee, s Warner Oland, Neil Hamilton, O.P. Heggie.
THE RETURN OF DR. FU MANCHU (Paramount, 1930) d Rowland V. Lee, s Warner Oland, Neil Hamilton, Jean Arthur, O.P. Heggie.
DAUGHTER OF THE DRAGON (Paramount, 1931) d Lloyd Corrigan, s Warner Oland, Sessue Hayakawa, Anna May Wong.
THE MASK OF FU MANCHU (Paramount, 1932) d Charles Vidor and Charles Brabin, s Boris Karloff, Lewis Stone, Myrna Loy.
DRUMS OF FU MANCHU (Republic, 1940) (15 chapters) d William Witney and John English, s Henry Brandon, William Royle, Robert Kellard, Gloria Franklin.
THE FACE OF FU MANCHU (Warner Brothers-Seven Arts, 1965) d Don Sharp, s Christopher Lee, Nigel Green.
THE BRIDES OF FU MANCHU (Warner Brothers-Seven Arts, 1965) d Don Sharp, s Christopher Lee, Douglas Wilmer.
THE VENGEANCE OF FU MANCHU (Warner Brothers-Seven Arts, 1968) d Jeremy Summers, s Christopher Lee, Tony Ferrer.
KISS AND TELL (Commonwealth United, 1968) [aka THE BLOOD OF FU MANCHU and AGAINST ALL ODDS] d Jess Franco, s Christopher Lee, Richard Greene.
CASTLE OF FU MANCHU (Commonwealth United, 1968) d Jess Franco, s Christopher Lee, Richard Greene.

MOTION PICTURE SERIES & SEQUELS 131

270. FUNNY GIRL
The story of showgirl Fanny Brice has ended up in two pictures.
FUNNY GIRL (Columbia, 1968) d William Wyler, s Barbra Streisand, Omar Sharif.
FUNNY LADY (Columbia, 1975) d Herbert Ross, s Barbra Streisand, James Caan.

271. FUTURE FORCE
FUTURE FORCE (Action International Pictures, 1988) [aka C.O.P.S.] d David A. Prior, s David Carradine.
FUTURE FORCE II (Action International Pictures, 1989) d David A. Prior, s David Carradine.

272. GAMBLER, THE
These Western adventures, based on the leading actor's best-selling song, are about gambler Brady Hawkes.
KENNY ROGERS AS THE GAMBLER (Kragen, 1980) (CBS-TV movie) d Dick Lowery, s Kenny Rogers, Christine Belford, Bruce Boxleitner.
KENNY ROGERS AS THE GAMBLER -- THE ADVENTURE CONTINUES (Lion Share Productions, 1983) (CBS-TV movie) d Dick Lowery, s Kenny Rogers, Linda Evans, Bruce Boxleitner.

273. GAME OF DEATH
These are martial arts films.
GAME OF DEATH (1979) d Robert Clouse, s Bruce Lee, Kareem Abdul-Jabbar.
GAME OF DEATH II (Paragon, 1981) d Ng See-Yuan, s Bruce Lee.

274. GAMERA
The title monster is a flame-breathing turtle who, in most of his outings, battles other monsters.
GAMERA THE INVINCIBLE (World Entertainment, 1966) d Noriyaki Yuasa, s Albert Dekker.
GAMERA VERSUS BARUGON (Daiei, 1966) d Shigeo Tanaka, s Kojiro Hongo.
GAMERA VERSUS GAOS (Daiei, 1967) d Noriyaki Yuasa, s Kojiro Hongo.
GAMERA VERSUS VIRAS (Daiei, 1968) d Noriyaki Yuasa, s Kojiro Hongo.
GAMERA VERSUS GUIRON (Daiei, 1969) d Noriyaki Yuasa, s Nobuhiro Kashima.
GAMERA VERSUS MONSTER X (Daiei, 1970) d Noriyaki Yuasa, s Tsotomo Takakoma.
GAMERA VERSUS ZIGRA (1971)

275. GAS HOUSE KIDS
These are B-grade adventure films in the vein of the BOWERY BOYS.
GAS HOUSE KIDS (PRC, 1946)

132 MOTION PICTURE SERIES & SEQUELS

GAS HOUSE KIDS GO WEST (PRC, 1947) d William Beaudine, s Chili Williams, John Sheldon, Carl "Alfalfa" Switzer.
GAS HOUSE KIDS IN HOLLYWOOD (PRC, 1947)

276. GATE, THE
Teenagers discover the gate to Hell in their backyard.
THE GATE (Alliance, 1987) d Tibor Takacs, s Stephen Dorff, Christa Denton.
GATE II (Alliance, 1989) d Tibor Takacs, s Louis Tripp, Pamela Segall.

277. GATHERING, THE
An aging businessman hopes to reconcile differences with his family, in the initial film; in the second there is a struggle to keep the family business holdings together.
THE GATHERING (Hanna-Barbera Productions, 1977) (ABC-TV movie) d Randal Kleiser, s Edward Asner, Maureen Stapleton.
THE GATHERING, PART II (Hanna-Barbera Productions, 1979) d Charles S. Dubin, s Maureen Stapleton.

278. 'GATOR BAIT
A Cajun alligator poacher, wrongfully accused of murder, has to prove her innocence.
'GATOR BAIT (Sebastian, 1973) d Ferd Sebastian and Beverly Sebastian, s Claudia Jennings.
'GATOR BAIT 2: CAJUN JUSTICE (Sebastian, 1988) d Ferd Sebastian and Beverly Sebastian, s Jan Mackenzie.

279. GATOR MCKLUSKY
A good 'ol boy moonshiner gets revenge.
WHITE LIGHTNING (United Artists, 1973) d Joseph Sargent, s Burt Reynolds, Jennifer Billingsly, Ned Beatty, Bo Hopkins.
GATOR (United Artists, 1976) d Burt Reynolds, s Burt Reynolds, Jack Weston, Lauren Hutton, Jerry Reed.

280. *GENE AUTRY AND SMILEY BURNETTE*
B-grade movies, the Autrys essentially feature Gene as himself, in a West which still uses horses but also has automobiles. This listing groups the pictures based on sidekicks, providing a modest sense of continuity among the films. Occasionally when Burnette assumes the role of Frog Millhouse, Joe Stauch Jr. turns up as *his* sidekick, Tadpole.
TUMBLING TUMBLEWEEDS (Republic, 1935) d Joseph Kane, s Gene Autry, Smiley Burnette, Ann Rutherford.
SAGEBRUSH TROUBADOR (Republic, 1935) d Joseph Kane, s Gene Autry, Smiley Burnette, Barbara Pepper.
MELODY TRAIL (Republic, 1935) d Joseph Kane, s Gene Autry, Smiley Burnette, Ann Rutherford.
THE SINGING VAGABOND (Republic, 1935) d Carl Pierson, s Gene Autry, Smiley Burnette, Ann Rutherford.

RED RIVER VALLEY (Republic, 1936) [aka MAN OF THE FRONTIER] d
    B. Reeves Eason, s Gene Autry, Smiley Burnette, Frances Grant.
COMIN' ROUND THE MOUNTAIN (Republic, 1936) d Mack V. Wright, s
    Gene Autry, Smiley Burnette, Ann Rutherford.
THE SINGING COWBOY (Republic, 1936) d Mack V. Wright, s Gene Autry,
    Smiley Burnette, Lois Wilde.
GUNS AND GUITARS (Republic, 1936) d Joseph Kane, s Gene Autry, Smiley
    Burnette, Dorothy Dix.
OH, SUSANNAH (Republic, 1936) d Joseph Kane, s Gene Autry, Smiley
    Burnette, Frances Grant.
RIDE, RANGER, RIDE (Republic, 1936) d Joseph Kane, s Gene Autry, Smiley
    Burnette, Kay Hughes.
THE BIG SHOW (Republic, 1936) d Mack V. Wright, s Gene Autry, Smiley
    Burnette, Kay Hughes.
THE OLD CORRAL (Republic, 1936) d Joseph Kane, s Gene Autry, Smiley
    Burnette, Hope Manning.
ROUND UP TIME IN TEXAS (Republic, 1937) d Joseph Kane, s Gene Autry,
    Smiley Burnette, Maxine Doyle.
GIT ALONG LITTLE DOGIES (Republic, 1937) d Joseph Kane, s Gene Autry,
    Smiley Burnette, Judith Allen.
ROOTIN' TOOTIN' RHYTHM (Republic, 1937) d Mack V. Wright, s Gene
    Autry, Smiley Burnette, Armida.
YODELIN' KID FROM PINE RIDGE (Republic, 1937) d Joseph Kane, s Gene
    Autry, Smiley Burnette, Betty Bronson.
PUBLIC COWBOY NO. 1 (Republic, 1937) d Joseph Kane, s Gene Autry,
    Smiley Burnette, Ann Rutherford.
BOOTS AND SADDLES (Republic, 1937) d Joseph Kane, s Gene Autry,
    Smiley Burnette, Judith Allen.
MANHATTAN MERRY-GO ROUND (Republic, 1937) d Charles Riesner, s
    Gene Autry, Smiley Burnette, Ann Dvorak.
SPRINGTIME IN THE ROCKIES (Republic, 1937) d Joseph Kane, s Gene
    Autry, Smiley Burnette, Polly Rowles.
THE OLD BARN DANCE (Republic, 1938) d Joseph Kane, s Gene Autry,
    Smiley Burnette, Helen Valkis.
GOLD MINE IN THE SKY (Republic, 1938) d Joseph Kane, s Gene Autry,
    Smiley Burnette, Carol Hughes.
MAN FROM MUSIC MOUNTAIN (Republic, 1938) d Joseph Kane, s Gene
    Autry, Smiley Burnette,
PRAIRIE MOON (Republic, 1938) d Ralph Staub, s Gene Autry, Smiley
    Burnette, Shirley Deane.
RHYTHMS OF THE SADDLE (Republic, 1938) d George Sherman, s Gene
    Autry, Smiley Burnette, Peggy Moran.
WESTERN JAMBOREE (Republic, 1938) d Ralph Staub, s Gene Autry,
    Smiley Burnette, Jean Rouverol.
HOME ON THE PRAIRIE (Republic, 1939) d Jack Townley, s Gene Autry,
    Smiley Burnette, June Storey.
MEXICALI ROSE (Republic, 1939) d George Sherman, s Gene Autry, Smiley

Burnette, Luana Walters.
BLUE MONTANA SKIES (Republic, 1939) d George Sherman, s Gene Autry, Smiley Burnette, June Storey.
MOUNTAIN RHYTHM (Republic, 1939) d B. Reeves Eason, s Gene Autry, Smiley Burnette, June Storey.
COLORADO SUNSET (Republic, 1939) d George Sherman, s Gene Autry, Smiley Burnette, June Storey.
IN OLD MONTEREY (Republic, 1939) d Joseph Kane, s Gene Autry, Smiley Burnette, George "Gabby" Hayes.
ROVIN' TUMBLEWEEDS (Republic, 1939) d George Sherman, s Gene Autry, Smiley Burnette, Mary Carlisle.
SOUTH OF THE BORDER (Republic, 1939) d George Sherman, s Gene Autry, Smiley Burnette, Lupita Tovar, June Storey.
RANCHO GRANDE (Republic, 1940) d Frank McDonald, s Gene Autry, Smiley Burnette, June Storey.
GAUCHO SERENADE (Republic, 1940) d Frank McDonald, s Gene Autry, Smiley Burnette, June Storey, Mary Lee.
CAROLINA MOON (Republic, 1940) d Frank McDonald, s Gene Autry, Smiley Burnette, June Storey, Mary Lee.
RIDE TENDERFOOT RIDE (Republic, 1940) d Frank McDonald, s Gene Autry, Smiley Burnette, June Storey, Mary Lee.
RIDIN' ON A RAINBOW (Republlic, 1941) d Lew Landers, s Gene Autry, Smiley Burnette, Mary Lee, Carol Adams.
BACK IN THE SADDLE (Republic, 1941) d Lew Landers, s Gene Autry, Smiley Burnette, Mary Lee, Jacqueline Wells.
THE SINGING HILL (Republic, 1941) d Lew Landers, s Gene Autry, Smiley Burnette, Virginia Dale, Mary Lee.
SUNSET IN WYOMING (Republic, 1941) d William Morgan, s Gene Autry, Smiley Burnette, Maris Wrizon.
UNDER FIESTA STARS (Republic, 1941) d Frank McDonald, s Gene Autry, Smiley Burnette, Carol Hughes, Joe Stauch Jr.
DOWN MEXICO WAY (Republic, 1941) d Joseph Santley, s Gene Autry, Smiley Burnette, Fay McKenzie.
SIERRA SUE (Republic, 1941) d William Morgan, s Gene Autry, Smiley Burnette, Fay McKenzie.
COWBOY SERENADE (Republic, 1942) d William Morgan, s Gene Autry, Smiley Burnette, Fay McKenzie.
HEART OF THE RIO GRANDE (Republic, 1942) d William Morgan, s Gene Autry, Smiley Burnette, Fay McKenzie, Joe Stauch Jr.
HOME IN WYOMIN' (Republic, 1942) d William Morgan, s Gene Autry, Smiley Burnette, Fay McKenzie, Joe Stauch Jr.
STARDUST ON THE SAGE (Republic, 1942) d William Morgan, s Gene Autry, Smiley Burnette, Louise Currie.
CALL OF THE CANYON (Republic, 1942) d Joseph Santley, s Gene Autry, Smiley Burnette, Ruth Terry, Joe Stauch Jr.
BELLS OF CAPISTRANO (Republic, 1942) d William Morgan, s Gene Autry, Smiley Burnette, Virginia Grey, Joe Stauch Jr.

WHIRLWIND (Columbia, 1951) d John English, s Gene Autry, Smiley Burnette, Gail Davis.
WINNING OF THE WEST (Columbia, 1953) d George Archainbaud, s Gene Autry, Smiley Burnette, Gail Davis.
ON TOP OF OLD SMOKEY (Columbia, 1953) d George Archainbaud, s Gene Autry, Smiley Burnette, Sheila Ryan, Gail Davis.
GOLDTOWN GHOST RIDERS (Columbia, 1953) d George Archainbaud, s Gene Autry, Smiley Burnette, Gail Davis.
PACK TRAIN (Columbia, 1953) d George Archainbaud, s Gene Autry, Smiley Burnette, Gail Davis, Sheila Ryan.
SAGINAW TRAIL (Columbia, 1953) d George Archainbaud, s Gene Autry, Smiley Burnette, Connie Marshall.
LAST OF THE PONY RIDERS (Columbia, 1953) d George Archainbaud, s Gene Autry, Smiley Burnette.

281. *GENE AUTRY AND STERLING HOLLOWAY*
SIOUX CITY SUE (Republic, 1946) d Frank McDonald, s Gene Autry, Sterling Holloway, Lynne Roberts.
TRAIL TO SAN ANTONE (Republic, 1947) d John English, s Gene Autry, Sterling Holloway, Peggy Stewart.
TWILIGHT ON THE RIO GRANDE (Republic, 1947) d Frank McDonald, s Gene Autry, Sterling Holloway, Adele Mra.
SADDLE PALS (Republic, 1947) d Lesley Selander, s Gene Autry, Sterling Holloway, Lynne Roberts.
ROBIN HOOD OF TEXAS (Republic, 1947) d Lesley Selander, s Gene Autry, Sterling Holloway, Lynne Roberts.

282. *GENE AUTRY AND PAT BUTTRAM*
Buttram in addition to sidekicking Autry in films, appeared for fifteen years on the MELODY RANCH radio shows and the GENE AUTRY SHOW on television.
THE STRAWBERRY ROAN (Columbia, 1948) d John English, s Gene Autry, Pat Buttram, Gloria Henry, Rufe Davis.
RIDERS IN THE SKY (Columbia, 1949) d John English, s Gene Autry, Pat Buttram, Gloria Henry.
MULE TRAIN (Columbia, 1950) d John English, s Gene Autry, Pat Buttram, Sheila Ryan.
BEYOND THE PURPLE HILLS (Columbia, 1950) d John English, s Gene Autry, Pat Buttram, Jo Dennison.
INDIAN TERRITORY (Columbia, 1950) d John English, s Gene Autry, Pat Buttram, Gail Davis.
THE BLAZING HILLS (Columbia, 1950) d John English, s Gene Autry, Pat Buttram, Lynne Roberts.
GENE AUTRY AND THE MOUNTIES (Columbia, 1951) d John English, s Gene Autry, Pat Buttram, Elena Verdugo.
TEXANS NEVER CRY (Columbia, 1951) d Frank McDonald, s Gene Autry, Pat Buttram, Gail Davis.

SILVER CANYON (Columbia, 1951) d John English, s Gene Autry, Pat Buttram, Gail Davis.
HILLS OF UTAH (Columbia, 1951) d John English, s Gene Autry, Pat Buttram, Elaine Riley.
VALLEY OF FIRE (Columbia, 1951) d John English, s Gene Autry, Pat Buttram, Gail Davis.
THE OLD WEST (Columbia, 1952) d George Archainbaud, s Gene Autry, Pat Buttram, Gail Davis.
NIGHT STAGE TO GALVESTON (Columbia, 1952) d George Archainbaud, s Gene Autry, Pat Buttram, Virginia Houston.
APACHE COUNTRY (Columbia, 1952) d George Archainbaud, s Gene Autry, Pat Buttram, Carolina Cotton.
BARBED WIRE (Columbia, 1952) d George Archainbaud, s Gene Autry, Pat Buttram, Anne James.
WAGON TEAM (Columbia, 1952) d George Archainbaud, s Gene Autry, Pat Buttram, Gail Davis.
BLUE CANADIAN SKIES (Columbia, 1952) d George Archainbaud, s Gene Autry, Pat Buttram, Gail Davis.

283. GENTLEMEN PREFER BLONDES
The pictures are based on Anita Loos's novel of golddiggers Lorelei Lee and Dorothy Shaw setting their sights on rich bachelors.
GENTLEMEN PREFER BLONDES (Paramount, 1928) d Malcolm St. Clair, s Ruth Taylor, Alice White.
GENTLEMEN PREFER BLONDES (20th Century-Fox, 1953) d Howard Hawks, s Jane Russell, Marilyn Monroe.
GENTLEMEN MARRY BRUNETTES (United Artists, 1955) d Richard Sale, s Jane Russell, Jeanne Crain.

284. *GEORGE O'BRIEN AND RAY WHITLEY*
These are B Westerns.
GUN LAW (RKO, 1938) d David Howard, s George O'Brien, Ray Whitley, Rita Oehmen.
BORDER G-MAN (RKO, 1938) d David Howard, s George O'Brien, Ray Whitley, Lorraine Johnson.
THE PAINTED DESERT (RKO, 1938) d David Howard, s George O'Brien, Ray Whitley, Lorraine Johnson.
THE RENEGADE RANGER (RKO, 1938) d David Howard, s George O'Brien, Ray Whitley, Tim Holt, Rita Hayworth.

285. *GEORGE O'BRIEN AND CHILL WILLS*
LAWLESS VALLEY (RKO, 1938) d David Howard, s George O'Brien, Chill Wills, Kay Sutton.
ARIZONA LEGION (RKO, 1939) d David Howard, s George O'Brien, Chill Wills, Lorraine Johnson.
TROUBLE IN SUNDOWN (RKO, 1939) d David Howard, s George O'Brien, Chill Wills, Ray Whitley, Rosiland Keith.

RACKETEERS OF THE RANGE (RKO, 1939) d D. Ross Lederman, s George O'Brien, Chill Wills, Marjorie Reynolds.
TIMBER STAMPEDE (RKO, 1939) d David Howard, s George O'Brien, Chill Wills, Marjorie Reynolds.
MARSHAL OF MESA CITY (RKO, 1939) d David Howard, s George O'Brien, Chill Wills, Virginia Vale.

286. GEORGE WHITE'S SCANDALS
The films are backstage show biz pix.
GEORGE WHITE'S SCANDALS (RKO, 1934) d George White, Thornton Freeland and Harry Lachman, s Rudy Vallee, Jimmy Durante, Alice Faye.
GEORGE WHITE'S 1935 SCANDALS (Fox, 1935) d George White, s Alice Faye, James Dunn, Ned Sparks.

287. GERT AND DAISY
Cockney sisters take charge of evacuee children who are wrecking a country manor -- and also expose criminals-- in the first film. The characters were created by Elsie and Doris Waters, first on record, then on BBC radio.
GERT AND DAISY'S WEEKEND (Butcher, 1941) d Maclean Rogers, s Elsie Waters, Doris Waters.
GERT AND DAISY CLEAN UP (Butcher, 1942) d Maclean Rogers, s Elsie Waters, Doris Waters.

288. GET-RICH-QUICK WALLINGFORD
J. Rufus Wallingford is a sharp businessman featured in George Randolph Chester-authored stories.
GET-RICH-QUICK WALLINGFORD (1921) d Frank Borzabe, s Sam Hardy
THE NEW ADVENTURES OF GET-RICH-QUICK WALLINGFORD (MGM, 1931) d Sam Wood, s William Haines.

289. GHOSTBUSTERS
The four heroes are professionals who eradicate spooks, ghouls and slimes from clients' properties. The success of the first picture also resulted in a Saturday morning TV cartoon series.
GHOSTBUSTERS (Columbia, 1984) d Ivan Reitman, s Bill Murray, Dan Akroyd, Harold Ramis, Sigourney Weaver, Rick Moranis, Ernie Hudson.
GHOSTBUSTERS II (Columbia, 1989) d Ivan Reitman, s Dan Akroyd, Bill Murray, Harold Ramis, Sigourney Weaver, Ernie Hudson, Annie Potts.

290. GHOULIES
Small reptilian monsters crawl out of the toilet to menace innocent people.
GHOULIES (1985) d Luca Bercovici, s Peter Liapis, Lisa Pelkan.
GHOULIES II (1987) d Albert Band, s Damon Martin, Royal Dano.

291. GIDGET

Californian Francine Lawrence is a girl and is a shade taller than a midget, hence she's a "Gidget." The premise is taken from the novel by Frederick Kohner. There was also a TV series on ABC, 1965-66, with Sally Field and a syndicated series, 1988-89.

GIDGET (Columbia, 1959) d Paul Wendkos, s Sandra Dee
GIDGET GOES HAWAIIAN (Columbia, 1961) d Paul Wendkos, s Deborah Walley
GIDGET GOES TO ROME (Columbia, 1963) d Paul Wendkos, s Cindy Carol
GIDGET GROWS UP (Screen Gems/Columbia Pictures Television, 1969) (ABC-TV movie) d James Sheldon, s Karen Valentine, Edward Mulhare.
GIDGET GETS MARRIED (Screen Gems/Columbia Pictures Television, 1969) (ABC-TV movie) d E.W. Swackhamer, s Monie Ellis, Michael Burns.
GIDGET'S SUMMER REUNION (1985) d Bruce Bilson, s Caryn Richman.

292. GIL LAMB

Vaudevillian and dancer Gil Lamb appeared in a number of Paramount musical comedies and a series of shorts. This list is incomplete.

PARDON MY WRENCH s Gil Lamb, Carol Hughes, Claire Carleton, Andy Clyde.
FRESH PAINTER s Gil Lamb, Carol Hughes, Claire Carleton, Andy Clyde
BABY MAKES TWO (1952) s Gil Lamb, Carol Hughes, Claire Carleton.

293. GILLIGAN'S ISLAND

In the CBS television series which aired 1964-67, the Skipper (Alan Hale Jr.) and Gilligan (Bob Denver), crew of the charter boat *Minnow,* are stranded on an island with their passengers: millionaires Thurston and Lovey Howell (Jim Backus and Natalie Schafer), Ginger (Tina Louise), the Professor (Russell Johnson) and Mary Ann (Dawn Wells). There was also a later animated version of GILLIGAN'S ISLAND on ABC, 1974-77. The films below reunite the original cast.

RESCUE FROM GILLIGAN'S ISLAND (Sherwood Schwartz Productions/Redwood Productions/Universal, 1978) (NBC-TV movie) d Leslie Martinson, s Bob Denver, Alan Hale Jr., Jim Backus, Natalie Schafer, Russell Johnson, Dawn Wells, Judith Baldwin.
THE CASTAWAYS ON GILLIGAN'S ISLAND (Sherwood Schwartz Productions/Redwood Productions/Universal, 1979) (NBC-TV movie) d Earl Bellamy, s Bob Denver, Alan Hale Jr.
THE HARLEM GLOBETROTTERS ON GILLIGAN'S ISLAND (Redwood Productions/Universal Television, 1981) d Peter Baldwin, s Bob Denver, Alan Hale Jr.

294. GINGER
These X-rated features star Ginger Lynn. (See also SEX ASYLUM.)
GINGER (Vivid, 1985) s Ginger Lynn, Tom Byron.
GINGER ON THE ROCKS (Vivid, 1985) s Ginger Lynn, Amber Lynn.
GINGER'S PRIVATE PARTY (Vivid, 1985) s Ginger Lynn, Tom Byron.
GINGER MAKES HISTORY (Vivid, 1985) s Ginger Lynn.
THE GINGER EFFECT (Vivid, 1986) s Ginger Lynn, Kristara Barrington.
GINGER AND SPICE (Vivid, 1987) s Ginger Lynn, Jamie Gillis.
GINGER SNAPS (Vivid, 1987) s Ginger Lynn, Herschel Savage.
GINGER'S GREATEST ALL-GIRL HITS (Vivid, 1987) s Ginger Lynn, Amber Lynn.

295. GIRL, THE GOLD WATCH & EVERYTHING, THE
The films are based on John D. MacDonald's fantasy novel *The Girl, The Gold Watch & Everything*. A magical watch can stop time.
THE GIRL, THE GOLD WATCH & EVERYTHING (Paramount Television, 1980) (Operation Prime Time TV movie) d William Wiard, s Robert Hays, Pam Dawber.
THE GIRL, THE GOLD WATCH & DYNAMITE (Paramount Television, 1981) (Operation Prime Time TV movie) d Hy Averback, s Lee Purcell, Philip MacHale.

296. GLOVE SLINGERS, THE
These comedy shorts, with a boxing background, were filmed 1939-43. The list is incomplete.
THE GLOVE SLINGERS (Vitaphone, 1939) d Jules White, s Noah Beery Jr., Shemp Howard, Dorothy Vaughn.
THE GREAT GLOVER
MITT ME TONIGHT
GLOVE AFFAIR
SOCKS APPEAL
FRESH AS A FRESHMAN

297. GODFATHER, THE
Mario Puzo's blockbuster novel of an aging Mafia don and his family provided the material for these pictures.
THE GODFATHER (Alfran/Paramount, 1972) d Francis Ford Coppola, s Marlon Brando, Al Pacino, James Caan.
THE GODFATHER, PART II (Coppola/Paramount, 1974) d Francis Ford Coppola, s Al Pacino, Robert Duvall, Diane Keaton.
THE GODFATHER III -- THE CONTINUING STORY (Zoetrope/Paramount, announced 1990) d Francis Ford Coppola, s Al Pacino, Diane Keaton, Talia Shire, Elie Wallach.

298. GODMOTHER, THE
These sex films spoof the above entry.
THE GODMOTHER I (VCA, 1988) s Ebony Ayes, Tony El-Lay.
THE GODMOTHER II (VCA, 1988) s Ebony Ayes, Ray Victory.

140 MOTION PICTURE SERIES & SEQUELS

299. GODS MUST BE CRAZY, THE
A bushman living in Africa's Kalahari desert discovers a Coke bottle, and sets out to throw it over the edge of the earth, in the first of these slapstick comedies.
THE GODS MUST BE CRAZY (TLC, 1981) d Jamie Uys, s Marius Weyers, Sandra Prinsloo, N!xau.
THE GODS MUST BE CRAZY II (Weintraub Entertainment Group, 1989) d Jamie Uys

300. GODZILLA
The Japanese made scores of monster movies including these with a prehistoric dinosaur hero awakened by atomic bomb tests.
GODZILLA, KING OF THE MONSTERS (Toho/Jewel, 1954) d Inoshiro Honda and Terry Morse, s Raymond Burr, Takashi Shimura.
GIGANTIS, THE FIRE MONSTER (Toho/Warner Brothres, 1955) d Motoyoshi and Hugo Grimaldi, s Hiroshi Koizumi, Setsuko Makayama.
KING KONG VS. GODZILLA (Universal, 1962) d Thomas Montgomery and Inoshiro Hodna, s Michael Keith, James Yagi.
GODZILLA VS. THE THING (American International, 1964) d Inoshiro Honda, s Okira Takarada.
GHIDRAH, THE THREE-HEADED MONSTER (Continental, 1965) d Inoshiro Honda, s Yosuke Natsuki.
MONSTER ZERO (Toho, 1965) d Inoshiro Honda, s Nick Adams, Akira Takarada.
GO SEA MONSTER (Toho, 1966) [aka GODZILLA VS. THE SEA MONSTER] d Jun Fukuda.
SON OF GODZILLA (1968) d Jun Fukuda, s Tadao Takashima, Akira Kubo.
DESTROY ALL MONSTERS (Toho, 1968) d Ishiro Honda, s Akira Kubo, Jun Tazaki.
GODZILLA'S REVENGE (Toho, 1969) d Ishiro Honda, s Kenji Sahara.
GODZILLA VERSUS THE SMOG MONSTER (American International, 1971) d Yoshimitu Banno, s Akira Yamauchi.
GODZILLA VS. GIGAN (1972) d Jun Fukuda, s Hiroshi Ishikawa.
GODZILLA VS. MEGALON (Cinema Shares International, 1973) d Jun Fukuda, s Katsuhiko Sasaki.
GODZILLA VERSUS THE COSMIC MONSTER (Toho, 1974) d Jun Fukuda, s Masaki Daimon.
GODZILLA VS. MEGAGODZILLA (Toho, 1975) d Jun Fukuda, s Masacki Daimon.
MONSTERS FROM THE UNKNOWN PLANET (Toho, 1975) d Ishiro Honda, s Katsuhiko Sasaki.
GODZILLA 1985 (Toho, 1985) d Kohji Hashimoto and R.J. Kizer, s Raymond Burr, Keiju Kobayashi.

301. GOING MY WAY
Father O'Malley's adventures in New York slum are told in these movies.
GOING MY WAY (Paramount, 1944) d Leo McCarey, s Bing Crosby, Bary

Fitzgerald.
THE BELLS OF ST. MARY's (RKO, 1945) d Leo McCarey, s Bing Crosby, Ingrid Bergman.

302. GOLDIE AND THE BOXER
A ten-year-old girl teams with a struggling pugilist.
GOLDIE AND THE BOXER (Orenthal Productions/Columbia, 1979) (NBC-TV movie) d David Miller, s O.J. Simpson, Melissa Michaelsen.
GOLDIE AND THE BOXER GO TO HOLLYWOOD (Orenthal Productions/Columbia, 1981) (NBC-TV movie) d David Miller, s O.J. Simpson, Melissa Michaelsen.

303. GOLEM, THE
The horror pictures are derived from Gustav Meyrikn's novel of a clay statue which comes to life.
THE GOLEM (Deutsche Bioscop, 1914) [aka THE MONSTER OF FATE] d Henrik Galeen, s Paul Wegener.
THE GOLEM: HOW HE CAME INTO THE WORLD (Pagu, 1920) d Paul Wegener, s Paul Wegener.
GOLEM (Barrandov/Metropolis, 1936) d Julien Duvivier, s Harry Baur.
IT (Seven Arts/Goldstar, 1967) [aka THE CURSE OF THE GOLEM and ANGER OF THE GOLEM] d Herbert J. Leder, s Roddy McDowall, Jill Haworth.

303A. GOOD MORNING, VIETNAM
There is reportedly in works for 1990-91 a sequel to the serio-comic portrait of Armed Forces Radio disc jockey Adrian Cronauer in Saigon during the Vietnam War.
GOOD MORNING, VIETNAM (Buena Vista, 1987) d Barry Levinson, s Robin Williams.

304. GOR
The swords-action films are based on the fantasy novels (which first appeared in 1966) by John Norman.
GOR (Cannon, 1987) d Fritz Kiersch, s Urbano Barberini, Rebecca Ferratti.
OUTLAW OF GOR (Cannon, 1987) d Jan "Bud" Condos, s Urbano Barberini, Rebecca Ferratti.

305. GRAVEYARD SHIFT
These are horror stories of cab driver who is really a vampire.
GRAVEYARD SHIFT (Cinema Ventures, 1987) d Gerard Ciccoritti, s Silvio Oliviero, Helen Papas.
THE UNDERSTUDY: THE GRAVEYARD SHIFT II (Cinema Ventures, 1989) d Gerard Ciccoritti, s Wendy Gazelle, Mark Soper.

306. GREASE
Musical summer frolic at Rydell High finds Mr. Tough-Guy romancing Miss

New-Girl-At-School.
GREASE (Paramount, 1978) d Randal Kleiser, s John Travolta, Olivia Newton-John.
GREASE 2 (Paramount, 1982) d Patricia Birch, s Maxwell Caulfield, Michelle Pfeiffer.

307. THE GREAT ESCAPE
World War II prisoners of war outwit their German captors. The original motion picture (based on Paul Brickell's book) was followed twenty-five years later by a television movie.
THE GREAT ESCAPE (United Artists, 1963) d John Sturges, s Steve McQueen, James Garner, Richard Attenborough, Charles Bronson.
THE GREAT ESCAPE II: THE UNTOLD STORY (NBC-TV movie, 1988) s Christopher Reeve.

308. GREAT GILDERSLEEVE, THE
Throckmorton P. Gildersleeve (Harold Peary) was an obnoxious character on the radio show FIBBER AND McGEE AND MOLLY. He eventually was given his own program on NBC from 1941-58.
THE GREAT GILDERSLEEVE (RKO, 1943) d Gordon Douglas, s Harold Peary, Nancy Gates.
GILDERSLEEVE'S BAD DAY (RKO, 1943) d Gordon Douglas, s Harold Peary, Barbara Hale
GILDERSLEEVE ON BROADWAY (RKO, 1943) d Gordon Douglas, s Harold Peary.
GILDERSLEEVE'S GHOST (RKO, 1944) d Gordon Douglas, s Harold Peary.

309. GREEN HORNET, THE
Britt Reid, crusading owner of a newspaper, is also a masked crime fighter. He first appeared in the American radio series broadcast 1936-52 and later in a TV show which aired 1966-67.
THE GREEN HORNET (Universal, 1940) (13 parts) d Ford Beebe and Ray Taylor, s Gordon Jones, Wade Boteler, Keye Luke, Anne Nagel.
THE GREEN HORNET STRIKES AGAIN (Universal, 1941) (13 chapters) d Ford Beebe and John Rawlins, s Warren Hull, Keye Luke, Wade Boteler, Anne Nagel.

310. GREETINGS
These are anti-establishment films; young men scheme to avoid the draft.
GREETINGS (West End Films/Sigma III, 1968) d Brian De Palma, s Jonathan Warden, Robert De Niro.
HI, MOM! (West End Films/Sigma III, 1970) d Brian De Palma, s Robert De Niro, Charles Durham.

311. GREMLINS
Watch out for those cute, cuddly little creatures.
GREMLINS (Warner Brothers, 1984) d Joe Dante, s Zach Galligan, Phoebe

Cates, Hoyt Axton.
GREMLINS II (Warner Brothers, announced 1990) d Joe Dante, s Zach Galligan, Phoebe Cates, John Glover.

312. GRIZZLY ADAMS
A man, at odds with the law, takes to the mountains. There was also a television series, THE LIFE AND TIMES OF GRIZZLY ADAMS, with Dan Haggerty as James "Grizzly" Adams, Denver Pyle as Mad Jack and Don Shanks as Nakuma. It ran on NBC 1977-78.
THE LIFE AND TIMES OF GRIZZLY ADAMS (Sunn Classics, 1976) d Richard Friedenberg, s Dan Haggerty, Don Shanks, Lisa Jones.
THE CAPTURE OF GRIZZLY ADAMS (Sunn Classics, 1982) (NBC movie) d Don Kessler, s Dan Haggerty, Kim Darby, Noah Beery.
THE LEGEND OF GRIZZLY ADAMS (Shapiro, 1987) d Don Shanks, s Don Shanks, Gene Edwards.

312A GUNSMOKE
America's longest-running television Western aired in thirty- and sixty-minute formats, in black-and-white and in color, over CBS from 1955-75. The adventures of Marshal Matt Dillon of Dodge City were first dramatized in 1952 on radio. Major characters included Kitty Russell, Doc Adams, Chester Goode and Festus Haggen.
GUNSMOKE: RETURN TO DODGE CITY (TV movie 1987) d Vincent McEveety, s James Arness, Amanda Blake.
GUNSMOKE II: THE LAST APACHE (TV movie 1990) s James Arness, Michael Learned.

313. GUNS OF NAVARONE, THE
The World War II tales -- only remotely related -- are based on Alistair MacLean novels. Allied forces on Aegean Sea island find a way to elude the Germans.
THE GUNS OF NAVARONE (Columbia, 1961) d Lee Thompson, s Gregory Peck, David Niven.
FORCE 10 FROM NAVARONE (American International, 1978) d Guy Hamilton, s Robert Shaw, Harrison Ford.

314. GUSSLE
This silent comedy series produced by Mack Sennett feature Sydney Chaplin, Charlie's older half-brother, as an overblown, occasionally vulgar, would-be dandy in baggy clothes. The listing may not be complete.
GUSSLE THE GOLFER (Keystone, 1914) s Sydney Chaplin, Mack Swain, Dixie Chene.
GUSSLE'S DAY OF REST (Keystone, 1915) d Charles Avery, s Sydney Chaplin, Cecil Arnold, Slim Summerville.
GUSSLE RIVALS JONAH (Keystone, 1915) d Charles Avery, d Charles Avery, s Sydney Chaplin.
GUSSLE'S BACKWARD PATH (Keystone, 1915) d Charles Avery, s Sydney

144 MOTION PICTURE SERIES & SEQUELS

Chaplin.
GUSSLE'S WAYWARD PATH (Keystone, 1915) s Sydney Chaplin.
GUSSLE'S BACKWARD WAY (Keystone, 1915) d Charles Avery, s Sydney Chaplin.
GUSSLE TIED TO TROUBLE (Keystone, 1915) d Charles Avery, s Sydney Chaplin

315. HALLOWEEN
A psychotic killer -- an escapee from an asylum -- strikes on Halloween.
HALLOWEEN (Compass International, 1978) d John Carpenter, s Donald Pleasance, Jamie Lee Curtis.
HALLOWEEN II (Universal, 1981) d Rick Rosenthal, s Jamie Lee Curtis, Donald Pleasance.
HALLOWEEN III: SEASON OF THE WITCH (Universal, 1983) d Tommy Lee Wallace, s Tom Atkins, Stacey Nelkin.
HALLOWEEN 4: THE RETURN OF MICHAEL MYERS (Galaxy, 1988) d Dwight H. Little, s Donald Pleasance.
HALLOWEEN 5: THE REVENGE OF MICHAEL MYERS (Galaxy, 1989) d Dominique Othen-Girard, s Donald Pleasance, Danielle Harris, Ellie Cornell.

316. HALL-ROOM BOYS, THE
These silent comedies produced in the early 1920s by Columbia feature Sidney Smith and Harry McCoy. The pictures were issued by Federated Film Exchange and are based on a newspaper comic strip begun in 1906 by H.A. McGill.

317. HAM AND BUD
This Kalem silent comedy series features Lloyd V. Hamilton and Bud Duncan. The list is incomplete.
HAM, THE PIANO MOVER (Kalem, 1914) s Lloyd V. Hamilton, Bud Duncan.
HAM AT THE GARBAGE GENTLEMAN'S BALL (Kalem, 1915) s Lloyd V. Hamilton, Bud Duncan.

318. HANK AND LANK
This Essanay silent comedy series features Augustus Carney and Victor Potel. The list is incomplete.
JOYRIDING (Essanay, 1910) s Augustus Carney, Victor Potel.

319. HAPPY HOOKER, THE
Based on Xaviera Hollander's bestselling novel, these movies are about a high-priced madam.
THE HAPPY HOOKER (Cannon, 1975) d Nicholas Sgarro, s Lynn Redgrave, Jean-Pierre Aumont.
THE HAPPY HOOKER GOES TO WASHINGTON (Cannon, 1977) d William A. Levey, s Joey Heatherton, George Hamilton.

MOTION PICTURE SERIES & SEQUELS 145

THE HAPPY HOOKER GOES TO HOLLYWOOD (Cannon, 1980) d Alan
   Roberst, s Martine Beswicke, Chris Lemmon.

319A. HAPPY HOOLIGAN
Fred Opper's newspaper comic strip Irishman, a tramp with a tin can hat, first appeared in Hearst Sunday sections in 1900. He was an early, popular silent film character.
HOOLIGAN ASSISTS THE MAGICIAN (Edison, 1900)
HAPPY HOOLIGAN APRIL-FOOLED (Edison, 1901)
HAPPY HOOLIGAN SURPRISED (Edison, 1901)
HAPPY HOOLIGAN TURNS A BURGLAR (Edison, 1902)
THE TWENTIETH CENTURY TRAP; OR, HAPPY HOOLIGAN AND HIS
   AIRSHIP (Edison, 1902)
HAPPY HOOLIGAN'S INTERRUPTED LUNCH (American Mutoscope &
   Biograph, 1903)
HAPPY HOOLIGAN (American Mutoscope & Biograph, 1903)
HAPPY HOOLIGAN IN A TRAP (American Mutoscope & Biograph, 1903)
HOOLIGAN AS A SAFE ROBBER (American Mutoscope & Biograph, 1903)
HOOLIGAN IN JAIL (American Mutoscope & Biograph, 1903)
HOOLIGAN'S CHRISTMAS DREAM (American Mutoscope & Biograph,
   1903)
HOOLIGAN'S ROLLER SKATES (American Mutoscope & Biograph, 1903)
POOR HOOLIGAN, SO HUNGRY, TOO (American Mutoscope & Biograph,
   1903)
HOOLIGAN'S THANKSGIVING DINNER (American Mutoscope &
   Biograph, 1904)

320. HARDBODIES
Successful businessmen rent a beach house and hope to use it to seduce teenage girls.
HARDBODIES (Columbia, 1984) d Mark Griffiths, s Grant Cramer, Gary
   Wood.
HARDBODIES 2 (First American, 1986) d Mark Griffiths, s Brad Zutaut.

321. HARLEM GLOBETROTTERS, THE
The famous basketball team, which still performs widely in exhibition games, plays itself in these pictures.
THE HARLEM GLOBETROTTERS (Columbia, 1951) d Phil Brown, s Thomas
   Gomez, Dorothy Dandridge.
THE HARLEM GLOBETROTTERS ON GILLIGAN'S ISLAND (1981 TV
   movie) d Peter Baldwin, Bob Denver, Alan Hale.

322. HARLEM RIDES THE RANGE
A Black cowboy -- one of the rare few -- is featured in these Western programmers.
HARLEM ON THE PRAIRIE (Associated Features, 1938) d Sam Newfield, s
   Herb Jeffries, Flourney E. Miller, Mantan Moreland, Connie Harris.

146 MOTION PICTURE SERIES & SEQUELS

THE BRONZE BUCKAROO (Sack Amusements, 1938) d Richard C. Kahn, s Herb Jeffries, Spencer Williams.
HARLEM RIDES THE RANGE (Hollywood Pictures, 1939) d Richard C. Kahn, s Herb Jeffries, Spencer Williams, Lucius Brooks.

323. HAROLD LLOYD

The silent (and later talkie) film comedian broke away from his LONESOME LUKE series for Hal Roach-Pathe by donning a pair of owl-glasses. The first feature film is A SAILOR-MADE MAN, the first talkie is WELCOME DANGER. (See also THE FRESHMAN listings.)

OVER THE FENCE (Hal Roach-Pathe, 1917) s Harold Lloyd.
PINCHED (Hal Roach-Pathe, 1917) s Harold Lloyd.
BY THE SAD SEA WAVES (Hal Roach-Pathe, 1917) s Harold Lloyd.
THE FLIRT (Hal Roach-Pathe, 1917) s Harold Lloyd.
ALL ABOARD (Hal Roach-Pathe, 1917) s Harold Lloyd.
MOVE ON (Hal Roach-Pathe, 1917) s Harold Lloyd.
BASHFUL (Hal Roach-Pathe, 1917) s Harold Lloyd.
THE TIP (Hal Roach-Pathe, 1917) s Harold Lloyd.
THE BIG IDEA (Hal Roach-Pathe, 1918) s Harold Lloyd.
THE LAMB (Hal Roach-Pathe, 1918) s Harold Lloyd.
HIT HIM AGAIN (Hal Roach-Pathe, 1918) s Harold Lloyd.
BEAT IT (Hal Roach-Pathe, 1918) s Harold Lloyd.
A GASOLINE WEDDING (Hal Roach-Pathe, 1918) s Harold Lloyd.
LOOK PLEASANT, PLEASE (Hal Roach-Pathe, 1918) s Harold Lloyd.
HERE COME THE GIRLS (Hal Roach-Pathe, 1918) s Harold Lloyd.
LET'S GO (Hal Roach-Pathe, 1918) s Harold Lloyd.
ON THE JUMP (Hal Roach-Pathe, 1918) s Harold Lloyd.
FOLLOW THE CROWD (Hal Roach-Pathe, 1918) s Harold Lloyd.
PIPE THE WHISKERS (Hal Roach-Pathe, 1918) s Harold Lloyd.
IT'S A WILD LIFE (Hal Roach-Pathe, 1918) s Harold Lloyd.
HEY THERE (Hal Roach-Pathe, 1918) s Harold Lloyd.
KICKED OUT (Hal Roach-Pathe, 1918) s Harold Lloyd.
THE NON-STOP KID (Hal Roach-Pathe, 1918) s Harold Lloyd.
TWO-GUN GUSSIE (Hal Roach-Pathe, 1918) s Harold Lloyd.
FIREMAN, SAVE MY CHILD (Hal Roach-Pathe, 1918) s Harold Lloyd.
THE CITY SLICKER (Hal Roach-Pathe, 1918) s Harold Lloyd.
SIC 'EM TOWSER (Hal Roach-Pathe, 1918) s Harold Lloyd.
SOMEWHERE IN TURKEY (Hal Roach-Pathe, 1918) s Harold Lloyd.
ARE CROOKS DISHONEST? (Hal Roach-Pathe, 1918) s Harold Lloyd.
AN OZARK ROMANCE (Hal Roach-Pathe, 1918) s Harold Lloyd.
KICKING THE GERM OUT OF GERMANY (Hal Roach-Pathe, 1918) s Harold Lloyd.
THAT'S HIM (Hal Roach-Pathe, 1918) s Harold Lloyd.
BRIDE AND GLOOM (Hal Roach-Pathe, 1918) s Harold Lloyd.
TWO SCRAMBLED (Hal Roach-Pathe, 1918) s Harold Lloyd.
BEES IN HIS BONNET (Hal Roach-Pathe, 1918) s Harold Lloyd.
SWING YOUR PARTNERS (Hal Roach-Pathe, 1918) s Harold Lloyd.

MOTION PICTURE SERIES & SEQUELS 147

WHY PICK ON ME? (Hal Roach-Pathe, 1918) s Harold Lloyd.
NOTHING BUT TROUBLE (Hal Roach-Pathe, 1918) s Harold Lloyd.
HEAR 'EM RAVE (Hal Roach-Pathe, 1918) s Harold Lloyd.
TAKE A CHANCE (Hal Roach-Pathe, 1918) s Harold Lloyd.
SHE LOVES ME NOT (Hal Roach-Pathe, 1918) s Harold Lloyd.
WANTED -- $5,000 (Hal Roach-Pathe, 1919) s Harold Lloyd.
GOING! GOING! GONE! (Hal Roach-Pathe, 1919) s Harold Lloyd.
ASK FATHER (Hal Roach-Pathe, 1919) s Harold Lloyd.
ON THE FIRE (Hal Roach-Pathe, 1919) s Harold Lloyd.
I'M ON MY WAY (Hal Roach-Pathe, 1919) s Harold Lloyd.
LOOK OUT BELOW! (Hal Roach-Pathe, 1919) s Harold Lloyd.
THE DUTIFUL DUB (Hal Roach-Pathe, 1919) s Harold Lloyd.
NEXT AISLE OVER (Hal Roach-Pathe, 1919) s Harold Lloyd.
A SAMMY IN SIBERIA (Hal Roach-Pathe, 1919) s Harold Lloyd.
JUST DROPPED IN (Hal Roach-Pathe, 1919) s Harold Lloyd.
CRACK YOUR HEELS (Hal Roach-Pathe, 1919) s Harold Lloyd.
RING UP THE CURTAIN (Hal Roach-Pathe, 1919) s Harold Lloyd.
YOUNG MR. JAZZ (Hal Roach-Pathe, 1919) s Harold Lloyd.
SI SENOR (Hal Roach-Pathe, 1919) s Harold Lloyd.
BEFORE BREAKFAST (Hal Roach-Pathe, 1919) s Harold Lloyd.
THE MARATHON (Hal Roach-Pathe, 1919) s Harold Lloyd.
BACK TO THE WOODS (Hal Roach-Pathe, 1919) s Harold Lloyd.
PISTOLS FOR BREAKFAST (Hal Roach-Pathe, 1919) s Harold Lloyd.
SWAT THE CROOK (Hal Roach-Pathe, 1919) s Harold Lloyd.
OFF THE TROLLEY (Hal Roach-Pathe, 1919) s Harold Lloyd.
SPRING FEVER (Hal Roach-Pathe, 1919) s Harold Lloyd.
BILLY BLAZES, ESQ. (Hal Roach-Pathe, 1919) s Harold Lloyd.
JUST NEIGHBORS (Hal Roach-Pathe, 1919) s Harold Lloyd.
AT THE OLD STAGE DOOR (Hal Roach-Pathe, 1919) s Harold Lloyd.
NEVER TOUCHED ME (Hal Roach-Pathe, 1919) s Harold Lloyd.
A JAZZED HONEYMOON (Hal Roach-Pathe, 1919) s Harold Lloyd.
COUNT YOUR CHANGE (Hal Roach-Pathe, 1919) s Harold Lloyd.
CHOP SUEY & CO. (Hal Roach-Pathe, 1919) s Harold Lloyd.
HEAP BIG CHIEF (Hal Roach-Pathe, 1919) s Harold Lloyd.
DON'T SHOVE (Hal Roach-Pathe, 1919) s Harold Lloyd.
THE RAJAH (Hal Roach-Pathe, 1919) s Harold Lloyd.
HE LEADS, OTHERS FOLLOW (Hal Roach-Pathe, 1919) s Harold Lloyd.
SOFT MONEY (Hal Roach-Pathe, 1919) s Harold Lloyd.
COUNT THE VOTES (Hal Roach-Pathe, 1919) s Harold Lloyd.
PAY YOUR DUES (Hal Roach-Pathe, 1919) s Harold Lloyd.
HIS ONLY FATHER (Hal Roach-Pathe, 1919) s Harold Lloyd.
BUMPING INTO BROADWAY (Hal Roach-Pathe, 1919) s Harold Lloyd.
CAPTAIN KIDD'S KIDS (Hal Roach-Pathe, 1919) s Harold Lloyd.
FROM HAND TO MOUTH (Hal Roach-Pathe, 1919) s Harold Lloyd.
HIS ROYAL SLYNESS (Hal Roach-Pathe, 1920) s Harold Lloyd.
HAUNTED SPOOKS (Hal Roach-Pathe, 1920) s Harold Lloyd.
AN EASTERN WESTERNER (Hal Roach-Pathe, 1920) s Harold Lloyd.

HIGH AND DIZZY (Hal Roach-Pathe, 1920) s Harold Lloyd.
GET OUT AND GET UNDER (Hal Roach-Pathe, 1920) s Harold Lloyd.
NUMBER PLEASE (Hal Roach-Pathe, 1920) s Harold Lloyd.
NOW OR NEVER (Hal Roach-Pathe, 1921) s Harold Lloyd.
AMONG THOSE PRESENT (Hal Roach-Pathe, 1921) s Harold Lloyd.
I DO (Hal Roach-Pathe, 1921) s Harold Lloyd.
NEVER WEAKEN (Hal Roach-Pathe, 1921) s Harold Lloyd.
A SAILOR-MADE MAN (Hal Roach-Associated Distributors, 1921) s Harold Lloyd.
GRANDMA'S BOY (Hal Roach-Pathe, 1922) s Harold Lloyd.
DOCTOR JACK (Hal Roach-Pathe, 1922) s Harold Lloyd.
SAFETY LAST (Hal Roach-Pathe, 1923) s Harold Lloyd.
WHY WORRY? (Hal Roach-Pathe, 1923) s Harold Lloyd.
GIRL SHY (Hal Roach-Pathe, 1924) s Harold Lloyd.
HOT WATER (Hal Roach-Pathe, 1924) s Harold Lloyd.
FOR HEAVEN'S SAKE (Lloyd-Paramount, 1926) s Harold Lloyd.
THE KID BROTHER (Lloyd-Paramount, 1927) s Harold Lloyd.
SPEEDY (Lloyd-Paramount, 1928) s Harold Lloyd.
WELCOME DANGER (Lloyd-Paramount, 1929) s Harold Lloyd.
FEET FIRST (Lloyd-Paramount, 1930) s Harold Lloyd.
MOVIE CRAZY (Lloyd-Paramount, 1932) s Harold Lloyd.
THE CAT'S PAW (Lloyd-Fox, 1934) s Harold Lloyd.
THE MILKY WAY (Paramount, 1936) s Harold Lloyd.
PROFESSOR, BEWARE! (Paramount, 1938) s Harold Lloyd.

324. HARRAD EXPERIMENT, THE
Robert H. Rimmer's "sociological" novel of rampant campus lovemaking is the basis for these pictures.
THE HARRAD EXPERIMENT (Cinerama, 1973) d Ted Post, s James Whitmore, Tippi Hedren.
THE HARRAD SUMMER (Cinerama, 1974) d Steven H. Stern, s Robert Reiser, Laurie Walters.

325. HARRY LANGDON
The baby-faced silent comedian acts childlike in an adult world. Listed are comedy shorts.
PICKING PEACHES (Mack Sennett/Pathe, 1924) s Harry Langdon.
SMILE, PLEASE (Mack Sennett/Pathe, 1924) s Harry Langdon.
SHANGHAIED LOVERS (Mack Sennett/Pathe, 1924) s Harry Langdon.
FLICKERING YOUTH (Mack Sennett/Pathe, 1924) s Harry Langdon.
THE CAT'S MEOW (Mack Sennett/Pathe, 1924) s Harry Langdon.
HIS NEW MAMA (Mack Sennett/Pathe, 1924) s Harry Langdon.
THE LUCK OF THE FOOLISH (Mack Sennett/Pathe, 1924) s Harry Langdon.
ALL NIGHT LONG (Mack Sennett/Pathe, 1924) s Harry Langdon.
THE FIRST HUNDRED YEARS (Mack Sennett/Pathe, 1924) s Harry Langdon.
FEET OF MUD (Mack Sennett/Pathe, 1924) s Harry Langdon.

MOTION PICTURE SERIES & SEQUELS 149

THE SEA SQUAWK (Mack Sennett/Pathe, 1924) s Harry Langdon.
HIS FIRST FLAME (Mack Sennett/Pathe, 1925) s Harry Langdon.
PLAIN CLOTHES (Mack Sennett/Pathe, 1925) s Harry Langdon.
REMEMBER WHEN? (Mack Sennett/Pathe, 1925) s Harry Langdon.
THE HANSOM CABMAN (Mack Sennett/Pathe, 1925) s Harry Langdon.
THERE HE GOES (Mack Sennett/Pathe, 1925) s Harry Langdon.
BOOBS IN THE WOODS (Mack Sennett/Pathe, 1925) s Harry Langdon.
HIS MARRIAGE WOW (Mack Sennett/Pathe, 1925) s Harry Langdon.
OVER HERE (Mack Sennett/Pathe, 1925) s Harry Langdon.
SKY SCRAPER (Mack Sennett/Pathe, 1925) s Harry Langdon.
WATCH OUT (Mack Sennett/Pathe, 1925) s Harry Langdon.
SATURDAY AFTERNOON (Mack Sennett/Pathe, 1925) s Harry Langdon.
FIDDLESTICKS (Mack Sennett/Pathe, 1926) s Harry Langdon.
SOLDIER MAN (Mack Sennett/Pathe, 1926) s Harry Langdon.
LUCKY STARS (Mack Sennett/Pathe, 1926) s Harry Langdon.
HOTTER THAN HOT (Hal Roach-MGM, 1929) d Lewis R. Foster, s Harry Langdon, Edgar Kennedy, Thelma Todd.
SKY BOY (Hal Roach-MGM, 1929) d Charles Rogers, s Harry Landgon, Thelma Todd.
SKIRT SHY (Hal Roach-MGM, 1929) d Charles Rogers, s Harry Langdon, May Wallace.
THE HEAD GUY (Hal Roach-MGM, 1930) d Fred Guiol, s Harry Langdon, Thelma Todd.
THE FIGHTING PARSON (Hal Roach-MGM, 1930) d Charles Rogers and Fred Guiol, s Harry Langdon, Thelma Todd.
THE BIG KICK (Hal Roach-MGM, 1930) d Warren Doane, s Harry Langdon, Nancy Dover.
THE SHRIMP (Hal Roach-MGM, 1930) d Charles Rogers, s Harry Langdon, Thelma Todd.
THE KING (Hal Roach-MGM, 1930) d James W. Horne, s Harry Langdon, Thelma Todd.
THE BIG FLASH (Educational, 1932) d Arvid E. Gillstrom, s Harry Langdon, Vernon Dent.
TIRED FEET (Educational, 1933) d Arvid E. Gillstrom, s Harry Langdon, Vernon Dent.
THE HITCH HIKER (Educational, 1933) d Arvid E. Gillstrom, s Harry Langdon, Vernon Dent.
KNIGHT DUTY (Educational, 1933) d Arvid E. Gillstrom, s Harry Langdon, Vernon Dent.
TIED FOR LIFE (Educational, 1933) d Arvid E. Gillstrom, s Harry Langdon, Vernon Dent.
HOOKS AND JABS (Educational, 1933) d Arvid E. Gillstrom, s Harry Langdon, Vernon Dent, Nell O'Day.
THE STAGE HAND (Educational, 1933) d Harry Edwards, s Harry Langdon, Marel Foster.
MARRIAGE HUMOR (Paramount, 1933) d Harry Edwards, s Harry Langdon, Vernon Dent.

ON ICE (Paramount, 1933) d Arvid E. Gillstrom, s Harry Langdon, Vernon Dent.
ROAMING ROMEO (Paramount, 1933) d Arvid E. Gillstrom, s Harry Langdon, Vernon Dent.
TRIMMED IN FURS (Educational, 1934) d Charle Lamont, s Harry Langdon, John Sheehan.
CIRCUS HOODOO (Paramount, 1934) d Arvid E. Gillstrom, s Harry Langdon, Vernon Dent.
PETTING PREFERRED (Paramount, 1934) d Arvid E. Gillstrom, s Harry Langdon, Vernon Dent.
COUNSEL ON DE FENCE (Columbia, 1934) d Arthur Ripley, s Harry Langdon, Renee Whitney.
SHIVERS (Columbia, 1934) d Arthur Ripley, s Harry Langdon, Florence Lake.
HIS BRIDAL SWEET (Columbia, 1935) d Alf Goulding, s Harry Langdon, Billy Gilbert.
THE LEATHER NECKER (Columbia, 1935) d Arthur Ripley, s Harry Langdon.
HIS MARRIAGE MIXUP (Columbia, 1935) d Preston Black, s Harry Langdon, Dorothy Granger.
I DON'T REMEMBER (Columbia, 1935) d Preston Black, s Harry Langdon.
A DOGGONE MIXUP (Columbia, 1938) d Charles Lamont, s Harry Langdon, Ann Doran.
SUE MY LAWYER (Columbia, 1938) d Jules White, s Harry Langdon, Ann Doran.
GOODNESS, A GHOST (RKO, 1940) d Harry D'Arcy, s Harry Langdon.
COLD TURKEY (Columbia, 1940) d Del Lord, s Harry Langdon, Ann Doran.
WHAT MAKES LIZZY DIZZY? (Columbia, 1942) d Jules White, s Harry Langdon, Elsie Ames.
TIREMAN, SPARE MY TIRES (Columbia, 1942) d Jules White, s Harry Langdon.
CARRY HARRY (Columbia, 1942) d Harry Edwards, s Harry Langdon.
PIANO MOONER (Columbia, 1942) d Harry Edwards, s Harry Landgon, Fifi D'Orsay.
BLITZ ON THE FRITZ (Columbia, 1943) d Jules White, s Harry Langdon, Louise Currie.
BLONDE AND GROOM (Columbia, 1943) d Harry Edwards, s Harry Langdon.
HERE COMES MR. ZERK (Columbia, 1943) d Jules White, s Harry Langdon.
TO HEIR IS HUMAN (Columbia, 1944) d Harold Godsoe, s Harry Langdon.
DEFECTIVE DETECTIVES (Columbia, 19414) d Harry Edwards, s Harry Langdon.
MOPEY DOPE (Columbia, 1944) d Del Lord, s Hary Langdon, El Brendel.
SNOOPER SERVICE (Columbia, 1945) d Harry Edwards, s Harry Langdon, El Brendel.
PISTOL PACKIN' NITWITS (Columbia, 1945) d Harry Edwards, s Harry Langdon, El Brendel.

MOTION PICTURE SERIES & SEQUELS 151

326. HARRY PALMER
The espionage novels by Len Deighton, upon which these pictures are based, offer a low-key intelligence agent.
THE IPCRESS FILE (Rank/Universal, 1965) d Sidney J. Furie, s Michael Caine, Nigel Green.
FUNERAL IN BERLIN (Lowndes/Paramount, 1966) d Guy Hamilton, s Michael Caine, Eva Renzi.
BILLION DOLLAR BRAIN (Lowndes/United Artists, 1967) d Ken Russell, s Michael Caine, Karl Malden.

327. HAVING BABIES
The pictures are about couples and their experiences in childbirth. They anticipated the short-lived JULIE FARR MD television series carried over ABC 1978-79.
HAVING BABIES (Jozak, 1976) (ABC-TV movie) d Robert Day, s Desi Arnaz Jr., Adrienne Barbeau.
HAVING BABIES II (Jozak, 1977) d Richard Michaels, s Tony Bill, Carol Lynley.
HAVING BABIES III (Jozak/Paramount, 1978) (ABC-TV movie) d Jackie Cooper, s Susan Sullivan, Dennis Howard, Patti Duke Astin.

328. HAWAII
James A. Michener's novel of New England missionaries venturing to remote islands serves as the basis for these pictures.
HAWAII (United Artists, 1966) d George Roy Hill, s Julie Andrews, Max von Sydow.
THE HAWAIIANS (United Artists, 1970) d Tom Gries, s Charlton Heston, Geraldine Chaplin.

329. HAWAII VICE
These pictures are rated X.
HAWAII VICE (CDI, 1988) s Kascha, Francois Papillon.
HAWAII VICE II (CDI, 1989) s Kascha, Francois Papillon.
HAWAII VICE III: BEYOND THE BADGE (CDI, 1989) s Kascha, Francois Papillon.

HAWKEYE
See **LEATHERSTOCKING**

329A. HEAVENLY TWINS, THE
These are silent films. The list may be incomplete.
THE HEAVENLY TWINS AT LUNCH (Edison, 1903).
THE HEAVENLY TWINS AT ODDS (Edison, 1903)

330. HEC RAMSEY
Hec Ramsey is a grizzled, old-time gunfighter who only begrudgingly gives in to newfangled ways of solving crimes. Ramsey appeared in 90-minute

programs over NBC, 1972-74, as part of the SUNDAY MYSTERY MOVIE. The first picture below is a is TV series pilot; the others are telefilms derived from that series.
HEC RAMSEY (Universal, 1972) (NBC-TV movie) [aka THE CENTURY TURNS] d Daniel Petrie, s Richard Boone, Rick Lenz.
MYSTERY OF CHALK HILL (Universal, 1973) (NBC-TV movie) s Richard Boone, Sharon Acker, Rick Lenz.
SCAR TISSUE (Universal, 1974) (NBC-TV movie) s Richard Boone, Sharon Acker, Rick Lenz.

331. HEIDI
Johanna Spyri's tale of a young girl who has adventures in the Swiss Alps inspired a number of pictures.
HEIDI (20th Century-Fox, 1937) d Allan Dwan, s Shirley Temple, Jean Hersholt.
HEIDI (1952) d Luigi Comencini, s Elsbeth Sigmund, Heirich Gretler.
HEIDI AND PETER (1955) d Franz Schnyder, s Heinrich Gretler, Elsbeth Sigmund.
A GIFT FOR HEIDI (1958) d George Templeton, s Sandy Descher
HEIDI (Omnibus-Biography Productions, 1968) (CBS-TV movie) d Delbert Mann, s Maximilian Schell, Jean Simmons, Jennifer Edwards.
HEIDI (Warner Brothers-7 Arts, 1967) d Werner Jacobs, s Eva Marie Singhammer, Gertraud Mittermayr.
THE NEW ADVENTURES OF HEIDI (Pierre Cossette Enterprises, 1978) (NBC-TV movie) d Ralph Senensky, s Katy Kurtzman, Burl Ives.
HEIDI's SONG (Paramount, 1982) (animated) d Robert Taylor, voices of Lorne Greene, Sammy Davis Jr., Margery Gray.
EROTIC ADVENTURES OF HEIDI
COURAGE MOUNTAIN: THE FURTHER ADVENTURES OF HEIDI (Trans World, 1989)

331A. HEINIE AND LOUIE
These are silent comedies featuring Jimmy Aubrey. The list is incomplete.
A MERRY CHASE
MONKEY SHINES

332. HELLRAISER
The first of these pictures is penned by English horror writer Clive Barker. The Cenobites -- dead souls who worship the Devil -- terrorize the young cast.
HELLRAISER (New World, 1987) d Clive Barker, s Andrew Robinson, Clare Higgins, Ashley Laurence.
HELLBOUND: HELLRAISER II (New World Pictures, 1988) d Tony Randel, s Clare Higgins, Ashley Laurence, Kenneth Cranham.

333. HELL'S ANGELS
The California motorcycle gang is depicted in a number of 1960s pictures.
WILD ANGELS (American International, 1966) d Roger Corman, s Peter

Fonda, Nancy Sinatra
HELL'S ANGELS ON WHEELS (U.S. Films, 1967) d Richard Rush, s Adam Roarke, Jack Nicholson.
DEVILS ANGELS (American International, 1967) d Daniel Heller, s John Cassavetes, Beverly Adams.
SAVAGE SEVEN (American International, 1968) d Richard Rush, s Robert Walker, Larry Bishop.
HELLS ANGELS 69 (American International, 1969) d Lee Madden.
ANGELS DIE HARD (New World, 1970) d Richard Compton, s Tom Baker, William Smith.
HARD RIDE (American International, 1971) d Burt Topper
THE HIGH RIDERS

334. HENRY ALDRICH
Clifford Goldsmith's play *What a Life* inspired both a radio and a film series about teenage/family life.
WHAT A LIFE (Paramount, 1939) d Ted Reed, s Jackie Cooper, Betty Field.
LIFE WITH HENRY (Paramount, 1941) d Ted Reed, s Jackie Cooper, Lila Ernst.
HENRY ALDRICH FOR PRESIDENT (Paramount, 1941) d Hugh Bennett, s James Lydon, Charles Smith.
HENRY AND DIZZY (Paramount, 1942) d Hugh Bennett, s Jimmy Lydon, Mary Anderson.
HENRY ALDRICH, EDITOR (Paramount, 1942) d Hugh Bennett, s Jimmy Lydon, Charles Smith.
HENRY ALDRICH GETS GLAMOUR (Paramount, 1943) d Hugh Bennett, s Jimmy Lydon, Charles Smith.
HENRY ALDRICH SWINGS IT (Paramount, 1943) d Hugh Bennett, s Jimmy Lydon, Charles Smith.
HENRY ALDRICH HAUNTS HOUSE (Paramount, 1943) d Hugh Bennett, s Jimmy Lydon, Charles Smith.
HENRY ALDRICH, BOY SCOUT (Paramount, 1944) d Hugh Bennett, s Jimmy Lydon, Charles Smith.
HENRY ALDRICH PLAYS CUPID (Paramount, 1944) d Hugh Bennett, s Jimmy Lydon, Charles Smith.
HENRY ALDRICH'S LITTLE SECRET (Paramount, 1944) d Hugh Bennett, s Jimmy Lydon, Charles Smith.

335. HENRY LATHAM
These folksy pictures set in a small town are derived from stories by D.D. Beauchamp.
HENRY, THE RAINMAKER (Monogram, 1949) d Jean Yarbrough, s Raymond Walburn, Walter Catlett.
LEAVE IT TO HENRY (Monogram, 1949) d Jean Yarbrough, s Raymond Walburn, Walter Catlett.

FATHER MAKES GOOD (Monogram, 1950) d Jean Yarbrough, s Raymond Walburn, Walter Catlett.
FATHER'S WILD GAME (Monogram, 1950) d Jean Yarbrough, s Raymond Walburn, Walter Catlett.
FATHER TAKES THE AIR (Monogram, 1951) d Jean Yarbrough, s Raymond Walburn, Walter Catlett.

336. HERCULE POIROT
Agatha Christie wrote a series of mysteries featuring the egg-head detective.
ALIBI (Twickenham, 1931) d Leslie Hiscott, s Austin Trevor.
BLACK COFFEE (Twickenham, 1931) d Leslie Hiscott, s Austin Trevor.
LORD EDGWARE DIES (Real Art, 1934) d Henry Edwards, s Austin Trevor.
THE ALPHABET MURDERS (MGM, 1966) d Frank Tashlin, s Tony Randall, Anita Ekberg.
MURDER ON THE ORIENT EXPRESS (EMI, 1974) d Sidney Lumet, s Albert Finney, Lauren Bacall.
DEATH ON THE NILE (1978) d John Guillermin, s Peter Ustinov, Bette Davis.
EVIL UNDER THE SUN (Universal, 1982) d Guy Hamilton, s Peter Ustinov, Jane Birkin.
AGATHA CHRISTIE'S "THIRTEEN AT DINNER" (1985 TV movie) d Lou Antonio, s Peter Ustinov, Faye Dunaway.
AGATHA CHRISTIE'S "DEAD MAN'S FOLLY" (1986 TV movie) [aka DEAD MAN'S FOLLY] d Clive Donner, s Peter Ustinov, Jean Stapleton.

337. HERCULES
The muscular hero of Greek legend appeared in a number of films.
HERCULES (Warner Brothers, 1959) d Pietro Francisci, s Steve Reeves, Sylva Koscina.
HERCULES UNCHAINED (1960) d Pietro Francisci, s Steve Reeves, Sylva Koscina.
HERCULES AGAINST ROME (1960) d Piero Pierott, s Alan Steel, Wandisa Guida.
HERCULES IN THE HAUNTED WORLD (Spa Cinematografica/Woolner Brothers, 1961) [aka HERCULES AT THE CENTER OF THE EARTH and HERCULES VS. THE VAMPIRES and THE VAMPIRES VS. HERCULES and WITH HERCULES TO THE CENTER OF THE EARTH] d Mario Bava, s Reg Park, Christopher Lee.
THE FURY OF HERCULES (1961) d V. Scega, s Brad Harris, Brigitte Corey.
HERCULES AGAINST THE SONS OF THE SUN (1963) d Osvaldo Civirani, s Mark Forest, Anna Pace.
HERCULES AND THE CAPTIVE WOMEN (1963) d Vittorio Cottafavi, s Reg Park, Fay Spain.
HERCULES AGAINST THE MOON MEN (1964) d Giacomo Gentilomo, s Alan Steel, Jany Clair.
HERCULES, SAMSON AND ULYSSES (MGM, 1965) d Pietro Francisci, s Kirk Morris, Richard Lloyd.

MOTION PICTURE SERIES & SEQUELS

HERCULES (Cannon, 1983) d Lewis Coates (Luigi Cozzi), s Lou Ferrigno, Mirella D'Angelo.
HERCULES II (Cannon, 1985) [aka THE ADVENTURES OF HERCULES] d Luigi Cozzi, s Lou Ferrigno, Milly Carlucci.

338. HEY FELLAS
Davis Distributing made these short comedies featuring a cast of juveniles.

339. HIGGINS FAMILY, THE
An advertising man heads the family in this series.
THE HIGGINS FAMILY (Republic, 1938) d Gus Meins, s James Gleason, Lucile Gleason.
MY WIFE'S RELATIVES (Republic, 1939)
SHOULD HUSBANDS WORK? (Republic, 1939)
THE COVERED TRAILER (Republic, 1939)
MONEY TO BURN (Republic, 1940)
GRANDPA GOES TO TOWN (Republic, 1940) d Gus Meins, s James Gleason, Lucille Gleason, Ralph Gleason.
EARL OF PUDDLESTONE (Republic, 1940)
MEET THE MISSUS (1940)
PETTICOAT POLITICS (Republic, 1941)

340. HIGHLANDER
An immortal 16th century Scotland being is pursued to modern-day America by his eternal arch-enemy.
HIGHLANDER (20th Century-Fox, 1986) d Russell Mulcahy, s Christopher Lambert, Roxanne Hart, Clancy Brown, Sean Connery.
HIGHLANDER 2 (Jaglom, 1990 announced) d Russell Mulcahy, s Christopher Lambert, Sean Connery.

341. HIGH NOON
The classic Western finds the marshal defending the town against outlaws.
HIGH NOON (United Artists, 1952) d Fred Zinnemann, s Gary Cooper, Grace Kelly.
HIGH NOON, PART II: THE RETURN OF WILL KANE (Charles Fries Productions, 1980) (CBS-TV movie) d Jerry Jameson, s Lee Majors, David Carradine.

342. HILDEGARDE WITHERS
The spinsterish amateur detective appeared in Stuart Palmer mystery books. For the 1950 picture below, her named was changed and she teamed with John J. Malone (see that series entry).
THE PENGUIN POOL MURDER (RKO, 1932) d George Archainbaud, s Edna May Oliver.
MURDER ON THE BLACKBOARD (RKO, 1934) s Edna May Oliver.
MURDER ON A HONEYMOON (RKO, 1935) s Edna May Oliver.
MURDER ON A BRIDLE PATH (RKO, 1936) s Helen Broderick

THE PLOT THICKENS (RKO, 1936) s Zasu Pitts.
40 NAUGHTY GIRLS (RKO, 1937)
MRS. O'MALLEY AND MR. MALONE (1950) s James Whitmore.
A VERY MISSING PERSON (TV movie, 1972) d Russell Mayberry, s Eve Arden.

343. HILLS HAVE EYES, THE
Savage mutants harass a family on a camping trip, in the first outing; in the second, passengers on a school bus face a menace.
THE HILLS HAVE EYES (Blood Relations/Vanguard, 1977) d Wes Craven, s Susan Lanier, Robert Houston.
THE HILLS HAVE EYES PART II (New Realm, 1985) d Wes Craven, s Michael Berryman, John Laughlin.

344. HISTORY OF WHITE PEOPLE IN AMERICA, THE
These are spoof documentaries on white traits, habits and preferences.
THE HISTORY OF WHITE PEOPLE IN AMERICA (1985) d Harry Shearer, s Martin Mull, Mary Kay Place.
THE HISTORY OF WHITE PEOPLE IN AMERICA, VOLUME II (1986) d Harry Shearer, s Fred Willard, Mary Kay Place, Martin Mull.

345. HIT PARADE, THE
These musical films have a radio station background.
THE HIT PARADE (Republic, 1937) d Gus Meins, s France Langford, Phil Regan.
HIT PARADE OF 1941 (Republic, 1940) d John S. Auer, s Kenny Baker, Frances Langford.
HIT PARADE OF 1943 (Republic, 1943) d John Carroll, s Susan Hayward.
HIT PARADE OF 1947 (Republic, 1947) d Frank McDonald, s Eddie Albert, Constance Moore.

346. HOGAN
The silent comedy series is from Mack Sennett's Keystone Studios.
HOGAN'S ANNUAL SPREE (Keystone, 1915) s Charles Murray.
HOGAN'S WILD OATS (Keystone, 1915) d Charles Avery, s Charles Murray.
HOGAN'S MUSSY JOB (Keystone, 1915) d Charles Avery, s Charles Murray.
HOGAN THE PORTER (Keystone, 1915) d Charles Avery, s Charles Murray.
HOGAN'S ROMANCE UPSET (Keystone, 1915) d Charles Avery, s Charles Murray.
HOGAN'S ARISTOCRATIC DREAM (Keystone, 1915) d Charles Avery, s Charles Murray.
HOGAN OUT WEST (Keystone, 1915) d Charles Avery, s Charles Murray.

347. HOLLYWOOD BOULEVARD
A would-be actress goes to work for schlock movie makers in the first entry.
HOLLYWOOD BOULEVARD (New World, 1976) d Joe Dante, s Allan

Arkush, Candice Rialson.
HOLLYWOOD BOULEVARD II (Concorde, 1989) d Steve Barnett, s Ginger Lynn Allen, Kelly Monteith.

348. HOLLYWOOD HIGH
Teen sexploitation: Juveniles cruise, party and carry on.
HOLLYWOOD HIGH (Peter Perryt, 1976) d Patrick Wright.
HOLLYWOOD HIGH, PART II (Lone Star, 1981) d Caruth C. Byrd and Lee Thomburg, s April May, Donna Lynn.

348A. HONEY, I SHRUNK THE KIDS
This Disney picture about youngsters' escapades in miniature was sufficiently successful that the studio has reportedly registered these possible titles for sequels: HONEY, I MADE THE KIDS INVISIBLE; HONEY; I LAUNCHED THE KIDS TO THE MOON; and HONEY, I XEROXED THE KIDS.
HONEY, I SHRUNK THE KIDS (Buena Vista, 1989) d Joe Johnston, s Rick Moranis, Jared Rushton, Matt Frewer.

349. HOO-RAY KIDS
This British series of comedy shorts stars youthful Jackie Ray.

350. *HOOT GIBSON AND SKEETER BILL ROBBINS*
These are B-Westerns.
WILD HORSE (Allied, 1931) d Richard Thorpe and Sidney Algier, s Hoot Gibson, Stepin Fetchit, Skeeter Bill Robbins, Alberta Vaughn.
HARD HOMBRE (Allied, 1931) d Otto Brower, s Hoot Gibson, Skeeter Bill Robbins, Lina Basquette.
THE LOCAL BAD MAN (Allied, 1931) d Otto Brower, s Hoot Gibson, Skeeter Bill Robbins, Sally Blaine.
A MAN'S LAND (Allied, 1932) d Phil Rosen, s Hoot Gibson, Skeeter Bill Robbins, Marion Shilling.
THE COWBOY COUNSELOR (Allied, 1932) d George Melford, s Hoot Gibson, Skeeter Bill Robbins, Sheila Mannors
THE BOILING POINT (Allied, 1932) d George Melford, s Hoot Gibson, Skeeter Bill Robbins, Helen Foster
DUDE BANDIT (Allied, 1932) d George Melford, s Hoot Gibson, Skeeter Bill Robbins, Gloria Shea.
THE FIGHTING PARSON (Allied, 1932) d Harry Fraser, s Hoot Gibson, Skeeter Bill Robbins, Marceline Day.

351. HOPALONG CASSIDY
Author Clarence E. Mulford's tobacco-chewing, rough-and-tough ranchhand (in eighteen books published 1905-41) was sanitized for a string of sixty-six Hollywood B-grade oaters featuring William Boyd and a series of sidekicks. Boyd also played the character in radio (with sidekick Andy Clyde) and television (with Edgar Buchanan) series.
HOP-A-LONG CASSIDY (Paramount, 1935), d Howard Bretherton, s William

158 MOTION PICTURE SERIES & SEQUELS

Boyd, Jimmy Ellison, Paula Stone, George Hayes.
THE EAGLE'S BROOD (Paramount, 1935) d Howard Bretherton, s William Boyd, Jimmy Ellison, William Farnum, George Hayes.
BAR 20 RIDES AGAIN (Paramount, 1935) d Howard Bretherton, s William Boyd, Jimmy Ellison, Jean Rouveral, George Hayes.
CALL OF THE PRAIRIE (Paramount, 1936) d Howard Bretherton, s William Boyd, Jimmy Ellison, Muriel Evans, George Hayes.
THREE ON THE TRAIL (Paramount, 1936) d Howard Bretherton, s William Boyd, Jimmy Ellison, Onslow Stevens, Evans, George "Windy" Hayes, Claude King.
HEART OF THE WEST (Paramount, 1936) d Howard Bretherton, s William Boyd, Jimmy Ellison, George "Windy" Hayes, Lynn Gilbert.
HOPALONG CASSIDY RETURNS (Paramount, 1936) d Nate Watt, s William Boyd, George "Windy" Hayes, Gail Sheridan.
TRAIL DUST (Paramount, 1936) d Nate Watt, s William Boyd, Jimmy Ellison, George "Windy" Hayes, Gwynne Shipman.
BORDERLAND (Paramount, 1937) d Nate Watt, s William Boyd, Jimmy Ellison, George "Windy" Hayes, Morris, Beach.
HILLS OF OLD WYOMING (Paramount, 1937) d Nate Watt, s William Boyd, George "Windy" Hayes, Russell Hayden.
NORTH OF THE RIO GRANDE (Paramount, 1937) d Nate Watt, s William Boyd, Russell Hayden.
RUSTLERS' VALLEY (Paramount, 1937) d Nate Watt, s William Boyd, George "Windy" Hayes, Russell Hayden.
HOPALONG RIDES AGAIN (Paramount, 1937) d Lesley Selander, s William Boyd, George "Windy" Hayes, Russell Hayden, Harry Worth.
TEXAS TRAIL (Paramount, 1937) d David Selman, s William Boyd, George "Windy" Hayes, Russell Hayden, Judith Allen, Alexander Cross.
CASSIDY OF BAR 20 (Paramount, 1938) d Lesley Selander, s William Boyd, Frank Darien, Russell Hayden.
HEART OF ARIZONA (Paramount, 1938) d Lesley Selander, s William Boyd, George "Windy" Hayes, Russell Hayden, Natalie Moorhead.
BAR 20 JUSTICE (Paramount, 1938) d Lesley Selander, s William Boyd, George "Windy" Hayes, Russell Hayden, Paul Sutton, Gwen Gaze.
PRIDE OF THE WEST (Paramount, 1938) d Lesley Selander, s William Boyd, George "Windy" Hayes, Russell Hayden, Charlotte Field.
IN OLD MEXICO (Paramount, 1938) d Edward D. Venturini, s William Boyd, George "Windy" Hayes, Russell Hayden, Betty Amann, Jane Clayton.
PARTNERS OF THE PLAINS (Paramount, 1938) d Lesley Selander, s William Boyd, Harvey Clark, Russell Hayden, Gwen Gaze.
THE FRONTIERSMAN (Paramount, 1938) d Lesley Selander, s William Boyd, George "Windy" Hayes, Russell Hayden, Evelyn Venable.
SUNSET TRAIL (Paramount, 1939) d Lesley Selander, s William Boyd, George "Windy" Hayes, Russell Hayden, Charlotte Wynters, Jane Clayton.
SILVER ON THE SAGE (Paramount, 1939) d Lesley Selander, s William Boyd, Russell Hayden, George "Windy" Hayes, Ruth Rogers, Stanley Ridges.

THE RENEGADE TRAIL (Paramount, 1939) d Lesley Selander, s William Boyd, George "Windy" Hayes, Russell Hayden.
RANGE WAR (Paramount, 1939) d Lesley Selander, s William Boyd, Russell Hayden, Willard Robertson, Matt Moore, Pedro De Cordoba, Betty Moran.
LAW OF THE PAMPAS (Paramount, 1939) d Nate Watt, s William Boyd, Sidney Toler, Steffi Duna, Russell Hayden.
SANTA FE MARSHAL (Paramount, 1940) d Lesley Selander, s William Boyd, Russell Hayden, Marjorie Rambeau.
THE SHOWDOWN (Paramont, 1940) d Howard Bretherton, s William Boyd, Russell Hayden, Jane (Jan) Clayton.
HIDDEN GOLD (Paramount, 1940) d Lesley Selander, s William Boyd, Russell Hayden, Minor Watson.
STAGECOACH WAR (Paramount, 1940) d Lesley Selander, s William Boyd, Russell Hayden, Julie Carter, J. Farrell MacDonald.
THREE MEN FROM TEXAS (Paramount, 1940) d Lesley Selander, s William Boyd, Russell Hayden, Andy Clyde, Esther Estrella.
DOOMED CARAVAN (Paramount, 1941) d Lesley Selander, s William Boyd, Russell Hayden, Andy Clyde, Minna Gombell.
IN OLD COLORADO (Paramount, 1941) d Howard Bretherton, s William Boyd, Russell Hayden, Andy Clyde, Margaret Hayes.
BORDER VIGILANTES (Paramount, 1941) d Derwin Abrahams, s William Boyd, Russell Hayden, Andy Clyde, Victor Jory.
PIRATES ON HORSEBACK (Paramount, 1941) d Lesley Selander, s William Boyd, Russell Hayden, Andy Clyde, Eleanor Stewart.
WIDE OPEN TOWN (Paramount, 1941) d Lesley Selander, s William Boyd, Russell Hayden, Andy Clyde, Bernice Kay.
OUTLAWS OF THE DESERT (Paramount, 1941) d Howard Bretherton s William Boyd, Brad King, Andy Clyde, Forest Stanley, Jean Phillips.
RIDERS OF THE TIMBERLINE (Paramount, 1941) d Lesley Selander, s William Boyd, King, Andy Clyde, J. Farrell MacDonald, Eleanor Stewart,.
TWILIGHT ON THE TRAIL (Paramount, 1941) d Howard Bretherton, s William Boyd, Andy Clyde, King, Wanda McKay.
STICK TO YOUR GUNS (Paramount, 1941) d Lesley Selander, s William Boyd, Andy Clyde, King, Jacqueline (Jennifer) Holt, Curtis, Weldon Heybrun.
SECRETS OF THE WASTELAND (Paramount, 1941) d Derwin Abrahams, s William Boyd, Andy Clyde, Barbara Britton.
UNDERCOVER MAN (United Artists, 1942) d Lesley Selander, s William Boyd, Andy Clyde, Jay Kirby, Antonio Moreno.
HOPPY SERVES A WRIT (United Artists, 1943) d George Archainbaud, s William Boyd, Andy Clyde, Jan Christy.
BORDER PATROL (United Artists, 1943) d Lesley Selander, s William Boyd, Andy Clyde, Claudia Drake, Duncan Renaldo.
COLD COMRADES (United Artists, 1943) d Lesley Selander, s William Boyd, Andy Clyde, Gayle Lord.
THE LEATHER BURNERS (United Artists, 1943) d Joseph Henabery, s William Boyd, Andy Clyde, Shelley Spencer.

160 MOTION PICTURE SERIES & SEQUELS

BAR 20 (United Artists, 1943) d Lesley Selander, s William Boyd, Andy Clyde, Dustin Farnum, Betty Blythe.
FALSE COLORS (United Artsts, 1943) d George Archainbaud, s William Boyd, Andy Clyde, Jimmy Rogers.
RIDERS OF THE DEADLINE (United Artists, 1943) d Lesley Selander, s William Boyd, Andy Clyde, Jimmy Rogers, Richard Krane.
LOST CANYON (United Artists, 1943) d Lesley Selander, s William Boyd, Andy Clyde.
TEXAS MASQUERADE (United Artists, 1944) d George Archainbaud, s William Boyd, Andy Clyde, Jimmy Rogers, Mady Correll.
LUMBERJACK (United Artists, 1944) d Lesley Selander, s William Boyd, Andy Clyde, Jimmy Rogers, Ellen Hall.
MYSTERY MAN (United Artists, 1944) d George Archainbaud, s William Boyd, Andy Clyde, Jimmy Rogers, Don Costello, Eleanor Stewart.
FORTY THIEVES (United Artists, 1944) d Lesley Selander, s William Boyd, Andy Clyde, Jimmy Rogers, Louise Currie.
FOOL'S GOLD (United Artists, 1946) d George Archainbaud, s William Boyd, Andy Clyde, Rand Brooks, Robert Emmett Keane, Jane Randolph.
THE DEVIL'S PLAYGROUND (United Artists, 1946) d George Archainbaud, s William Boyd, Andy Clyde, Rand Brooks, Elaine Riley.
UNEXPECTED GUEST (United Artists, 1947) d George Archainbaud, s William Boyd, Brooks, Andy Clyde, Una O'Connor, Patricia Tate.
DANGEROUS VENTURE (United Artists, 1947) d George Archainbaud, s William Boyd, Andy Clyde, Rand Brooks, Fritz Leiber.
THE MARAUDERS (United Artists, 1947) d George Archainbaud, s William Boyd, Andy Clyde, Rand Brooks, Dorinda Clifton.
HOPPY'S HOLIDAY (United Artists, 1947) d George Archainbaud, s William Boyd, Andy Clyde, Rand Brooks, Mary Ware.
SILENT CONFLICT (United Artists, 1948) d George Archainbaud, s William Boyd, Andy Clyde, Rand Brooks, Virginia Belmont.
THE DEAD DON'T DREAM (United Artists, 1948) d George Archainbaud, s William Boyd, Andy Clyde, Rand Brooks, Mary Ware.
SINISTER JOURNEY (United Artists, 1948) d George Archainbaud, s William Boyd, Andy Clyde, Rand Brooks, Elaine Riley.
BORROWED TROUBLE (United Artists, 1948) d George Archainbaud, s William Boyd, Andy Clyde, Rand Brooks, Elaine Riley.
FALSE PARADISE (United Artists, 1948) d George Archainbaud, s William Boyd, Andy Clyde, Brooks, Elaine Riley.
STRANGE GAMBLE (United Artists, 1948) d George Archainbaud, s William Boyd, Andy Clyde, Rand Brooks, Elaine Riley.

352. HOTEL FOR WOMEN

A young woman whose architect boyfriend isn't that keen on their romance turns her attention to a modeling career.
HOTEL FOR WOMEN (20th Century-Fox, 1939) d Gregory Ratoff, s Ann Sothern, Linda Darnell, James Elison.
FREE, BLONDE AND 21 (20th Century-Fox, 1940) d Ricardo Cortex, s Lynn Bari, Mary Beth Hughes, Joan Davis.

353. HOUSE
A horror novelist returns to his boyhood home to write about Vietnam experiences and finds the building is haunted.
HOUSE (New World, 1986) d Steve Miner, s William Katt, George Wendt.
HOUSE II: THE SECOND STORY (New World, 1987) d Ethan Wiley, s Ayre Gross, Jonathan Stark.

354. HOWLING
Each of these werewolf pictures was filmed on a different continent. The first entry is based on a book by Gary Brandner. It is about a news anchorwoman who discovers that her encounter group is full of lycanthropes.
THE HOWLING (Avco Embassy, 1981) d Joe Dante, s Dee Wallace, Patrick Macnee.
HOWLING II: YOUR SISTER IS A WEREWOLF (1985) d Philippe Mora, s Christopher Lee, Annie McEnroe.
HOWLING III (Australian, 1987) d Philippe Mora, s Barry Otto, Imogen Annesley.
HOWLING IV: THE ORIGINAL NIGHTMARE (Allied Entertainment, 1988) d John Hough, s Romy Windsor, Michael T. Weiss.
HOWLING V (Allied Entertainment, announced 1989) d Neal Sundstrom, s Philip Davis, Victoria Catlin.

HUBBY
See **BILLY BEVAN**

355. HUGGETTS FAMILY, THE
The books *Here Come the Huggetts* and *The Huggetts Abroad* by Mabel and Denis Constanduros, about a suburban family, inspired these pictures.
HOLIDAY CAMP (Universal International, 1947) d Ken Annakin, s Jack Warner, Kathleen Harrison.
HERE COME THE HUGGETTS (General Film, 1948) d Ken Annakin, s Jack Warner, Kathleen Harrison.
VOTE FOR HUGGETT (General Film, 1948) s Jack Warner, Kathleen Harrison.
THE HUGGETTS ABROAD (General Film, 1949) s Jack Warner, Kathleen Harrison.

356. *HUGH HERBERT*
The short subjects feature a bumbling hero. The list is incomplete.
SHAMPOO THE MAGICIAN (RKO, 1932) s Hugh Herbert, Roscoe Ates, Dorothy Granger.
A NIGHT AND A BLONDE
WIFE DECOY
WHO'S HUGH
DARK AND GRUESOME (1947)
A PINCH IN TIME (1948)

162 MOTION PICTURE SERIES & SEQUELS

HULK, THE
    See **THE INCREDIBLE HULK**

357. HUMAN CONDITION, THE
This trilogy follows the Japanese hero Kaji during World War II.
NO GREATER LOVE (1958) d Masaki Kobayashi, s Tatsuya Nakadai, Michiyo Aratama.
THE ROAD TO ETERNITY (1959) d Masaki Kobayashi, s Tatsuya Nakadai.
A SOLDIER'S PRAYER (1961) d Masaki Kobayashi, s Tatsuya Nakadai.

358. HUSTLER, THE
These poolroom tales are based on Walter Tevis's novel. Fast Eddie Felson challenges Minnesota Fats, in the first, and nurtures a successor in the sequel.
THE HUSTLER (20th Century Fox, 1961) d Robert Rossen, s Paul Newman, Jackie Gleason, Piper Laurie.
THE COLOR OF MONEY (Touchstone, 1986) d Martin Scorsese, s Paul Newman, Tom Cruise, Helen Shaver.

359. HUTCH
These are silent movies.
HURRICANE HUTCH (1921) d George B. Seitz.
GO GET 'EM HUTCH (1921) d George B. Seitz.

360. I AM CURIOUS
The films are based on original screenplays by Vilgot Sjoman, published by Grove Press.
I AM CURIOUS (YELLOW) (Grove Press, 1969) d Vilgot Sjoman, s Lena Nyman.
I AM CURIOUS (BLUE) (Grove Press, 1970) d Vilgot Sjoman, s Lena Nyman.

361. I, A WOMAN
The films are derived from books by Siv Holm.
I, A WOMAN (Audubon, 1966) d Mac Ahlberg.
I, A WOMAN II (Chevron, 1975) d Mac Ahlberg.
I, A WOMAN III: THE DAUGHTER (Chevron, 1975) d Mac Ahlberg.

362. I LOVE A MYSTERY
From the radio show (1939-52) created by Carleton E. Morse, adventurers Jack Packard, Doc Long and Reggie York form the A-1 Detective Agency to handle any and all cases. (The pictures drop the Reggie character.)
I LOVE A MYSTERY (Columbia, 1945) s Jim Bannon, Barton Yarborough.
THE DEVIL'S MASK (Columbia, 1946) s Jim Bannon, Barton Yarborough.
THE UNKNOWN (Columbia, 1946) s Jim Bannon, Barton Yarborough.

363. INCREDIBLE HULK, THE
David Banner, who overdosed on radiation in a laboratory experiment, transforms into the huge, green Hulk in times of stress. Bill Bixby and Lou

MOTION PICTURE SERIES & SEQUELS 163

Ferrigno played the dual-personna in a CBS television series which ran from 1978-82. The characters originated in Marvel comic books in 1962.
THE INCREDIBLE HULK (Universal, 1977) (CBS-TV broadcast) d Kenneth Johnson, s Bill Bixby, Susan Sullivan, Lou Ferrigno.
THE RETURN OF THE HULK (Universal, 1977) (CBS-TV broadcast) d Alan Levi, s Bill Bixby, Laurie Prang, Lou Ferrigno.
THE INCREDIBLE HULK RETURNS (Universal, 1987) (CBS-TV broadcast) s Bill Bixby, Lou Ferrigno.
THE TRIAL OF THE INCREDIBLE HULK (Universal, 1989) (CBS-TV broadcast) s Bill Bixby, Lou Ferrigno.

364. INDIANA JONES
A 1930s archaeologist, afraid of snakes but little else, tracks exotic artifacts in these latter-day, ambitious recreations of 1930s action serials.
RAIDERS OF THE LOST ARK (Paramount, 1981) d Steven Spielberg, s Harrison Ford, Karen Allen.
INDIANA JONES AND THE TEMPLE OF DOOM (Paramount, 1984) d Steven Spielberg, s Harrison Ford, Kate Capshaw.
INDIANA JONES AND THE LAST CRUSADE (Paramount, 1989) d Steven Spielberg, s Harrison Ford, Sean Connery.

365. INNER SANCTUM
The series evolved from a mystery radio show. The stories, with twist endings, are introduced by a face in a crystal ball.
CALLING DR. DEATH (Universal, 1943) s Lon Chaney Jr.
WEIRD WOMAN (Universal, 1944) s Lon Chaney Jr.
DEAD MAN'S EYES (Universal, 1944) s Lon Chaney Jr.
THE FROZEN GHOST (Universal, 1945) s Lon Chaney Jr.
STRANGE CONFESSION (Universal, 1945) s Lon Chaney Jr.
PILLOW OF DEATH (Universal, 1945) s Lon Chaney Jr.

366. INNOCENTS, THE
Henry James' story *The Turn of the Screw* and William Archibald's play of the same title inspired these pictures. A governess at an English country estate finds there are eerie goings on. The second picture, a prequel, shows how the children came to be possessed.
THE INNOCENTS (20th Century-Fox, 1961) d Jack Clayton, s Deborah Kerr, Martin Stephens, Pamela Franklin.
THE NIGHTCOMERS (Schmitar/Kastner-Kanter-Ladd, 1972) d Michael Winner, s Marlon Brando, Stephanie Beachman.

367. INSATIABLE
Marilyn Chambers plays fashion model Sandra Chase in these X-rated pictures.
INSATIABLE (Caballero, 1980) d Godfrey Daniels, s Marilyn Chambers.
INSATIABLE II (Caballero, 1984) d Godfrey Daniels, s Marilyn Chambers.

164 MOTION PICTURE SERIES & SEQUELS

INSPECTOR CLOUSEAU
See **PINK PANTHER**

368. INSPECTOR HANAUD
A.E.W. Mason's literary (and cinematic) policeman Gabriel Hanaud is a middle-aged member of the French Surete.
AT THE VILLA ROSE (Stoll, 1920) d Maurice Elvey, s Manora Thew, Langhorne Burton, Teddy Arundell.
AT THE VILLA ROSE (Twickenham, 1930) [aka MYSTERY AT THE VILLA ROSE] d Leslie Hiscott, s Norah Baring, Austin Trevor.
THE HOUSE OF THE ARROW (Twickenham, 1930) d Leslie Hiscott, s Denis Neilson, Benita Hume.
AT THE VILLA ROSE (Associated British Picture, 1939) d Walter Summers, s Kenneth Kent, Judy Kelly.
THE HOUSE OF THE ARROW (Associated British Picture, 1940) d Harold French, s Kenneth Kent, Diana Churchill.
THE HOUSE OF THE ARROW (Associated British Picture, 1953) d Michael Anderson, s Oscar Homolka, Yvonne Furneaux.

369. INSPECTOR HORNLEIGH
The police comedy-dramas are based on Hans Priwin's MONDAY NIGHT AT EIGHT radio series character and his associate, Sergeant Bingham.
INSPECTOR HORNLEIGH (20th Century-Fox, 1938) d Eugene Forde, s Gordon Harker, Wally Patch.
INSPECTOR HORNLEIGH ON HOLIDAY (20th Century-Fox, 1939) d Louis Levy, s Gordon Harker, Alastair Sim.
MAIL TRAIN (20th Century-Fox, 1940) [aka INSPECTOR HORNLEIGH GOES TO IT] d Walter Forde, s Gordon Harker, Alastair Sim.

370. INSPECTOR MAIGRET
Georges Simenon's detective shows up in a number of French films as well as a TV series shown 1950s-60s in England with Rupert Davies and another in 1988 with Richard Harris.
TEMPTATION HARBOR (Monogram, 1947) d Lance Comfort, s Robert Newton, Simone Simon, William Hartnell.
THE MAN ON THE EIFFEL TOWER (British Lion, 1948) d Burgess Meredith, s Charles Laughton.
STRANGERS IN THE HOUSE (Lopert, 1949)
THE MAN WHO WATCHED THE TRAINS GO BY (Eros Limited, 1952)
THE PARIS EXPRESS (George Schoefer, 1953)
THE SNOW WAS BLACK (Continental, 1956)
MAIGRET SETS A TRAP (1957) d Jean Delannoy, s Jean Gabin.
INSPECTOR MAIGRET (Lopert, 1958)
MAIGRET SEES RED

371. INTERNS, THE

Richard Frede's novel about new doctors at a major city hospital provides the background to these films.
THE INTERNS (Columbia, 1962) d David Swift, s Michael Callan, Cliff Robertson.
THE NEW INTERNS (Columbia, 1964) d John Rich, s Barbara Eden, Telly Savalas, George Segal.

372. IN THE LINE OF DUTY
These are Hong Kong-made martial arts films.
IN THE LINE OF DUTY
IN THE LINE OF DUTY II
IN THE LINE OF DUTY III
IN THE LINE OF DUTY PART 4 (D&B Films, 1989) s Cynthia Khan, Michael Wong.

373. INTIMATE REALITIES
The X-rated films purport to be interviews with sex stars who then act out vignettes.
INTIMATE REALITIES 1 (VCA, 1983) d Richard Wright, s Serena.
INTIMATE REALITIES 2 (VCA, 1984) d John Christopher, s Kay Parker, Reic Edwards.

374. INVISIBLE MAN, THE
These pictures were inspired by H.G. Wells' 1897 novel of a scientist named Griffin who discovers the secret of invisibility and as a result is driven mad. There have been two television series featuring the character.
THE INVISIBLE MAN (Universal, 1933) d James Whale, s Claude Rains, Gloria Stuart.
THE INVISIBLE MAN RETURNS (Universal, 1940) d Joe May, s Sir Cedric Hardwicke, Vincent Price.
THE INVISIBLE WOMAN (Universal, 1941) d A. Edward Sutherland, s Virginia Bruce, John Barrymore.
INVISIBLE AGENT (Universal, 1942, d Edwin L. Marin, s Ilona Massey, Jon Hall.
THE INVISIBLE MAN'S REVENGE (Universal, 1944) d Ford Beebe, s Jon Hall, Alan Curtis.
ABBOTT AND COSTELLO MEET THE INVISIBLE MAN (Universal, 1951) d Charles Lamong, s Bud Abbott, Lou Costello, Nancy Guild, Arthur Franx.
THE INVISIBLE MAN (Silverton Productions/Universal, 1975) (NBC-TV broadcast) D Robert Michael Lewis, s David McCallum, Melinda Fee.
THE INVISIBLE WOMAN (Redwood Productions/Universal Television, 1983) (NBC-TV broadcast) d Alan J. Levi, s Bob Denver, Jonathan Banks, Alexa Hamilton.
THE INVISIBLE MAN (BBC Television, 1984) s Pip Donaghy.

375. IRON EAGLE

166 MOTION PICTURE SERIES & SEQUELS

Studying documents in the case, Ronald Reagan gives a hand to the Dead End Kids in ANGELS WASH THEIR FACES (1938).

A retired Air Force colonel teams with a teenager to rescue the latter's fighter pilot father from Middle Eastern captors, in the first picture. In the second, Gen. "Chappy" Sinclair organizes an American-Soviet air strike against a Mideast missile silo.
IRON EAGLE (Tri-Star, 1986) d Sidney J. Furie, s Louis Gossett Jr., Jason Gedrick.
IRON EAGLE II (Tri-Star, 1988) d Sidney J. Furie, s Louis Gossett Jr., Mark Humphrey.

375A. IS MARRIAGE SACRED?
This circa 1917 silent film series stars E.H. Calvert.

376. IT'S ALIVE
Mutant babies thirst for blood.
IT'S ALIVE! (Warner Brothers, 1974) d Larry Cohen, s Joyn Ryan, Sharron Farrell.
IT LIVES AGAIN (Warner Brothers, 1978) d Larry Cohen, s Frederick Forrest, Kathleen Lloyd.
IT'S ALIVE III: ISLAND OF THE ALIVE (Warner Brothers, 1986) d Larry Cohen, s Michael Moriarty, Karen Black.

377. JACK 'N JILL
A married couple experiments to spice up their sex life, in these X-raters.
JACK 'N JILL (Quality X, 1979) d Mark Ubell, s Samantha Fox, Jack Wrangler.
JACK 'N JILL PART II (VCA, 1984) d Chuck Vincent, s Samantha Fox, Jack Wrangler.

378. JAMES BOND
Ian Fleming's series of novels about a British secret agent (published 1953-66 and followed by sequels by other writers) has been converted into a successful series of motion pictures. Such Fleming villains as Auric Goldfinger, Ernst Blofield and Dr. No are handsomely translated to the screen, as are Bond allies Miss Moneypenny and M and dalliances Tatiana Romanova, Pussy Galore and Kissy Suzuki.
DR. NO (United Artists, 1962) d Terence Young, s Sean Connery, Ursula Andress, Joseph Wiseman.
FROM RUSSIA WITH LOVE (United Artists, 1963) d Terence Young, s Sean Connery, Daniela Bianchi.
GOLDFINGER (United Artists, 1964) d Guy Hamilton, s Sean Connery, Gert Frobe, Honor Blackman.
THUNDERBALL (United Artists, 1965) d Terence Young, s Sean Connery, Claudine Auger.
CASINO ROYALE (Columbia, 1967) d John Huston, Ken Hughes, Val Guest, Robert Parrish and Jose McGrath, s Peter Sellers, Ursula Andress, David Niven, Orson Welles, Woody Allen.
YOU ONLY LIVE TWICE (United Artists, 1967) d Lewis Gilbert, s Sean Connery, Akiko Wakabayashi, Mie Hama.
ON HER MAJESTY'S SECRET SERVICE (United Artists, 1969) d Peter Hunt, s George Lazenby, Diana Rigg.
DIAMONDS ARE FOREVER (United Artists, 1971) d Guy Hamilton, s Sean Connery, Jill St. John, Charles Gray.
LIVE AND LET DIE (United Artists, 1973) d Guy Hamilton, s Roger Moore, Jane Seymour.
THE MAN WITH THE GOLDEN GUN (United Artists, 1974) d Guy Hamilton, s Roger Moore, Christopher Lee.
THE SPY WHO LOVED ME (United Artists, 1977) d Lewis Gilbert, s Roger Moore, Barbara Bach, Curt Jurgens.
MOONRAKER (United Artists, 1979) d Lewis Gilbert, s Roger Moore, Lois Chiles, Richard Kiel.
FOR YOUR EYES ONLY (United Artists, 1981) d John Glen, s Roger Moore, Carole Bouquet.
OCTOPUSSY (MGM/United Artists, 1983) d John Glen, s Roger Moore, Maud Adams.
NEVER SAY NEVER AGAIN (Warner Brothers, 1983) d Irving Kershner, s Sean Connery, Max von Sydow.
A VIEW TO A KILL (MGM/UA, 1985) d John Glen, s Roger Moore, Christopher Walken, Tanya Roberts.

THE LIVING DAYLIGHTS (MGM/UA, 1987) d John Glen, s Timothy Dalton, Maryam d'Abo.
LICENSE TO KILL (MGM/UA, 1989) d John Glen, s Timothy Dalton, Carey Lowell.

379. JANE BOND
A female secret agent is featured in these X-rated pictures.
JANE BOND (Vidco, 1985) d Bob Kirk, s Heather Wayne.
JANE BOND MEETS OCTOPUSSY (Vidco, 1986) d Jack Remy, s Amber Lynn, Tony Martino.
JANE BOND MEETS GOLDEN ROD (Vidco, 1987) s Amber Lynn, Robert Bullock.
JANE BOND MEETS THUNDERBALLS (Vidco, 1987) s Stacey Donovan, Robert Bullock.

380. JANE MARPLE
Agatha Christie's spinsterish sleuth has prompted several motion pictures and has appeared in a television series. Marple first showed up in Christie's *Murder at the Vicarage* (1930) and her final cases were issued in 1979.
MURDER SHE SAID (MGM, 1962) d George Pollock, s Margaret Rutherford, Arthur Kennedy.
MURDER AT THE GALLOP (MGM, 1963), d George Pollock, s Margaret Rutherford, Robert Morley.
MURDER MOST FOUL (MGM, 1964) d George Pollock, s Margaret Rutherford, Ron Moody.
MURDER AHOY! (MGM, 1964) d George Pollock, s Margaret Rutherford, Lionel Jeffries.
THE ALPHABET MURDERS (MGM, 1966) s Frank Tashlin, s Tony Randall, Anita Ekberg, Margaret Rutherford.
THE MIRROR CRACK'D (AFD, 1980) d Guy Hamilton, Angela Lansbury, Elizabeth Taylor.
AGATHA CHRISTIE'S "A CARIBBEAN MYSTERY" (Stan Margulies/Warner Brothers, 1983) (CBS-TV movie) d Robert Lewis, s Helen Hayes, Barnard Hughes.
MURDER WITH MIRRORS (1985) (TV movie) d Dick Lowry, s Helen Hayes, Bette Davis, John Mills, Leo McKern.

380A. JARR FAMILY
These early silent films (circa 1914) featured Paul Kelly.

JASON
    See **FRIDAY THE 13TH**

381. JASON
The classic Greek hero is featured in these pictures.
JASON AND THE GOLDEN FLEECE (Columbia, 1961)

JASON AND THE ARGONAUTS (Columbia, 1962) d Don Chaffey, s Todd Armstrong, Gary Raymond, Nancy Kovack.

382. JAWS
A killer shark terrorizes a beach community.
JAWS (Universal, 1975) d Steven Spielberg, s Roy Scheider, Robert Shaw, Richard Dreyfuss.
JAWS 2 (Universal, 1978) d Jeannot Szward, s Roy Scheider, Lorraine Gary.
JAWS 3-D (Universal, 1983) d Joe Alves, s Dennis Quaid, Bess Armstrong.
JAWS THE REVENGE (Universal, 1987) d Joseph Sargent, s Lorraine Gary, Lance Guest.

383. J. EDGAR HOOVER
The films are based on the exploits of the late FBI director.
DAUGHTER OF SHANGHAI (Paramount, 1937) d Robert Florey, s Anna May Wong, Charles Bickford, Buster Crabbe.
KING OF ALCATRAZ (Paramount, 1938) d Robert Florey, s J. Carrol Naish, Gail Patrick.
HUNTED MEN (Paramount, 1938)
ILLEGAL TRAFFIC (Paramount, 1938)
TIP OFF GIRLS (Paramount, 1938)
PERSONS IN HIDING (Paramount, 1939)
QUEEN OF THE MOB (Paramount, 1940)
PAROLE FIXER (Paramount, 1940)

384. JEEVES
P.G. Wodehouse's twit Bertie Wooster and his gentleman's gentleman Jeeves appeared in ten novels and thirty-five short stories. The characters have also been featured in two plays and two radio shows.
THANK YOU, JEEVES (20th Century-Fox, 1936) [aka THANK YOU, MR. JEEVES] d Arthur Grenville, s David Niven, Arthur Treacher.
STEP LIVELY, JEEVES (20th Century-Fox, 1937) d Eugene Ford, s Arthur Treacher.

385. THE JERK
The hero is stupid.
THE JERK (Universal, 1979) d Carl Reiner, s Steve Martin, Bernadette Peters.
THE JERK, TOO (Share Productions/Universal Television, 1984) (NBC-TV movie) d Michael Schultz, s Mark Blankfield, Ray Walston.

386. JESSE JAMES
All of the films listed are about the Western outlaw, however only the first are related by studio/actor.
JESSE JAMES (20th Century-Fox, 1939) d Henry King, s Tyrone Power, Henry Fonda, Nancy Kelly.

THE RETURN OF FRANK JAMES (20th Century-Fox, 1940) d Fritz Lang, s Henry Fonda, Gene Tierney.
JESSE JAMES AT BAY (Republic, 1941) d Joseph Kane, s Roy Rogers, George "Gabby" Hayes, Sally Payne.
JESSE JAMES JR. (Republic, 1942) d George Sherman, s Don Barry, Lynn Merrick.
JESSE JAMES RIDES AGAIN (Republic, 1947) (13 chapters) [aka ADVENTURES OF FRANK AND JESSE JAMES] d Fred C. Bannon, s Clayton Moore, Linda Stirling.
I SHOT JESSE JAMES (Lippert, 1949) d Samuel Fuller, s Preston Foster, John Ireland, Barbara Britton.
THE JAMES BROTHERS OF MISSOURI (Republic, 1950) (12 chapters) d Fred C. Brannon, s Keith Richards, Robert Bice.
KANSAS RAIDERS (Universal-International, 1950) d Ray Enright, s Audie Murphy.
JESSE JAMES VS. THE DALTONS (Columbia, 1954) d William Castle, s Brett King, Barbara Lawrence.
JESSE JAMES' WOMEN (United Artists, 1954) d Donald Bary, s Don Barry, Jack Buetel.
JESSE JAMES MEETS FRANKENSTEIN'S DAUGHTER (Embassy, 1966) d William Beaudine, s John Lupton, Estelia.
A TIME FOR DYING (Corinth, 1971) Budd Boetticher, s Audie Murphy, Richard Lapp, Anne Randall.

387. J.G. REEDER
The hero of these pictures (based on Edgar Wallace books) also appeared in THE MIND OF MR. REEDER on Thames Television in 1972 with Hugh Burden.
MR. REEDER IN ROOM 13 (British National, 1938) s Will Fyffe.
THE MIND OF MR. REEDER (Grand National, 1939) s Will Fyffe.

388. JIGGS AND MAGGIE
Based on George McManus's comic strip *Bringing Up Father*, Jiggs and Maggie are an Irish couple always bickering.
BRINGING UP FATHER (1928) d Jack Conway, s J. Farrell MacDonald, Polly Moran.
BRINGING UP FATHER (Monogram, 1936) s Joe Yule, Renie Riano.
JIGGS AND MAGGIE IN COURT (Monogram, 1948)
JIGGS AND MAGGIE IN JACKPOT JITTERS (Monogram, 1949)
JIGGS AND MAGGIE IN SOCIETY (Monogram, 1949)
JIGGS AND MAGGIE OUT WEST (Monogram, 1950) d William Beaudine, s Joe Yule, Renie Riano, Tim Ryan, Jim Bannon, George McManus.

389. *JIMMY WAKELY AND CANNONBALL TAYLOR*
These are B Westerns.
RIDIN' DOWN THE TRAIL (Monogram, 1947) d Howard Bretherton, s Jimmy Wakley, Dub "Cannonball" Taylor, Beverly Jons.

SONG OF THE DRIFTER (Monogram, 1948) d Frank Wishbar, s Jimmy Wakely, Dub "Cannonball" Taylor, Mildred Coles.
OKLAHOMA BLUES (Monogram, 1948) d Lambert Hillyer, s Jimmy Wakely, Dub "Cannonball" Taylor, Virginia Belmont.
THE RANGERS RIDE (Monogram, 1948) d Derwin Abrahams, s Jimmy Wakely, Dub "Cannonball" Taylor, Virginia Belmont.
RANGE RENEGADES (Monogram, 1948) d Lambert Hillyer, s Jimmy Wakely, Dub "Cannonball" Taylor, Jennifer Holt.
COWBOY CAVALIER (Monogram, 1948) d Derwin Abrahams, s Jimmy Wakely, Dub "Cannonball" Taylor, Jan Bryant.
PARTNERS OF THE SUNSET (Monogram, 1948) d Lambert Hillyer, s Jimmy Wakely, Dub "Cannonball" Taylor, Christine Larson.
SILVER TRAILS (Monogram, 1948) d Christy Cabanne, s Jimmy Wakely, Dub "Cannonball" Taylor, Whip Wilson, Christine Larson.
OUTLAW BRAND (Monogram, 1948) d Lambert Hillyer, s Jimmy Wakely, Dub "Cannonball" Taylor, Christine Larson, Kay Morley.
COURTIN' TROUBLE (Monogram, 1948) d Ford Beebe, s Jimmy Wakely, Dub "Cannonball" Taylor, Virginia Belmont.
GUN RUNNER (Monogram, 1949) d Lambert Hillyer, s Jimmy Wakely, Dub "Cannonball" Taylor, Mae Clark.
GUN LAW JUSTICE (Monogram, 1949) d Lambert Hillyer, s Jimmy Wakely, Dub "Cannonball" Taylor, Jane Adams.
ACROSS THE RIO GRANDE (Monogram, 1949) d Oliver Drake, s Jimmy Wakely, Dub "Cannonball" Taylor, Reno Browne.
BRAND OF FEAR (Monogram, 1949) d Oliver Drake, s Jimmy Wakely, Dub "Cannonball" Taylor, Gail Davis.
ROARING WESTWARD (Monogram, 1949) d Oliver Drake, s Jimmy Wakely, Dub "Cannonball" Taylor, Lois Hall.
LAWLESS CODE (Monogram, 1949) d Oliver Drake, s Jimmy Wakely, Dub "Cannonball" Taylor, Ellen Hall.

390. *JIMMY WAKELY AND LASSES WHITE*
SONG OF THE RANGE (Monogram, 1944) d Wallace Fox, s Jimmy Wakley, Lee "Lasses" White, Kay Forrester.
SPRINGTIME IN TEXAS (Monogram, 1945) d Oliver Drake, s Jimmy Wakley, Lee "Lasses" White, Marion Harmon.
SADDLE SERENADE (Monogram, 1945) d Oliver Drake, s Jimmy Wakley, Lee "Lasses" White, Nancy Brinkman.
RIDERS OF THE DAWN (Monogram, 1945) d Oliver Drake, s Jimmy Wakley, Lee "Lasses" White, Iris Clive.
MOON OVER MONTANA (Monogram, 1946) d Oliver Drake, s Jimmy Wakley, Lee "Lasses" White, Jennifer Holt.
WEST OF THE ALAMO (Monogram, 1946) d Oliver Drake, s Jimmy Wakley, Lee "Lasses" White, Iris Clive.
TRAIL TO MEXICO (Monogram, 1946) d Oliver Drake, s Jimmy Wakley, Lee "Lasses" White, Delores Castelli.

SONG OF THE SIERRAS (Monogram, 1946) d Oliver Drake, s Jimmy Wakley, Lee "Lasses" White, Jean Carlin, Iris Clive.
RAINBOW OVER THE ROCKIES (Monogram, 1947) d Oliver Drake, s Jimmy Wakley, Lee "Lasses" White, Pat Starling.
SIX GUN SERENADE (Monogram, 1947) d Ford Beeve., s Jimmy Wakley, Lee "Lasses" White.
SONG OF THE WASTELAND (Monogram, 1947) d Thomas Carr, s Jimmy Wakley, Lee "Lasses" White, Dottye Brown.

391. JOEL AND GARDA SLOANE
The pictures are screwball comedy-mysteries.
FAST COMPANY (MGM, 1938) d Edward Buzzell, s Melvyn Douglas, Florence Rice.
FAST AND FURIOUS (MGM, 1939) d Busby Berkeley, s Franchot Tone, Ann Sothern.
FAST AND LOOSE (MGM, 1939) d Edwin L. Marin, s Robert Montgomery, Rosalind Russell.

392. JOE McDOAKES
Warner Brothers filmed these short comedies featuring George O'Hanlon.
SO YOU WANT TO GIVE UP SMOKING (Warner Brothers, 1942) d Richard L. Bare, s George O'Hanlon.
SO YOU THINK YOU NEED GLASSES (Warner Brothers, 1942) d Richard L. Bare, s George O'Hanlon.
SO YOU THINK YOU'RE ALLERGIC (Warner Brothers, 1945) d Richard L. Bare, s George O'Hanlon.
SO YOU WANT TO PLAY THE HORSES (Warner Brothers, 1946) d Richard L. Bare, s George O'Hanlon.
SO YOU WANT TO KEEP YOUR HAIR (Warner Brothers, 1946) d Richard L. Bare, s George O'Hanlon.
SO YOU THINK YOU'RE A NERVOUS WRECK (Warner Brothers, 1946) d Richard L. Bare, s George O'Hanlon.
SO YOU'RE GOING TO BE A FATHER (Warner Brothers, 1947) d Richard L. Bare, s George O'Hanlon.
SO YOU WANT TO BE IN PICTURES (Warner Brothers, 1947) d Richard L. Bare, s George O'Hanlon.
SO YOU'RE GOING ON A VACATION (Warner Brothers, 1947) d Richard L. Bare, s George O'Hanlon.
SO YOU WANT TO BE A SALESMAN (Warner Brothers, 1947) d Richard L. Bare, s George O'Hanlon.
SO YOU WANT TO HOLD YOUR WIFE (Warner Brothers, 1947) d Richard L. Bare, s George O'Hanlon.
SO YOU WANT AN APARTMENT (Warner Brothers, 1948) d Richard L. Bare, s George O'Hanlon.
SO YOU WANT TO BE A GAMBLER (Warner Brothers, 1948) d Richard L. Bare, s George O'Hanlon.

SO YOU WANT TO BUILD A HOUSE (Warner Brothers, 1948) d Richard L. Bare, s George O'Hanlon.
SO YOU WANT TO BE A DETECTIVE (Warner Brothers, 1948) d Richard L. Bare, s George O'Hanlon.
SO YOU WANT TO BE IN POLITICS (Warner Brothers, 1948) d Richard L Bare, s George O'Hanlon.
SO YOU WANT TO BE ON THE RADIO (Warner Brothers, 1948) d Richard L. Bare, s George O'Hanlon.
SO YOU WANT TO BE A BABY-SITTER (Warner Brothers, 1949) d Richard L. Bare, s George O'Hanlon.
SO YOU WANT TO BE POPULAR (Warner Brothers, 1949) d Richard L. Bare, s George O'Hanlon.
SO YOU WANT TO BE A MUSCLEMAN (Warner Brothers, 1949) d Richard L. Bare, s George O'Hanlon, Phyllis Coates.
SO YOU'RE HAVING IN-LAW TROUBLE (Warner Brothers, 1949) d Richard L. Bare, s George O'Hanlon.
SO YOU WANT TO GET RICH QUICK (Warner Brothers, 1949) d Richard L. Bare, s George O'Hanlon.
SO YOU WANT TO BE AN ACTOR (Warner Brothers, 1949) d Richard L. Bare, s George O'Hanlon.
SO YOU WANT TO THROW A PARTY (Warner Brothers, 1950) d Richard L. Bare, s George O'Hanlon.
SO YOU THINK YOU'RE NOT GUILTY (Warner Brothers, 1950) d Richard L. Bare, s George O'Hanlon.
SO YOU WANT TO HOLD YOUR HUSBAND (Warner Brothers, 1950) d Richard L. Bare, s George O'Hanlon, Phyllis Coates.
SO YOU WANT TO MOVE (Warner Brothers, 1950) d Richard L. Bare, s George O'Hanlon.
SO YOU WANT A RAISE (Warner Brothers, 1950) d Richard L. Bare, s George O'Hanlon.
SO YOU'RE GOING TO HAVE AN OPERATION (Warner Brothers, 1950) d Richard L. Bare, s George O'Hanlon.
SO YOU WANT TO BE A HANDYMAN (Warner Brothers, 1951) d Richard L. Bare, s George O'Hanlon.
SO YOU WANT TO BE A COWBOY (Warner Brothers, 1951) d Richard L. Bare, s George O'Hanlon.
SO YOU WANT TO BE A PAPERHANGER (Warner Brothers, 1951) d Richard L. Bare, s George O'Hanlon.
SO YOU WANT TO BUY A USED CAR (Warner Brothers, 1951) d Richard L. Bare, s George O'Hanlon.
SO YOU WANT TO BE A BACHELOR (Warner Brothers, 1951) d Richard L. Bare, s George O'Hanlon.
SO YOU WANT TO BE A PLUMBER (Warner Brothers, 1951) d Richard L. Bare, s George O'Hanlon.
SO YOU WANT TO GET IT WHOLESALE (Warner Brothers, 1952) d Richard L. Bare, s George O'Hanlon.

SO YOU WANT TO ENJOY LIFE (Warner Brothers, 1952) d Richard L. Bare, s George O'Hanlon.
SO YOU'RE GOING TO A CONVENTION (Warner Brothers, 1952) d Richard L. Bare, s George O'Hanlon.
SO YOU NEVER TELL A LIE (Warner Brothers, 1952) d Richard L. Bare, s George O'Hanlon.
SO YOU'RE GOING TO THE DENTIST (Warner Brothers, 1952) d Richard L. Bare, s George O'Hanlon.
SO YOU WANT TO WEAR THE PANTS (Warner Brothers, 1952) d Richard L. Bare, s George O'Hanlon.
SO YOU WANT TO BE A MUSICIAN (Warner Brothers, 1953) d Richard L. Bare, s George O'Hanlon.
SO YOU WANT TO LEARN TO DANCE (Warner Brothers, 1953) d Richard L. Bare, s George O'Hanlon.
SO YOU WANT A TELEVISION SET (Warner Brothers, 1953) d Richard L. Bare, s George O'Hanlon, Phyllis Coates.
SO YOU LOVE YOUR DOG (Warner Brothers, 1953) d Richard L. Bare, s George O'Hanlon.
SO YOU THINK YOU CAN'T SLEEP (Warner Brothers, 1953) d Richard L. Bare, s George O'Hanlon.
SO YOU WANT TO BE AN HEIR (Warner Brothers, 1953) d Richard L. Bare, s George O'Hanlon.
SO YOU'RE HAVING NEIGHBOR TROUBLE (Warner Brothers, 1954) d Richard L. Bare, s George O'Hanlon.
SO YOU WANT TO BE YOUR OWN BOSS (Warner Brothers, 1954) d Richard L. Bare, s George O'Hanlon.
SO YOU WANT TO GO TO A NIGHTCLUB (Warner Brothers, 1954) d Richard L. Bare, s George O'Hanlon.
SO YOU WANT TO BE A BANKER (Warner Brothers, 1954) d Richard L. Bare, s George O'Hanlon.
SO YOU'RE TAKIN IN A ROOMER (Warner Brothers, 1954) d Richard L. Bare, s George O'Hanlon.
SO YOU WANT TO KNOW YOUR RELATIVES (Warner Brothers, 1955) d Richard L. Bare, s George O'Hanlon.
SO YOU DON'T TRUST YOUR WIFE (Warner Brothers, 1955) d Richard L. Bare, s George O'Hanlon.
SO YOU WANT TO BE A GLADIATOR (Warner Brothers, 1955) d Richard L. Bare, s George O'Hanlon.
SO YOU WANT TO BE ON A JURY (Warner Brothers, 1955) d Richard L. Bare, s George O'Hanlon.
SO YOU WANT TO BUILD A MODEL RAILROAD (Warner Brothers, 1955) d Richard L. Bare, s George O'Hanlon.
SO YOU WANT TO BE A V.P. (Warner Brothers, 1955) d Richard L. Bare, s George O'Hanlon.
SO YOU WANT TO BE A POLICEMAN (Warner Brothers, 1955) d Richard L. Bare, s George O'Hanlon.

MOTION PICTURE SERIES & SEQUELS 175

SO YOU THINK THE GRASS IS GREENER (Warner Brothers, 1956) d
    Richard L. Bare, s George O'Hanlon, Jane Frazee.
SO YOU WANT TO BE PRETTY (Warner Brothers, 1956) d Richard L. Bare,
    s George O'Hanlon.
SO YOU WANT TO PLAY THE PIANO (Warner Brothers, 1956) d Richard
    L. Bare, s George O'Hanlon.
SO YOUR WIFE WANTS TO WORK (Warner Brothers, 1956) d Richard L.
    Bare, s George O'Hanlon.

393. JOE PALOOKA
The stories, taken from Ham Fisher's comic strip, have a boxing background.
Palooka first appeared in 1920. Other characters included Humphrey, Bateese,
Senator Weidebottom, Jerry Leemy and Ann Howe.
PALOOKA (Reliance, 1934) [aka JOE PALOOKA] d Benjamin Stoloff, s
    Jimmy Durante, Stu Erwin, Lupe Velez.
JOE PALOOKA, CHAMP (Monogram, 1946) d Reginald Le Borg, s Leon
    Errol, Joe Kirkwood, Elyse Knox.
GENTLEMAN JOE PALOOKA (Monogram, 1946)
JOE PALOOKA IN THE KNOCKOUT (Monogram, 1947)
JOE PALOOKA IN FIGHTING MAD (Monogram, 1948)
JOE PALOOKA IN WINNER TAKE ALL (Monogram, 1948)
A JOE NAMED PALOOKA (Monogram, 1948)
JOE PALOOKA IN THE COUNTERPUNCH (Monogram, 1949)
JOE PALOOKA IN THE BIG FIGHT (Monogram, 1949)
JOE PALOOKA MEETS HUMPHREY (Monogram, 1950)
JOE PALOOKA IN HUMPHREY TAKES A CHANCE (Monogram, 1950)
JOE PALOOKA IN THE SQUARED CIRCLE (Monogram, 1950)
JOE PALOOKA IN THE TRIPLE CROSS (Monogram, 1951)

394A. *JOHN DOOLEY*
These silent pictures featured John Dooley.

394. JOHN J. MALONE
Craig Rice's fictional Chicago lawyer appeared in mysteries along with press
agent Jake Justus and his socialite wife Helene. The last entry also features a
re-named HILDEGARDE WITHERS.
HAVING A WONDERFUL CRIME (RKO, 1945) d Eddie Sutherland, s Pat
    O'Brien, George Murphy, Carole Landis.
THE LUCKY STIFF (United Artists, 1949) d Lewis R. Foster, s Brian
    Donlevy, Dorothy Lamour.
MRS. O'MALLEY AND MR. MALONE (MGM, 1950) s James Whitmore.

395. *JOHNNY MACK BROWN AND FUZZY KNIGHT*
These are B Westerns.
THE OREGON TRAIL (Universal, 1939) d Ford Beebe, s Johnny Mack
    Brown, Fuzzy Knight, Louise Stanley.

DESPERATE TRAILS (Universal, 1939) d Albert Ray, s Johnny Mack Brown, Fuzzy Knight, Frances Robinson.
OKLAHOMA FRONTIER (Universal, 1939) d Ford Beebe, s Johnny Mack Brown, Fuzzy Knight, Anne Gwynne.
CHIP OF THE FLYING U (Universal, 1939) d Ralph Staub, s Johnny Mack Brown, Fuzzy Knight, Doris Weston.
RIDERS OF PASCO BASIN (Universal, 1940) d Ray Taylor, s Johnny Mack Brown, Fuzzy Knight, Frances Robinson.
BADMAN FROM RED BUTTE (Universal, 1940) d Ray Taylor, s Johnny Mack Brown, Fuzzy Knight, Anne Gwynne.
SON OF ROARING DAWN (Universal, 1940) d Ford Beebe, s Johnny Mack Brown, Fuzzy Knight, Nell O'Day.
RAGTIME COWBOY JOE (Universal, 1940) d Ray Taylor, s Johnny Mack Brown, Fuzzy Knight, Nell O'Day.
LAW AND ORDER (Universal, 1940) d Ray Taylor, s Johnny Mack Brown, Fuzzy Knight, Nell O'Day.
PONY POST (Universal, 1940) d Ray Taylor, s Johnny Mack Brown, Fuzzy Knight, Nell O'Day.
BOSS OF BULLION CITY (Universal, 1941) d Ray Taylor, s Johnny Mack Brown, Fuzzy Knight, Nell O'Day.
BURY ME NOT ON THE LONE PRAIRIE (Universal, 1941) d Ray Taylor, s Johnny Mack Brown, Fuzzy Knight, Nell O'Day.
LAW OF THE RANGE (Universal, 1941) d Ray Taylor, s Johnny Mack Brown, Fuzzy Knight, Nell O'Day.
RAWHIDE RANGERS (Universal, 1941) d Ray Taylor, s Johnny Mack Brown, Fuzzy Knight, Nell O'Day.
MAN FROM MONTANA (Universal, 1941) d Ray Taylor, s Johnny Mack Brown, Fuzzy Knight, Nell O'Day.
THE MASKED RIDER (Universal, 1941) d Ford Beebe, s Johnny Mack Brown, Fuzzy Knight, Nell O'Day.
ARIZONA CYCLONE (Universal, 1941) d Joseph H. Lewis, s Johnny Mack Brown, Fuzzy Knight, Nell O'Day.
FIGHTING BILL FARGO (Universal, 1941) d Ray Taylor, s Johnny Mack Brown, Fuzzy Knight, Nell O'Day.
STAGECOACH BUCKAROO (Universal, 1942) d Ray Taylor, s Johnny Mack Brown, Fuzzy Knight, Nell O'Day.
THE SILVER BULLET (Universal, 1942) d Joseph H. Lewis, s Johnny Mack Brown, Fuzzy Knight, Jennifer Holt.
BOSS OF HANGTOWN MESA (Universal, 1942) d Joseph H. Lewis, s Johnny Mack Brown, Fuzzy Knight, Helen Deverell.
DEEP IN THE HEART OF TEXAS (Universal, 1942) d Elmer Clifton, s Johnny Mack Brown, Fuzzy Knight, Jennifer Holt.
LITTLE JOE THE WRANGLER (Universal, 1942) d Lewis Collins, s Johnny Mack Brown, Fuzzy Knight, Jennifer Holt.
TENTING TONIGHT ON THE OLD CAMPGROUND (Universal, 1943) d Lewis Collins, s Johnny Mack Brown, Fuzzy Knight, Jennifer Holt.

CHEYENNE ROUNDUP (Universal, 1943) d Ray Taylor, s Johnny Mack Brown, Fuzzy Knight, Jennifer Holt.
RAIDERS OF SAN JOAQUIN (Universal, 1943) d Lewis Collins, s Johnny Mack Brown, Fuzzy Knight, Jennifer Holt.
THE LONE STAR TRAIL (Universal, 1943) d Ray Taylor, s Johnny Mack Brown, Fuzzy Knight, Jennifer Holt.

396. *JOHNNY MACK BROWN AND RAYMOND HATTON*
THE STRANGER FROM PECOS (Monogram, 1943) d Lambert Hillyer, s Johnny Mack Brown, Raymond Hatton, Christine MacIntyre.
SIX GUN GOSPEL (Monogram, 1943) d Lambert Hillyer, s Johnny Mack Brown, Raymond Hatton, Inna Gest.
OUTLAWS OF STAMPEDE PASS (Monogram, 1943) d Wallace Fox, s Johnny Mack Brown, Raymond Hatton, Ellen Hall.
THE TEXAS KID (Monogram, 1943) d Lambert Hillyer, s Johnny Mack Brown, Raymond Hatton, Shirley Patterson.
RAIDERS OF THE BORDER (Monogram, 1944) d John P. McCarthy, s Johnny Mack Brown, Raymond Hatton, Ellen Hall.
PARTNERS OF THE TRAIL (Monogram, 1944) d Lambert Hillyer, s Johnny Mack Brown, Raymond Hatton, Christine McIntyre.
LAWMEN (Monogram, 1944) d Lambert Hillyer, s Johnny Mack Brown, Raymond Hatton, Jan Wiley.
RANGE LAND (Monogram, 1944) d Lambert Hillyer, s Johnny Mack Brown, Raymond Hatton, Sarah Padden.
WEST OF THE RIO GRANDE (Monogram, 1944) d Lambert Hillyer, s Johnny Mack Brown, Raymond Hatton, Christine McIntyre.
LAND OF THE OUTLAWS (Monogram, 1944) d Lambert Hillyer, s Johnny Mack Brown, Raymond Hatton, Nan Holiday.
LAND OF THE VALLEY (Monogram, 1944) d Howard Bretherton, s Johnny Mack Brown, Raymond Hatton, Lynne Carver.
GHOST GUNS (Monogram, 1944) d Lambert Hillyer, s Johnny Mack Brown, Raymond Hatton, Evelyn Finley.
THE NAVAJO TRAIL (Monogram, 1945) d Howard Bretherton, s Johnny Mack Brown, Raymond Hatton, Jennifer Holt.
GUNSMOKE (Monogram, 1945) d Howard Bretherton, s Johnny Mack Brown, Raymond Hatton, Jennifer Holt.
STRANGER FROM SANTA FE (Monogram, 1945) d Lambert Hillyer, s Johnny Mack Brown, Raymond Hatton, Beatrice Gray.
FLAME OF THE WEST (Monogram, 1945) d Lambert Hillyer, s Johnny Mack Brown, Raymond Hatton, Joan Woodbury.
THE LOST TRAIL (Monogram, 1945) d Lambert Hillyer, s Johnny Mack Brown, Raymond Hatton, Jennifer Holt.
FRONTIER FEUD (Monogram, 1945) d Lambert Hillyer, s Johnny Mack Brown, Raymond Hatton, Christine McIntyre.
BORDER BANDITS (Monogram, 1946) d Lambert Hillyer, s Johnny Mack Brown, Raymond Hatton, Rosa Del Rosario.

DRIFTING ALONG (Monogram, 1946) d Derwin Abrahams, s Johnny Mack Brown, Raymond Hatton, Lynne Carver.
THE HAUNTED MINE (Monogram, 1946) d Derwin Abrahams, s Johnny Mack Brown, Raymond Hatton, Linda Johnson.
UNDER ARIZONA SKIES (Monogram, 1946) d Lambert Hillyer, s Johnny Mack Brown, Raymond Hatton, Reno Blair.
THE GENTLEMAN FROM TEXAS (Monogram, 1946) d Lambert Hillyer, s Johnny Mack Brown, Raymond Hatton, Reno Blair.
TRIGGER FINGERS (Monogram, 1946) d Lambert Hillyer, s Johnny Mack Brown, Raymond Hatton, Jennifer Holt.
SHADOWS ON THE RANGE (Monogram, 1946) d Lambert Hillyer, s Johnny Mack Brown, Raymond Hatton, Jan Bryant.
SILVER RANGE (Monogram, 1946) d Lambert Hillyer, s Johnny Mack Brown, Raymond Hatton, Jan Bryant.
RAIDERS OF THE SOUTH (Monogram, 1947) d Lambert Hillyer, s Johnny Mack Brown, Raymond Hatton, Evelyn Brent.
VALLEY OF FEAR (Monogram, 1947) d Lambert Hillyer, s Johnny Mack Brown, Raymond Hatton, Christine McIntyre.
TRAILING DANGER (Monogram, 1947) d Lambert Hillyer, s Johnny Mack Brown, Raymond Hatton, Peggy Wynne.
LAND OF THE LAWLESS (Monogram, 1947) d Lambert Hillyer, s Johnny Mack Brown, Raymond Hatton, Christine McIntyre.
THE LAW COMES TO GUNSIGHT (Monogram, 1947) d Lambert Hillyer, s Johnny Mack Brown, Raymond Hatton, Reno Blair.
CODE OF THE SADDLE (Monogram, 1947) d Thomas Carr, s Johnny Mack Brown, Raymond Hatton, Kay Morley.
FLASHING GUNS (Monogram, 1947) d Lambert Hillyer, s Johnny Mack Brown, Raymond Hatton, Jan Bryant.
PRAIRIE EXPRESS (Monogram, 1947) d Lambert Hillyer, s Johnny Mack Brown, Raymond Hatton, Virginia Belmont.
GUN TALK (Monogram, 1947) d Lambert Hillyer, s Johnny Mack Brown, Raymond Hatton, Christine McIntyre.
OVERLAND TRAILS (Monogram, 1948) d Lambert Hillyer, s Johnny Mack Brown, Raymond Hatton, Virginia Belmont.
CROSSED TRAILS (Monogram, 1948) d Lambert Hillyer, s Johnny Mack Brown, Raymond Hatton, Lynne Carver.
FRONTIER AGENT (Monogram, 1948) d Lambert Hillyer, s Johnny Mack Brown, Raymond Hatton, Reno Blair.
TRIGGER MAN (Monogram, 1948) d Howard Bretherton, s Johnny Mack Brown, Raymond Hatton, Virginia Carroll.
BACK TRAIL (Monogram, 1948) d Christy Cabanne, s Johnny Mack Brown, Raymond Hatton, Mildred Coles.
THE FIGHTING RANGER (Monogram, 1948) d Lambert Hillyer, s Johnny Mack Brown, Raymond Hatton, Christine Larson.
THE SHERIFF OF MEDICINE BOW (Monogram 1948) d Lambert Hillyer, s Johnny Mack Brown, Raymond Hatton, Evelyn Finley.

MOTION PICTURE SERIES & SEQUELS

GUNNING FOR JUSTICE (Monogram, 1948) d Ray Taylor, s Johnny Mack Brown, Raymond Hatton, Evelyn Finley.
HIDDEN DANGER (Monogram, 1948) d Ray Taylor, s Johnny Mack Brown, Raymond Hatton, Max Terhune, Christine Larson.
LAW OF THE WEST (Monogram, 1949) d Ray Taylor, s Johnny Mack Brown, Raymond Hatton, Gerry Patterson.
TRAIL'S END (Monogram, 1949) d Lambert Hillyer, s Johnny Mack Brown, Raymond Hatton, Kay Morley.

397. *JOHNNY MACK BROWN AND MAX TERHUNE*
WEST OF EL DORADO (Monogram, 1949) d Ray Taylor, s Johnny Mack Brown, Max Terhune, Reno Browne.
WESTERN RENEGADES (Monogram, 1949) d Wallace Fox, s Johnny Mack Brown, Max Terhune, Jane Adams.

398. *JOHNNY MACK BROWN AND JIMMY ELLISON*
OKLAHOMA JUSTICE (Monogram, 1951) d Lewis Collins, s Johnny Mack Brown, Jimmy Ellison, Phyllis Coates.
WHISTLING HILLS (Monogram, 1951) d Derwin Abrahams, s Johnny Mack Brown, Jimmy Ellison, Noel Neill.
TEXAS LAWMEN (Monogram, 1951) d Lewis Collins, s Johnny Mack Brown, Jimmy Ellison.
TEXAS CITY (Monogram, 1952) d Lewis Collins, s Johnny Mack Brown, Jimmy Ellison.
MAN FROM THE BLACK HILLS (Monogram, 1952) d Thomas Carr, s Johnny Mack Brown, Jimmy Ellison.
DEAD MAN'S TRAIL (Monogram, 1952) d Lewis Collins, s Johnny Mack Brown, Jimmy Ellison, Barbara Allen.

399. JOHNNY WADD
Porno film actor John C. Holmes takes on this private detective personna for a number of pictures. The list may be incomplete.
JOHNNY WADD (VCX) s John C. Holmes.
TELL THEM JOHNNY WADD IS HERE (Freeway, 1976) d Bob Chinn, s John C. Holmes, Annette Haven.
THE RETURN OF JOHNNY WADD (Penguin, 1985) d Pat Roggins, s John C. Holmes, Mai Lin, Kimberly Carson.

400. JOHN PAUL REVERE
These are B-grade oaters with the main character a sheriff.
PRIDE OF THE PLAINS (Republic, 1944) d Wallace Fox, s Robert Livingston, Smiley Burnette.
BENEATH WESTERN SKIES (Republic, 1944) d Spencer Gordon Bennet, s Robert Livingston, Smiley Burnette.
THE LARAMIE TRAIL (Republic, 1944) d John English, s Robert Livingston, Smiley Burnette, Linda Brent.

180 MOTION PICTURE SERIES & SEQUELS

401. JONES FAMILY, THE
Jed Prouty is the father, Spring Byington is the mother, Florence Roberts is grandma, Kenneth Howell, George Ernest, Billy Mahan, June Carlson and June Lang are the kids. The first entry was based on a play by Katharine Cavanaugh. (An earlier JONES FAMILY features different actors in YOUNG AS YOU FEEL [1931] and BUSINESS AND PLEASURE [1932].)
EVERY SATURDAY NIGHT (Twentieth Century-Fox, 1936) s Jed Prouty, Spring Byington.
EDUCATING FATHER (Twentieth Century-Fox, 1936) s Jed Prouty, Spring Byington.
BACK TO NATURE (Twentieth Century-Fox, 1936) s Jed Prouty, Spring Byington.
OFF TO THE RACES (Twentieth Century-Fox, 1937) s Jed Prouty, Spring Byington.
BIG BUSINESS (Twentieth Century-Fox, 1937) s Jed Prouty, Spring Byington.
HOT WATER (Twentieth Century-Fox, 1937) s Jed Prouty, Spring Byington.
BORROWING TROUBLE (Twentieth Century-Fox, 1937) s Jed Prouty, Spring Byington.
LOVE ON A BUDGET (Twentieth Century-Fox, 1938) s Jed Prouty, Spring Byington.
A TRIP TO PARIS (Twentieth Century-Fox, 1938) s Jed Prouty, Spring Byington.
SAFETY IN NUMBERS (Twentieth Century-Fox, 1938) s Jed Prouty, Spring Byington.
DOWN ON THE FARM (Twentieth Century-Fox, 1938) s Jed Prouty, Spring Byington.
EVERYBODY'S BABY (Twentieth Century-Fox, 1939) s Jed Prouty, Spring Byington.
THE JONES FAMILY IN HOLLYWOOD (Twentieth Century-Fox, 1939) d Malcolm St. Clair, s Jed Prouty, Spring Byington, Buster Keaton.
THE JONES FAMILY IN QUICK MILLIONS (Twentieth Century-Fox, 1939) d Malcolm St. Clair, s Jed Prouty, Spring Byington, Buster Keaton.
TOO BUSY TO WORK (Twentieth Century-Fox, 1939) s Jed Prouty, Spring Byington.
ON THEIR OWN (Twentieth Century-Fox, 1940) s Jed Prouty, Spring Byington.

402. JONESY SERIES
The silent films circa 1908-11 feature Harry Myers.

403. JOSEY WALES
A Civil War veteran returns home to find his family murdered. With the help of an old Indian, he seeks revenge. The films are based on the books by Forrest Carter.
THE OUTLAW - JOSEY WALES (Warner Brothers, 1976) d Clint Eastwood, s Clint Eastwood, Chief Dan George, Sondra Locke.

THE RETURN OF JOSEY WALES (1986) d Michael Parks, s Michael Parks, Rafael Campos.

404. JOSSER
The hero is hapless Jimmy Josser.
P.C. JOSSER (Gainsborough, 1931) d Milton Rosner, s Ernie Lotinga, Jack Frost.
DR. JOSSER KC (British International Pictures, 1931) d Norman Lee, s Ernie Lotinga, Jack Hobbs.
JOSSER JOINS THE NAVY (British International Pictures, 1932) d Norman Lee, s Ernie Lotinga, Cyril McLaglen.
JOSSER ON THE RIVER (British International Pictures, 1932) s Ernie Lotinga.
JOSSER IN THE ARMY (British International Pictures, 1932) d Norman Lee, s Ernie Lotinga, Betty Norton.
JOSSER ON THE FARM (British International Pictures, 1934) d T. Hayes Haunter, s Ernie Lotinga.

405. JUNGLE JIM
Alex Raymond's syndicated newspaper comic strip (which began in 1934) inspired this series. There was also a 1955 syndicated television series with Weismuller.
JUNGLE JIM (Universal, 1937) (12-chapter serial) d Ford Beebe and Cliff Smith, s Grant Withers, Betty Jane Rhodes.
JUNGLE JIM (Columbia, 1948) d William Berke, s Johnny Weismuller, Virginia Grey, George Reeves.
THE LOST TRIBE (Columbia, 1949) d William Berke, s Johnny Weismuller, Myrna Dell.
CAPTIVE GIRL (Columbia, 1950) d William Berke, s Johnny Weismuller, Buster Crabbe.
MARK OF THE GORILLA (Columbia, 1950) d William Berke, s Johnny Weismuller, Trudy Marshall.
PYGMY ISLAND (Columbia, 1950) d William Berke, s Johnny Weismuller, Ann Savage.
FURY OF THE CONGO (Columbia, 1951) d William Berke, s Johnny Weismuller, Sherry Moreland.
JUNGLE MANHUNT (Columbia, 1951) d Lew Landers, s Johnny Weismuller, Bob Waterfield, Sheila Ryan.
JUNGLE JIM IN THE FORBIDDEN LAND (Columbia, 1952) d Lew Landers, s Johnny Weismuller, Angela Greene.
VOODOO TIGER (Columbia, 1952) d Spencer G. Bennet, s Johnny Weismuller, Jean Byron.
SAVAGE MUTINY (Columbia, 1953) d Spencer G. Bennet, s Johnny Weismuller, Angela Greene.
VALLEY OF THE HEADHUNTERS (Columbia, 1953) d William Berke, s Johnny Weismuller, Christine Larson.

KILLER APE (Columbia, 1953) d Spencer G. Bennet, s Johnny Weismuller, Carol Thurston.
JUNGLE MAN-EATERS (Columbia, 1954) d Lee Sholem, s Johnny Weismuller, Karin Booth.
CANNIBAL ATTACK (Columbia, 1954) d Lee Sholem, s Johnny Weismuller, s Johnny Weismuller, Judy Walsh.
JUNGLE MOON MEN (Columbia, 1955) d Charles S. Gould, s Johnny Weismuller, Jean Byron.
DEVIL GODDESS (Columbia, 1955) d Spencer G. Bennet, s Johnny Weismuller, Angela Stevens.

406. JUNGLE WOLF
Soldiers of fortune are featured in these pictures.
JUNGLE WOLF
RETURN FIRE: JUNGLE WOLF II (Romarc, 1988) d Neil Callaghan, s Adam West, Ron Marchini.

407. JUNIOR G-MEN
Billy, Gyp, Terry and Lug uncover a kindnapping plot in the first picture. Ace Holden, Bolts Larson, Stick Munsey and Greaseball Plunkett, junkyard workers, uncover an espionage plot in the second outing. The entries evolved from LITTLE TOUGH GUYS.
JUNIOR G-MEN (Universal, 1940) (twelve episodes) d Ford Beebe and John Rawlins, s Billy Hallop, Huntz Hall, Gabriel Dell.
JUNIOR G-MEN OF THE AIR (Universal, 1942) (thirteen episodes) d Ray Taylor and Lewis D. Collins, s Billy Hallop, Gene Reynolds, Lionel Atwill.

408. JUVENILE COMEDIES
These are OUR GANG imitations from the 1920s.

409. KARATE KID, THE
A lonely and bullied teenager Daniel learns karate from his Japanese mentor Miyagi.
THE KARATE KID (Columbia, 1984) d John G. Avildson, s Ralph Macchio, Noriyuki (Pat) Morita, Elisabeth Shue.
THE KARATE KID, PART II (Columbia, 1986) d John G. Avildsen, s Ralph Macchio, Noriyuki (Pat) Morita.
THE KARATE KID, PART III (Columbia, 1989) d John G. Avildsen, s Ralph Macchio, Noriyuki (Pat) Morita.

409A. KATZENJAMMER KIDS, THE
Hans and Fritz, the trouble-making Katzenjammer Kids, first appeared in Rudolph Dirks' newspaper comic strip of the same name in 1897. Other characters include Mama, the Captain and the Inspector.
KATZENJAMMER KIDS AND THE SCHOOL MARM (American Mutoscope & Biograph, 1903)

MOTION PICTURE SERIES & SEQUELS 183

THE KATZENJAMMER KIDS HAVE A LOVE AFFAIR (American
Mutoscope & Biograph, 1903)
KATZENJAMMER KIDS (Selig, 1912)

410. *KAY KYSER*
The bandleader popular on the radio quiz show KAY KAISER'S KOLLEGE
OF MUSICAL KNOWLEDGE also appeared in musical films. Featured in the
band is Ish Kabibble.
THAT'S RIGHT YOU'RE WRONG (RKO, 1939) d David Butler, s Kay Kyser,
    Adolphe Menjoy, Lucille Ball.
YOU'LL FIND OUT (RKO, 1940) d David Butler, s Kay Kyser, Boris Karloff,
    Bela Lugosi.
PLAYMATES (RKO, 1941) d David Butler, s Kay Kyser and his Band, John
    Barrymore.
MY FAVORITE SPY (RKO, 1942) d Tay Garnett, s Kay Kyser, Ginny Simms.
STAGE DOOR CANTEEN (United Artists, 1943) d Frank Borzage, s Cheryl
    Walker, Lon McCallister, Kay Kyser and his Band.
AROUND THE WORLD (RKO, 1943) d Allan Dwan, s Kay Kyser, Ish
    Kabibble, Ginny Simms.
SWING FEVER (MRM, 1944) d Tim Whelan, s Kay Kyser and his Band,
    Marilyn Maxwell.
CAROLINA BLUES (Columbia, 1944) d Leigh Jason, s Kay Kyser and his
    Band, Ann Miller.

411. *KEN CURTIS AND GUY KIBBEE*
These are B Westerns.
COWBOY BLUES (Columbia, 1946) d Ray Nazarro, s Ken Curtis, Big Boy
    Williams, Guy Kibbee, Jeff Donnell, Carolina Cotton.
SINGING ON THE TRAIL (Columbia, 1946) d Ray Nazarro, s Ken Curtis, Big
    Boy Williams, Guy Kibbee, Jeff Donnell.
LONE STAR MOONLIGHT (Columbia, 1946) d Ray Nazarro, s Ken Curtis,
    Guy Kibbee, Joan Barton.
OVER THE SANTA FE TRAIL (Columbia, 1947) d Ray Nazarro, s Ken
    Curtis, Big Boy Williams, Guy Kibbee, Jennifer Holt.

412. KEYSTONE COPS, THE
Mack Sennett's Keystone Studios from 1912-20 featured slapstick lawmen, led
variously by Fred Mace, Chester Conklin and Ford Sterling as Chief Teheezal
in a number of wild chase and trick effects comedies. The Cops -- whose
numbers included Roscoe "Fatty Arbuckle," Edgar Kennedy, Mack Sennett,
Frank Hayes, Fred Fishback, Mack Swain -- did not have a series of their own,
and the following listing is incomplete. The players also converted to the
Keystone Fire Department for such pictures as THE PLUMBER (1914) and
BATH TUB PERILS (1916).
THE BANGVILLE POLICE (Keystone, 1913) d Henry Lehrman, s Fred Mace
PEEPING PETE A BANDIT (Keystone, 1913) d Mack Sennett, s Ford
    Sterling.

A MUDDY ROMANCE (Keystone, 1913) d Mack Sennett, s Mabel Normand, Ford Sterling.
IN THE CLUTCHES OF A GANG (Keystone, 1914) d George Nichols, s Ford Sterling, Hank Mann, Roscoe Arbuckle, Rube Miller, Al St. John.
LOVE, LOOT AND CRASH (Keystone, 1915) s Chester Conklin, Charles Chase, Dora Rogers.
FATTY JOINS THE FORCE (Keystone, 1913) d George Nichols, s Roscoe "Fatty" Arbuckle.
THE ALARM (Keystone, 1914) d Roscoe Arbuckle, s Roscoe "Fatty" Arbuckle, Mabel Normand.
THE LOVE THIEF (Keystone, 1914) s Chester Conklin.
THE NOISE OF BOMBS (Keystone, 1914) s Charles Murray, Edgar Kennedy.
GETTING ACQUAINTED (Keystone, 1914) d Charles Chaplin.
CINDERS OF LOVE (Keystone, 1916) d Walter Wright, s Chester Conklin, Slim Summervile.
A DASH OF COURAGE (Keystone, 1916) d Charles Chase, s Harry Gribbon, Wallace Beery.
STARS AND BARS (Keystone-Triangle, 1917) d Victor Heerman, s Ford Sterling, Harry Gribbon.
ABBOTT AND COSTELLO MEET THE KEYSTONE KOPS (Universal, 1955) s Bud Abbott, Lou Costello, Fred Clark, Lynn Bari.

413. KIDDIE KUTE KOMEDIES
Eureka Productions made a series of short comedies with a cast of juvenile actors and actresses.

414. KIDDIE TROUPERS, THE
These short comedies were variations on OUR GANG.

415. KID GALAHAD
A bellhop becomes a boxer.
KID GALAHAD (Warner Brothers, 1937) [aka BATTLING BELLHOP] d Michael Curtiz, s Edward G. Robinson, Bette Davis.
THE KID COMES BACK (Warner Brothers, 1937) s Wayne Morris, Barton MacLane.
KID GALAHAD (United Artists/Mirisch, 1962) d Phil Karlson, s Elvis Presley, Lola Albright.

416. KID NOAH
Pinellas Films made a series of short comedies with kid performers.

417. KILLER TOMATOES
Campy, low-budget science fiction fare, the plot obvious from the titles.
ATTACK OF THE KILLER TOMATOES (NAI Entertainment, 1980) d John DeBello, s David Miller, Sharon Taylor.

RETURN OF THE KILLER TOMATOES (1988) d John DeBEllo, s Chad Finletter.

418. KILL OR BE KILLED
The first title is a martial arts/revenge film, the followup involves a plot to take over the world
KILL OR BE KILLED (Film Ventures International, 1980) d Ivan Hall, s James Ryan, Norman Combes, Charlotte Michelle.
KILL AND KILL AGAIN (Film Ventures International, 1981) d Ivan Hall, s James Ryan, Anneline Kriel.

419. KING KONG
The first two giant ape pix boast Willis O'Brien special effects. Kong is "rescued" from his wilderness island and brought to New York for show business exploitation.
KING KONG (RKO, 1939) d Merian C. Cooper and Ernest B. Schoedsack, s Fay Wray, Bruce Cabot, Robert Armstrong.
SON OF KONG (RKO, 1933) d Ernest B. Schoedsack, s Robert Armstrong, Helen Mack, Victor Wong.
KING KONG VS. GODZILLA (Universal, 1963) d Thomas Montgomery, Inoshiro Honda, s Michael Keith, James Yagi.
KING KONG ESCAPES (Universal, 1968) d Inoshiro Honda, s Rhodes Reason, Mie Hama.
KING KONG (Paramount, 1976) d John Guillermin, s Jeff Bridges, Jessica Lang.
KING KONG LIVES (DEG, 1986) d John Guillermin, s Brian Kerwin, Linda Hamilton.

420. KING OF THE ROYAL MOUNTED
These pictures are based on the newspaper comic strip (launched in 1935) supposedly written by Zane Grey.
KING OF THE ROYAL MOUNTED (20th Century-Fox, 1936) d Howard Bretherton, s Robert Kent, Rosalind Keith.
KING OF THE ROYAL MOUNTED (Republic, 1940) (twelve chapters) [aka YUKON PATROL] d William Witney and John English, s Allan Lane, Robert Strange.
KING OF THE MOUNTIES (Republic, 1942) (twelve chapters) d William Witney, s Allan Lane, Peggy Drake.

421. KLEVER KOMEDIES
Victor Moore appeared in these one-reel comedies. The list is not complete.
BUNGALOWING (Paramount, 1917) s Victor Moore.
COMMUTING (Paramount, 1917) s Victor Moore.
MOVING (Paramount, 1917) s Victor Moore.
FLIVVERING (Paramount, 1917) s Victor Moore.

422. KOJAK

Lt. Theo Kojak is a lollipop-loving homicide detective who appeared in a weekly television series over CBS 1974-78. Kojak returned to regular television in movie-length episodes in 1989. Other characters include his supervisor, Frank McNeil (Dan Frazer), Lt. Bobby Crocker (Kevin Dobson) and Det. Stavros (George Savalas).

THE MARCUS-NELSON MURDERS (Universal, 1973) (CBS-TV movie) [aka KOJAK AND THE MARCUS-NELSON MURDERS] d Joseph Sargent, s Telly Savalas, Marjoe Gortner.

KOJAK: THE BELARUS FILE (1985 TV movie) d Robert Markowitz, s Telly Savalas, Suzanne Pleshette, Dan Frazer, George Savalas.

KOJAK: THE PRICE OF JUSTICE (1987 TV movie) d Alan Metzger, s Telly Savalas, Kate Nelligan.

KOJAK: ARIANA (TV movie, 1989) s Telly Savalas, Andre Braugher.

KOJAK: FATAL FLAW (TV movie, 1989) s Telly Savalas, Angie Dickinson.

KOJAK: FLOWERS FOR MATTY (ABC-TV movie, 1990) s Telly Savalas, Glynnis O'Connor.

KOJAK: IT'S ALWAYS SOMETHING (ABC-TV movie, 1990) s Telly Savalas, Kevin Dobson.

423. KUKU COMEDIES
These silent comedies feature Dot Farley and Sammy Burns. The list is incomplete.

SAMMY'S SCANDALOUS SCHEMES (Vogue, 1915) d Gilbert P. Hamilton, s Sammy Burns, Dot Farley.

SAMMY VS. CUPID (Mutual, 1915) s Sammy Burns.

424. KUNG FU
Caine, a Buddhist monk, raised in China, roamed the West in an ABC television series which aired 1972-75.

KUNG FU (Warner Brothers, 1972) (ABC-TV movie) d Jerry Thorpe, s David Carradine, Barry Sullivan, Keye Luke.

KUNG FU: THE MOVIE (TV movie, 1986) d Richard Lang, s David Carradine, Kerri Keane.

425. KUNG FU WARLORDS
These are martial arts films.

KUNG FU WARLORDS (World Northal, 1983)

KUNG FUN WARLORDS PART II (World Northal, 1983) d Chang Chen.

Pee-Wee Herman is in real life Paul Reubens; he has appeared in two feature-length films.

426. LA CAGE AUX FOLLES
In the first entry, a straight son wants his homosexual nightclub-owner father to act in proper manner before his girlfriend's folks. But the elder's female impersonator companion becomes jealous.
LA CAGE AUX FOLLES (UA, 1978) [aka BIRDS OF A FEATHER] d
   Edouard Molinara, s Ugo Tognazzi, Michel Serrault.
LA CAGE AUX FOLLES II (UA, 1980) d Edouard Molinaro, s Ugo Tognazzi,
   Michel Serrault, Marcel Bozzuffi, Paola Borboni.
LA CAGE AUX FOLLES 3: THE WEDDING (1985) d Georges Lautner, s
   Ugo Tognazzi, Michel Serrault.

427. L.A. CRACKDOWN
A female undercover cop breaks a crack ring.
L.A. CRACKDOWN (1988) d Joseph Merhi, s Pamela Dixon.
L.A. CRACKDOWN II (1988) d Joseph Merhi, s Pamela Dixon.

428. LADY CHATTERLEY
The D.H. Lawrence novel *Lady Chatterley's Lover* inspired these pictures.
LADY CHATTERLEY'S LOVER (Cohen/Seat/Columbia, 1956) d Marc
   Allegret, s Danielle Darrieux, Leo Genn.
YOUNG LADY CHATTERLEY (Pro International, 1977) d Alan Roberts, s
   Harlee McBride, Peter Ratray.
LADY CHATTERLEY'S LOVER (Cannon/Producteurs Associes, 1981) d Just
   Jaeckin, s Sylvia Kristel, Nichlas Clay.
YOUNG LADY CHATTERLEY II (1985) s Harlee McBride.

429. LAND TIME FORGOT, THE
Edgar Rice Burroughs wrote a series of novels about a lost civilization, upon which these films are based.
THE LAND THAT TIME FORGOT (American International, 1975) d Kevin
   Connor, s Doug McClure, John McEnery, Susan Pehnaligon.
THE PEOPLE THAT TIME FORGOT (American International, 1977) d Kevin
   Connor, s Patrick Wayne, Doug McClure, Sarah Douglas.

430. *LARRY SEMON*
Larry Semon regularly played a grinning, white-faced, baggy-pants dumbbell in silent comedies for Vitagraph.
BOAST AND BOLDNESS (Vitagraph, 1917) d Larry Semon, s Larry Semon.
WORRIES AND WOBBLES (Vitagraph, 1917) d Larry Semon, s Larry
   Semon.
SHELLS AND SHIVERS (Vitagraph, 1917) d Larry Semon, s Larry Semon.
CHUMPS AND CHANCES (Vitagraph, 1917) d Larry Semon, s Larry Semon.
GALL AND GOLF (Vitagraph, 1917) d Larry Semon, s Larry Semon.
SLIPS AND SLACKERS (Vitagraph, 1917) d Larry Semon, s Larry Semon.
RISKS AND ROUGHNECKS (Vitagraph, 1917) d Larry Semon, s Larry
   Semon.
PLANS AND PAJAMAS (Vitagraph, 1917) d Larry Semon, s Larry Semon.

PLAGUES AND PUPPY LOVE (Vitagraph, 1917) d Larry Semon, s Larry Semon.
SPORTS AND SPLASHES (Vitagraph, 1917) d Larry Semon, s Larry Semon.
TOUGHLUCK AND TIN LIZZIES (Vitagraph, 1917) d Larry Semon, s Larry Semon.
ROUGH TOUGHS AND ROOFTOPS (Vitagraph, 1917) d Larry Semon, s Larry Semon.
SPOOKS AND SPASMS (Vitagraph, 1917) d Larry Semon, s Larry Semon.
NOISY NAGGERS AND NOSEY NEIGHBORS (Vitagraph, 1917) d Larry Semon, s Larry Semon.
GUNS AND GREASERS (Vitagraph, 1918) d Larry Semon, s Larry Semon.
BABES AND BOOBS (Vitagraph, 1918) d Larry Semon, s Larry Semon.
ROOMS AND RUMORS (Vitagraph, 1918) d Larry Semon, s Larry Semon.
MEDDLERS AND MOONSHINE (Vitagraph, 1918) d Larry Semon, s Larry Semon.
STRIPES AND STUMBLES (Vitagraph, 1918) d Larry Semon, s Larry Semon.
RUMMIES AND RAZORS (Vitagraph, 1918) d Larry Semon, s Larry Semon.
WHISTLES AND WINDOWS (Vitagraph, 1918) d Larry Semon, s Larry Semon.
SPIES AND SPILLS (Vitagraph, 1918) d Larry Semon, s Larry Semon.
ROMANS AND RASCALS (Vitagraph, 1918) d Larry Semon, s Larry Semon.
SKIDS AND SCALAWAGS (Vitagraph, 1918) d Larry Semon, s Larry Semon.
BOODLE AND BANDITS (Vitagraph, 1918) d Larry Semon, s Larry Semon.
HINDOOS AND HAZARDS (Vitagraph, 1918) d Larry Semon, s Larry Semon.
BATHING BEAUTIES AND BIG BOOBS (Vitagraph, 1918) d Larry Semon, s Larry Semon.
DUNCES AND DANGER (Vitagraph, 1918) d Larry Semon, s Larry Semon.
MUTTS AND MOTORS (Vitagraph, 1918) d Larry Semon, s Larry Semon.
HUNS AND HYPHENS (Vitagraph, 1918) d Larry Semon, s Larry Semon.
BEARS AND BAD MEN (Vitagraph, 1918) d Larry Semon, s Larry Semon.
FRAUDS AND FRENZIES (Vitagraph, 1918) d Larry Semon, s Larry Semon.
HUMUS AND HUSBANDS (Vitagraph, 1918) d Larry Semon, s Larry Semon.
PLUCK AND PLOTTERS (Vitagraph, 1918) d Larry Semon, s Larry Semon.
TRAPS AND TANGLES (Vitagraph, 1919) d Larry Semon, s Larry Semon.
SCAMPS AND SCANDALS (Vitagraph, 1919) d Larry Semon, s Larry Semon.
SOAPSUDS AND SAPHEADS (Vitagraph, 1919) d Larry Semon, s Larry Semon.
WELL, I'LL BE... (Vitagraph, 1919) d Larry Semon, s Larry Semon.
PASSING THE BUCK (Vitagraph, 1919) d Larry Semon, s Larry Semon.
THE STAR BOARDER (Vitagraph, 1919) d Larry Semon, s Larry Semon.
HIS HOME SWEET HOME (Vitagraph, 1919) d Larry Semon, s Larry Semon.
THE SIMPLE LIFE (Vitagraph, 1919) d Larry Semon, s Larry Semon.
BETWEEN THE ACTS (Vitagraph, 1919) d Larry Semon, s Larry Semon.
DULL CARE (Vitagraph, 1919) d Larry Semon, s Larry Semon.
DEW DROP INN (Vitagraph, 1919) d Larry Semon, s Larry Semon.

THE HEADWAITER (Vitagraph, 1919) d Larry Semon, s Larry Semon.
THE GROCERY CLERK (Vitagraph, 1920) d Larry Semon, s Larry Semon.
THE FLY COP (Vitagraph, 1920) d Larry Semon, Norman Taurog and Mort Peebles, s Larry Semon.
SCHOOL DAYS (Vitagraph, 1920) d Larry Semon, Norman Taurog and Mort Peebles, s Larry Semon.
SOLID CONCRETE (Vitagraph, 1920) d Larry Semon, s Larry Semon.
THE SUITOR (Vitagraph, 1920) d Larry Semon and Norman Taurog, s Larry Semon.
THE SPORTSMAN (Vitagraph, 1921) d Larry Semon and Norman Taurog, s Larry Semon.
THE HICK (Vitagraph, 1921) d Larry Semon and Norman Taurog, s Larry Semon.
THE RENT COLLECTOR (Vitagraph, 1921) d Larry Semon and Norman Taurog, s Larry Semon.
THE BAKERY (Vitagraph, 1921) d Larry Semon and Norman Taurog, s Larry Semon.
THE FALL GUY (Vitagraph, 1921) d Larry Semon and Norman Taurog, s Larry Semon.
THE BELL HOP (Vitagraph, 1921) d Larry Semon and Norman Taurog, s Larry Semon.
THE SAWMILL (Vitagraph, 1922) d Larry Semon and Norman Taurog, s Larry Semon.
THE SHOW (Vitagraph, 1922) d Larry Semon and Norman Taurog, s Larry Semon.
A PAIR OF KINGS (Vitagraph, 1922) d Larry Semon and Norman Taurog, s Larry Semon.
GOLF (Vitagraph, 1922) d Larry Semon and Tom Buckingham, s Larry Semon.
THE SLEUTH (Vitagraph, 1922) d Larry Semon and Tom Buckingham, s Larry Semon.
THE COUNTER JUMPER (Vitagraph, 1922) d Larry Semon, s Larry Semon.
NO WEDDING BELLS (Vitagraph, 1923) d Larry Semon, s Larry Semon.
THE BARNYARD (Vitagraph, 1923) d Larry Semon, s Larry Semon.
MIDNIGHT CABARET (Vitagraph, 1923) d Larry Semon, s Larry Semon.
THE GOWN SHOP (Vitagraph, 1923) d Larry Semon, s Larry Semon.
LIGHTNING LOVE (Vitagraph, 1923) d Larry Semon and James Davis, s Larry Semon.
HORSESHOES (Vitagraph, 1923) d Larry Semon and James Davis, s Larry Semon.
TROUBLE BREWING (Vitagraph, 1924) d Larry Semon and James Davis, s Larry Semon.
HER BOY FRIEND (Educational, 1924) d Noel Smith, s Larry Semon.
KID SPEED (Educational, 1924) d Larry Semon and Noel Smith, s Larry Semon.
THE DOME DOCTOR (Educational, 1925) d Larry Semon, s Larry Semon.
THE CLOUDHOPPER (Educational, 1925) d Larry Semon, s Larry Semon.
THE STUNTMAN (Educational, 1927) d Larry Semon, s Larry Semon.

OH WHAT A MAN (Educational, 1927) d Larry Semon, s Larry Semon.
DUMMIES (Educational, 1928) d Larry Semon, s Larry Semon.
A SIMPLE SAP (Educational, 1927) d Larry Semon and Hampton Del Ruth, s Larry Semon.
THE GIRL IN THE LIMOUSINE (First National, 1924) d Larry Semon, s Larry Semon.
THE PERFECT CLOWN (1925) s Larry Semon.
STOP, LOOK AND LISTEN (Pathe, 1926) s Larry Semon.
SPUDS (Pathe, 1927) s Larry Semon.

431. LASH LARUE
The B Western cowboy was known as the King of the Bullwhip.
LAW OF THE LASH (PRC, 1947) d Ray Taylor, s Lath LaRue, Al "Fuzzy" St. John, Mary Scott.
BORDER FEUD (PRC, 1947) d Ray Taylor, s Lash LaRue, Al "Fuzzy" St. John, Gloria Marlen.
PIONEER JUSTICE (PRC, 1947) d Ray Taylor, s Lash LaRue, Al "Fuzzy" St. John, Jennifer Holt.
GHOST TOWN RENEGADES (PRC, 1947) d Ray Taylor, s Lash LaRue, Al "Fuzzy" St. John, Jennifer Holt.
STAGE TO MESA CITY (PRC, 1947) d Ray Taylor, s Lash LaRue, Al "Fuzzy" St. John, Jennifer Holt.
RETURN OF THE LASH (PRC, 1947) d Ray Taylor, s Lash LaRue, Al "Fuzzy" St. John, Mary Maynard.
THE FIGHTING VIGILANTES (PRC, 1947) d Ray Taylor, s Lash LaRue, Al "Fuzzy" St. John, Jennifer Holt.
CHEYENNE TAKES OVER (PRC, 1947) d Ray Taylor, s Lash LaRue, Al "Fuzzy" St. John, Nancy Gates.
DEAD MAN'S GOLD (Screen Guild, 1948) d Ray Taylor, s Lash LaRue, Al "Fuzzy" St. John, Suzi Crandall.
MARK OF THE LASH (Screen Guild, 1948) d Ray Taylor, s Lash LaRue, Al "Fuzzy" St. John, Suzi Crandall.
FRONTIER REVENGE (Screen Guild, 1948) d Ray Taylor, s Lash LaRue, Al "Fuzzy" St. John, Peggy Stewart.
OUTLAW COUNTRY (Screen Guild, 1949) d Ray Taylor, s Lash LaRue, Al "Fuzzy" St. John, Nancy Saunders.
SON OF BILLY THE KID (Screen Guild, 1949) d Ray Taylor, s Lash LaRue, Al "Fuzzy" St. John, Marion Colby, June Carr.
SON OF A BADMAN (Screen Guild, 1949) d Ray Taylor, s Lash LaRue, Al "Fuzzy" St. John, Noel Neill.
THE DALTONS' WOMEN (Howcos, 1950) d Thomas Carr, s Lash LaRue, Al "Fuzzy" St. John, Pamela Blake.
KING OF THE BULLWHIP (Western Adventure, 1951) d Ron Ormond, s Lash La Rue, Al "Fuzzy" St. John, Anne Gwynne.
THE THUNDERING TRAIL (Western Adventure, 1951) d Ron Ormond, s Lash La Rue, Al "Fuzzy" St. John, Sally Anglim.

THE VANISHING OUTPOST (Western Adventure, 1951) d Ron Ormond, s
    Lash La Rue, Al "Fuzzy" St. John, Sue Hussey.
THE BLACK LASH (Western Adventure, 1952) d Ron Ormond, s Lash La
    Rue, Al "Fuzzy" St. John, Peggy Stewart.
THE FRONTIER PHANTOM (Western Adventure, 1952) d Ron Ormond, s
    Lash La Rue, Al "Fuzzy" St. John, Virginia Herrick.

432. LASSIE
Eric Mowbray Knight's 1940 novel of a poor family forced to sell its beloved collie also inspired a long-running television program which aired 1954-71 and a recent syndicated version 1990-. There was also a Lassie radio series 1947-50.
LASSIE COME HOME (Loew's, 1943) d Fred M. Wilcox, s Roddy McDowall,
    Donald Crisp.
SON OF LASSIE (MGM, 1945) d Sylvan Simon, s Peter Lawford, Donald
    Crisp, June Lockhart.
COURAGE OF LASSIE (MGM, 1946) d Fred M. Wilcox, s Elizabeth Taylor,
    Frank Morgan.
HILLS OF HOME (MGM, 1948) d Fred M. Wilcox, s Edmund Gwenn, Donald
    Crisp.
THE SUN COMES UP (MGM, 1949) d Richar Thorpe, s Jeanette MacDonald,
    Lloyd Nolan.
CHALLENGE TO LASSIE (MGM, 1949) d Richard Thorpe, s Edmund
    Gwenn, Donald Crisp.
THE PAINTED HILLS (MGM, 1951) d Harold F. Kress, s Paul Kelly, Bruce
    Cowling.
LASSIE'S GREAT ADVENTURE (20th Century-Fox, 1963) d William
    Beaudine, s June Lockhart, Hugh Reilly, Jon Provost.
THE MAGIC OF LASSIE (International Picture Show, 1978) d Don Chaffey, s
    James Stewart, Mickey Rooney.

433. LAST PICTURE SHOW, THE
The pictures are based on Larry McMurtry's novels of small-town Texas.
THE LAST PICTURE SHOW (Columbia, 1971) d Peter Bogdanovich, s
    Timothy Bottoms, Jeff Bridges, Cybill Shepherd.
TEXASVILLE (Majestic Films, announced 1990) d Peter Bogdanovich, s
    Timothy Bottoms, Jeff Bridges, Cybill Shepherd.

434. *LAUREL AND HARDY*
Stan Laurel and Oliver Hardy -- skinny and chubby comedians -- appeared in a series of classic silent and sound comedies. The list does not include compilations. The two first appeared together in a Stan Laurel short, LUCKY DOG (G.M. Anderson-Metro, 1917).
FORTY-FIVE MINUTES FROM HOLLYWOOD (Hal Roach-Pathe, 1926) d
    Hal Roach, s Stan Laurel, Oliver Hardy.
DUCK SOUP (Hal Roach-Pathe, 1927) d Hal Roach, s Stan Laurel, Oliver
    Hardy.

SLIPPING WIVES (Hal Roach-Pathe, 1927) d Fred Guiol, s Stan Laurel, Oliver Hardy.
LOVE 'EM AND WEEP (Hal Roach-Pathe, 1927) d Fred Guiol, s Stan Laurel, Oliver Hardy, James Finlayson, Mae Busch.
WHY GIRLS LOVE SAILORS (Hal Roach-Pathe, 1927) d Fred Guiol, s Stan Laurel, Oliver Hardy.
WITH LOVE AND HISSES (Hal Roach-Pathe, 1927) d Fred Guiol, s Stan Laurel, Oliver Hardy, James Finlayson.
SAILORS BEWARE (Hal Roach-Pathe, 1927) d Fred Guiol, s Stan Laurel, Oliver Hardy, Anita Garvin.
DO DETECTIVES THINK? (Hal Roach-Pathe, 1927) d Fred Guiol, s Stan Laurel, Oliver Hardy, James Finlayson.
FLYING ELEPHANTS (Hal Roach-Pathe, 1927) d Frank Butler, s Stan Laurel, Oliver Hardy, James Finlayson, Viola Ritchard.
SUGAR DADDIES (Hal Roach-MGM, 1927) d Fred Guiol, s Stan Laurel, Oliver Hardy, James Finlayson, Eugene Pallette, Edna Marion.
CALL OF THE CUCKOOS (Hal Roach-MGM, 1927) d Clyde Bruckman, s Stan Laurel, Oliver Hardy, Charlie Chase.
THE SECOND HUNDRED YEARS (Hal Roach-MGM, 1927) d Fred Guiol, s Stan Laurel, Oliver Hardy, Tiny Sanford.
HATS OFF (Hal Roach-MGM, 1927) d Hal Yates, s Stan Laurel, Oliver Hardy.
PUTTING PANTS ON PHILIP (Hal Roach-MGM, 1927) d Clyde Bruckman, s Stan Laurel, Oliver Hardy, Harvey Clark.
THE BATTLE OF THE CENTURY (Hal Roach-MGM, 1927) d Clyde Bruckman, s Stan Laurel, Oliver Hardy, Charlie Hall.
LEAVE 'EM LAUGHING (Hal Roach-MGM, 1928) d Clyde Bruckman, s Stan Laurel, Oliver Hardy, Edgar Kennedy.
THE FINISHING TOUCH (Hal Roach-MGM, 1928) d Clyde Bruckman, s Stan Laurel, Oliver Hardy, Edgar Kennedy.
FROM SOUP TO NUTS (Hal Roach-MGM, 1928) d E. Livingston Kennedy (Edgar Kennedy), s Stan Laurel, Oliver Hardy, Anita Garvin.
YOU'RE DARN TOOTIN' (Hal Roach-MGM, 1928) d Edgar Kennedy, s Stan Laurel, Oliver Hardy, Charles Hall.
THEIR PURPLE MOMENT (Hal Roach-MGM, 1928) d James Parrott, s Stan Laurel, Oliver Hardy, Anita Garvin.
SHOULD MARRIED MEN GO HOME? (Hal Roach-MGM, 1928) d James Parrott, s Stan Laurel, Oliver Hardy, Edgar Kennedy, Viola Ritchard.
EARLY TO BED (Hal Roach-MGM, 1928) d Emmett Flynn, s Stan Laurel, Oliver Hardy.
TWO TARS (Hal Roach-MGM, 1928) d James Parrott, s Stan Laurel, Oliver Hardy, Edgar Kennedy.
HABEAS CORPUS (Hal Roach-MGM, 1928) d Leo McCarey, s Stan Laurel, Oliver Hardy.
WE FAW DOWN (Hal Roach-MGM, 1928) [aka WE SLIP UP] d Leo McCarey, s Stan Laurel, Oliver Hardy.

LIBERTY (Hal Roach-MGM, 1929) d Leo McCarey, s Stan Laurel, Oliver Hardy, Jean Harlow.
WRONG AGAIN (Hal Roach-MGM, 1929) d Leo McCarey, s Stan Laurel, Oliver Hardy, Anders Randolph.
THAT'S MY WIFE (Hal Roach-MGM, 1929) d Lloyd French, s Stan Laurel, Oliver Hardy, Dorothy Christie.
BIG BUSINESS (Hal Roach-MGM, 1929) d James Horne, s Stan Laurel, Oliver Hardy, James Finlayson.
DOUBLE WHOOPEE (Hal Roach-MGM, 1929) d Leo McCarey, s Stan Laurel, Oliver Hardy, Jean Harlow, Charle Hall.
BERTH MARKS (Hal Roach-MGM, 1929) d Lewis Foster, s Stan Laurel, Oliver Hardy.
MEN O'WAR (Hal Roach-MGM, 1929) d Lewis Foster, s Stan Laurel, Oliver Hardy, James Finlayson.
A PERFECT DAY (Hal Roach-MGM, 1929) d James Parrott, s Stan Laurel, Oliver Hardy, Edgar Kennedy.
THEY GO BOOM (Hal Roach-MGM, 1929) d James Parrott, s Stan Laurel, Oliver Hardy.
BACON GRABBERS (Hal Roach-MGM, 1929) d Lewis Foster, s Stan Laurel, Oliver Hardy, Edgar Kennedy, Jean Harlow.
ANGORA LOVE (Hal Roach-MGM, 1929) d Lewis Foster, s Stan Laurel, Oliver Hardy, Edgar Kennedy.
UNACCUSTOMED AS WE ARE (Hal Roach-MGM, 1929) d Lewis Foster, s Stan Laurel, Oliver Hardy, Mae Busch, Thelma Todd.
HOLLYWOOD REVIEW OF 1929 (MGM, 1929) s Stan Laurel, Oliver Hardy, Marie Dressler, Lionel Barrymore, Buster Keaton.
HOOSEGOW (Hal Roach-MGM, 1929) d James Parrott, s Stan Laurel, Oliver Hardy, James Finlayson.
NIGHT OWLS (Hal Roach-MGM, 1930) d James Parrott, s Stan Laurel, Oliver Hardy, Edgar Kennedy.
BLOTTO (Hal Roach-MGM, 1930) d James Parrott, s Stan Laurel, Oliver Hardy, Dorothy Christie.
ROGUE SONG (Hal Roach-MGM, 1930) d Lionel Barrymore, s Stan Laurel, Oliver Hardy, Lawrence Tibbett, Catherine Dale Owen.
BE BIG (Hal Roach-MGM, 1930) d James Parrott, s Stan Laurel, Oliver Hardy, Anita Garvin.
BRATS (Hal Roach-MGM, 1930) d James Parrott, s Stan Laurel, Oliver Hardy.
BELOW ZERO (Hal Roach-MGM, 1930) d James Parrott, s Stan Laurel, Oliver Hardy, Charles Hall.
THE LAUREL & HARDY MURDER CASE (Hal Roach-MGM, 1930) d James Parrott, s Stan Laurel, Oliver Hardy, Stanley Blystone, Tiny Sanford.
HOG WILD (Hal Roach-MGM, 1930) d James Parrott, s Stan Laurel, Oliver Hardy, Fay Holderness.
ANOTHER FINE MESS (Hal Roach-MGM, 1930) d James Parrott, s Stan Laurel, Oliver Hardy, Thelma Todd, James Finlayson.

CHICKENS COMES HOME (Hal Roach-MGM, 1931) d James Horne, s Stan Laurel, Oliver Hardy, Mae Busch, James Finlayson.
LAUGHING GRAVY (Hal Roach-MGM, 1931) d James Horne, s Stan Laurel, Oliver Hardy, Charles Hall.
OUR WIFE (Hal Roach-MGM, 1931) d James Horne, s Stan Laurel, Oliver Hardy, James Finlayson, Ben Turpin.
COME CLEAN (Hal Roach-MGM, 1931) d James Horne, s Stan Laurel, Oliver Hardy, Mae Busch, Gertrude Astor.
PARDON US (Hal Roach-MGM, 1931) [aka GAOL BIRDS] d James Parrott, s Stan Laurel, Oliver Hardy, James Finlayson.
ONE GOOD TURN (Hal Roach-MGM, 1931) d James Horne, s Stan Laurel, Oliver Hardy, James Finlayson, Billy Gilbert.
BEAU HUNKS (Hal Roach-MGM, 1931) d James Horne, s Stan Laurel, Oliver Hardy, Charles Middleton.
HELPMATES (Hal Roach-MGM, 1931) d James Parrott, s Stan Laurel, Oliver Hardy.
ANY OLD PORT (Hal Roach-MGM, 1932) d James Horne, s Stan Laurel, Oliver Hardy, Jacqueline Wells.
THE MUSIC BOX (Hal Roach-MGM, 1932) d James Parrott, s Stan Laurel, Oliver Hardy, Billy Gilbert, Charlie Hall.
THE CHIMP (Hal Roach-MGM, 1932) d James Parrott, s Stan Laurel, Oliver Hardy, Billy Gilbert.
COUNTY HOSPITAL (Hal Roach-MGM, 1932) d James Parrott, s Stan Laurel, Oliver Hardy, Billy Gilbert.
SCRAM (Hal Roach-MGM, 1932) d Raymond McCarey, s Stan Laurel, Oliver Hardy.
PACKUP YOUR TROUBLES (Hal Roach-MGM, 1932) d Raymond McCarey and George Marshall, s Stan Laurel, Oliver Hardy, Donald Dillaway, Mary Carr.
THEIR FIRST MISTAKE (Hal Roach-MGM, 1932) d George Marshall, s Stan Laurel, Oliver Hardy, Mae Busch, Billy Gilbert.
TOWED IN A HOLE (Hal Roach-MGM, 1933) d George Marshall, s Stan Laurel, Oliver Hardy, Billy Gilbert.
TWICE TWO (Hal Roach-MGM, 1933) d James Parrrott, s Stan Laurel, Oliver Hardy.
ME AND MY PAL (Hal Roach-MGM, 1933) d Charles Rogers and Lloyd French, s Stan Laurel, Oliver Hardy.
FRA DIAVOLO (Hal Roach-MGM, 1933) [aka THE DEVIL'S BROTHER] d Hal Roach and Charles Rogers, s Dennis King, Thelma Todd, Stan Laurel, Oliver Hardy.
THE MIDNIGHT PATROL (Hal Roach-MGM, 1933) d Lloyd French, s Stan Laurel, Oliver Hardy, Charles Rogers.
BUSY BODIES (Hal Roach-MGM, 1933) d Lloyd French, s Stan Laurel, Oliver Hardy.
DIRTY WORK (Hal Roach-MGM, 1933) d Lloyd French, s Stan Laurel, Oliver Hardy.

SONS OF THE DESERT (Hal Roach-MGM, 1933) [aka FRATERNALLY YOURS] d William A. Sesiter, s Stan Laurel, Oliver Hardy, Charlie Chase, Mae Busch.
THE PRIVATE LIFE OF OLIVER THE EIGHTH (Hal Roach-MGM, 1934) d Lloyd French, s Stan Laurel, Oliver Hardy, Mae Busch.
HOLLYWOOD PARTY (MGM, 1934) d Richard Boleslawski, s Stan Laurel, Oliver Hardy.
GOING BYE BYE (Hal Roach-MGM, 1934) d Charles Rogers, s Stan Laurel, Oliver Hardy, Walter Long, Mae Busch.
THEM THAR HILLS (Hal Roach-MGM, 1934) d Charles Rogers, s Stan Laurel, Oliver Hardy, Mae Busch, Charlie Hall, Billy Gilbert.
BABES IN TOYLAND (Hal Roach-MGM, 1934) [aka MARCH OF THE WOODEN SOLDIERS] d Gus Meins and Charles Rogers, s Charlotte Henry, Harry Kleinbach, Stan Laurel, Oliver Hardy.
THE LIVE GHOST (Hal Roach-MGM, 1934) d Charles Rogers, s Stan Laurel, Oliver Hardy, Mae Busch, Walter Long.
TIT FOR TAT (Hal Roach-MGM, 1934) d Charles Rogers, s Stan Laurel, Oliver Hardy, Mae Busch, Charlie Hall.
THE FIXER UPPERS (Hal Roach-MGM, 1934) d Charles Rogers, s Stan Laurel, Oliver Hardy, Mae Busch, Charles Middleton.
THICKER THAN WATER (Hal Roach-MGM, 1934) d James Horne, s Stan Laurel, Oliver Hardy, Daphne Pollard.
BONNIE SCOTLAND (Hal Roach-MGM, 1935) d James Horne, s Stan Laurel, Oliver Hardy, June Lang.
THE BOHEMIAN GIRL (Hal Roach-MGM, 1936) d James Horne and Charles Rogers, s Stan Laurel, Oliver Hardy, Antonio Morena, Jacqueline Wells.
OUR RELATIONS (Hal Roach-MGM, 1936) d Harry Lachman, s Stan Laurel, Oliver Hardy, Alan Hale.
WAY OUT WEST (Stan Laurel Productions for Hal Roach-MGM, 1937) d James Horne, s Stan Laurel, Oliver Hardy, Sharon Lynne, James Finlayson.
PICK A STAR (Hal Roach-MGM, 1937) d Edward Sedgwick, s Stan Laurel, Oliver Hardy, Jack Haley, Patsy Kelly.
SWISS MISS (Hal Roach-MGM, 1938) d John G. Blystone, s Stan Laurel, Oliver Hardy, Della Lind, Walter Woolf.
BLOCKHEADS (Stan Laurel Productions for Hal Roach-MGM, 1938) d John G. Blystone, s Stan Laurel, Oliver Hardy.
THE FLYING DEUCES (RKO Radio, 1939) d Edward Sutherland, s Stan Laurel, Oliver Hardy, Jean Parker.
A CHUMP AT OXFORD (Hal Roach-United Artists, 1940) d Alfred Goulding, s Stan Laurel, Oliver Hardy, Forrester Harvey, James Finlayson.
SAPS AT SEA (Hal Roach-United Artists, 1940) d Gordon Douglas, s Stan Laurel, Oliver Hardy, James Finlayson.
GREAT GUNS (20th Century-Fox, 1941) d Monty Banks, s Stan Laurel, Oliver Hary, Sheila Ryan.

A-HAUNTING WE WILL GO (20th Century-Fox, 1942) d Alfred Werker, s Stan Laurel, Oliver Hardy.
AIR RAID WARDENS (MGM, 1943) d Edward Sedgwick, s Stan Laurel, Oliver Hardy, Edgar Kennedy.
JITTERBUGS (20th Century-Fox, 1943) d Malcolm St. Clair, s Stan Laurel, Oliver Hardy, Vivian Blaine.
THE DANCING MASTERS (20th Century-Fox, 1943) d Malcolm St. Clair, s Stan Laurel, Oliver Hardy, Trudy Marshal.
THE BIG NOISE (20th Century-Fox, 1944) d Malcolm St. Clair, s Stan Laurel, Oliver Hardy, Doris Merrick.
NOTHING BUT TROUBLE (20th Century-Fox, 1944) d Sam Taylor, s Stan Laurel, Oliver Hardy, Mary Boland.
THE BULLFIGHTERS (20th Century-Fox, 1945) d Malcolm St. Clair, s Stan Laurel, Oliver Hardy, Margo Woode.
ATOLL K (Fortezza Films and Les Films Sirius, 1952) [aka ROBINSON CRUSOELAND and UTOPIA] d John Berry and Leo Joannon, s Stan Laurel, Oliver Hardy, Suzy Delair, Max Elloy.

435. LAWYER, THE
These movies were pilots for the PETROCELLI TV show (1974-75 on NBC).
THE LAWYER (NBC TV movie, 1970) d Sidney J. Furie, s Barry Newman, Harold Gould, Diana Muldaur.
NIGHT GAMES (Paramount Television, 1974) (NBC-TV movie) d Don Taylor, s Barry Newman, Susan Howard.

436. LEATHER PUSHER
This series of two-reel action pictures, circa 1930, features Kane Richmond.

437. LEATHERSTOCKING
Author James Fenimore Cooper's pioneer scout Leatherstocking (also known as Natty Bumppo, Hawkeye, Pathfinder and Deerslayer) was featured with his Mohican companion Chingachgook in five novels and also appeared in a number of movies. There was a Canadian television series in 1956 with John Hart, HAWKEYE AND THE LAST OF THE MOHICANS, and there was a BBC-TV serialization aired over PBS in the United States, THE LAST OF THE MOHICANS, in 1971. (A similar character is OLD SHATTERHAND; see that entry.)
LEATHERSTOCKING (Biograph, 1909) s James Kirkwood, Linda Arvidson.
THE LAST OF THE MOHICANS (Thanhouser, 1911)
DEERSLAYER (Vitagraph, 1913)
THE LAST OF THE MOHICANS (Associated Producers, 1920) d Maurice Tourneur and Clarence Brown, s Wallace Beery, Albert Roscoe, Barbara Bedford.
THE DEERSLAYER (Cameo, 1923) d Arthur Wellin, s Emil Mamelok, Bela Lugosi, Herta Heden.
LEATHERSTOCKING (Pathe, 1924) d George Seitz.

THE LAST OF THE MOHICANS (Mascot, 1932) [twelve chapters] d Ford Beebe, s Harry Carey, Hobart Bosworth.
THE LAST OF THE MOHICANS (United Artists, 1936) d George B. Seitz, s Randolph Scott, Binnie Barnes, Heather Angel.
THE PIONEERS (Monogram, 1941) d Al Herman, s Tex Ritter, Wanda McKay, Red Foley & His Saddle Pals.
THE DEERSLAYER (Republic, 1943) d Lew Landers, s Bruce Kellogg, Jean Parker, Larry Parks.
LAST OF THE REDMEN (Columbia, 1947) d George Sherman, s Michael O'Shea, Rich Vallin, Buster Crabbe.
THE PRAIRIE (Screen Guild, 1947) d Frank Wisbar, s Lenore Aubert, Alan Baxter, Russ Vincent.
IROQUOIS TRAIL (United Artists, 1950) d Phil Karlson, s George Montgomery, Brenda Marshall, Monte Blue.
THE PATHFINDER (Columbia, 1953) d Sidney Salkow, s George Montgomery, Helena Carter, Jay Silverheels.
THE DEERSLAYER (20th Century-Fox, 1957) d Kurt Newmann, s Lex Barker, Forrest Tucker, Cathy O'Donnell.
THE LONG RIFLE AND THE TOMAHAWK (ITC, 1964) d Sam Newfield and Sidney Salkow, s John Hart, Lon Chaney, John Vernon. Compilation of three episodes of the HAWKEYE AND THE LAST OF THE MOHICANS television series.
THE PATHFINDER AND THE MOHICAN (ITC, 1964) d Sam Newfield, s John Hart, Lon Chaney, Jonathan White. Compilation of three episodes of the HAWKEYE AND THE LAST OF THE MOHICANS television series.
ALONG THE MOHAWK TRAIL (ITC, 1964) d Sam Newfield, s John Hart, Lon Chaney, Bill Walsh. Compilation of three episodes of the HAWKEYE AND THE LAST OF THE MOHICANS television series.
THE REDMAN AND THE RENEGADES (ITC, 1964) d Sam Newfield, s John Hart, Lon Chaney, George Barnes. Compilation of three episodes of the HAWKEYE AND THE LAST OF THE MOHICANS television series.
THE LAST OF THE MOHICANS (International German/Balcazar Cineproduzione, 1965) d Harald Reinl, s Jaochim Fuchsberger, Karin Dor, Carl Lange.
LAST OF THE MOHICANS (NBC-TV/Schick Sunn Classics, 1977) d James L. Conway, s Steve Forrest, Ned Romero, Andrew Prine.
THE DEERSLAYER (NBC-TV/Schick Sunn Classics, 1978) d Dick Friedenbert, s Steve Forrest, Ned Romero, John Anderson.

438. LEGEND OF NIGGER CHARLEY, THE
Plantation life and slavery in the old South are depicted in these movies.
THE LEGEND OF NIGGER CHARLEY (Paramount, 1972) d Martin Goldman, s Fred Williamson, D'Urville Martin.
THE SOUL OF NIGGER CHARLIE (Paramount, 1973) d Larry G. Spangler, s Fred Williamson, D'Urville Martin, Denise Nichols.

439. LETHAL WEAPON
These stylish action films showcase a psychopathic cop with a methodical partner.
LETHAL WEAPON (Warner Brothers, 1987) d Richard Donner, s Mel Gibson, Danny Glover.
LETHAL WEAPON 2 (Warner Brothers, 1989) d Richard Donner, s Mel Gibson, Danny Glover.

440. LEW ARCHER
Ross MacDonald (Kenneth Millar) wrote a series of mystery novels featuring the persistent private eye. Brian Keith played the hero in a television series on NBC.
HARPER (Warner Brothers, 1966) d Jack Smight, s Paul Newman, Lauren Bacall.
THE DROWNING POOL (Warner Brothers, 1975) d Stuart Rosenberg, s Paul Newman, Joanne Woodward.

441. LICENSED TO KILL
British secret agent Charles Vine has to protect a Swedish inventor, in the first picture.
LICENSED TO KILL (Alistair Film/Embassy, 1965) d Lindsay Shonteff, s Tom Adams, Karel Staepanek, Veronica Hurst.
WHERE THE BULLETS FLY (Puck Films/Embassy, 1966) d John Gilling, s Tom Adams, Dawn Addams.

442. LIFE WITH THE LYONS
Based on the British radio series, the Lyons family is so batty -- in the first film -- that a new landlord refuses to sign a lease.
LIFE WITH THE LYONS (Hammer, 1954) d Val Guest, s Bebe Daniels, Ben Lyon, Barbara Lyon, Richard Lyon, Horace Percival.
THE LYONS IN PARIS (Hammer, 1955) d Val Guest, s Bebe Daniels, Ben Lyon, Barbara Lyon, Richard Lyon.

443. LIGHTNING BILL CARSON
These B Western films are about a government agent played by Tim McCoy.
LIGHTNIN' BILL CARSON (Puritan, 1936) d Sam Newfield, s Tim McCoy, Lois January.
LIGHTNING CARSON RIDES AGAIN (Victory, 1938) d Sam Newfield, s Tim McCoy, Joan Barclay.
SIX-GUN TRAIL (Victory, 1938) d Sam Newfield, s Tim McCoy, Nora Lane.
CODE OF THE CACTUS (Victory, 1939) d Sam Newfield, s Tim McCoy, Dorothy Short.
TEXAS WILDCATS (Victory, 1939) d Sam Newfield, s Tim McCoy, Joan Barclay.
OUTLAW'S PARADISE (Victory, 1939) d Sam Newfield, s Tim McCoy, Joan Barclay.

FIGHTING RENEGADE (Victory, 1939) d Sam Newfield, s Tim McCoy, Joyce Bryant.
STRAIGHT SHOOTER (Victory, 1939) d Sam Newfield, s Tim McCoy, Julie Sheldon.

444. LILIES OF THE FIELD
A handyman is conned into building a chapel for a group of nuns.
LILIES OF THE FIELD (UA, 1963) d Ralph Nelson, s Sidney Poitier, Lilia Skala.
CHRISTMAS LILIES OF THE FIELD (1979) (TV movie) d Ralph Nelson, s Billy Dee Williams, Maria Schel.

445. LINDA LOVELACE
The actress is best known for X-rated fare such as DEEP THROAT. Here she plays herself.
LINDA LOVELACE MEETS MISS JONES (LMMJ, 1975) d Angelo Spaveni, s Linda Lovelace.
LINDA LOVELACE FOR PRESIDENT (General Film, 1975) d Claudio Guzman, s Linda Lovelace.

446. LITTLE ANNIE ROONEY
The films are based on the comic strip, begun in 1929, about a twelve-year-old girl and her adventures.
LITTLE ANNIE ROONEY (United Artists, 1925) d William Beaudine, s Mary Pickford.
MISS ANNIE ROONEY (United Artists, 1942) d Edwin L. Marin, s Shirley Temple.

447. LITTLE BILLY
Keystone Studios produced a series of short subjects featuring Paul Jacobs as Little Billy, a child comedian. The list is incomplete. The series later switched to the Sterling banner at Universal.
LITTLE BILLY'S TRIUMPH (Keystone, 1914) d Robert Thornby, s Paul Jacobs.
LITTLE BILLY'S STRATEGY (Keystone, 1914) d Robert Thornby, s Paul Jacobs.
LITTLE BILLY'S CITY COUSIN (Keystone, 1914) d Robert Thornby, s Paul Jacobs.

448. LITTLE FOXES, THE
Lillian Hellman's play of the Hubbard family, post-Civil War schemers, inspired these films.
THE LITTLE FOXES (RKO, 1941) d William Wyler, s Bette Davis, Herbert Marshall, Charles Dingle.
ANOTHER PART OF THE FOREST (Universal-International Pictures, 1948) d Michael Gordon, s Frederic March, Ann Blyth.

449. LITTLE GIRLS BLUE
These are adult films about a schoolgirl's fantasies.
LITTLE GIRLS BLUE (VCX, 1978) d Joanna Williams, s K.C. Winters, Tamara Morgan.
LITTLE GIRLS BLUE PART II (VCX, 1983) d Joanna Williams, s Kathleen Kristel, Barbara Clouds.

450. LITTLE HOUSE ON THE PRAIRIE
Laura Ingalls Wilder wrote a series of books about family life on the American prairies a century ago. There was an NBC television series which was broadcast 1976-83, of which these pictures are a part.
LITTLE HOUSE ON THE PRAIRIE (NBC Productions, 1974) (NBC-TV movie) d Michael Landon, s Michael Landon, Karen Grassle, Melissa Gilbert.
LITTLE HOUSE: LOOK BACK TO YESTERDAY (NBC Productions, TV-movie, 1983) d Victor French, s Melissa Gilbert, Dean Butler, Victor French, Michael Landon.
LITTLE HOUSE; THE LAST FAREWELL (NBC Productions, TV movie, 1984) d Michael Landon, s Michael Landon, Karen Grassle, Melissa Gilvert, Dean Butler.

451. LITTLE ORPHAN ANNIE
Harold Gray in 1924 created a newspaper comic strip about an orphan girl and her dog Sandy and a bald benefactor Daddy Warbucks. A radio show aired 1931-43. There have also been two stage plays based on the character.
LITTLE ORPHAN ANNIE (RKO, 1932) d John Robertson, s May Robson, Mitzi Green, Edgar Kennedy.
ANNIE (Columbia, 1982) d John Huston, s Aileen Quinn, Carol Burnett.

452. LITTLE ORPHAN DUSTY
These are sex films.
LITTLE ORPHAN DUSTY (TVX, 1976) d Bob Chinn, s Rhonda Jo Petty.
LITTLE ORPHAN DUSTY PART II (Caballero, 1982) d Jacov Jacovi, s Rhonda Jo Petty, John C. Holmes.

453. LITTLE TOUGH GUYS
The gang adventures of Tom, Pig, Ape and String are featured in these movies, which were distributed simultaneous with the EASTSIDE KIDS series. (See also BOWERY BOYS, DEAD END KIDS and JUNIOR G-MEN.)
LITTLE TOUGH GUYS (Universal, 1938) d Harold Young, s Billy Halop, Huntz Hall, Gabriel Dell, Bernard Punsley, David Gorcey.
CALL A MESSENGER (Universal, 1939) d Arthur Lubin, s Billy Halop, Huntz Hall, David Gorcey.
YOU'RE NOT SO TOUGH (Universal, 1940) d Joe May, s Billy Halop, Huntz Hall, Gabriel Dell, Bernard Punsley, Bobby Jordan.
GIVE US WINGS (Universal, 1940) d Charles Lamont, s Billy Halop, Huntz Hall, Gabriel Dell, Bernard Punsley, Bobby Jordan.

HIT THE ROAD (Universal, 1941) d Joe May, s Billy Halop, Huntz Hall, Gabriel Dell, Bernard Punsley.
SEA RAIDERS (Universal, 1941) d Ford Beebe and John Rawlins, s Billy Halop, Huntz Hall, Gabriel Dell, Bernard Punsley.
MOB TOWN (Universal, 1941) d William Nigh, s Billy Halop, Huntz Hall, Gabriel Dell, Bernard Punsley.
TOUGH AS THEY COME (Universal, 1942) d William Nigh, s Billy Halop, Huntz Hall, Gabriel Dell, Bernard Punsley.
MUG TOWN (Universal, 1943) d Ray Taylor, s Billy Halop, Huntz Hall, Gabriel Dell, Bernard Punsley.
KEEP 'EM SLUGGING (Universal, 1943) d Christy Cabanne, s Bobby Jordan, Huntz Hall, Gabriel Dell.

454. LITTLE WOMEN
Louisa May Alcott wrote several 19th century novels of Meg, Jo, Beth and Amy and their childhood and maturity in Concord, Massachusetts.
LITTLE WOMEN (Moss, 1917) d Alexander Butler and G.B. Samuelson, s Ruby Miller, Mary Lincoln, Muriel Myers, Daisy Bussell.
LITTLE WOMEN (Paramount/Artcraft, 1918) d Harley Knoles, s Dorothy Bernard, Isabel Lamon, Lillian Hall.
LITTLE WOMEN (RKO, 1933) d George Cukor, s Katharine Hepburn, Frances Dee, Jean Parker, Joan Bennett.
LITTLE MEN (Mascot, 1935) d Phil Rosen, s Ralph Morgan, Erin O'Brien-Moore.
LITTLE MEN (RKO, 1940) d Norman Z. MacLeod, s Kay Francis, Jack Oakie, George Bancroft.
LITTLE WOMEN (MGM, 1949) d Mervyn LeRoy, s June Allyson, Janet Leigh, Margaret O'Brien, Elizabeth Taylor.

455. LIVING DEAD
After the success of NIGHT OF THE LIVING DEAD, George Romero and partners came to a parting of the ways, they retaining the rights to the words LIVING DEAD, he to the DEAD designation. (See NIGHT OF THE LIVING DEAD.)
NIGHT OF THE LIVING DEAD (Image Ten, 1968) d George A. Romero, s Duane Jones, Judith O'Dea.
RETURN OF THE LIVING DEAD (Hemdale/Vox, 1985) d Dan O'Bannon, s Clu Gulager, James Karen.

456. LONE RANGER, THE
A Texas Ranger left for dead is revived by an Indian. Donning a mask, he vows to fight for truth and justice in the early American West. The duo appeared on radio (1933-55), television (1949-57 and 1990-), juvenile novels (1936-57), comic books (1948-62, 1969-77) and a newspaper comic strip (1938-71). Wrather entries below are strung-together television episodes.

THE LONE RANGER (Republic, 1938) (fifteen chapters) d William Witney and John English, s Lee Powell, Herman Briz, Chief Thundercloud, Lynne Roberts.
THE LONE RANGER RIDES AGAIN (Republic, 1939) (fifteen chapters) d William Witney and John English, s Robert Livingston, Chief Thundercloud, Duncan Renaldo.
THE LEGEND OF THE LONE RANGER (Apex, 1949) d George B. Seitz Jr., sClayton Moore, Jay Silverheels, Glenn Strange.
THE LONE RANGER (Warner Brothers, 1956) d Stuart Heisler, s Clayton Moore, Jay Silverheels, Lyle Bettger, Bonita Granville.
THE LONE RANGER AND THE LOST CITY OF GOLD (United Artists, 1958) d Lesley Selander, s Clayton Moore, Jay Silverheels, Douglas Kennedy.
COUNT THE CLUES (Wrather, 1956) d Earl Bellamy and Oscar Rudolph, s Clayton Moore, Jay Silverheels.
THE LAWLESS (Wrather, 1956) d Earl Bellamy and Oscar Rudolph, s Clayton Moore, Jay Silverheels.
JUSTICE OF THE WEST (Wrather, 1956) d Earl Bellamy and Oscar Rudolph, s Clayton Moore, Jay Silverheels.
THE SEARCH (Wrather, 1956) d Earl Bellamy, s Clayton Moore, Jay Silverheels.
TRACKERS (Wrather, 1956) d Earl Bellamy and Oscar Rudolph, s Clayton Moore, Jay Silverheels.
MORE THAN MAGIC (Wrather, 1956) d Earl Bellamy and Oscar Rudolph, s Clayton Moore, Jay Silverheels.
NOT ABOVE SUSPICION (Wrather, 1956) d Earl Bellamy and Oscar Rudolph, s Clayton Moore, Jay Silverheels.
ONE MASK TOO MANY (Wrather, 1956) d Earl Bellamy and Oscar Rudolph, s Clayton Moore, Jay Silverheels.
TALE OF GOLD (Wrather, 1956) d Earl Bellamy, s Clayton Moore, Jay Silverheels.
THE TRUTH (Wrather, 1956) d Earl Bellamy and Oscar Rudolph, s Clayton Moore, Jay Silverheels.
VENGEANCE VOW (Wrather, 1956) d Earl Bellamy, s Clayton Moore, Jay Silverheels.
THE LEGEND OF THE LONE RANGER (Universal/Associated Film, 1981) d William A. Fraker, s Klinton Spilsbury, Michael Horse, Jason Robards.

457. LONE RIDER
These are B Westerns featuring a masked avenger.
THE LONE RIDER RIDES ON (PRC, 1941) d Sam Newfield, s George Houston, Al "Fuzzy" St. John, Hillary Brooke.
THE LONE RIDER CROSSES THE RIO (PRC, 1941) d Sam Newfield, s George Houston, Al "Fuzzy" St. John, Roquell Verrin.
THE LONE RIDER IN GHOST TOWN (PRC, 1941) d Sam Newfield, s George Houston, Al "Fuzzy" St. John, Alaine Brandes.

THE LONE RIDER IN FRONTIER FURY (PRC, 1941) d Sam Newfield, s George Houston, Al "Fuzzy" St. John, Hillary Brooke.
THE LONE RIDER AMBUSHED (PRC, 1941) d Sam Newfield, s George Houston, Al "Fuzzy" St. John, Maxine Leslie.
THE LONE RIDER FIGHTS BACK (PRC, 1941) d Sam Newfield, s George Houston, Al "Fuzzy" St. John, Dorothy Short.
THE LONE RIDER AND THE BANDIT (PRC, 1941) d Sam Newfield, s George Houston, Al "Fuzzy" St. John, Vicki Lester.
THE LONE RIDER IN BORDER ROUNDUP (PRC, 1942) d Sam Newfield, s George Houston, Dennis Moore, Al "Fuzzy" St. John, Patricia Knox.
THE LONE RIDER IN CHEYENNE (PRC, 1942) d Sam Newfield, s George Houston, Al "Fuzzy" St. John, Ella Neal.
THE LONE RIDER IN TEXAS JUSTICE (PRC, 1942) d Sam Newfield, s George Houston, Al "Fuzzy" St. John, Claire Rochelle.
OUTLAWS OF BORDER PASS (PRC, 1942) dSam Newfield, s George Houston, Al "Fuzzy" St. John, Marjorie Manners.
WILD HORSE RUSTLERS (PRC, 1943) d Sam Newfield, s Robert Livingston, Al "Fuzzy" St. John, Linda Johnson.
DEATH RIDES THE PLAINS (PRC, 1943) d Sam Newfield, s Robert Livingston, Al "Fuzzy" St. John, Nica Doret.
WOLVES OF THE RANGE (PRC, 1943) d Sam Newfield, s Robert Livingston, Al "Fuzzy" St. John, Frances Gladwin.
LAW OF THE SADDLE (PRC, 1943) d Melville DeLay, s Robert Livingston, Al "Fuzzy" St. John, Betty Miles.
RAIDERS OF RED GAP (PRC, 1943) d Sam Newfield, s Robert Livingston, Al "Fuzzy" St. John, Myrna Dell.

458. LONESOME LUKE
Harold Lloyd appeared in more than 150 one- and two-reel silent short comedies made between 1915-19, a good number of them in the Lonesome Luke personna which preceeded his "glasses" character (see also HAROLD LLOYD). This list is incomplete.
LONESOME LUKE, SOCIAL GANGSTER (Hal Roach/Pathe, 1915) s Harold Lloyd.
LUKE LEANS TO THE LITERARY (Hal Roach/Pathe, 1916) d Hal Roach, s Harold Lloyd.
LUKE LUGS LUGGAGE (Hal Roach/Pathe, 1916) d Hal Roach, s Harold Lloyd.
LUKE LOLLS IN LUXURY (Hal Roach/Pathe, 1916) d Hal Roach, s Harold Lloyd.
LUKE THE CANDY CUT-UP (Hal Roach/Pathe, 1916) d Hal Roach, s Harold Lloyd.
LUKE FOILS THE VILLAIN (Hal Roach/Pathe, 1916) d Hal Roach, s Harold Lloyd.
LUKE AND THE RURAL ROUGHNECKS (Hal Roach/Pathe, 1916) d Hal Roach, s Harold Lloyd.

204 MOTION PICTURE SERIES & SEQUELS

LUKE PIPES THE PIPPINS (Hal Roach/Pathe, 1916) d Hal Roach, s Harold Lloyd.
LONESOME LUKE, CIRCUS KING (Hal Roach/Pathe, 1916) d Hal Roach, s Harold Lloyd.
LUKE'S DOUBLE (Hal Roach/Pathe, 1916) d Hal Roach, s Harold Lloyd.
LUKE AND THE BOMB THROWERS (Hal Roach/Pathe, 1916) d Hal Roach, s Harold Lloyd.
LUKE'S LATE LUNCHERS (Hal Roach/Pathe, 1916) d Hal Roach, s Harold Lloyd.
LUKE LAUGHS LAST (Hal Roach/Pathe, 1916) d Hal Roach, s Harold Lloyd.
LUKE'S FATAL FLIVVER (Hal Roach/Pathe, 1916) d Hal Roach, s Harold Lloyd.
LUKE'S SOCIETY MIXUP (Hal Roach/Pathe, 1916) d Hal Roach, s Harold Lloyd.
LUKE'S WASHFUL WAITING (Hal Roach/Pathe, 1916) d Hal Roach, s Harold Lloyd.
LUKE RIDES ROUGHSHOD (Hal Roach/Pathe, 1916) d Hal Roach, s Harold Lloyd.
LUKE, CRYSTAL GAZER (Hal Roach/Pathe, 1916) d Hal Roach, s Harold Lloyd.
LUKE'S LOST LAMB (Hal Roach/Pathe, 1916) d Hal Roach, s Harold Lloyd.
LUKE DOES THE MIDWAY (Hal Roach/Pathe, 1916) d Hal Roach, s Harold Lloyd.
LUKE JOINS THE NAVY (Hal Roach/Pathe, 1916) d Hal Roach, s Harold Lloyd.
LUKE AND THE MERMAIDS (Hal Roach/Pathe, 1916) d Hal Roach, s Harold Lloyd.
LUKE'S SPEEDY CLUB LIFE (Hal Roach/Pathe, 1916) d Hal Roach, s Harold Lloyd.
LUKE'S PREPAREDNESS PREPARATION (Hal Roach/Pathe, 1916) d Hal Roach, s Harold Lloyd.
LUKE AND THE BANT-TAILS (Hal Roach/Pathe, 1916) d Hal Roach, s Harold Lloyd.
LUKE, THE CHAUFFEUR (Hal Roach/Pathe, 1916) d Hal Roach, s Harold Lloyd.
LUKE, GLADIATOR (Hal Roach/Pathe, 1916) d Hal Roach, s Harold Lloyd.
LUKE, PATIENT PROVIDER (Hal Roach/Pathe, 1916) d Hal Roach, s Harold Lloyd.
LUKE'S NEWSIE KNOWKOUT (Hal Roach/Pathe, 1916) d Hal Roach, s Harold Lloyd.
LUKE'S MOVIE MUDDLE (Hal Roach/Pathe, 1916) d Hal Roach, s Harold Lloyd.
LUKE, RANK IMPERSONATOR (Hal Roach/Pathe, 1916) d Hal Roach, s Harold Lloyd.
LUKE'S FIREWORKS FIZZLE (Hal Roach/Pathe, 1916) d Hal Roach, s Harold Lloyd.

LUKE LOCATES THE LOOT (Hal Roach/Pathe, 1916) d Hal Roach, s Harold Lloyd.
LUKE'S SHATTERED SLEEP (Hal Roach/Pathe, 1916) d Hal Roach, s Harold Lloyd.
LUKE'S LOST LIBERTY (Hal Roach/Pathe, 1917) d Hal Roach, s Harold Lloyd.
LOMESOME LUKE'S LIVELY LIFE (Hal Roach/Pathe, 1917) d Hal Roach, s Harold Lloyd.
LUKE'S BUSY DAY (Hal Roach/Pathe, 1917) d Hal Roach, s Harold Lloyd.
LUKE'S TROLLEY TROUBLES (Hal Roach/Pathe, 1917) d Hal Roach, s Harold Lloyd.
LONESOME LUKE ON TIN CAN ALLEY (Hal Roach/Pathe, 1917) d Hal Roach, s Harold Lloyd.
LONESOME LUKE'S HONEYMOON (Hal Roach/Pathe, 1917) d Hal Roach, s Harold Lloyd.
LONESOME LUKE -- PLUMBER (Hal Roach/Pathe, 1917) d Hal Roach, s Harold Lloyd.
STOP! LUKE! LISTEN! (Hal Roach/Pathe, 1917) d Hal Roach, s Harold Lloyd.
LONESOME LUKE -- MESSENGER (Hal Roach/Pathe, 1917) d Hal Roach, s Harold Lloyd.
LONESOME LUKE -- MECHANIC (Hal Roach/Pathe, 1917) d Hal Roach, s Harold Lloyd.
LONESOME LUKE'S WILD WOMEN (Hal Roach/Pathe, 1917) d Hal Roach, s Harold Lloyd.
LONESOME LUKE LOSES PATIENTS (Hal Roach/Pathe, 1917) d Hal Roach, s Harold Lloyd.
LONESOME LUKE FROM LONDON TO LARAMIE (Hal Roach/Pathe, 1917) d Hal Roach, s Harold Lloyd.
LUKE'S LAST LIBERTY (Hal Roach/Pathe, 1917) d Hal Roach, s Harold Lloyd.
LUKE'S BUSY DAYS (Hal Roach/Pathe, 1917) d Hal Roach, s Harold Lloyd.
LUKE'S TROLLEY TROUBLE (Hal Roach/Pathe, 1917) d Hal Roach, s Harold Lloyd.
LONESOME LUKE -- LAWYER (Hal Roach/Pathe, 1917) d Hal Roach, s Harold Lloyd.
LUKE WINS YE LADYE FAIRE (Hal Roach/Pathe, 1917) d Hal Roach, s Harold Lloyd.
LONESOME LUKE'S LIVELY LIFE (Hal Roach/Pathe, 1917) d Hal Roach, s Harold Lloyd.

459. LONE STAR SERIES
John Wayne frequently plays the character Singin' Sandy in these B Westerns.
RIDERS OF DESTINY (Monogram, 1933) d Robert N. Bradbury, s John Wayne, Cecilia Parker, George "Gabby" Hayes.
SAGEBRUSH TRAIL (Monogram, 1933) d Armand Schaefer, s John Wayne, Nancy Shubert.

WEST OF THE DIVIDE (Monogram, 1933) d Robert N. Bradbury, s John
    Wayne, Virginia Brown Faire, George "Gabby" Hayes.
LUCKY TEXAN (Monogram, 1934) d Robert N. Bradbury, s John Wayne,
    Barbara Sheldon, George "Gabby" Hayes.
BLUE STEEL (Monogram, 1934) d Robert N. Bradbury, s John Wayne,
    Eleanor Hunt, George "Gabby" Hayes.
THE MAN FROM UTAH (Monogram, 1934) d Robert N. Bradbury, s John
    Wayne, Polly Ann Young, George "Gabby" Hayes.
RANDY RIDES ALONE (Monogram, 1934) d Harry Fraser, s John Wayne,
    Alberta Vaughn, George "Gabby" Hayes.
THE STAR PACKER (Monogram, 1934) d Robert N. Bradbury, s John Wayne,
    George "Gabby" Hayes, Verna Hillie.
THE TRAIL BEYOND (Monogram, 1934) d Robert N. Bradbury, s John
    Wayne, Verna Hillie, Noah Beery.
'NEATH ARIZONA SKIES (Monogram, 1934) d Harry Fraser, s John Wayne,
    George "Gabby" Hayes, Sheila Terry.
LAWLESS FRONTIER (Monogram, 1934) d Robert N. Bradbury, s John
    Wayne, George "Gabby" Hayes, Sheila Terry.
TEXAS TERROR (Monogram, 1935) d Robert N. Bradbury, s John Wayne,
    George "Gabby" Hayes, Lucille Browne.
RAINBOW VALLEY (Monogram, 1935) d Robert N. Bradbury, s John
    Wayne, George "Gabby" Hayes, Lucille Browne.
PARADISE CANYON (Monogram, 1935) d Carl Pierson, s John Wayne,
    Marion Burns.
THE DAWN RIDERS (Monogram, 1935) d Robert N. Bradbury, s John
    Wayne, Marion Burns.
DESERT TRAIL (Monogram, 1935) d Collin Lewis, s John Wayne, Mary
    Kornman.

460. LONE STAR SERIES
Paired in these programmer Westerns are Jack Randall and Frank Yaconelli.
WILD HORSE CANYON (Monogram, 1938) d Robert Hill, s Jack Randall,
    Frank Yaconelli, Dorothy Short.
DRIFTING WESTWARD (Monogram, 1939) d Robert Hill, s Jack Randall,
    Frank Yaconelli, Edna Duran.
TRIGGER SMITH (Monogram, 1939) d Alan James, s Jack Randall, Frank
    Yaconelli, Joyce Bryant.
ACROSS THE PLAINS (Monogram, 1939) d Spencer Bennett, s Jack Randall,
    Frank Yaconelli, Joyce Bryant.
PIONEER DAYS (Monogram, 1940) d Harry S. Webb, s Jack Randall, Frank
    Yaconelli, June Wilkins.
THE CHEYENNE KID (Monogram, 1940) d Raymond K. Johnson, s Jack
    Randall, Frank Yaconelli, Louise Stanley.
WILD HORSE RANGE (Monogram, 1940) d Raymond K. Johnson, s Jack
    Randall, Frank Yaconelli, Phyllis Ruth.

461. LONE WOLF, THE

Louis Joseph Vance created the ex-jewel thief turned gentleman crime solver Michael Lanyard for seven books written 1914-34.
THE LONE WOLF (Selznick, 1917) s Bert Lytell.
THE FALSE FACES (Paramount, 1919) s Henry B. Walthall.
THE LONE WOLF'S DAUGHTER (Hodkinson, 1919)
THE LONE WOLF (Associated Exchange, 1924) s Jack Holt.
THE LONE WOLF RETURNS (Columbia, 1926) d Ralph Ince, s Bert Lytell, Billie Dove.
ALIAS THE LONE WOLF (Columbia, 1927) d Edward H. Griffiths, s Bert Lytell, Lois Wilson.
THE LONE WOLF'S DAUGHTER (Columbia, 1929) s Bert Lytell, Gertrude Olmstead.
LAST OF THE LONE WOLF (Columbia, 1930) d Richard Boleslavsky, s Bert Lytell, Patsy Ruth Miller.
CHEATERS AT PLAY (Fox, 1932) d Hamilton MacFadden, s Thomas Meighan, Charlotte Greenwood.
THE LONE WOLF RETURNS (Columbia, 1935) d R. William Neill, s Melvyn Douglas, Gail Patrick.
THE LONE WOLF IN PARIS (Columbia, 1938) d Albert S. Rogell, s Francis Lederer, Frances Drake.
THE LONE WOLF SPY HUNT (Columbia, 1939) d Peter Godfrey, s Warren William, Ida Lupino.
THE LONE WOLF STRIKES (Columbia, 1940) d Sidney Salkow, s Warren Williams, Joan Perry.
THE LONE WOLF MEETS A LADY (Columbia, 1940) d Sidney Salkow, s Warren Williams, Jean Muir.
THE LONE WOLF TAKES A CHANCE (Columbia, 1941) d Sidney Salkow, s Warren William, June Storey.
THE LONE WOLF KEEPS A DATE (Columbia, 1941) d Sidney Salkow, s Warren William, Frances Robinson.
SECRETS OF THE LONE WOLF (Columbia, 1941) d Edward Dmytryk, s Warren William, Ruth Ford.
ONE DANGEROUS NIGHT (Columbia, 1943) d Michael Gordon, s Warren William, Marguerite Chapman.
PASSPORT TO SUEZ (Columbia, 1943) d Andre DeToth, s Warren William, Ann Savage.
THE NOTORIOUS LONE WOLF (Columbia, 1946) s Gerald Mohr, Janis Carter.
THE LONE WOLF IN LONDON (Columbia, 1947) d Leslie Goodwins, s Gerald Mohr, Nancy Saunders.
THE LONE WOLF IN MEXICO (Columbia, 1947) d D. Ross Lederman, s Gerald Mohr, Sheila Ryan.
THE LONE WOLF AND HIS LADY (Columbia, 1949) d John Hoffman, s Ron Randell.

462. LOOSE ENDS
These are sex films.

LOOSE ENDS (4-Play, 1985) d Bruce Seven, s Janey Robbins, Erica Boyer, Harry Reems.
LOOSE ENDS II (4-Play, 1986) d Bruce Seven, s Penny Morgan, Marc Wallice.
LOOSE ENDS III (4-Play, 1987) s Erica Boyer, Tom Byron.
LOOSE ENDS IV (4-Play, 1988) s Bionca, John Leslie.
LOOSE ENDS V (4-Play, 1988) s Barbii, John Leslie.

463. LORD PETER WIMSEY
Dorothy L. Sayers' gentleman detective Lord Peter Wimsey has also been featured on Public Television's MYSTERY (BBC-originated, 1970-75) with Ian Carmichael and with Edward Petherbridge (in another BBC mini-series).
THE SILENT PASSENGER (Associated British, 1935) d Reginald Denham, s Peter Haddon, John Loder, Mary Newland.
THE HAUNTED HONEYMOON (MGM, 1940) [aka BUSMAN'S HONEYMOON] d Arthur Woods, s Robert Montgomery, Constance Cummings.

464. LONGEST DAY, THE
The Cornelius Ryan book *The Longest Day*, about the Allied invasion of Normandy, inspired the first picture, while George Bar's *Epitaph for an Enemy* was the basis for the second.
THE LONGEST DAY (20th Century-Fox, 1962) d Ken Annakin, Andrew Marton and Bernhard Wicki, s John Wayne, Robert Mitchum, Robert Ryan.
UP FROM THE BEACH (20th Century-Fox, 1965) d Robert Parrish, s Cliff Robertson, Red Buttons, Irina Demick.

465. LOVE BOAT, THE
The television program THE LOVE BOAT, which aired over ABC from 1977-86, had a regular shipboard crew of Captain Merrill Stubing (Gavin MacLeod), Dr. Adam Bricker (Bernie Kopell), "Gopher" Smith (Fred Grandy), cruise director Julie McCoy (Lauren Tewes) and others. It also spotlighted guests' romantic adventures each week.
THE LOVE BOAT (Douglas S. Cramer, 1976) (ABC-TV movie) d Alan Myerson and Richard Kinon, s Don Adams, Tom Bosley.
THE LOVE BOAT II (Aaron Spelling Productions, 1977) (ABC-TV movie) d Hy Averback, s Ken Berry, Bert Convy.
THE LOVE BOAT: A VALENTINE VOYAGE (CBS-TV movie, 1990)

466. LOVE BUG, THE
A lovable Volkswagen Beetle is the hero.
THE LOVE BUG (Buena Vista, 1969) d Robert Stevenson, s Dean Jones, Michelle Lee, Buddy Hackett.
HERBIE RIDES AGAIN (Buena Vista, 1974) d Robert Stevenson, s Helen Hayes, Ken Berry.

HERBIE GOES TO MONTE CARLO (Buena Vista, 1977) d Vincent McEveety, s Dean Jones, Don Knotts, Julie Sommars.
HERBIE GOES BANANAS (Buena Vista, 1980) d Vincent McEveety, s Charlie Martin Smith, Steven W. Burns.

467. LOVE STORY
These pictures are based on Erich Segal's tragic romance novel about Oliver Barrett IV and Jenny Cavileri.
LOVE STORY (Paramount, 1970) Arthur Hiller, s Ali MacGraw, Ryan O'Neal.
OLIVER'S STORY (Paramount, 1978) d John Korty, s Ryan O'Neal, Candice Bergen.

467A. LT. DARING
These are British silent films.
LT. DARING AND THE SECRET SERVICE AGENTS (1912) s Percy Moran.
LT. DARING AND THE DANCING GIRL (1912) s Percy Moran.
LT. DARING AND THE PLANS OF THE MINEFIELD (1912) s Percy Moran.

468. LUST IN SPACE
These are X-rated pictures set on the planet Zitcom.
LUST IN SPACE (Paradise, 1985) d Miles Kidder, s Lana Burner, Harry Reems.
LUST IN SPACE II (Paradise, 1985) s Lana Burner, Harry Reems.

On a vine tour of the jungle is a decidedly off-beat Jane (Bo Derek) and her muscular Tarzan (Miles O'Keeffe) in TARZAN, THE APE MAN (1981).

469. MA AND PA KETTLE
When Betty MacDonald's novel *The Egg and I* (1945) was made into a film, two secondary bumpkin characters played by Marjorie Main and Percy Kilbride stole the show and were soon given a series of their own.

THE EGG AND I (Universal, 1947) d Chester Erskine, s Claudette Colbert, Fred MacMurray, Marjorie Main, Percy Kilbride.
MA AND PA KETTLE (Universal, 1949) d Charles Lamont, s Marjorie Main, Percy Kilbride.
MA AND PA KETTLE GO TO TOWN (Universal, 1950) d Charles Lamont, s Marjorie Main, Percy Kilbride.
MA AND PA KETTLE BACK ON THE FARM (Universal, 1951) d Edward Sedgwick, s Marjorie Main, Percy Kilbride.
MA AND PA KETTLE AT THE FAIR (Universal, 1952) d Charles Barton, s Marjorie Main, Percy Kilbride.
MA AND PA KETTLE ON VACATION (Universal, 1953) d Charles Barton, s Marjorie Main, Percy Kilbride.
MA AND PA KETTLE AT HOME (Universal, 1954) d Charles Barton, s Marjorie Main, Percy Kilbride.
MA AND PA KETTLE AT WAIKIKI (Universal, 1955) d Lee Sholem, s Marjorie Main, Percy Kilbride.
THE KETTLES IN THE OZARKS (Universal, 1956) d Charles Lamont, s Marjorie Main, Arthur Hunnicutt.
THE KETTLES ON OLD MACDONALD'S FARM (Universal, 1957) d Virgil Vogel, s Marjorie Main, Parker Fennelly.

470. MABEL
Silent screen actress Mabel Normand (1894-1930) was featured in a series of comedies, some of which she co-directed with Mack Sennett or Charlie Chaplin. Later entries team her with Roscoe "FATTY" Arbuckle. The list may be incomplete.

MABEL'S ADVENTURES (Keystone, 1912) d Mack Sennett, s Mabel Normand.
MABEL'S STRATAGEM (Keystone, 1912) d Mack Sennett, s Mabel Normand.
MABEL'S LOVERS (Keystone, 1912) d Mack Sennett, s Mabel Normand.
SAVING MABEL'S DAD (Keystone, 1913) s Mabel Normand.
MABEL'S AWFUL MISTAKE (Keystone, 1913) d Mack Sennett, s Mabel Normand, Mack Sennett.
MABEL'S HEROES (Keystone, 1913) d Mack Sennett, s Mabel Normand.
MABEL'S NEW HERO (Keystone, 1913) d Mack Sennett, s Mabel Normand.
MABEL'S DRAMATIC CAREER (Keystone, 1913) d Mack Sennett, s Mabel Normand.
FOR LOVE OF MABEL (Keystone, 1913) d Mack Sennett, s Mabel Normand.
MABEL'S STORMY LOVE AFFAIR (Keystone, 1914) d Mabel Normand, s Mabel Normand.

MABEL'S BARE ESCAPE (Keystone, 1914) d Mabel Normand, s Mabel Normand.
MABEL'S STRANGE PREDICAMENT (1914) d Mabel Normand, s Mabel Normand, Harry McCoy, Chester Conklin, Hank Mann.
MABEL AT THE WHEEL (Keystone, 1914) d Mack Sennett and Mabel Normand, s Mabel Normand, Harry McCoy.
MABEL'S NERVE (Keystone, 1914) d Mabel Normand, s Mabel Normand.
MABEL'S BUSY DAY (Keystone, 1914) d Mabel Normand and Charles Chaplin, s Mabel Normand.
MABEL'S MARRIED LIFE (Keystone, 1914) d Mabel Normand and Charles Chaplin, s Mabel Normand, Harry McCoy, Hank Mann.
MABEL'S NEW JOB (Keystone, 1914) s Mabel Normand.
MABEL'S LATEST PRANK (Keystone, 1914) d Mabel Normand, s Mabel Normand.
MABEL'S BLUNDER (Keystone, 1914) d Mabel Normand, s Mabel Normand.
HELLO, MABEL (Keystone, 1914) s Mabel Normand.
MABEL'S AND FATTY'S WASH DAY (Keystone, 1915) d Mabel Normand and Eddie Dillon, s Mabel Normand, Roscoe "Fatty" Arbuckle.
MABEL'S AND FATTY'S SIMPLE LIFE (Keystone, 1915) d Mabel Normand and Eddie Dillon, s Mabel Normand, Roscoe "Fatty" Arbuckle.
FATTY AND MABEL'S MARRIED LIFE (Keystone, 1915) s Roscoe "Fatty" Arbuckle, Mabel Normand.
MABEL, FATTY AND THE LAW (Keystone, 1915) s Mabel Normand, Roscoe "Fatty" Arbuckle.
WISHED ON MABEL (Keystone, 1915) s Mabel Normand.
FATTY AND MABEL VIEWING THE WORLD'S FAIR AT SAN FRANCISCO (Keystone, 1915) d Mabel Normand and Roscoe "Fatty" Arbuckle, s Mabel Normand, Roscoe "Fatty" Arbuckle.
FATTY AND MABEL AT THE SAN DIEGO EXPOSITION (Keystone, 1915) s Mabel Normand, Roscoe "Fatty" Arbuckle.
MABEL'S WILFUL WAY (Keystone, 1915) s Mabel Normand.
MABEL LOST AND WON (Keystone, 1915) s Mabel Normand.
FATTY AND MABEL ADRIFT (Triangle, 1916) s Mabel Normand, Roscoe "Fatty" Arbuckle.
OH! MABEL BEHAVE (Photocraft, 1922) s Mabel Normand.

471. MACISTE
The muscleman was featured in a number of Italian films. In English-languages releases, his name is sometimes changed to Atlas or Goliath. The listing may be incomplete.
CABIRI (1914) d Giobanni Pastrone, s Bartolomeo Pagano.
THE MARVELOUS MACISTE (1915)
MACISTE IN HELL (Excelsior, 1931)
MACISTE -- THE MIGHTY (1960) d Carlo Campogalliani, s Mark Forrest.
MACISTE, STRONGEST MAN IN THE WORLD (1961) d Antonio Leonviola, s Mark Forrest.

MACISTE AGAINST THE VAMPIRES (Ambrosiana Cinematografica, 1961) [aka MACISTE VS. THE VAMPIRE and GOLIATH AND THE ISLAND OF VAMPIRES and THE VAMPIRES and GOLIATH AND THE VAMPIRES] d Sergio Corbucci, s Gordon Scott, Gianna Maria Canale.
MACISTE AGAINST HERCULES IN THE VALE OF WOE (1962) d Mario Mattoli.
MACISTE IN HELL (Panda/Industria Cinematografica Italiana, 1962) [aka THE WITCH'S CURSE] d Riccardo Freda, s Kirk Morris, Helene Chanel.
MACISTE IN KING SOLOMON'S MINES (1964) d Martin Andrews, s Reg Park.

472. MACON COUNTY LINE
Louisiana troublemakers are falsely accused of murder.
MACON COUNTY LINE (American International, 1974) d Richard Compton, s Alan Vint, Jesse Vint, Cheryl Waters, Max Baer.
RETURN TO MACON COUNTY (American International, 1975) d Richard Compton, s Nick Nolte, Don Johnson, Robin Mattson.

473. MAD MAX
Post-apocalyptic adventures find gangs roving the highways and a lone cop, his family wiped out, seeking revenge.
MAD MAX (American International/Filmways, 1979) d George Miller, s Mel Gibson.
MAD MAX 2 (Warner Brothers, 1981) [aka THE ROAD WARRIOR] d George Miller, s Mel Gibson, Bruce Spence.
MAD MAX BEYOND THUNDERDOME (Warner Brothers, 1985) d George Miller and George Ogilvie, s Mel Gibson, Tina Turner.

474. MAD MISSION
Made in Hong Kong, these are martial arts/adventure pictures.
MAD MISSION
MAD MISSION II
MAD MISSION III
MAD MISSION IV
MAD MISSION V (Terracotta, 1989)

475. MAGNIFICENT SEVEN, THE
These American Westerns, based on Japanese film THE SEVEN SAMURAI, have an assemblage of gunmen riding to save a Mexican village.
THE SEVEN SAMURAI (Toho, 1954) d Akira Kurosawa, s Toshiro Mifune, Takoshi Shimura, Yoshio Inaba.
THE MAGNIFICENT SEVEN (United Artists, 1960) d John Sturges, s Yul Brynner, Steve McQueen.
RETURN OF THE SEVEN (United Artists, 1966) d Burt Kennedy, s Yul Brynner, Robert Fuller.

GUNS OF THE MAGNIFICENT SEVEN (United Artists, 1969) d Paul Wendkos, s George Kennedy.
THE MAGNIFICENT SEVEN RIDE! (United Artists, 1972) d George McCowan, s Lee Van Cleef, Stefanie Powers.

476. MAISIE
This series grew from Wilson Collison's novel *Dark Dame* (1935) about a brassy showgirl from Brooklyn. The character also appeared on radio in 1945 and 1949.
MAISIE (MGM, 1939) d Edwin L. Marin, s Robert Young, Ann Sothern.
CONGO MAISIE (MGM, 1940) d Henry Potter, s Ann Sothern, John Carroll.
GOLD RUSH MAISIE (MGM, 1940) d Edwin L. Marin, s Ann Sothern, Lee Bowman.
MAISIE WAS A LADY (MGM, 1941) [aka CASH AND CARRY] d Edwin L. Marin, s Ann Sothern, Lew Ayres.
RINGSIDE MAISIE (MGM, 1941) d Edwin L. Marin, s Ann Sothern, George Murphy.
MAISIE GETS HER MAN (MGM, 1942) [aka SHE GETS HER MAN] d Roy Del Ruth, s Ann Sothern, Red Skelton.
SWING SHIFT MAISIE (MGM, 1943) [aka THE GIRL IN OVERALLS] d Norman McLeod, s Ann Sothern, James Craig.
MAISIE GOES TO RENO (MGM, 1944) [aka YOU CAN'T DO THAT TO ME] d Harry Beaumont, s Ann Sothern, John Hodiak.
UP GOES MAISIE (MGM, 1946) d Harry Beaumont, s Ann Sothern, George Murphy.
UNDERCOVER MAISIE (1947) [aka UNDERCOVER GIRL]

476A. MAJOR LEAGUE
There is reportedly in the works for 1990-91 a sequel to this movie about an inept Cleveland Indians baseball team, billed "A comedy with bats and balls."
MAJOR LEAGUE (Paramount, 1989) d David S. Ward, s Tom Beringer, Charlie Sheen, Margaret Whitton.

477. MALTESE FALCON, THE
Dashiell Hammett's private eye story, thrice filmed, inspired only a spoof sequel, though bits of Sam Spade have been worked into other pictures, notably PLAY IT AGAIN, SAM.
THE MALTESE FALCON (Warner Brothers, 1931) d Roy Del Ruth, s Bebe Daniels, Ricardo Cortez.
SATAN MET A LADY (Warner Brothers, 1936) d William Dieterle, s Bette Davis, Warren William.
THE MALTESE FALCON (Warner Brothers, 1941) d John Huston, s Humphrey Bogart, Mary Astor, Peter Lorre, Sydney Greenstreet.
THE BLACK BIRD (Columbia, 1975) d David Giler, s George Segal.

477A. MAN AGAINST THE MOB
Mob squad detective Frank Doakey battles Los Angeles crime circa 1945.

MAN AGAINST THE MOB (NBC TV movie 1989) d Steven Hilliard Stern, s George Peppard.
MAN AGAINST THE MOB: THE CHINATOWN MURDERS (NBC-TV movie, 1989) d Michael Pressman, s George Peppard, Ursula Andress.

478. MAN AND A WOMAN, A
A widow and a widower fall in love.
A MAN AND A WOMAN (American Artists, 1966) d Claude Lelouch, s Anouk Aimee, Jean-Louis Trintignant.
A MAN AND A WOMAN: 20 YEARS LATER (Warner Brothers, 1986) d Claude Lelouch, s Anouk Aimee, Jean-Louis Trintignant.

479. MAN CALLED HORSE, A
These westerns, based on novel by Dorothy M. Johnson, are about an aristocratic Englishman who lives with and becomes a leader of a tribe of Native Americans.
A MAN CALLED HORSE (National General, 1970) d Elliot Silverstein, s Richard Harris, Judith Anderson.
RETURN OF A MAN CALLED HORSE (United Artists, 1976) d Irvin Kershner, s Richard Harris.
TRIUMPHS OF A MAN CALLED HORSE (Jensen Farley, 1984) d John Hough, s Richard Harris.

480. MANDINGO
Kyle Onstott's novel and Jack Kirkland's play about slave breeding on a Louisiana plantation in the 1840s provide the plots for these movies.
MANDINGO (Paramount, 1975) d Richard Fleischer, s James Mason, Susan George.
DRUM (United Artists, 1976) d Steve Carver, s Warren Oates, Isela Vega, Ken Norton.

481. MANDRAKE THE MAGICIAN
Lee Falk's comic strip prestidigitator first appeared in 1934. His sidekick is a giant Black man, Lothar.
MANDRAKE THE MAGICIAN (Columbia, 1939) (twelve episodes) d Sam Nelson and Norman Demins, s Warren Hull, Doris Weston, Al Kikume.
MANDRAKE (TV movie, 1979) d Harry Falk, s Anthony Herrera, Simone Griffeth, Ji-Tu Cumbuka.

482. MAN FROM SNOWY RIVER, THE
Based on an Australian poem by A.B. "Banjo" Paterson, the first film is about a strong-willed man who falls in love with a rich cattleman's daughter.
THE MAN FROM SNOWY RIVER (20th Century-Fox, 1982) d George Miller, s Kirk Douglas, Tom Burlinson, Sigrid Thornton, Jack Thompson.
RETURN TO SNOWY RIVER PART II (Buena Vista, 1988) d Geoff Burrowes, s Tom Burlinson, Sigrid Thornton.

483. MAN FROM U.N.C.L.E., THE
The TV spy series which was televised over NBC from 1964-68 featured secret government agents Napoleon Solo (Robert Vaughn) and Ilya Kuryakin (David McCallum). A number of the TV episodes were strapped together for theatrical screening overseas.
TO TRAP A SPY (MGM, 1966) d Don Medford, s Robert Vaughn, David McCallum, Leo G. Carroll.
THE SPY WITH MY FACE (MGM, 1966) d John Newland, s Robert Vaughn, David McCallum, Leo G. Carroll.
THE KARATE KILLERS (MGM, 1966) s Robert Vaughn, David McCallum, Leo G. Carroll.
THE SPY IN THE GREEN HAT (MGM, 1966) s Robert Vaughn, David McCallum, Leo G. Carroll.
ONE OF OUR SPIES IS MISSING (MGM, 1966) d E. Darrell Hallenbeck, s Robert Vaughn, David McCallum, Leo G. Carroll.
THE HELICOPTER SPIES (MGM, 1966) s Robert Vaughn, David McCallum, Leo G. Carroll.
HOW TO STEAL THE WORLD (MGM, 1966) s Robert Vaughn, David McCallum, Leo G. Carroll.
ONE SPY TOO MANY (MGM, 1966) s Robert Vaughn, David McCallum, Leo G. Carroll.
RETURN OF THE MAN FROM U.N.C.L.E. (1983 TV movie) d Ray Austin, s Robert Vaughn, David McCallum, Patrick MacNee.

483A. MANIAC COP
A violent killer is on the loose.
MANIAC COP (Shapiro Glickenhaus, 1988) d William Lustig, s Tom Atkins, Bruce Campbell.
MANIAC COP II (Movie House Sales, announced 1990) d William Lustig.

484. MAN WITH NO NAME, THE
The spaghetti Westerns are derived from the Japanese Samurai picture YOJIMBO and feature an unnamed, violent hero who in the initial Clint Eastwood outing cleans up a Mexican border town.
YOJIMBO (Toho, 1961) d Akira Kurosawa, s Toshiro Mifune, Eljiro Tono.
A FISTFUL OF DOLLARS (United Artists, 1964) d Sergio Leone, s Clint Eastwood, Gian Maria Volonte.
FOR A FEW DOLLARS MORE (United Artists, 1965) d Sergio Leone, s Clint Eastwood, Lee Van Cleef.
THE GOOD, THE BAD, THE UGLY (United Artists, 1967) d Sergio Leone, s Clint Eastwood, Lee Van Cleef, Eli Walach.

485. MARCUS WELBY, M.D.
ABC-TV aired a medical series from 1969-76 featuring Robert Young as Dr. Marcus Welby, a veteran general practitioner in California, with James Brolin as Dr. Steven Kiley and Elena Verdugo as nurse Consuelo Lopez.

MARCUS WELBY, M.D. (Universal, 1969) (ABC-TV movie [aka A
    MATTER OF HUMANITIES] d David Lowell Rich, s Robert Young,
    James Brolin.
THE RETURN OF MARCUS WELBY, M.D. (Universal, 1984) (ABC-TV
    movie) d Alexander Singer, s Robert Young, Darren McGavin.
MARCUS WELBY, M.D.: A HOLIDAY AFFAIR (1988 TV movie) d Steven
    Gethers, s Robert Young, Alexis Smith, Craig Stevens.

486. MARILYN CHAMBERS' PRIVATE FANTASIES
These are X-rated films.
MARILYN CHAMBERS' PRIVATE FANTASIES 1 (Creative Image, 1983) s
    Marilyn Chambers, Annette Haven.
MARILYN CHAMBERS' PRIVATE FANTASIES 2
MARILYN CHAMBERS' PRIVATE FANTASIES 3 (Caballero, 1984) d Ned
    Morehead, s Gaylee Marie, Nick Random.
MARILYN CHAMBERS' PRIVATE FANTASIES 4 (Caballero, 1985) d Jack
    Remy, s Marilyn Chambers, Harry Reems.
MARILYN CHAMBERS' PRIVATE FANTASIES 5 (Caballero, 1985) d Jack
    Remy, s Marilyn Chambers, Traci Lords.

487. MARK OF THE DEVIL
The horror films are about an eighteenth century witch hunter.
MARK OF THE DEVIL (Hallmark, 1972) d Michael Armstrong, s Herbert
    Lom, Udo Kier.
MARK OF THE DEVIL, PART 2 (Hallmark, 1975) d Adrian Hoven.

488. *MARX BROTHERS, THE*
Groucho is the leering ringleader, Harpo is the silent one, Chico is the schemer
and sometimes Zeppo is the romantic lead. The quartet got its start on stage.
THE COCOANUTS (Paramount, 1929) d Robert Florey and Joseph Santley, s
    Groucho Marx, Harpo Marx, Chico Marx, Zeppo Marx, Margaret
    Dumont.
ANIMAL CRACKERS (Paramount, 1930) d Victor Herrman, s Groucho Marx,
    Harpo Marx, Chico Marx, Zeppo Marx, Thelma Todd.
MONKEY BUSINESS (Paramount, 1931) d Norman Z. McLeod, s Groucho
    Marx, Harpo Marx, Chico Marx, Zeppo Marx, Thelma Todd.
HORSE FEATHERS (Paramount, 1932) d Norman Z. McLeod, s Groucho
    Marx, Harpo Marx, Chico Marx, Zeppo Marx, Thelma Todd.
DUCK SOUP (Paramount, 1933) d Leo McCarey, s Groucho Marx, Harpo
    Marx, Chico Marx, Zeppo Marx, Margaret Dumont.
A NIGHT AT THE OPERA (MGM, 1935) d Sam Wood, s Groucho Marx,
    Harpo Marx, Chico Marx, Margaret Dumont.
A DAY AT THE RACES (MGM, 1937) d Sam Wood, s Groucho Marx, Harpo
    Marx, Chico Marx, Margaret Dumont.
ROOM SERVICE (RKO, 1938) d William A. Seiter, s Groucho Marx, Harpo
    Marx, Chico Marx, Lucille Ball, Ann Miller.

AT THE CIRCUS (MGM, 1939) d Edward Buzzell, s Groucho Marx, Harpo Marx, Chico Marx, Margaret Dumont.
GO WEST (MGM, 1940) d Edward Buzzell, s Groucho Marx, Harpo Marx, Chico Marx.
THE BIG STORE (MGM, 1941) d Charles Riesner, s Groucho Marx, Harpo Marx, Chico Marx, Margaret Dumont.
A NIGHT IN CASABLANCA (David Loew-United Artists, 1946) s Groucho Marx, Harpo Marx, Chico Marx, Sig Rumann.
LOVE HAPPY (United Artists, 1949) d David Miller, s Groucho Marx, Harpo Marx, Chico Marx.

489. MASQUERS CLUB, THE
These are two-reel comedies.
STOUT HEARTS AND WILLING HANDS (1931) d Bryan Foy, s Frank Fay, Lew Cody.
OH! OH! CLEOPATRA (1931) s Wheeler and Woolsey, Dorothy Burgess.
WIDE OPEN SPACES (1932) s Ned Sparks, Antonio Moreno.
RULE'EM AND WEEP (1932) s Sam Hardy, Glenn Tryon.
TWO LIPS AND JULEPS; OR, SOUTHERN LOVE AND NORTHERN EXPOSURE (1932) s Conway Tearle, Helen Millard.
THE BRIDE'S BEREAVEMENT; OR, SNAKE IN THE GRASS (1932) s Charles Ray, Montagu Love.
LOST IN LIMEHOUSE; OR, LADY ESMERELDA'S PREDICAMENT (1933) s Laura LaPlante.
THE MOONSHINER'S DAUGHTER; OR, ABROAD IN OLD KENTUCKY (1933) s Mary Carr, Russell Simpson.
THRU THIN AND TICKET; OR, WHO'S ZOO IN AFRICA (1933)

490. MATT HELM
Donald Hamilton's espionage books, which by 1989 numbered twenty-five, are about an agent for a secret American governmental organization. Helm's specialty is eradication. The film versions go for yucks over realism.
THE SILENCERS (Columbia, 1966) d Phil Karlson, s Dean Martin, Stella Stevens.
MURDERER'S ROW (Columbia, 1966) d Henry Levin, s Dean Martin, Ann-Margaret.
THE AMBUSHERS (Columbia, 1967) d Henry Levin, s Dean Martin, Senta Berger.
THE WRECKING CREW (Columbia, 1968) d Phil Karlson, s Dean Martin, Elke Sommer.
MATT HELM (Columbia Pictures television, 1975) (ABC-TV movie) d Buzz Kulik, s Anthony Franciosa, Ann Turkel.

490A. MAX
The French actor and director Max Linder (1883-1925) was an internationally popular comedian typically appearing as a dandy. Listed here are his Max titles only.

MAX TAKES A BATH (Pathe, 1907) s Max Linder.
MAX IN A MUSEUM (Pathe, 1907) s Max Linder.
MAX AND HIS MOTHER-IN-LAW'S FALSE TEETH (Pathe, 1907) s Max Linder.
MAX'S HANGING (Pathe, 1907) s Max Linder.
MAX -- AERONAUT (Pathe, 1907) s Max Linder.
MAX'S NEW LANDLORD (Pathe, 1907) s Max Linder.
MAX -- PHOTOGRAPHER (Pathe, 1907) s Max Linder.
MAX IN A DILEMMA (Pathe, 1910) s Max Linder.
MAX IS ABSENT-MINDED (Pathe, 1910) s Max Linder.
MAX'S ASTIGMATISM (Pathe, 1910) s Max Linder.
HOW MAX WENT AROUND THE WORLD (Pathe, 1911) s Max Linder.
MAX -- VICTIM OF QUINQUINA (Pathe, 1911) s Max Linder.
MAX IN THE ALPS (Pathe, 1911) s Max Linder.
MAX TAKES UP SPORTS (Pathe, 1911) s Max Linder.
MAX ON SKIS (Pathe, 1911) s Max Linder.
MAX -- TOREODOR (Pathe, 1911) s Max Linder.
MAX, JOCKEY FOR LOVE (Pathe, 1911) s Max Linder.
MAX'S NEIGHBORLY NEIGHBOR (Pathe, 1911) s Max Linder.
MAX EMBARRASSED (Pathe, 1911) s Max Linder.
MAX IS FORCED TO WORK (Pathe, 1911) s Max Linder.
MAX IN THE MOVIES (Pathe, 1911) s Max Linder.
MAX HYPNOTIZED (Pathe, 1911) s Max Linder.
MAX SEARCHES FOR A SWEETHEART (Pathe, 1911) s Max Linder.
MAX IS DISTRAUGHT (Pathe, 1911) s Max Linder.
MAX IS ALMOST MARRIED (Pathe, 1911) s Max Linder.
MAX WEARS TIGHT SHOES (Pathe, 1911) s Max Linder.
MAX IS STUCK UP (Pathe, 1911) s Max Linder.
MAX -- PEDICURIST (Pathe, 1911) s Max Linder.
MAX TEACHES THE TANGO; OR, TOO MUCH MUSTARD (Pathe, 1911) s Max Linder.
MAX IN THE ARMS OF HIS FAMILY (Pathe, 1911) s Max Linder.
MAX VIRTUOSO (Pathe, 1912) s Max Linder.
MAX GETS THE REWARD (Pathe, 1912) s Max Linder.
MAX'S VACATION (Pathe, 1912) s Max Linder.
MAX'S MARRIAGE (Pathe, 1912) s Max Linder.
MAX'S HONEYMOON (Pathe, 1912) s Max Linder.
MAX MAKES A CONQUEST (Pathe, 1912) s Max Linder.
MAX IS JEALOUS (Pathe, 1912) s Max Linder.
MAX DOES NOT SPEAK ENGLISH (Pathe, 1912) s Max Linder.
MAX MAKES MUSIC (Pathe, 1912) s Max Linder.
MAX'S DOUBLE (Pathe, 1912) s Max Linder.
MAX -- MAGICIAN (Pathe, 1912) s Max Linder.
MAX'S DUEL (Pathe, 1912) s Max Linder.
MAX AND THE STATUE (Pathe, 1912) s Max Linder.
WHO KILLED MAX? (Pathe, 1912) s Max Linder.
MAX CREATES A FASHION (Pathe, 1912) s Max Linder.

MAX AND JANE GO TO THE THEATER (Pathe, circa 1913) s Max Linder.
MAX PLAYS IN DRAMA (Pathe, circa 1913) s Max Linder.
MAX DOES NOT LIKE CATS (Pathe, circa 1913) s Max Linder.
MAX ATTENDS AN INAUGURATION (Pathe, circa 1913) s Max Linder.
MAX'S HAT (Pathe, circa 1913) s Max Linder.
MAX IS DECORATED (Pathe, circa 1914) s Max Linder.
MAX AND JANE MAKE A DESSERT (Pathe, circa 1914) s Max Linder.
MAX AND THE CLUTCHING HAND (Pathe, 1915) s Max Linder.
MAX BETWEEN FIRES (Pathe, 1915) s Max Linder.
MAX COMES ACROSS (Pathe, 1917) s Max Linder.
MAX WANTS A DIVORCE (Pathe, 1917) s Max Linder.
MAX AND HIS TAXI (Pathe, 1917) s Max Linder.
MAX IS FORCED TO WORK (1920) s Max Linder.
MAX, THE HEADWAITER (1920) s Max Linder.

491. McCLOUD
A Taos marshal is transplanted to the Big Apple in the NBC television series which aired 1970-77. In the last entry here, McCloud has become a Senator from New Mexico and has been called to London to solve his niece's murder.
McCLOUD: WHO KILLED MISS U.S.A.? (TV movie, 1969) [aka PORTRAIT OF A DEAD GIRL] d Richard Colla, s Dennis Weaver, Craig Stevens, Diana Muldaur.
THE RETURN OF SAM McCLOUD (TV movie, 1989) s Dennis Weaver, Terry Carter.

492. McDOUGAL ALLEY KIDS
Bray Production made these juvenile comedies.

493. McHALE'S NAVY
ABC aired McHALE'S NAVY from 1962-66. A World War II PT boat is headed by McHale (Ernest Borgnine). The crew includes Ensign Charles Parker (Tim Conway) and Capt. Wallace B. Binghamton (Joe Flynn).
McHALE'S NAVY (Universal, 1964) d Edward J. Montague, s Ernest Borgnine, Joe Flynn, Jean Willes, Tim Conway.
McHALE'S NAVY JOINS THE ARMY (Univeral, 1965) d Edward J. Montague, s Joe Flynn, Tim Conway, Gary Vinson.

494. MEATBALLS
Summer camp brings out the zany and lusty in its counselors and kids.
MEATBALLS (Paramount, 1979) d Ivan Reitman, s Bill Murray, Harvey Atkin.
MEATBALLS PART II (Tri-Star Pictures, 1984) d Ken Wiederhorn, s Richard Mulligan, John Mengatti.
MEATBALLS III (1987) d George Menduluk, s Sally Kellerman, Patrick Dempsey.

495. MEET THE GIRLS

Out-of-work entertainers stow away on a ship in order to get home. They become mixed up with jewel thieves.
MEET THE GIRLS (20th Century-Fox, 1938) d Eugene Forde, s Lynn Bari, June Lang.
PARDON OUR NERVE (20th Century-Fox, 1939) d Bruce Humberstone, s Lynn Bari, June Lang.

496. MELVIN PURVIS, G-MAN
The pictures are about a famous gangbuster who pursued Machine Gun Kelly, Pretty Boy Floyd, etc., in the 1930s.
MELVIN PURVIS: G-MAN (American-International Pictures, 1974) (ABC-TV movie) [aka THE LEGEND OF MACHINE GUN KELLY] d Dan Curtis, s Dale Robertson, Harris Yulin.
THE KANSAS CITY MASSACRE (ABC Circle Films, 1975) (ABC-TV movie) d Dan Curtis, s Dale Robertson, Bo Hopkins.

497. MERLIN JONES
A teenager becomes a mind reader in the first of these Walt Disney films.
THE MISADVENTURES OF MERLIN JONES (Buena Vista, 1964) d Robert Stevenson, s Tommy Kirk, Annette Funicello.
THE MONKEY'S UNCLE (Buena Vista, 1967) d Andrew V. McLaglen, s Tommy Kir, Annette Funicello.

498. MEXICAN SPITFIRE
The fiery personality of Lupe Velez, a Mexican movie star, inspired these pictures. The heroine is called Carmelita.
THE GIRL FROM MEXICO (RKO, 1939) d Leslie Goodwin, s Lupe Velez, Leon Errol.
MEXICAN SPITFIRE (RKO, 1939) d Leslie Goodwin, s Lupe Velez, Leon Errol.
MEXICAN SPITFIRE OUT WEST (RKO, 1940) d Leslie Goodwin, s Lupe Velez, Leon Errol.
MEXICAN SPITFIRE'S BABY (RKO, 1941) d Leslie Goodwin, s Lupe Velez, Leon Errol.
MEXICAN SPITFIRE AT SEA (RKO, 1941) d Leslie Goodwin, s Lupe Velez, Leon Errol.
MEXICAN SPITFIRE SEES A GHOST (RKO, 1942) d Leslie Goodwin, s Lupe Velez, Leon Errol.
MEXICAN SPITFIRE'S ELEPHANT (RKO, 1942) d Leslie Goodwin, s Lupe Velez, Leon Errol.
MEXICAN SPITFIRE'S BLESSED EVENT (RKO, 1943) d Leslie Goodwin, s Lupe Velez, Leon Errol.

499. MIAMI SPICE
These are adult pictures.
MIAMI SPICE (Caballero, 1987) s Amber Lynn, Randy West.
MIAMI SPICE II (Caballero, 1987) s Amber Lynn, John Leslie.

500. MICHAEL SHAYNE
Brett Halliday's tough, red-headed Miami private eye appeared in a series of mystery novels beginning in 1939.
MICHAEL SHAYNE, PRIVATE DETECTIVE (20th Century-Fox, 1940) d Eugene Forde, s Lloyd Nolan, Marjorie Weaver.
SLEEPERS WEST (20th Century-Fox, 1941) d Eugene Forde, s Lloyd Nolan, Lynn Bari.
DRESSED TO KILL (20th Century-Fox, 1941) d Eugene Forde, s Lloyd Nolan, Sheila Ryan, William Demarest.
BLUE, WHITE AND PERFECT (20th Century-Fox, 1941) d Herbert I. Leeds, s Lloyd Nolan, Mary Beth Hughes, George Reeves.
THE MAN WHO WOULDN'T DIE (20th Century-Fox, 1942) d Herbert I. Leeds, s Lloyd Nolan, Marjorie Weaver.
JUST OFF BROADWAY (20th Century-Fox, 1942) d Herbert I. Leeds, s Lloyd Nolan, Marjorie Weaver.
TIME TO KILL (20th Century-Fox, 1942) d Herbert I. Leeds, s Lloyd Nolan, Janis Carter, Marjorie Weaver.
MURDER IS MY BUSINESS (PRC, 1946) d Sam Newfield, s Hugh Beaumont, Cheryl Walker.
LARCENY IN HER HEART (PRC, 1946) d Sam Newfield, s Hugh Beaumont, Cheryl Walker.
BLONDE FOR A DAY (PRC, 1946) d Sam Newfield, s Hugh Beaumont, Kathryn Adams.
THREE ON A TICKET (PRC, 1947) d Sam Newfield, s Hugh Beaumont, Cheryl Walker.
TOO MANY WINNERS (PRC, 1947) d William Beaudine, s Hugh Beaumont, Trudy Marshall.

501. MICKEY McGUIRE
From Fontaine Fox's comic strip *Toonerville Trolley* (which began in 1915), these films feature Mickey Rooney.
MICKEY IN LOVE (1928) s Mickey Rooney.
MICKEY'S WILD WEST (1928) s Mickey Rooney.
MICKEY'S TRIUMPH (1928) s Mickey Rooney.
MICKEY'S MOVIES (1928) s Mickey Rooney.
MICKEY THE DETECTIVE (1928) s Mickey Rooney.
MICKEY, I LOVE YOU (1928) s Mickey Rooney.
MICKEY'S RIVALS (1928) s Mickey Rooney.
MICKEY'S BIG GAME HUNT (1928) s Mickey Rooney.
ORCHIDS AND ERMINE (1928) s Mickey Rooney.

501A. MIDNIGHT EXPRESS
Billy Hayes, in a Turkish prison for smuggling hashish, is anxious to escape.
MIDNIGHT EXPRESS (1978) d Alan Parker, s Brad Davis, John Hurt, Randy Quaid.
MIDNIGHT EXPRESS II: THE RETURN (Sotela Pictures, announced 1990)

502. MIKE AND IKE
This series of comedy short series from Universal in the late 1920s features Charles King.

503. MIKE AND JAKE
The silent comedies feature Max Asher (1880-1957) teamed with Harry McCoy (1894-1937), and later Bobby Vernon (1897-1939). The list may be incomplete.
MIKE AND JAKE AMONG THE CANNIBALS (1913) s Max Asher
MIKE AND JAKE IN THE WILD WEST (1913) s Max Asher
MIKE AND JAKE AT THE BEACH (1913) s Max Asher, Harry McCoy, Louise Fazenda, Bobby Vernon.
MIKE AND JAKE PUGILISTS (1913) s Max Asher, Harry McCoy
MIKE AND JAKE IN SOCIETY (1913) s Max Asher
MIKE AND JAKE LIVE CLOSE TO NATURE (1914) s Max Asher
MIKE AND JAKE JOIN THE ARMY (1914) s Max Asher

504. MIKE HAMMER
Mickey Spillane's fists-and-bullets private eye has been featured in a dozen best-selling novels published beginning in 1950. There have been two television series featuring the character, one in the 1950s with Darren McGavin, one in the 1980s with Stacy Keach.
I, THE JURY (United Artists, 1953) d Harry Essex, s Biff Elliot.
KISS ME DEADLY (United Artists, 1955), d Robert Aldrich, s Ralph Meeker.
MY GUN IS QUICK (United Artists, 1957) d Phil Victor, s Robert Bray, Whitney Blake.
THE GIRL HUNTERS (Colorama, 1963) d Roy Rowland, s Mickey Spillane, Shirley Eaton, Lloyd Nolan.
MICKEY SPILLANE'S MARGIN FOR MURDER (Hamner Productions, 1981) (CBS-TV movie) d Daniel Haller, s Kevin Dobson, Charles Hallahan, Cindy Pickett.
MURDER ME, MURDER YOU (Columbia Pictures Television, 1983) (CBS-TV movie) [aka MICKEY SPILLANE'S MURDER ME, MURDER YOU] d Gary Nelson, s Stacy Keach, Tanya Roberts, Don Stroud.

505. MIRACLE WORKER, THE
William Gibson wrote a popular play of deaf and blind Helen Keller and her teacher Anne Sullivan. The first entry below is the work as it was featured on *Playhouse 90* in 1957. The third film listed continues Helen's career through college.
THE MIRACLE WORKER (United Artists, 1962) d Arthur Penn, s Anne Bancroft, Patty Duke.
THE MIRACLE WORKER (NBC TV movie, 1979) d Paul Aaron, s Patty Duke Astin, Melissa Gilbert.
HELEN KELLER -- THE MIRACLE CONTINUES (20th Century-Fox, 1984) (TV movie) d Alan Gibson, s Blythe Danner, Mare Winningham.

506. MIRANDA
From Peter Blackmore's play, a physician takes a mermaid to London.
MIRANDA (Gainsborough-Box, 1948) d Ken Annakin, s Glynis Johns, Googie Withers, Griffith Jones.
MAD ABOUT MEN (General Film, 1954) d Ralph Thomas, s Glynis Johns, Anne Crawford, Donald Sinden.

507. MISSING IN ACTION
A soldier-of-fortune, Col. James Braddock, blasts the Commies.
MISSING IN ACTION (Cannon, 1984) d Joseph Zito, s Chuck Norris.
MISSING IN ACTION 2 -- THE BEGINNING (Cannon, 1985) d Lance Hool, s Chuck Norris.
BRADDOCK: MISSING IN ACTION III (Cannon, 1988) d A. Norris, s Chuck Norris, Aki Aleong.

508. MISTER ROBERTS
Roberts, serving aboard a cargo ship during World War II, yearns for action. Thomas Heggen and Joshua Logan wrote the play upon which the films are based.
MISTER ROBERTS (Warner Brothers, 1955) d John Ford, Mervyn LeRoy, s Henry Fonda, Jack Lemmon, William Powell, James Cagney.
ENSIGN PULVER (Warner Brothers, 1964) d Joshua Logan, s Robert Walker Jr., Burl Ives.

509. MODESTY BLAISE
Peter O'Donnell's action heroine has appeared with her companion Willie Garvin in an internationally syndicated newspaper comic strip and several books since 1963.
MODESTY BLAISE (20th Century-Fox, 1963) d Joseph Losey, s Monica Vitti, Terence Stamp.
MODESTY BLAISE (Paramount, 1982) (TV movie) s Ann Turkel.

510. MONSIEUR LECOQ
The films are based on books by Emile Gaboriau.
MONSIEUR LECOQ, DETECTIVE (Eclair Films, 1914) [aka THE TRAGEDY AT PEPPER-BOX INN]
FILE 113 (Gaumond Productions, 1932) s Lew Cody.

511. *MONTE HALE AND ADRIAN BOOTH*
These are B Westerns.
HOME ON THE RANGE (Republic, 1946) d R.G. Springsteen, s Monte Hale, Adrian Booth.
MAN FROM RAINBOW VALLEY (Republic, 1946) d R.G. Springsteen, s Monte Hale, Adrian Booth, Emmett Lynn.
OUT CALIFORNIA WAY (Republic, 1946) d Lesley Selander, s Monte Hale, Adrian Booth.

LAST FRONTIER UPRISING (Republic, 1947) d Lesley Selander, s Monte Hale, Adrian Booth.
ALONG THE OREGON TRAIL (Republic, 1947) d R.G. Springsteen, s Monte Hale, Adrian Booth.
UNDER COLORADO SKIES (Republic, 1947) d R.G. Springsteen, s Monte Hale, Adrian Booth, Paul Hurst.

512. *MONTE HALE AND PAUL HURST*
UNDER COLORADO SKIES (Republic, 1947) d R.G. Springsteen, s Monte Hale, Adrian Booth, Paul Hurst.
CALIFORNIA FIREBRAND (Republic, 1948) d Phillip Ford, s Monte Hale, Paul Hurst, Adrian Booth.
SONG OF GOD'S COUNTRY (Republic, 1948) d R.G. Springsteen, s Monte Hale, Paul Hurst, Pamela Blake.
PRINCE OF THE PLAINS (Republic, 1949) d Phillip Ford, s Monte Hale, Paul Hurst, Shirley Davis.
LAW OF THE GOLDEN WEST (Republic, 1949) d Phillip Ford, s Monte Hale, Paul Hurst, Gail Davis.
OUTCASTS OF THE TRAIL (Republic, 1949) d Phillip Ford, s Monte Hale, Paul Hurst, Jeff Donnell.
SOUTH OF RIO (Republic, 1949) d Phillip Ford, s Monte Hale, Paul Hurst, Kay Christopher.
SAN ANTONE AMBUSH (Republic, 1949) d Phillip Ford, s Monte Hale, Paul Hurst, Bette Daniels.
RANGER OF THE CHEROKEE STRIP (Republic, 1949) d Phillip Ford, s Monte Hale, Paul Hurst, Alice Talton.
PIONEER MARSHALL (Republic, 1949) d Phillip Ford, s Monte Hale, Paul Hurst, Nan Leslie.
THE VANISHING WESTERNER (Republic, 1950) d Phillip Ford, s Monte Hale, Paul Hurst, Aline Towne.
THE OLD FRONTIER (Republic, 1950) d Phillip Ford, s Monte Hale, Paul Hurst, Claudia Barrett.
THE MISSOURIANS (Republic, 1950) d George Blair, s Monte Hale, Paul Hurst, Lyn Thomas.

513. MONTY PYTHON
Monty Python is a troupe of British comedians.
MONTY PYTHON AND THE HOLY GRAIL (Cinema 5, 1974) d Terry Gilliam, s Terry Jones, Graham Chapman, John Cleese.
MONTY PYTHON MEETS BEYOND THE FRINGE (New Line, 1978) d Roger Graef.
MONTY PYTHON LIVE AT THE HOLLYWOOD BOWL (1982) d Terry Hughes, s Graham Chapman, John Cleese, Terry Gilliam.
MONTY PYTHON'S LIFE OF BRIAN (Warner Brothers/Orion, 1979) d Terry Jones, s John Cleese, Eric Idle, Graham Chapman, Terry Gilliam.
MONTY PYTHON'S THE MEANING OF LIFE (Universal, 1983) d Terry Jones, s John Cleese, Eric Idle.

514. MORTON OF THE MOUNTED
These are second feature northerns.
COURAGE OF THE NORTH (Stage & Screen, 1935) d Robert Emmett Tansey, s John Preston, Dynamite the Wonder Horse, Captain King of the Dogs, June Love.
TIMBER TERRORS (Stage & Screen, 1935) d Robert Emmett Tansey, s Dynamite the Wonder Horse, Captain King of the Dogs, Marla Bratton.

515. MOUNTIE CORPORAL ROD WEBB
Mountie Corporal Rod Webb is the leading figure in these Canadian adventures which are based on James Oliver Curwood northlands novels.
TRAIL OF THE YUKON (Monogram, 1949) d William X. Crowley, s Kirby Grant, Suzanne Dalbert, Chinook the Dog.
WOLF HUNTERS (Monogram, 1949) d Oscar (Budd) Boetticher, s Kirby Grant, Jan Clayton, Chinook the Dog.
CALL OF THE KLONDIKE (Monogram, 1950) d Frank McDonald, s Kirby Grant, Anne Gwynne, Chinook the Dog.
SNOW DOG (Monogram, 1950) d Frank McDonald, s Kirby Grant, Elena Verdugo, Chinook the Dog.
NORTHWEST TERRITORY (Monogram, 1951) d Frank McDonald, s Kirby Grant, Gloria Saunders, Chinook the Dog.
YUKON MANHUNT (Monogram, 1951) d Frank McDonald, s Kirby Grant, Gail Davis, Chinook the Dog.
YUKON GOLD (Monogram, 1952) d Frank McDonald, s Kirby Grant, Martha Hyer, Chinook the Dog.
FANGS OF THE ARCTIC (Monogram, 1953) d Rex Bailey, s Kirby Grant, Lorna Hansen, Chinook the Dog.
NORTHERN PATROL (Monogram, 1953) d Rex Bailey, s Kirby Grant, Marion Car, Chinook the Dog.
YUKON VENGEANCE (Allied Artists, 1954) d William Beaudine, s Kirby Grant, Monte Hale.

516. MOUSE THAT ROARED, THE
From Leonard Wibberley's novel, the Duchy of Grand Fenwick invades the United States in order to secure foreign aid.
THE MOUSE THAT ROARED (Columbia, 1959) d Jack Arnold, s Peter Sellers, Jean Seberg.
THE MOUSE ON THE MOON (United Artists, 1963) d Richard Lester, s Margaret Rutherford, Bernard Cribbins, Ron Moody, Terry-Thomas.

517. MR. AVERAGE MAN
Two-reel comedies beginning in 1931 featured Edgar Kennedy as an average Joe, henpecked by wife and mother-in-law. They ran for 17 years until the actor's death. The pictures are also called the EDGAR KENNEDY SERIES.
ROUGH HOUSE RHYTHM (RKO, 1931) d Harry Sweet, s Edgar Kennedy, Franklin Pangborn, Florence Lake.

LEMON MERINGUE (RKO, 1931) d Harry Sweet, s Edgar Kennedy, Florence Lake.
THANKS AGAIN (RKO, 1931) d Harry Sweet, s Edgar Kennedy, Florence Lake.
CAMPING OUT (RKO, 1931) d Harry Sweet, s Edgar Kennedy, Florence Lake.
BON VOYAGE (RKO, 1932) d Harry Sweet, s Edgar Kennedy, Florence Lake.
MOTHER-IN-LAW'S DAY (RKO, 1932) d Harry Sweet, s Edgar Kennedy, Florence Lake.
GIGGLE WATER (RKO, 1932) d Harry Sweet, s Edgar Kennedy, Florence Lake.
THE GOLF CHUMP (RKO, 1932) d Harry Sweet, s Edgar Kennedy, Florence Lake.
PARLOR, BEDROOM AND WRATH (RKO, 1932) d Harry Sweet, s Edgar Kennedy, Florence Lake.
FISH FEATHERS (RKO, 1932) d Harry Sweet, s Edgar Kennedy, Florence Lake.
ART IN THE RAW (RKO, 1933) d Harry Sweet, s Edgar Kennedy, Florence Lake.
THE MERCHANT OF MENACE (RKO, 1933) d Harry Sweet, s Edgar Kennedy, Florence Lake.
GOOD HOUSEWRECKING (RKO, 1933) d Harry Sweet, s Edgar Kennedy, Florence Lake.
QUIET, PLEASE (RKO, 1933) d George Stevens, s Edgar Kennedy, Florence Lake.
WHAT FUR (RKO, 1933) d George Stevens, s Edgar Kennedy, Florence Lake.
GRIN AND BEAR IT (RKO, 1933) d George Stevens, s Edgar Kennedy, Florence Lake.
LOVE ON A LADDER (RKO, 1934) d Sam White, s Edgar Kennedy, Florence Lake.
WRONG DIRECTION (RKO, 1934) d Alf Goulding, s Edgar Kennedy, Florence Lake.
IN-LAWS ARE OUT (RKO, 1934) d Sam White, s Edgar Kennedy, Florence Lake.
A BLASTED EVENT (RKO, 1934) d Alf Goulding, s Edgar Kennedy, Florence Lake.
POISONED IVORY (RKO, 1934) d Alf Goulding, s Edgar Kennedy, Florence Lake.
BRIC-A-BRAC (RKO, 1935) d Sam White, s Edgar Kennedy, Florence Lake.
SOUTH SEASICKNESS (RKO, 1935) d Arthur Ripley, s Edgar Kennedy, Florence Lake.
SOCK ME TO SLEEP (RKO, 1935) d Ben Holmes, s Edgar Kennedy, Florence Lake.
EDGAR HAMLET (RKO, 1935) d Arthur Ripley, s Edgar Kennedy, Florence Lake.

IN LOVE AT 40 (RKO, 1935) d Arthur Ripley, s Edgar Kennedy, Florence Lake.
HAPPY THO MARRIED (RKO, 1935) d Arthur Ripley, s Edgar Kennedy, Florence Lake.
GASOLOONS (Rko, 1936) d Arthur Ripley, s Edgar Kennedy, Florence Lake.
WILL POWER (RKO, 1936) d Arthur Ripley, s Edgar Kennedy, Florence Lake.
HIGH BEER PRESSURE (RKO, 1936) d Leslie Goodwins, s Edgar Kennedy, Florence Lake.
DUMMY ACHE (RKO, 1936) d Leslie Goodwins, s Edgar Kennedy, Florence Lake.
VOCALIZING (RKO, 1936) d Leslie Goodwins, s Edgar Kennedy.
HILLBILLY GOAT (RKO, 1937) d Leslie Goodwins, s Edgar Kennedy, Si Jenks, Fern Emmett.
BAD HOUSEKEEPING (RKO, 1937) d Leslie Goodwins, s Edgar Kennedy, Vivien Oakland.
LOCKS AND BONDS (RKO, 1937) d Leslie Goodwins, s Edgar Kennedy, Bill Franey.
DUMB'S THE WORD (RKO, 1937) d Leslie Goodwins, s Edgar Kennedy, Vivien Oakland.
TRAMP TROUBLE (RKO, 1937) d Leslie Goodwins, s Edgar Kennedy, Vivien Oakland.
MORNING, JUDGE (RKO, 1937) d Leslie Goodwins, s Edgar Kennedy, Agnes Ayres.
EDGAR AND THE GOLIATH (RKO, 1937) d Leslie Goodwins, s Edgar Kennedy, Florence Lake.
EARS OF EXPERIENCE (RKO, 1938) d Leslie Goodwins, s Edgar Kennedy, Florence Lake.
FALSE ROOMERS (RKO, 1938) d Leslie Goodwins, s Edgar Kennedy, Constance Bergen.
KENNEDY'S CASTLE (RKO, 1938) d Leslie Goodwins, s Edgar Kennedy, Vivian Tobin.
FOOL COVERAGE (RKO, 1938) d Leslie Goodwins, s Vivien Oakland.
BEAUX AND ERRORS (RKO, 1938) d Charles E. Roberts, s Edgar Kennedy, Vivien Oakland.
A CLEAN SWEEP (RKO, 1938) d Charles E. Roberts, s Edgar Kennedy, Vivien Oakland.
MAID TO ORDER (RKO, 1939) d Charles E. Roberts, s Edgar Kennedy, Vivien Oakland.
CLOCK WISE (RKO, 1939) d Charles E. Roberts, s Edgar Kennedy, Vivien Oakland.
BABY DAZE (RKO, 1939) d Charles E. Roberts, s Edgar Kennedy, Vivien Oakland.
FEATHERED PESTS (RKO, 1939) d Charles E. Roberts, s Edgar Kennedy, Vivien Oakland.
ACT YOUR AGE (RKO, 1939) d Charles E. Roberts, s Edgar Kennedy, Vivien Oakland.

KENNEDY THE GREAT (RKO, 1939) d Charles E. Roberts, s Edgar Kennedy, Vivien Oakland.
SLIGHTLY AT SEA (RKO, 1940) d Harry D'Arcy, s Edgar Kennedy, Vivien Oakland.
MUTINY IN THE COUNTY (RKO, 1940) d Harry D'Arcy, s Edgar Kennedy, Vivien Oakland.
'TAINT LEGAL (RKO, 1940) d Harry D'Arcy, s Edgar Kennedy, Vivien Oakland.
SUNK BY THE CENSUS (RKO, 1940) d Harry D'Arcy, s Edgar Kennedy, Vivien Oakland.
TRAILER TRAGEDY (RKO, 1940) d Harry D'Arcy, s Edgar Kennedy, Vivien Oakland.
DRAFTED IN THE DEPOT (RKO, 1940) d Lloyd French, s Edgar Kennedy, Vivien Oakland.
MAD ABOUT MOONSHINE (RKO, 1941) d Harry D'Arcy, s Edgar Kennedy, Vivien Oakland.
IT HAPPENED ALL NIGHT (RKO, 1941) d Charles E. Roberts, s Edgar Kennedy, Vivien Oakland.
AN APPLE IN HIS EYE (RKO, 1941) d Harry D'Arcy, s Edgar Kennedy, Vivien Oakland.
WESTWARD HO-HUM (RKO, 1941) d Clem Beauchamp, s Edgar Kennedy, Sally Payne.
I'LL FIX THAT (RKO, 1941) d Charles E. Roberst, s Edgar Kennedy, Sally Payne.
A QUIET FOURTH (RKO, 1941) d Harry D'ARcy, s Edgar Kennedy, Sally Payne.
HEART BURN (RKO, 1942) d Harry D'Arcy, s Edgar Kennedy, Sally Payne.
INFERIOR DECORATOR (RKO, 1942) d Clem Beauchamp, s Edgar Kennedy, Sally Payne.
COOKS AND CROOKS (RKO, 1942) d Henry James, s Edgar Kennedy, Sally Payne.
TWO FOR THE MONEY (RKO, 1942) d Lloyd French, s Edgar Kennedy, Florence Lake.
ROUGH ON RENTS (RKO, 1942) d Ben Holmes, s Edgar Kennedy, Florence Lake.
DUCK SOUP (RKO, 1942) d Ben Holmes, s Edgar Kennedy, Florence Lake.
HOLD YOUR TEMPER (RKO, 1943) d Lloyd French, s Edgar Kennedy, Irene Ryan.
INDIAN SIGNS (RKO, 1943) d Charles E. Roberts, s Edgar Kennedy, Irene Ryan.
HOT FOOT (RKO, 1943) d Ben Holmes, s Edgar Kennedy, Dot Farley.
NOT ON MY ACCOUNT (RKO, 1943) d Charles E. Roberts, s Edgar Kennedy, Pauline Drake.
UNLUCKY DOG (RKO, 1943) d Ben HOlmes, s Edgar Kennedy, Pauline Drake.
PRUNES AND POLITICS (RKO, 1944) d Ben Holmes, s Edgar Kennedy, Pauline Drake.

LOVE YOUR LANDLORD (RKO, 1944) d Charles E. Roberts, s Edgar Kennedy, Florence Lake.
RADIO RAMPAGE (RKO, 1944) d Charles E. Roberts, s Edgar Kennedy, Florence Lake.
THE KITCHEN CYNIC (RKO, 1944) d Hal Yates, s Edgar Kennedy, Florence Lake.
FEATHER YOUR NEST (RKO, 1944) d Hal Yates, s Edgar Kennedy, Florence Lake.
ALIBI BABY (RKO, 1945) d Hal Yates, s Edgar Kennedy, Florence Lake.
SLEEPLESS TUESDAY (RKO, 1945) d Hal Yates, s Edgar Kennedy, Florence Lake.
WHAT, NO CIGARETTES? (RKO, 1945) d Hal Yates, s Edgar Kennedy, Florence Lake.
IT'S YOUR MOVE (RKO, 1945) d Hal Yates, s Edgar Kennedy, Florence Lake.
YOU DRIVE ME CRAZY (RKO, 1945) d Hal Yates, s Edgar Kennedy, Florence Lake.
THE BIG BEEF (RKO, 1945) d Charles E. Roberts, s Edgar Kennedy, Florence Lake.
MOTHER-IN-LAW'S DAY (RKO, 1945) d Hal Yates, s Edgar Kennedy, Florence Lake.
TROUBLE OR NOTHING (RKO, 1946) d Hal Yates, s Edgar Kennedy, Florence Lake.
WALL STREET BLUES (RKO, 1946) d Hal Yates, s Edgar Kennedy, Florence Lake.
MOTOR MANIACS (RKO, 1946) d Wallace Grissell, s Edgar Kennedy, Florence Lake.
NOISY NEIGHBORS (RKO, 1946) d Hal Yates, s Edgar Kennedy, Florence Lake.
I'LL BUILD IT MYSELF (RKO, 1946) d Hal Yales, s Edgar Kennedy, Florence Lake.
SOCIAL TERRORS (RKO, 1946) d Charles E. Roberts, s Edgar Kennedy, Florence Lake.
DO OR DIET (RKO, 1947) d Hal Yates, s Edgar Kennedy, Florence Lake.
HEADING FOR TROUBLE (RKO, 1947) d Hal Yates, s Edgar Kennedy, Florence Lake.
HOST TO A GHOST (RKO, 1947) d Hal Yates, s Edgar Kennedy, Florence Lake.
TELEVISION TURMOIL (RKO, 1947) d Hal Yates, s Edgar Kennedy, Florence Lake.
MIND OVER MOUSE (RKO, 1947) d Hal Yates, s Edgar Kennedy, Florence Lake.
BROTHER KNOWS BEST (RKO, 1948) d Hal Yates, s Edgar Kennedy, Florence Lake.
NO MORE RELATIVES (RKO, 1948) d Hal Yates, s Edgar Kennedy, Florence Lake.

HOW TO CLEAN HOUSE (RKO, 1948) d Charles E. Roberts, s Edgar Kennedy, Florence Lake.
DIG THAT GOLD (RKO, 1948) d Hal Yates, s Edgar Kennedy, Florence Lake.
HOME CANNING (RKO, 1948) d Hal Yates, s Edgar Kennedy, Florence Lake.
CONTEST CRAZY (RKO, 1948) d Hal Yates, s Edgar Kennedy, Florence Lake.

518. MR. BELVEDERE
Based on the book *Belvedere* by Gwen Davenport (1947), the stories offer a self-centered genius who accepts a child care position in suburban town.
SITTING PRETTY (20th Century-Fox, 1948) d Walter Lang, s Robert Young, Maureen O'Hara, Clifton Webb.
MR. BELVEDERE GOES TO COLLEGE (20th Century-Fox, 1949) d Elliott Nugent, s Clifton Webb, Shirley Temple.
MR. BELVEDERE RINGS THE BELL (1951) d Henry Koster, s Clifton Webb, Joanne Dru.

519. MR. BOGGS
The pictures are based on Clarence Budington Kelland's *American Magazine* story *Face the Facts*.
MR. BOGGS STEPS OUT (Grand National, 1937)
MR. BOGGS BUYS A BARREL (Grand National, 1937)

520. MR. DISTRICT ATTORNEY
Based on radio show (1939-51), the pictures are about a crusading lawman.
MR. DISTRICT ATTORNEY (Republic, 1941)
THE CARTER CASE (Republic, 1941)
SECRETS OF THE UNDERGROUND (Republic, 1943)

521. MR. HULOT
French filmmaker Jacques Tati (1908-1982) directed and plays the main character, a charming eccentric who wears a rain coat, smokes a pipe and bumbles his way through a resort community, a modern office or an auto show, depending on the picture. (Mr. Hulot has a walk-on in BED AND BOARD, which is part of Francois Truffaut's ANTOINE DOINEL series.)
MR. HULOT'S HOLIDAY (Cady/GAU-Images, 1954) [aka MONSIEUR HULOT'S HOLIDAY] d Jacques Tati, s Jacques Tati, Nathalie Pascaud, Louis Perrault.
MY UNCLE (Spectra-Gray-Alter-Cady Film del Centauro/Continental, 1958) [aka MON ONCLE] d Jacques Tati, s Jacques Tati, Jean-Pierre Zola, Adrienne Servanti, Alain Becourt.
PLAYTIME (Spectra/Continental, 1973) d Jacques Tati, s Jacques Tati, Barbara Dennek, Jacqueline Lecomte, Valerie Camille.
TRAFFIC (Corona/Columbia, 1972) [aka TRAFIC] d Jacques Tati, s Jacques Tati, Maria Kimberly, Marcel Fravel, Honore Bostel.

521A. MR. JACK
This is a silent comedy series.
MR. JACK CAUGHT IN THE DRESSING ROOM (American Mutoscope & Biograph, 1904)
MR. JACK ENTERTAINS IN HIS OFFICE (American Mutoscope & Biograph, 1904)
MR. JACK IN HIS DRESSING ROOM (American Mutoscope & Biograph, 1904)

522. MR. JONES
These silent comedies may actually be two separate series: the first from Edison 1899, the second, 1908-09, largely directed by D.W. Griffith (1875-1948).
JONES AND HIS PAL IN TROUBLE (Edison 1899)
JONES' INTERRUPTED SLEIGH RIDE (Edison, 1899)
JONES MAKES A DISCOVERY (Edison, 1899)
JONES RETURNS FROM THE CLUB (Edison, 1899)
MR. JONES AT THE BALL (Biograph, 1908) d D.W. Griffith, s Florence Lawrence, John Compson.
MRS. JONES ENTERTAINS (Biograph, 1908) d D.W. Griffith, s Florence Lawrence, John Cumpson.
JONES AND HIS NEIGHBORS (Biograph, 1909) s Florence Lawrence, John Compson, Flora Finch, Mack Sennett.
MR. JONES HAS A CARD PARTY (Biograph, 1909) d D.W. Griffith, s Florence Lawrence, John Cumpson.
MR. JONES' BURGLAR (Biograph, 1909) s Florence Lawrence, John Compson.
MRS. JONES' LOVER (Biograph, 1909)
JONES AND THE LADY BOOK AGENT (Biograph, 1909) d D.W. Griffith, s Florence Lawrence, John Cumpson.
THE JONESES HAVE AMATEUR THEATRICALS (Biograph, 1909) d D.W. Griffith, s Florence Lawrence, John Cumpson.
JONES AND HIS NEW NEIGHBORS (Biograph, 1909) d D.W. Griffith, s Florence Lawrence, John Cumpson.
MRS. JONES' LOVER, OR, "I WANT MY HAT!" (Biograph, 1909) d D.W. Griffith, s Florence Lawrence, John Cumpson.
MR. JONES' BURGLAR (Biograph, 1909) d D.W. Griffith, s Florence Lawrence, John Cumpson.

523. MR. MOTO
John P. Marquand wrote a series of espionage novels featuring I.A. Moto; these are the film versions.
THINK FAST, MR. MOTO (20th Century-Fox, 1937) d Norman Foster, s Peter Lorre, Virginia Field.
THANK YOU MR. MOTO (20th Century-Fox, 1938) d Norman Foster, s Peter Lorre, Thomas Beck.

MR. MOTO'S GAMBLE (20th Century-Fox, 1938) d James Tinling, s Peter Lorre, Keye Luke.
MR. MOTO TAKES A CHANCE (20th Century-Fox, 1938) d Norman Foster, s Peter Lorre, Rochelle Hudson.
THE MYSTERIOUS MR. MOTO (20th Century-Fox, 1938) d Norman Foster, s Peter Lorre, Mary Maguire.
MR. MOTO'S LAST WARNING (20th Century-Fox, 1939) d Norman Foster, s Peter Lorre, Ricardo Cortez.
MR. MOTO IN DANGER ISLAND (20th Century-Fox, 1939) [aka DANGER ISLAND] d Herbert I. Leeds, s Peter Lorre, Jean Hersholt.
MR. MOTO TAKES A VACATION (20th Century-Fox, 1939) d Norman Foster, s Peter Lorre, Joseph Schildkraut.
THE RETURN OF MR. MOTO (20th Century-Fox, 1965) d Ernest Morris, s Henry Silva, Terence Longdon.

524. MRS. MINIVER
From Jan Struther novel, this is the story of a typical British village family.
MRS. MINIVER (MGM, 1942) d William Wyler, s Greer Garson, Walter Pidgeon, Teresa Wright.
THE MINIVER STORY (MGM, 1950) d H.C. Potter, s Greer Garson, Walter Pidgeon, John Hodiak, Leo Genn.

525. MRS. SUNDANCE
The pictures are offshoots of the movie BUTCH CASSIDY AND THE SUNDANCE KID.
MRS. SUNDANCE (20th Century-Fox Television, 1974) (ABC-TV movie) d Marvin Chomsky, s Elizabeth Montgomery, Robert Foxworth, L.Q. Jones.
WANTED: THE SUNDANCE WOMAN (20th Century-Fox Television, 1976) (ABC-TV movie) [aka MRS. SUNDANCE RIDES AGAIN] d Lee Philips, s Katharine Ross, Steve Forrest, Stella Stevens.

526. MR. WONG
Chinese detective Wong solves puzzling crimes.
MR. WONG, DETECTIVE (Monogram, 1938) d William Nigh, s Boris Karloff, Grant Withers, Maxine Jennings.
MYSTERY OF MR. WONG (Mongram, 1939)
MR. WONG IN CHINATOWN (Monogram, 1939)d William Nigh, s Boris Karloff, Grant Withers.
THE FATAL HOUR (Mongram, 1940) d William Nigh, s Boris Karloff, Marjorie Reynolds.
DOOMED TO DIE (Mongram, 1940) d William Nigh, s Boris Karloff, Grant Withers, Marjorie Reynolds.
PHANTOM OF CHINATOWN (Mongram, 1941) d Phil Rosen, s Keye Luke, Lotus Long, Grant Withers.

526A. MUGGSY

These are silent movies.
MUGGSY BECOMES A HERO (Biograph, 1910) s Mary Pickford.
MUGGSY'S FIRST SWEETHEART (Biograph, 1910) s Mary Pickford.

527. MUMMY, THE
The shrouded character (variously known as Im-Ho-Kharis or simply The Mummy) is played by a number of popular horror film actors.
THE MUMMY (Universal, 1932) d Karl Freund, s Boris Karloff.
MUMMY'S BOYS (RKO, 1936) d Fred Guiol, s Bert Wheeler Robert Woolsey.
THE MUMMY'S HAND (Universal, 1940) d Christy Cabanne, s Dick Foran, Tom Tyler, Peggy Moran.
THE MUMMY'S TOMB (Universal, 1942) d Harold Young, s Lon Chaney Jr., Dick Foran, Elyse Knox.
THE MUMMY'S GHOST (Universal, 1944) d Reginald Le Borg, s Lon Chaney Jr., John Carradine.
THE MUMMY'S CURSE (Universal, 1945), d Leslie Goodwins, s Lon Chaney Jr., Peter Coe, Virginia Christine.
ABBOTT AND COSTELLO MEET THE MUMMY (Universal, 1955) d Charles Lamont, s Bud Abbott, Lou Costello, Marie Windsor.
ATTACK OF THE MAYAN MUMMY (Cinematagrafica Calderon, 1957) [aka THE MUMMY STRIKES and THE MUMMY] d Rafael Portillo, s Ramon Gay, Rosita Arenas.
THE MUMMY (Hammer/Universal, 1959) [aka TERROR OF THE MUMMY] d Terence Fisher, s Peter Cushing, Christopher Lee.
THE CURSE OF THE MUMMY'S TOMB (Hammer/Columbia, 1964) d Michael Carreras, s Terence Morgan, Fred Clark.
THE MUMMY'S SHROUD (Hammer/20th Century-Fox, 1967), d John Gilling, s Andre Morell.
BLOOD FROM THE MUMMY'S TOMB (Hammer/American International, 1972) d Seth Holt, s Andrew Keir, Valerie Leon.
THE MUMMY'S VENGEANCE (Lotus/Sara, 1973) [aka THE MUMMY'S REVENGE and THE VENGEANCE OF THE MUMMY] d Carlos Aured, s Paul Naschy, Jack Taylor.

528. MUNSTERS, THE
The television show featuring Herman Munster (a Frankenstein-type creature), his wife Lily, Grandpa (a vampire) and the rest of their family (CBS, 1964-66 and in syndication 1989-) inspired the following pictures.
MUNSTER, GO HOME (Universal, 1966) d Earl Bellamy, s Fred Gwynne, Yvonne De Carlo.
THE MUNSTERS' REVENGE (Universal/NBC1981) (NBC-TV broadcast) d Don Weis, s Fred Gwynne, Yvonne De Carlo, Al Lewis.

529. MUPPETS, THE
Jim Henson's puppet characters were also featured in their own television program and on SESAME STREET.

234 MOTION PICTURE SERIES & SEQUELS

THE MUPPET MOVIE (Associated, 1979), d James Frawley, s Kermit the
  Frog, Miss Piggy.
THE MUPPETS TAKE MANHATTAN (Tri-Star Pictures, 1984), d Frank Oz,
  s Kermit the Frog, Miss Piggy, Fozzie Bear, Gonzo.
SESAME STREET PRESENTS FOLLOW THAT BIRD (Warner Brothers,
  1985) d Ken Kwapis, s Big Bird, Bert and Ernie, Oscar the Grouch.

530. MURDER GOES TO COLLEGE
Newman Sim Perkins and private eye Hank Hyer find the murderer of a college professor, in the first film.
MURDER GOES TO COLLEGE (Paramount, 1937) d Charles Reisner, s
  Roscoe Karns, Marhsa Hunt, Lynne Overman.
PARTNERS IN CRIME (Paramount, 1937) d Ralph Murray, s Lynne
  Overman, Roscoe Karns, Muriel Hutchinson.

531. MUTT AND JEFF
There were twenty-five silent comedies in this series made beginning in 1911 and featuring the tall and short characters from the Ham Fisher newspaper comic strip.

532. MY FRIEND IRMA
From Cy Howard's radio series, these are slapstick tales of a dumb blonde, her brighter roommate and the men in their lives.
MY FRIEND IRMA (Paramount, 1949) d George Marshall, s Marie Wilson,
  John Lund, Dean Martin, Jerry Lewis.
MY FRIEND IRMA GOES WEST (Paramount, 1950) d Hal Walker, s Marie
  Wilson, Jerry Lewis.

533. MY AMERICAN COUSIN
The coming-of-age stories are set in Novia Scotia (first entry) and California and are about a teenaged girl's infatuation with her James Dean-like cousin.
MY AMERICAN COUSIN (Spectrafilm, 1985) d Sandy Wilson, s Margaret
  Langrick, John Wildman, Richard Donat.
AMERICAN BOYFRIENDS (1989) d Sandy Wilson, s Margaret Langrick,
  John Wildman.

534. MY FRIEND FLICKA
Horse stories.
MY FRIEND FLICKA (20th Century-Fox, 1943) d Harold Schuster, s Roddy
  McDowall, Preston Foster.
THUNDERHEAD, SON OF FLICKA (20th Century-Fox, 1945) d Louis King,
  s Roddy McDowall, Preston Foster.
GREEN GRASS OF WYOMING (TCF, 1948) d Louis King, s Peggy Cummins,
  Charles Coburn.

535. NANCY DREW
The pseudonymous Carolyn Keene's girls' book detective inspired this series. The books first appeared in 1930 and now number more than 100. There was also a television series featuring the character, with Pamela Sue Martin and, later, Janet Louise Johnson (ABC 1977-78).
NANCY DREW, DETECTIVE (Warner Brothers, 1938) d William Clemens, s Bonita Granville, John Litel, Frankie Thomas.
NANCY DREW -- REPORTER (Warner Brothers, 1939) d William Clemens, s Bonita Granville, John Litel, Frankie Thomas.
NANCY DREW -- TROUBLE SHOOTER (Warner Brothers, 1939) d William Clemens, s Bonita Granville, John Litel, Frankie Thomas.
NANCY DREW AND THE HIDDEN STAIRCASE (Warner Brothers, 1939) d William Clemens, s Bonita Granville, John Litel, Frankie Thomas.

536. NATIONAL LAMPOON'S VACATION
A typical (?) American family has more holiday mishaps than one might imagine in these comedies.
NATIONAL LAMPOON'S VACATION (Warner Brothers, 1983) d Harold Ramis, s Chevy Chase, Beverly D'Angelo.
NATIONAL LAMPOON'S EUROPEAN VACATION (Warner Brothers, 1985) d Amy Heckerling, s Chevy Chase, Beverly D'Angelo.
NATIONAL LAMPOON'S CHRISTMAS VACATION (Warner Brothers, 1989) d Jeremiah Chechik, s Chevy Chase, Beverly D'Angelo, Randy Quaid.

537. NATIONAL VELVET
The first film dramatizes Enid Bagnold's story of Velvet Brown winning a horse in a raffle and readying it for the Grand National steeplechase. In the sequel, Velvet helps a niece train for the Olympics.
NATIONAL VELVET (MGM, 1944) d Clarence Brown, s Mickey Rooney, Elizabeth Taylor, Donald Crisp, Anne Revere.
INTERNATIONAL VELVET (MGM, 1978) d Bryan Forbes, s Tatum O'Neal, Christopher Plummer.

538. NERO WOLFE
Rex Stout's portly, housebound private investigator and his right-hand Archie Goodwin, who appeared in mystery novels beginning in 1934, have also appeared in a television series (with William Conrad in 1981) and a radio program (with Sydney Greenstreet in 1943-51).
MEET NERO WOLFE (Columbia, 1936) d Herbert Biberman, s Edward Arnold, Lionel Stander.
THE LEAGUE OF FRIGHTENED MEN (Columbia, 1937) d Alfred E. Green, s Walter Connolly, Lionel Stander.
NERO WOLFE (Paramount Television, 1979) (ABC-TV movie) d Frank Gilroy, s Thayer David, Anne Baxter, Tom Mason, Brooke Adams.

539. NEVERENDING STORY, THE

Young Oliver visualizes what he is reading in these fantasy films.
THE NEVERENDING STORY (Warner Brothers, 1984) d Wolfgang
    Petersen, s Noah Hathaway, Barrett Oliver, Tami Stronach.
THE NEVERENDING STORY II (announced 1990) d George Miller, s
    Jonathan Brandis, Kenny Morrison.

540. NEWLYWEDS AND THEIR BABY, THE
The RKO short subject series (nine titles), adapted in the 1920s from the George McManus newspaper cartoons, feature variously Robert Neil, Polly Moran, Robert Hutton, Elizabeth Frazer and Donald McBride. Sunny McKeen plays Baby Snookums.The list is incomplete.
NEWLYWEDS' HOUSE GUEST
PRIZE MAID

541. NICK CARTER
The ace private investigator began appearing in dime novels in 1886, continued his adventures in the pulps and is still thriving as a secret agent in a paperback series (numbering more than 250 entries) today.
NICK CARTER (Itala Films, 1908)
NICK CARTER -- BANDITS IN EVENING DRESS (Itala Films, 1908)
NICK CARTER -- SLEEPING PILLS (Itala Films, 1909)
NICK CARTER IN DANGER (Itala Films, 1909)
NICK CARTER AS AN ACROBAT (Eclair Films, 1910)
NICK CARTER -- THE MYSTERY OF THE WHITE BED (Eclair Films,
    1911)
NICK CARTER AND THE BLACK-COATED THIEVES (Eclair Films, 1915)
NICK CARTER (International Cine, 1921) (Fifteen-chapter serial) s Tom
    Carrigan.
NICK CARTER, MASTER DETECTIVE (MGM, 1939) d Jacques Tourneur, s
    Walter Pidgeon, Rita Johnson.
PHANTOM RAIDERS (MGM, 1940) d Jacques Tourneur, s Walter Pidgeon,
    Donald Meek.
SKY MURDER (MGM, 1940) d George Seitz, s Walter Pidgeon, Donald
    Meek.
CHICK CARTER, DETECTIVE (Columbia, 1946) d Derwin Abrahams, s Lyle
    Talbot.
THE ADVENTURES OF NICK CARTER (Universal, 1972) (NBC-TV movie)
    d Paul Krasny, s Robert Conrad, Shelley Winters, Broderick Crawford.

542. NIGHTMARE ON ELM STREET, A
Freddy Krueger haunts dreams in these horror films. There was also a syndicated TV series, FREDDY'S NIGHTMARES, beginning in 1989.
A NIGHTMARE ON ELM STREET (New Line, 1984) d Wes Craven, s John
    Saxon, Ronnee Blakley.
A NIGHTMARE ON ELM STREET 2: FREDDY'S REVENGE (New Line,
    1985) d Jack Sholder, s Mark Patton, Kim Yers, Robert Englund.

A NIGHTMARE ON ELM STREET 3: DREAM WARRIORS (New Line, 1987) d Chuck Russell, s Heather Langenkamp, Robert Englund.
A NIGHTMARE ON ELM STREET 4: THE DREAM MASTER (New Line, 1988) d Renny Harlin, s Robert Englund.
A NIGHTMARE ON ELM STREET 5: THE DREAM CHILD (New Line, 1989) d Stephen Hopkins, s Robert Englund, Lisa Wilcox.

543. NIGHT OF THE LIVING DEAD
After the success of the first grisly entry, George A. Romero and his partners came to a parting of ways, they taking the LIVING DEAD designation, Romero keeping DEAD. (See also LIVING DEAD entry.) The fourth entry here is based on the 1968 script.
NIGHT OF THE LIVING DEAD (Continental, 1968) d George A. Romero, s Duane Jones, Judith O'Dea.
DAWN OF THE DEAD (United Film Distribution, 1979) d George A. Romero, s David Emge, Ken Foree.
DAY OF THE DEAD (Laurel, 1985) d George A. Romero, s Lori Cardille, Terry Alexander.
NIGHT OF THE LIVING DEAD (21st Century Film, announced 1990) d Tom Savini.

544. NIGHT STALKER, THE
Carl Kolchak, a luckless reporter, stumbles across modern-day vampires and other weirdies in the tele-features and TV series (KOLCHAK: THE NIGHT STALKER on ABC, 1974-75).
THE NIGHT STALKER (ABC, 1972) (ABC-TV movie) d John Llewellyn Moxey, s Darren McGavin, Carol Lynley.
THE NIGHT STRANGLER (ABC Circle, 1973) (ABC-TV movie) d Dan Curtis, s Darren McGavin, Jo Ann Pflug.

544A. NIPPER
These pictures were produced in England.
NIPPER AND THE CURATE (1915) s Lupino Lane.
NIPPER'S BANK HOLIDAY (1915) s Lupino Lane.
NIPPER'S BUSY HOLIDAY (1915) s Lupino Lane.

545. NO. 1 OF THE SECRET SERVICE
Agent Charles Bind is agent No. 1 of the Secret Service.
NO. 1 OF THE SECRET SERVICE (Shonteff/Hemdale, 1978) d Lindsay Shonteff, s Nick Henson, Richard Todd.
LICENSED TO LOVE AND KILL (Shonteff/Palm Springs, 1979) d Lindsay Shonteff, s Gareth Hunt, Nick Tate.

546. NO RETREAT, NO SURRENDER
A teenager learns kung fu from the ghost of Bruce Lee.
NO RETREAT, NO SURRENDER (1985) d Corey Yuen, s Kurt McKinney.

NO RETREAT, NO SURRENDER II (Seasonal Films, 1987) d Corey Yuen, s Cynthia Rothrock, Loren Avedon, Max Thayer.

547. NORTHWEST MOUNTED POLICE ADVENTURES
B Northerns showcase Kermit Maynard as a scarlet-jacketed lawman.
THE FIGHTING TROOPER (Ambassador, 1934) d Ray Taylor, s Kermit Maynard, Barbara Worth.
NORTHERN FRONTIER (Ambassador, 1935) d Sam Newfield, s Kermit Maynard, Eleanor Hunt.
WILDERNESS MAIL (Ambassador, 1935) d Forrest Sheldon, s Kermit Maynard, Syd Saylor, Doris Brook.
CODE OF THE MOUNTED (Ambassador, 1935) d Sam Newfield, s Kermit Maynard, Lillian Miles.
THE RED BLOOD OF COURAGE (Ambassador, 1935) d Jack English, s Kermit Maynard, Ann Sheridan.
TRAILS OF THE WILD (Ambassador, 1935) d Sam Newfield, s Kermit Maynard, Al "Fuzzy" Knight.
HIS FIGHTING BLOOD (Ambassador, 1935) d John English, s Kermit Maynard, Polly Ann Young.
TIMBER WAR (Ambassador, 1935) d Sam Newfield, s Kermit Maynard, Lucille Lund.
SONG OF THE TRAIL (Ambassador, 1936) d Russell Hopton, s Kermit Maynard, Al "Fuzzy" Knight, Evelyn Brent.
WILDCAT TROOPER (Ambassador, 1936) dElmer Clifton, s Kermit Maynard, Al "Fuzzy" Knight, Lois Wilde.
PHANTOM PATROL (Ambassador, 1936) d Charles Hutchinson, s Kermit Maynard, Joan Barclay.
VALLEY OF TERROR (Ambassador, 1937) d Al Herman, s Kermit Maynard, Harley Wood.
WHISTLING BULLETS (Ambassador, 1937) d John English, s Kermit Maynard, Harley Wood.
THE FIGHTING TEXAN (Ambassador, 1937) d Charles Abbott, s Kermit Maynard, Elaine Shepard.
GALLOPING DYNAMITE (Ambassador, 1937) d Harry Fraser, s Kermit Maynard, Ariane Allen.
ROUGH RIDIN' RHYTHM (Ambassador, 1937) d J.P. McGowan, s Kermit Maynard, Beryl Wallace, Betty Mack.
ROARING SIX GUNS (Ambassador, 1937) d J.P. McGowan, s Kermit Maynard, Mary Hayes.

548. NOSFERATU
The vampire featured in these films is an early cinematic version of DRACULA.
NOSFERATU (Prana, 1922) [aka NOSFERATU -- A SYMPHONY OF HORROR, NOSFERATU THE VAMPIRE, TERROR OF DRACULA, DRACULA, NOSFERATU -- THE TWELFTH HOUR] d F.W. Murnau, s Max Schreck, Alexander Granach.

NOSFERATU THE VAMPYRE (20th Century-Fox, 1979) d Werner Herzog, s Klaus Kinski, Isabelle Adjani.
NOSFERATU IN VENICE (Scena, 1987) d Augusto Caminito, s Klaus Kinski, Christopher Plummer.

549. NURSE SARAH KEATE
The spinsterish nurse of Mignon G. Eberhart's mystery novels is paired in solving crimes with police detective Lance O'Leary.
WHILE THE PATIENT SLEPT (First National, 1935) d Ray Enright, s Aline MacMahon, Guy Kibbee, Allen Jenkins.
THE MURDER OF DR. HARRIGAN (First National, 1936) d Frank McDonald, s Kay Linaker, Ricardo Cortez.
MURDER BY AN ARISTOCRAT (First National, 1936) d Frank McDonald, s Marguerite Churchill, Lyle Talbot.
THE GREAT HOSPITAL MYSTERY (20th Century-Fox, 1937) d James Tinling, s Jane Darwell, Sally Blane.
THE PATIENT IN ROOM 18 (Warner Brothers/First National, 1938) d Crane Wilbur, s Ann Sheridan, Patric Knowles.
MYSTERY HOUSE (Warner Brothers/First National, 1938) d Noel Smith, s Dick Purcell, Ann Sheridan.
THE WHITE COCKATOO (Warner Brothers, 1935) dAlan Crosland, s Jean Muir, Ricardo Cortez.

550. OH, GOD
The comedies feature the venerable cigar-chewing comedian George Burns as the Lord.
OH GOD! (Warner Brothers, 1977) d Carl Reiner, s George Burns, John Denver, Teri Garr.
OH GOD! BOOK II (Warner Brothers, 1980) d Gilbert Cates, s George Burns, Suzanne Pleshette.
OH, GOD! YOU DEVIL (Warner Brothers, 1984) d Paul Bogart, s George Burns, Ted Wass.

550A. OLD MAID
This is an early silent comedy series.
THE OLD MAID IN THE HORSE CAR (Edison, 1901)
THE OLD MAID HAVING HER PICTURE TAKEN (Edison, 1901)
THE OLD MAID'S DISAPPOINTMENT (Edison, 1902)
THE OLD MAID AND THE BURGLAR (American Mutoscope & Biograph, 1903)
THE OLD MAID'S PICTURE (American Mutoscope & Biograph, 1903)
THE OLD MAID AND THE FORTUNE TELLER (Edison, 1904)

551. OLD MAN IN THE CORNER, THE
Baroness Emmuska Orczy's armchair detective was featured in a series of twelve short British films, four of which are listed here.
THE KENSINGTON MYSTERY (1924) s Rolf Leslie, Renee Wakefield.

THE BRIGHTON MYSTERY (1924) s Rolf Leslie, Renee Wakefield.
THE NORTHERN MYSTERY (1924) s Rolf Leslie, Renee Wakefield.
THE YORK MYSTERY (1924) s Rolf Leslie, Renee Wakefield.

552. OLD MOTHER RILEY
An Irish washerwoman and daughter Kitty were featured in a stage play written by Arthur Lucan, and also in a BBC radio series and television program with Brian Murphy and Maureen Lipman. Arthur Lucan plays the lead, Kitty Macshane plays the daughter. A match industrialist dies and leaves his fortune to his family with the condition that it take in the first person they see selling matches -- who turns out to be loud Old Mother Riley.
OLD MOTHER RILEY (Renown, 1937) [aka THE RETURN OF OLD
    MOTHER RILEY and THE ORIGINAL OLD MOTHER RILEY] d
    Oswald Mitchell, s Arthur Lucan, Kitty McShane.
OLD MOTHER RILEY IN PARIS (Renown, 1938) [aka OLD MOTHER
    RILEY CATCHES A QUISLING] d Oswald Mitchell, s Arthur Lucan,
    Kitty McShane, Jerry Verno.
OLD MOTHER RILEY MP (Renown, 1939)d Oswald Mitchell, s Arthur
    Lucan, Kitty McShane, Torin Thatcher.
OLD MOTHER RILEY JOINS UP (Renown, 1939) d Maclean Rogers, s
    Arthur Lucan, Kitty McShane, Bruce Seton.
OLD MOTHER RILEY IN SOCIETY (Renown, 1940) d John Baxter, s Arthur
    Lucan, Kitty McShane, John Stuart.
OLD MOTHER RILEY IN BUSINESS (Renown, 1940) d John Baxter, s
    Arthur Lucan, Kitty McShane, Cyril Chamberlain.
OLD MOTHER RILEY'S GHOSTS (Anglo-American, 1941) d John Baxter, s
    Arthur Lucan, Kitty McShane, John Stuart.
OLD MOTHER RILEY'S CIRCUS (Allied Artists, 1941) d Thomas Bentley, s
    Arthur Lucan, Kitty McShane, John Londgen.
OLD MOTHER RILEY, DETECTIVE (Renown, 1943) d Lance Comfort, s
    Arthur Lucan, Kitty McShane, Ivan Brandt.
OLD MOTHER RILEY OVERSEAS (Renown, 1943) d Oswald Mitchell, s
    Arthur Lucan, Kitty McShane, Morris Harvey.
OLD MOTHER RILEY AT HOME (Renown, 1945) d Oswald Mitchell, s
    Arthur Lucan, Kitty McShane, Freddie Forbes.
OLD MOTHER RILEY, HEADMISTRESS (Renown, 1950) d John Harlow, s
    Arthur Lucan, Kitty McShane, Enid Hewitt.
OLD MOTHER RILEY'S JUNGLE TREASURE (Renown, 1951) d Maclean
    Rogers, s Arthur Lucan, Kitty McShane, Garry Marsh.
OLD MOTHER RILEY (Renown, 1952) [aka OLD MOTHER RILEY'S NEW
    VENTURE] d John Harlow, s Arthur Lucan, Kitty McShane.
OLD MOTHER RILEY MEETS THE VAMPIRE (Renown, 1952) [aka MY
    SON THE VAMPIRE and MOTHER RILEY MEETS THE VAMPIRE
    and VAMPIRE OVER LONDON and KING ROBOT and MOTHER
    RILEY RUNS RIOT and DRACULA'S DESIRE] d John Gilling, s
    Arthur Lucan, Kitty McShane, Bela Lugosi.

MOTION PICTURE SERIES & SEQUELS 241

553. OLD SHATTERHAND
These pioneer tales, which greatly resemble James Fenimore Cooper's LEATHERSTOCKING stories, are actually based on German Karl May's 1890s novels. The frontiersman Old Shatterhand is also known as Old Surehand in the Granger versions, Old Firehand in the Cameron editions. Companion Winnetou is a staunch Native American companion.
APACHE GOLD (Columbi, 1963) [aka WINNETOU THE WARRIOR and WINNETOU PART I] d Harald Reinl, s Lex Barker, Pierre Brice.
LAST OF THE RENEGADES (Constantin, 1964) [aka WINNETOU II] d Harald Reinl, s Lex Barker, Pierre Brice.
TREASURE OF SILVER LAKE (Rialtox/Jadran Film, 1965) d Harald Reinl, s Lex Barker, Pierre Brice.
AMONG VULTURES (Rialto Film, 1966) [aka FRONTIER HELLCAT] d Alfred Vohrer, s Stewart Granger, Pierre Brice, Elke Sommer.
THE DESPERADO TRAIL (Constantin, 1966) [aka WINNETOU III] d Harald Reinl, s Lex Barker, Pierre Brice.
WINNETOU AND SHATTERHAND IN THE VALLEY OF DEATH (Super International, 1968) d Harald Renil, s Lex Barker, Pierre Brice.
RAMPAGE AT APACHE WELLS (Columbia, 1966) d Harald Philipp, s Stewart Granger, Pierre Brice.
SHATTERHAND (Goldstone, 1968) [aka OLD SHATTERHAND] d Hugo Fregonese, s Lex Barker, Pierre Brice, Daliah Lavi.
THUNDER AT THE BORDER (Columbia, 1967) d Alfred Vohrer, s Rod Cameron, Pierre Brice.
FLAMING FRONTIER (Warner Brothers-Seven Arts, 1968) [aka OLD SUREHAND] d Alfred Vohrer, s Stewart Granger, Pierre Brice.
HALF BREED (Hampton, 1973) d Harald Philipp, s Lex Barker, Pierre Brice.

554. OLSON AND JOHNSON
The vaudeville comedians bring their stage antics to cinema in these films.
OH SAILOR BEHAVE! (Warner Brothers, 1930) d Archie Mayo, s Irene Delroy, Charles King, Ole Olsen, Chic Johnson.
FIFTY MILLION FRENCHMEN (Warner Brothers, 1931) d Lloyd Bacon, s William Gaxton, Helen Broderick, Ole Olsen, Chic Johnson.
GOLD DUST GERTIE (Warner Brothers, 1931) d Lloyd Bacon, s Winnie Lightner, Arthur Hoyt, Ole Olsen, Chic Johnson.
COUNTRY GENTLEMEN (Republic, 1937) d Ralph Staub, s Joyce Compton, Lila Lee, Ole Olsen, Chic Johnson.
ALL OVER TOWN (Republic, 1937) d James W. Horne, s Mary Howard, Harry Stockwell, Ole Olsen, Chic Johnson.
HELLZAPOPPIN (Universal, 1941) d H.C. Potter, s Martha Raye, Mischa Auer, Ole Olsen, Chic Johnson.
CRAZY HOUSE (Universal, 1943) d Edward Cline, s Martha O'Driscoll, Patric Knowles, Ole Olsen, Chic Johnson.
GHOST CATCHERS (Univeral, 1944) d Edward L. Cline, s Gloria Jean, Ole Olsen, Chic Johnson.

SEE MY LAWYER (Universal, 1945) d Edward L. Cline, s Alan Curtis, Ole Olsen, Chic Johnson.

555. O'MALLEY
Patrolman Jim O'Malley, whose beat is near a grade school, befriends kids and a teacher and also uncovers a bootlegging hideout only to let a thug go to protect the teacher.
THE MAKING OF O'MALLEY (First National, 1925) d Lambert Hillyer, s Milton Sills, Dorothy Mackaill.
THE GREAT O'MALLEY (Warner Brothers, 1937) d William Dieterle, s Pat O'Brien, Sybil Jason, Humphrey Bogart.

556. OMEN, THE
The anti-Christ Damien terrorizes his stepparents and others. He ages as the series progresses, and in the third picture he heads Thorn Industries.
THE OMEN (20th Century-Fox, 1976) d Richard Donner, s Gregory Peck, Lee Remick.
DAMIEN -- OMEN II (20th Century-Fox, 1978) d Don Taylor. s William Holden, Lee Grant, Lew Ayres.
THE FINAL CONFLICT (20th Century-Fox, 1981) d Graham Baker, s Sam Neill, Rossano Brazzi.

557. ONE POLICE PLAZA
A New York police lieutenant bucks authority to solve a crime.
ONE POLICE PLAZA (1986) (TV movie) d Jerry Jameson, s Robert Conrad.
THE RED SPIDER (1988) d Jerry Jameson, s James Farention, Jennifer O'Neill.

559. OTHER SIDE OF THE MOUNTAIN, THE
Olympic-hopeful skier Jill Kinmont suffers an accident which leaves her paralyzed.
THE OTHER SIDE OF THE MOUNTAIN (Jack Bond, 1975) d Larry Peerce, s Marilyn Hassett, Beau Bridges.
THE OTHER SIDE OF THE MOUNTAIN PART 2 (Universal, 1978) d Larry Peerce, s Marilyn Hassett, Timothy Bottoms.

560. OUR GANG
These Hal Roach comedies, with an interracial cast of youngsters, were later called LITTLE RASCALS. The pictures are silents through SMALL TALK (1929).
OUR GANG (Roach Pathe, 1922) d Robert F McGowan, s Ernie "Sunshine Sammy" Morrison, Jackie Condon, Peggy Cartwright, Dinah the Mule.
FIRE FIGHTERS (Roach Pathe, 1922) d Robert F. McGowan and Tom McNamara, Jackie "Rosie" Condon, Peggy Cartwright, Monty O'Grady, Allen "Farina" Hoskins, Ernie "Booker T" Morrison, Winston Doty, Dinah the Mule.

MOTION PICTURE SERIES & SEQUELS 243

YOUNG SHERLOCKS (Roach Pathe, 1922) d Robert F. McGowan and Tom McNamara, Jackie Condon, Peggy Cartwright, Mickey Daniels, Allen "Farina" Hoskins, Mary Kornman. Dinah the Mule.
ONE TERRIBLE DAY (Roach Pathe, 1922) d Robert F. McGowan and Tom McNamara, s Jack Davis, Mickey Daniels, Ernie "Booker T" Morrison, Jackie Condon, Allen "Farina" Hoskins, Peggy Cartwright, Winston Doty.
A QUIET STREET (Roach Pathe, 1922) d Robert F. McGowan and Tom McNamara, s Jack Davis, Mickey Daniels, Ernie "Booker T" Morrison, Jackie Condon, Peggy Cartwright, Dinah the Mule.
SATURDAY MORNING (Roach Pathe, 1922) d Robert F. McGowan and Tom McNamara, s Jack Davis, Mickey Daniels, Ernie "Sorghum" Morrison, Allen "Maple" Hoskins, Jackie Condon, Dinah the Mule.
THE BIG SHOW (Roach Pathe, 1923) d Robert F. McGowan, s Jackie Davis, Mickey Daniels, Allen "Farina" Hoskins.
THE COBBLER (Roach Pathe, 1923) d Tom McNamara, s Mickey Daniels, Jack Davis, Ernie "Sunshine Sammy" Morrison, Pete the Pup.
THE CHAMPEEN (Roach Pathe, 1923) d Robert F. McGowan, s Mickey Daniels, Ernie "Sunshine Sammy" Morrison, Joe Cobb.
BOYS TO BOARD (Roach Pathe, 1923) d Tom McNamara, s Ernie "Sunshine Sammy" Morrison, Jack Davis, Joe Cobb.
A PLEASANT JOURNEY (Roach Pathe, 1923) d Robert F. McGowan, s Ernie Morrison, Mickey Daniels, Mary Kornman.
GIANTS VS. YANKS (Roach Pathe, 1923) d Robert F. McGowan, s Mickey Daniels, Allen "Farina" Hoskins, Joe Cobb, Dinah the Mule.
BACK STAGE (Roach Pathe, 1923) d Robert F. McGowan, s Mickey Daniels, Joe Cobb, Allen "Farina" Hoskins.
DOGS OF WAR (Roach Pathe, 1923) d Robert F. McGowan, s Mickey Daniels, Mary Kornman.
LODGE NIGHT (Roach Pathe, 1923) d Robert F. McGowan, s Joe Cobb, Jack Davis, Ernie Morrison.
STAGE FRIGHT (Roach Pathe, 1923) d Robert F. McGowan, s Joe Cobb, Ernie "Sunshine Sammy" Morrison, Mary Kornman.
SUNDAY CALM (Roach Pathe, 1923) d Robert F. McGowan, s Ernie Morrison, Jackie Condon, Jack Davis.
NO NOISE (Roach Pathe, 1923) d Robert F. McGowan, s Mickey Daniels, Mary Kornman.
DERBY DAY (Roach Pathe, 1923) d Robert F. McGowan, s Ernie "Sunshine Sammy" Morrison, Allen "Farina" Hoskins, Mickey Daniels.
TIRE TROUBLE (Roach Pathe, 1923) d Robert F. McGowan, s Mickey Daniels, Joe Cobb.
BIG BUSINESS (Roach Pathe, 1924) d Robert F. McGowan, s Mickey Daniels, Mary Kornman.
THE BUCCANEERS (Roach Pathe, 1924) d Robert F. McGowan and Mark Haldane, s Mickey Daniels, Mary Kornman, Pal the Dog.
FAST COMPANY (Roach Pathe, 1924) d Robert F. McGowan, s Mickey Daniels, Joe Cobb.

SEEIN' THINGS (Roach Pathe, 1924) d Robert F. McGowan, s Ernie Morrison, Florence Morrison, Mickey Daniels.
COMMENCEMENT DAY (Roach Pathe, 1924) d Robert F. McGowan and Mark Haldane, s Mary Kornman, Joe Cobb.
IT'S A BEAR (Roach Pathe, 1924) d Robert F. McGowan, s Mickey Daniels, Mary Kornman.
CRADLE ROBBERS (Roach Pathe, 1924) d Robert F. McGowan, s Joe Cobb, Mickey Daniels.
JUBILO, JR. (Roach Pathe, 1924) d Robert F. McGowan, s Mickey Daniels, Mary Kornman.
HIGH SOCIETY (Roach Pathe, 1924) d Robert F. McGowan, s Mickey Daniels, Mary Kornman.
THE SUN DOWN LIMITED (Roach Pathe, 1924) d Robert F. McGowan, s Mickey Daniels, Mary Kornman.
EVERY MAN FOR HIMSELF (Roach Pathe, 1924) d Robert F. McGowan, s Mickey Daniels, Mary Kornman.
THE MYSTERIOUS MYSTERY! (Roach Pathe, 1924) d Robert F. McGowan, s Mickey Daniels, Joe Cobb, Eugene Jackson, Sing Joy.
THE BIG TOWN (Roach Pathe, 1925) d Robert F. McGowan, s Mickey Daniels, Mary Kornman.
CIRCUS FEVER (Roach Pathe, 1925) d Robert F. McGowan, s Mickey Daniels, Mary Kornman.
DOG DAYS (Roach Pathe, 1925) d Robert F. McGowan, s Mickey Daniels, Mary Kornman.
THE LOVE BUG (Roach Pathe, 1925) d Robert F. McGowan, s Mickey Daniels, Mary Kornman.
ASK GRANDMA (Roach Pathe, 1925) d Robert F. McGowan, s Mickey Daniels, Mary Kornman.
SHOOTIN' INJUNS (Roach Pathe, 1925) d Robert F. McGowan, s Mickey Daniels, Mary Kornman, Joe Cobb, Eugene Jackson.
OFFICIAL OFFICERS (Roach Pathe, 1925) d Robert F. McGowan, s Mickey Daniels, Mary Kornman.
MARY, QUEEN OF TOTS (Roach Pathe, 1925) d Robert F. McGowan, s Mickey Daniels, Mary Kornman.
BOYS WILL BE JOYS (Roach Pathe, 1925) d Robert F. McGowan, s Mickey Daniels, Mary Kornman.
BETTER MOVIES (Roach Pathe, 1925) d Robert F. McGowan, s Mickey Daniels, Mary Kornman.
YOUR OWN BACK YARD (Roach Pathe, 1925) d Robert F. McGowan, s Mickey Daniels, Mary Kornman, Allen "Farina" Hoskins, Johnny Downs.
ONE WILD RIDE (Roach Pathe, 1925) d Robert F. McGowan, s Mickey Daniels, Mary Kornman.
GOOD CHEER (Roach Pathe, 1925) d Robert F. McGowan, s Mickey Daniels, Mary Kornman, Joe Cobb, Pal the Dog.
BURIED TREASURE (Roach Pathe, 1925) d Robert F. McGowan, s Mickey Daniels, Mary Kornman, Jay R. "Specks" Smith.

MONKEY BUSINESS (Roach Pathe, 1926) d Robert F. McGowan, s Mickey Daniels, Mary Kornman.
BABY CLOTHES (Roach Pathe, 1926) d Robert F. McGowan, s Mickey Daniels, Mary Kornman.
UNCLE TOM'S UNCLE (Roach Pathe, 1926) d Robert F. McGowan, s Mickey Daniels, Mary Kornman, Jannie Hoskins, Bobby "Bonedust" Young.
THUNDERING FLEAS (Roach Pathe, 1926) d Robert F. McGowan, s Mickey Daniels, Mary Kornman.
SHIVERING SPOOKS (Roach Pathe, 1926) d Robert F. McGowan, s Joe Cobb, Mary Kornman.
THE FOURTH ALARM (Roach Pathe, 1926) d Robert F. McGowan, s Joe Cobb, Mary Kornman.
WAR FEATHERS (Roach Pathe, 1926) d Robert F. McGowan, s Joe Cobb, Johnny Downs.
SEEING THE WORLD (Roach Pathe, 1927) d Robert F. McGowan, s Joe Cobb, Jean Darling.
TELLING WHOPPERS (Roach Pathe, 1926) d Robert F. McGowan and Anthony Mack, s Johnny Downs, Jay R. Smith, Scooter Lowry, Joe Cobb.
BRING HOME THE TURKEY (Roach Pathe, 1927) d Robert F. McGowan and Anthony Mack, s Jean Darling, Peggy Eames, Scooter Lowry, Joe Cobb.
TEN YEARS OLD (Roach Pathe, 1927) d Anthony Mack, s Joe Cobb, Allen "Farina" Hoskins.
LOVE MY DOG (Roach Pathe, 1927) d Robert F. McGowan, s Allen Hoskins, Jackie Condon.
TIRED BUSINESS MEN (Roach Pathe, 1927) d Anthony Mack and Charles Oelze, s Allen "Farina" Hoskins, Jean Darling.
BABY BROTHER (Roach Pathe, 1927) d Anthony Mack and Charles Oelze, s Joe Cobb, Jay R. Smith.
CHICKEN FEED (Roach Pathe, 1927) d Anthony Mack and Charles Oelze, s Johnny Downs, Joe Cobb, Scooter Lowry.
OLYMPIC GAMES (Roach Pathe, 1927) d Robert F. McGowan, s Bobby "Wheezer" Hutchins, Joe Cobb.
THE GLORIOUS FOURTH (Roach Pathe, 1927) d Robert F. McGowan, s Joe Cobb, Allen "Farina" Hoskins, Pete the Pup.
PLAYING HOOKEY (Roach Pathe, 1927) d Anthony Mack, s Allen "Farina" Hoskins, Jackie Condon.
THE SMILE WINS (Roach Pathe, 1927) d Robert F. McGowan, s Allen "Farina" Hoskins.
YALE VS. HARVARD (Roach MGM, 1927) d Robert F. McGowan, s Joe Cobb, Allen "Farina" Hoskins, Jean Darling.
THE OLD WALLOP (Roach MGM, 1927) d Robert F. McGowan, s Joe Cobb, Allen "Farina" Hoskins, Jean Darling, Bobby "Wheezer" Hutchins.
HEEBEE JEEBEES (Roach MGM, 1927) d Anthony Mack, s Joe Cobb, Allen "Farina" Hoskins, Jean Darling, Bobby "Wheezer" Hutchins.

DOG HEAVEN (Roach MGM, 1927) d Robert F. McGowan, s Joe Cobb, Allen "Farina" Hoskins, Jean Darling, Bobby "Wheezer" Hutchins.
SPOOK SPOOFING (Roach MGM, 1928) d Robert F. McGowan, s Joe Cobb, Allen "Farina" Hoskins, Jean Darling, Bobby "Wheezer" Hutchins.
RAINY DAYS (Roach MGM, 1928) d Robert F. McGowan, s Joe Cobb, Allen "Farina" Hoskins, Jean Darling, Bobby "Wheezer" Hutchins.
EDISON, MARCONI & CO. (Roach MGM, 1928) d Anthony Mack, s Joe Cobb, Allen "Farina" Hoskins, Jean Darling, Bobby "Wheezer" Hutchins.
BARNUM & RINGLING, INC. (Roach MGM, 1928) d Robert F. McGowan, s Joe Cobb, Allen "Farina" Hoskins, Jean Darling, Bobby "Wheezer" Hutchins, Oliver Hardy, Pete the Pup.
FAIR AND MUDDY (Roach MGM, 1928) d Robert F. McGowan, s Joe Cobb, Allen "Farina" Hoskins, Jean Darling, Bobby "Wheezer" Hutchins.
CRAZY HOUSE (Roach MGM, 1928) d Robert F. McGowan, s Joe Cobb, Allen "Farina" Hoskins, Jean Darling, Bobby "Wheezer" Hutchins.
GROWING PAINS (Roach MGM, 1928) d Robert F. McGowan, s Joe Cobb, Allen "Farina" Hoskins, Jean Darling, Bobby "Wheezer" Hutchins, Pete the Pup.
OLD GRAY HOSS (Roach MGM, 1928) d Anthony Mack, s Joe Cobb, Allen "Farina" Hoskins, Jean Darling, Bobby "Wheezer" Hutchins.
SCHOOL BEGINS (Roach MGM, 1928) d Anthony Mack, s Jean Darling, Bobby "Wheezer" Hutchins.
THE SPANKING AGE (Roach MGM, 1928) d Robert F. McGowan, s Joe Cobb, Allen "Farina" Hoskins, Jean Darling, Bobby "Wheezer" Hutchins.
ELECTION DAY (Roach MGM, 1929) d Anthony Mack, s Joe Cobb, Allen "Farina" Hoskins, Bobby "Wheezer" Hutchins.
NOISY NOISES (Roach MGM, 1929) d Robert F. McGowan, s Joe Cobb, Jean Darling.
THE HOLY TERROR (Roach MGM, 1929) d Anthony Mack, s Mary Ann Jackson, Joe Cobb.
WIGGLE YOUR EARS (Roach MGM, 1929) d Robert F. McGowan, s Harry Spear, Mary Ann Jackson.
FAST FREIGHT (Roach MGM, 1929) d Anthony Mack, s Allen "Farina" Hoskins, Joe Cobb.
LITTLE MOTHER (Roach MGM, 1929) d Robert F. McGowan, s Bobby "Wheezer" Hutchins, Mary Ann Jackson.
CAT, DOG & CO. (Roach MGM, 1929) d Anthony Mack, s Bobby "Wheezer" Hutchins, Joe Cobb.
SATURDAY'S LESSON (Roach MGM, 1929) d Robert F. McGowan, s Allen "Farina" Hoskins, Joe Cobb.
SMALL TALK (Roach MGM, 1929) d Robert F. McGowan, s Bobby "Wheezer" Hutchins, Mary Ann Jackson.
RAILROADIN' (Roach MGM, 1929) d Robert F. McGowan, s Allen "Farina" Hoskins, Joe Cobb.

BOXING GLOVES (Roach MGM, 1929) d Anthony Mack, s Joe Cobb, Norman "Chubby" Chaney, Mary Ann Jackson.
LAZY DAYS (Roach MGM, 1929) d Robert F. McGowan, s Joe Cobb, Norman "Chubby" Chaney, Mary Ann Jackson.
BOUNCING BABIES (Roach MGM, 1929) d Robert McGowan, s Norman "Chubby" Chaney, Mary Ann Jackson, Jackie Cooper.
MOAN & GROAN, INC. (Roach MGM, 1929) d Robert F. McGowan, s Allen "Farina" Hoskins, Mary Ann Jackson.
SHIVERING SHAKESPEARE (Roach MGM, 1929) d Anthony Mack, s Jackie Cooper, Edith Fellows, Douglas "Turkie Egg" Greer.
THE FIRST SEVEN YEARS (Roach MGM, 1930) d Robert F. McGowan, s Donald "Speck" Haines, Mary Ann Jackson, Jackie Cooper.
WHEN THE WIND BLOWS (Roach MGM, 1930) d James W. Horne, s Jackie Cooper, Mary Ann Jackson.
BEAR SHOOTERS (Roach MGM, 1930) d Robert F. McGowan, s Donald "Spud" Janney, Bobby "Wheezer" Hutchins.
A TOUGH WINTER (Roach MGM, 1930) d Robert F. McGowan, s Allen "Farina" Hoskins, Mary Ann Jackson.
PUPS IS PUPS (Roach MGM, 1930) d Robert F. McGowan, s Bobby "Wheezer" Hutchins, Allen "Farina" Hoskins.
TEACHER'S PET (Roach MGM, 1930) d Robert F. McGowan, s Jackie Cooper, Norman "Chubby" Chaney.
SCHOOL'S OUT (Roach MGM, 1930) d Robert F. McGowan, s Jackie Cooper, Matthew "Stymie" Beard.
HELPING GRANDMA (Roach MGM, 1930) d Robert F. McGowan, s Matthew "Stymie" Beard, Mary Ann Jackson.
LOVE BUSINESS (Roach MGM, 1931) d Robert F. McGowan, s Jackie Cooper.
LITTLE DADDY (Roach MGM, 1931) d Jackie Cooper, Norman "Chubby" Chaney.
BARGAIN DAY (Roach MGM, 1931) d Robert F. McGowan, s Matthew "Stymie" Beard, Shirley Jean Rickert.
FLY MY KITE (Roach MGM, 1931) d Robert F. McGowan, s Allen "Farina" Hutchins, Norman "Chubby" Chaney.
BIG EARS (Roach MGM, 1931) d Robert F. McGowan, s Bobby "Wheezer" Hutchins, Matthew "Stymie" Beard.
SHIVER MY TIMBERS (Roach MGM, 1931) d Robert F. McGowan, s Matthew "Stymie" Beard, Bobby "Wheezer" Hutchins.
DOGS IS DOGS (Roach MGM, 1931) d Robert F. McGowan, s Bobby "Wheezer" Hutchins, Matthew "Stymie" Beard, Sherwood "Spud" Bailey.
READIN' AND WRITIN' (Roach MGM, 1932) d Robert F. McGowan, s Kendall "Breezy Brisbane" McComas, Matthew "Stymie" Beard.
FREE EATS (Roach MGM, 1932) d Raymond McCarey, s Bobby "Wheezer" Hutchins.
SPANKY (Roach MGM, 1932) d Robert F. McGowan, s George "Spanky" McFarland, Kendall "Breezy Brisbane" McComas.

CHOO-CHOO (Roach MGM, 1932) d Robert F. McGowan, s George "Spanky" McFarland, Kendall "Breezy Brisbane" McComas, Matthew "Stymie" Beard.
THE POOCH (Roach MGM, 1932) d Robert F. McGowan, s George "Spanky" McFarland, Kendall "Breezy Brisbane" McComas, Dorothy DeBorba.
HOOK AND LADDER (Roach MGM, 1932) d Robert F. McGowan, s George "Spanky" McFarland, Dickie Moore.
FREE WHEELING (Roach MGM, 1932) d Robert F. McGowan, s George "Spanky" McFarland, Matthew "Stymie" Beard.
BIRTHDAY BLUES (Roach MGM, 1932) d Robert F. McGowan, s George "Spanky" McFarland, Carlena Beard, Douglas Greer.
A LAD AN' A LAMP (Roach MGM, 1932) d Robert F. McGowan, s George "Spanky" McFarland, Dickie Moore.
FISH HOOKY (Roach MGM, 1932) d Robert F. McGowan, s George "Spanky" McFarland, Bobbie "Cotton" Beard, Donald Haines.
FORGOTTEN BABIES (Roach MGM, 1932) d Robert F. McGowan, s George "Spanky" McFarland, Dickie Moore.
THE KID FROM BORNEO (Roach MGM, 1933) d Robert F. McGowan, s George "Spanky" McFarland, Matthew "Stymie" Beard.
MUSH AND MILK (Roach MGM, 1933) d Robert F. McGowan, s George "Spanky" McFarland, Tommy Bond.
BEDTIME WORRIES (Roach MGM, 1933) d Robert F. McGowan, s George "Spanky" McFarland, Mathew "Stymie" Beard.
WILD POSES (Roach MGM, 1933) d Robert F. McGowan, s George "Spanky" McFarland, Jerry Tucker, Tommy Bond.
HI'-NEIGHBOR! (Roach MGM, 1934) d Gus Meins, s George "Spanky" McFarland, Wally Albright, Matthew "Stymie" Beard.
FOR PETE'S SAKE! (Roach MGM, 1933) d Gus eins, s George "Spanky" McFarland, Wally Albright, Scotty Beckett.
THE FIRST ROUND-UP (Roach MGM, 1933) d Gus Meins, s George "Spanky" McFarland, Scotty Beckett.
HONKY DONKEY (Roach MGM, 1933) d Gus Meins, s George "Spanky" McFarland, Scotty Beckett, Willie Mae "Buckwheat" Taylor.
MIKE FRIGHT (Roach MGM, 1934) d Gus Meins, s George "Spanky" McFarland, Scotty Beckett, Tommy Bond.
WASHEE IRONEE (Roach MGM, 1934) d Gus Meins, s George "Spanky" McFarland, Wally "Waldo" Albright, Matthew "Stymie" Beard.
MAMA'S LITTLE PIRATE (Roach MGM, 1934) d Gus Meins, s George "Spanky" McFarland, Scotty Beckett.
SHRIMPS FOR A DAY (Roach MGM, 1934) d Gus Meins, s George "Spanky" McFarland, Scotty Beckett, Matthew "Stymie" Beard.
ANNIVERSARY TROUBLE (Roach MGM, 1935) d Gus Meins, s George "Spanky" McFarland, Billie "Buckwheat" Thomas.
BEGINNER'S LUCK (Roach MGM, 1935) d Gus Meins, s George "Spanky" McFarland, Billie "Buckwheat" Thomas.

TEACHER'S BEAU (Roach MGM, 1935) d Gus Meins, s George "Spanky" McFarland, Billie "Buckwheat" Thomas, Carl "Alfalfa" Switzer, Scotty Beckett.
SPRUCIN' UP (Roach MGM, 1935) d Gus Meins, s George "Spanky" McFarland, Billie "Buckwheat" Thomas, Carl "Alfalfa" Switzer, Scotty Beckett.
THE LUCKY CORNER (Roach MGM, 1936) d Gus Meins, s George "Spanky" McFarland, Billie "Buckwheat" Thomas, Carl "Alfalfa" Switzer, Scotty Beckett.
LITTLE PAPA (Roach MGM, 1936) d Gus Meins, s George "Spanky" McFarland, Billie "Buckwheat" Thomas, Carl "Alfalfa" Switzer, Scotty Beckett.
LITTLE SINNER (Roach MGM, 1936) d Gus Meins, s George "Spanky" McFarland, Billie "Buckwheat" Thomas, Carl "Alfalfa" Switzer, Eugene "Porky" Lee.
OUR GANG FOLLIES OF 1936 (Roach MGM, 1936) d Gus Meins, s George "Spanky" McFarland, Billie "Buckwheat" Thomas, Carl "Alfalfa" Switzer, Eugene "Porky" Lee, Darla Hood.
DIVOT DIGGERS (Roach MGM, 1936) d Robert F. McGowan, s George "Spanky" McFarland, Billie "Buckwheat" Thomas, Carl "Alfalfa" Switzer, Eugene "Porky" Lee, Darla Hood.
THE PINCH SINGER (Roach MGM, 1936) d Fred Newmeyer, s George "Spanky" McFarland, Billie "Buckwheat" Thomas, Carl "Alfalfa" Switzer, Eugene "Porky" Lee, Darla Hood.
SECOND CHILDHOOD (Roach MGM, 1936) d Gus Meins, s George "Spanky" McFarland, Billie "Buckwheat" Thomas, Carl "Alfalfa" Switzer, Eugene "Porky" Lee, Darla Hood.
ARBOR DAY (Roach MGM, 1936) d Fred Newmeyer, s George "Spanky" McFarland, Billie "Buckwheat" Thomas, Carl "Alfalfa" Switzer, Eugene "Porky" Lee, Darla Hood.
BORED OF EDUCATION (Roach MGM, 1936) d Gordon Douglas, s George "Spanky" McFarland, Billie "Buckwheat" Thomas, Carl "Alfalfa" Switzer, Eugene "Porky" Lee, Darla Hood.
TWO TOO YOUNG (Roach MGM, 1936) d Gordon Douglas, s George "Spanky" McFarland, Billie "Buckwheat" Thomas, Carl "Alfalfa" Switzer, Eugene "Porky" Lee.
PAY AS YOU EXIT (Roach MGM, 1936) d Gordon Douglas, s George "Spanky" McFarland, Billie "Buckwheat" Thomas, Carl "Alfalfa" Switzer, Eugene "Porky" Lee, Darla Hood.
SPOOKY HOOKY (Roach MGM, 1936) d Goordon Douglas, s George "Spanky" McFarland, Billie "Buckwheat" Thomas, Carl "Alfalfa" Switzer, Eugene "Porky" Lee.
GENERAL SPANKY (Roach MGM, 1936) d Fred Newmeyer and Gordon Douglas, s George "Spanky" McFarland, Billie "Buckwheat" Thomas, Carl "Alfalfa" Switzer, Eugene "Porky" Lee.

REUNION IN RHYTHM (Roach MGM, 1937) d Gordon Douglas, s George "Spanky" McFarland, Billie "Buckwheat" Thomas, Darla Hood, Carl "Alfalfa" Switzer, Eugene "Porky" Lee.

GLOVE TAPS (Roach MGM, 1937) d Gordon Douglas, s George "Spanky" McFarland, Billie "Buckwheat" Thomas, Darla Hood, Carl "Alfalfa" Switzer, Eugene "Porky" Lee, Tommy "Butch" Bond.

HEARTS ARE THUMPS (Roach MGM, 1937) d Gordon Douglas, s George "Spanky" McFarland, Billie "Buckwheat" Thomas, Darla Hood, Carl "Alfalfa" Switzer, Eugene "Porky" Lee, Darwood "Waldo" Kaye.

THREE SMART BOYS (Roach MGM, 1937) d Gordon Douglas, s George "Spanky" McFarland, Billie "Buckwheat" Thomas, Darla Hood, Carl "Alfalfa" Switzer, Eugene "Porky" Lee.

RUSHIN' BALLET (Roach MGM, 1937) d Gordon Douglas, s George "Spanky" McFarland, Billie "Buckwheat" Thomas, Darla Hood, Carl "Alfalfa" Switzer, Eugene "Porky" Lee.

ROAMIN' HOLIDAY (Roach MGM, 1937) d Gordon Douglas, s George "Spanky" McFarland, Billie "Buckwheat" Thomas, Darla Hood, Carl "Alfalfa" Switzer, Eugene "Porky" Lee.

NIGHT 'N' GALES (Roach MGM, 1937) d Gordon Douglas, s George "Spanky" McFarland, Billie "Buckwheat" Thomas, Darla Hood, Carl "Alfalfa" Switzer, Eugene "Porky" Lee.

FISHY TALES (Roach MGM, 1937) d Gordon Douglas, s George "Spanky" McFarland, Billie "Buckwheat" Thomas, Darla Hood, Carl "Alfalfa" Switzer, Eugene "Porky" Lee.

FRAMING YOUTH (Roach MGM, 1937) d Gordon Douglas, s George "Spanky" McFarland, Billie "Buckwheat" Thomas, Darla Hood, Carl "Alfalfa" Switzer, Eugene "Porky" Lee.

THE PIGSKIN PALOOKA (Roach MGM, 1937) d Gordon Douglas, s George "Spanky" McFarland, Billie "Buckwheat" Thomas, Darla Hood, Carl "Alfalfa" Switzer, Eugene "Porky" Lee.

MAIL AND FEMALE (Roach MGM, 1937) d Gordon Douglas, s George "Spanky" McFarland, Billie "Buckwheat" Thomas, Darla Hood, Carl "Alfalfa" Switzer, Eugene "Porky" Lee, Alvin "Spike" Buckelew.

OUR GANG FOLLIES OF 1938 (Roach MGM, 1937) d Gordon Douglas, s George "Spanky" McFarland, Billie "Buckwheat" Thomas, Darla Hood, Carl "Alfalfa" Switzer, Eugene "Porky" Lee.

CANNED FISHING (Roach MGM, 1938) d Gordon Douglas, s George "Spanky" McFarland, Billie "Buckwheat" Thomas, Carl "Alfalfa" Switzer, Eugene "Porky" Lee.

BEAR FACTS (Roach MGM, 1938) d Gordon Douglas, s George "Spanky" McFarland, Billie "Buckwheat" Thomas, Darla Hood, Carl "Alfalfa" Switzer, Eugene "Porky" Lee.

THREE MEN IN A TUB (Roach MGM, 1938) d Gordon Douglas, s George "Spanky" McFarland, Billie "Buckwheat" Thomas, Darla Hood, Carl "Alfalfa" Switzer, Eugene "Porky" Lee.

MOTION PICTURE SERIES & SEQUELS 251

CAME THE BRAWN (Roach MGM, 1938) d Gordon Douglas, s George "Spanky" McFarland, Billie "Buckwheat" Thomas, Darla Hood, Carl "Alfalfa" Switzer, Eugene "Porky" Lee , Sidney "Woim" Kibrick.
FEED 'EM AND WEEP (Roach MGM, 1938) d Gordon Douglas, s Darla Hood, Carl "Alfalfa" Switzer, Eugene "Porky" Lee.
THE AWFUL TOOTH (Roach MGM, 1938) d Nate Watt, s Darla Hood, Carl "Alfalfa" Switzer, Eugene "Porky" Lee, Billie "Buckwheat" Thomas.
HIDE AND SHRIEK (Roach MGM, 1938) d Gordon Douglas, s Darla Hood, Carl "Alfalfa" Switzer, Eugene "Porky" Lee.
THE LITTLE RANGER (MGM, 1938) d Gordon Douglas, s Carl "Alfalfa" Switzer, Darla Hood, Billie "Buckwheat" Thomas, Shirley "Muggsy" Coates.
PARTY FEVER (MGM, 1938) d George Sidney, s Carl "Alfalfa" Switzer, Darla Hood, Billie "Buckwheat" Thomas.
ALADDIN'S LANTERN (MGM, 1938) d Gordon Douglas, s Carl "Alfalfa" Switzer, Darla Hood, Billie "Buckwheat" Thomas.
MEN IN FRIGHT (MGM, 1938) d Gordon Douglas, s Carl "Alfalfa" Switzer, Darla Hood, Billie "Buckwheat" Thomas, George "Spanky" McFarland.
FOOTBALL ROMEO (MGM, 1938) d George Sidney, s Carl "Alfalfa" Switzer, Darla Hood, Billie "Buckwheat" Thomas.
PRACTICAL JOKERS (MGM, 1938) d George Sidney, s Carl "Alfalfa" Switzer, Darla Hood, Billie "Buckwheat" Thomas, George "Spanky" McFarland.
ALFALFA'S AUNT (MGM, 1939) d George Sidney, s Carl "Alfalfa" Switzer, Darla Hood, Billie "Buckwheat" Thomas, George "Spanky" McFarland.
TINY TROUBLES (MGM, 1939) d George Sidney, s Carl "Alfalfa" Switzer, Darla Hood, Billie "Buckwheat" Thomas, George "Spanky" McFarland, Eugene "Porky" Lee.
DUEL PERSONALITIES (MGM, 1939) d George Sidney, s Carl "Alfalfa" Switzer, Darla Hood, Billie "Buckwheat" Thomas, George "Spanky" McFarland.
CLOWN PRINCES (MGM, 1939) d George Sidney, s Carl "Alfalfa" Switzer, Darla Hood, Billie "Buckwheat" Thomas, George "Spanky" McFarland.
COUSIN WILBUR (MGM, 1939) d George Sidney, s Carl "Alfalfa" Switzer, Darla Hood, Billie "Buckwheat" Thomas, George "Spanky" McFarland.
JOY SCOUTS (MGM, 1939) d Edward Cahn, s Carl "Alfalfa" Switzer, Darla Hood, Billie "Buckwheat" Thomas, George "Spanky" McFarland.
DOG DAZE (MGM, 1939) d George Sidney, s Carl "Alfalfa" Switzer, Darla Hood, Billie "Buckwheat" Thomas, George "Spanky" McFarland.
AUTO ANTICS (MGM, 1939) d Edward Cahn, s Carl "Alfalfa" Switzer, Darla Hood, Billie "Buckwheat" Thomas, George "Spanky" McFarland.
CAPTAIN SPANKY'S SHOW BOAT (MGM, 1939) d Edward Cahn, s Carl "Alfalfa" Switzer, Darla Hood, Billie "Buckwheat" Thomas, George "Spanky" McFarland.
DAD FOR A DAY (MGM, 1939) d Edward Cahn, s Carl "Alfalfa" Switzer, Darla Hood, Billie "Buckwheat" Thomas, George "Spanky" McFarland.

TIME OUT FOR LESSONS (MGM, 1939) d Edward Cahn and Bud Murray, s Carl "Alfalfa" Switzer, Darla Hood, Billie "Buckwheat" Thomas, George "Spanky" McFarland.

ALFALFA'S DOUBLE (MGM, 1940) d Edward Cahn, s Carl "Alfalfa" Switzer, Darla Hood, Billie "Buckwheat" Thomas, George "Spanky" McFarland, Mickey Gubitosi.

BUBBLING TROUBLES (MGM, 1940) d Edward Cahn, s Carl "Alfalfa" Switzer, Darla Hood, Billie "Buckwheat" Thomas, George "Spanky" McFarland.

THE BIG PREMIERE (MGM, 1940) d Edward Cahn, s Carl "Alfalfa" Switzer, Darla Hood, Billie "Buckwheat" Thomas, George "Spanky" McFarland.

ALL ABOUT HASH (MGM, 1940) d Edward Cahn, s Carl "Alfalfa" Switzer, Darla Hood, Billie "Buckwheat" Thomas, George "Spanky" McFarland.

THE NEW PUPIL (MGM, 1940) d Edward Cahn, s Carl "Alfalfa" Switzer, Darla Hood, Billie "Buckwheat" Thomas, George "Spanky" McFarland.

GOIN' FISHIN' (MGM, 1940) d Edward Cahn, s Carl "Alfalfa" Switzer, Darla Hood, Billie "Buckwheat" Thomas, George "Spanky" McFarland.

GOOD BAD BOYS (MGM, 1940) d Edward Cahn, s Carl "Alfalfa" Switzer, Darla Hood, Billie "Buckwheat" Thomas, George "Spanky" McFarland, Mickey Gubitosi.

WALDO'S LAST STAND (MGM, 1940) d Edward Cahn, and Steven Granger s Darwood "Waldo" Kaye, Carl "Alfalfa" Switzer, Darla Hood, Billie "Buckwheat" Thomas, George "Spanky" McFarland.

KIDDIE CURE (MGM, 1940) d Edward Cahn, s Carl "Alfalfa" Switzer, Darla Hood, Billie "Buckwheat" Thomas, George "Spanky" McFarland, Billy "Froggy" Laughlin.

FIGHTIN' FOOLS (MGM, 1941) d Edward Cahn, s George "Spanky" McFarland, Billy "Froggy" Laughlin.

BABY BLUES (MGM, 1941) d Edward Cahn, s George "Spanky" McFarland, Billy "Froggy" Laughlin.

YE OLDE MINSTRELS (MGM, 1941) d Edward Cahn, s George "Spanky" McFarland, Billy "Froggy" Laughlin, Darla Hood.

COME BACK, MISS PIPPS (MGM, 1941) d Edward Cahn, s George "Spanky" McFarland, Billy "Froggy" Laughlin, Billie "Buckwheat" Thomas.

1-2-3 GO! (MGM, 1941) d Edward Cahn, s George "Spanky" McFarland, Billy "Froggy" Laughlin.

ROBOT WRECKS (MGM, 1941) d Edward Cahn, s George "Spanky" McFarland, Billy "Froggy" Laughlin.

HELPING HANDS (MGM, 1941) d Edward Cahn, s George "Spanky" McFarland, Billy "Froggy" Laughlin.

WEDDING WORRIES (MGM, 1941) d Edward Cahn, s George "Spanky" McFarland, Billy "Froggy" Laughlin, Darla Hood.

MELODIES OLD AND NEW (MGM, 1941) d Edward Cahn, s George "Spanky" McFarland.

GOING TO PRESS (MGM, 1942) d Edward Cahn, s George "Spanky" McFarland, Billy "Froggy" Laughlin.

DON'T LIE (MGM, 1942) d Edward Cahn, s George "Spanky" McFarland, Billy "Froggy" Laughlin.
SURPRISED PARTIES (MGM, 1942) d Edward Cahn, s George "Spanky" McFarland, Billy "Froggy" Laughlin.
DOIN' THEIR BIT (MGM, 1942) d Edward Cahn, s George "Spanky" McFarland, Billy "Froggy" Laughlin.
ROVER'S BIG CHANCE (MGM, 1942) d Herbert Glazer, s George "Spanky" McFarland, Billy "Froggy" Laughlin, Bobby "Mickey" Blake.
MIGHTY LAK A GOAT (MGM, 1942) d Herbert Glazer, s George "Spanky" McFarland, Billie "Buckwheat" Thomas.
UNEXPECTED RICHES (MGM, 1942) d Herbert Glazer, s George "Spanky" McFarland, Billy "Froggy" Laughlin, Bobby "Mickey" Blake.
BENJAMIN FRANKLIN JR. (MGM, 1943) d Herbert Glazer, s Bobby "Mickey" Blake, Billy "Froggy" Laughlin.
FAMILY TROUBLES (MGM, 1943) d Herbert Glazer, s Bobby "Mickey" Blake, Billy "Froggy" Laughlin.
ELECTION DAZE (MGM, 1943) d Herbert Glazer, s Bobby "Mickey" Blake, Billy "Froggy" Laughlin.
CALLING ALL KIDS (MGM, 1943) d Herbert Glazer, s Bobby "Mickey" Blake, Billy "Froggy" Laughlin.
FARM HANDS (MGM, 1943) d Herbert Glazer, s Bobby "Mickey" Blake, Billy "Froggy" Laughlin.
LITTLE MISS PINKERTON (MGM, 1943) d Herbert Glazer, s Bobby "Mickey" Blake, Billy "Froggy" Laughlin, Billie "Buckwheat" Thomas.
THREE SMART GUYS (MGM, 1943) d Edward Cahn s Bobby "Mickey" Blake, Billy "Froggy" Laughlin.
RADIO BUGS (MGM, 1944) d Cyril Enfield, s Bobby "Mickey" Blake, Billy "Froggy" Laughlin.
DANCING ROMEO (MGM, 1944) d Cyril Enfield, s Bobby "Mickey" Blake, Billy "Froggy" Laughlin, Janet Burston.
TALE OF A DOG (MGM, 1944) d Cyril Enfield, s Bobby "Mickey" Blake, Billy "Froggy" Laughlin, Janet Burston, Billie "Buckwheat" Thomas.

561. OUTLAW LADIES
These pictures are rated X.
OUTLAW LADIES (Quality, 1981) d Henri Pachard, s John Leslie, Marlene Willoughby.
OUTLAW LADIES II (VCA, 1988) s Sharon Kane, Joey Silvera.

562. OVER-THE-HILL GANG, THE
A retired Texas Ranger and his pards clean up a town.
THE OVER-THE-HILL GANG (Thomas/Spelling Productions, 1969) (ABC-TV movie) d Jean Yarbrough, s Pat O'Brien, Walter Brennan, Chill Wills, Edgar Buchanan, Gypsy Rose Lee, Andy Devine, Jack Elam.
THE OVER-THE-HILL GANG RIDES AGAIN (Thomas/Spelling Productions, 1970) (ABC-TV movie) d George McGowan, s Walter Brennan, Fred Astaire, Edgar Buchanan, Andy Devine, Chill Wills.

563. PALEFACE, THE
A timid cowboy is backed up by sharpshooting woman.
PALEFACE (Paramount, 1948) d Norman Z. McLeod, s Bob Hope, Jane Russell.
SON OF PALEFACE (Paramount, 1952) d Frank Tashlin, s Bob Hope, Jane Russell, Roy Rogers.

564. PANCHO VILLA
The Mexican revolutionary Francisco "Pancho" Villa (1978-1923) evades a military expedition under the command of Gen. John Pershing in 1916.
PANCHO VILLA RETURNS (Hispano Continental, 1950) d Miguel Contrevas Torres, s Leo Carillo.
PANCHO VILLA (Scotia International, 1975) d Eugenio Martin, s Telly Savalas, Clint Walker.

565. PANTHER
Jason Blade is a martial artist.
THE STRIKE OF THE PANTHER (International Film Marketing, 1988) d Brian Trenchard-Smith, s Ed Staszak, Rowena Wallace.
DAY OF THE PANTHER (International Film Marketing, 1988) d Brian Trenchard-Smith, s Ed Staszak, James Beattie.

565A. PARENTHOOD
There is said to be pending a sequel to this film about "model parents" coping with kids and careers.
PARENTHOOD (Universal, 1989) d Ron Howard, s Steve Martin, Mary Steenburgen, Tom Hulce, Rick Moranis.
PROBLEM CHILD (Announced 1990)

566. PARKER
Professional criminals are spotlighted in a series of novels by Richard Stark (Donald E. Westlake), written 1962-74.
POINT BLANK (MGM, 1967) d John Boorman, s Lee Marvin, Angie Dickinson
MADE IN USA (Pathe Contemporary, 1967) d Jean-Luc Godard s Anna Karina.
THE OUTFIT (1973) d John Flynn, s Robert Dufall.
SLAYGROUND (Universal, 1984) d Terry Bedford, s Peter Coyote, Mel Smith, Billie Whitelaw.

PATHFINDER
See LEATHERSTOCKING

567. PARDON MON AFFAIRE
A happily married man pursues a beautiful model in the first of these French farces.

PARDON MON AFFAIRE (1976) d Yves Robert, s Jean Rochefort, Claude Brasseur.
PARDON MON AFFAIRE, TOO! (1977) [aka WE WILL ALL MEET IN PARADISE] d Yves Robert, s Jean Rochefort, Claude Brasseur.

568. PATTON
Gen. George S. Patton Jr., "Old Blood and Guts" (1885-1945), specializes in armored warfare tactics during World War II.
PATTON (20th Century-Fox, 1970) d Franklin Schaffner, s George C. Scott, Karl Malden.
THE LAST DAYS OF PATTON (TV movie, 1986) d Delbert Mann, s George C. Scott, Eva Marie Saint.

569. PAUL TEMPLE
The detective appeared in the Francis Durbridge-penned BBC radio series in the 1940s, in a TV series with Francis Matthews in the 1960s and in a newspaper comic strip and books.
CALLING PAUL TEMPLE (Butchers Films, 1948) s John Bentley.
PAUL TEMPLE'S TRIUMPH (Butchers Films, 1950) s John Bentley.
PAUL TEMPLE RETURNS (Butchers Films, 1952) s John Bentley.

569A. PEARL
The silent serial queen Pearl White appears in these films.
PEARL AND THE POET (1913) s Pearl White.
PEARL AND THE TRAMP (1913) s Pearl White.
PEARL AS A DETECTIVE (1913) s Pearl White.
PEARL'S HERO (1913) s Pearl White.
PEARL'S MISTAKE (1913) s Pearl White.

570. PECK'S BAD BOY
An accident-prone youth is featured in these pictures.
PECK'S BAD BOY (1921) d Sam Wood, s Jackie Coogan, Wheeler Oakman, Doris May.
PECK's BAD BOY (Fox, 1934) d Edward Cline, s Jackie Cooper, Jackie Searle, Dorothy Peterson.
PECK'S BAD BOY WITH THE CIRCUS (1938) d Edward Cline, s Tommy Kelly, Ann Gillis, Edgar Kennedy.

571. PEE-WEE HERMAN
Cartoonish Pee-wee has also has his own Saturday morning television program.
PEE-WEE'S BIG ADVENTURE (1985) d Tim Burton, s Pee-wee Herman (Paul Reubens), Elizabeth Daily.
BIG-TOP PEE-WEE (Paramount, 1988) d Randall Kleiser, s Pee-wee Herman (Paul Reubens), Kris Kristofferson.

572. PENITENTIARY

A young black man, wrongly imprisoned, takes up boxing.
PENITENTIARY (Jerry Gross Organization, 1979) d Jamaa Fanaka, s Leon Isaac Kennedy, Thommy Pollard.
PENITENTIARY II (MGM/UA, 1982) d Jamaa Fanaka, s Leon Isaac Kennedy, Ernie Hudson.
PENITENTIARY III (1987) d Jamaa Fanaka, s Leon Isaac Kennedy, Anthony Geary.

573. PENROD
Booth Tarkington's young hero first appeared in three novels published 1914-29. Penrod is slightly out of synch with his family.
PENROD (First National, 1922) d Marshall Neilan, s Wesley Barry, Tully Marshall, Claire McDowell.
PENROD AND SAM (First National, 1931) d William Beaudine, s Leon Janney, Matt Moore, Dorothy Peterson.
PENROD AND SAM (First National, 1937) d William McGann, s Billy Mauch, Frank Craven, Spring Byington.
PENROD AND HIS TWIN BROTHER (Warner Brothers/First National, 1938) d William Mcgann, s Billy Mauch, Bobby Mauch, Frank Craven, Spring Byington.
PENROD'S DOUBLE TROUBLE (Warner Brothers 1938) d Lewis Seiler, s Billy Mauch, Bobby Mauch, Dick Purcell.
ON MOONLIGHT BAY (Warner Brothers, 1951) d Roy Del Ruth, s Doris Day, Gordon MacRae, Leon Ames.
BY THE LIGHT OF THE SILVERY MOON (Warner Brothers, 1953) d David Butler, s Doris Day, Gordon MacRae, Leon Ames.

574. PERILS OF PAULINE, THE
Heiress Pauline Marvin is a girl in non-stop danger, in the first picture. In the second, Pauline Hargaves and her scientist father are in China. The third is a bio-pic about Pearl White and the fourth is a spoof.
THE PERILS OF PAULINE (1914) (15 chapters) s Pearl White.
PERILS OF PAULINE (Universal, 1934) s Evalyn Knapp, Robert Allen, James Durkin.
PERILS OF PAULINE (Paramount, 1947) d George Marshall, s Betty Hutton.
THE PERILS OF PAULINE (Universal, 1967) d Herbert Leonard and Joshua Shelley, s Pamela Austin, Pat Boone.

575. PERRY MASON
Erle Stanley Gardner's prose counselor, Perry Mason, along with secretary Della Street, private eye Paul Drake, district attorney Hamilton Burger and Police Detective Tragg have been featured in two television series as well, airing over CBS, 1957-66 (Raymond Burr in title role) and 1973-74 (Monte Markham). The books first appeared in 1933.
THE CASE OF THE HOWLING DOG (Warner Brothers, 1934) d Alan Crosland, s Warren William, Mary Astor.

THE CASE OF THE CURIOUS BRIDE (Warner Brothers, 1935) d Michael Curtiz, s Warren William, Margaret Lindsay.
THE CASE OF THE LUCKY LEGS (Warner Brothers, 1935) d Archie L. Mayo, s Warren William, Genevieve Tobin.
THE CASE OF THE VELVET CLAWS (Warner Brothers, 1936) d William Clemens, s Warren William, Winifred Shaw.
THE CASE OF THE BLACK CAT (Warner Brothers, 1936) d William McGann, s Ricardo Cortez, Gary Owen.
THE CASE OF THE STUTTERING BISHOP (Warner Brothers, 1937) d William Clemens, s Donald Woods, Ann Dvorak
PERRY MASON RETURNS (NBC-TV movie, 1985) d Ron Satlof, s Raymond Burr, Barbara Hale, William Katt.
PERRY MASON: THE CASE OF THE NOTORIOUS NUN (NBC-TV movie, 1986) d Ron Satlof, s Raymond Burr, Barbara Hale, William Katt.
PERRY MASON: THE CASE OF THE SHOOTING STAR (NBC-TV movie, 1986) d Ron Satlof, s Raymond Burr, Barbara Hale, William Katt.
PERRY MASON: THE CASE OF THE LOST LOVE (NBC-TV movie, 1987) d Ron Satlof, s Raymond Burr, Barbara Hale, William Katt.
PERRY MASON: THE CASE OF THE SINISTER SPIRIT (NBC-TV movie, 1987) d Richard Lang, s Raymond Burr, Barbara Hale, William Katt.
PERRY MASON: THE CASE OF THE MURDERED MADAM (NBC-TV movie, 1987) d Richard Satlof, s Raymond Burr, Barbara Hale, William Katt.
PERRY MASON: THE CASE OF THE SCANDALOUS SCOUNDREL (NBC-TV movie, 1987) d Christian I Nyby II, s Raymond Burr, Barbara Hale, William Katt.
PERRY MASON: THE CASE OF THE AVENGING ACE (NBC-TV movie, 1988) d Christian I. Nyby II, s Raymond Burr, Barbara Hale, William Katt.
PERRY MASON: THE CASE OF THE LADY IN THE LAKE (NBC-TV movie, 1988) s Raymond Burr, Barbara Hale.
PERRY MASON: THE CASE OF THE LETHAL LESSON (NBC-TV movie, 1988) s Raymond Burr, Barbara Hale, William Katt.
PERRY MASON: THE CASE OF THE MUSICAL MURDER (NBC-TV movie, 1989) s Raymond Burr, Barbara Hale.
PERRY MASON: THE CASE OF THE ALL-STAR ASSASSIN (TV movie, 1989) s Raymond Burr, Barbara Hale.
PERRY MASON: THE CASE OF THE POISONED PEN (TV movie, 1990) s Raymond Burr, Barbara Hale, Barbara Babcock.

576. PERSONAL TOUCH
These pictures are intended for adults only.
PERSONAL TOUCH (Arrow, 1982) s Sharon Mitchell.
PERSONAL TOUCH II (Arrow, 1983) d Bobby Hollander, s Shauna Grant.
PERSONAL TOUCH III (Arrow, 1984) s Lisa de Leeuw, Jerry Davis.

577. PETER DULUTH

258 MOTION PICTURE SERIES & SEQUELS

Patrick Quentin's fictional detective hero Peter Duluth is a theatrical producer who stumbles onto crimes. His wife Iris is an actress. They were featured in nine mystery novels.
HOMICIDE FOR THREE (Republic, 1948) d George Blair, s Warren Douglas, Audrey Long.
BLACK WIDOW (20th Century-Fox, 1954) d Nunnally Johnson, s Van Heflin, Gene Tierney.

578. PETE SMITH "FISHERMAN'S PARADISE"
These are comedy two-reelers.
FISHERMAN'S PARADISE (MGM, 1931) s Pete Smith.
PEARLS AND DEVIL-FISH (MGM, 1931) d Harold Austin, s Pete Smith.
SHARKS AND SWORDFISH (MGM, 1931) s Pete Smith.
PISCATORIAL PLEASURES (MGM, 1931) d Harold Austin, s Pete Smith.
TROUT FISHING (MGM, 1932) d Irving Reis, s Pete Smith.
COLOR SCALES (MGM, 1932) d Zion Myers, s Pete Smith.

579. PETE SMITH "SPORTS CHAMPIONS"
SPLASH! (MGM, 1931) d Zion Myers and Jules White, s Pete Smith.
WILD AND WOOLY (MGM, 1931) d Charles Dorian, s Pete Smith.
WHIPPET RACING (MGM, 1931) d Ward Wing, s Pete Smith.
LESSON IN GOLF (MGM, 1932) d Dudley Murphy, s Pete Smith.
DIVE IN (MGM, 1932) d Ray McCarey, s Pete Smith.
OLYMPIC EVENTS (MGM, 1932) d Ray McCarey, s Pete Smith.
ATHLETIC DAZE (MGM, 1932) d Ray McCarey, s Pete Smith.
FLYING SPIKES (MGM, 1932) d Ray McCarey, s Pete Smith.
TIMBER TOPPPERS (MGM, 1932) d Ray McCarey, s Pete Smith.
SNOW BIRDS (MGM, 1932) d Jules White, s Pete Smith.
DESERT REGATTA (MGM, 1932) d Jules White, s Pete Smith.
PIGSKIN (MGM, 1932) d Ray McCarey and Dick Hanley, s Pete Smith.
BLOCK AND TACKLE (MGM, 1932) d Dick Hanley, s Pete Smith.
SWING HIGH (MGM, 1932) d Jack Cummings, s Pete Smith.
FOOTBALL FOOTWORK (MGM, 1932) d Felix E. Feist and Dick Hanley, s Pete Smith.
CHALK UP (MGM, 1932) d Zion Myers and Willie Hoppe, s Pete Smith.
MOTORCYCLE MANIA (MGM, 1933) d Jack Cummings, s Pete Smith.
BONE CRUSHERS (MGM, 1933) d Ward Wing, s Pete Smith.
ALLEZ OOP (MGM, 1933) d Jack Cummings, s Pete Smith.
THROTTLE PUSHERS (MGM, 1933) d Jules White, s Pete Smith.

580. PETE SMITH "GOOFY MOVIES"
GOOFY MOVIES 1 (MGM, 1933) s Pete Smith.
GOOFY MOVIES 2 (MGM, 1934) s Pete Smith.
GOOFY MOVIES 3 (MGM, 1934) s Pete Smith.
GOOFY MOVIES 4 (MGM, 1934) s Pete Smith.
GOOFY MOVIES 5 (MGM, 1934) s Pete Smith.
GOOFY MOVIES 6 (MGM, 1934) s Pete Smith.

MOTION PICTURE SERIES & SEQUELS

GOOFY MOVIES 7 (MGM, 1934) s Pete Smith.
GOOFY MOVIES 8 (MGM, 1934) s Pete Smith.
GOOFY MOVIES 9 (MGM, 1934) s Pete Smith.
GOOFY MOVIES 10 (MGM, 1934) s Pete Smith.

581. PETE SMITH'S "MGM ODDITIES"
HANDLEBARS (MGM, 1933) d Jules White, s Pete Smith.
MICROSCOPIC MYSTERIES (MGM, 1933) d Hugo Lund, s Pete Smith.
MENU (MGM, 1933) d Nick Grinde, s Pete Smith.
HAPPY WARRIORS (MGM, 1933) d Jules White, s Pete Smith.
FINE FEATHERS (MGM, 1933) d Jules White, s Pete Smith.
ROPING WILD BEARS (MGM, 1934) d W. Earle Frank, s Pete Smith.
VITAL VICTUALS (MGM, 1934) d Nick Grinde, s Pete Smith.
TRICK GOLF (MGM, 1934) s Pete Smith.
NIPUPS (MGM, 1934) d Marty Brooks, s Pete Smith.
FLYING HUNTERS (MGM, 1934) d Lauron A. Draper, s Pete Smith.
ATTENTION, SUCKERS (MGM, 1934) d Jack Cummings, s Pete Smith.
TAKING CARE OF BABY (MGM, 1934) d Jack Cummings, s Pete Smith.
PRO FOOTBALL (MGM, 1934) d Ray McCarey, s Pete Smith.
PICHIANNI TROUPE (MGM, 1934) s Pete Smith.
STRIKES AND SPARES (MGM, 1934) d Felix E. Feist, s Pete Smith.
DARTMOUTH DAYS (MGM, 1934) d Maurice Rapf, s Pete Smith.
RUGBY (MGM, 1934) d Ray McCarey, s Pete Smith.
MOTORCYCLE COSSACKS (MGM, 1935) d Antonio Samaniego, s Pete Smith.
DONKEY BASEBALL (MGM, 1935) d John Waters, s Pete Smith.
SPORTING NUTS (MGM, 1935) s Pete Smith.
FIGHTIN' FISH (MGM, 1935) s Pete Smith.
CHAIN LETTER DIMES (MGM, 1935) d Al Ray, s Pete Smith.
PRINCE, KING OF DOGS (MGM, 1935) d Felix E. Feist, s Pete Smith.

582. PETE SMITH'S "MGM SPECIALS"
INFLATION (MGM, 1933) d Zion Myers, s Pete Smith.
AUDIOSCOPIKS (MGM, 1935) s Pete Smith.
NEW AUDIOSCOPIKS (MGM, 1938) s Pete Smith.
THIRD-DIMENSIONAL MURDER (MGM, 1941) d George Sidney, s Pete Smith.

583. PETE SMITH'S "SPORTS PARADE"
BASKETBALL TECHNIQUE (MGM, 1935) d Ray McCarey, s Pete Smith.
FOOTBALL TEAMWORK (MGM, 1935) d Felix E. Feist, s Pete Smith.
GYMNASTICS (MGM, 1935) d Charles T. Trego, s Pete Smith.
WATER SPORTS (MGM, 1935) d Ray McCarey, s Pete Smith.
CREW RACING (MGM, 1935) d David Miller, s Pete Smith.
AIR HOPPERS (MGM, 1936) d Joseph Boyle, s Pete Smith.
TABLE TENNIS (MGM, 1936) d David Miller, s Pete Smith, Coleman Clark.
RACING CANINES (MGM, 1936) d David Miller, s Pete Smith.

AQUATIC ARTISTRY (MGM, 1936) d David Miller, s Pete Smith, Gus Smith.
POLO (MGM, 1936) d George Sidney, s Pete Smith.
HARNESSED RHYTHM (MGM, 1936) d Jacques Tourneur, s Pete Smith.
DARE-DEVILTRY (MGM, 1936) d David Miller, s Pete Smith.

584. PETE SMITH'S "MGM MINIATURES" & "MGM MUSICAL REVUE"
TRAINED HOOFS (MGM, 1935) d David Miller, s Pete Smith.
LET'S DANCE (MGM, 1936) d David Miller, s Pete Smith.
WEST POINT OF THE SOUTH (MGM, 1936) d Richard Rosson, s Pete Smith.
JONKER DIAMOND (MGM, 1936) d Jacques Tourneur, s Pete Smith.
LA FIESTA DE SANTA BARBARA (MGM, 1935) d Louis Lewyn, s Pete Smith.

585. PETE SMITH "SPECIALTIES"
KILLER DOG (MGM, 1936) d Jacques Tourneur, s Pete Smith.
BEHIND THE HEADLINES (MGM, 1936) d Edward Cahn, s Pete Smith.
OLYMPIC SKI CHAMPIONS (MGM, 1936) s Pete Smith.
SPORTS ON ICE (MGM, 1936) s Pete Smith.
HURLING (MGM, 1936) d David Miller, s Pete Smith.
WANTED: A MASTER (MGM, 1936) d Gunther Von Fritsch and Arthur Ornitz, s Pete Smith.
DEXTERITY (MGM, 1937) d David Miller, s Pete Smith.
GILDING THE LILY (MGM, 1937) d David Miller, s Pete Smith.
BAR-RAC'S NIGHT OUT (MGM, 1937) d Earl Frank, s Pete Smith.
PENNY WISDOM (MGM, 1937) d David Miler, s Pete Smith, Prudence Penny.
TENNIS TACTICS (MGM, 1937) d David Miller, s Pete Smith.
GRAND BOUNCE (MGM, 1937) d Jacques Tourneur, s Pete Smith.
GOLF MISTAKES (MGM, 1937) d Felix E. Feist, s Pete Smith.
PIGSKIN CHAMPIONS (MGM, 1937) d Charles Clarke, s Pete Smith, Green Bay Packers.
EQUESTRIAN ACROBATICS (MGM, 1937) d David Miller, s Pete Smith.
JUNGLE JUVENILES (MGM, 1937) d John A. Haeseler, s Pete Smith.
SKI SKILL (MGM, 1937) s Pete Smith.
CANDID CAMERAMANIACS (MGM, 1937) d Hal Yates, s Pete Smith.
DECATHLON CHAMPION (MGM, 1937) d Felix E. Feist, s Pete Smith.
FRIEND INDEED (MGM, 1938) d Fred Zinnemann, s Pete Smith.
JUNGLE JUVENILES No. 2 (MGM, 1938) d John A. Haeseler, s Pete Smith.
THREE ON A ROPE (MGM, 1938) d Willard Vander Veer, s Pete Smith.
LA SAVATE (MGM, 1938) d David Miller, s Pete Smith.
PENNY'S PARTY (MGM, 1938) d David Miller, s Pete Smith.
MODELING FOR MONEY (MGM, 1938) d David Miller.
SURF HEROES (MGM, 1938) d Charles T. Trego, s Pete Smith.

THE STORY OF DR. CARVER (MGM, 1938) d Fred Zinnemann, s Pete Smith.
ANESTHESIA (MGM, 1938) d Will Jason, s Pete Smith.
FOLLOW THE ARROW (MGM, 1938) d Felix E. Feist, s Pete Smith, Sally Payne.
FISTICUFFS (MGM, 1938) d David Miller, s Pete Smith, Max Baer.
FOOTBALL THRILLS OF 1937 (MGM, 19338) s Pete Smith.
GRID RULES (MGM, 1938) d Edward Cahn, s Pete Smith.
HOT ON ICE (MGM, 1938) d Willard Vander Veer, s Pete Smith.
MAN'S GREATEST FRIEND (MGM, 1938) d Joe Newman, s Pete Smith.
PENNY'S PICNIC (MGM, 1938) d Will Jason, s Pete Smith, Prudence Penny.
DOUBLE DIVING (MGM, 1939) d Felix E. Feist, s Pete Smith.
HEROES AT LEISURE (MGM, 1939) d Charles T. Trego, s Pete Smith.
MARINE CIRCUS (MGM, 1939) d James A. FitzPatrick, s Pete Smith.
WEATHER WIZARDS (MGM, 1939) d Fred Zinnemann, s Pete Smith.
RADIO HAMS (MGM, 1939) d Felix E. Feist, s Pete Smith.
PEOTRY OF NATURE (MGM, 1939) d Mervyn Freeman, s Pete Smith.
CULINARY CARVING (MGM, 1939) d Felix E. Feist, s Pete Smith, Sally Payne.
TAKE A CUE (MGM, 1939) d Felix E. Feist, s Pete Smith.
FOOTBALL THRILLS OF 1938 (MGM, 1939) s Pete Smith.
SET 'EM UP (MGM, 1939) d Felix E. Feist, s Pete Smith.
LET'S TALK TURKEY (MGM, 1939) d Felix E. Feist, s Pete Smith.
SKI BIRDS (MGM, 1939) d Charles T. Trego, s Pete Smith.
ROMANCE OF THE POTATO (MGM, 1939) d Sammy Lee, s Pete Smith.
MAINTAIN THE RIGHT (MGM, 1940) d Joe Newman, s Pete Smith.
WHAT'S YOUR I.Q. NO. 1 (MGM, 1940) s Pete Smith.
STUFFIE (MGM, 1940) d Fred Zinnemann, s Pete Smith.
THE DOMINEERING MALE (MGM, 1940) d John Hines, s Pete Smith.
SPOTS BEFORE YOUR EYES (MGM, 1940) d John Hines, s Pete Smith.
WHAT'S YOUR I.Q. NO. 2 (MGM, 1940) d George Sidney, s Pete Smith.
CAT COLLEGE (MGM, 1940) d Joe Newman, s Pete Smith.
SOCIAL SEA LIONS (MGM, 1940) d John Hines, s Pete Smith.
PLEASE ANSWER (MGM, 1940) d Roy Rowland, s Pete Smith.
FOOTBALL THRILLS OF 1939 (MGM, 1940) s Pete Smith.
QUICKER'N A WINK (MGM, 1940) d George Sidney, s Pete Smith.
WEDDING BELLS (MGM, 1940) d Roy Mack, s Pete Smith, Sally Payne.
SEA FOR YOURSELF (MGM, 1940) d Charles T. Trego, s Pete Smith.
PENNY TO THE RESCUE (MGM, 1941) d Will Jason, s Pete Smith.
QUIZ BIZ (MGM, 1941) d Will Jason, s Pete Smith.
MEMORY TRICKS (MGM, 1941) d Will Jason, s Pete Smith.
AERONAUTICS (MGM, 1941) d Francis Corby, s Pete Smith.
LIONS ON THE LOOSE (MGM, 1941) d Marjorie Freeman, s Pete Smith.
CUBAN RHYTHM (MGM, 1941) d Will Jason, s Pete Smith.
WATER BUGS (MGM, 1941) d Will Jason, s Pete Smith.
FOOTBALL THRILLS OF 1940 (MGM, 1941) s Pete Smith.
FLICKER MEMORIES (MGM, 1941) d George Sidney, s Pete Smith.

ARMY CHAMPIONS (MGM, 1941) d Paul Vogel, s Pete Smith.
FANCY ANSWERS (MGM, 1941) d Basil Wrangell, s Pete Smith.
HOW TO HOLD YOUR HUSBAND - BACK (MGM, 1941) d John Hines, s Pete Smith.
AQUA ANTICS (MGM, 1942) d Louis Lewyn, s Pete Smith.
WHAT ABOUT DADDY? (MGM, 1942) d Will Jason, s Pete Smith.
ACRO-BATTY (MGM, 1942) d Louis Lewyn, s Pete Smith.
VICTORY QUIZ (MGM, 1942) d Will Jason, s Pete Smith.
PETE SMITH'S SCRAPBOOK (MGM, 1942) s Pete Smith.
BARBEE-CUES (MGM, 1942) d Will Jason, s Pete Smith.
SELF-DEFENSE (MGM, 1942) d Philip Anderson, s Pete Smith.
IT'S A DOG'S LIFE (MGM, 1942) d Robert Wilmot, s Pete Smith.
VICTORY VITTLES (MGM, 1942) d Will Jason, s Pete Smith.
FOOTBALL THRILLS OF 1941 (MGM, 1942) s Pete Smith.
CALLING ALL PA'S (MGM, 1942) d Will Jason, s Pete Smith.
MARINES IN THE MAKING (MGM, 1942) d Herbert Polesie, s Pete Smith.
FIRST AID (MGM, 1943) d Will Jason, s Pete Smith.
HOLLYWOOD DAREDEVILS (MGM, 1943) d Louis Lewyn, s Pete Smith.
FALA (MGM, 1943) d Gunther V. Ftitsch, s Pete Smith.
WILD HORSES (MGM, 1943) s Pete Smith.
SKY SCIENCE (MGM, 1943) d Will Jason, s Pete Smith.
DOG HOUSE (MGM, 1943) d Robert Wilmot, s Pete Smith.
SEEING HANDS (MGM, 1943) d Gunther V. Fritsch, s Pete Smith.
SEVENTH COLUMN (MGM, 1943) d Will Jason, s Pete Smith.
SCRAP HAPPY (MGM, 1943) d Will Jason, s Pete Smith.
FIXIN' TRICKS (MGM, 1943) d Will Jason, s Pete Smith.
FOOTBALL THRILLS OF 1942 (MGM, 1943) s Pete Smith.
TIPS ON TRIPS (MGM, 1943) d Will Jason, s Pete Smith.
WATER WISDOM (MGM, 1943) s Pete Smith.
PRACTICAL JOKER (MGM, 1944) d Will Jason, s Pete Smith.
HOME MAID (MGM, 1944) d Will Jason, s Pete Smith.
GROOVIE MOVIE (MGM, 1944) d Will Jason, s Pete Smith.
SPORTSMAN'S MEMORIES (MGM, 1944) s Pete Smith.
MOVIE PESTS (MGM, 1944) d Will Jason, s Pete Smith.
SPORTS QUIZ (MGM, 1944) d Will Jason, s Pete Smith.
FOOTBALL THRILLS OF 1943 (MGM, 1944) s Pete Smith.
SAFETY SLEUTH (MGM, 1944) d Will Jason, s Pete Smith.
TRACK AND FIELD QUIZ (MGM, 1945) s Pete Smith.
HOLLYWOOD SCOUT (MGM, 1945) d Phil Anderson, s Pete Smith.
FOOTBALL THRILLS OF 1944 (MGM,, 1945) s Pete Smith.
GUEST PESTS (MGM, 1945) d Will Jason, s Pete Smith.
BUS PESTS (MGM, 1945) d Chuck Riesner, s Pete Smith.
BADMINTON (MGM, 1945) d Philip Anderson, s Pete Smith.
SPORTS STICKLERS (MGM, 1945) s Pete Smith.
FALA AT HYDE PARK (MGM, 1946) d Gunther V. Fritsch.
GETTIN' CLAMOR (MGM, 1946) d Philip Anderson, s Pete Smith.
STUDIO VISIT (MGM, 1946) s Pete Smith.

EQUESTRIAN QUIZ (MGM, 1946) s Pete Smith.
TREASURES FROM TRASH (MGM, 1946) d David Barclay, s Pete Smith.
FOOTBALL THRILLS NO. 9 (MGM, 1946) s Pete Smith.
SURE CURES (MGM, 1946) d David Barclay, s Pete Smith.
I LOVE MY HUSBAND, BUT! (MGM, 1946) d David Barclay, s Pete Smith.
PLAYING BY EAR (MGM, 1946) d David Barclay, s Pete Smith.
ATHLETIQUIZ (MGM, 1947) d David Barclay, s Pete Smith.
DIAMOND DEMON (MGM, 1947) d David Barclay, s Pete Smith, Johnny Price.
EARLY SPORTS QUIZ (MGM, 1947) d David Barclay, s Pete Smith.
I LOVE MY WIFE (MGM, 1947) d David Barclay, s Pete Smith.
NEIGHBOR PESTS (MGM, 1947) d David Barclay, s Pete Smith.
PET PEEVES (MGM, 1947) d David Barclay, s Pete Smith.
FOOTBALL THRILLS NO. 10 (MGM, 1947) s Pete Smith.
SURFBOARD RHYTHM (MGM, 1947) d David Barclay, s Pete Smith.
WHAT D'YA KNOW (MGM, 1947) d David Barclay, s Pete Smith.
HAVE YOU EVER WONDERED (MGM, 1947) d David Barclay, s Pete Smith.
BOWLING TRICKS (MGM, 1948) d David Barclay, s Pete Smith.
I LOVE MY MOTHER-IN-LAW, BUT! (MGM, 1948) d David Barclay, s Pete Smith.
NOW YOU SEE IT (MGM, 1948) d Richard L. Cassell, s Pete Smith.
YOU CAN'T WIN (MGM, 1948) d David Barclay, s Pete Smith, Dave O'Brien.
JUST SUPPOSE (MGM, 1948) d David Barclay, s Pete Smith.
FOOTBALL THRILLS NO. 11 (MGM, 1948) s Pete Smith.
WHY IS IT? (MGM, 1948) d David Barclay, s Pete Smith.
PIGSKIN SKILL (MGM, 1948) d Carl Dudley, s Pete Smith.
ICE ACES (MGM, 1948) d David Barclay, s Pete Smith.
LET'S COGITATE (MGM, 1948) d David Barclay, s Pete Smith.
SUPER CUE MAN (MGM, 1949) d David Barclay, s Pete Smith.
WHAT I WANT NEXT (MG, 1949) d David Barclay, s Pete Smith.
SCIENTIFIQUIZ (MGM, 1949) s Pete Smith.
THOSE GOOD OLD DAYS (MGM, 1949) d David Barclay, s Pete Smith.
FISHING FOR FUN (MGM, 1949) d Lewis Ossi, s Pete Smith.
FOOTBALL THRILLS NO. 12 (MGM, 1949) s Pete Smith.
WATER TRIX (MGM, 1949) d Charles T. Trego, s Pete Smith.
HOW COME? (MGM, 1949) d David Barclay, s Pete Smith.
WE CAN DREAM, CAN'T WE? (MGM, 1949) d David Barclay, s Pete Smith.
SPORTS ODDITIES (MGM, 1949) s Pete Smith.
PEST CONTROL (MGM, 1950) d David Barclay, s Pete Smith.
CRASHING THE MOVIES (MGM, 1950) s Pete Smith.
WRONG SON (MGM, 1950) d Gunther V. Fritsch, s Pete Smith.
DID'JA KNOW (MGM, 1950) d David Barclay, s Pete Smith.
THAT'S HIS STORY (MGM, 1950) d David Barclay, s Pete Smith.
A WIFE'S LIFE (MGM, 1950) d David Barclay, s Pete Smith.
WRONG WAY BUTCH (MGM, 1950) d David Barclay, s Pete Smith.
FOOTBALL THRILLS NO. 13 (MGM, 1950) s Pete Smith.

TABLE TOPPERS (MGM, 1950) d David Barclay, s Pete Smith.
CURIOUS CONTESTS (MGM, 1950) s Pete Smith.
WANTED: ONE EGG (MGM, 1950) d David Barclay, s Pete Smith.
SKY SKIERS (MGM, 1951) d Charles T. Trego, s Pete Smith.
FIXIN' FOOL (MGM, 1951) d David Barclay, s Pete Smith.
CAMERA SLEUTH (MGM, 1951) d David Barclay, s Pete Smith.
BANDAGE BAIT (MGM, 1951) d David Barclay, s Pete Smith.
FOOTBALL THRILLS NO. 14 (MGM, 1951) s Pete Smith.
THAT'S WHAT *YOU* THINK (MGM, 1951) d David Barclay, s Pete Smith.
IN CASE YOU'RE CURIOUS (MGM, 1951) d David Barclay, s Pete Smith.
FISHING FEATS (MGM, 1951) d Charles T. Trego, s Pete Smith.
MUSIQUIZ (MGM, 1951) d David Barclay, s Pete Smith.
REDUCING (MGM, 1952) d David Barclay, s Pete Smith.
MEALTIME MAGIC (MGM, 1952) d Will Jason, s Pete Smith.
GYMNASTIC RHYTHM (MGM, 1952) s Pete Smith.
IT COULD HAPPEN TO YOU (MGM, 1952) d David Barclay, s Pete Smith.
PEDESTRIAN SAFETY (MGM, 1952) d David Barclay, s Pete Smith.
FOOTBALL THRILLS NO. 15 (MGM, 1952) s Pete Smith.
SWEET MEMORIES (MGM, 1952) d David Barclay, s Pete Smith.
I LOVE CHILDREN, BUT! (MGM, 1952) d David Barclay, s Pete Smith.
AQUATIC KIDS (MGM, 1953) s Pete Smith.
THE MOSCONI STORY (MGM, 1953) d David Barclay, s Pete Smith, Willie Mosconi.
THE POSTMAN (MGM, 1953) s Pete Smith.
DOGS'N DUCKS (MGM, 1953) s Pete Smith.
ANCIENT CURES (MGM, 1953) s Pete Smith.
CASH STASHERS (MGM, 1953) d David Barclay, s Pete Smith.
IT WOULD SERVE 'EM RIGHT (MGM, 1953) d David Barclay, s Pete Smith.
THIS IS A LIVING (MGM, 1953) s Pete Smith.
LANDLORDING IT (MGM, 1953) d David Barclay, s Pete Smith.
THINGS WE CAN DO WITHOUT (MGM, 1953) d David Barclay, s Pete Smith.
FILM ANTICS (MGM, 1954) d David Barclay, s Pete Smith.
AIN'T IT AGGRAVATIN' (MGM, 1954) d David Barclay, s Pete Smith.
FISH TALES (MGM, 1954) d David Barclay, s Pete Smith.
DO SOMEONE A FAVOR (MGM, 1954) d David Barclay, s Pete Smith.
OUT FOR FUN (MGM, 1954) d David Barclay, s Pete Smith.
SAFE AT HOME (MGM, 1954) d David Barclay, s Pete Smith.
THE CAMERA CAUGHT IT (MGM, 1954) s Pete Smith.
ROUGH RIDING (MGM, 1954) s Pete Smith.
THE MAN AROUND THE HOUSE (MGM, 1955) d David Barclay, s Pete Smith.
KEEP YOUNG (MGM, 1955) s Pete Smith.
SPORTS TRIX (MGM, 1955) s Pete Smith.
JUST WHAT I NEEDED (MGM, 1955) d David Barclay, s Pete Smith.
GLOBAL QUIZ (MGM, 1955) s Pete Smith.
ANIMALS IN ACTION (MGM, 1955) s Pete Smith.

HISTORICAL ODDITIES (MGM, 1955) s Pete Smith.
FALL GUY (MGM, 1955) s Pete Smith.

PETROCELLI
See **LAWYER**

586. PEYTON PLACE
The soap opera movies are derived from the Grace Metalious novels. A TV show of the same title ran from 1964-69 on ABC, featuring Dorothy Malone, Mia Farrow and Ed Nelson.
PEYTON PLACE (20th Century-Fox, 1957) d Mark Robson, s Lana Turner, Hope Lang, Arthur Kennedy.
RETURN TO PEYTON PLACE (20th Century-Fox, 1961) d Jose Ferrer, s Jeff Changler, Eleanor Parker, Carol Lynley.
MURDER IN PEYTON PLACE (20th Century-Fox, 1977) (CBS-TV movie) d Bruce Kessler, s Christopher Connelly, Dorothy Malone, Ed Nelson.
PEYTON PLACE: THE NEXT GENERATION (1985) d Larry Elikann, s Christopher Connelly, James Douglas, Dorothy Malone.

587. PHANTASM
These are gorey horror films with a character known as the Tall Man enslaving graveyard zombies.
PHANTASM (1979) d Don Coscarelli, s Michael Baldwin, Bill Thornbury.
PHANTASM II (Cannon, 1988) d Lloyd Fonvielle, s Tommy Lee Jones, Virginia Madsen.

588. PHILIP MARLOWE
Raymond Chandler created the California private eye character in a series of pulp magazine stories and crime novels.
MURDER MY SWEET (RKO 1944) [aka FAREWELL MY LOVELY] d Edward Dymtryk, s Dick Powell, Claire Trevor.
THE BIG SLEEP (Warner Brothers, 1946) d Howard Hawks, s Humphrey Bogart, Lauren Bacall.
THE LADY IN THE LAKE (MGM, 1946) d Robert Montgomery, s Robert Montgomery, Audrey Totter.
THE BRASHER DOUBLOON (20th Century-Fox, 1947) [aka THE HIGH WINDOW] d John Brahm, s George Montgomery, Nancy Guild.
MARLOWE (MGM, 1969) d Paul Bogart, s James Garner, Gayle Hunnicutt.
THE LONG GOODBYE (United Artists, 1973) d Robert Altman, s Elliott Gould, Nina van Pallandt.
FAREWELL, MY LOVELY (Avco Embassy, 1975) d Dick Richards, s Robert Mitchum, Charlotte Rampling.
THE BIG SLEEP (United Artists, 1978) d Michael Winner, s Robert Mitchum, Sarah Miles.

589. PHILO VANCE

A.A. Van Dine (Willard Huntington Wright [1988-1939]) penned a series of mystery novels featuring an erudite investigator. These are the film versions.
THE CANARY MURDER CASE (Paramount, 1929) d Malcolm St. Clair, s William Powell, Louis Brooks.
THE GREENE MURDER CASE (Paramount, 1929) d Frank Tuttle, s William Powell, Jean Arthur.
THE BISHOP MURDER CASE (MGM, 1930) d Nick Grinde and David Burton, s Basil Rathbone, Leila Hyams.
THE BENSON MURDER CASE (Paramount, 1930) d Frank Tuttle, s William Powell, Natalie Moorhead.
THE KENNEL MURDER CASE (Warner Brothers, 1933) d Michael Curtiz, s William Powell, Mary Astor.
THE DRAGON MURDER CASE (Warner Brothers-First National, 1934) d H. Bruce Humberstone, s Warren William, Margaret Lindsay.
THE CASINO MURDER CASE (MGM, 1935) d Edwin L. Marin, s Paul Lukas, Rosalind Russell.
THE GARDEN MURDER CASE (MGM, 1936) d Edwin L. Marin, s Edmund Lowe, Virginia Bruce.
THE SCARAB MURDER CASE (Paramount, 1936) d Michael Hankinson, s Wilfrid Hyde-White, Kathleen Kelly.
NIGHT OF MYSTERY (Paramount, 1937) d E.A. Dupont, s Grant Richards, Helen Burgess.
THE GRACIE ALLEN MURDER CASE (Paramount, 1939) d Alfred E. Green, s Warren William, Gracie Allen.
CALLING PHILO VANCE (Warner Brothers, 1940) d William Clemens, s James Stephenson, Margot Stevenson.
PHILO VANCE RETURNS (PRC, 1947) d William Beaudine, s William Wright, Terry Austin.
PHILO VANCE'S GAMBLE (PRC, 1947) d Basil Wrangell, s Alan Curtis, Terry Austin.
PHILO VANCE'S SECRET MISSION (PRC, 1947) d Reginald Le Borg, s Alan Curtis, Sheila Ryan.

590. PHONE SEX GIRLS
These are adult pictures.
PHONE SEX GIRLS (Video Team, 1987) s Samantha Strong, Herschel Savage.
PHONE SEX GIRLS II (Video Team, 1988) s Samantha Strong, Mike Norner.

591. PHYSICAL
These films carry an X rating.
PHYSICAL (Select-A-Tape) s Julie Anderson.
PHYSICAL II (Superior Video, 1985) s Traci Lords, Tom Byron.

591A. PIMPLE
These silent films were made in Great Britain. Fred Evans plays the title character.

PIMPLE DOES THE TURKEY TROT (1912) s Fred Evans, Joe Evans.
PIMPLE'S BATTLE OF WATERLOO (1913) s Fred Evans, Joe Evans.
PIMPLE'S CLUTCHING HAND (1913) s Fred Evans, Joe Evans.
PIMPLE'S IVANHOE (1913) s Fred Evans, Joe Evans.
SEXTON PIMPLE s Fred Evans, Joe Evans.
PIMPLE'S MIDSUMMER'S NIGHT'S DREAM (1915) s Fred Evans, Joe Evans.
PIMPLE'S MILLION DOLLAR MYSTERY (1915) s Fred Evans, Joe Evans.
PIMPLE'S ROYAL DIVORCE (1915) s Fred Evans, Joe Evans.
PIMPLE'S THREE WEEKS (1915) s Fred Evans, Joe Evans.
PIMPLE AS HAMLET (1916) s Fred Evans, Joe Evans.
PIMPLE'S BETTER 'OLE (1918) s Fred Evans, Joe Evans.
HOW LT. PIMPLE CAPTURED THE KAISER s Fred Evans, Joe Evans.
LT. PIMPLE ON SECRET SERVICE s Fred Evans, Joe Evans.

592. PINK PANTHER, THE
The cast of the first picture, about a cat burglar after a prized jewel, features a bungling Surete inspector named Clouseau (played by Peter Sellers), who stole the picture and returned for several sequels.
THE PINK PANTHER (United Artists, 1964) d Blake Edwards, s Peter Sellers, David Niven, Capucin, Claudia Cardinale.
A SHOT IN THE DARK (United Artists, 1964) d Blake Edwards, s Peter Sellers, Elke Sommer, George Sanders, Herbert Lom, Burt Kwouk.
INSPECTOR CLOUSEAU (United Artists, 1968) d Bud Yorkin, s Alan Arkin, Delia Boccardo.
THE RETURN OF THE PINK PANTHER (United Artists, 1975) d Blake Edwards, s Peter Sellers, Christopher Plummer.
THE PINK PANTHER STRIKES AGAIN (United Artists, 1976) d Blake Edwards, s Peter Sellers, Herbert Lom.
REVENGE OF THE PINK PANTHER (United Artists, 1978) d Blake Edwards, s Peter Sellers, Herbert Lom, Burt Kwouk.
THE TRAIL OF THE PINK PANTHER (MGM/UA, 1982) d Blake Edwards, s Peter Sellers, David Niven, Herbert Lom.
CURSE OF THE PINK PANTHER (MGM/UA, 1983) d Blake Edwards, s Peter Sellers, Joanna Lumley, David Niven.

593. PINOCCHIO
These children's tales are about a puppet who comes to life. They are based on the Collodi original story.
PINOCCHIO (Walt Disney, 1940) d Ben Sharpsteen, Hamilton Luske, animated with voices Dickie Jones, Christian Rub.
PINOCCHIO IN OUTER SPACE (Universal, 1965) d Ray Goosens, voices Arnold Stang, Jess Cain.
PINOCCHIO'S STORYBOOK ADVENTURES (First Ameridan, 1979) d Ron Merk.
PINOCCHIO AND THE EMPEROR OF THE NIGHT (Filmation/New World, 1987) d Hal Sutherland, voices Edward Asner, Tom Bosley.

594. PIPPI LONGSTOCKING
Astrid Lindgren's children's books about a red-haired imp inspired these movies.
PIPPI LONGSTOCKING (G.G. Communications) d Olle Hellbom, s Inger Nillson.
PIPPI IN THE SOUTH SEAS (G.G. Communications, 1974) d Olle Hellbom, s Inger Nilsson, Par Sundberg, Maria Perrson.
PIPPI GOES ON BOARD (G.G. Communications, 1978) d Olle Hellbom, s Inger Nilsson.
PIPPI ON THE RUN (G.G. Communications) d Olle Hellbom, s Inger Nillson.
THE NEW ADVENTURES OF PIPPI LONGSTOCKING (Columbia Pictures, 1988) d Ken Annakin, s Tami Erin, Eileen Brennan, Dennis Dugan.

595. PIRANHA
The hero and heroine unwittingly release experimental piranha which spawn in fresh water and devour victims left and right.
PIRANHA (New World, 1978) d Joe Dante, s Bradford Dillman, Heather Menzies, Keenan Wynn, Kevin McCarthy.
PIRANHA II: THE SPAWNING (Saturn International Pictures, 1983) d James Cameron, s Tricia O'Neil, Steve Marachuk.

596. PLANET OF THE APES
Pierre Boulle wrote a science fiction novel about a post-apocalyptic race of ape-like beings discovered by American astronauts. There was also a television series which was broadcast by CBS in 1974.
PLANET OF THE APES (20th Century-Fox, 1968) d Franklin J. Schaffner, s Charlton Heston, Roddy McDowall, Kim Hunter.
BENEATH THE PLANE OF THE APES (20th Century-Fox), d Ted Post, s James Franciscus, Kim Hunter, Maurice Evans.
ESCAPE FROM THE PLANET OF THE APES (20th Century-Fox, 1971), d Don Taylor, s Roddy McDowall, Kim Hunter.
CONQUEST OF THE PLANET OF THE APES (20th Century-Fox, 1972) d J. Lee Thompson, s Roddy McDowall, Don Murray, Natalie Trundy.
BATTLE FOR THE PLANET OF THE APES (20th Century-Fox, 1973) d J. Lee Thompson, s Roddy McDowall, Natalie Trundy.

597. PLEASURE HUNT, THE
In these adult pix a child-bride follows her husband's "pleasure map."
THE PLEASURE HUNT (Now Showing, 1984) d Lawrence T. Cole, s Ginger Lynn.
PLEASURE HUNT II (Now Showing, 1985) d Lawrence T. Cole, s Ginger Lynn.

597A. PLUMP AND RUNT
See POKE AND JABBS for description.

598. POKE AND JABBS
This silent comedy series featured the hobo slapstick of Bobbie Burns and Walter Stull for General Film, circa 1916-18. After Burns left the series, Billy Ruge arrived and the characters became Finn and Haddie. When Stull left, Oliver Hardy came in and the characters were called Plump and Runt.

599. POLICE ACADEMY
These comedy films depict a farcical force of extremely bungling cops.
POLICE ACADEMY (Ladd/Warner Brothers, 1984) d Hugh Wilson, s Steve Guttenberg, G.W. Baily.
POLICE ACADEMY 2: THEIR FIRST ASSIGNMENT (1985) d Jerry Paris, s. Steve Guttenberg, Bubba Smith.
POLICE ACADEMY 3: BACK IN TRAINING (1986) d Jerry Paris, s Steve Guttenberg, Bubba Smith.
POLICE ACADEMY 4: CITIZENS ON PATROL (1987) d Jim Drake, s Steve Guttenberg, Bubba Smith.
POLICE ACADEMY 5: ASSIGNMENT MIAMI BEACH (1988) d Alan Myerson, s Bubba Smith, George Gaynes.
POLICE ACADEMY 6 (Warner Brothers, 1989) d Peter Bonerz, s Bubba Smith, Michael Winslow, Marion Ramsey.

600. POLTERGEIST
A young family's home is occupied by unfriendly spirits.
POLTERGEIST (MGM/UA, 1982) d Tobe Hooper, s Craig T. Nelson, JoBeth Williams.
POLTERGEIST II (MGM/UA, 1986) d Brian Gibson, s JoBeth Williams, Craig T. Nelson.
POLTERGEIST III (MGM/UA, 1988) d Gary Sherman, s Tom Skeritt, Nancy Allen.

601. POOR WHITE TRASH
A Yankee architect clashes with Louisiana developers, in the first; in the second, a Vietnam vet goes on a rampage.
POOR WHITE TRASH (United Artists, 1957) [aka BAYOU] d Harold Daniels, s Peter Graves, Lita Milan.
POOR WHITE TRASH, PART 2 (Dimension, 1976) [aka SCUM OF THE EARTH] d S.F. Brownrigg.

602. PORKY'S
These are adventures of raunchy nerds in a Florida high school. Porky is the owner of a brothel.
PORKY'S (20th Century-Fox, 1981) d Bob Clark, s Dan Monahan, Mark Herrier.
PORKY'S II: THE NEXT DAY (20th Century-Fox, 1983) d Bob Clark, s Dan Monahan, Wyatt Knight.
PORKY'S REVENGE (Astral Bellvue Pathe, 1985) d James Komack, s Dan Monahan, Wyatt Knight.

603. POSEIDON ADVENTURE, THE
A capsized luxury liner creates a challenge for would-be rescuers.
THE POSEIDON ADVENTURE (20th Century-Fox, 1972) d Ronald Neame, s Gene Hackman, Ernest Borgnine.
BEYOND THE POSEIDON ADVENTURE (Warner Brothers, 1979) d Irwin Allen, s Michael Caine, Sally Field.

604. POTASH AND PERLMUTTER
Silent comedies.
POTASH AND PERLMUTTER (1923) s Alexander Carr
IN HOLLYWOOD WITH POTASH AND PERLMUTTER (1924) s Alexander Carr, Vera Gordon.
PARTNERS AGAIN (1926) s Alexander Carr

605. PRETTY PEACHES
These are adult flicks about a scatterbrained woman who suffers amnesia.
PRETTY PEACHES (Mitchell Brothers, 1979) d Alex de Renzy, s Desiree Cousteau, Joey Silvera.
PRETTY PEACHES 2 (VCA, 1987) s Siobhan Hunter, Herschel Savage.

605A. PRISCILLA
This is a silent film series.
PRISCILLA AND THE UMBRELLA (Biograph, 1911)
PRISCILLA'S ENGAGEMENT KISS (Biograph, 1911)
PRISCILLA'S APRIL FOOL JOKE (Biograph, 1911)
PRISCILLA'S CAPTURE (Biograph, 1912)

606. PROM NIGHT
A mad killer stalks kids at a Hamilton High dance. A girl returns from her grave, in the second outing, to get revenge.
PROM NIGHT (Prom Night Productions, 1980) d Paul Lynch, s Jamie Lee Curtis, Leslie Nielsen.
HELLO, MARY LOU: PROM NIGHT II (Simcon/Norstar, 1987) d Bruce Pittman, s Lisa Schrage, Wendy Lyon.
PROM NIGHT III: THE LAST KISS (Announced, 1990) s Courtney Taylor.

607. PSYCHO
Norman Bates is the mother-dominated proprietor of a remote motel in the classic Alfred Hitchcock-directed suspense film.
PSYCHO (Paramount, 1960) d Alfred Hitchcock, s Anthony Perkins, Janet Leigh, Vera Miles, Martin Balsam, John Gavin.
PSYCHO II (Universal, 1983) d Richard Franklin, s Anthony Perkins, Vera Miles, Meg Tilly, Robert Loggia.
PSYCHO III (1986) d Anthony Perkins, s Anthony Perkins, Diana Scarwid, Jeff Fahey.

608. PUBLIC ENEMY
Gangsters and molls are brought to justice.
THE PUBLIC ENEMY (Warner Brothers, 1931) d William A. Wellman, s
 James Cagney, Edward Woods, Jean Harlow.
PUBLIC ENEMY'S WIFE (Warner Brothers, 1936) d Nick Grinde, s Margaret
 Linsay, Pat O'Brien.

608A. PUPPETMASTER
PUPPETMASTER
PUPPETMASTER II (Full Moon Productions, scheduled 1990)

609. QUATERMASS
Quatermass is a professor who deals with antagonistic foes from outer space. He was featured in three BBC television serials.
THE CREEPING UNKNOWN (United Artists, 1956) [aka THE
 QUATERMASS EXPERIMENT] d Val Guest, s Brian Donlevy,
 Margia Dean.
QUATERMASS II [aka ENEMY FROM SPACE] (United Artists, 1957) d
 Val Guest, s Brian Donlevy, Michael Ripper.
QUATERMASS AND THE PIT (Hammer/20th Century-Fox, 1968) [aka
 FIVE MILLION YEARS TO EARTH] d Roy Ward Baker, s James
 Donald, Barbara Shelley.
QUATERMASS CONCLUSION (Easton, 1980) d Piers Haggard, s John Mills.

610. QUEEN OF THE PIRATES
Pirates.
QUEEN OF THE PIRATES (Columbia, 1960) d Mario Costa, s Gianna Maria
 Canale.
TIGER OF THE SEVEN SEAS (Embassy, 1962) d Luigi Capuano, s Gianna
 Maria Canale, Anthony Steel.

A confident (but naked) Inspector Clouseau (Peter Sellers) attempts to escape from a nudist camp with beautiful (and equally clothesless) Elke Sommer in the crime comedy A SHOT IN THE DARK (1964).

272 MOTION PICTURE SERIES & SEQUELS

611. RAFFLES
The Amateur Cracksman was featured in books by E.W. Hornung, written in the period 1892-1905.
RAFFLES (1905) d G.M. Anderson.
RAFFLES (1910)
RAFFLES (1914)
RAFFLES, THE AMATEUR CRACKSMAN (Hiller-Wilk, 1917) d George Irving, s John Barrymore.
RAFFLES (1920)
RAFFLES, THE AMATEUR CRACKSMAN (Universal, 1925) d King Baggott, s House Peters.
RAFFLES (United Artists, 1930) d Harry D'Arrast, George Fitzmaurice, s Ronald Colman, Kay Francis.
THE RETURN OF RAFFLES (1932) s George Barraud.
RAFFLES (United Artist, 1940) d Sam Wood, s David Niven, Olivia De Havilland.
RAFFLES (1960)

612. RAMBO
David Morrell's 1972 novel *The First Blood* is about John Rambo, a Vietnam vet who vents his rage at American injustice. The movies take the character back to Vietnam to free POWs and to Afghanistan to rescue a former superior officer.
FIRST BLOOD (Orion, 1982) d Ted Kotcheff, s Sylvester Stallone, Richard Crenna.
RAMBO: FIRST BLOOD PART II (Tri-Star, 1985) d George P. Cosmatos, s Sylvester Stallone, Richard Crenna.
RAMBO III (Tri-Star, 1988) d Peter Macdonald, s Sylvester Stallone, Richard Crenna.

613. RAMBONE
These X-rated pictures feature "actor" Dick Rambone. The list may be incomplete.
RAMBONE: THE FIRST TIME (Jack-of-Hearts, 1985) s Mai Lin, Dick Rambone, Jack Hammer.
RAMBONE MEETS THE DOUBLE PENETRATORS (Wet, 1986) s Dick Rambone, Keli Richards.
RAMBONE THE DESTROYER (Wet, 1986) d William Whett, s Patti Petite, Dick Rambone.
RAMBONE DOES HOLLYWOOD (Wet, 1986) s Buffy Davis, Dick Rambone.

613A. RANCH GIRL
These are silent westerns. The list may be incomplete.
THE RANCH GIRL'S LEGACY (Essanay, 1910) s G.B. Anderson.
THE CORPORATION AND THE RANCH GIRL (Essanay, 1911) s G.B. Anderson

THE RANCH GIRL'S TRAIL (Essanay, 1912) s G.B. Anderson.

614. RANGE BUSTERS
This is a Western series featuring a trio of actors. Ray "Crash" Corrigan previously appeared in twenty-four of the THREE MESQUITEERS saddles-and-sixguns series.
THE RANGE BUSTERS (Monogram, 1940) d S. Roy Luby, s Ray Corrigan, Dusty King, Max Terhune, Luana Walters.
TRAILING DOUBLE TROUBLE (Monogram, 1940) d Roy Luby, s Ray Corrigan, Dusty King, Max Terhune, Lita Conway.
WEST OF PINTO BASIN (Monogram, 1940) d S. Roy Luby, s Ray Corrigan, Dusty King, Max Terhune, Gwen Gaze.
TRAIL OF THE SILVER SPURS (Monogram, 1941) d S. Roy Luby, s Ray Corrigan, Dusty King, Max Terhune, Dorothy Short.
THE KID'S LAST RIDE (Monogram, 1941) d S. Roy Luby, s Ray Corrigan, Dusty King, Max Terhune, Sheila Darcy, Marian Kirby.
WRANGLER'S ROOST (Monogram, 1941) d S. Roy Luby, s Ray Corrigan, Dusty King, Max Terhune, Gwen Gaze.
FUGITIVE VALLEY (Monogram, 1941) d S. Roy Luby, s Ray Corrigan, Dusty King, Max Terhune, Julie Duncan.
SADDLE MOUNTAIN ROUNDUP (Monogram, 1941) d S. Roy Luby, s Ray Corrigan, Dusty King, Max Terhune, Lita Conway.
TONTO BASIN OUTLAWS (Monogram, 1941) d S. Roy Luby, s Ray Corrigan, Dusty King, Max Terhune, Gwen Gaze.
THUNDER RIVER FEUD (Monogram, 1942) d S. Roy Luby, s Ray Corrigan, Dusty King, Max Terhune, Jan Wiley.
ROCK RIVER RENEGADES (Monogram, 1942) d S. Roy Luby, s Ray Corrigan, Dusty King, Max Terhune, Christine McIntyre.
BOOT HILL BANDITS (Monogram, 1942) d S. Roy Luby, s Ray Corrigan, Dusty King, Max Terhune, Jean Brooks.
TEXAS TROUBLE SHOOTERS (Monogram, 1942) d S. Roy Luby, s Ray Corrigan, Dusty King, Max Terhune, Julie Duncan.
ARIZONA STAGECOACH (Monogram, 1942) d S. Roy Luby, s Ray Corrigan, Dusty King, Max Terhune, Nell O'Day.
TEXAS TO BATAAN (Monogram, 1942) d Robert Tansey, s Dusty King, David Sharpe, Max Terhune, Marjorie Manners.
TRAIL RIDERS (Monogram, 1942) d Robert Tansey, s Dusty King, David Sharpe, Max Terhune, Evelyn Finley.
TWO FISTED JUSTICE (Monogram, 1943) d Robert Tansey, s Dusty King, David Sharpe, Max Terhune, Gwen Gaze.
HAUNTED RANCH (Monogram, 1943) d Robert Tansey, s Dusty King, David Sharpe, Max Terhune, Julie Duncan.
LAND OF HUNTED MEN (Monogram, 1943) d S. Roy Luby, s Ray Corrigan, Dennis Moore, Max Terhune, Phyllis Adair.
COWBOY COMMANDOS (Monogram, 1943) d S. Roy Luby, s Ray Corrigan, Dennis Moore, Max Terhune, Evelyn Finley.

BLACK MARKET RUSTLERS (Monogram, 1943) d S. Roy Luby, s Ray Corrigan, Dennis Moore, Max Terhune, Evelyn Finley.
BULLETS AND SADDLES (Monogram, 1943) d Anthony Marshall, s Ray Corrigan, Dennis Moore, Max Terhune, Julie Duncan.

615. RASTUS
These films feature Negro performers as buffoons.
HOW RASTUS GOT HIS PORK CHOPS (Lubin, 1908)
HOW RASTUS GOT HIS TURKEY (ca 1910)
RASTUS IN ZULULAND (ca 1910)
RASTUS AND CHICKEN (ca 1910-11)
PICKANINNIES AND WATERMELON (ca 1910-11)
CHICKEN THIEF (ca 1910-11)

616. RAT, THE
From Ivor Novello and Constance Collier's play, Pierre Boucheron, alias The Rat, bilks the rich but is reformed by an orphan girl.
THE RAT (Gainsborough, 1925) d Graham Cutts, s Ivor Novello, Mae Marsh.
THE TRIUMPH OF THE RAT (Gainsborough, 1926) d Graham Cutts, s Ivor Novello, Isobel Jeans.
THE RETURN OF THE RAT (Gainsborough, 1929) d Graham Cutts, s Ivor Novello, Isabel Jeans.
THE RAT (Imperator/Radio, 1937) d Jack Raymond, s Ruth Chatterton, Anton Walbrook.

616A. RE-ANIMATOR
H.P. Lovecraft's horror prose inspired this stylish but gorey picture about a young medical student who brings the dead back to life.
RE-ANIMATOR (1985) d Stuart Gordon, s Bruce Abbott, Barbara Crampton.
RE-ANIMATOR II: THE SEQUEL (Announced 1990-91)

617. RED RYDER
The series is based on Fred Harmon's newspaper comic strip and comic books set in the old West with Red, Little Beaver and the Dutchess. The strip first appeared in 1938. Red was also heard on radio beginning in 1942.
ADVENTURES OF RED RYDER (Republic, 1940) d William Witney and John English, s Don "Red" Barry, Noah Beery, Tommy Cook.
TUCSON RAIDERS (Republic, 1944) d Spencer Bennett, s Wild Bill Eliott, Gabby Hayes, Bobby Blake, Peggy Stewart.
MARSHAL OF RENO (Republic, 1944) d Wallace Grissell, s Wild Bill Elliott, Gabby Hayes, Bobby Blake.
THE SAN ANTONIO KID (Republic, 1944) d Howard Bertherton, s Wild Bill Elliott, Bobby Blake, Linda Stirling.
CHEYENNE WILDCAT (Republic, 1944) d Lesley Selander, s Wild Bill Elliott, Bobby Blake, Peggy Stewart.
VIGILANTES OF DODGE CITY (Republic, 1944) d Wallace Grissell, s Wild Bill Elliott, Bobby Blake, Linda Stirling.

SHERIFF OF LAS VEGAS (Republic, 1944) d Lesley Selander, s Wild Bill Elliott, Bobby Blake, Peggy Stewart.
THE GREAT STAGECOACH ROBBERY (Republic, 1945) d Lesley Selander, s Wild Bill Elliott, Bobby Blake, Sylvia Arslan.
LONE TEXAS RANGER (Republic, 1945) d Spencer Bennett, s Wild Bill Elliott, Bobby Blake, Helen Talbot.
PHANTOM OF THE PLAINS (Republic, 1945) d Lesley Selander, s Wild Bill Elliott, Bobby Blake, Virginia Christine.
MARSHAL OF LAREDO (Republic, 1945) d R.G. Springsteen, s Wild Bill Elliott, Bobby Blake, Peggy Stewart.
COLORADO PIONEERS (Republic, 1945) d R.G. Springsteen, s Wild Bill Elliott, Bobby Blake.
WAGON WHEELS WESTWARD (Republic, 1945) d R.G. Springsteen, s Wild Bill Elliott, Bobby Blake, Linda Stirling.
CALIFORNIA GOLD RUSH (Republic, 1946) d R.G. Springsteen, s Wild Bill Elliott, Bobby Blake, Peggy Stewart.
SUN VALLEY CYCLONE (Republic, 1946) d R.G. Springsteen, s Wild Bill Elliott, Bobby Blake.
CONQUEST OF CHEYENNE (Republic, 1946) d R.G. Springsteen, s Wild Bill Elliott, Bobby Blake, Peggy Stewart.
SHERIFF OF REDWOOD VALLEY (Republic, 1946) d R.G. Springsteen, s Wild Bill Elliott, Bobby Blake, Peggy Stewart.
SANTA FE UPRISING (Republic, 1946) d R.G. Springsteen, s Rocky Lane, Bobby Blake.
STAGECOACH TO DENVER (Republic, 1946) d R.G. Springsteen, s Rocky Lane, Bobby Blake, Peggy Stewart.
VIGILANTES OF BOOMTOWN (Republic, 1947) d R.G. Springsteen, s Rocky Lane, Bobby Blake, Peggy Stewart.
HOMESTEADERS OF PARADISE VALLEY (Republic, 1947) d R.G. Springsteen, s Rocky Lane, Ann Todd.
OREGON TRAIL SCOUTS (Republic, 1947) d R.G. Springsteen, s Rocky Lane, Bobby Blake.
RUSTLERS OF DEVIL'S CANYON (Republic, 1947) d R.G. Springsteen, s Rocky Lane, Bobby Blake, Peggy Stewart.
MARSHAL OF CRIPPLE CREEK (Republic, 1947) d R.G. Springsteen, s Rocky Lane, Bobby Blake.
RIDE, RYDER, RIDE (Eagle Lion, 1949) d Lewis Collins, s Jim Bannon, Peggy Stewart, Don Kay Reynolds.
ROLL, THUNDER, ROLL (Eagle Lion, 1949) d Lewis Colins, s Jim Bannon, Nancy Gates, Don Kay Reynolds.
THE FIGHTING REDHEAD (Eagle Lion, 1949) d Lewis Collins, s Jim Bannon, Peggy Stewart, Don Kay Reynolds.
COWBOY AND THE PRIZEFIGHTER (Eagle Lion, 1949) d Lewis Collins, s Jim Bannon, Karen Randle, Don Kay Reynolds.

618. RED STALLION
A youth raises a horse for racing.

RED STALLION (Eagle Lion, 1947) d Lesley Selander, s Robert Paige, Noreen Nash.
RED STALLION IN THE ROCKIES (Eagle Lion, 1949) d Ralph Murphy, s Arthur Franz, Wallace Ford.

619. REG'LAR KIDS, THE
These M.J. Winkler short comedies feature a cast of children.

620. RENFREW OF THE MOUNTIES
James Newill plays the title character in a series of B-grade action pictures based on Laurie York Erskine's Canadian novels. Renfrew was also featured in radio (1936-40) and television programs (1953).
RENFREW OF THE ROYAL MOUNTED (Grand National, 1937) d Al Herman, s James Newill, Carol Hughes.
ON THE GREAT WHITE TRAIL (Grand National, 1938) [aka RENFREW OF THE ROYAL MOUNTED ON THE GREAT WHITE TRAIL and RENFREW ON THE GREAT WHITE TRAIL] d Al Herman, s James Newill, Terry Walker.
CRASHING THRU' (Grand National/Monogram, 1939) d Elmer Clifton, s James Newill, Warren Hull.
FIGHTING MAD (Monogram, 1939) [aka RENFREW OF THE ROYAL MOUNTED IN FIGHTING MAD] d Sam Newfield, s James Newill, Sally Blane.
YUKON FLIGHT (Monogram, 1940) [aka RENFREW OF THE ROYAL MOUNTED IN YUKON FLIGHT] d Ralph Staub, s James Newill, Louise Stanley.
DANGER AHEAD (Monogram, 1940) d Ralph Staub, s James Newill, Dorothea Kent.
MURDER ON THE YUKON (Monogram, 1940) d Louis Gasnier, s James Newill, Polly Ann Young.
SKY BANDITS (Monogram, 1940) d Ralph Staub, s James Newill, Dave O'Brien.

621. RETURN OF THE LIVING DEAD
These pictures are spoofs of George Romero's zombie films including NIGHT OF THE LIVING DEAD.
THE RETURN OF THE LIVING DEAD (International Cinefilm, 1985) [aka DEAD PEOPLE and MESSIAH OF EVIL and REVENGE OF THE SCREAMING DEAD and THE SECOND COMING] d Dan O'Bannon, s Clu Gulager, James Karen.
RETURN OF THE LIVING DEAD PART II (Lorimar, 1988) d Ken Wiederhorn, s James Karen, Thom Mathews.

622. REVENGE OF THE NERDS
Nerdy college freshmen form their own fraternity and have their last laugh on the jocks.

REVENGE OF THE NERDS (20th Century-Fox, 1984) d Jeff Kanew, s Robert Carradine.
REVENGE OF THE NERDS II: NERDS IN PARADISE (20th Century-Fox, 1987) d Joe Roth, s Robert Carradine.

623. *REX ALLEN AND BUDDY EBSEN*
B Westerns teamed Rex Allen with two sidekicks (see also next entry).
UNDER MEXICALI STARS (Republic, 1950) d George Blair, s Rex Allen, Buddy Ebsen, Dorothy Patrick.
SILVER CITY BONANZA (Republic, 1952) d George Blair, s Rex Allen, Buddy Ebsen, Mary Ellen Kay.
RODEO KING AND THE SENORITA (Republic, 1952) d Philip Ford, s Rex Allen, Buddy Ebsen, Mary Ellen Kay.
UTAH WAGON TRAIN (Republic, 1951) s Rex Allen, Buddy Ebsen, Penny Edwards.

624. *REX ALLEN AND SLIM PICKINS*
COLORADO SUNDOWN (Republic, 1952) d William Witney, s Rex Allen, Slim Pickins, Mary Ellen Kay.
THE LAST MUSKETEER (Republic, 1952) d William Witney, s Rex Allen, Slim Pickins, Mary Ellen Kay.
BORDER SADDLEMATES (Republic, 1952) d William Witney s Rex Allen, Slim Pickins, Mary Ellen Kay.
OLD OKLAHOMA PLAINS (Republic, 1952) d William Witney, s Rex Allen, Slim Pickins, Elaine Edwards.
SOUTH PACIFIC TRAIL (Republic, 1952) d William Witney, s Rex Allen, Slim Pickins, Estelita Rodriguez.
OLD OVERLAND TRAIL (Republic, 1953) d William Witney s Rex Allen, Slim Pickins, Virginia Hall.
IRON MOUNTAIN TRAIL (Republic, 1953) d William Witney s Rex Allen, Slim Pickins, Nan Leslie.
DOWN LAREDO WAY (Republic, 1953) d William Witney, s Rex Allen, Slim Pickins, Donna Drake.
SHADOWS OF TOMBSTONE (Republic, 1953) d William Witney, s Rex Allen, Slim Pickins, Jeanne Cooper.
RED RIVER SHORE (Republic, 1953) d Harry Keller, s Rex Allen, Slim Pickins, Lyn Thomas.
PHANTOM STALLION (Republic, 1954) d Harry Keller, s Rex Allen, Slim Pickins, Carla Balenda.

625. *REX BELL AND BUZZ BARTON*
Poverty Row low-budget Westerns team Bell and Barton.
FIGHTING PIONEERS (Resolute, 1935) d Harry Fraser, s Rex Bell, Buzz Barton.
GUNFIRE (Resolute, 1935) d Harry Fraser, s Rex Bell, Buzz Barton.
SADDLE ACES (Resolute, 1935) d Harry Fraser, s Rex Bell, Buzz Barton.
THE TONTO KID (Resolute, 1935) d Harry Fraser, s Rex Bell, Buzz Barton.

626. RICHEST GIRL IN THE WORLD, THE
Dorothy Hunter wants a man who will love her for herself, and not her riches.
THE RICHEST GIRL IN THE WORLD (RKO, 1934) d William A. Seiter, s
 Miriam Hopkins, Henry Stephenson, Joel McCrea.
BRIDE BY MISTAKE (RKO, 1944) d Richard Wallace, s Alan Marshal,
 Laraine Day.

627. RIDERS OF THE PURPLE SAGE
Zane Grey's gunslinger Lassiter first made a prose appearance in *Riders of the Purple Sage* (1912) and its sequel *The Rainbow Trail* (1915).
RIDERS OF THE PURPLE SAGE (Fox, 1918) s William Farnum.
THE RAINBOW TRAIL (Fox, 1918) s William Farnum
RIDERS OF THE PURPLE SAGE (Fox, 1925) d Lynn Reynolds, s Tom Mix,
 Beatrice Burnham.
THE RAINBOW TRAIL (1925) d Lynn Reynolds, s Tom Mix, Anne Cornwall.
RIDERS OF THE PURPLE SAGE (Fox, 1931) d Hamilton MacFadden, s
 George O'Brien, Marguerite Churchill.
THE RAINBOW TRAIL (1932)
RIDERS OF THE PURPLE SAGE (20th Century-Fox, 1941) d James Tinling,
 s George Montgomery, Mary Howard.

627A RIDDLE RIDER, THE
These are silent films about a vigilante.
THE RIDDLE RIDER (Universal, 1924) s William Desmond, Eileen Sedgwick.
THE RETURN OF THE RIDDLE RIDER (Universal) s William Desmond,
 Eileen Sedgwick.

628. RIFIFI
Criminals plot surefire robberies -- which end up with a hitch.
RIFIFI (United Motion Pictures, 1956) d Jules Dassin, s Jean Servais, Carl
 Mohner.
RIFIFI IN TOKYO (MGM, 1962) d Jacques Deray, s Karl Boehm.
RIFF RAFF GIRLS (Continental, 1962) [aka RIFIFI FOR GIRLS] d Alex
 Joffe, s Nadja Tiller, Robert Hossein.
UPPER HAND (Paramount, 1967) [aka RIFIFI IN PARIS] d Denys de la
 Patelliere, s Jean Gabin.

629. *RIN-TIN-TIN*
The German shepherd was also featured in television series with cavalry of Old West, over ABC-TV 1954-59. The last listing below was culled from segments of that show. The dog also appeared on radio and in new TV show on Family Channel beginning in 1988.
THE MAN FROM HELL'S RIVER (1922)
WHERE THE NORTH BEGINS (1923)
FIND YOUR MAN (1924)
LIGHTHOUSE BY THE SEA (1924)

CLASH OF THE WOLVES (Warner Brothers, 1924) d Noel Mason, s Rin-Tin-Tin, June Marlowe, Charles Farrell.
TRACKED IN THE SNOW COUNTRY (1925)
WHILE LONDON SLEEPS (1926)
THE NIGHT CRY (Warner Brothers, 1926) d Herman C. Raymaker, s Rin-Tin-Tin, John Harron, June Marlowe.
HERO OF THE BIG SNOWS (1926)
TRACKED BY THE POLICE (Warner Brothers, 1927) d Ray Enright, s Rin-Tin-Tin, Jason Robards, Virginia Browne Faire.
JAWS OF STEEL (1927)
HILLS OF KENTUCKY (1927)
A DOG OF THE REGIMENT (1927)
RINTY OF THE DESERT (1928)
LAND OF THE SILVER FOX (1928)
RACE FOR LIFE (1928)
TIGER ROSE (1929)
LIGHTNING WARRIOR (1929)
THE MILLION DOLLAR COLLAR (1929)
SHOW OF SHOWS (1929)
FROZEN RIVER (1929)
THE LONE DEFENDER (Mascot, 1930) (12 chapters) d Richard Thorpe, s Rin-Tin-Tin, Walter Miller, June Marlowe.
ROUGH WATERS (1929)
MAN HUNTER (1930)
THE LIGHTNING WARRIOR (Mascot, 1931) (12-chapter serial) d Armand L. Schaefer and Benjamin Kline, s Rin-Tin-Tin, Frankie Darro, George Brent.
HUMAN TARGETS (Big 4, 1932) d J.P. McGowan, s Rin-Tin-Tin Jr., Buzz Barton, Francis X. Bushman Jr.
WOLF DOG (1933) (serial) s Rinty Jr.
THE LAW OF THE WILD (Mascot, 1934) (12 chapters) d B. Reeves Eason and Armand L. Schaefer, s Rex, Rin-Tin-Tin Jr., Ben Turpin, Bob Custer, Lucille Browne.
SKULL AND CROWN (Reliable, 1935) d Elmer Clifton, s Rin-Tin-Tin Jr., Regis Toomey.
THE TEST (Reliable, 1935) d Bernard B. Ray, s Rin-Tin-Tin Jr., Grant Withers, Grace Ford.
VENGEANCE OF RANNAH (Reliable, 1936) d Franklin Shamray, s Bob Custer, Rin-Tin-Tin Jr.
CARYL OF THE MOUNTAINS (Reliable, 1936) d Bernard B. Ray, s Rin-Tin-Tin Jr., Francis X. Bushman Jr., Lois Wild.
THE SILVER TRAIL (Reliable, 1937) d Raymond Samuels, s Rin-Tin-Tin Jr., Rex Lease, Mary Russell.
DEATH GOES NORTH (Warwick, 1939) d Frank McDonald, s Rin-Tin-Tin Jr., Edgar Edwards, Dorothy Bradshaw.
FANGS OF THE WILD (Astor/Metropolitan, 1941) d Raymond K. Johnson, s Rin-Tin-Tin Jr., Dennis Moore, Luana Walters.

LAW OF THE WOLF (Ziehm, 1941) d Raymond K. Johnson, s Rin-Tin-Tin III, Dennis Moore, Luana Walters.
THE RETURN OF RIN TIN TIN (Romay Pictures, 1947) d Max Nosseck, s Rin-Tin-Tin III, Donald Woods, Bobby Blake.
THE CHALLENGE OF RIN TIN TIN (Burt Leonard Productions, 1957) d Robert G. Walker, s Rin-Tin-Tin V, James Brown, Lee Aaker.

630. RITZ BROTHERS, THE
The comedy team of Harry, Jimmy and Al Ritz is featured in the listings below.
HOTEL ANCHOVY (Educational-Fox, 1934) d Al Christie, s Ritz Brothers, Doris Hill.
SING, BABY, SING (20th Century-Fox, 1936) d Sidney Lanfield, s Alice Faye, Adolphe Menjou, Ritz Brothers.
ONE IN A MILLION (20th Century-Fox, 1937) d Sidney Lanfield, s Sonja Henie, Adolphe Menjou, Don Ameche, Ritz Brothers.
ON THE AVENUE (20th Century-Fox, 1937) d Roy Del Ruth, s Dick Powell, Madeleine Carroll, Ritz Brothers.
LIFE BEGINS AT COLLEGE (20th Century-Fox, 1937) [aka LIFE BEGINS IN COLLEGE] d William Seiter, s Joan Davis, Tony Martin, Ritz Brothers.
THE GOLDWYN FOLLIES (Samuel Goldwyn-United Artists, 1938) d George Marshall, s Adolphe Menjou, Zorina, Ritz Brothers.
KENTUCKY MOONSHINE (20th Century-Fox, 1938) d David Butler, s Tony Martin, Marjorie Weaver, Ritz Brothers.
STRAIGHT, PLACE AND SHOW (20th Century-Fox, 1938) d David Butler, s Richard Arlen, Ethel Merman, Ritz Brothers.
THE THREE MUSKETEERS (20th Century-Fox, 1939) d Allan Dwan, s Don Ameche, Ritz Brothers.
THE GORILLA (20th Century-Fox, 1939) d Allan Dwan, s Anita Louise, Patsy Kelly, Ritz Brothers.
PACK UP YOUR TROUBLES (20th Century-Fox, 1939) d H. Bruce Humberstone, s Jane Withers, Ritz Brothers.
ARGENTINE NIGHTS (Universal, 1940) d Albert S. Rogell, s Andrews Sisters, Ritz Brothers.
BEHIND THE EIGHT-BALL (Universal, 1942) d Stanley Roberts, s Carol Bruce, Dick Foran, Ritz Brothers.
HI-YA, CHUM (Universal, 1943) d Harold Young, s Jane Frazee, Robert Paige, Ritz Brothers.
NEVER A DULL MOMENT (Universal, 1943) d Edward Lilley, s Frances Langford, Stuart Crawford, Ritz Brothers.

631. ROAD TO...
The comedies team jokester Bob Hope, singer Bing Crosby and beauty Dorothy Lamour.
ROAD TO SINGAPORE (Warner Brothers, 1940) d Victor Schertzinger, s Bob Hope, Bing Crosby, Dorothy Lamour.

ROAD TO ZANZIBAR (Paramount, 1941) d Victor Schertzinger, s Bob Hope, Bing Crosby, Dorothy Lamour.
ROAD TO MOROCCO (Paramount, 1942) d David Butler, s Bob Hope, Bing Crosby, Dorothy Lamour.
ROAD TO UTOPIA (Paramount, 1945) d Hal Walker, s Bob Hope, Bing Crosby, Dorothy Lamour.
ROAD TO RIO (Paramount, 1947) d Norman Z. McLeod, s Bob Hope, Bing Crosby, Dorothy Lamour.
ROAD TO BALI (Paramount, 1952) d Hal Walker, s Bob Hope, Bing Crosby, Dorothy Lamour.
THE ROAD TO HONG KONG (United Artists, 1962) d Norman Panama, s Bob Hope, Bing Crosby, Dorothy Lamour.

632. ROBE, THE
The effects of Christ's crucifixion on young tribune Marcellius Gallio and his slave Demetrius are dramatized in these films.
THE ROBE (20th Century-Fox, 1953) d Henry Koster, s Richard Burton, Jean Simmons, Victor Mature.
DEMETRIUS AND THE GLADIATORS (20th Century-Fox, 1954) d Delmer Daves, s Victor Mature, Susan Hayward, Michael Rennie.

633. *ROBERT BENCHLEY*
The short subjects feature after dinner speaker and humorist Robert Benchley.
THE TREASURER'S REPORT (Fox, 1928) d Thomas Chalmers, s Robert Benchley.
THE SEX LIFE OF THE POLYP (Fox, 1928) d Thomas Chalmers, s Robert Benchley.
THE SPELLBINDER (Fox, 1928) d Thomas Chalmers, s Robert Benchley.
LESSON NO. 1 (Fox, 1929) d James Parrott, s Robert Benchley.
FURNACE TROUBLE (Fox, 1929) d James Parrott, s Robert Benchley.
STEWED, FRIED AND BOILED (Fox, 1929) d James Parrott, s Robert Benchley, Sylvia Fields.
YOUR TECHNOCRACY AND MINE (Universal, 1933) s Robert Benchley.
HOW TO BREAK 90 AT CROQUET (RKO, 1935, d Lee Marcus, s Robert Benchley.
HOW TO SLEEP (MGM, 1935) d Nick Grinde, s Robert Benchley.
HOW TO BEHAVE (MGM, 1936) d Arthur Ripley, s Robert Benchley.
HOW TO TRAIN A DOG (MGM, 1936) d Arthur Ripley, s Robert Benchley.
HOW TO VOTE (MGM, 1936) d Felix E. Feist, s Robert Benchley.
HOW TO BE A DETECTIVE (MGM, 1936) d Felix E. Feist, s Robert Benchley.
THE ROMANCE OF DIGESTION (MGM, 1937) d Felix E. Feist, s Robert Benchley.
HOW TO START THE DAY (MGM, 1937) d Roy Rowland, s Robert Benchley.
A NIGHT AT THE MOVIES (MGM, 1937) d Roy Rowland, s Robert Benchley, Gwen Lee.

HOW TO FIGURE INCOME TAX (MGM, 1938) d Roy Rowland, s Robert Benchley.
MUSIC MADE SIMPLE (MGM, 1938) d Roy Rowland, s Robert Benchley.
AN EVENING ALONE (MGM, 1938) d Roy Rowland, s Robert Benchley.
HOW TO RAISE A BABY (MGM, 1938) d Roy Rowland, s Robert Benchley.
THE COURTSHIP OF THE NEWT (MGM, 1938) d Roy Rowland, s Robert Benchley.
HOW TO READ (MGM, 1938) d Roy Rowland, s Robert Benchley.
HOW TO WATCH FOOTBALL (MGM, 1938) d Roy Rowland, s Robert Benchley.
OPENING DAY (MGM, 1938) d Roy Rowland, s Robert Benchley.
MENTAL POISE (MGM, 1938) d Roy Rowland, s Robert Benchley.
HOW TO SUB-LET (MGM, 1938) d Roy Rowland, s Robert Benchley.
AN HOUR FOR LUNCH (MGM, 1939) d Roy Rowland, s Robert Benchley.
DARK MAGIC (MGM, 1939) d Roy Rowland, s Robert Benchley.
HOME EARLY (MGM, 1939) d Roy Rowland, s Robert Benchley.
HOW TO EAT (MGM, 1939) d Roy Rowland, s Robert Benchley.
THE DAY OF REST (MGM, 1939) d Basil Wrangell, s Robert Benchley.
SEE YOUR DOCTOR (MGM, 1939) d Basil Wrangell, s Robert Benchley.
THAT INFERIOR FEELING (MGM, 1940) d Basil Wrangell, s Robert Benchley.
HOME MOVIES (MGM, 1940) d Basil Wrangell, s Robert Benchley.
THE TROUBLE WITH HUSBANDS (Paramount, 1940) d Leslie Roush, s Robert Benchley.
WAITING FOR BABY (Paramount, 1940) d Leslie Roush, s Robert Benchley.
CRIME CONTROL (Paramount, 1941) d Leslie Roush, s Robert Benchley.
THE FORGOTTEN MAN (Paramount, 1941) d Leslie Roush, s Robert Benchley.
HOW TO TAKE A VACATION (Paramount, 1941) d Leslie Roush, s Robert Benchley.
NOTHING BUT NERVES (Paramount, 1942) d Leslie Roush, s Robert Benchley.
THE WITNESS (Paramount, 1942) d Leslie Roush, s Robert Benchley.
KEEPING IN SHAPE (Paramount, 1942) d Leslie Roush, s Robert Benchley.
THE MAN'S ANGLE (Paramount, 1942) d Leslie Roush, s Robert Benchley.
MY TOMATO (Paramount, 1943) d Leslie Roush, s Robert Benchley.
NO NEWS IS GOOD NEWS (Paramount, 1943) d Leslie Roush, s Robert Benchley.
IMPORTANT BUSINESS (Paramount, 1944) d Leslie Roush, s Robert Benchley.
WHY, DADDY? (Paramount, 1944) d Leslie Roush, s Robert Benchley.
BOOGIE WOOGIE (Paramount, 1945) d Leslie Roush, s Robert Benchley.
I'M A CIVILIAN HERE MYSELF (Navy, 1945) s Robert Benchley.

634. ROBIN HOOD
Sherwood Forest is the setting for the tales of the legendary outlaw who robs from the rich and gives to the poor. Among his band are Friar Tuck, Little John

and Maid Marion. Their frequent nemesis is the Sheriff of Nottingham. THE ADVENTURES OF ROBIN HOOD also appeared on CBS 1955-58 with Richard Greene and ROBIN OF SHERWOOD aired over Showtime and PBS, 1986-88.

ROBIN HOOD AND HIS MERRY MEN (1908)
ROBIN HOOD (Edison, 1912) s Alec B. Francis.
ROBIN HOOD (Triangle, 1913) s Gerda Holmes, William Russell.
ROBIN HOOD (United Artists, 1922) d Allan Dwan, s Douglas Fairbanks, Enid Bennett, William Lowery.
LADY ROBIN HOOD (1925) s Boris Karloff.
THE MERRY MEN OF SHERWOOD (1931)
THE ADVENTURES OF ROBIN HOOD (First National, 1938) d Michael Curtiz and William Keighley, s Erroll Flynn, Olivia de Havilland, Basil Rathbone.
THE BANDIT OF SHERWOOD FOREST (Columbia, 1946) d George Sherman and Henry Levin, s Cornel Wilde, Anita Louise, Edgar Buchanan.
THE PRINCE OF THIEVES (Columbia, 1948) d Howard Bretherton, s Jon Hall, Patricia Morison, Adele Jergens, Alan Mowbray.
ROGUES OF SHERWOOD FOREST (Columbia, 1950) d Gordon Douglas, s John Derek, Diana Lynn, George Macready.
THE STORY OF ROBIN HOOD AND HIS MERRIE MEN (Disney/RKO, 1952) d Ken Annakin, s Richard Todd, Joan Rice, Peter Finch.
TALES OF ROBIN HOOD (1952)
MISS ROBIN HOOD (Union Film, 1952)
MEN OF SHERWOOD FOREST (Hammer, 1954) d Val Guest, s Don Taylor, Eileen Moore, Reginald Beckwith.
SON OF ROBIN HOOD (1959)
SWORD OF SHERWOOD FOREST (Hammer/Yeoman, 1960) d Terence Fisher, s Richard Greene, Peter Cushing, Sarah Branch.
TRIUMPH OF ROBIN HOOD (1962)
ROBIN AND THE SEVEN HOODS (1964)
ROBIN HOOD AND THE PIRATES (1964)
ROBIN HOOD (1966)
CHALLENGE FOR ROBIN HOOD (Hammer, 1967) d C. Pennington-Richards, s Barrie Ingham, James Hayter, Leon Greene.
THE RIBALD TALES OF ROBIN HOOD (1969)
A CHALLENGE FOR ROBIN HOOD (20th Century-Fox, 1969) d Dean Selmier.
ROBIN HOOD (Disney, 1973) (animated) d Wolfgang Reitherman, voices of Brian Bedford, Phil Harris, Monica Evans.
ROBIN HOODNIK (1975)
ROBIN AND MARIAN (1976) d Richard Lester, s Sean Connery, Audrey Hepburn, Robert Shaw.
THE AFFAIRS OF ROBIN HOOD (Lima, 1981) d Richard Kanter.
ROBIN HOOD AND THE SORCERER (BBC TV adaptation, 1983) d Ian Sharp, s Michael Praed, Anthony Valentine.

ROBIN HOOD AND THE SORCERER (Showtime TV movie, 1984) d Ian Sharp, s Michael Praed, Nickolas Grace, Judi Trott.
THE ZANY ADVENTURES OF ROBIN HOOD (CBS TV movie, 1984) d Ray Austin, s George Segal, Morgan Fairchild.
ROBIN HOOD: THE SWORDS OF WAYLAND (BCC TV adaptation, 1986) d Robert Young, s Michael Praed, Rula Lenska, Nickolas Grace.
ROBIN HOOD: HERNE'S SON (BCC TV adaptation, 1986) d Robert Young, s Jason Connery, Oliver Cotton.

635. ROBINSON CRUSOE
Daniel Defoe's shipwrecked island-walker has only his man Friday for companionship.
ROBINSON CRUSOE (Rex/Universal, 1913) s Robert Z. Leonard.
ADVENTURES OF ROBINSON CRUSOE (Universal, 1922) (Serial)
ROBINSON CRUSOE (Epic, 1927) d M.A. Wetherell, s M.A. Wetherell, Fay Compton, Herbert Waithe.
MR. ROBINSON CRUSOE (United Artists, 1932) d Edward Sutherland, s Douglas Fairbanks, Maria Alba.
ROBINSON CRUSOE OF CLIPPER ISLAND (1936) (Serial) [aka ROBINSON CRUSOE OF MYSTERY ISLAND] d Mark V. Wright, s Ray Taylor, Mala, Rex, Buck, Mamo Clark.
THE ADVENTURES OF ROBINSON CRUSOE (United Artists.1952) d Luis Bunuel, s Dan O'Herlihy, Jaime Fernandez.
ROBINSON CRUSOE ON MARS (Paramount, 1964) d Byron Haskin, s Paul Mantee.
LT. ROBIN CRUSOE, U.S.N. (Disney, 1966) d Byron Paul, s Dick Van Dyke, Nancy Kwan.
ROBINSON CRUSOE (BBC-TV, 1974) (NBC-TV movie broadcast) d James Mactaggart, s Stanley Baker, Ram John Holder.
MAN FRIDAY (Avco Embassy, 1975) d Jack Gold, s Peter O'Toole, Richard Roundtree.

636. ROBOCOP
The futuristic crime pictures offer a mechanical law officer.
ROBOCOP (Orion, 1987) d Paul Verhoeven, s Peter Weller, Nancy Allen.
ROBOCOP II (announced 1990)

637. ROBOFOX
The films are strictly for adults.
ROBOFOX (Fantasy, 1987) s Angela Baron, Randy West.
ROBOFOX II (Fantasy, 1988) s Angela Baron, Randy West.

638. ROCK 'N' ROLL HIGH SCHOOL
Students rebel against authority, with lots of music.
ROCK 'N' ROLL HIGH SCHOOL (New World, 1979) d Allan Arkush, s P.J. Soles, Vincent Van Patten, Clint Howard.

ROCK 'N' ROLL HIGH SCHOOL FOREVER (Concorde, announced 1990) d Deborah Brock, s Corey Feldman, Paul Bartel.

639. ROCK, PRETTY BABY
A high schooler wants to become a bandleader; his father wants him to go to medical school. There's lots of music.
ROCK, PRETTY BABY (Universal, 1956) d Richard Bartlett, s John Saxon, Sal Mineo.
SUMMER LOVE (Universal, 1958) d Charles Haas, s John Saxon, Molly Bee, Rod McKuen.

640. ROCKY
A two-bit boxer gets an impossible chance at fighting the champ, and never looks back.
ROCKY (United Artists, 1976) d John G. Avildsen, s Sylvester Stallone, Talia Shire, Burt Young, Carl Weathers, Burgess Meredith.
ROCKY II (United Artists, 1979) d Sylvester Stallone, s Sylvester Stallone, Talia Shire, Burt Young, Carl Weathers, Burgess Meredith.
ROCKY III (MGM/UA, 1982) d Sylvester Stallone, s Sylvester Stallone, Talia Shire, Burt Young, Carl Weathers, Burgess Meredith.
ROCKY IV (United Artists, 1985) d Sylvester Stallone, s Sylvester Stallone, Dolph Lundgren, Carl Weathers, Talia Shire, Brigitte Nielsen, Talia Shire.
ROCKY V (United Artists, announced, 1990) d John Avildson, s Sylvester Stallone.

641. ROCKY HORROR PICTURE SHOW, THE
The musical flick spoofs horror films.
THE ROCKY HORROR PICTURE SHOW (20th Century-Fox, 1975) d Jim Sharman, s Tim Curry, Susan Sarandon.
SHOCK TREATMENT (20th Century-Fox, 1981) d Jim Sharman, s Jessica Harper, Cliff De Young.

642. *ROD CAMERON AND FUZZY KNIGHT*
B Westerns pair the veteran Canadian-born actor with one of the more popular sidekicks.
BOSS OF BOOMTOWN (Universal, 1944) d Ray Taylor, s Rod Cameron, Fuzzy Knight, Ray Whitley, Vivian Austin.
TRIGGER TRAIL (Universal, 1944) d Lewis Collins, s Rod Cameron, Fuzzy Knight, Ray Whitley, Eddie Dew, Vivian Austin.
RIDERS OF THE SANTA FE (Universal, 1944) d Wallace Fox, s Rod Cameron, Fuzzy Knight, Ray Whitley, Eddie Dew, Jennifer Holt.
THE OLD TEXAS TRAIL (Universal, 1944) d Lewis Collins, s Rod Cameron, Fuzzy Knight, Ray Whitley, Eddie Dew, Marjorie Clemments, Virginia Christine.

BEYOND THE PECOS (Universal, 1945) d Lambert Hillyer, s Rod Cameron, Fuzzy Knight, Ray Whitley, Eddie Dew, Marjorie Clemments, Virginia Christine.
RENEGADES OF THE RIO GRANDE (Universal, 1945) d Howard Bretherton, s Rod Cameron, Fuzzy Knight, Ray Whitley, Eddie Dew, Jennifer Holt.

643. ROMANCING THE STONE
A writer of romantic literature finds herself in real adventure in Colombia, aided by an American adventurer and a pesky fortune seeker.
ROMANCING THE STONE (20th Century-Fox, 1984) d Robert Zemeckis, s Kathleen Turner, Michael Douglas, Danny DeVito.
THE JEWEL OF THE NILE (20th Century-Fox, 1985) d Lewis Teague, s Kathleen Turner, Michael Douglas, Danny DeVito.

644. ROOKIES
These are the misadventures of a group of military recruits during World War II.
ADVENTURES OF A ROOKIE (RKO, 1943) d Leslie Goodwins, s Wally Brown, Alan Carney, Richard Martin.
ROOKIES IN BURMA (RKO, 1943) d Leslie Goodwins, s Wally Brown, Alan Carney, Erford Gage.

645. ROOM AT THE TOP
Joe Lampton has love problems.
ROOM AT THE TOP (Remus, 1959) d Jack Clayton, s Simone Signoret, Laurence Harvey, Heather Sears.
LIFE AT THE TOP (Romulus/Columbia, 1965) d Ted Kotcheff, s Laurence Harvey, Jean Simmons, Honor Blackman.

646. ROSEMARY'S BABY
The devil's seed is planted in an unsuspecting young woman, who falls under the supervision of a coven of witches.
ROSEMARY'S BABY (Paramount, 1968) d Roman Polanski, s Mia Farrow.
LOOK WHAT'S HAPPENED TO ROSEMARY'S BABY (TV movie, 1976) d Sam O'Steen, s Stephen McHattie, Patty Duke Astin, Broderick Crawford.

647. *ROY ROGERS AND ANDY DEVINE*
The B-western hero plays himself in most of his films; they are divided here by sidekick.
BELLS OF SAN ANGELO (Republic, 1947) d William Witney, s Roy Rogers, Dale Evans, Andy Devine.
SPRINGTIME IN THE SIERRAS (Republic, 1947) d William Witney, s Roy Rogers, Jane Frazee, Andy Devine.
ON THE OLD SPANISH TRAIL (Republic, 1947) d William Witney, s Roy Rogers, Jane Frazee, Andy Devine.

MOTION PICTURE SERIES & SEQUELS 287

THE GAY RANCHERO (Republic, 1948) d William Witney, s Roy Rogers, Jane Frazee, Andy Devine.
UNDER CALIFORNIA STARS (Republic, 1948) d William Witney, s Roy Rogers, Jane Frazee, Andy Devine.
EYES OF TEXAS (Republic, 1948) d William Witney, s Roy Rogers, Lynne Roberts, Andy Devine.
NIGHT TIME IN NEVADA (Republic, 1948) d William Witney, s Roy Rogers, Adele Mara, Andy Devine.
GRAND CANYON TRAIL (Republic, 1948) d William Witney, s Roy Rogers, Jane Frazee, Andy Devine.
THE FAR FRONTIER (Republic, 1948) d William Witney, s Roy Rogers, Gail Davis, Andy Devine.

648. *ROY ROGERS AND GABBY HAYES*
SOUTHWARD HO (Republic, 1939) d Joseph Kane, s Roy Rogers, Mary Hart, George "Gabby" Hayes.
IN OLD CALIENTE (Republic, 1939) d Joseph Kane, s Roy Rogers, Mary Hart, George "Gabby" Hayes.
WALL STREET COWBOY (Republic, 1939) d Joseph Kane, s Roy Rogers, Ann Baldwin, George "Gabby" Hayes.
THE ARIZONA KID (Republic, 1939) d Joseph Kane, s Roy Rogers, George "Gabby" Hayes, Sally March.
SAGA OF DEATH VALLEY (Republic, 1939) d Joseph Kane, s Roy Rogers, George "Gabby" Hayes, Doris Day.
DAYS OF JESSE JAMES (Republic, 1939) d Joseph Kane, s Roy Rogers, George "Gabby" Hayes, Pauline Moore.
YOUNG BUFFALO BILL (Republic, 1940) d Joseph Kane, s Roy Rogers, George "Gabby" Hayes, Pauline Moore, Chief Thundercloud.
THE DARK COMMAND (Republic, 1940) d Raoul Walsh, s John Wayne, Claire Trevor, Roy Rogers, George "Gabby" Hayes.
THE CARSON CITY KID (Republic, 1940) d Joseph Kane, s Roy Rogers, George "Gabby" Hayes, Pauline Moore.
THE RANGER AND THE LADY (Republic, 1940) d Joseph Kane, s Roy Rogers, George "Gabby" Hayes, Jacqueline Wells.
COLORADO (Republic, 1940) d Joseph Kane, s Roy Rogers, George "Gabby" Hayes, Pauline Moore.
YOUNG BILL HICKOK (Republic, 1940) d Joseph Kane, s Roy Rogers, George "Gabby" Hayes, Jacqueline Wells.
ROBIN HOOD OF THE PECOS (Republic, 1941) d Joseph Kane, s Roy Rogers, George "Gabby" Hayes, Marjorie Reynolds.
IN OLD CHEYENNE (Republic, 1941) d Joseph Kane, s Roy Rogers, George "Gabby" Hayes, Joan Woodbury.
SHERIFF OF TOMBSTONE (Republic, 1941) d Joseph Kane, s Roy Rogers, George "Gabby" Hayes, Elyse Knox.
NEVADA CITY (Republic, 1941) d Joseph Kane, s Roy Rogers, George "Gabby" Hayes, Sally Payne.

BAD MAN OF DEADWOOD (Republic, 1941) d Joseph Kane, s Roy Rogers, George "Gabby" Hayes, Carol Adams.
JESSE JAMES AT BAY (Republic, 1941) d Joseph Kane, s Roy Rogers, George "Gabby" Hayes, Sally Payne.
RED RIVER VALLEY (Republic, 1941) d Joseph Kane, s Roy Rogers, George "Gabby" Hayes, Sally Payne.
MAN FROM CHEYENNE (Republic, 1942) d Joseph Kane, s Roy Rogers, George "Gabby" Hayes, Sally Payne.
SOUTH OF SANTA FE (Republic, 1942) d Joseph Kane, s Roy Rogers, George "Gabby" Hayes, Linda Hayes.
SUNSET IN THE DESERT (Republic, 1942) d Joseph Kane, s Roy Rogers, George "Gabby" Hayes, Lynne Carver.
ROMANCE ON THE RANGE (Republic, 1942) d Joseph Kane, s Roy Rogers, George "Gabby" Hayes, Sally Payne.
SONS OF THE PIONEERS (Republic, 1942) d Joseph Kane, s Roy Rogers, George "Gabby" Hayes, Bob Nolan and the Sons of the Pioneers.
SUNSET SERENADE (Republic, 1942) d Joseph Kane, s Roy Rogers, George "Gabby" Hayes, Helen Parrish.
HEART OF THE GOLDEN WEST (Republic, 1942) d Joseph Kane, s Roy Rogers, George "Gabby" Hayes, Smiley Burnette.
RIDIN' DOWN THE CANYON (Republic, 1942) d Joseph Kane, s Roy Rogers, George "Gabby" Hayes, Linda Hayes.
LIGHTS OF OLD SANTA FE (Republic, 1944) d Joseph Kane, s Roy Rogers, George "Gabby" Hayes, Dale Evans.
UTAH (Republic, 1945) d John English, s Roy Rogers, George "Gabby" Hayes, Dale Evans.
BELLS OF ROSARITA (Republic, 1945) d Frank McDonald, s Roy Rogers, George "Gabby" Hayes, Dale Evans.
THE MAN FROM OKLAHOMA (Republic, 1945) d Frank McDonald, s Roy Rogers, George "Gabby" Hayes, Dale Evans.
SUNSET IN EL DORADO (Republic, 1945) d Frank McDonald, s Roy Rogers, George "Gabby" Hayes, Dale Evans.
DON'T FENCE ME IN (Republic, 1945) d John English, s Roy Rogers, George "Gabby" Hayes, Dale Evans.
ALONG THE NAVAJO TRAIL (Republic, 1945) d Frank McDonald, s Roy Rogers, George "Gabby" Hayes, Dale Evans.
SONG OF ARIZONA (Republic, 1946) d Frank McDonald, s Roy Rogers, George "Gabby" Hayes, Dale Evans.
MY PAL TRIGGER (Republic, 1946) d Frank McDonald, s Roy Rogers, George "Gabby" Hayes, Dale Evans.
ROLL ON, TEXAS MOON (Republic, 1946) d William Witney, s Roy Rogers, George "Gabby" Hayes, Dale Evans.
HOME IN OKLAHOMA (Republic, 1946) d William Witney, s Roy Rogers, George "Gabby" Hayes, Dale Evans.
HELDORADO (Republic, 1946) d William Witney, s Roy Rogers, George "Gabby" Hayes, Dale Evans.

649. ROY ROGERS AND GORDON JONES
NORTH OF THE GREAT DIVIDE (Republic, 1950) d William Witney, s Roy Rogers, Penny Edwards, Gordon Jones.
TRAIL OF ROBIN HOOD (Republic, 1950) d William Witney, s Roy Rogers, Penny Edwards, Gordon Jones.
SPOILERS OF THE PLAINS (Republic, 1951) d William Witney, s Roy Rogers, Penny Edwards, Gordon Jones.
HEART OF THE ROCKIES (Republic, 1951) d William Witney, s Roy Rogers, Penny Edwards, Gordon Jones.

650. ROY ROGERS AND RAYMOND HATTON
ROUGH RIDERS' ROUNDUP (Republic, 1939) d Joseph Kane, s Roy Rogers, Mary Hart, Raymond Hatton.
FRONTIER PONY EXPRESS (Republic, 1939) d Joseph Kane, s Roy Rogers, Mary Hart, Raymond Hatton.

651. ROY ROGERS AND PAT BRADY
MAN FROM MUSIC MOUNTAIN (Republic, 1943) d Joseph Kane, s Roy Rogers, Pat Brady, Ann Gillis.
DOWN DAKOTA WAY (Republic, 1949) d William Witney, s Roy Rogers, Dale Evans, Pat Brady.
THE GOLDEN STALLION (Republic, 1949) d William Witney, s Roy Rogers, Dale Evans, Pat Brady.
BELLS OF CORONADO (Republic, 1950) d William Witney, s Roy Rogers, Dale Evans, Pat Brady.
TWILIGHT IN THE SIERRAS (Republic, 1950) d William Witney, s Roy Rogers, Dale Evans, Pat Brady.
TRIGGER JR. (Republic, 1950) d William Witney, s Roy Rogers, Dale Evans, Pat Brady.

652. ROY ROGERS AND PINKY LEE
IN OLD AMARILLO (Republic, 1951) d William Witney, s Roy Rogers, Penny Edwards, Pinky Lee.
SOUTH OF CALIENTE (Republic, 1951) d William Witney, s Roy Rogers, Dale Evans, Pinky Lee.
PALS OF THE GOLDEN WEST (Republic, 1951) d William Witney, s Roy Rogers, Dale Evans, Pinky Lee.

653. ROY ROGERS AND SMILEY BURNETTE
UNDER WESTERN STARS (Republic, 1938) d Joseph Kane, s Roy Rogers, Smiley Burnette, Carol Hughes.
BILLY THE KID RETURNS (Republic, 1938) d Joseph Kane, s Roy Rogers, Smiley Burnette, Lynn Roberts.
IDAHO (Republic, 1943) d Joseph Kane, s Roy Rogers, Smiley Burnette, Virginia Grey.
KING OF THE COWBOYS (Republic, 1943) d Joseph Kane, s Roy Rogers, Smiley Burnette, Peggy Moran.

SILVER SPURS (Republic, 1943) d Joseph Kane, s Roy Rogers, Smiley Burnette, Phyllis Brooks.

654. *ROY ROGERS AND TEDDY BEAR*
COWBOY AND THE SENORITA (Republic, 1944, d Joseph Kane, s Roy Rogers, Big Boy Williams, Fuzzy Knight, Dale Evans, Mary Lee.
HANDS ACROSS THE BORDER (Republic, 1944) d Joseph Kane, s Roy Rogres, Big Boy Williams, Ruth Terry.

655. ROUGH RIDERS, THE
These Westerns team popular celluloid cowboys.
ARIZONA BOUND (Monogram, 1941) d Spencer Bennett, s Buck Jones, Tim McCoy, Raymond Hatton, Luana Walters.
THE GUNMAN FROM BODIE (Monogram, 1941) d Spencer Bennett, s Buck Jones, Tim McCoy, Raymond Hatton, Christine McIntyre.
FORBIDDEN TRAILS (Monogram, 1941) d R.N. Bradbury, s Buck Jones, Tim McCoy, Raymond Hatton, Christine McIntyre.
BELOW THE BORDER (Monogram, 1942) d Howard Bretherton, s Buck Jones, Tim McCoy, Raymond Hatton, Linda Brent.
GHOST TOWN LAW (Monogram, 1942) d Howard Bretherton, s Buck Jones, Tim McCoy, Raymond Hatton, Virginia Carpenter.
DOWN TEXAS WAY (Monogram 1942) d Howard Brtherton, s Buck Jones, Tim McCoy, Raymond Hatton, Luana Walters.
RIDERS OF THE WEST (Monogram, 1942) d Howard Bretherton, s Buck Jones, Tim McCoy, Raymond Hatton, Christine McIntyre.
WEST OF THE LAW (Monogram, 1942) d Howard Bretherton, s Buck Jones, Tim McCoy, Raymond Hatton, Evelyn Cook.

656. ROUGH RIDIN' KIDS
These Westerns feature youngsters on the range.
BUCKAROO SHERIFF OF TEXAS (Republic, 1951) d Philip Ford, s Michael Chapin, Eilene Janssen.
THE DAKOTA KID (Republic, 1951) d Philip Ford, s Michael Chapin, Eilene Janssen.
ARIZONA MANHUNT (Republic, 1951) d Fred C. Brannon, s Michael Chapin, Eilene Janssen.
WILD HORSE AMBUSH (Republic, 1952) d Fred C. Brannon, s Michael Chapin, Eilene Janssen.

657. *RUSSELL HAYDEN AND DUB TAYLOR*
B Westerns combine the talents of two veteran actors.
THE LONE PRAIRIE (Columbia, 1942) d William Berke, s Russell Hayden, Dub Taylor, Lucille Lambert.
A TORNADO IN THE SADDLE (Columbia, 1942) d William Berke, s Russell Hayden, Dub Taylor, Alma Carroll.
RIDERS OF THE NORTHWEST MOUNTED (Columbia, 1943) d William Berke, s Russell Hayden, Dub Taylor, Adele Mara.

SADDLES AND SAGEBRUSH (Columbia, 1943) d William Berke, s Russell Hayden, Dub Taylor, Ann Savage.
SILVER CITY RAIDERS (Columbia, 1943) d William Berke, s Russell Hayden, Dub Taylor, Alma Carroll.
THE VIGILANTES RIDE (Columbia, 1944) d William Berke, s Russell Hayden, Dub Taylor, Shirley Patterson.
WYOMING HURRICANE (Columbia, 1944) d William Berke, s Russell Hayden, Dub Taylor, Alma Carroll.
THE LAST HORSEMAN (Columbia, 1944) d William Berke, s Russell Hayden, Dub Taylor, Ann Savage.

658. RUSTY
Characters created by Al Martin appear in these pictures.
RUSTY RIDES ALONE (Columbia, 1933) d D. Ross Lederman, s Tim McCoy, Barbara Weeks, Dorothy Burgess.
THE ADVENTURES OF RUSTY (Columbia, 1945)
FOR THE LOVE OF RUSTY (Columbia, 1947)
RUSTY LEADS THE WAY (Columbia, 1948)
RUSTY SAVES A LIFE (Columbia, 1949)
RUSTY'S BIRTHDAY (Columbia, 1949)

659. RUTH
The pictures feature a silent serial heroine.
THE ADVENTURES OF RUTH (1919) (serial) s Ruth Roland.
RUTH OF THE ROCKIES (1919) (serial) s Ruth Roland.
RUTH OF THE RANGE (1920) (serial) s Ruth Roland.

A wrathful Freddy Kreuger inspires horrible dreams in NIGHTMARE ON ELM STREET.

292 MOTION PICTURE SERIES & SEQUELS

660. SABATA
The hero of these spaghetti Westerns is a gambler/gunslinger.
SABATA (United Artists, 1970) d Frank Kramer, s Lee Van Cleef, William Berger.
ADIOS, SABATA (United Artists, 1971) d Frank Kramer, s Yul Brynner, Dean Reed.
THE RETURN OF SABATA (United Artists, 1972) d Frank Kramer, s Lee Van Cleef, Reiner Schone.

661. SAINT, THE
Leslie Charteris wrote a series of novels and short stories featuring Simon Templar, a modern, gentleman ROBIN HOOD. Roger Moore played the character in a series which NBC-TV aired in 1966-69 (featuring Roger Moore). CBS offered RETURN OF THE SAINT in its late movie lineup in 1978, with British-made episodes providing Ian Ogilvy in the title role. Yet a third, syndicated version began airing in 1989, with initial entries listed below. (See also THE FALCON.)
THE SAINT IN NEW YORK (RKO, 1938) d Ben Holmes, s Louis Haward, Kay Sutton
THE SAINT STRIKES BACK (RKO, 1939) d John Farrow, s George Sanders, Wendy Barrie.
THE SAINT IN LONDON (RKO, 1939) d John Paddy Carstairs, s George Sanders, Sally Gray.
THE SAINT'S DOUBLE TROUBLE (RKO, 1940) d Jack Hively, s George Sanders, Helene Whitney.
THE SAINT TAKES OVER (RKO, 1940) d Jack Hively, s George Sanders, Wendy Barrie.
THE SAINT IN PALM SPRINGS (RKO, 1941) d Jack Hively, s George Sanders, Wendy Barrie.
THE SAINT'S VACATION (RKO, 1941) d Leslie Fenton, s Hugh Sinclair, Sally Gray.
THE SAINT MEETS THE TIGER (Republic, 1943) d Paul Stein, s Hugh Sinclair, Jean Gillie.
THE SAINT'S GIRL FRIDAY (RKO, 1954) [aka GIRL FRIDAY] d Seymour Friedman, s Louis Hayward, Naomi Chance.
THE BRAZILIAN CONNECTION (TV movie, 1989) s Simon Dutton, Gayle Hunnicutt.
THE BLUE DULAC (TV movie, 1989) s Simon Dutton, John Astin.
THE SOFTWARE MURDERS (TV movie, 1989) s Simon Dutton, Pamela Sue Martin.
THE BIG BANG (TV movie, 1989) s Simon Dutton, Morgan Brittany.
WRONG NUMBER (TV movie, 1989) s Simon Dutton, Vince Edwards.
FEAR IN FUN PARK (TV movie, 1989) s Simon Dutton, Rebecca Gilling.

662. SALT AND PEPPER
Club owners Charles Salt and Christopher Pepper become involved in a plot to overthrow the government, in the first entry.

SALT AND PEPPER (United Artists, 1968) d Richard D. Donner, s Sammy Davis Jr., Peter Lawford.
ONE MORE TIME (United Artists, 1970) d Jerry Lewis, s Sammy Davis Jr., Peter Lawford.

663. SANDERS OF THE RIVER
From the Edgar Wallace novel, these are tales of British colonial struggles among tribesmen in Africa.
SANDERS OF THE RIVER (United Artists, 1935) d Zoltan Korda, s Paul Robeson, Leslie Banks, Nina Mae McKinney.
DEATH DRUMS ALONG THE RIVER (Big Ben/Hallam, 1963) d Lawrence Huntington, s Richard Todd, Marianne Koch.
COAST OF SKELETONS (Seven Arts, 1964) d Robert Lynn, s Richard Todd, Dale Robertson.

664. SCARAMOUCHE
A Rafael Sabatini novel inspired these swashbucklers set during the period of the French Revolution.
SCARAMOUCHE (Metro, 1923) d Rex Ingram, s Ramon Novarro, Alice Terry.
SCARAMOUCHE (MGM, 1952) d George Sidney, s Stewart Granger, Eleanor Parker.
THE LOVES AND TIMES OF SCARAMOUCHE (Avco-Embassy, 1976) d Enzo G. Castellari, s Michael Sarrazin, Ursula Andress.

665. SCARLET PIMPERNEL, THE
Based on the novel by Baroness Orczy, these pictures are about Sir Percy Blakeney, master of disguise and leader of a band which saves aristocrats from French Revolution execution.
THE SCARLET PIMPERNEL (Fox, 1917)
THE ELUSIVE PIMPERNEL (1919)
THE SCARLET DAREDEVIL (World Wide, 1928)
THE SCARLET PIMPERNEL (London Films, 1934) d Harold Young, s Leslie Howard, Merle Oberon.
THE RETURN OF THE SCARLET PIMPERNEL (London Films, 1937) d Hanz Schwartz, s Barry Barnes, Sophie Stewart.
PIMPERNEL SMITH (British National, 1941) [aka MISTER V] d Leslie Howard, s Leslie Howard, Francis L. Sullivan, Mary Morris.
THE ELUSIVE PIMPERNEL (London Films, 1950) d Michael Powell and Emeric Pressburger, s David Niven, Margaret Leighton.
THE SCARLET PIMPERNEL (London Films, 1982) (CBS-TV broadcast) d Clive Donner, s Anthony Andrews, Jane Seymour.

666. SCATTERGOOD BAINES
The crafty Yankee hardware store owner first appeared in four short stories in *The Saturday Evening Post* beginning in 1917, then switched to *American* magazine for another 120 stories through 1954. In the second motion picture,

typically, Scattergood travels to New York to help a local boy deal with crooked promoters. The character, created by Clarence Budington Kelland, was also featured on radio.

SCATTERGOOD BAINES (Pyramid/RKO 1941) d Christy Cabanne, s Guy Kibbee, Carol Hughes, John Archer, Francis "Dink" Trout.

SCATTERGOOD MEETS BROADWAY (Pyramid/RKO 1941) d Christy Cabanne, s Guy Kibbe, Emma Dunn, Joyce Compton, Bradley Page.

SCATTERGOOD PULLS THE STRINGS (Pyramid/RKO 1941) d Christy Cabanne, s Guy Kibbee, Bobs Watson, Susan Peters.

SCATTERGOOD RIDES HIGH (Pyramid/RKO, 1941) d Christy Cabanne, s Guy Kibbee, Jed Prouty, Dorothy Moore.

SCATTERGOOD SURVIVES A MURDER (Pyramid/RKO 1942) d Christy Cabanne, s Guy Kibbee, John Archer, Margaret Hayes.

CINDERELLA SWINGS IT (RKO 1942) d Christy Cabanne, s Guy Kibbee, Gloria Warren, Helen Parrish.

667. SECRET AGENT X-9

The newspaper espionage comic strip written and drawn by Alex Raymond beginning in 1934 inspired these pictures.

SECRET AGENT X-9 (Universal, 1937) (12 chapters) d Ford Beebe and Cliff Smith, s Scott Kolk, Jean Rogers.

SECRET AGENT X-9 (Universal, 1945) (13 chapters) d Ray Taylor and Lewis Collins, s Lloyd Bridges, Keye Luke, Jan Wiley.

668. SENSATIONAL JANINE

These pictures are rated X.

SENSATIONAL JANINE (Caballero, 1979) d Hans Billian, s Patricia Rhomberg.

SENSATIONAL JANINE II (Caballero) s Patricia Rhomberg.

669. SEX ASYLUM

This X-rated fare has a young woman admitting herself to an asylum for treatment of her sexual urges. See also GINGER.

GINGER'S SEX ASYLUM (Vivid, 1986) d Bruce Seven, s Ginger Lynn, Harry Reems.

SEX ASYLUM II: SHEER BEDLAM (Vivid, 1986) d Bruce Seven, s Amber Lynn, Candie Evans, Tom Byron.

SEX ASLYUM III (Vivid, 1987) s Tracey Adams, Erica Boyer, Randy West, Mike Horner.

670. SEX LIVES OF THE RICH AND FAMOUS

These pictures are X-rated

SEX LIVES OF THE RICH AND FAMOUS, PART 1 (VCA, 1989) s Eva Allen, Peter North.

SEX LIVES OF THE RICH AND FAMOUS, PART 2 (VCA, 1989) s Eva Allen, Peter North.

671. SEXTON BLAKE
Blake is a criminologist popular in British boys' fiction beginning in 1893 in publications such as *Halfpenny Marvel* and *Union Jack,* and today still appearing in paperback novels. The character has appeared also in theater and television.

SEXTON BLAKE (1909)
SEXTON BLAKE VS BARON KETTLER (1912)
THE STOLEN HEIRLOOMS (Walturdaw Productions, 1915) s Henry Lorraine.
THE FURTHER EXPLOITS OF SEXTON BLAKE (1919)
THE CLUE OF THE SECOND GOBLET (1928)
BLAKE THE LAWBREAKER (1928)
SEXTON BLAKE, GAMBLER (1928)
SILKEN THREADS (1928)
THE GREAT OFFICE MYSTERY (1928)
THE MYSTERY OF THE SILENT DEATH (1928)
SEXTON BLAKE AND THE BEARDED DOCTOR (MGM/Fox, 1935) d George A. Cooper, s George Curson, Tony Sympson.
SEXTON BLAKE AND THE MADEMOISELLE (MGM/Fox, 1935) d Alex Bryce, s George Curson, Tony Sympson, Lorraine Grey.
SEXTON BLAKE AND THE HOODED TERROR (MGM/Fox, 1938) d George King, s George Curson, Tony Sympson, Tod Slaughter, Greta Gynt.
MEET SEXTON BLAKE (British National, 1944) d John Harlow, s David Farrar, John Varley, Magda Kun.
THE ECHO MURDERS (British National, 1945) d John Harlow, s David Farrar, Dennis Price, Pamela Stirling.
MURDER AT SITE THREE (Francis Tearle Productions, 1959) s Geoffrey Toone.

672. SHADOW, THE
Walter B. Gibson in 1931 created the pulp magazine cloaked crime-fighter called The Shadow, who would appear in 326 novel-length tales over the next two decades. The character, who frequently adopted the persona of Lamont Cranston, a wealthy playboy, was also featured on radio. The Shadow in 1931 hosted a series of six Universal Pictures filmettes in the Shadow Detective Series: BURGLAR TO THE RESCUE; TRAPPED; SEALED LIPS; HOUSE OF MYSTERY; THE RED SCARE; and THE CIRCUS SHOW-UP.

THE SHADOW STRIKES (Grand National, 1937) d Lynn Shores, s Rod La Rocque, Lynn Anders.
INTERNATIONAL CRIME (Grand National, 1938) d Charles Lamont, s Rod La Rocque.
THE SHADOW (Columbia, 1940) (fifteen-chapter serial) d James Horne, s Victor Jory, Veda Ann Borg, Roger Moore.
THE SHADOW RETURNS (Monogram, 1946) d Phil Rosen, s Kane Richmond, Barbara Reed.

BEHIND THE MASK (Monogram) d Phil Karlson, s Kane Richmond, Barbara Reed.
THE MISSING LADY (Monogram, 1946) d Phil Karlson, s Kane Richmond, Barbara Reed.
INVISIBLE AVENGER (Republic, 1958) [aka BOURBON STREET SHADOWS] d James Wong Howe and John Sledge, s Richard Derr, Mark Daniels, Helen Westcott.

673. SHAFT
A black private detective, John Shaft, is featured in these stylish but violent pictures based on Ernest Tidyman's books (seven titles, 1970-75). There was also a TV series starring Richard Roundtree, airing over CBS in 1973-74..
SHAFT (MGM, 1971) d Gordon Parks, s Richard Roundtree, Moses Gunn.
SHAFT'S BIG SCORE! (MGM, 1972) d Gordon Parks, s Richard Roundtree, Moses Gunn.
SHAFT IN AFRICA (MGM, 1973) d John Guillermin, s Richard Roundtree, Frank Finlay, Vonetta McGee.

674. THE SHAGGY DOG
Caught in an ancient spell, a teenager turns into a shaggy mutt.
THE SHAGGY DOG (Disney, 1959) d Charles Barton, s Fred MacMurray, Jean Hagen, Tommy Kirk, Annette Funicello.
THE SHAGGY D.A. (Disney, 1976) d Robert Stevenson, s Dean Jones, Suzanne Pleshette.
THE RETURN OF THE SHAGGY DOG (Disney, 1987) (TV movie) d Stuart Gillard, s Gary Kroeger, Todd Waring, Michelle Little.

675. SHAMROCK AND LUCKY
This series of B Westerns pairs actors Jimmy Ellison and Russell Hayden.
HOSTILE COUNTRY (Lippert, 1950) d Thomas Carr, s Jimmy Ellison, Russell Hayden, Fuzzy Knight, Raymond Hatton, Betty Adams.
MARSHAL OF HELDORADO (Lippert, 1950) d Thomas Carr, s Jimmy Ellison, Russell Hayden, Fuzzy Knight, Raymond Hatton, Betty Adams.
COLORADO RANGER (Lippert, 1950) d Thomas Carr, s Jimmy Ellison, Russell Hayden, Fuzzy Knight, Raymond Hatton, Betty Adams.
WEST OF THE BRAZOS (Lippert, 1950) d Thomas Carr, s Jimmy Ellison, Russell Hayden, Fuzzy Knight, Raymond Hatton, Betty Adams.
CROOKED RIVER (Lippert, 1950) d Thomas Carr, s Jimmy Ellison, Russell Hayden, Fuzzy Knight, Raymond Hatton, Betty Adams.
FAST ON THE DRAW (Lippert, 1950) d Thomas Carr, s Jimmy Ellison, Russell Hayden, Fuzzy Knight, Raymond Hatton, Betty Adams.

676. SHE
H. Rider Haggard's fantasy novel about a queen ruling a lost city in Africa inspired silent and talkie films.
SHE (1917)

SHE (1926)
SHE (RKO, 1935) d Irving Pichel and Lansing C. Holden, s Helen Gahagan, Randolph Scott.
SHE (MGM, 1965) d Robert Day, s Ursula Andress, John Richardson.
THE VENGEANCE OF SHE (20th Century-Fox, 1968) d Cliff Owen, s John Richardson, Olinka Berova.

676A. SHERIFF, THE
G.M. "BRONCO BILLY" Anderson starred in these silent sagebrush pix. The list may be incomplete.
THE SHERIFF'S SACRIFICE (Essanay, 1910)
THE SHERIFF'S CHUM (Essanay, 1911)
THE SHERIFF'S BROTHER (Essanay, 1911)
THE SHERIFF'S LUCK (Essnay, 1912)
THE SHERIFF'S INHERITANCE (Essnay, 1912)
THE SHERIFF'S CHILD (Essanay, 1913)
THE SHERIFF'S STORY (Essanay, 1913)

676B. SHERIFF NELL
These are silent films with a Western setting.
SHERIFF NELL'S COME BACK (Keystone, 1915, s Polly Moran.
SHERIFF NELL'S TUSSLE (Keystone/Triangle, 1918) s Ben Turpin.

677. SHERLOCK HOLMES
Arthur Conan Doyle's consulting detective and his doctor companion solve crime puzzles in Victorian London. The list includes American, British, Australian and Canadian productions. There was also a TV series featuring Ronald Howard, syndicated in 1954.
SHERLOCK HOLMES BAFFLED (American Mutoscope & Biograph, 1903)
THE ADVENTURES OF SHERLOCK HOLMES (Vitagraph, 1905) [aka HELD FOR A RANSOM} d J. Stuart Blackton, s Maurice Costello.
SHERLOCK HOLMES RETURNS (ca 1906)
RIVAL SHERLOCK HOLMES (Ambrosio, 1907)
SHERLOCK HOLMES (Nordisk Film, 1908) s Forrest Holger Madsen.
THE LATEST TRIUMPH OF SHERLOCK HOLMES (Gaumont, 1909)
SHERLOCK HOLMES AND THE GREAT MURDER MYSTERY (Crescent Film Manufacturing, 1909)
SHERLOCK HOLMES: THE SPECKLED BAND (Eclair, 1912) d Georges Treville, s Georges Treville.
SHERLOCK HOLMES: SILVER BLAZE (Eclair, 1912) d Georges Treville, s Georges Treville.
SHERLOCK HOLMES: THE BERYL CORONET (Eclair, 1912) d Georges Treville, s Georges Treville.
SHERLOCK HOLMES: THE MUSGRAVE RITUAL (Eclair, 1912) d Georges Treville, s Georges Treville.
SHERLOCK HOLMES: THE REIGATE SQUIRES (Eclair, 1912) d Georges Treville, s Georges Treville.

SHERLOCK HOLMES: THE STOLEN PAPERS (Eclair, 1912) d Georges Treville, s Georges Treville.
SHERLOCK HOLMES: THE MYSTERY OF BOSCOMBE VALE (Eclair, 1912) d Georges Treville, s Georges Treville.
SHERLOCK HOLMES: THE COPPER BEECHES (Eclair, 1912) d Georges Treville, s Georges Treville.
SHERLOCK HOLMES SOLVES THE SIGN OF THE FOUR (Thanhouser, 1913) [aka THE SIGN OF FOUR] s Harry Behnam.
A STUDY IN SCARLET (Moss/Samuelson Film Manufacturing, 1914) d George Pearson, s James Bragington, Fred Paul.
A STUDY IN SCARLET (Gold Seal/Universal, 1914) d Francis Ford, s Francis Ford, Jack Francis.
THE HOUND OF THE BASKERVILLES (Vitascope, 1914) (two parts) d Rudolph Meinert, s Alwin Neuss, Friedrich Kuehne.
THE HOUND OF THE BASKERVILLES (Greenbaum, 1914) (two parts, continuation of above entry) d Richard Oswald, s Alwin Neuss, Friedrich Kuehne.
SHERLOCK HOLMES (Essanay, 1916) d Arthur Berthelet, s William Gillette, Edward Fielding, Ernest Maupain.
THE VALLEY OF FEAR (Moss/Samuelson Film Manufacturing, 1916) d Alexander Butler, s H.A. Saintsbury, Arthur M. Cullin.
BLACK SHERLOCK HOLMES (1918) s Sam Robinson.
THE HOUND OF THE BASKERVILLES (Greenbaum, 1920) (two parts, continuation of 1914-15 film of same title) d Willy Zehn, s Willy Kayser-Titz, Lu Juergens.
THE ADVENTURES OF SHERLOCK HOLMES: THE DYING DETECTIVE (Stoll Picture Productions, 1921) d Maurice Elvey, s Eille Norwood, Hubert Willis, Mme d'Esterre.
THE ADVENTURES OF SHERLOCK HOLMES: THE DEVIL'S FOOT (Stoll Picture Productions, 1921) d Maurice Elvey, s Eille Norwood, Hubert Willis, Mme d'Esterre.
THE ADVENTURES OF SHERLOCK HOLMES: A CASE OF IDENTITY (Stoll Picture Productions, 1921) d Maurice Elvey, s Eille Norwood, Hubert Willis, Mme d'Esterre.
THE ADVENTURES OF SHERLOCK HOLMES: THE YELLOW FACE (Stoll Picture Productions, 1921) d Maurice Elvey, s Eille Norwood, Hubert Willis, Mme d'Esterre.
THE ADVENTURES OF SHERLOCK HOLMES: THE RED-HEADED LEAGUE (Stoll Picture Productions, 1921) d Maurice Elvey, s Eille Norwood, Hubert Willis, Mme d'Esterre.
THE ADVENTURES OF SHERLOCK HOLMES: THE RESIDENT PATIENT (Stoll Picture Productions, 1921) d Maurice Elvey, s Eille Norwood, Hubert Willis, Mme d'Esterre.
THE ADVENTURES OF SHERLOCK HOLMES:A SCANDAL IN BOHEMIA (Stoll Picture Productions, 1921) d Maurice Elvey, s Eille Norwood, Hubert Willis, Mme d'Esterre.

THE ADVENTURES OF SHERLOCK HOLMES:THE MAN WITH THE TWISTED LIP (Stoll Picture Productions, 1921) d Maurice Elvey, s Eille Norwood, Hubert Willis, Mme d'Esterre.
THE ADVENTURES OF SHERLOCK HOLMES:THE BERYL CORONET (Stoll Picture Productions, 1921) d Maurice Elvey, s Eille Norwood, Hubert Willis, Mme d'Esterre.
THE ADVENTURES OF SHERLOCK HOLMES:THE NOBLE BACHELOR (Stoll Picture Productions, 1921) d Maurice Elvey, s Eille Norwood, Hubert Willis, Mme d'Esterre.
THE ADVENTURES OF SHERLOCK HOLMES:THE COPPER BEECHES (Stoll Picture Productions, 1921) d Maurice Elvey, s Eille Norwood, Hubert Willis, Mme d'Esterre.
THE ADVENTURES OF SHERLOCK HOLMES:THE EMPTY HOUSE (Stoll Picture Productions, 1921) d Maurice Elvey, s Eille Norwood, Hubert Willis, Mme d'Esterre.
THE ADVENTURES OF SHERLOCK HOLMES:THE TIGER OF SAN PEDRO (Stoll Picture Productions, 1921) d Maurice Elvey, s Eille Norwood, Hubert Willis, Mme d'Esterre.
THE ADVENTURES OF SHERLOCK HOLMES:THE PRIORY SCHOOL (Stoll Picture Productions, 1921) d Maurice Elvey, s Eille Norwood, Hubert Willis, Mme d'Esterre.
THE ADVENTURES OF SHERLOCK HOLMES:THE SOLITARY CYCLIST (Stoll Picture Productions, 1921) d Maurice Elvey, s Eille Norwood, Hubert Willis, Mme d'Esterre.
THE HOUND OF THE BASKERVILLES (Stoll Picture Productions, 1921) d Maurice Elvey, s Eille Norwood, Hubert Willis, Mme Esterre, Catina Campbell, Rex McDougall.
THE FURTHER ADVENTURES OF SHERLOCK HOLMES: CHARLES AUGUSTUS MILVERTON (Stoll Picture Productions, 1922) d George Ridgewell, s Eille Norwood, Hubert Willis, Mme d'Esterre.
THE FURTHER ADVENTURES OF SHERLOCK HOLMES: THE ABBEY GRANGE (Stoll Picture Productions, 1922) d George Ridgewell, s Eille Norwood, Hubert Willis, Mme d'Esterre.
THE FURTHER ADVENTURES OF SHERLOCK HOLMES: THE NORWOOD BUILDER (Stoll Picture Productions, 1922) d George Ridgewell, s Eille Norwood, Hubert Willis, Mme d'Esterre.
THE FURTHER ADVENTURES OF SHERLOCK HOLMES: THE REIGATE SQUIRES (Stoll Picture Productions, 1922) d George Ridgewell, s Eille Norwood, Hubert Willis, Mme d'Esterre.
THE FURTHER ADVENTURES OF SHERLOCK HOLMES: THE NAVAL TREATY (Stoll Picture Productions, 1922) d George Ridgewell, s Eille Norwood, Hubert Willis, Mme d'Esterre.
THE FURTHER ADVENTURES OF SHERLOCK HOLMES: THE SECOND STAIN (Stoll Picture Productions, 1922) d George Ridgewell, s Eille Norwood, Hubert Willis, Mme d'Esterre.

THE FURTHER ADVENTURES OF SHERLOCK HOLMES: THE RED CIRCLE (Stoll Picture Productions, 1922) d George Ridgewell, s Eille Norwood, Hubert Willis, Mme d'Esterre.
THE FURTHER ADVENTURES OF SHERLOCK HOLMES: THE SIX NAPOLEONS (Stoll Picture Productions, 1922) d George Ridgewell, s Eille Norwood, Hubert Willis, Mme d'Esterre.
THE FURTHER ADVENTURES OF SHERLOCK HOLMES: BLACK PETER (Stoll Picture Productions, 1922) d George Ridgewell, s Eille Norwood, Hubert Willis, Mme d'Esterre.
THE FURTHER ADVENTURES OF SHERLOCK HOLMES: THE BRUCE-PARTINGTON PLANS (Stoll Picture Productions, 1922) d George Ridgewell, s Eille Norwood, Hubert Willis, Mme d'Esterre.
THE FURTHER ADVENTURES OF SHERLOCK HOLMES: THE STOCKBROKER'S CLERK (Stoll Picture Productions, 1922) d George Ridgewell, s Eille Norwood, Hubert Willis, Mme d'Esterre.
THE FURTHER ADVENTURES OF SHERLOCK HOLMES: THE BOSCOMBE VALLEY MYSTERY (Stoll Picture Productions, 1922) d George Ridgewell, s Eille Norwood, Hubert Willis, Mme d'Esterre.
THE FURTHER ADVENTURES OF SHERLOCK HOLMES: THE MUSGRAVE RITUAL (Stoll Picture Productions, 1922) d George Ridgewell, s Eille Norwood, Hubert Willis, Mme d'Esterre.
THE FURTHER ADVENTURES OF SHERLOCK HOLMES: THE GOLDEN PINCE-NEZ (Stoll Picture Productions, 1922) d George Ridgewell, s Eille Norwood, Hubert Willis, Mme d'Esterre.
THE FURTHER ADVENTURES OF SHERLOCK HOLMES: THE GREEK INTERPRETER (Stoll Picture Productions, 1922) d George Ridgewell, s Eille Norwood, Hubert Willis, Mme d'Esterre.
SHERLOCK HOLMES (Goldwyn, 1922) d Albert Parker, s John Barrymore, Roland Young.
THE LAST ADVENTURES OF SHERLOCK HOLMES: SILVER BLAZE (Stoll Picture Productions, 1923) d George Ridgwell, s Eille Norwood, Hubert Willis, Mme d'Esterre.
THE LAST ADVENTURES OF SHERLOCK HOLMES: THE LAST ADVENTURES OF SHERLOCK HOLMES: THE SPECKLED BAND (Stoll Picture Productions, 1923) d George Ridgwell, s Eille Norwood, Hubert Willis, Mme d'Esterre.
THE LAST ADVENTURES OF SHERLOCK HOLMES: THE "GLORIA SCOTT" (Stoll Picture Productions, 1923) d George Ridgwell, s Eille Norwood, Hubert Willis, Mme d'Esterre.
THE LAST ADVENTURES OF SHERLOCK HOLMES: THE BLUE CARBUNCLE (Stoll Picture Productions, 1923) d George Ridgwell, s Eille Norwood, Hubert Willis, Mme d'Esterre.
THE LAST ADVENTURES OF SHERLOCK HOLMES: THE ENGINEER'S THUMB (Stoll Picture Productions, 1923) d George Ridgwell, s Eille Norwood, Hubert Willis, Mme d'Esterre.

THE LAST ADVENTURES OF SHERLOCK HOLMES: HIS LAST BOW (Stoll Picture Productions, 1923) d George Ridgwell, s Eille Norwood, Hubert Willis, Mme d'Esterre.
THE LAST ADVENTURES OF SHERLOCK HOLMES: THE CARDBOARD BOX (Stoll Picture Productions, 1923) d George Ridgwell, s Eille Norwood, Hubert Willis, Mme d'Esterre.
THE LAST ADVENTURES OF SHERLOCK HOLMES: THE DISAPPEARANCE OF LADY FRANCES CARFAX (Stoll Picture Productions, 1923) d George Ridgwell, s Eille Norwood, Hubert Willis, Mme d'Esterre.
THE LAST ADVENTURES OF SHERLOCK HOLMES: THE THREE STUDENTS (Stoll Picture Productions, 1923) d George Ridgwell, s Eille Norwood, Hubert Willis, Mme d'Esterre.
THE LAST ADVENTURES OF SHERLOCK HOLMES: THE MISSING THREE-QUARTER (Stoll Picture Productions, 1923) d George Ridgwell, s Eille Norwood, Hubert Willis, Mme d'Esterre.
THE LAST ADVENTURES OF SHERLOCK HOLMES: THE MYSTERY OF THOR BRIDGE (Stoll Picture Productions, 1923) d George Ridgwell, s Eille Norwood, Hubert Willis, Mme d'Esterre.
THE LAST ADVENTURES OF SHERLOCK HOLMES: THE MAZARIN STONE (Stoll Picture Productions, 1923) d George Ridgwell, s Eille Norwood, Hubert Willis, Mme d'Esterre.
THE LAST ADVENTURES OF SHERLOCK HOLMES: THE DANCING MEN (Stoll Picture Productions, 1923) d George Ridgwell, s Eille Norwood, Hubert Willis, Mme d'Esterre.
THE LAST ADVENTURES OF SHERLOCK HOLMES: THE CROOKED MAN (Stoll Picture Productions, 1923) d George Ridgwell, s Eille Norwood, Hubert Willis, Mme d'Esterre.
THE LAST ADVENTURES OF SHERLOCK HOLMES: THE FINAL PROBLEM (Stoll Picture Productions, 1923) d George Ridgwell, s Eille Norwood, Hubert Willis, Mme d'Esterre.
THE HOUND OF THE BASKERVILLES (Suedfilm/Erda, 1929) d Richard Oswald, s Caryle Blackwell, George Seroff.
THE RETURN OF SHERLOCK HOLMES (Paramount, 1929) d Basil Dean, s Clive Brook, H. Reeves-Smith.
THE SLEEPING CARDINAL (Warner Brothers, 1931) [aka SHERLOCK HOLMES' FATAL HOUR] d Leslie Hiscott, s Arthur Wontner, Ian Fleming, Minnie Rayner.
THE SPECKLED BAND (W&F, 1931) d Jack Raymond, s Raymond Massey, Athole Stewart.
THE HOUND OF THE BASKERVILLES (Gaumont-British, 1932) d V. Gareth Gundrey, s Robert Rendel, Frederick Lloyd.
THE MISSING REMBRANDT (PDC, 1932) d Leslie Hiscott, s Arthur Wontner, Ian Fleming.
THE SIGN OF FOUR (Associated Radio, 1932) d Graham Cutts, s Arthur Wontner, Ian Hunter.

SHERLOCK HOLMES (Fox, 1932) d William K. Howard, s Clive Brook, Reginald Owen.
A STUDY IN SCARLET (World Wide, 1933) d Edwin L. Marin, s Reginald Owen, Warburton Gamble.
THE RADIO MURDER MYSTERY (1933) s Richard Gordon.
THE TRIUMPH OF SHERLOCK HOLMES (Gaumont-British, 1935) d Leslie S. Hiscott, s Arthur Wontner, Ian Fleming.
SILVER BLAZE (Associated British, 1937) [aka MURDER AT THE BASKERVILLES] d Thomas Bentley, s Arthur Wontner, Ian Fleming.
THE HOUND OF THE BASKERVILLES (20th Century-Fox, 1939) d Sidney Lanfield, s Basil Rathbone, Nigel Bruce.
THE ADVENTURES OF SHERLOCK HOLMES (20th Century-Fox, 1939) d Alfred Werker, s Basil Rathbone, Nigel Bruce, Ida Lupino.
SHERLOCK HOLMES AND THE VOICE OF TERROR (Universal, 1942) d John Rawlins, s Basil Rathbone, Nigel Bruce.
SHERLOCK HOLMES AND THE SECRET WEAPON (Universal, 1942) d Roy William Neill, s Basil Rathbone, Nigel Bruce.
SHERLOCK HOLMES IN WASHINGTON (Universal, 1943) d Roy William Neill, s Basil Rathbone, Nigel Bruce.
SHERLOCK HOLMES FACES DEATH (Universal, 1943) d Roy William Neill, s Basil Rathbone, Nigel Bruce.
SHERLOCK HOLMES AND THE SPIDER WOMAN (Universal, 1944) [aka SPIDER WOMAN] d Roy William Neill, s Basil Rathbone, Nigel Bruce.
THE PEARL OF DEATH (Universal, 1944) d Roy William Neill, s Basil Rathbone, Nigel Bruce.
THE HOUSE OF FEAR (Universal, 1945) d Roy William Neill, s Basil Rathbone, Nigel Bruce.
THE WOMAN IN GREEN (Universal, 1945) d Roy William Neill, s Basil Rathbone, Nigel Bruce.
PURSUIT TO ALGIERS (Universal, 1945) d Roy William Neill, s Basil Rathbone, Nigel Bruce.
TERROR BY NIGHT (Universal, 1946) d Roy William Neill, s Basil Rathbone, Nigel Bruce.
DRESSED TO KILL (Universal, 1946) [aka SHERLOCK HOLMES AND THE SECRET CODE] d Roy William Neill, s Basil Rathbone, Nigel Bruce.
ADVENTURE OF THE SPECKLED BAND (Marshall Grant Realm-Tele Productions, 1949) s Alan Napier.
THE MAN WITH THE TWISTED LIP (Grand National, 1951) d Richard M. Grey, s John Longden, Campbell Singer.
THE HOUND OF THE BASKERVILLES (Hammer/United Artists, 1959) d Terence Fisher, s Peter Cushing, Andre Morell.
A STUDY IN TERROR (Compton/Tekli/Sir Nigel, 1965) d James Hill, s John Neville, Donald Houston.
THE DOUBLE-BARRELED DETECTIVE STORY (1965) s Jerome Raphel
THE PRIVATE LIFE OF SHERLOCK HOLMES (United Artists, 1970) d Billy Wilder, s Robert Stephens, Colin Blakely.

THEY MIGHT BE GIANTS (Universal, 1971) d Anthony Harvey, s Joanne Woodward, George C. Scott.
THE HOUND OF THE BASKERVILLES (Universal, 1972) (ABC-TV movie) d Barry Crane, s Stewart Granger, Bernard Fox.
MURDER IN NORTHUMBERLAND (1974) s Keith McConnell.
THE ADVENTURE OF SHERLOCK HOLMES' SMARTER BROTHER (20th Century-Fox, 1975) d Gene Wilder, s Douglas Wilmer, Thorley Walters, Gene Wilder.
SHERLOCK HOLMES (1975) s Harry Reems.
THE RETURN OF THE WORLD'S GREATEST DETECTIVE (Universal, 1976) (NBC-TV movie) d Dean Hargrove, s Larry Hagman, Jenny O'Hara.
SHERLOCK HOLMES IN NEW YORK (20th Century-Fox Television, 1976) (NBC-TV movie) d Boris Sagal, s Roger Moore, Patrick Macnee.
THE SEVEN-PER-CENT SOLUTION (Universal, 1976) d Herbert Ross, s Nicol Williamson, Robert Duvall.
MURDER BY DEATH (1976) s Keith McConnell.
A CASE OF ROYAL MURDER (1977)
THE HOUND OF THE BASKERVILLES (Michael White, 1977) d Paul Morrissey, s Peter Cook, Dudley Moore.
THE CASE OF THE MOUNTING FORTUNE (1978) s Trevor Ainsley.
MURDER BY DECREE (Avco Embassy, 1979) d Bob Clark, s Christopher Plummer, James Mason.
THE CASE OF THE FANTASTICAL PASSBOOK (1979) s Jeremy Young.
SHERLOCK HOLMES AND THE BASKERVILLE CURSE (Eddy Graham, 1981) (animated) voice Peter O'Toole.
THE SIGN OF FOUR (Eddy Graham, 1981) (animated) voice Peter O'Toole.
A STUDY IN SCARLET (Eddy Graham, 1981) (animated) voice Peter O'Toole.
A VALLEY OF FEAR (Eddy Graham, 1981) (animated) voice Peter O'Toole.
SHERLOCK HOLMES (TV stage presentation on HBO, 1981) d Gary Halverson, Peter H. Hunt, s Frank Langella, Richard Woods.
THE SIGN OF FOUR (TV movie, 1983) d Desmond Davis, s Ian Richardson, David Healy.
THE HOUND OF THE BASKERVILLES (Mapleton, 1983) d Douglas Hickox, s Ian Richardson, Donald Churchill.
SHERLOCK HOLMES AND THE BASKERVILLE CURSE (1984) (animated) d Eddy Graham.
THE MASKS OF DEATH (British TV film, 1984) d Roy Ward Baker, s Peter Cushing, John Mills.
YOUNG SHERLOCK HOLMES (Paramount, 1985) d Barry Levinson, s Nicholas Rowe, Alan Cox.
THE RETURN OF SHERLOCK HOLMES (1987) (TV movie) d Kevin Conner, s Margaret Colin, Michael Pennington.
WITHOUT A CLUE (Orion, 1988) d Thom Eberhardt, s Michael Caine, Ben Kingsley.

678. SHEIK, THE
A woman falls in love with a desert chieftain.
THE SHEIK (Paramount, 1921) d George Melford, s Rudolph Valentino, Agnes Ayres.
SON OF THE SHEIK (United Artists, 1926) d George Fitzmaurice, s Rudolph Valentino, Vilma Banky.

679. SHE'S SO FINE
These films are rated X.
SHE'S SO FINE (VCA, 1985) s Taija Rae, Joey Silvera.
SHE'S SO FINE II (VCA, 1988) s Sharon Kane, Joey Silvera.

680. SHORT CIRCUIT
A government robot, No. 5, develops a mind of its own and with the help of sympathetic humans, ventures into the real world.
SHORT CIRCUIT (Tri-Star, 1986) d John Badham, s Ally Sheedy, Steve Guttenberg.
SHORT CIRCUIT II (Tri-Star, 1988) d Kenneth Johnson, s Fisher Stevens, Michael McKean, Cynthia Gibb.

681. SHOW GIRL
Based on the Joseph Patrick McEvoy play: Dixie Dugan gets her bigtime chance.
SHOW GIRL (First National, 1928) d Alfred Santell, s Alice White, Donald Reed.
SHOW GIRL IN HOLLYWOOD (First National, 1930) d Mervyn LeRoy, s Alice White, Jack Mulhall.

682. SILENT NIGHT, DEADLY NIGHT
A psychotic dresses as Santa Claus in this "splatter movie" series. In the second picture, the killer of the first entry (Dr. Newbury) is replaced by a younger brother. In the third, the doctor is brought out of a six-year coma.
SILENT NIGHT, DEADLY NIGHT (Tri-Star, 1984) d Charles E. Sellier Jr., s Lilyan Chauvan, Gilmer McCormick.
SILENT NIGHT, DEADLY NIGHT PART II (Silent Night Releasing, 1987) d Lee Harry, s Eric Freeman, James L. Newman, Linnea Quigley.
SILENT NIGHT, DEADLY NIGHT III: BETTER WATCH OUT (Quiet Films, 1989) d Monte Hellman, s Richard Beymer, Bill Moseley, Samantha Scully.

683. SILK
Jenny "Silk" Sleighton is a tough cop investigating drug traffickers in Hawaii.
SILK (Concorde, 1986) d Cirio H. Santiago, s Cec Verrell.
SILK 2 (New Horizons, announced 1990) d Cirio H. Santiago, s Monique Gabrielle, Maria Claire.

684. SIMON DRAKE

A reporter, fired for not following up an important crime story lead, phones in a phoney tip which turns out to be real.
THE MAN IS NEWS (Pinebrook/Paramount, 1938) d Donald MacDonald, s Barry K. Barnes, Valerie Hobson.
THIS MAN IN PARIS (Pinebrook/Paramount, 1939) d David MacDonald, s Barry K. Barnes, Valerie Hobson.

685. SINBAD THE SAILOR
Arabian Nights and daring-do.
SINBAD THE SAILOR (RKO, 1947) d Richard Wallace, s Douglas Fairbanks Jr., Maureen O'Hara.
SON OF SINBAD (RKO, 1955) d Ted Tetzlaff, s Dale Robertson, Sally Forrest.
SEVENTH VOYAGE OF SINBAD (Columbia, 1958) d Nathan Juran, s Kerwin Mathews, Kathryn Grant.
CAPTAIN SINBAD (MGM, 1963) d Byron Haskin, s Guy Williams, Heidi Bruhl.
THE GOLDEN VOYAGE OF SINBAD (Columbia, 1974) d Gordon Hessler, s John Phillip Law, Caroline Munro.
SINBAD AND THE EYE OF THE TIGER (Columbia, 1977) d Sam Wanamaker, s Patrick Wayne, Jane Seymour.

686. SINS OF THE WEALTHY
These pictures are rated X.
SINS OF THE WEALTHY I (Classic Editions, 1986) s Krista Lane, Dick Rambone.
SINS OF THE WEALTHY II (Classic Editions, 1987) s Krista Lane, Paul Thomas.

687. SIX-MILLION DOLLAR MAN, THE
An injured test pilot, Steve Austin, is outfitted with bionic body parts and becomes a top government agent, in the television series featuring Lee Majors which aired over ABC 1974-78. An off-shoot series is about the BIONIC WOMAN (Lindsay Wagner), shown on ABC and ABC, 1976-78. Richard Anderson plays Oscar Goldman on both programs.
THE SIX MILLION DOLLAR MAN (Universal, 1973) (ABC-TV movie) [aka CYBORG: THE SIX-MILLION DOLLAR MAN] d Richard Irving, s Lee Majors, Darren McGavin.
THE RETURN OF THE SIX-MILLION-DOLLAR MAN AND THE BIONIC WOMAN (1987 TV movie) d Ray Austin, s Lee Majors, Lindsay Wagner, Richard Anderson.
THE BIONIC SHOWDOWN (1989 TV movie) s Lee Majors, Lindsay Wagner.

688. SKINNER
Meek clerk Skinner, pretending he got the raise which his boss refused him, doesn't anticipate his wife going on a buying binge.

SKINNER'S DRESS SUIT (Essanay, 1917)
SKINNER'S BUBBLE (Essanay, 1917) s Bryant Washburn.
SKINNER'S BABY (Essanay, 1917) s Bryant Washburn.
SKINNER'S DRESS SUIT (Universal, 1926) d William A. Seiter, s Reginald Denny, Laura La Plante.
SKINNER'S BIG IDEA (FBO, 1928) d Lynn Shores, s Bryant Washburn, William Orlamond, James Bradbury Sr.
SKINNER STEPS OUT (Universal, 1929) d William James Craft, s Glenn Tryon, Merna Kennedy.

689. SKINNY
These are silent comedy films from Hal Roach's studio.
SKINNY GETS A GOAT (1917) d Hal Roach.
SKINNY'S FALSE ALARM (1917) d Hal Roach.
SKINNY'S SHIPWRECKED SAND-WITCH (1917) d Hal Roach.

690. SLAUGHTER
An ex-Green Beret goes after syndicate killers.
SLAUGHTER (American-International, 1972) d Jack Starrett, s Jim Brown, Stella Stevens.
SLAUGHTER'S BIG RIP-OFF (American-International, 1973) d Gordon Douglas, s Jim Brown, Ed McMahon.

691. SLEEPAWAY CAMP
In the first picture, a crazy villain slaughters twenty-five camp kids. In the second, a puritanical counselor disposes of naughty youths.
SLEEPAWAY CAMP (United Film, 1983) d Robert Hiltzik
SLEEPAWAY CAMP II: UNHAPPY CAMPERS (Nelson, 1988) d Michael A. Simpson, s Pam Springsteen, Renee Estevez.
SLEEPAWAY CAMP III: TEENAGE WASTELAND (Nelson, 1989) d Michael A. Simpson, s Pamela Springsteen, Tracy Griffith, Michael J. Pollard.

692. SLIM CALLAGHAN
The detective character was created by novelist by Peter Cheyney. Callaghan novels were published from 1938-1946.
UNEASY TERMS (British National, 1948) s Michael Rennie.
MEET MR. CALLAGHAN (Eros Films, 1954) s Derrick de Marney.

692A. SLIPPERY SLIM
Victor Potel is featured in this series of silent films, offshoots of the SNAKEVILLE pictures.

693. SLUMBER PARTY MASSACRE
Blood and gore; a mass murderer escapes an asylum and kills girls with a power drill.

SLUMBER PARTY MASSACRE (Pacific Film, 1982) d Amy Jones, s Michele Michaels, Robin Stille.
SLUMBER PARTY MASSACRE II (Concorde, 1987) d Deborah Brock, s Crystal Bernard, Kimberly McArthur.

694. SMILEY
The initial Australian film is about a young boy seeking a bicycle and becoming entangled with thugs. It is based on the book by Moore Raymond. The character in the second picture, also based on a Raymond book, tries to win the right to have a gun.
SMILEY (London Films, 1957) d Anthony Kimmins, s Ralph Richardson, John McCallum, Chips Rafferty.
SMILEY GETS A GUN (20th Century-Fox, 1959) d Anthony Kimmins, s Sybil Thorndike, Keith Calvert, Bruce Archer, Chips Rafferty.

695. SMILEY
John Le Carre's espionage series character George Smiley has also been featured in a television mini-series.
THE SPY WHO CAME IN FROM THE COLD (Paramount, 1965) d Martin Ritt, s Richard Burton, Claire Bloom.
THE DEADLY AFFAIR (Columbia, 1967) d Sidney Lumet, s James Mason, Simone Signoret.
THE LOOKING GLASS WAR (Columbia, 1970) d Frank R. Pierson, s Christopher Jones, Ralph Richardson, Paul Rogers.

696. SMITH
This is a Mack Sennett silent comedy series.
SMITH'S VACATION (1926)
SMITH'S LANDLORD (1926)
SMITH'S PICNIC (1926)
SMITH'S CUSTOMER (1927)
SMITH'S SURPRISE (1927)
SMITH'S NEW HOME (1927)
SMITH'S KINDERGARTEN (1927)
SMITH'S CANDY SHOP (1927)
SMITH'S PONY (1927)
SMITH'S COOK (1927)
SMITH'S COUSIN (1927)
SMITH'S MODISTE SHOP (1927)
SMITH'S HOLIDAY (1928)
SMITH'S ARMY LIFE (1928)
SMITH'S FARM DAYS (1928)
SMITH'S RESTAURANT (1928)
SMITH'S CATALINA ROWBOAT RACE (1928) [aka CATALINA ROWBOAT RACE]

697. SMITH AND DALE

308 MOTION PICTURE SERIES & SEQUELS

The vaudeville comedy team also appeared in other films. These are shorts.
A NAG IN THE BAG (Columbia, 1939) d Charley Chase, s Joe Smith, Charlie Dale.
MUTINY ON THE BODY (Columbia, 1939) d Charley Chase, s Joe Smith, Charlie Dale.

698. SMOKEY AND THE BANDIT
A redneck sheriff chases a bootlegger.
SMOKEY AND THE BANDIT (Universal, 197) d Hal Needham, s Burt Reynolds, Sally Field, Jackie Gleason.
SMOKEY AND THE BANDIT II (Universal, 1980) d Hal Needham, s Burt Reynolds, Jackie Gleason, Jerry Reed.
SMOKEY AND THE BANDIT PART 3 (Universal, 1983) d Dick Lowry, s Jackie Gleason, Jery Reed.

698A. SNAKE EATER
These are crime films.
SNAKE EATER (Cinepix, 1988) d George Erschbamer, s Lorenzo Lamas, Josie Bell.
DRUGBUSTERS: SNAKE EATER II (Cinepix, announced 1990) [aka SNAKE EATER'S REVENGE] d George Erschbamer, s Lorenzo Lamas, Michelle Scarabelli.

699. SNAKE EYES
The films are for adults only.
SNAKE EYES (Command, 1987) s Laurie Smith, Jerry Butler.
SNAKE EYES II (Command, 1987) s Laurie Smith, Jerry Butler.

700. SNAKE FIST
These are martial arts pictures.
SNAKE FIST VS. THE DRAGON (21st Century, 1980)
SNAKE FIST, FIGHTER (21st Century, 1981) d Chin Hsin.

701. SNAKEVILLE
This town was the setting for a series of corny silent comedy films including those featuring ALKALI IKE (Augustus Carney). Other characters included Mustang Pete, Coyote Simpson and Rawhide Bill (both Fred Church), SLIPPERY SLIM (Victor Potel) and Doc Killem (David Kirkland) as well as Sophie Clutts (Margaret Joslin). Roy Clements directed most entries. The list is likely incomplete.
SNAKEVILLE HEN MEDIC (1920) s Ben Turpin
SNAKEVILLE'S CHAMPION (1920) s Ben Turpin
SNAKEVILLE DEBUTANTE (1920) s Ben Turpin

702. SNOW WHITE
The classic children's fairy tale from the Brothers Grimm was several times filmed.

MOTION PICTURE SERIES & SEQUELS 309

SNOW WHITE AND THE SEVEN DWARFS (Disney, 1938) animated.
SNOW WHITE AND THE THREE STOOGES (20th Century-Fox, 1961) d Walter Lang, s Three Stooges, Patricia Medina, Carol Heiss.
NEW ADVENTURES OF SNOW WHITE (NMD, 1980) d Rolf Thiel.

703. *SNUB POLLARD*
Harry "Snub" Pollard played supporting roles in Harold Lloyd silent comedies before being given his own series. A small man with a drooping mustache, he frequently is depicted as a henpecked husband.
START SOMETHING (Hal Roach, 1919) d Charles Parrott, s Snub Pollard.
ALL AT SEA (Hal Roach, 1919) d Charles Parrott, s Snub Pollard.
CALL FOR MR. CAVE MAN (Hal Roach, 1919) d Charles Parrott, s Snub Pollard.
GIVING THE BRIDE AWAY (Hal Roach, 1919) d Charles Parrott, s Snub Pollard.
ORDER IN COURT (Hal Roach, 1919) d Charles Parrott, s Snub Pollard.
IT'S A HARD LIFE (Hal Roach, 1919) d Charles Parrott, s Snub Pollard.
HOW DRY I AM (Hal Roach, 1919) d Charles Parrott, s Snub Pollard.
LOOKING FOR TROUBLE (Hal Roach, 1919) d Charles Parrott, s Snub Pollard.
TOUGH LUCK (Hal Roach, 1919) d Charles Parrott, s Snub Pollard.
THE FLOOR BELOW (Hal Roach, 1919) d Charles Parrott, s Snub Pollard.
RED HOT HOTTENTOTS (Hal Roach, 1920) d Charles Parrott, s Snub Pollard.
WHY GO HOME? (Hal Roach, 1920) d Charles Parrott, s Snub Pollard.
SLIPPER SLICKERS (Hal Roach, 1920) d Charles Parrott, s Snub Pollard.
THE DIPPY DENTIST (Hal Roach, 1920) d Charles Parrott, s Snub Pollard.
ALL LIT UP (Hal Roach, 1920) d Charles Parrott, s Snub Pollard.
GETTING HIS GOAT (Hal Roach, 1920) d Charles Parrott, s Snub Pollard.
WALTZ ME AROUND (Hal Roach, 1920) d Charles Parrott, s Snub Pollard.
RAISE THE RENT (Hal Roach, 1920) d Charles Parrott, s Snub Pollard.
FIND THE GIRL (Hal Roach, 1920) d Charles Parrott, s Snub Pollard.
FRESH PAINT (Hal Roach, 1920) d Charles Parrott, s Snub Pollard.
FLAT BROKE (Hal Roach, 1920) d Charles Parrott, s Snub Pollard.
CUT THE CARDS (Hal Roach, 1920) d Charles Parrott, s Snub Pollard.
THE DINNER HOUR (Hal Roach, 1920) d Charles Parrott, s Snub Pollard.
CRACKED WEDDING BELLS (Hal Roach, 1920) d Charles Parrott, s Snub Pollard.
SPEED TO SPARE (Hal Roach, 1920) d Charles Parrott, s Snub Pollard.
SHOOT ON SIGHT (Hal Roach, 1920) d Charles Parrott, s Snub Pollard.
DON'T WEAKEN (Hal Roach, 1920) d Charles Parrott, s Snub Pollard.
DRINK HEARTY (Hal Roach, 1920) d Charles Parrott, s Snub Pollard.
NEARLY A MAID (Hal Roach, 1920) d Charles Parrott, s Snub Pollard.
TROTTING THROUGH TURKEY (Hal Roach, 1920) d Charles Parrott, s Snub Pollard.
ALL DRESSED UP (Hal Roach, 1920) d Charles Parrott, s Snub Pollard.
GRAB THE GHOST (Hal Roach, 1920) d Charles Parrott, s Snub Pollard.

ALL IN A DAY (Hal Roach, 1920) d Charles Parrott, s Snub Pollard.
ANY OLD PORT (Hal Roach, 1920) d Charles Parrott, s Snub Pollard.
DON'T ROCK THE BOAT (Hal Roach, 1920) d Charles Parrott, s Snub Pollard.
THE HOME STRETCH (Hal Roach, 1920) d Charles Parrott, s Snub Pollard.
CALL A TAXI (Hal Roach, 1920) d Charles Parrott, s Snub Pollard.
LIVE AND LEARN (Hal Roach, 1920) d Charles Parrott, s Snub Pollard.
RUN 'EM RAGGED (Hal Roach, 1920) d Charles Parrott, s Snub Pollard.
A LONDON BOBBY (Hal Roach, 1920) d Charles Parrott, s Snub Pollard.
MONEY TO BURN (Hal Roach, 1920) d Charles Parrott, s Snub Pollard.
GO AS YOU PLEASE (Hal Roach, 1920) d Charles Parrott, s Snub Pollard.
ROCK-A-BY-BABY (Hal Roach, 1920) d Charles Parrott, s Snub Pollard.
DOING TIME (Hal Roach, 1920) d Charles Parrott, s Snub Pollard.
FELLOW CITIZENS (Hal Roach, 1920) d Charles Parrott, s Snub Pollard.
WHEN THE WIND BLOWS (Hal Roach, 1920) d Charles Parrott, s Snub Pollard.
INSULTING THE SULTAN (Hal Roach, 1920) d Charles Parrott, s Snub Pollard.
THE DEARLY DEPARTED (Hal Roach, 1920) d Charles Parrott, s Snub Pollard.
CASH CUSTOMERS (Hal Roach, 1920) d Charles Parrott, s Snub Pollard.
PARK YOUR CAR (Hal Roach, 1920) d Charles Parrott, s Snub Pollard.
THE MORNING AFTER (Hal Roach, 1921) d Charles Parrott, s Snub Pollard.
WHIRL O' THE WEST (Hal Roach, 1921) d Charles Parrott, s Snub Pollard.
OPEN ANOTHER BOTTLE (Hal Roach, 1921) d Charles Parrott, s Snub Pollard.
HIS BEST GIRL (Hal Roach, 1921) d Charles Parrott, s Snub Pollard.
MAKE IT SNAPPY (Hal Roach, 1921) d Charles Parrott, s Snub Pollard.
FELLOW ROMANS (Hal Roach, 1921) d Charles Parrott, s Snub Pollard.
RUSH ORDERS (Hal Roach, 1921) d Charles Parrott, s Snub Pollard.
BUBBLING OVER (Hal Roach, 1921) d Charles Parrott, s Snub Pollard.
NO CHILDREN (Hal Roach, 1921) d Charles Parrott, s Snub Pollard.
OWN YOUR OWN HOME (Hal Roach, 1921) d Charles Parrott, s Snub Pollard.
BIG GAME (Hal Roach, 1921) d Charles Parrott, s Snub Pollard.
SAVE YOUR MONEY (Hal Roach, 1921) d Charles Parrott, s Snub Pollard.
BLUE SUNDAY (Hal Roach, 1921) d Charles Parrott, s Snub Pollard.
WHERE'S THE FIRE (Hal Roach, 1921) d Charles Parrott, s Snub Pollard.
THE HIGH ROLLERS (Hal Roach, 1921) d Charles Parrott, s Snub Pollard.
YOU'RE NEXT (Hal Roach, 1921) d Charles Parrott, s Snub Pollard.
THE BIKE BUG (Hal Roach, 1921) d Charles Parrott, s Snub Pollard.
AT THE RINGSIDE (Hal Roach, 1921) d Charles Parrott, s Snub Pollard.
NO STOP-OVER (Hal Roach, 1921) d Charles Parrott, s Snub Pollard.
WHAT A WHOPPER (Hal Roach, 1921) d Charles Parrott, s Snub Pollard.
TEACHING THE TEACHER (Hal Roach, 1921) d Charles Parrott, s Snub Pollard.
SPOT CASH (Hal Roach, 1921) d Charles Parrott, s Snub Pollard.

NAME THE DAY (Hal Roach, 1921) d Charles Parrott, s Snub Pollard.
THE JAIL BIRD (Hal Roach, 1921) d Charles Parrott, s Snub Pollard.
LATE LODGERS (Hal Roach, 1921) d Charles Parrott, s Snub Pollard.
GONE TO THE COUNTRY (Hal Roach, 1921) d Charles Parrott, s Snub Pollard.
LAW AND ORDER (Hal Roach, 1921) d Charles Parrott, s Snub Pollard.
FIFTEEN MINUTES (Hal Roach, 1921) d Charles Parrott, s Snub Pollard.
ON LOCATION (Hal Roach, 1921) d Charles Parrott, s Snub Pollard.
HOCUS-POCUS (Hal Roach, 1921) d Charles Parrott, s Snub Pollard.
PENNY-IN-THE-SLOT (Hal Roach, 1921) d Charles Parrott, s Snub Pollard.
THE JOY RIDER (Hal Roach, 1921) d Charles Parrott, s Snub Pollard.
THE HUSTLER (Hal Roach, 1921) d Charles Parrott, s Snub Pollard.
SINK OR SWIM (Hal Roach, 1921) d Charles Parrott, s Snub Pollard.
SHAKE 'EM UP (Hal Roach, 1921) d Charles Parrott, s Snub Pollard.
CORNER POCKET (Hal Roach, 1921) d Charles Parrott, s Snub Pollard.
LOSE NO TIME (Hal Roach, 1922) d Charles Parrott, s Snub Pollard.
CALL THE WITNESS (Hal Roach, 1922) d Charles Parrott, s Snub Pollard.
YEARS TO COME (Hal Roach, 1922) d Charles Parrott, s Snub Pollard.
BLOE 'EM UP (Hal Roach, 1922) d Charles Parrott, s Snub Pollard.
STAGE STRUCK (Hal Roach, 1922) d William Watson, s Snub Pollard.
DOWN AND OUT (Hal Roach, 1922) d Ralph Cedar, s Snub Pollard.
PARDON ME (Hal Roach, 1922) d Ralph Cedar, s Snub Pollard.
THE BOW WOWS (Hal Roach, 1922) d Ralph Cedar, s Snub Pollard.
HOT OFF THE PRESS (Hal Roach, 1922) d Ralph Cedar, s Snub Pollard.
THE ANVIL CHORUS (Hal Roach, 1922) d Ralph Cedar, s Snub Pollard.
JUMP YOUR JOB (Hal Roach, 1922) d Ralph Cedar, s Snub Pollard.
FULL O'PEP (Hal Roach, 1922) d Charles Parrott, s Snub Pollard.
KILL THE NERVE (Hal Roach, 1922) d Ralph Cedar, s Snub Pollard.
DAYS OF OLD (Hal Roach, 1922) d William Watson, s Snub Pollard.
LIGHT SHOWERS (Hal Roach, 1922) d William Watson, s Snub Pollard.
DO ME A FAVOR (Hal Roach, 1922) d William Watson, s Snub Pollard.
IN THE MOVIES (Hal Roach, 1922) d William Watson, s Snub Pollard.
PUNCH THE CLOCK (Hal Roach, 1922) d William Beaudine, s Snub Pollard.
STRICTLY MODERN (Hal Roach, 1922) d William Beaudine, s Snub Pollard.
HALE AND HEARTY (Hal Roach, 1922) d Al Santell, s Snub Pollard.
SOME BABY (Hal Roach, 1922) d Ralph Cedar, s Snub Pollard.
THE DUMB BELL (Hal Roach, 1922) d William Watson, s Snub Pollard.
BED OF ROSES (Hal Roach, 1922) d William Watson, s Snub Pollard.
THE STONE AGE (Hal Roach, 1922) d William Watson, s Snub Pollard.
365 DAYS (Hal Roach, 1922) d William Watson, s Snub Pollard.
THE OLD SEA DOG (Hal Roach, 1922) d William Watson, s Snub Pollard.
HOOK, LINE AND SINKER (Hal Roach, 1922) d William Watson, s Snub Pollard.
NEARLY RICH (Hal Roach, 1922) d William Watson, s Snub Pollard.
THE GREEN CAT (Hal Roach, 1922) d William Watson, s Snub Pollard.
DIG U (Hal Roach, 1923) d Craig Hutchinson, s Snub Pollard.
A TOUGH WINTER (Hal Roach, 1923) d William Watson, s Snub Pollard.

BEFORE THE PUBLIC (Hal Roach, 1923) d William Watson, s Snub Pollard.
WHERE AM I? (Hal Roach, 1923) d William Watson, s Snub Pollard.
CALIFORNIA OR BUST (Hal Roach, 1923) d Craig Hutchinson, s Snub Pollard.
SOLD AT AUCTION (Hal Roach, 1923) d William Watson, s Snub Pollard.
THE COURTSHIP OF MILES SANDWICH (Hal Roach, 1923) d William Watson, s Snub Pollard.
JACK FROST (Hal Roach, 1923) d William Watson, s Snub Pollard.
THE MYSTERY MAN (Hal Roach, 1923) d Hugh Fay, s Snub Pollard.
THE WALKOUT (Hal Roach, 1923) d George Jeske, s Snub Pollard.
IT'S A GIFT (Hal Roach, 1923) d Hugh Fay, s Snub Pollard.
DEAR OL' PAL (Hal Roach, 1923) d William Watson, s Snub Pollard.
JOIN THE CIRCUS (Hal Roach, 1923) d George Jeske, s Snub Pollard.
FULLY INSURED (Hal Roach, 1923) d George Jeske, s Snub Pollard.
IT'S A BOY (Hal Roach, 1923) d George Jeske, s Snub Pollard.
THE BIG IDEA (Hal Roach, 1924) d George Jeske, s Snub Pollard.
WHY MARRY? (Hal Roach, 1924) d Ward Hayes, s Snub Pollard.
GET BUSY (Hal Roach, 1924) d Ward Hayes, s Snub Pollard.
ARE HUSBANDS HUMAN? (Hal Roach, 1925) d William Watson, s Snub Pollard.
DO YOUR DUTY (Hal Roach, 1925) d Ralph Cedar, s Snub Pollard.
THE OLD WARHORSE (Hal Roach, 1925) d George Jeske, s Snub Pollard.
THE DOUGHBOY (Weiss Brothers Artclass, 1926) d Jim Davis, s Snub Pollard.
THE YOKEL (Weiss Brothers Artclass, 1926) d Jim Davis, s Snub Pollard.
THE FIRE (Weiss Brothers Artclass, 1926) d Jim Davis, s Snub Pollard.
ALL WET (Weiss Brothers Artclass, 1926) d Jim Davis, s Snub Pollard.
THE BUM'S RUSH (Weiss Brothers Artclass, 1926) d Jim Davis, s Snub Pollard.
THICK AND THIN (Weiss Brothers Artclass, 1926) d Jim Davis, s Snub Pollard.
ONCE OVER (Weiss Brothers Artclass, 1926) d Jim Davis, s Snub Pollard.
DOUBLE TROUBLE (Weiss Brothers Artclass, 1926) d Jim Davis, s Snub Pollard.

SNUFFY SMITH
See **BARNEY GOOGLE**

704. SOMEWHERE
This British military comedy series is known for its vulgarity and popular stars.
SOMEWHERE IN ENGLAND (Mancunian, 1940) d John E. Blakely, s Frank Randle, Harry Korris, Robbie Vincent, Winki Turner, Dan Young.
SOMEWHERE IN CAMP (Mancunian, 1942) d John E. Blakeley, s Harry Korris, Frank Randle.
SOMEWHERE ON LEAVE (Mancunian, 1942) d John E. Blakeley, s Frank Randle, Harry Korris.

SOMEWHERE IN CIVVIES (1943) d Maclean Rogers, s Frank Randle, George Donnan.
SOMEWHERE IN POLITICS (Mancunian, 1949) d John E. Blakeley, s Frank Randle, Tessie O'Shea.

705. SOPHIE LANG
The lady jewel thief, dealing with a foreign rival in the first picture, decides to go straight in the second.
THE NOTORIOUS SOPHIE LANG (Paramount, 1934) d Ralph Murphy, s Gertrude Michael, Paul Cavanagh.
THE RETURN OF SOPHIE LANG (Paramount, 1936) d George Archainbaud, s Gertrude Michael, Sir Guy Standing.
SOPHIE LANG GOES WEST (Paramount, 1937)

706. SORORITY
The low-budget horror flicks are about college girls who become ravenous dates.
SORORITY BABES IN THE SLIMEBALL BOWL-O-RAMA (1988) d David DeCoteau, s Linnea Quigley, Michelle Bauer.
NIGHTMARE SISTERS (Cinema Home Video, 1989) [aka SORORITY SISTERS] d David DeCoteau, s Linnea Quigley, Brinke Stevens.

707. SOUNDER
William H. Armstrong wrote the novel upon which the pictures are based. Nathan Lee Morgan steals a ham to feed his poor sharecropping family, is caught and imprisoned, leaving the mother to pull the family together.
SOUNDER (20th Century-Fox, 1972) d Martin Ritt, s Cicely Tyson, Paul Winfield.
SOUNDER: PART 2 (Gamma III, 1976) d William Graham, s Harold Sylvester, Ebony Wright.

708. SPIDER, THE
The vengeful crimefighter originally appeared in some 118 pulp magazine adventures from 1933-43, penned by Norvell Page and Reginald T. Maitland.
THE SPIDER'S WEB (Columbia, 1936) (15 chapters) d Ray Taylor and James W. Horne, s Warren Hull, Iris Meredith.
THE SPIDER RETURNS (Columbia, 1941) (15 chapter) d James W. Horne, s Warren Hull, Mary Ainslee, Dave O'Brien.

709. SPIDERMAN
The Marvel Comics character, bitten by a radioactive spider, now has the ability to climb walls. The character was introduced in 1962 as written by Stan Lee and drawn by Steve Ditko.
SPIDERMAN (Charles Fries Productions, 1977) (CBS-TV movie) d E.W. Swackhamer, s Nicholas Hammond, David White.
THE CHINESE WEB (TV movie, 1978) d Don McDougall, s Nicholas Hammond, Robert F. Simpson.

314 MOTION PICTURE SERIES & SEQUELS

SPIDERMAN (21st Century Film, announced for 1990)

710. SPIDER WOMAN, THE
The villainess kills her victims with spiders. She survives a sparring match with SHERLOCK HOLMES in the first entry below.
THE SPIDER WOMAN (Universal, 1943) d Roy William Neill, s Basil Rathbone, Nigel Bruce, Gale Sondergaard.
THE SPIDER WOMAN STRIKES BACK (Universal, 1946) d Arthur Lubin, s Gale Sondergaard, Brenda Joyce, Rondo Hatton.

711. SQUIBS
In the play by Clifford Seyler and George Pearson, Cockney Squibs Hopkins is a spitfire.
SQUIBS (Welsh/Pearson, 1921) d George Pearson, s Betty Balfour, Hugh E. Wright, Fred Groves.
SQUIBS WINS THE CALCUTTA SWEEP (Welsh/Pearson, 1922) d George Pearson, s Betty Balfour, Fred Groves.
SQUIBS, MP (Welsh/Pearson, 1923) d George Pearson, s Betty Balfour, Hugh E. Wright, Fred Groves.
SQUIBS HONEYMOON (Welsh/Pearson, 1923) d George Pearson, s Betty Balfour, Hugh E. Wright, Fred Groves.
SQUIBS (Twickenham, 1935) d Henry Edwards, s Betty Balfour, Gordon Harker, Stanley Holloway.

712. STAR TREK
The crew of the *Enterprise* came to movies from television. The adventures of Capt. James T. Kirk (William Shatner), Mr. Spock (Leonard Nimoy), Dr. Leonard McCoy (DeForest Kelley), Sulu (George Takei), Scott (James Doohan), Uhura (Nichelle Nichols), Chekov (Walter Koenig) and the rest were broadcast on NBC 1966-69, then enjoyed great popularity in syndication. A subsequent series, STAR TREK: THE NEXT GENERATION, began in syndication in 1987.
STAR TREK: THE MOTION PICTURE (Paramount, 1979) d Robert Wise, s William Shatner, Leonard Nimoy, DeForest Kelley, James Doohan, Nichelle Nichols, Walter Koenig, George Takei.
STAR TREK II: THE WRATH OF KHAN (Paramount, 1982) d Nicholas Meyer, s William Shatner, Leonard Nimoy, DeForest Kelley, James Doohan, Nichelle Nichols, Walter Koenig, George Takei.
STAR TREK III: THE SEARCH FOR SPOCK (Paramount, 1984) d Leonard Nimoy, s William Shatner, Leonard Nimoy, DeForest Kelley, James Doohan, Nichelle Nichols, Walter Koenig, George Takei.
STAR TREK IV: THE VOYAGE HOME (Paramount, 1986) d Leonard Nimoy, s William Shatner, Leonard Nimoy, DeForest Kelley, James Doohan, Nichelle Nichols, Walter Koenig, George Takei.
STAR TREK V: THE FINAL FRONTIER (Paramount, 1989) d William Shatner, s William Shatner, Leonard Nimoy, DeForest Kelley, James Doohan, Nichelle Nichols, Walter Koenig, George Takei.

713. STAR WARS
This outer space fantasy finds young Luke Skywalker helping a rebel princess who has escaped from a distant galaxy. The villain is heavy-breathing Darth Vader. The lovable sidekicks are the robot and android, R2D2 and C3PO. Han Solo is a space-hopping soldier-for-hire.
STAR WARS (20th Century-Fox, 1977) d George Lucas, s Mark Hamill, Harrison Ford, Carrie Fisher.
THE EMPIRE STRIKES BACK (20th Century-Fox, 1980) d Irvin Kershner, s Mark Hamill, Harrison Ford, Carrie Fisher.
RETURN OF THE JEDI (20th Century-Fox, 1983) d Richard Marquand, s Mark Hamill, Harrison Ford, Carrie Fisher.

714. STAR WORMS
STAR WORMS
STAR WORMS II: ATTACK OF THE PLEASURE PODS (Troma, 1989 announced) d Lin Sten.

715. STEPFATHER, THE
A Casper Milktoast turns out to be a psychopath.
THE STEPFATHER (New Century, 1987) d Joseph Ruben, s Terry O'Quinn, Jill Schoelen.
STEPFATHER II (ITC, 1989) d Jeff Burr, s Terry O'Quinn, Meg Foster.

716. STEPFORD WIVES, THE
Ira Levin's suspense novel is the source of these films about women in suburban New England community in a permanent, controlled, blissful state.
THE STEPFORD WIVES (Columbia, 1975) d Bryan Forbes, s Katharine Ross, Paula Prentiss.
REVENGE OF THE STEPFORD WIVES (Edgar J. Sherick Associates, 1980) (NBC-TV movie) d Robert Fuest, s Sharon Gless, Julie Kavner.
THE STEPFORD CHILDREN (1987) d Alan J. Levi, s Barbara Eden, Don Murray.

717. STEPTOE AND SON
A British TV series about junkmen who live in a dilapidated London house inspired the American TV series SANFORD AND SON and two motion pictures.
STEPTOE AND SON (EMI, 1972) d Cliff Owen, s Harry H. Corbett and Wilfred Brambell.
STEPTOE AND SON RIDE AGAIN (EMI, 1973) s Harry H. Corbett and Wilfred Brambell.

718. STING, THE
It's Chicago in the 1920s, and a pair of con men set up an elaborate scam to get revenge on a big-time gambler.

THE STING (Universal, 1973) d George Roy Hill, s Paul Newman, Robert Redford.
THE STING II (Universal, 1983) d Jeremy Paul Kagan, s Jackie Gleason, Mac Davis, Teri Garr.

719. STREETFIGHTER
These are martial arts films.
THE RETURN OF THE STREETFIGHTER (New Line, 1975)
THE STREETFIGHTER'S LAST REVENGE (New Line, 1979)

720. STREET WARRIORS
Teenagers rape, rob and pillage.
STREET WARRIORS (1977) d Anthony Loma, s Victor Petit, Frank Branc.
STREET WARRIORS II (1981) d Anthony Loma, s Angel Fernandez Franco.

721. STRIPPED TO KILL
Undercover cops investigate the murder of a stripper.
STRIPPED TO KILL (Concorde, 1987) d Katt Shea Ruben, s Kay Lenz, Greg Evigan.
STRIPPED TO KILL II: LIVE GIRLS (MGM/UA, 1989) d Katt Shea Ruben, s Maria Ford, Eb Lottimer.

722. *STRONGHEART*
This German shepherd was the first dog featured in dramatic feature films. His first role was in THE SILENT CALL, based on Hal G. Everts' *Saturday Evening Post* story *The Cross Pull*. The list is incomplete.
THE SILENT CALL (1921)
BRAWN OF THE NORTH
THE LOVE MASTER
WHITE FANG
THE RETURN OF BOSTON BLACKIE (1927)
THE WARNING (1927)

723. ST. XWHERE
These X-rated pictures spoof the popular television program ST. ELSEWHERE.
ST. XWHERE (Vidco, 1987) s Danielle, Jerry Butler.
ST. XWHERE 2 (Vidco, 1988) s Britt Morgan, Jesse Eastern.

724. SUMMER OF '42
Teenagers grow up during the war years.
SUMMER OF '42 (Warner Brothers, 1971) d Robert Mulligan, s Jennifer O'Neill, Gary Grimes, Jerry Houser.
CLASS OF '44 (Warner Brothers, 1973) d Paul Bogart, s Gary Grimes, Jerry Houser.

725. *SUNSET CARSON AND PEGGY STEWART*

B Westerns team Carson and Stewart.
FIREBRANDS OF ARIZONA (Republic, 1944) d Lesley Selander, s Sunset Carson, Peggy Stewart, Smiley Burnette.
CODE OF THE PRAIRIE (Republic, 1944) d Lesley Selander, s Sunset Carson, Peggy Stewart, Smiley Burnette.
SHERIFF OF CIMARRON (Republic, 1945) d Yakima Canutt, s Sunset Carson, Peggy Stewart, Olin Howlin.
SANTA FE SADDLEMATES (Republic, 1945) d Thomas Carr, s Sunset Carson, Peggy Stewart, Olin Howlin.
OREGON TRAIL (Republic, 1945) d Thomas Carr, s Sunset Carson, Peggy Stewart.
BANDITS OF THE BADLANDS (Republic, 1945) d Thomas Carr, s Sunset Carson, Peggy Stewart.
ROUGH RIDERS OF CHEYENNE (Republic, 1945) d Thomas Carr, s Sunset Carson, Peggy Stewart.
THE CHEROKEE FLASH (Republic, 1945) d Thomas Carr, s Sunset Carson, Peggy Stewart.
DAYS OF BUFFALO BILL (Republic, 1946) d Thomas Carr, s Sunset Carson, Peggy Stewart.
RED RIVER RENEGADES (Republic, 1946) d Thomas Carr, s Sunset Carson, Peggy Stewart.
ALIAS BILLY THE KID (Republic, 1946) d Thomas Carr, s Sunset Carson, Peggy Stewart.

726. SUPERFLY
A Harlem drug dealer is featured in these darkly comic adventures.
SUPERFLY (Warner Brothers, 1972) d Gordon Parks Jr., s Ron O'Neal.
SUPERFLY T.N.T. (Paramount, 1973) d Ron O'Neal, s Ron O'Neal, Roscoe Lee Browne.

727. SUPERGIRLS
These are adult films.
SUPERGIRLS DO GENERAL HOSPITAL (VCA, 1985) d Jackson St. Louis, s Raven, Ginger Lynn.
SUPERGIRLS DO THE NAVY (VCA, 1985) s Kristara Barrington.

728. SUPERMAN
The pictures are based on a DC comic book character, an outer space hero who came to Earth from Krypton in 1938. The original tales were written and drawn by Jerry Siegel and Joe Shuster. Conscientious about his superpowers, the hero disguises himself as a reporter by day, working at *The Daily Planet* with boss Perry White, fellow reporter Lois Lane and sidekick Jimmy Olson.
SUPERMAN (Columbia, 1948) (fifteen-episode serial) d Spencer Bennett and Thomas Carr, s Kirk Alyn, Noel Neill.
ATOM MAN VS. SUPERMAN (Columbia, 1950) d Spencer Bennet, s Kirk Alyn, Noel Neill, Lyle Talbot.

SUPERMAN AND THE MOLE MEN (1951) d Lee Sholem, s George Reeves, Phyllis Coates.
SUPERMAN (Warner Brothers, 1978) d Richard Donner, s Christopher Reeve, Margot Kidder, Marlon Brando.
SUPERMAN II (Warner Brothers, 1980) d Richard Lester, s Christopher Reeve, Margot Kidder, Gene Hackman.
SUPERMAN III (Warner Brothers, 1983) d Richard Lester, s Christopher Reeve, Richard Pryor, Annette O'Toole.
SUPERGIRL (Tri-Star, 1984) d Jeannot Szwarc, s Helen Slater.
SUPERMAN IV: THE QUEST FOR PEACE (1987) d Sidney J. Furie, s Christopher Reeve, Gene Hackman, Jackie Cooper.

729. SWAMP THING
A DC comic book about a research scientist who has been transformed into a muck creature prompted the movies.
SWAMP THING (Embassy, 1982) d Wes Craven, s Louis Jourdan, Adrienne Barbeau.
THE RETURN OF SWAMP THING (Millimeter Films, 1989) d Jim Wynorski, s Louis Jourdan, Heather Locklear.

730. SWEDISH EROTICA
This is a long-running series of X-rated films, numbering nearly seventy, with varying casts and predictable subject matter. The titles, which began in 1978 from BMC, are simply numbered.

Annette Funicello was teamed with Frankie Avalon for a half dozen 1960s sand and surfing films including BEACH PARTY and BIKINI BEACH.

DRACULA, Bram Stoker's gothic vampire, is one of the most-filmed novels of all time. Frank Langella appears as the title character in 1979.

Were the Arabian Nights like this? Caroline Munro appears in exotic pose in THE GOLDEN VOYAGE OF SINBAD (1973).

In profile: the best remembered screen Sherlock Holmes, Basil Rathbone.

731. SWEEDIE
Silent comedy series featuring Wallace Beery as a Swedish maid. E. Mason Hopper directed many of the entries. The list may be incomplete.
SWEEDIE AND THE SWATTER (Essanay, 1914) s Wallace Beery.
SWEEDIE LEARNS TO SWIM (Essanay, 1914) s Wallace Beery.
SWEEDIE AT THE FAIR (Essanay, 1914) s Wallace Beery.
COUNTESS SWEEDIE (Essanay, 1914) s Wallace Beery.
SWEEDIE'S SUICIDE (Essanay, 1915) s Wallace Beery.
SWEEDIE AND HER DOG (Essanay, 1915) s Wallace Beery.
SWEEDIE'S HOPELESS LOVE (Essanay, 1915) s Wallace Beery.
SWEEDIE GOES TO COLLEGE (Essanay, 1915) s Wallace Beery, Gloria Swanson.
SWEEDIE IN VAUDEVILLE (Essanay, 1915) s Wallace Beery.

732. SWEENEY
From the TV series, Flying Squad Inspector Regan investigates crime.
SWEENEY (Euston Films, 1977) d David Wickes, s John Thaw, Dennis Waterman.
SWEENEY 2 (Euston Films, 1978) d Tom Clegg, s John Thaw, Dennis Waterman, Denholm Elliott.

733. SWITCH HITTERS
These are X-rated pictures.
SWITCH HITTERS (Intropics, 1987) s Stacey Donovan, Randy West.
SWITCH HITTERS II (Intropics, 1987) s Nina Hartley, Big Jim Bentley.
SWITCH HITTERS III (Intropics, 1988) s Samantha Strong, Mike Horner.

734. TABOO
A married couple explores various sexual avenues in the first entry in this X-rated series.
TABOO (VCX, 1980) d Kirdy Stevens, s Kay Parker.
TABOO II (Visual Entertainment, 1983) d Kirdy Stevens, s Kay Parker, Eric Edwards.
TABOO III: THE FINAL CHAPTER (Standard Video, 1985) d Kirdy Stevens, s Kay Parker, Jerry Butler.
TABOO IV: THE YOUNGER GENERATION (Standard Video, 1985) d Kirdy Stevens, s Ginger Lynn, Jamie Gillis.

735. TABOO, AMERICAN STYLE
The X-rated soap opera depict sexual misadventures in a millionaire household.
TABOO AMERICAN STYLE, PART 1: THE RUTHLESS BEGINNING (VCA, 1985) d Henri Pachard, s Raven, Paul Thomas, Taija Rae.
TABOO AMERICAN STYLE, PART 2: THE STORY CONTINUES (VCA, 1985) d Henri Pachard, s Raven, Paul Thomas, Taija Rae.
TABOO AMERICAN STYLE, PART 3: NINA BECOMES AN ACTRESS (VCA, 1985) d Henri Pachard, s Raven, Paul Thomas, Taija Rae.
TABOO AMERICAN STYLE, PART 4: THE EXCITING CONCLUSION (VCA, 1985) d Henri Pachard, s Raven, Paul Thomas, Taija Rae.

736. TAILSPIN TOMMY
The newspaper comic strip air adventurer first appeared in 1928 as written by Glen Chaffin and drawn by Hal Forrest. These are cinematic versions.
TAILSPIN TOMMY (Universal, 1934) (12-episode serial) d Louis Friedlander, s Maurice Murphy, Patricia Farr, Noah Beery Jr.
TAILSPIN TOMMY IN THE GREAT AIR MYSTERY (Universal, 1935) d Ray Taylor, s Clark Williams, Noah Beery Jr., Jean Rogers.

737. TAKIN' IT OFF
These R-rated farces involve exotic dancers.
TAKIN' IT OFF (Vestron, 1984) d Ed Hansen, s Kitten Natividad.
TAKING IT ALL OFF (Vestron, 1987) d Ed Hansen, s Kitten Natividad.

738. TALES FROM THE CRYPT
The episodic horror films are reminiscent of 1950s EC comic books.
TALES FROM THE CRYPT (Amicus/Metromedia Producers, 1972) d Freddie Francis, s Ralph Richardson, Geoffrey Bayldon.
VAULT OF HORROR (Amicus/Metromedia Producers, 1973) [aka FURTHER TALES FROM THE CRYPT] d Roy Ward Baker, s Daniel Massey, Anna Massey.

739. TALK DIRTY TO ME
This is an X-rated series. In the first picture, the main character brags that he can have any woman jumping into the sack with him within three days. In the

sixth entry, a radio talk show host -- a sex therapist -- hears listeners' fantasies.
TALK DIRTY TO ME (Caballero, 1980) d Anthony Spinelli, s Richard Pacheco, Juliet Anderson.
TALK DIRTY TO ME II (Caballero, 1983) d Tim McDonald, s John Leslie, Bridgett Monet.
TALK DIRTY TO ME, PART III (Dreamland Video, 1984) d Ned Morehead, s Traci Lords, John Leslie.
TALK DIRTY TO ME ONE IV (Dreamland, 1986) d Ned Morehead, s John Leslie, Taija Rae.
TALK DIRTY TO ME PART V (Dreamland, 1987) s Tracey Adams, John Leslie.
TALK DIRTY TO ME PART 6 (Dreamland, 1989) s Tracey Adams, Shanna McCullough.

740. TALL BLOND MAN WITH ONE BLACK SHOE, THE
In these comedies, a tall blond man is mistaken for a spy with a death warrant on his head.
THE TALL BLOND MAN WITH ONE BLACK SHOE (1972) d Yves Roberts, s Pierre Richard, Bernard Biler, Mirelle Darc.
THE RETURN OF THE TALL BLOND MAN WITH ONE BLACK SHOE (1974) d Yves Robert, s Pierre Richard, Mirelle Darc.
THE MAN WITH ONE RED SHOE (20th Century-Fox, 1985) d Stan Dragoti, s Tom Hanks, Dabney Coleman.

741. TAMMY
A teenage girl finds romance. The movies are based on Cid Ricketts Sumer's novels *Tammy Out of Time* and *Tammy Tell Me True*.
TAMMY AND THE BACHELOR (Universal, 1957) d Joseph Pevney, s Debbie Reynolds, Walter Brennan, Leslie Nielsen.
TAMMY TELL ME TRUE (Universal, 1961) d Harry Keller, s Sandra Dee, John Gavin.
TAMMY AND THE DOCTOR (Universal, 1963) d Harry Keller, s Sandra Dee, Peter Fonda.
TAMMY AND THE MILLIONAIRE (Universal, 1967) d Sidney Miller, Ezra Stone and Leslie Goodwins, s Debbie Watson, Frank McGrath, Denver Pyle.

742. TARZAN OF THE APES
Edgar Rice Burroughs wrote twenty-eight books about the jungle lord. American and British films only are listed. NATURE IN THE WRONG (1932) starring Charlie Chase and TARZOON, SHAME OF THE JUNGLE (1975), animated with the voice of Johnny Weismuller Jr., were parodies; TARZAN AND BOY (1955), TARZ AND JANE AND BOY AND CHEETA (1975) and TARZAN AND THE VALLEY OF LUST (1976) are adult films. There were also Tarzan pictures made in India, Czechoslovakia, Germany, Singapore, Brazil, Spain, Italy, Jamaica.

TARZAN OF THE APES (1918) d Scott Sidney, s Elmo Lincoln, Enid Markey.
THE ROMANCE OF TARZAN (1918) s Elmo Lincoln.
THE REVENGE OF TARZAN (1920) s Gene Pollar.
THE SON OF TARZAN (1920) s P. Dempsey Tabler.
THE ADVENTURES OF TARZAN (1921) s Elmo Lincoln.
TARZAN AND THE GOLDEN LION (1927) s James Pierce.
TARZAN THE MIGHTY (1928) (serial) s Frank Merrill.
TARZAN THE TIGER (Universal, 1929) (10-episode serial) d Henry McRae, s Frank Merrill, Natalie Kingston, Lillian Worth.
TARZAN THE APE MAN (MGM, 1932) d Edward S. Van Dyke, s Johnny Weismuller, Maureen O'Sullivan.
TARZAN THE FEARLESS (Principal, 1933) (fifteen chapters) d Robert F. Hill, s Buster Crabbe, Jaqueline Wells.
TARZAN AND HIS MATE (MGM, 1934) d Cedric Gibbon and Jack Conway, s Johnny Weismuller, Maureen O'Sullivan.
THE NEW ADVENTURES OF TARZAN (Tarzan Pictures, 1935) (twelve episodes) [aka TARZAN IN GUATEMALA and TARZAN AND THE GREEN GODDESS] d Edward Kull and W.F. McGaugh, s Herman Brix, Ula Holt, Frank Baker.
TARZAN ESCAPES (MGM, 1936) d Richard Thorpe, s Johnny Weismuller, Maureen O'Sullivan.
TARZAN'S REVENGE (20th Century-Fox, 1938) d Ross Lederman, s Glenn Morris, Eleanor Holm.
TARZAN FINDS A SON! (MGM, 1939) d Richard Thorpe, s Johnny Weismuller, Maureen O'Sullivan, Johnny Sheffield.
TARZAN'S SECRET TREASURE (MGM, 1941) d Richard Thorpe, s Johnny Weismuller, Maureen O'Sullivan, Johnny Sheffield.
TARZAN'S NEW YORK ADVENTURE (MGM, 1942) d Richard Thorpe, s Johnny Weismuller, Maureen O'Sullivan, Johnny Sheffield.
TARZAN TRIUMPHS (RKO, 1943) d William Thiele, s Johnny Weismuller.
TARZAN'S DESERT MYSTERY (RKO, 1943) d William Thiele, s Johnny Weismuller.
TARZAN AND THE AMAZONS (RKO, 1945) s Johnny Weismuller, Nancy Kelly.
TARZAN AND THE LEOPARD WOMEN (RKO, 1946) d Kurt Neumann, s Johnny Weismuller, Brenda Joyce, Johnny Sheffield.
TARZAN AND THE HUNTRESS (RKO, 1947) d Kurt Neumann, s Johnny Weismuller, Brenda Joyce, Johnny Sheffield.
TARZAN AND THE MERMAIDS (RKO, 1948) d Robert Florey, s Johnny Weismuller, Brenda Joyce, Linda Christian.
TARZAN'S FIGHT FOR LIFE (RKO, 1948) d H. Bruce Humberstone, s Gordon Scott, Eve Brent.
TARZAN'S MAGIC FOUNTAIN (RKO, 1949) d Lee Sholem, s Lex Barker, Brenda Joyce.
TARZAN AND THE SLAVE GIRL (RKO, 1950) d Lee Sholem, s Lex Barker, Vanessa Brown.

TARZAN'S PERIL (RKO, 1951) d Byron Haskin, s Lex Barker, Virginia Huston.
TARZAN'S SAVAGE FURY (RKO, 1952) d Cyril Endfield, s Lex Barker, Dorothy Hart.
TARZAN AND THE SHE-DEVIL (RKO, 1953) d Kurt Neumann, s Lex Barker, Joyce MacKenzie.
TARZAN'S HIDDEN JUNGLE (RKO, 1955) d Harold Schuster, s Gordon Scott, Vera Miles.
TARZAN AND THE LOST SAFARI (Loew's, 1957) d H. Bruce Humberstone, s Gordon Scott, Yolande Donlan.
TARZAN'S FIGHT FOR LIFE (Sol Lesser, 1958) d H. Bruce Humberstone, s Gordon Scott.
TARZAN AND THE TRAPPERS (1958) d H. Bruce Humberstone, s Gordon Scott, Eve Brent.
TARZAN'S GREATEST ADVENTURE (Paramount, 1959) d John Guillermin, s Gordon Scott.
TARZAN THE APE MAN (MGM, 1959) d Joseph M. Newman, s Denny Miller, Joanna Barnes.
TARZAN THE MAGNIFICENT (Paramount, 1960) d Robert Day, s Gordon Scott, Jock Mahoney.
TARZAN GOES TO INDIA (MGM, 1962) d John Guillermin, s Jock Mahoney.
TARZAN'S THREE CHALLENGES (MGM, 1963) d Robert Day, s Jock Mahoney.
TARZAN AND JANE REGAINED SORT OF... (1964) d Andy Warhol, s Taylor Mead.
TARZAN AND THE VALLEY OF GOLD (American International, 1967) d Robert Day, s Mike Henry.
TARZAN AND THE GREAT RIVER (Paramount, 1967) d Robert Day, s Mike Henry.
TARZAN AND THE JUNGLE BOY (Paramount, 1968) d Robert Gordon, s Mike Henry.
TARZAN'S JUNGLE REBELLION (1970) d William Witney, s Ron Ely.
TARZAN'S DEADLY SILENCE (National General, 1970) d Robert L. Friend, s Ron Ely.
TARZ & JANE & BOY & CHEETA (Fine Brothers/Ded Films, 1976) d Hans Johnson.
TARZAN THE APEMAN (MGM/United Artists, 1981) d John Derek, s Bo Derek, Miles O'Keefe.
GREYSTOKE: THE LEGEND OF TARZAN, LORD OF THE APES (Warner Brothers, 1984) d Hugh Hudson, s Christopher Lambert, Ralph Richardson, Ian Holm, James Fox, Cheryl Campbell.
TARZAN IN MANHATTAN (TV movie, 1989) d Michael Schultz, s Joe Lara, Kim Crosby.

743. TAXI BOYS, THE
Hal Roach teamed Billy Gilbert and Ben Blue in effort to find another Laurel and Hardy. The listing is incomplete.

324 MOTION PICTURE SERIES & SEQUELS

WHAT PRICE TAXI
STRANGE INNERTUBE
WRECKETY WRECK
CALL HER SAUSAGE

744. TEENAGE FANTASIES
X-rated, as you might expect.
TEENAGE FANTASIES (VCX, 1974) s Renee Bond.
TEENAGE FANTASIES PART II (Arrow, 1974) s John Holmes, Renee Bond.

745. TEEN WOLF
A teenager's lycanthropic tendencies make him a hit at school. The movie inspired an animated children's television series. The second film below follows the similar adventures of a cousin.
TEEN WOLF (Atlantic, 1985) d Rod Daniel, s Michael J. Fox, James
    Hampton.
TEEN WOLF TOO (Atlantic, 1987) d Christopher Leitch, s Jason Bateman,
    Kim Darby.

745A. TEN NIGHTS IN A BARROOM
This dramatic, silent film series takes its inspiration from T.S. Arthur's 1854 temperance novel *Ten Nights in a Bar Room and What I Saw There*.
TEN NIGHTS IN A BARROOM: DEATH OF LITTLE MAY (American
    Mutoscope & Biograph, 1903)
TEN NIGHTS IN A BARROOM: DEATH OF SLADE (American Mutoscope
    & Biograph, 1903)
TEN NIGHTS IN A BARROOM: THE FATAL BLOW (American Mutoscope
    & Biograph, 1903)
TEN NIGHTS IN A BARROOM: MURDER OF WILLIE (American
    Mutoscope & Biograph, 1903)
TEN NIGHTS IN A BARROOM: VISION OF MARY (American Mutoscope
    & Biograph, 1903)

746. TEXAS CHAINSAW MASSACRE, THE
The unrelenting, gorey, darkly comic horror films are about a rampant chainsaw killer.
THE TEXAS CHAINSAW MASSACRE (Bryanston, 1974) d Tobe Hooper, s
    Marilyn Burns, Gunner Hansen.
THE TEXAS CHAINSAW MASSACRE 2 (Cannon, 1986) d Tobe Hooper, s
    Dennis Hooper, Caroline Williams.
LEATHERFACE: THE TEXAS CHAINSAW MASSACRE 3 (New Line,
    1989) d Jeff Burr, s Kate Hodge, William Butler.

747. TEXAS RANGERS, THE
The B Western series spotlights the famous Lone Star State police organization.

THE UNKNOWN RANGER (Columbia, 1936) d Spencer G. Bennett, s Bob Allen, Martha Tibbetts.
RIO GRANDE RANGER (Columbia, 1936) d Spencer G. Bennett, s Bob Allen, Iris Meredith.
RANGER COURAGE (Columbia, 1937) d Spencer G. Bennett, s Bob Allen, Martha Tibbetts.
LAW OF THE RANGER (Columbia, 1937) d Spencer G. Bennett, s Bob Allen, Elaine Shepard.
RECKLESS RANGER (Columbia, 1937) d Spencer G. Bennett, s Bob Allen, Louise Small.
THE RANGERS STEP IN (Columbia, 1937) d Spencer G. Bennett, s Bob Allen, Eleanor Stewart.

748. TEXAS RANGERS, THE
B Westerns.
THE RANGERS TAKE OVER (PRC, 1942) d Al Herman, s James Newill, Dave O'Brien, Guy Wilkerson, Iris Meredith.
BAD MEN OF THUNDER GAP (PRC, 1943) d Al Herman, s James Newill, Dave O'Brien, Guy Wilkerson, Janet Shaw.
WEST OF TEXAS (PRC, 1943) [aka SHOOTIN' IRONS] d Oliver Drake, s James Newill, Dave O'Brien, Guy Wilkerson, Frances Gladwin.
BORDER BUCKAROOS (PRC, 1943) d Oliver Drake, s James Newill, Dave O'Brien, Guy Wilkerson, Christine McIntyre.
FIGHTING VALLEY (PRC, 1943) d Oliver Drake, s James Newill, Dave O'Brien, Guy Wilkerson, Patti McCarty.
TRAIL OF TERROR (PRC, 1943) d Oliver Drake, s James Newill, Dave O'Brien, Guy Wilkerson, Patricia Knox.
RETURN OF THE RANGERS (PRC, 1943) d Elmer Clifton, s James Newill, Dave O'Brien, Guy Wilkerson, Nell O'Day.
BOSS OF RAWHIDE (PRC, 1943) d Elmer Clifton, s James Newill, Dave O'Brien, Guy Wilkerson, Nell O'Day.
GUNSMOKE MESA (PRC, 1944) d Harry Fraser, s James Newill, Dave O'Brien, Guy Wilkerson, Patti McCarty.
OUTLAW ROUNDUP (PRC, 1944) d Harry Fraser, s James Newill, Dave O'Brien, Guy Wilkerson, Helen Chapman.
GUNS OF THE LAW (PRC, 1944) d Elmer Clifton, s James Newill, Dave O'Brien, Guy Wilkerson.
THE PINTO BANDIT (PRC, 1944) d Elmer Clifton s James Newill, Dave O'Brien, Guy Wilkerson, Mady Lawrence.
SPOOK TOWN (PRC, 1944) d Elmer Clifton, s James Newill, Dave O'Brien, Guy Wilkerson, Mady Lawrence.
BRAND OF THE DEVIL (PRC, 1944) d Harry Fraser, s James Newill, Dave O'Brien, Guy Wilkerson, Ellen Hall.
GANGSTERS OF THE FRONTIER (PRC, 1944) d Elmer Clifton, s Tex Ritter, Dave O'Brien, Guy Wilkerson, Patti McCarty.
DEAD OR ALIVE (PRC, 1944) d Elmer Clifton, s Tex Ritter, Dave O'Brien, Guy Wilkerson, Marjorie Clements.

THE WHISPERING SKULL (PRC, 1944) s Tex Ritter, Dave O'Brien, Guy Wilkerson.
MARKED FOR MURDER (PRC, 1945) d Elmer Clifton, s Tex Ritter, Dave O'Brien, Guy Wilkerson, Marilyn McConnell.
ENEMY OF THE LAW (PRC, 1945) d Harry Fraser, s Tex Ritter, Dave O'Brien, Guy Wilkerson, Kay Hughes.
THREE IN THE SADDLE (PRC, 1945) d Harry Fraser, s Tex Ritter, Dave O'Brien, Guy Wilkerson, Lorraine Miller.
FRONTIER FUGITIVES (PRC, 1945) d Harry Fraser, s Tex Ritter, Dave O'Brien, Guy Wilkerson, Lorraine Miller.
FLAMING BULLETS (PRC, 1945) d Harry Fraser, s Tex Ritter, Dave O'Brien, Guy Wilkerson, Patricia Knox.

749. *TEX RITTER AND ARKANSAS SLIM ANDREWS*
B Westerns
RHYTHM OF THE RIO GRANDE (Monogram, 1940) d Al Herman, s Tex Ritter, Arkansas Slim Andrews, Suzan Dale.
PALS OF THE SILVER SAGE (Monogram, 1940) d Al Herman, s Tex Ritter, Arkansas Slim Andrews, Clarissa Curtis.
COWBOY FROM SUNDOWN (Monogram, 1940) d Spencer Bennett, s Tex Ritter, Arkansas Slim Andrews, Roscoe Ates, Patsy Moran.
THE GOLDEN TRAIL (Monogram, 1940) d Al Herman, s Tex Ritter, Arkansas Slim Andrews, Patsy Moran
RAINBOW OVER THE RANGE (Monogram, 1940) d Al Herman, s Tex Ritter, Arkansas Slim Andrews, Dorothy Fay.
ARIZONA FRONTIER (Monogram, 1940) d Al Herman, s Tex Ritter, Arkansas Slim Andrews, Evelyn Finley.
TAKE ME BACK TO OKLAHOMA (Monogram, 1940) d Al Herman, s Tex Ritter, Arkansas Slim Andrews.
ROLLIN' HOME TO TEXAS (Monogram, 1940) d Al Herman, s Tex Ritter, Arkansas Slim Andrews, Virginia Carpenter.
RIDIN' THE CHEROKEE TRAIL (Monogram, 1941) d Spencer G. Bennett, s Tex Ritter, Arkansas Slim Andrews.
THE PIONEERS (Monogram, 1941) d Al Herman, s Tex Ritter, Arkansas Slim Andrews, Wanda McKay.

750. *TEX RITTER AND SNUB POLLARD*
HEADIN' FOR THE RIO GRANDE (Grand National, 1936) d R.N. Bradbury, s Tex Ritter, Syd Saylor, Snub Pollard, Eleanor Stewart.
HITTIN' THE TRAIL (Grand National, 1937) d R.N. Bradbury, s Tex Ritter, Snub Pollard, Heber Snow.
RIDERS OF THE ROCKIES (Grand National, 1937) d R.N. Bradbury, s Tex Ritter, Snub Pollard, Hank Worden, Louise Stanley.
TEX RIDES WITH THE BOY SCOUTS (Grand National, 1938) d Ray Taylor, s Tex Ritter, Snub Pollard, Marjorie Reynolds.
FRONTIER TOWN (Grand National, 1938) d Ray Taylor, s Tex Ritter, Snub Pollard, Hank Worden, Anne Evers.

ROLLIN' PLAINS (Grand National, 1938) d Al Herman, s Tex Ritter, Snub Pollard, Harriet Bennett.
UTAH TRAIL (Grand National, 1938) d Al Herman, s Tex Ritter, Snub Pollard, Horace Murphy, Adele Pearce.
STARLIGHT OVER TEXAS (Monogram, 1938) d Al Herman, s Tex Ritter, Horace Murphy, Snub Pollard, Carmen Laroux.
WHERE THE BUFALO ROAM (Monogram, 1938) d Al Herman, s Tex Ritter, Horace Murphy, Snub Pollard, Dorothy Short.
SONG OF THE BUCKAROO (Monogram, 1939) d Al Herman, s Tex Ritter, Horace Murphy, Snub Pollard, Jinx Falkenberg, Mary Ruth.

751. THELMA TODD AND ZASU PITTS
Comic short subjects pairing gorgeous, refined Thelma Todd with first ditsy Zasu Pitts and later (see next entry) wisacre Patsy Kelly were made by the Hal Roach studio. As the series wound down, Todd was succeeded by Pert Kelton then Lyda Roberti.
LET'S DO THINGS (Roach MGM, 1931) d Hal Roach, s Thelma Todd, Zasu Pitts, George Byron.
CATCH AS CATCH CAN (Roach MGM, 1931) d Marshall Neilan, s Thelma Todd, Zasu Pitts, Guinn "Big Boy" Williams.
THE PAJAMA PARTY (Roach MGM, 1931) d Hal Roach, s Thelma Todd, Zasu Pitts.
WAR MAMA (Roach MGM, 1931) d Marshall Neilan, s Thelma Todd, Zasu Pitts, Charles Judels.
ON THE LOOSE (Roach MGM, 1931) d Hal Roach, s Thelma Todd, Zasu Pitts, Stan Laurel, Oliver Hardy.
SEAL SKINS (Roach MGM, 1932) d Gil Pratt, s Thelma Todd, Zasu Pitts, Billy Gilbert.
RED NOSES (Roach MGM, 1932) d James W. Norne, s Thelma Todd, Zasu Pitts, Billy Gilbert.
STRICTLY UNRELIABLE (Roach MGM, 1932) d George Marshall, s Thelma Todd, Zasu Pitts, Billy Gilbert.
THE OLD BULL (Roach MGM, 1932) d George Marshall, s Thelma Todd, Zasu Pitts, Otto Fries.
SHOW BUSINESS (Roach MGM, 1932) d Jules White, s Thelma Todd, Zasu Pitts, Anita Garvin.
ALUM AND EVE (Roach MGM, 1932) d George Marshall, s Thelma Todd, Zasu Pitts.
SNEAK EASILY (Roach MGM, 1932) d Gus Meins, s Thelma Todd, Zasu Pitts, Robert Burns.
ASLEEP IN THE FLEET (Roach MGM, 1933) d Gus Meins, s Thelma Todd, Zasu Pitts, Billy Gilbert.
MAIDS A LA MODE (Roach MGM, 1933) d Gus Meins, s Thelma Todd, Zasu Pitts, Billy Gilbert.
THE BARGAIN OF THE CENTURY (Roach MGM, 1933) d Charley Chase, s Thelma Todd, Zasu Pitts.

752. THELMA TODD AND PATSY KELLY

BEAUTY AND THE BUS (Roach MGM 1933) d Gus Meins, s Thelma Todd, Patsy Kelly, Don Barclay.
BACKS TO NATURE (Roach MGM, 1933) d Gus Meins, s Thelma Todd, Patsy Kelly, Don Barclay.
AIR FRIGHT (Roach MGM, 1933) d Gus Meins, s Thelma Todd, Patsy Kelly, Don Barclay.
BABES IN THE GOODS (Roach MGM, 1934) d Gus Meins, s Thelma Todd, Patsy Kelly, Jack Barty.
SOUP AND FISH (Roach MGM, 1934) d Gus Meins, s Thelma Todd, Patsy Kelly, Gladys Gale.
MAID IN HOLLYWOOD (Roach MGM, 1934) d Gus Meins, s Thelma Todd, Patsy Kelly, Eddie Foy Jr.
I'LL BE SUING YOU (Roach MGM, 1934) d Gus Meins, s Thelma Todd, Patsy Kelly, Eddie Foy Jr.
THREE CHUMPS AHEAD (Roach MGM, 1934) d Gus Meins, s Thelma Todd, Patsy Kelly, Benny Baker.
ONE HORSE FARMERS (Roach MGM, 1934) d Gus Meins, s Thelma Todd, Patsy Kelly, James C. Morton.
OPENED BY MISTAKE (Roach MGM, 1934) d James Parrott, s Thelma Todd, Patsy Kelly.
DONE IN OIL (Roach MGM, 1934) d Gus Meins, s Thelma Todd, Patsy Kelly.
BUM VOYAGE (Roach MGM, 1934) d Nick Grinde, s Thelma Todd, Patsy Kelly.
TREASURE BLUES (Roach MGM, 1935) d James Parrott, s Thelma Todd, Patsy Kelly.
SING, SISTER, SING (Roach MGM, 1935) d James Parrott, s Thelma Todd, Patsy Kelly.
THE TIN MAN (Roach MGM, 1935) d James Parrott, s Thelma Todd, Patsy Kelly.
THE MISSES STOOGE (Roach MGM, 1935) d James Parrott, s Thelma Todd, Patsy Kelly.
SLIGHTLY STATIC (Roach MGM, 1935) d William Terhune, s Thelma Todd, Patsy Kelly.
TWIN TRIPLETS (Roach MGM, 1935) d William Terhune, s Thelma Todd, Patsy Kelly.
HOT MONEY (Roach MGM, 1935) d James W. Horne, s Thelma Todd, Patsy Kelly.
TOP FLAT (Roach MGM, 1935) d William Terhune and Jack Jevne, s Thelma Todd, Patsy Kelly.
ALL-AMERICAN TOOTHACHE (Roach MGM, 1936) d Gus Meins, s Thelma Todd, Patsy Kelly.
PAN HANDLERS (Roach MGM, 1936) d William Terhune, s Pert Kelton, Patsy Kelly.
AT SEA ASHORE (Roach MGM, 1936) d William Terhune, s Patsy Kelly, Lyda Roberti.

HILL TILLIES (Roach MGM, 1936) d Gus Meins, s Patsy Kelly, Lyda Roberti.

753. THIN MAN, THE
Dashiell Hammett's 1934 novel about Nick and Nora Charles, a stylish private detective and his socialite wife, inspired a movie series. Their dog, a perennial crossword puzzle clue, is Asta.
THE THIN MAN (MGM, 1934) d W.S. Van Dyke, s William Powell, Myrna Loy.
AFTER THE THIN MAN (MGM, 1935) d W.S. Van Dyke, s William Powell, Myrna Loy.
ANOTHER THIN MAN (MGM, 1939) d W.S. Van Dyke, s William Powell, Myrna Loy.
SHADOW OF THE THIN MAN (MGM, 1941) d W.S. Van Dyke, s William Powell, Myrna Loy.
THE THIN MAN GOES HOME (MGM, 1944) d Richard Thorpe, s William Powell, Myrna Loy.
SONG OF THE THIN MAN (MGM, 1947) d Edward Buzzell, s William Powell, Myrna Loy.

754. THOMAS EDISON
The American inventor (1847-1931) of a stock ticker tape, light bulb and motion picture projector is depicted in these pictures.
YOUNG TOM EDISON (MGM, 1940) d Norman Taurog, s Mickey Rooney, Fay Bainter.
EDISON THE MAN (MGM, 1940) d Clarence Brown, s Spencer Tracy, Rita Johnson.
TOM EDISON - THE BOY WHO LIT UP THE WORLD (1983) d Henning Schellerup, s David Huffman, Adam Arkin.

755. THREE COCKEYED SAILORS
In the first film, British tars stranded in South America, slightly inebriated, mistakenly board a German battleship and ultimately capture it. In the second picture, pair of sailors and a Wren are transported back in time.
THREE COCKEYED SAILORS (Ealing, 1940) [aka SAILORS THREE] d Walter Forde, s Tommy Trinder, Michael Wilding, Claude Hulbert.
FIDDLERS THREE (Ealing, 1944) d Henry Watt, s Tommy Trinder, Sonnie Hale, Diana Wrecker.

756. THREE MESQUITEERS
William Colt MacDonald's Western novels about a trio of range pards Stony Brooke, Tucson Smith and Lullaby Joslin is the basis for a series of B pictures.
POWERSMOKE RANGE (RKO Radio, 1935) d Wallace Fox, s Harry Carey, Hoot Gibson, Guinn Williams, Tom Tyler.
THE THREE MESQUITEERS (Republic, 1936) d Ray Taylor, s Ray Corrigan, Bob Livingston, Syd Saylor.

GHOST TOWN GOLD (Republic, 1936) d Joseph Kane, s Bob Livingston, Ray Corrigan, Max Terhune.
ROARIN' LEAD (Republic, 1936) d Mack V. Wright and Sam Newfield, s Bob Livingston, Ray Corrigan, Max Terhune.
RIDERS OF THE WHISTLING SKULL (Republic, 1937) d Mack V. Wright, s Bob Livingston, Ray Corrigan, Max Terhune.
HIT THE SADDLE (Republic, 1937) d Mack V. Wright, s Bob Livingston, Ray Corrigan, Max Terhune.
GUNSMOKE RANCH (Republic, 1937), d Joseph Kane, s Bob Livingston, Ray Corrigan, Max Terhune.
COME ON COWBOYS (Republic, 1937) d Joseph Kane, s Bob Livingston, Ray Corrigan, Max Terhune.
RANGE DEFENDERS (Republic, 1937) d Mack V. Wright, s Bob Livingston, Ray Corrigan, Max Terhune.
HEART OF THE ROCKIES (Republic, 1937) d Joseph Kane, s Bob Livingston, Ray Corrigan, Max Terhune.
THE TRIGGER TRIO (Republic, 1937) d William Witney, s Bob Livingston, Ray Corrigan, Ralph Byrd.
WILD HORSE RODEO (Republic, 1938) d George Sherman, s Bob Livingston, Ray Corrigan, Max Terhune.
THE PURPLE VIGILANTES (Republic, 1938) d George Sherman, s Bob Livingston, Ray Corrigan, Max Terhune.
CALL THE MESQUITEERS (Republic, 1938) d John English, s Bob Livingston, Ray Corrigan, Max Terhune.
OUTLAWS OF SONORA (Republic, 1938) d George Sherman, s Bob Livingston, Ray Corrigan, Max Terhune.
RIDERS OF THE BLACK HILLS (Republic, 1938) d George Sherman, s Bob Livingston, Ray Corrigan, Max Terhune.
HEROES OF THE HILLS (Republic, 1938) d George Sherman, s Bob Livingston, Ray Corrigan, Max Terhune.
PALS OF THE SADDLE (Republic, 1938) d George Sherman, s John Wayne, Ray Corrigan, Max Terhune.
OVERLAND STAGE RAIDERS (Republic, 1938) d George Sherman, s John Wayne, Ray Corrigan, Max Terhune.
SANTA FE STAMPEDE (Republic, 1938) d George Sherman, s John Wayne, Ray Corrigan, Max Terhune.
RED RIVER RANGE (Republic, 1938) d George Sherman, s John Wayne, Ray Corrigan, Max Terhune.
THE NIGHT RIDERS (Republic, 1939) d George Sherman, s John Wayne, Ray Corrigan, Max Terhune.
THREE TEXAS STEERS (Republic, 1939) d George Sherman, s John Wayne, Ray Corrigan, Max Terhune.
WYOMING OUTLAW (Republic, 1939) d George Sherman, s John Wayne, Ray Corrigan, Raymond Hatton.
NEW FRONTIER (Republic, 1939) d George Sherman, s John Wayne, Ray Corrigan, Raymond Hatton.

THE KANSAS TERRORS (Republic, 1939) d George Sherman, s Robert Livingston, Raymond Hatton, Duncan Renaldo.
COWBOYS FROM TEXAS (Republic, 1939) d George Sherman, s Robert Livingston, Raymond Hatton, Duncan Renaldo.
HEROES OF THE SADDLE (Republic, 1940) d William Witney, s Robert Livingston, Raymond Hatton, Duncan Renaldo.
PIONEERS OF THE WEST (Republic, 1940) d William Witney, s Robert Livingston, Raymond Hatton, Duncan Renaldo.
COVERED WAGON DAYS (Republic, 1940) d Lester Orlebeck, s Robert Livingston, Raymond Hatton, Duncan Renaldo.
ROCKY MOUNTAIN RANGERS (Republic, 1940) d George Sherman, s Robert Livingston, Raymond Hatton, Duncan Renaldo.
OKLAHOMA RENEGADES (Republic, 1940) d Nate Watt, s Robert Livingston, Raymond Hatton, Duncan Renaldo.
UNDER TEXAS SKIES (Republic, 1940) d George Sherman, s Robert Livingston, Bob Steele, Rufe Davis.
THE TRAIL BLAZERS (Republic, 1940) d George Sherman, s Robert Livingston, Bob Steele, Rufe Davis.
LONE STAR RAIDERS (Republic, 1940) s George Sherman, s Robert Livingston, Bob Steele, Rufe Davis.
PRAIRIE PIONEERS (Republic, 1941) d Lester Orlebeck, s Robert Livingston, Bob Steele, Rufe Davis.
PALS OF THE PECOS (Republic, 1941) d Lester Orlebeck, s Robert Livingston, Bob Steele, Rufe Davis.
SADDLEMATES (Republic, 1941) d Lester Orlebeck, s Robert Livingston, Bob Steele, Rufe Davis.
GANGS OF SONORA (Republic, 1941) d John English, s Robert Livingston, Bob Steele, Rufe Davis.
OUTLAWS OF THE CHEROKEE TRAIL (Republic, 1941), d Les Orlebeck, s Bob Steele, Tom Tyler, Rufe Davis.
GAUCHOS OF EL DORADO (Republic, 1941) d Lester Orlebeck, s Bob Steele, Tom Tyler, Rufe Davis.
WEST OF CIMARRON (Republic, 1941) d Les Orlebeck, s Bob Steele, Tom Tyler, Rufe Davis.
CODE OF THE OUTLAW (Republic, 1942) d John English, s Bob Steele, Tom Tyler, Rufe Davis.
RAIDERS OF THE RANGE (Republic, 1942) d John English, s Bob Steele, Tom Tyler, Rufe Davis.
WESTWARD, HO (Republic, 1942) d John English, s Bob Steele, Tom Tyler, Rufe Davis.
THE PHANTOM PLAINSMAN (Republic, 1942) d John English, s Bob Steele, Tom Tyler, Rufe Davis.
SHADOWS ON THE SAGE (Republic, 1942) d John English, s Bob Steele, Tom Tyler, Jimmie Dodd.
VALLEY OF HUNTED MEN (Republic, 1942) d John English, s Bob Steele, Tom Tyler, Jimmie Dodd.

THUNDERING TRAILS (Republic, 1943) d John English, s Bob Steele, Tom Tyler, Jimmie Dodd.
THE BLOCKED TRAIL (Republic, 1943) d Elmer Clifton, s Bob Steele, Tom Tyler, Jimmie Dodd.
SANTA FE SCOUTS (Republic, 1943) d Howard Bretherton, s Bob Steele, Tom Tyler, Jimmie Dodd.
RIDERS OF THE RIO GRANDE (Republic, 1943) d Albert De Mond, s Bob Steele, Tom Tyler, Jimmie Dodd.

757. THREE MUSKETEERS, THE
Alexander Dumas senior (1802-1870) wrote some 300 books, including swashbucklers about Athos, Porthos, Aramis and D'Artagnan.
THE THREE MUSKETEERS (Fairbanks/United Artists, 1921) d Fred Niblo, s Douglas Fairbanks, Leon Barry, George Siegmann, Eugene Pallette.
THE IRON MASK (United Artists, 1929) d Allan Dwan, s Douglas Fairbanks, Belle Bennett.
THE THREE MUSKETEERS (RKO, 1935) d Rowland V. Lee, s Walter Abel, Paul Lukas.
THE THREE MUSKETEERS (20th Century-Fox, 1939) d Allan Dwan, s Don Ameche, Ritz Brothers.
THE MAN IN THE IRON MASK (United Artists, 1939) d James Whale, s Louis Hayward, Joan Bennett.
THE SINGING MUSKETEER (20th Century-Fox, 1944)
THE THREE MUSKETEERS (MGM, 1948) d George Sidney, s Lana Turner, Gene Kelly, June Allyson, Van Heflin.
THE LADY IN THE IRON MASK (20th Century-Fox, 1952)
THE THREE MUSKETEERS (20th Century-Fox, 1974) d Richard Lester, s Oliver Reed, Raquel Welch.
THE FOUR MUSKETEERS (20th Century-Fox, 1975) d Richard Lester, s Oliver Reed, Raquel Welch, Richard Chamberlain.
THE MAN IN THE IRON MASK (ITC Entertainment, 1977) (NBC-TV movie) d Mike Newell, s Richard Chamberlain, Patrick McGoohan, Jenny Agutter.
THE RETURN OF THE MUSKETEERS (Universal, 1989) d Richard Lester, s Richard Chamberlain, Michael York, C. Thomas Howell.

758. THREE RIVERS TRILOGY
The films are based on James Oliver Curwood's Canadian Mounted Police novels.
RIVER'S END (First National, 1920) d Marshall Neillan, s Lewis Stone, Jane Novak.
THE VALLEY OF SILENT MEN (Cosmpolitan/Paramount, 1922) d Frank Borzage, s Alma Rubens, Lew Cody.
THE FLAMING FOREST (Cosmopolitan, 1926) d Reginald Barker, s Antonio Moreno, Renee Adoree.
THE RIVER'S END (Warner Brothers, 1931) d Michael Curtiz, s Charles Bickford, Evelyn Knapp.

THE RIVER'S END (Warner Brothers, 1940) [aka DOUBLE IDENTITY] d Ray Enright, s Dennis Morgan, Elizabeth Earl.

759. THREE SMART GIRLS
The Craig sisters, Penny, Joan and Kay, try to break up their divorced father's new romance, in this series opener.
THREE SMART GIRLS (Universal, 1936) d Henry Koster, s Deanna Durbin, Nan Grey, Barbara Read, Binnie Barnes, Alice Brady, Ray Milland.
THREE SMART GIRLS GROW UP (Universal, 1939) d Henry Koster, s Deanna Durbin, Nan Grey, Helen Parrish, Charles Winninger.
HERS TO HOLD (Universal, 1943) d Frank Ryan, s Deanna Durbin, Joseph Cotton.

760. THREE STOOGES, THE
Moe Howard, Larry Fine and variously Jerry "Curly" Howard, Shemp Howard, Joe Besser and Joe DeRita were featured in a lengthy series of slapstick comedy shorts, later feature films.
WOMAN HATERS (Columbia, 1934) d Archie Gottler, s Moe Howard, Larry Fine, Jerry "Curly" Howard.
PUNCH DRUNKS (Columbia, 1934) d Lou Breslow, s Moe Howard, Larry Fine, Jerry "Curly" Howard.
MEN IN BLACK (Columbia, 1934) d Raymond McCarey, s Moe Howard, Larry Fine, Jerry "Curly" Howard.
THREE LITTLE PIGSKINS (Columbia, 1934) d Raymond McCarey, s Moe Howard, Larry Fine, Jerry "Curly" Howard, Lucille Ball.
HORSES COLLARS (Columbia, 1935) d Clyde Bruckman, s Moe Howard, Larry Fine, Jerry "Curly" Howard.
RESTLESS KNIGHTS (Columbia, 1935) d Charles Lamont, s Moe Howard, Larry Fine, Jerry "Curly" Howard.
POP GOES THE EASEL (Columbia, 1935) d Del Lord, s Moe Howard, Larry Fine, Jerry "Curly" Howard, Leo White.
UNCIVIL WARRIORS (Columbia, 1935) d Del Lord, s Moe Howard, Larry Fine, Jerry "Curly" Howard.
PARDON MY SCOTCH (Columbia, 1935) d Del Lord, s Moe Howard, Larry Fine, Jerry "Curly" Howard.
HOI POLLOI (Columbia, 1935) d Del Lord, s Moe Howard, Larry Fine, Jerry "Curly" Howard.
THREE LITTLE BEERS (Columbia, 1935) d Del Lord, s Moe Howard, Larry Fine, Jerry "Curly" Howard.
ANTS IN THE PANTRY (Columbia, 1936) d Preston Black, s Moe Howard, Larry Fine, Jerry "Curly" Howard.
MOVIE MANIACS (Columbia, 1936) d Del Lord, s Moe Howard, Larry Fine, Jerry "Curly" Howard, Bud Jamison.
HALF-SHOT SHOOTERS (Columbia, 1936) d Preston Black, s Moe Howard, Larry Fine, Jerry "Curly" Howard, Vernon Dent.
DISORDER IN THE COURT (Columbia, 1936) d Preston Black, s Moe Howard, Larry Fine, Jerry "Curly" Howard.

A PAIN IN THE PULLMAN (Columbia, 1936) d Del Lord, s Moe Howard, Larry Fine, Jerry "Curly" Howard.
FALSE ALARMS (Columbia, 1936) d Del Lord, s Moe Howard, Larry Fine, Jerry "Curly" Howard.
WHOOPS I'M AN INDIAN (Columbia, 1936) d Del Lord, s Moe Howard, Larry Fine, Jerry "Curly" Howard, Bud Jamison.
SLIPPERY SILKS (Columbia, 1936) d Preston Black, s Moe Howard, Larry Fine, Jerry "Curly" Howard, Vernon Dent.
GRIPS, GRUNTS AND GROANS (Columbia, 1937) d Preston Black, s Moe Howard, Larry Fine, Jerry "Curly" Howard.
DIZZY DOCTORS (Columbia, 1937) d Del Lord, s Moe Howard, Larry Fine, Jerry "Curly" Howard.
THREE DUMB CLUCKS (Columbia, 1937) d Del Lord, s Moe Howard, Larry Fine, Jerry "Curly" Howard.
BACK TO THE WOODS (Columbia, 1937) d Preston Black, s Moe Howard, Larry Fine, Jerry "Curly" Howard.
GOOFS AND SADDLES (Columbia, 1937) d Del Lord, s Moe Howard, Larry Fine, Jerry "Curly" Howard.
CASH AND CARRY (Columbia, 1937) d Del Lord, s Moe Howard, Larry Fine, Jerry "Curly" Howard.
PLAYING THE PONIES (Columbia, 1937) d Charles Lamont, s Moe Howard, Larry Fine, Jerry "Curly" Howard.
THE SITTER-DOWNERS (Columbia, 1937) d Del Lord, s Moe Howard, Larry Fine, Jerry "Curly" Howard.
TERMITES OF 1938 (Columbia, 1938) d Del Lord, s Moe Howard, Larry Fine, Jerry "Curly" Howard.
WEE WEE, MONSIEUR (Columbia, 1938) d Del Lord, s Moe Howard, Larry Fine, Jerry "Curly" Howard, Bud Jamison.
TASSELS IN THE AIR (Columbia, 1938) d Charley Chase, s Moe Howard, Larry Fine, Jerry "Curly" Howard.
FLAT FOOT STOOGES (Columbia, 1938) d Charley Chase, s Moe Howard, Larry Fine, Jerry "Curly" Howard, Chester Conklin.
HEALTHY, WEALTHY AND DUMB (Columbia, 1938) d Del Lord, s Moe Howard, Larry Fine, Jerry "Curly" Howard.
VIOLENT IS THE WORD FOR CURLY (Columbia, 1938) d Charley Chase, s Moe Howard, Larry Fine, Jerry "Curly" Howard.
THREE MISSING LINKS (Columbia, 1938) d Jule White, s Moe Howard, Larry Fine, Jerry "Curly" Howard.
MUTTS TO YOU (Columbia, 1938) d Charley Chase, s Moe Howard, Larry Fine, Jerry "Curly" Howard, Bess Flowers.
THREE LITTLE SEW AND SEWS (Columbia, 1939) d Del Lord, s Moe Howard, Larry Fine, Jerry "Curly" Howard.
WE WANT OUR MUMMY (Columbia, 1939) d Del Lord, s Moe Howard, Larry Fine, Jerry "Curly" Howard.
A-DUCKING THEY DID GO (Columbia, 1939) d Del Lord, s Moe Howard, Larry Fine, Jerry "Curly" Howard.

YES, WE HAVE NO BONANZA (Columbia, 1939) d Del Lord, s Moe Howard, Larry Fine, Jerry "Curly" Howard.
SAVED BY THE BELLE (Columbia, 1939) d Charley Chase, s Moe Howard, Larry Fine, Jerry "Curly" Howard.
CALLING ALL CURS (Columbia, 1939) d Jules White, s Moe Howard, Larry Fine, Jerry "Curly" Howard.
OILY TO BED, OILY TO RISE (Columbia, 1939) d Jules White, s Moe Howard, Larry Fine, Jerry "Curly" Howard.
THREE SAPPY PEOPLE (Columbia, 1939) d Jules White, s Moe Howard, Larry Fine, Jerry "Curly" Howard.
YOU NAZTY SPY (Columbia, 1940) d Jules White, s Moe Howard, Larry Fine, Jerry "Curly" Howard, Dick Curtis, Don Beddoe.
ROCKIN' THROUGH THE ROCKIES (Columbia, 1940) d Jules White, s Moe Howard, Larry Fine, Jerry "Curly" Howard.
A-PLUMBING WE WILL GO (Columbia, 1940) d Del Lord, s Moe Howard, Larry Fine, Jerry "Curly" Howard.
NUTTY BUT NICE (Columbia, 1940) d Jules White, s Moe Howard, Larry Fine, Jerry "Curly" Howard.
HOW HIGH IS UP? (Columbia, 1940) d Del Lord, s Moe Howard, Larry Fine, Jerry "Curly" Howard.
FROM NURSE TO WORSE (Columbia, 1940) d Jules White, s Moe Howard, Larry Fine, Jerry "Curly" Howard.
NO CENSUS, NO FEELING (Columbia, 1940) d Del Lord, s Moe Howard, Larry Fine, Jerry "Curly" Howard.
CUCKOO CAVALIERS (Columbia, 1940) d Jules White, s Moe Howard, Larry Fine, Jerry "Curly" Howard.
BOOBS IN ARMS (Columbia, 1940) d Jules White, s Moe Howard, Larry Fine, Jerry "Curly" Howard.
SO LONG, MR. CHUMPS (Columbia, 1941) d Jules White, s Moe Howard, Larry Fine, Jerry "Curly" Howard.
DUTIFUL BUT DUMB (Columbia, 1941) d Del Lord, s Moe Howard, Larry Fine, Jerry "Curly" Howard.
ALL THE WORLD'S A STOOGE (Columbia, 1941) d Del Lord, s Moe Howard, Larry Fine, Jerry "Curly" Howard.
I'LL NEVER HEIL AGAIN (Columbia, 1941) d Jules White, s Moe Howard, Larry Fine, Jerry "Curly" Howard, Mary Ainslee.
AN ACHE IN EVERY STAKE (Columbia, 1941) d Del Lord, s Moe Howard, Larry Fine, Jerry "Curly" Howard.
IN THE SWEET PIE AND PIE (Columbia, 1941) d Jules White, s Moe Howard, Larry Fine, Jerry "Curly" Howard.
SOME MORE OF SAMOA (Columbia, 1941) d Del Lord, s Moe Howard, Larry Fine, Jerry "Curly" Howard.
LOCO BOY MAKES GOOD (Columbia, 1942) d Jules White, s Moe Howard, Larry Fine, Jerry "Curly" Howard.
CACTUS MAKES PERFECT (Columbia, 1942) d Del Lord, s Moe Howard, Larry Fine, Jerry "Curly" Howard.

WHAT'S THE MATADOR? (Columbia, 1942) d Jules White, s Moe Howard, Larry Fine, Jerry "Curly" Howard.
MATRI-PHONY (Columbia, 1942) d Harry Edwards, s Moe Howard, Larry Fine, Jerry "Curly" Howard.
THREE SMART SAPS (Columbia, 1942) d Jules White, s Moe Howard, Larry Fine, Jerry "Curly" Howard.
EVEN AS I.O.U. (Columbia, 1942) d Del Lord, s Moe Howard, Larry Fine, Jerry "Curly" Howard.
SOCK-A-BYE BABY (Columbia, 1942) d Jules White, s Moe Howard, Larry Fine, Jerry "Curly" Howard.
THEY STOOGE TO CONGA (Columbia, 1943) d Del Lord, s Moe Howard, Larry Fine, Jerry "Curly" Howard.
DIZZY DETECTIVES (Columbia, 1943) d Jules White, s Moe Howard, Larry Fine, Jerry "Curly" Howard.
SPOOK LOUDER (Columbia, 1943) d Del Lord, s Moe Howard, Larry Fine, Jerry "Curly" Howard.
BACK FROM THE FRONT (Columbia, 1943) d Jules White, s Moe Howard, Larry Fine, Jerry "Curly" Howard.
THREE LITTLE TWERPS (Columbia, 1943) d Harry Edwards, s Moe Howard, Larry Fine, Jerry "Curly" Howard.
HIGHER THAN A KITE (Columbia, 1943) d Del Lord, s Moe Howard, Larry Fine, Jerry "Curly" Howard.
I CAN HARDLY WAIT (Columbia, 1943) d Jules White, s Moe Howard, Larry Fine, Jerry "Curly" Howard.
DIZZY PILOTS (Columbia, 1943) d Jules White, s Moe Howard, Larry Fine, Jerry "Curly" Howard.
PHONY EXPRESS (Columbia, 1943) d Del Lord, s Moe Howard, Larry Fine, Jerry "Curly" Howard.
A GEM OF A JAM (Columbia, 1943) d Del Lord, s Moe Howard, Larry Fine, Jerry "Curly" Howard.
CRASH GOES THE HASH (Columbia, 1944) d Jules White, s Moe Howard, Larry Fine, Jerry "Curly" Howard.
BUSY BUDDIES (Columbia, 1944) d Del Lord, s Moe Howard, Larry Fine, Jerry "Curly" Howard.
THE YOKE'S ON ME (Columbia, 1944) d Jules White, s Moe Howard, Larry Fine, Jerry "Curly" Howard.
IDLE ROOMERS (Columbia, 1944) d Del Lord, s Moe Howard, Larry Fine, Jerry "Curly" Howard.
GENTS WITHOUT CENTS (Columbia, 1944) d Jules White, s Moe Howard, Larry Fine, Jerry "Curly" Howard.
NO DOUGH, BOYS (Columbia, 1944) d Jules White, s Moe Howard, Larry Fine, Jerry "Curly" Howard.
THREE PESTS IN A MESS (Columbia, 1945) d Del Lord, s Moe Howard, Larry Fine, Jerry "Curly" Howard.
BOOBY DUPES (Columbia, 1945) d Del Lord, s Moe Howard, Larry Fine, Jerry "Curly" Howard.

IDIOTS DELUXE (Columbia, 1945) d Jules White, s Moe Howard, Larry Fine, Jerry "Curly" Howard.
IF A BODY MEETS A BODY (Columbia, 1945) d Jules White, s Moe Howard, Larry Fine, Jerry "Curly" Howard.
MICRO-PHONIES (Columbia, 1945) d Edward Bernds, s Moe Howard, Larry Fine, Jerry "Curly" Howard.
BEER BARREL POLECATS (Columbia, 1946) d Jules White, s Moe Howard, Larry Fine, Jerry "Curly" Howard.
A BIRD IN THE HEAD (Columbia, 1946) d Edward Bernds, s Moe Howard, Larry Fine, Jerry "Curly" Howard.
UNCIVIL WARBIRDS (Columbia, 1946) d Jules White, s Moe Howard, Larry Fine, Jerry "Curly" Howard.
THREE TROUBLEDOERS (Columbia, 1946) d Edward Bernds, s Moe Howard, Larry Fine, Jerry "Curly" Howard.
MONKEY BUSINES (Columbia, 1946) d Edward Bernds, s Moe Howard, Larry Fine, Jerry "Curly" Howard.
THREE LOAN WOLVES (Columbia, 1946) d Jules White, s Moe Howard, Larry Fine, Jerry "Curly" Howard.
G.I. WANNA GO HOME (Columbia, 1946) d Jules White, s Moe Howard, Larry Fine, Jerry "Curly" Howard.
RHYTHM AND WEEP (Columbia, 1946) d Jules White, s Moe Howard, Larry Fine, Jerry "Curly" Howard.
THREE LITTLE PIRATES (Columbia, 1946) d Edward Bernds, s Moe Howard, Larry Fine, Jerry "Curly" Howard.
HALF-WITS HOLIDAY (Columbia, 1947) d Jules White, s Moe Howard, Larry Fine, Jerry "Curly" Howard.
FRIGHT NIGHT (Columbia, 1947) d Edward Bernds, s Moe Howard, Larry Fine, Shemp Howard.
OUT WEST (Columbia, 1947) d Edward Bernds, s Moe Howard, Larry Fine, Shemp Howard.
HOLD THAT LION (Columbia, 1947) d Jules White, s Moe Howard, Larry Fine, Shemp Howard.
BRIDELESS GROOM (Columbia, 1947) d Edward Bernds, s Moe Howard, Larry Fine, Shemp Howard.
SING A SONG OF SIX PANTS (Columbia, 1947) d Jules White, s Moe Howard, Larry Fine, Shemp Howard.
ALL GUMMED UP (Columbia, 1947) d Jules White, s Moe Howard, Larry Fine, Shemp Howard.
SHIVVERING SHERLOCKS (Columbia, 1948) d Del Lord, s Moe Howard, Larry Fine, Shemp Howard.
PARDON MY CLUTCH (Columbia, 1948) d Edward Bernds, s Moe Howard, Larry Fine, Shemp Howard.
SQUAREHEADS OF THE ROUND TABLE (Columbia, 1948) d Edward Bernds, s Moe Howard, Larry Fine, Shemp Howard.
FIDDLERS THREE (Columbia, 1948) d Jules White, s Moe Howard, Larry Fine, Shemp Howard.

338 MOTION PICTURE SERIES & SEQUELS

HEAVENLY DAZE (Columbia, 1948) d Jules White, s Moe Howard, Larry Fine, Shemp Howard.
HOT SCOTS (Columbia, 1948) d Edward Bernds, s Moe Howard, Larry Fine, Shemp Howard.
I'M A MONKEY'S UNCLE (Columbia, 1948) d Jules White, s Moe Howard, Larry Fine, Shemp Howard.
MUMMY'S DUMMIES (Columbia, 1948) d Edward Bernds, s Moe Howard, Larry Fine, Shemp Howard.
CRIME ON THEIR HANDS (Columbia, 1948) d Edward Bernds, s Moe Howard, Larry Fine, Shemp Howard.
THE GHOST TALKS (Columbia, 1949) d Jules White, s Moe Howard, Larry Fine, Shemp Howard.
WHO DONE IT? (Columbia, 1949) d Edward Bernds, s Moe Howard, Larry Fine, Shemp Howard.
HOCUS POCUS (Columbia, 1949) d Jules White, s Moe Howard, Larry Fine, Shemp Howard.
FUELIN' AROUND (Columbia, 1949) d Edward Bernds, s Moe Howard, Larry Fine, Shemp Howard.
MALICE IN THE PALACE (Columbia, 1949) d Jules White, s Moe Howard, Larry Fine, Shemp Howard.
VAGABOND LOAFERS (Columbia, 1949) d Edward Bernds, s Moe Howard, Larry Fine, Shemp Howard.
DUNKED IN THE DEEP (Columbia, 1949) d Jules White, s Moe Howard, Larry Fine, Shemp Howard.
PUNCHY COWPUNCHERS (Columbia, 1950) d Edward Bernds, s Moe Howard, Larry Fine, Shemp Howard.
HUGS AND MUGS (Columbia, 1950) d Jules White, s Moe Howard, Larry Fine, Shemp Howard.
DOPEY DICKS (Columbia, 1950) d Edward Bernds, s Moe Howard, Larry Fine, Shemp Howard.
LOVE AT FIRST BITE (Columbia, 1950) d Jules White, s Moe Howard, Larry Fine, Shemp Howard.
SELF-MADE MAIDS (Columbia, 1950) d Hugh McColum, s Moe Howard, Larry Fine, Shemp Howard.
THREE HAMS ON RYE (Columbia, 1950) d Jules White, s Moe Howard, Larry Fine, Shemp Howard.
STUDIO STOOPS (Columbia, 1950) d Edward Bernds, s Moe Howard, Larry Fine, Shemp Howard.
SLAP HAPPY SLEUTHS (Columbia, 1950) d Hugh McCollum, s Moe Howard, Larry Fine, Shemp Howard.
A SNITCH IN TIME (Columbia, 1950) d Edward Bernds, s Moe Howard, Larry Fine, Shemp Howard.
THREE ARABIAN NUTS (Columbia, 1951) d Edward Bernds, s Moe Howard, Larry Fine, Shemp Howard.
BABY SITTERS JITTERS (Columbia, 1951) d Jules White, s Moe Howard, Larry Fine, Shemp Howard.

DON'T THROW THAT KNIFE (Columbia, 1951) d Jules White, s Moe Howard, Larry Fine, Shemp Howard.
SCRAMBLED BRAINS (Columbia, 1951) d Jules White, s Moe Howard, Larry Fine, Shemp Howard.
MERRY MAVERICKS (Columbia, 1951) d Edward Bernds, s Moe Howard, Larry Fine, Shemp Howard.
THE TOOTH WILL OUT (Columbia, 1951) d Edward Bernds, s Moe Howard, Larry Fine, Shemp Howard.
HULA LA LA (Columbia, 1951) d Hugh McCollum, s Moe Howard, Larry Fine, Shemp Howard.
THE PEST MAN WINS (Columbia, 1951) d Jules White, s Moe Howard, Larry Fine, Shemp Howard.
A MISSED FORTUNE (Columbia, 1952) d Jules White, s Moe Howard, Larry Fine, Shemp Howard.
LISTEN, JUDGE (Columbia, 1952) d Edward Bernds, s Moe Howard, Larry Fine, Shemp Howard.
CORNY CASANOVAS (Columbia, 1952) d Jules White, s Moe Howard, Larry Fine, Shemp Howard.
HE COOKED HIS GOOSE (Columbia, 1952) d Jules White, s Moe Howard, Larry Fine, Shemp Howard.
GENTS IN A JAM (Columbia, 1952) d Edward Bernds, s Moe Howard, Larry Fine, Shemp Howard.
THREE DARK HORSES (Columbia, 1952) d Jules White, s Moe Howard, Larry Fine, Shemp Howard.
CUCKOO ON A CHOO CHOO (Columbia, 1952) d Jules White, s Moe Howard, Larry Fine, Shemp Howard.
UP IN DAISY'S PENTHOUSE (Columbia, 1953) d Jules White, s Moe Howard, Larry Fine, Shemp Howard.
BOOTY AND THE BEAST (Columbia, 1953) d Jules White, s Moe Howard, Larry Fine, Shemp Howard.
LOOSE LOOT (Columbia, 1953) d Jules White, s Moe Howard, Larry Fine, Shemp Howard.
TRICKY DICKS (Columbia, 1953) d Jules White, s Moe Howard, Larry Fine, Shemp Howard.
SPOOKS (Columbia, 1953) d Jules White, s Moe Howard, Larry Fine, Shemp Howard.
PARDON MY BACKFIRE (Columbia, 1953) d Jules White, s Moe Howard, Larry Fine, Shemp Howard.
RIP SEW AND STITCH (Columbia, 1953) d Jules White, s Moe Howard, Larry Fine, Shemp Howard, Vernon Dent.
BUBBLE TROUBLE (Columbia, 1953) d Jules White, s Moe Howard, Larry Fine, Shemp Howard.
GOOF ON THE ROOF (Columbia, 1953) d Jules White, s Moe Howard, Larry Fine, Shemp Howard.
INCOME TAX SAPPY (Columbia, 1954) d Jules White, s Moe Howard, Larry Fine, Shemp Howard.

MUSTY MUSKETEERS (Columbia, 1954) d Jules White, s Moe Howard, Larry Fine, Shemp Howard.
PALS AND GALS (Columbia, 1954) d Jules White, s Moe Howard, Larry Fine, Shemp Howard.
KNUTZY KNIGHTS (Columbia, 1954) d Jules White, s Moe Howard, Larry Fine, Shemp Howard.
SHOT IN THE FRONTIER (Columbia, 1954) d Jules White, s Moe Howard, Larry Fine, Shemp Howard.
SCOTCHED IN SCOTLAND (Columbia, 1954) d Jules White, s Moe Howard, Larry Fine, Shemp Howard.
FLING IN THE RING (Columbia, 1955) d Jules White, s Moe Howard, Larry Fine, Shemp Howard.
OF CASH AND HASH (Columbia, 1955) d Jules White, s Moe Howard, Larry Fine, Shemp Howard.
GYPPED IN THE PENTHOUSE (Columbia, 1955) d Jules White, s Moe Howard, Larry Fine, Shemp Howard.
BEDLAM IN PARADISE (Columbia, 1955) d Jules White, s Moe Howard, Larry Fine, Shemp Howard.
STONE AGE ROMEOS (Columbia, 1955) d Jules White, s Moe Howard, Larry Fine, Shemp Howard.
WHAM BAM SLAM (Columbia, 1955) d Jules White, s Moe Howard, Larry Fine, Shemp Howard.
HOT ICE (Columbia, 1955) d Jules White, s Moe Howard, Larry Fine, Shemp Howard.
BLUNDER BOYS (Columbia, 1955) d Jules White, s Moe Howard, Larry Fine, Shemp Howard.
HUSBANDS BEWARE (Columbia, 1955) d Jules White, s Moe Howard, Larry Fine, Shemp Howard.
CREEPS (Columbia, 1956) d Jules White, s Moe Howard, Larry Fine, Shemp Howard.
FLAGPOLE JITTERS (Columbia, 1956) d Jules White, s Moe Howard, Larry Fine, Shemp Howard.
FOR CRIMIN' OUT LOUD (Columbia, 1956) d Jules White, s Moe Howard, Larry Fine, Shemp Howard.
RUMPUS IN THE HAREM (Columbia, 1956) d Jules White, s Moe Howard, Larry Fine, Shemp Howard.
HOT STUFF (Columbia, 1956) d Jules White, s Moe Howard, Larry Fine, Shemp Howard, Christine McIntyre.
SCHEMING SCHEMERS (Columbia, 1956) d Jules White, s Moe Howard, Larry Fine, Shemp Howard.
COMMOTION ON THE OCEAN (Columbia, 1956) d Jules White, s Moe Howard, Larry Fine, Shemp Howard.
HOOFS AND GOOFS (Columbia, 1957) d Jules White, s Moe Howard, Larry Fine, Joe Besser.
MUSCLE UP A LITTLE CLOSER (Columbia, 1957) d Jules White, s Moe Howard, Larry Fine, Joe Besser.

A MERRY MIX-UP (Columbia, 1957) d Jules White, s Moe Howard, Larry Fine, Joe Besser.
SPACE SHIP SAPPY (Columbia, 1957) d Jules White, s Moe Howard, Larry Fine, Joe Besser.
GUNS A-POPPIN (Columbia, 1957) d Jules White, s Moe Howard, Larry Fine, Joe Besser.
HORSING AROUND (Columbia, 1957) d Jules White, s Moe Howard, Larry Fine, Joe Besser, Tony the Wonder Horse.
RUSTY ROMEOS (Columbia, 1957) d Jules White, s Moe Howard, Larry Fine, Joe Besser.
OUTER SPACE JITTERS (Columbia, 1957) d Jules White, s Moe Howard, Larry Fine, Joe Besser, Emil Sitka.
QUIZ WHIZ (Columbia, 1958) d Jules White, s Moe Howard, Larry Fine, Joe Besser.
FIFI BLOWS HER TOP (Columbia, 1958) d Jules White, s Moe Howard, Larry Fine, Joe Besser.
PIES AND GUYS (Columbia, 1958) d Jules White, s Moe Howard, Larry Fine, Joe Besser.
SWEET AND HOT (Columbia, 1958) d Jules White, s Moe Howard, Larry Fine, Joe Besser.
FLYING SAUCER DAFFY (Columbia, 1958) d Jules White, s Moe Howard, Larry Fine, Joe Besser, Emil Sitka.
OIL'S WELL THAT ENDS WELL (Columbia, 1958) d Jules White, s Moe Howard, Larry Fine, Joe Besser.
TRIPLE CROSSING (Columbia, 1959) d Jules White, s Moe Howard, Larry Fine, Joe Besser.
SAPPY BULLFIGHTERS (Columbia, 1959) d Jules White, s Moe Howard, Larry Fine, Joe Besser, Greta Thyssen.
HAVE ROCKET, WILL TRAVEL (Columbia, 1959) d David Lowell Rich, s Moe Howard, Larry Fine, Curly Joe DeRita.
SNOW WHITE AND THE THREE STOOGES (Columbia, 1961) d Walter Lang, s Moe Howard, Larry Fine, Curly Joe DeRita, Carol Heiss.
THE THREE STOOGES MEET HERCULES (Columbia, 1962) d Edward Bernds, s Moe Howard, Larry Fine, Curly Joe DeRita, Vicki Trickett, Quinn Redeker.
THE THREE STOOGES IN ORBIT (Columbia, 1962) d Edward Bernds, s Moe Howard, Larry Fine, Curly Joe DeRita, Emil Sitka, Carol Christensen.
THE THREE STOOGES GO AROUND THE WORLD IN A DAZE (Columbia, 1963) d Norman Maurer, s Moe Howard, Larry Fine, Curly Joe DeRita, Jay Sheffield, Joan Freeman.
THE OUTLAWS IS COMING (Columbia, 1965) d Norman Maurer, s Moe Howard, Larry Fine, Curly Joe DeRita, Adam West, Nancy Kovack.

761. THUNDER WARRIOR, THE
An American Indian lawman wipes out corruption.

342 MOTION PICTURE SERIES & SEQUELS

THUNDER WARRIOR (Trans World, 1983) d Larry Ludman, s Mark Gregory, Bo Svenson.
THUNDER WARRIOR II (Trans World, 1985) d Larry Ludman, s Mark Gregory, Karen Reel, Bo Svenson.
THUNDER WARRIOR III (Trans World, 1988) d Larry Ludman, s Mark Gregory.

762. TIGER
A love triangle, in the first picture, is between a dancer, a maharajah and an architect. The two films, set in India, were re-edited and released as JOURNEY TO THE LOST CITY.
THE TIGER OF ESCHNAPUR (1958) d Fritz Lang, s Debra Paget, Paul Hubschmid, Walteher Reyer.
THE INDIAN TOMB (1959) d Fritz Lang, s Debra Paget, Paul Hubschmid, Walther Reyer.

763. TILLIE
Silent comedies featuring Marie Dressler are known for their slapstick pandemonium. The initial outing was based on the stage play *Tillie's Nightmare*, which also featured Dressler, and tells of a farm girl brought to the city by a no-good.
TILLIE'S PUNCTURED ROMANCE (Mack Sennett, 1914) s Marie Dressler, Charlie Chaplin, Mabel Normand, Keystone Cops.
TILLIE'S TOMATO SURPRISE (Lubin, 1915) s Marie Dressler.
TILLIE WAKES UP (Peerless-World, 1917) s Marie Dressler.

764. *TIM HOLT AND RICHARD MARTIN*
B Westerns.
THUNDER MOUNTAIN (RKO, 1947) d Lew Landers, s Tim Holt, Richard "Chito" Martin, Martha Hyer.
UNDER THE TONTO RIM (RKO, 1947) d Lew Landers, s Tim Holt, Richard "Chito" Martin, Nan Leslie.
WILD HORSE MESA (RKO, 1947) d Wallace Grissell, s Tim Holt, Richard "Chito" Martin, Nan Leslie.
WESTERN HERITAGE (RKO, 1948) d Wallace Grissell, s Tim Holt, Richard "Chito" Martin, Nan Leslie.
GUNS OF HATE (RKO, 1948) d Lesley Selander, s Tim Holt, Richard "Chito" Martin, Nan Leslie.
THE ARIZONA RANGER (RKO, 1948) d John Rawlins, s Tim Holt, Richard "Chito" Martin, Nan Leslie.
INDIAN AGENT (RKO, 1948) Lesley Selander, s Tim Holt, Richard "Chito" Martin, Lee "Lasses" White, Nan Leslie.
GUN SMUGGLERS (RKO, 1948) d Frank McDonald, s Tim Holt, Richard "Chito" Martin, Martha Hyer.
BROTHERS OF THE SADDLE (RKO, 1949) d Lesley Selander, s Tim Holt, Richard "Chito" Martin, Virginia Cox, Carol Forman.

MOTION PICTURE SERIES & SEQUELS 343

RUSTLERS (RKO, 1949) d Lesley Selander, s Tim Holt, Richard "Chito" Martin, Martha Hyer, Lois Andrews.
STAGECOACH KID (RKO, 1949) d Lew Landers, s Tim Holt, Richard "Chito" Martin, Jeff Donnell.
MASKED RAIDERS (RKO, 1949) d Lesley Selander, s Tim Holt, Richard "Chito" Martin, Marjorie Lord.
THE MYSTERIOUS DESPERADO (RKO, 1949) d Lesley Selander, s Tim Holt, Richard "Chito" Martin, Movita.
RIDERS OF THE RANGE (RKO, 1950) d Lesley Selander, s Tim Holt, Richard "Chito" Martin, Jacqueline White.
DYNAMITE PASS (RKO, 1950) d Lew Landers, s Tim Holt, Richard "Chito" Martin, Lynne Roberts.
STORM OVER WYOMING (RKO, 1950) d Lesley Selander, s Tim Holt, Richard "Chito" Martin, Noreen Nash.
RIDER FROM TUCSON (RKO, 1950) d Lesley Selander, s Tim Holt, Richard "Chito" Martin, Elaine Riley.
BORDER TREASURE (RKO, 1950) d George Archainbaud, s Tim Holt, Richard "Chito" Martin, Jane Nigh.
RIO GRANDE PATROL (RKO, 1950) d Lesley Selander, s Tim Holt, Richard "Chito" Martin, Jane Nigh.
LAW OF THE BADLANDS (RKO, 1951) d Lesley Selander, s Tim Holt, Richard "Chito" Martin, Joan Dixon.
SADDLE LEGION (RKO, 1951) d Lesley Selander, s Tim Holt, Richard "Chito" Martin, Dorothy Malone.
GUN PLAY (RKO, 1951) d Lesley Selander, s Tim Holt, Richard "Chito" Martin, Joan Dixon.
PISTOL HARVEST (RKO, 1951) d Lesley Selander, s Tim Holt, Richard "Chito" Martin, Joan Dixon.
HOT LEAD (RKO, 1951) d Stuart Gilmore, s Tim Holt, Richard "Chito" Martin, Joan Dixon.
OVERLAND TELEGRAPH (RKO, 1951) d Lesley Selander, s Tim Holt, Richard "Chito" Martin, Gail Davis.
TRAIL GUIDE (RKO, 1952) d Lesley Selander, s Tim Holt, Richard "Chito" Martin, Linda Douglas.
ROAD AGENT (RKO, 1952) d Lesley Selander, s Tim Holt, Richard "Chito" Martin, Noreen Nash.
TARGET (RKO, 1952) d Stuart Gilmore, s Tim Holt, Richard "Chito" Martin, Linda Douglas.
DESERT PASSAGE (RKO, 1952) d Lesley Selander, s Tim Holt, Richard "Chito" Martin, Joan Dixon, Dorothy Patrick.

764A. TISH
Mary Roberts Rinehart's spinsterish Tish and two companions appeared in a number of adventures in the pages of *The Saturday Evening Post,* and in motion pictures.
LIKE A WOLF ON THE FOLD (Essanay, 1913)
THE SIMPLE LIFERS (Essanay, 1913)

TISH'S SPY (Essanay, 1915)
TISH (MGM, 1942) d Sylvan Simon, s Marjorie Main, Zasu Pitts.

765. TOFF, THE
Prolific British mystery writer John Creasey created the dapper crime solver Richard Rollinson in 1938.
SALUTE THE TOFF (Butchers Films, 1951) s John Bentley.
HAMMER THE TOFF (Butchers Films, 1952) s John Bentley.

766. *TOM KEENE AND ARKANSAS SLIM ANDREWS*
B Westerns.
WANDERERS OF THE WEST (Monogram, 1941) d Robert Hill, S Tom Keene, Slim Andrews, Betty Miles.
DYNAMITE CANYON (Monogram, 1941) d Robert E. Tansey, s Tom Keene, Slim Andrews.
THE DRIFTIN' KID (Monotram, 1941) d Robert E. Tansey, s Tom Keene, Slim Andrews, Betty Miles.
RIDIN' THE SUNSET TRAIL (Monogram, 1941) d Robert E. Tansey, s Tom Keene, Slim Andrews.

767. TOM SAWYER AND HUCKLEBERRY FINN
The youthful Mississippi River adventurers were created by Western novelist and humorist Mark Twain (Samuel Clemens).
TOM SAWYER (1917) s Robert Gordon, Clara Horton.
HUCK AND TOM (1918)
HUCKLEBERRY FINN (Paramount, 1920) s Esther Ralson
TOM SAWYER (Paramount, 1930) d John Cromwell, s Jackie Coogan, Mitzie Green, Junior Durkin.
HUCKLEBERRY FINN (Paramount, 1931) d Norman Taurog, s Jackie Coogan, Mitzie Green, Junior Durkin.
TOM SAWYER (United Artists, 1938) d Norman Taurog, s Tommy Kelly, May Robson, Jackie Moran, Walter Brennan.
TOM SAWYER, DETECTIVE (Paramount, 1939) d Louis King, s Billy Cook, Donald O'Connor.
HUCKLEBERRY FINN (MGM, 1939) d Richard Thorpe, s Mickey Rooney, Walter Connolly, William Frawley.
HUCKLEBERRY FINN (MGM, 1960) d Michael Curtiz, s Eddie Hodges, Archie Moore, Tony Randall.
TOM SAWYER (1970) d Don Taylor, s Johnnie Whitaker, Celeste Holm, Warren Oates.
TOM SAWYER (United Artists, 1973) d James Neilson, s Josh Albee, Jeff Tyler, Jane Wyatt, Buddy Ebsen.
TOM SAWYER (Universal/Hal Roach, 1973) (CBS-TV movie) d James Neilson, s Josh Albee, Jeff Tyler, Buddy Ebsen.
HUCKLEBERRY FINN (United Artists, 1974) d J. Lee Thompson, s Jeff East, Paul Winfield.

MOTION PICTURE SERIES & SEQUELS 345

HUCKLEBERRY FINN (ABC Circle Films, 1975) (ABC-TV movie) d Robert Totten, s Ron Howard, Donny Most, Antonio Fargas, Jack Elam.
THE ADVENTURES OF HUCKLEBERRY FINN (Schick Sunn Classics/Taft International, 1981) (NBC-TV movie) d Jack B. Hively, s Kurt Ida, Dan Monahan, Brock Peters.
RASCALS AND ROBBERS -- THE SECRET ADVENTURES OF TOM SAWYER AND HUCK FINN (CBS Entertainment, 1982) (CBS-TV movie) d Dick Lowry, s Patrick Creadon, Anthony Michael Hall.
THE ADVENTURES OF MARK TWAIN (1985) (clay animated) d Will Vinton, voices James Whitmore, Chris Ritchie.
ADVENTURES OF HUCKLEBERRY FINN (PBS American Playhouse broadcast, 1985) d Peter H. Hunt, s Patrick Day, Jim Dale, Frederick Forrest, Samm-Art Williams, Butterfly McQueen.

768. TONY ROME
The private detective hero was created by novelist Marvin H. Albert.
TONY ROME (20th Century-Fox, 1967) d Gordon Douglas, s Frank Sinatra, Richard Conte.
LADY IN CEMENT (20th Century-Fox, 1968) d Gordon Douglas, s Frank Sinatra, Raquel Welch.

768A. TOODLES
These are silent comedy pictures.
TOODLES' TEA PARTY (American Mutoscope & Biograph, 1903)
TOODLES AND HER STRAWBERRY TART (American Mutoscope & Biograph, 1903)
TOODLES RECITES A RECITATION (American Mutoscope & Biograph, 1903)

769. TOPPER
In Thorne Smith's novel, fun-loving Marion and George Kirby die in a car accident and return to help out a friend, Cosmo Topper, as ghosts.
TOPPER (MGM, 1937) d Norman Z. McLeod, s Constance Bennett, Cary Grant, Roland Young.
TOPPER TAKES A TRIP (United Artists, 1939) d Norman Z. McLeod, s Constance Bennett, Roland Young, Billie Burke.
TOPPER RETURNS (United Artists, 1941) d Roy Del Ruth, s Joan Blondell, Roland Young, Carole Landis.

780. TORA-SAN
One of Japan's longest running film series (the forty-first entry is listed below) offer the comic misadventures of a traveling peddlar. They have been in production since 1969. Shown in this country in some ethnic communities, the entry below was the first given general release.
TORA-SAN GOES TO VIENNA (Kino International, 1989) d Yoji Yamada, s Kiyoshi Atsumi, Chieko Baisho.

346 MOTION PICTURE SERIES & SEQUELS

781. TORCHY BLANE
The female reporter for the *Star* first appeared in Frederick Nebel's short story *No Hard Feelings*. The heroine's frequent nemesis is Police Lt. Steve McBride.
SMART BLONDE (Warner Brothers, 1936) d Frank McDonald, s Glenda Farrell, Barton MacLane.
FLY-AWAY BABY (Warner Brothers, 1937) d Frank McDonald, s Glenda Farrell, Barton MacLane.
THE ADVENTUROUS BLONDE (Warner Brothers, 1937) d Frank McDonald, s Glenda Farrell, Barton MacLane.
BLONDES AT WORK (Warner Brothers, 1938) d Frank McDonald, s Glenda Farrell, Barton MacLane.
TORCHY BLANE IN PANAMA (Warner Brothers, 1938) d William Clemens, s Lola Lane, Paul Kelly.
TORCHY GETS HER MAN (Warner Brothers, 1938) d William Beaudine, s Glenda Farrell, Barton MacLane.
TORCHY BLANE IN CHINATOWN (Warner Brothers, 1939) d William Beaudine, s Glenda Farrell, Barton MacLane.
TORCHY RUNS FOR MAYOR (Warner Brothers, 1939) d Ray McCarey, s Glenda Farrell, Barton MacLane.
TORCHY PLAYS WITH DYNAMITE (Warner Brothers, 1939) d Noel Smith, s Jane Wyman, Allen Jenkins.

782. *TORI*
These X-rated films feature "actress" Tori Welles.
TORRID (Wave, 1989) s Tori Welles, Joey Silvera.
TORRID HOUSE (Vivid, 1989) s Tori Welles, Robert Bullock.
TORRID WITHOUT A CAUSE (Vivid, 1989) s Tori Welles, Randy West.
TRUE CONFESSIONS OF TORI WELLES (Vivid, 1989) s Tori Welles, Randy West.

783. TOXIC AVENGER, THE
The nerdy hero from Tromaville, New Jersey, falls into a chemical company's vat and turns into a misshapen fright. In the third outing, he has to raise money to restore his girlfriend's sight.
THE TOXIC AVENGER (Troma, 1985) d Michael Herz, s Samuel Weil, Andree Miranda.
THE TOXIC AVENGER PART II (Troma, 1988) d Michael Herz and Lloyd Kaufman, s Phoebe Legere, Ron Fazio.
THE TOXIC AVENGER PART III: THE LAST TEMPTATION OF TOXIE (Troma, 1989) d Michael Herz and Lloyd Kaufman, s Ron Fazio, John Altamura, Phoebe Legere, Rick Collins.

784. TRAIL BLAZERS, THE
The Westerns team veteran cowpokes.
WILD HORSE STAMPEDE (Monogram, 1943) d Alan James, s Ken Maynard, Hoot Gibson, Betty Miles.

THE LAW RIDES AGAIN (Monogram, 1943) d Alan James, s Ken Maynard, Hoot Gibson, Betty Miles.
BLAZING GUNS (Monogram, 1943) d Robert Tansey, s Ken Maynard, Hoot Gibson, Kay Forrester.
DEATH VALLEY RANGERS (Monogram, 1943) d Robert Tansey, s Ken Maynard, Hoot Gibson, Bob Steele, Betty Miles.
WESTWARD BOUND (Monogram, 1944) d Robert Tansey, s Ken Maynard, Hoot Gibson, Bob Steele, Betty Miles.
ARIZONA WHIRLWIND (Monogram, 1944) d Robert Tansey, s Ken Maynard, Hoot Gibson, Bob Steele, Myrna Dell.
OUTLAW TRAIL (Monogram, 1944), d Robert Tansey, s Bob Steele, Hoot Gibson, Chief Thundercloud, Jennifer Holt.
SONORA STAGECOACH (Monogram, 1944) d Robert Tansey, s Bob Steele, Hoot Gibson, Chief Thundercloud, Betty Miles.
MARKED TRAILS (Monogram, 1944) d J.P. McCarthy, s Hoot Gibson, Bob Steele, Veda Ann Borg.

785. TRANCERS
Jack Deth is a futuristic police officer who is sent back in time.
TRANCERS (Empire, 1985) [aka FUTURE COP] d Charles Band, s Tim Thomerson, Helen Hunt.
TRANCERS II (Band Company, announced 1990) d Danny Bilson, s Tim Thomerson.

786. TRANSACTION
These pictures are rated X.
TRANSACTION (Wet, 1986) s Lois Ayres, Steve Drake.
TRANSACTION II (Wet, 1987) s Emmanuel, Jacques Waine.

787. TRAVIS McGEE
John D. MacDonald's fictional detective/adventurer lives on a houseboat called the *Busted Flush* in Florida.
DARKER THAN AMBER (National General, 1970) d Robert Clouse, s Rod Taylor, Suzy Kendall.
TRAVIS McGEE (Hajeno Productions, 1983) (ABC-TV movie) [aka TRAVIS McGEE -- THE EMPTY COPPER SEA] d Andrew V. McLaglen, s Sam Elliott, Gene Evans.

788. TREASURE ISLAND
Robert Louis Stevenson adventure tale of young Jim Hawkins who becomes involved with pirates including Long John Silver. There have also been an Australian TV series (THE ADVENTURES OF LONG JOHN SILVER, 1955) and two British series (TREASURE ISLAND, 1978, and JOHN SILVER'S RETURN TO TREASURE ISLAND, 1986).
TREASURE ISLAND (MGM, 1934) d Victor Fleming, s Wallace Beery, Jackie Cooper, Lionel Barrymore.

TREASURE ISLAND (RKO, 1950) d Byron Haskin, s Bobby Driscoll, Robert Newton.
LONG JOHN SILVER (Distributors Corporation of America, 1954) d Byron Haskin, s Robert Newton, Connie Gilchrist.
RETURN TO TREASURE ISLAND (United Artists, 1954) d E.A. Dupont, s Tab Hunter, Dawn Addams.
TREASURE ISLAND (National General, 1972) d John Hough, s Orson Welles, Kim Burfield.
TREASURE ISLAND (TNT television movie, 1990) s Charleton Heston, Christian Bale.

789. TRINITY
Half-brothers Trinity and Bambino are featured in these spoof/violent Westerns.
THEY CALL ME TRINITY (Avco Embassy, 1971) d E.B. Clucher (Enzo Barboni), s Terence Hill, Bud Spencer.
TRINITY IS STILL MY NAME (Avco Embassy, 1972) d E.B. Clucher (Enzo Barboni), s Terence Hill, Bud Spencer.

790. TROUBLE WITH ANGELS, THE
Jane Trahey's novel *Life With Mother Superior,* about new entrants at St. Francis Convent, prompted these pictures.
THE TROUBLE WITH ANGELS (Columbia, 1966) d Ida Lupino, s Rosalind Russell, Hayley Mills, June Harding.
WHERE ANGELS GO -- TROUBLE FOLLOWS (Columbia, 1968) d James Neilson, s Rosalind Russell, Stella Stevens, Susan Saint James.

791. TRUE GRIT
Charles Portis's Western novel provided the characters of an aged marshal who helps a youthful but spunky girl track her father's killer.
TRUE GRIT (Paramount, 1969) d Henry Hathaway, s John Wayne, Kim Darby, Glen Campbell.
ROOSTER COGBURN (Universal, 1975) d Stuart Millar, s John Wayne, Katharine Hepburn, Strother Margin.
TRUE GRIT (A FURTHER ADVENTURE) (Paramount Television, 1978) (ABC-TV movie) d Richard T. Heffron, s Warren Oates, Lisa Pelikan.

792. TUGBOAT ANNIE
Norman Reilly Raine's feisty Secoma towboat captain appeared in 68 stories in *The Saturday Evening Post.* She also had her own syndicated television program in 1958.
TUGBOAT ANNIE (MGM, 1933) d Mervyn LeRoy, s Marie Dressler, Wallace Beery.
TUGBOAT ANNIE SAILS AGAIN (Warner Brothers, 1940) d Lewis Seiler, s Marjorie Rambeau, Alan Hale, Ronald Reagan.
CAPTAIN TUGBOAT ANNIE (Republic, 1945) d Phil Rosen, s Jane Darwell, Edgar Kennedy.

793. 20,000 LEAGURES UNDER THE SEA

Jules Verne wrote the science fiction/adventure novel of Captain Nemo and the *Nautilus*.

MYSTERIOUS ISLAND (1929)
20,000 LEAGUES UNDER THE SEA (Disney, 1954) d Richard Fleischer, s Kirk Douglas, James Mason.
MYSTERIOUS ISLAND (Columbia, 1951) (15 episodes) d Spencer Bennet, s Richard Crane, Marshall Reed.
MYSTERIOUS ISLAND (Columbia, 1961) [aka JULES VERNE'S MYSTERIOUS ISLAND] d Cy Endfield, s Michael Craig, Joan Greenwood.
CAPTAIN NEMO AND THE UNDERWATER CITY (MGM, 1969) d James Hill, s Robert Ryan, Chuck Connors.
THE MYSTERIOUS ISLAND OF CAPTAIN NEMO (1974) d Juan Antonio Bardem and Henri Colpi, s Omar Sharif, Philippe Nicaud.
AMAZING CAPTAIN NEMO (1978) s Jose Ferrer, Burgess Meredith.

794. TWO BLACK CROWS, THE

White performers in blackface were popular in vaudeville. Not listed are a series of shorts for Educational Films.

WHY BRING THAT UP? (Paramount, 1929) s Charles E. Mack, George Moran.
ANYBODY'S WAR (Paramount) s Charles E. Mack, Bert Swor.
HYPNOTIZED (Sono-Art World Pictures) d Mack Sennett, Charles E. Mack, George Moran.

795. 2001: A SPACE ODYSSEY

The films are based on Arthur C. Clarke's novel *The Sentinel*, about the future, space travel, man vs. machines.

2001: A SPACE ODYSSEY (MGM, 1968) d Stanley Kubrick, s Keir Dullea, William Sylvester.
2010 (MGM/UA, 1984) d Peter Hyams, s Roy Scheider, John Lithgow.

FLASH GORDON (Buster Crabbe) has his hands full both with beautiful Dale Arden (Jean Rogers) and with Ming the Merciless (Charles Middleton) in the 1936 serial.

350 MOTION PICTURE SERIES & SEQUELS

795A. UNCLE JOSH
Edison's early and popular gramophone comedian made the transition from aural character to silent one in films.
UNCLE JOSH IN A SPOOKY HOTEL (Edison, 1900)
UNCLE JOSH'S NIGHTMARE (Edison, 1900)
UNCLE JOSH AT THE MOVING PICTURE (Edison, 1902)

796. UNNATURAL ACT
These X-rated films involving ghosts and sex.
UNNATURAL ACT (Dreamland, 1984) d Tim McDonald, s Desiree Lane, John Leslie.
AN UNNATURAL ACT II (Dreamland, 1986) d Ned Morehead, s Nina Hartley.

797. UP FRONT
Bill Mauldin's World War II stories of GIs Willie and Joe were translated to cinema.
UP FRONT (Universal, 1951) d Alexander Hall, s David Wayne, Tom Ewell, Mariana Berti.
BACK AT THE FRONT (Universal, 1952) [aka WILLIE AND JOE IN BACK AT THE FRONT] d George Sherman, s Tom Ewell, Harvey Lembeck.

798. UP IN THE AIR
Pageboys solve a radio station murder in the first of these programmers.
UP IN THE AIR (Monogram, 1940) d Howard Bretherton, s Frankie Darro, Marjorie Reynolds, Mantan Moreland.
THERE GOES KELLY (Monogram, 1945) d Phil Karlstein, s Jackie Moran, Wanda McKay.

799. UP THE CREEK
An incompetant lieutenant is assigned to a mothballed cruiser.
UP THE CREEK (Warner Brothers, 1958) d Val Guest, s David Tomlinson, Peter Sellers, Wilfrid Hyde-White.
FURTHER UP THE CREEK (Columbia, 1958) d Val Guest, s David Tomlinson, Frankie Howard, Shirley Eton.

800. UPTOWN SATURDAY NIGHT
In the first picture, pals try to retrieve a winning lottery ticket. In the second film, lodge brothers hypnotize a beanpole into becoming a boxer, hoping to rake in the bets. In the third, conmen help a social worker in the ghetto.
UPTOWN SATURDAY NIGHT (Warner Brothers, 1974) d Sidney Poitier, s Sidney Poitier, Bill Cosby, Harry Belafonte, Flip Wilson.
LET'S DO IT AGAIN (Warner Brothers, 1975) d Sidney Poitier, s Sidney Poitier, Bill Cosby, Jimmie Walker.
A PIECE OF THE ACTION (Warner Brothers, 1977) d Sidney Poitier, s Sidney Poitier, Bill Cosby, James Earl Jones.

MOTION PICTURE SERIES & SEQUELS 351

801. US BUNCH COMEDIES, THE
Youngsters populate the cast of these comedies.

802. V
Extraterrestrials invade earth, professing to be peace-loving but in actuality seeking to dominate humanity. After these two pictures there was a television mini-series and a regular series over NBC (1984-85)
V (Warner Brothers Television, 1983) (NBC-TV movie) d Kenneth Johnson, s
    Marc Singer, Faye Grant.
V -- THE FINAL BATTLE (Warner Brothers Television, 1984) (NBC-TV
    movie) d Richard T. Heffron, s Jane Badler, Michael Durrell.

803. VALLEY OF THE DOLLS
The first and third films are based on the racy Jacqueline Susann novel of three young women in show business. The second entry is R-rated and related in title only.
VALLEY OF THE DOLLS (20th Century-Fox, 1967) d Mark Robson, s
    Barbara Parkins, Patty Duke, Sharon Tate.
BEYOND THE VALLEY OF THE DOLLS (20th Century-Fox, 1970) d Russ
    Meyer, s Dolly Reed, Cynthia Myers.
JACQUELINE SUSANN'S "VALLEY OF THE DOLLS 1981" (20th Century-
    Fox Television, 1981) (CBS-TV movie) dWalter Graumann, s
    Catherine Hicks, Lisa Hartman.

804. VAMPIRE, THE
Hungarian Count Karol de Lavud arrives in the Mexican Sierra Negra in the first installment.
THE VAMPIRE (Cinematogravica Absa, 1957) [aka EL VAMPIRO] d
    Fernando Mendez, s German Robles, Abel Salazar.
THE VAMPIRE'S COFFIN (Cinematografica, 1957) [aka EL RETORNO
    DEL VAMPIRO] d Fernando Mendez, s German Robles, Abel Salazar.

805. VERA VAGUE
These comedy shorts feature radio actress Barbara Jo Allen as a spinster. The list is incomplete.
DOCTOR, FEEL MY PULSE (1944)
THE JURY GOES ROUND AND ROUND

806. VILLAGE OF THE DAMNED
George Wyndham wrote a novel -- the basis of these pictures -- about an English village in which strange, emotionless children are born and seek power.
VILLAGE OF THE DAMNED (MGM, 1960) d Wolf Rilla, s George Sanders,
    Barbara Shelley.
CHILDREN OF THE DAMNED (MGM, 1964) d Anton Leader, s Ian Hendry,
    Alan Badel.

807. VIRGIL TIBBS
John Ball's fictional black police officer, who appeared in five mystery novels (1965-80), was translated to the screen in this series. Beginning in 1988 there was also an IN THE HEAT OF THE NIGHT television series with Carroll O'Connor and Howard Rollins.
IN THE HEAT OF THE NIGHT (United Artists, 1967) d Norman Jewison, s Sidney Poitier, Rod Steiger.
THEY CALL ME MISTER TIBBS! (United Artists, 1970) d Gordon Douglas, s Sidney Poitier, Barbara McNair.
THE ORGANIZATION (United Artists, 1971) d Don Medford, s Sidney Poitier, Barbara McNair.
IN THE HEAT OF THE NIGHT (NBC TV movie, 1988) s Carroll O'Connor, Howard Rollins.

808. WADDY AND ARTY
Arthur Houseman and William Wadsworth teamed for a series of one-reel comedies beginning in 1914 for Edison. The list is incomplete.
ON THE LAZY LINE (Edison, 1914) d C. Jay Williams, s Arthur Houseman, William Wadsworth, Herbert Prior.

809. WALKING TALL
The action-dramas about determined Southern Sheriff Buford Pusser and his battle against corruption are based on a real-life incident. An NBC-TV series featured Bo Svenson in the lead role in 1981.
WALKING TALL (Cinerama, 1973) d Phil Karlson, s Joe Don Baker, Elizabeth Hartman.
PART TWO, WALKING TALL (American International, 1975) d Earl Bellamy, s Bo Svenson, Luke Askew.
FINAL CHAPTER -- WALKING TALL (American International, 1977) d Jack Starrett, s Bo Svenson, Margaret Blye.
A REAL AMERICAN HERO (1978 TV movie) d Lou Antonio, s Brian Dennely, Forrest Tucker.

810. WALLY BENTON
A meek radio actor becomes a formidable detective called The Fox in these pictures, based on the play *Whistling in the Dark* by Lawrence Gross and Edward Childs.
WHISTLING IN THE DARK (MGM, 1933) d Ernest Truex, s Red Skelton.
WHISTLING IN THE DARK (MGM, 1941) d S. Sylvan Simon, s Red Skelton.
WHISTLING IN DIXIE (MGM, 1942) d S. Sylvan Simon, s Red Skelton.
WHISTLING IN BROOKLYN (MGM, 1943) d S. Sylvan Simon, s Red Skelton, Ann Rutherford, Jean Rogers.

811. WALTONS, THE
Earl Hamner Jr. created this series about a Blue Ridge Mountain family during the Depression. The characters are John and Oliva Walton (Ralph Waite and Michael Learned), Grandpa (Will Geer) and Grandma (Ellen Corby), John Boy

MOTION PICTURE SERIES & SEQUELS 353

(Richard Thomas), Mary Ellen (Judy Norton-Taylor) and the rest of the clan. The stories are folksy and human. THE WALTONS was an NBC television series 1972-81. The first film below is a pilot; others came after the regular series' end.
THE HOMECOMING -- A CHRISTMAS STORY (Lorimar, 1971) (ABC-TV movie) d Fielder Cook, s Patricia Neal, Edgar Bergen, Richard Thomas.
A WEDDING ON WALTONS MOUNTAIN (Amanda Productions/Lorimar, 1982) (NBC-TV movie) d Lee Philips, s Ralph Waite, Ellen Corby.
MOTHER'S DAY ON WALTONS MOUNTAIN (Amanda Productions/Lorimar, 1982) (NBC-TV movie) d Gwen Arner, s Ralph Waite, Michael Learned.
A DAY FOR THANKS ON WALTONS MOUNTAIN (Amanda Productions/Lorimar, 1982) (NBC-TV movie) d Hary Haris, s Ralph Waite, Jon Walmsley, Judy Norton-Taylor.

811A. WATCHERS, THE
Based on a Dean R. Koontz novel, these pictures are about a boy and a super-intelligent dog.
THE WATCHERS (Universal, 1988) d Jon Hess, s Corey Halm.
THE WATCHERS II: THE OUTSIDER (Concorde, announced 1990)

811B. WEARY WILLIE
This is an early silent comedy series.
WEARY WILLIE AND THE GARDENER (Edison, 1901)
WEARY WILLIE KIDNAPS A CHILD (Edison, 1904)

812. WEAVER FAMILY AND ELVIRY, THE
The Arkansas Travelers of Grand Ole Opry fame made a series of corny pictures. The hillbilly Weavers are Leon (as Abner), Frank (Cicero) and June (Elviry).
DOWN IN ARKANSAW (Republic, 1938) d Nick Grinde, s Leon Weaver, Frank Weaver, June Weaver.
JEEPERS CREEPERS (Republic, 1939) d Frank McDonald, s Leon Weaver, Frank Weaver, June Weaver.
IN OLD MISSOURI (Republic, 1940) d Frank McDonald, s Leon Weaver, Frank Weaver, June Weaver.
GRAND OLE OPRY (Republic, 1940) d Frank McDonald, s Leon Weaver, Frank Weaver, June Weaver.
FRIENDLY NEIGHBORS (Republic, 1940) d Nick Grinde, s Leon Weaver, Frank Weaver, June Weaver.
ARKANSAS JUDGE (Republic, 1941) d Frank McDonald, s Leon Weaver, Frank Weaver, June Weaver.
MOUNTAIN MOONLIGHT (Republic, 1940) [aka MOVING IN SOCIETY] d Nick Grinde, s Leon Weaver, Frank Weaver, June Weaver.
TUXEDO JUNCTION (Republic, 1941) d Frank McDonald, s Leon Weaver, Frank Weaver, June Weaver.

SHEPHERD OF THE OZARKS (Republic, 1942) d Frank McDonald, s Leon Weaver, Frank Weaver, June Weaver.
THE OLD HOMESTEAD (Republic, 1942) d Frank McDonald, s Leon Weaver, Frank Weaver, June Weaver.
MOUNTAIN RHYTHM (Republic, 1942) [aka HARVEST DAYS] d Frank McDonald, s Leon Weaver, Frank Weaver, June Weaver.

813. WEDNESDAY'S CHILD
Leopold L. Atlas's play about a child forced to testify at his parents' divorce trial and then going on to military boarding school is the basis for these pictures.
WEDNESDAY'S CHILD (RKO, 1934) d John S. Robertson, s Frankie Thomas, Edward Arnold, Karen Morley.
CHILD OF DIVORCE (RKO, 1946) d Richard O. Fleischer, s Sharyn Moffet, Regis Toomey, Madge Meredith.

WEREWOLF
See **WOLF MAN**

814. WESTWORLD
A futuristic vacation resort is manned by robots, which decide to take over.
WESTWORLD (MGM, 1973) d Michael Crichton, s Richard Benjamin, Yul Brynner.
FUTUREWORLD (American International, 1976) d Richard T. Heffron, s Peter Fonda, Blythe Danner, Arthur Hill, Yul Brynner.

815. WHAT HAPPENED TO MARY?
The Ladies World magazine in 1912 developed a mythical heroine (illustrated on its covers by Charles Dana Gibson) with a silent motion picture tie-in from the Edison studios. While presented as a serial, the chapters were actually independent stories. The list is incomplete.
THE ESCAPE FROM BONDAGE (Edison, 1912) s Mary Fuller.
ALONE IN NEW YORK (Edison, 1912) s Mary Fuller.

816. WHERE NO VULTURES FLY
A game warden tries to halt the slaughter of endangered animals in Africa.
WHERE NO VULTURES FLY (Ealing, 1952) d Harry Watt, s Anthony Steel, Dinah Sheridan.
WEST OF ZANZIBAR (Ealing, 1954) d Harry Watt, s Anthony Steel, Sheila Sim.

817. WHERE THE BOYS ARE
The annual spring invasion of Fort Lauderdale by college students (as depicted in the titular Glendon Swarthout novel) offers the plotline for these pictures.
WHERE THE BOYS ARE (MGM, 1960) d Henry Levin, s Dolores Hart, George Hamilton.

MOTION PICTURE SERIES & SEQUELS 355

WHERE THE BOYS ARE '84 (ITC, 1984) d Hy Averback, s Lisa Hartman, Lorna Luft.

818.WHIP WILSON AND ANDY CLYDE
The B Westerns feature a whip-carrying cowboy and his sidekick.
CRASHING THRU (Monogram, 1949) d Ray Taylor, s Whip Wilson, Andy Clyde, Christine Larson.
SHADOWS OF THE WEST (Monogram, 1949) d Ray Taylor, s Whip Wilson, Andy Clyde, Reno Browne.
HAUNTED TRAILS (Monogram, 1949) d Lambert Hillyer, s Whip Wilson, Andy Clyde, Reno Browne.
RIDERS OF THE DUSK (Monogram, 1949) d Lambert Hillyer, s Whip Wilson, Andy Clyde, Reno Browne.
RANGE LAND (Monogram, 1949) d Lambert Hillyer, s Whip Wilson, Andy Clyde, Reno Browne.
FENCE RIDERS (Monogram, 1950) d Wallace Fox, s Whip Wilson, Andy Clyde, Reno Browne.
GUNSLINGERS (Monogram, 1950) d Wallace Fox, s Whip Wilson, Andy Clyde, Reno Browne.
ARIZONA TERRITORY (Monogram, 1950) d Wallace Fox, s Whip Wilson, Andy Clyde, Nancy Saunders.
SILVER RAIDERS (Monogram, 1950) d Wallace Fox, s Whip Wilson, Andy Clyde, Virginia Herrick.
CHEROKEE UPRISING (Monogram, 1950) d Lewis Collins, s Whip Wilson, Andy Clyde, Lois Hall.
OUTLAWS OF TEXAS (Monogram, 1950) d Thomas Carr, s Whip Wilson, Andy Clyde, Phyllis Coates.
ABILENE TRAIL (Monogram, 1951) d Lewis Collins, s Whip Wilson, Andy Clyde, Noel Neill.

819. WHIP WILSON AND FUZZY KNIGHT
WANTED DEAD OR ALIVE (Monogram, 1951) d Thomas Carr, s Whip Wilson, Fuzzy Knight, Christine McIntyre.
CANYON RAIDERS (Monogram, 1951) d Lewis Collins, s Whip Wilson, Fuzzy Knight, Phyllis Coates.
NEVADA RAIDERS (Monogram, 1951) d Lewis Collins, s Whip Wilson, Fuzzy Knight, Phyllis Coates.
STAGECOACH DRIVER (Monogram, 1951) d Lewis Collins, s Whip Wilson, Fuzzy Knight, Gloria Winters.
LAWLESS COWBOYS (Monogram, 1951) d Lewis Collins, s Whip Wilson, Fuzzy Knight, Pamela Duncan.
STAGE TO BLUE RIVER (Monogram, 1951) d Lewis Collins, s Whip Wilson, Fuzzy Knight, Phyllis Coates.
NIGHT RAIDERS (Monogram, 1952) d Howard Bretherton, s Whip Wilson, Fuzzy Knight, Lois Hall.
THE GUNMAN (Monogram, 1952) d Lewis Collins, s Whip Wilson, Fuzzy Knight, Phyllis Coates.

MONTANA INCIDENT (Monogram, 1952) d Lewis Collins, s Whip Wilson, Fuzzy Knight, Peggy Stewart.

820. WHISPERING SMITH
The movies are taken from the book by F.H. Spearman. A soft-spoken special agent in the Wild West pursues criminals.
WHISPERING SMITH SPEAKS (20th Century-Fox, 1935)
WHISPERING SMITH (Paramount, 1948) d Leslie Fenton, s Alan Ladd, Brenda Marshall.
WHISPERING SMITH VERSUS SCOTLAND YARD (RKO, 1952) [aka WHISPERING SMITH HITS LONDON] d Francis Searle, s Richard Carlson, Greta Gynt.

821. WHISTLER, THE
A CBS radio show called THE WHISTLER (1942-55 with Bill Forman) inspired these movies. The host is a mysterious figure who whistles a haunting tune as he walks along. Richard Dix is featured alternatingly as a hero and villain. Cornell Woolrich provided several of the plots.
THE WHISTLER (Columbia, 1944) d William Castle, s Richard Dix, Gloria Stuart.
MARK OF THE WHISTLER (Columbia, 1944) d William Castle, s Richard Dix, Janis Carter.
POWER OF THE WHISTLER (Columbia, 1945) d Lew Landers, s Richard Dix, Janis Carter.
VOICE OF THE WHISTLER (Columbia, 1945) d William Castle, s Richard Dix, Lynn Merrick.
MYSTERIOUS INTRUDER (Columbia, 1946) d William Castle, s Richard Dix, Nina Vale.
SECRET OF THE WHISTLER (Columbia, 1946) d George Sherman, s Richard Dix, Leslie Brooks.
THE 13TH HOUR (Columbia, 1948) d William Clemens, s Richard Dix, Karen Morley.
THE RETURN OF THE WHISTLER (Columbia, 1948) d Ross Lederman, s Michael Duane, Lenore Aubert.

822. WICKED SENSATIONS
These pictures are rated X.
WICKED SENSATIONS (Caballero, 1981) d Ron Chrones, s Annette Haven, John Leslie.
WICKED SENSATIONS 2 (Dreamland, 1989) s Ona Zee, Randy West.

823. *WILD BILL ELLIOTT AND DUB TAYLOR*
These B Westerns pair Elliott and Dub Taylor. Other Elliott sidekicks follow.
PIONEERS OF THE FRONTIER (Columbia, 1940) d Sam Nelson, s Wild Bill Elliott, Dub Taylor, Linda Winters.
THE MAN FROM TUMBLEWEEDS (Columbia, 1940) d Joseph H. Lewis, s Wild Bill Elliott, Dub Taylor, Iris Meredith.

MOTION PICTURE SERIES & SEQUELS 357

THE RETURN OF WILD BILL (Columbia, 1940) d Joseph H. Lewis, s Wild Bill Elliott, Dub Taylor, Iris Meredith.
PRAIRIE SCHOONERS (Columbia, 1940) d Sam Nelson, s Wild Bill Elliott, Dub Taylor, Evelyn Young.
BEYOND THE SACRAMENTO (Columbia, 1940) d Lambert Hillyer, s Wild Bill Elliott, Dub Taylor, Evelyn Keyes.
WILDCAT OF TUCSON (Columbia, 1940) d Lambert Hillyer, s Wild Bill Elliott, Dub Taylor, Evelyn Young.
ACROSS THE SIERRAS (Columbia, 1941) d D. Ross Lederman, s Wild Bill Elliott, Dub Taylor, Luana Walters.
NORTH FROM THE LONE STAR (Columbia, 1941) d Lambert Hillyer, s Wild Bill Elliott, Dub Taylor, Dorothy Fay.
THE RETURN OF DANIEL BOONE (Columbia, 1941) d Lambert Hillyer, s Wild Bill Elliott, Dub Taylor, Betty Miles.
HANDS ACROSS THE ROCKIES (Columbia, 1941) d Lambert Hillyer, s Wild Bill Elliott, Dub Taylor, Mary Daily.
THE SON OF DAVY CROCKETT (Columbia, 1941) d Lambert Hillyer, s Wild Bill Elliott, Dub Taylor, Iris Meredith.

824. *WILD BILL ELLIOTT AND GABBY HAYES*
CALLING WILD BILL ELLIOTT (Republic, 1943) d Spencer Bennett, s Wild Bill Elliott, George "Gabby" Hayes, Anne Jeffreys.
THE MAN FROM THUNDER RIVER (Republic, 1943) d John English, s Wild Bill Elliott, George "Gabby" Hayes, Anne Jeffreys.
DEATH VALLEY MANHUNT (Republic, 1943) d John English, s Wild Bill Elliott, George "Gabby" Hayes, Anne Jeffreys.
WAGON TRACKS WEST (Republic, 1943) d Howard Bretherton, s Wild Bill Elliott, George "Gabby" Hayes, Anne Jeffreys.
OVERLAND MAIL ROBBERY (Republic, 1943) d John English, s Wild Bill Elliott, George "Gabby" Hayes, Anne Jeffreys.
HIDDEN VALLEY OUTLAWS (Republic, 1944) d Howard Bretherton, s Wild Bill Elliott, George "Gabby" Hayes, Anne Jeffreys.

825.*WILD BILL ELLIOTT AND TEX RITTER*
KING OF DODGE CITY (Columbia, 1941) d Lambert Hillyer, s Wild Bill Elliott, Tex Ritter, Dub Taylor, Judith Linden.
ROARING FRONTIERS (Columbia, 1941) d Lambert Hillyer, s Wild Bill Elliott, Tex Ritter, Ruth Ford.
LONE STAR VIGILANTES (Columbia, 1942) d Wallace Fox, s Wild Bill Elliott, Tex Ritter, Virginia Carpenter, Luana Walters.
BULLETS FOR BANDITS (Columbia, 1942) d Robert Lee Johnson, s Wild Bill Elliott, Tex Ritter, Dorothy Short.
NORTH OF THE ROCKIES (Columbia, 1942) d Lambert Hillyer, s Wild Bill Elliott, Tex Ritter, Shirley Patterson.
THE DEVIL'S TRAIL (Columbia, 1942) d Lambert Hillyer, s Wild Bill Elliott, Tex Ritter, Eileen O'Hearn.

PRAIRIE GUNSMOKE (Columbia, 1942) d Lambert Hillyer, s Wild Bill Elliott, Tex Ritter, Virginia Carroll.
VENGEANCE OF THE WEST (Columbia, 1942) d Lambert Hillyer, s Wild Bill Elliott, Tex Ritter, Adele Mara.

826. WILD BILL HICKOK AND JINGLES
These programmers are made up of episodes of the television Western THE ADVENTURES OF WILD BILL HICKOK (syndicated and on CBS and ABC, 1951-58). The leading players also appeared in a radio version of the program.
BORDER CITY RUSTLERS (Allied Artists, 1953) d Frank McDonald, s Guy Madison, Andy Devine.
THE TITLED TENDERFOOT (Allied Artists, 1955) d Frank McDonald, s Guy Madison, Andy Devine.

827. WILDERNESS FAMILY, THE
A modern couple with two children, tired of suburban hassles, take to the outdoors.
ADVENTURES OF THE WILDERNESS FAMILY (Pacific International, 1975) d Stewart Raffill, s Robert Logan, Susan D. Shaw.
FURTHER ADVENTURES OF THE WILDERNESS FAMILY (Pacific International, 1978) [aka WILDERNESS FAMILY, PART 2] d Frank Zuniga, s Robert Logan, Susan D. Shaw.
MOUNTAIN FAMILY ROBINSON (Pacific International, 1979) d John Cotter, s Robert Logan, Susan D. Shaw.

828. WILD GEESE, THE
Mercenaries rescue a kidnapped African leader in the first entry of this series.
THE WILD GEESE (Allied Artists, 1978) d Andrew V. McLaglen, s Richard Burton, Roger Moore.
WILD GEESE II (Frontier/Thorn--EMI, 1985) d Peter Hunt, s Scott Glenn, Barbara Carrera.

829. WILD THINGS
These are adult pictures.
WILD THINGS (Cal Vista, 1985) s Elle Rio, Herschel Savage.
WILD THINGS II (Cal Vista, 1986) d Alex deRenzy, s Amber Lynn, Joey Silvera.

830. WILD WILD WEST, THE
These TV movies derived from a secret agent-Western TV series of the same name featuring characters James T. West and Artemus Gordon. The program aired on CBS 1965-70.
THE WILD WILD WEST REVISITED (CBS Entertainment, 1979) (CBS-TV movie) d Burt Kennedy, s Robert Conrad, Ross Martin.
MORE WILD WILD WEST (CBS Entertainment, 1980) (CBS-TV movie) d Burt Kennedy, s Robert Conrad, Ross Martin.

MOTION PICTURE SERIES & SEQUELS 359

831. WILLARD
Stephen Filbert's novel *Ratman's Notebooks* inspired these films. Lonely Willard Stiles's only friends are pet rats which he trains as killers. Ben, of the second film, is a lead rat.
WILLARD (Cinerama, 1971) d Daniel Mann, s Bruce Davison, Ernest
  Borgnine.
BEN (Cinerama, 1972) d Phil Karlson, s Lee H. Montgomery, Joseph
  Campanella.

832. WILLIAM
The grubby sub-teenager featured in comic stories by Richmal Crompton was translated to films (in addition to a BBC radio series 1945 to circa 1950 and a television series 1976-77).
JUST WILLIAM'S LUCK (United Artists, 1947) d Val Guest, s William
  Graham.
WILLIAM COMES TO TOWN (United Artists, 1948) d Val Guest, s William
  Graham.

832A. WILLIE WESTINGHOUSE
These are silent-era comedies.
WILLIE'S FIRST SMOKE (Edison, 1899)
WILLIE'S HAT (American Mutoscope & Biograph, 1902)
WILLIE'S CAMERA (American Mutoscope & Biograph, 1902)
WILLIE WESTINGHOUSE AND THE DOCTOR'S BATTERY (American
  Mutoscope & Biograph, 1903)
WILLIE'S VACATION (Paley & Steiner, 1904)
WILLIE BECOMES AN ARTIST (Biograph, 1912) s Eddie Dillon.

833. WILLIE WORK
Harold Lloyd played this comic character for a series of short comedies for Hal Roach before adopting the LONESOME LUKE personna. The list may be incomplete. (See also HAROLD LLOYD.)
WILLIE (1914) s Harold Lloyd.
WILLIE'S HAIRCUT (1914) s Harold Lloyd.
WILLIE GOES TO SEA (1915) s Harold Lloyd.

834. WILL ROGERS TRAVELOGUES
The folksy humorist made a number of silent and feature films. Listed here are a series of short "travel" subjects.
WITH WILL ROGERS IN DUBLIN (C.S. Clancy/Pathe, 1927) s Will Rogers.
HIKING THROUGH HOLLAND WITH WILL ROGERS (C.S. Clancy/Pathe,
  1927) s Will Rogers.
WITH WILL ROGERS IN PARIS (C.S. Clancy/Pathe, 1927) s Will Rogers.
ROAMING THE EMERALD ISLE WITH WILL ROGERS (C.S.
  Clancy/Pathe, 1927) s Will Rogers.
HUNTING FOR GERMANS IN BERLIN WITH WILL ROGERS (C.S.
  Clancy/Pathe, 1927) s Will Rogers.

360 MOTION PICTURE SERIES & SEQUELS

THROUGH SWITZERLAND AND BAVARIA WITH WILL ROGERS (C.S. Clancy/Pathe, 1927) s Will Rogers.
WHIRLING AROUND FRANCE WITH WILL ROGERS (C.S. Clancy/Pathe, 1927) s Will Rogers.
WITH WILL ROGERS IN LONDON (C.S. Clancy/Pathe, 1927) s Will Rogers.
EXPLORING ENGLAND WITH WILL ROGERS (C.S. Clancy/Pathe, 1927) s Will Rogers.
REELING DOWN THE RHINE WITH WILL ROGERS (C.S. Clancy/Pathe, 1928) s Will Rogers.
OVER THE BOUNDING BLUE WITH WILL ROGERS (C.S. Clancy/Pathe, 1928) s Will Rogers.

835. WIZARD OF OZ, THE
The 1939 film version of L. Frank Baum's fantasy of a Kansas farmgirl's adventures in Oz has become a classic. Baum wrote more than a dozen Oz novels.
THE WIZARD OF OZ (Selig, 1910)
DOROTHY AND THE SCARECROW (Selznick, 1910)
LAND OF OZ (Selznick, 1910)
THE PATCHWORK GIRL OF OZ (Paramount, 1914) s Mildred Harris.
HIS MAJESTY, THE SCARECROW OF OZ (Baum, 1914) s Mildred Harris.
THE MAGIC CLOAK OF OZ (Baum, 1914) s Mildred Harris.
THE RAGGED GIRL OF OZ (Baum, 1919)
THE WIZARD OF OZ (Cadwick, 1925) d Larry Semon, s Larry Semon, Bryant Washburn, Dorothy Dwan.
THE WIZARD OF OZ (MGM, 1939) d Victor Fleming, s Judy Garland, Ray Bolger, Bert Lahr.
THE WONDERFUL LAND OF OZ (1969)
JOURNEY BACK TO OZ (1974) (animated) d Hal Sutherland, voices Liza Minnelli, Milton Berle, Margaret Hamilton.
OZ (1976)
THE WIZ (Universal, 1978) d Sidney Lumet, s Diana Ross, Michael Jackson.
20th CENTURY OZ (1978)
RETURN TO OZ (Buena Vista, 1985) d Walter Murch, s Nicol Williamson, Jean Marsh.

836. WIZARDS OF THE LOST KINGDOM
A master swordsman saves a sorcerer's son.
WIZARDS OF THE LOST KINGDOM (Concorde, 1985) d Hector Olivera, s Bo Svenson.
WIZARDS OF THE LOST KINGDOM II (Concorde, 1989) d Charles Griffith, s David Carradine, Lana Clarkson.

837. WOLF MAN, THE
These lycanthropic pictures, along with those featuring the FRANKENSTEIN MONSTER, the INVISIBLE MAN, DRACULA and the MUMMY, were very popular in the 1940s and '50s.

WEREWOLF OF LONDON (Universal, 1935) d Stuart Walker, s Henry Hull, Warner Oland, Valerie Hobson
THE WOLF MAN (Universal, 1941) d George Waggner, s Claude Raines, Warren William, Ralph Bellamy, Bela Lugosi.
FRANKENSTEIN MEETS THE WOLF MAN (Universal, 1943) d Roy William Neill, s Lon Chaney Jr., Bela Lugosi, Ilona Massey.
THE RETURN OF THE VAMPIRE (Columbia, 1943) d Lew Landers, s Bela Lugosi, Frieda Inescort.
CRY OF THE WEREWOLF (Columbia, 1944), d Henry Levin, s Nina Foch, Stephen Crane.
HOUSE OF FRANKENSTEIN (Universal, 1944) d Erle C. Kenton, s Boris Karloff, J. Carrol Naish, Lon Chaney Jr., John Carradine.
HOUSE OF DRACULA (Universal, 1945) d Erle C. Kenton, s Lon Chaney Jr., John Carradine.
SHE-WOLF OF LONDON (Universal, 1946) d Jean Yarbrough, s June Lockhart, Don Porter.
ABBOTT AND COSTELLO MEET FRANKENSTEIN (Universal, 1948) d Charles Barton, s Bud Abbott, Lou Costello, Lon Chaney Jr., Bela Lugosi.
THE WEREWOLF (Columbia, 1956) d Fred F. Sears, s Steven Rich, Don Megowan.
I WAS A TEENAGE WEREWOLF (American International, 1957) d Gene Fowler Jr., s Michael Landon, Yvonne Lime.
THE CURSE OF THE WEREWOLF (Universal, 1961) [aka THE WOLFMAN] d Terence FIsher, s Clifford Evans, Oliver Reed.
WEREWOLF IN A GIRL'S DORMITORY (MGM, 1963) d Richard Benson, s Barbara Lass, Carl Schell, Curt Lowens.
FURY OF THE WOLF MAN (1970) d Jose Maria Zabalza, s Paul Naschy, Perla Cristal.
WEREWOLVES ON WHEELS (Fanfare, 1971) d Michael Levesque.
WEREWOLF OF WASHINGTON (Diplomat, 1973) d Milton Moses Ginsberg, s Dean Stockwell, Biff McGuire.
AMERICAN WEREWOLF IN LONDON (Universal, 1981) d John Landis, s David Naughton, Jenny Agutter.

838. WOMEN'S PENITENTIARY
There's sex and violence behind bars as lesbian guards torment their prisoners.
WOMEN'S PENITENTIARY (MCM Entertainment) d Bob Oliver, s Sherri Vernon, Dixie Lane.
WOMEN'S PENITENTIARY II (MCM Entertainment, 1989) d Gerry De Leon, s Pam Grier, Judy Brown.

839. *WHEELER AND WOOLSEY*
Comedians Bert Wheeler and Robert Woolsey team for a series of pictures.
RIO RITA (RKO, 1929) d Luther Reed, s Bert Wheeler, Robert Woolsey, Bebe Daniels, John Boles.

THE CUCKOOS (RKO, 1930) d Paul Sloane, s Bert Wheeler, Robert Woolsey, June Clyde.
DIXIANA (RKO, 1930) d Luther Reed, s Bert Wheeler, Robert Woolsey, Bebe Daniels.
HALF SHOT AT SUNRISE (RKO, 1930) d Paul Sloane, s Dorothy Lee, Bert Wheeler, Robert Woolsey.
HOOK, LINE AND SINKER (RKO, 1930) d Edward Cline, s Bert Wheeler, Robert Woolsey.
CRACKED NUTS (RKO, 1931) d Edward Cline, s Bert Wheeler, Robert Woolsey, Dorothy Lee, Edna May Oliver.
CAUGHT PLASTERED (RKO, 1931) d William A. Seiter, s Bert Wheeler, Robert Woolsey, Dorothy Lee.
OH! OH! CLEOPATRA (RKO, 1931) d Joseph Santley, s Bert Wheeler, Robert Woolsey, Dorothy Burgess.
PEACH O'RENO (RKO, 1931) d William A. Seiter, s Bert Wheeler, Robert Woolsey, Dorothy Lee, Zelma O'Neal.
GIRL CRAZY (RKO, 1932) d William A. Seiter, s Bert Wheeler, Robert Woolsey, Eddie Quillan.
THE SLIPPERY PEARLS (RKO, 1932) s Bert Wheeler, Robert Woolsey, Wallace Beery, Buster Keaton.
HOLD 'EM JAIL (RKO, 1932) d Norman Taurog, s Bert Wheeler, Robert Woolsey, Betty Grable.
SO THIS IS AFRICA (Columbia, 1933) d Edward Cline, s Raquel Torres, Esther Muir, Bert Wheeler, Robert Woolsey.
DIPLOMANIACS (RKO, 1933) d William A. Seiter, s Bert Wheeler, Robert Woolsey, Marjorie White.
HIPS HIPS HOORAY (RKO, 1934) d Mark Sandrich, s Dorothy Lee, Thelma Todd, Bert Wheeler, Robert Woolsey.
COCKEYED CAVALIERS (RKO, 1934) d Mark Sandrich, s Thelma Todd, Dorothy Lee, Bert Wheeler, Robert Woolsey.
KENTUCKY KERNELS (RKO, 1934) d George Stevens, s Bert Wheeler, Robert Woolsey, Mary Carlisle.
THE NITWITS (RKO, 1935) d George Stevens, s Bert Wheeler, Robert Woolsey, Betty Grable.
THE RAINMAKERS (RKO, 1935) d Fred Guiol, s Bert Wheeler, Robert Woolsey, Dorothy Lee.
SILLY BILLIES (RKO, 1936) d Fred Guiol, s Bert Wheeler, Robert Woolsey, Dorothy Lee.
MUMMY'S BOYS (RKO, 1936) d Fred Guiol, s Bert Wheeler, Robert Woolsey, Barbara Pepper.
ON AGAIN, OFF AGAIN (RKO, 1937) d Edward Cline, s Bert Wheeler, Robert Woolsey, Marjorie Lord.
HIGH FLYERS (RKO, 1937) s Edward Cline, s Bert Wheeler, Robert Woolsey, Lupe Velez.

840. WONDER WOMAN

MOTION PICTURE SERIES & SEQUELS 363

Diana Prince, who fights crime in the DC comic books as Wonder Woman, also had her own television series with Lynda Carter. Writer William Moulton Marston created the heroine under the penname Charles Moulton in 1941. Lynda Carter played the heroine in a series for ABC and later CBS, 1976-79.
WONDER WOMAN (Warner Brothers, 1974) (ABC-TV movie) d Vincent McEveety, s Cathy Lee Crosby, Kaz Garas.
THE NEW ORIGINAL WONDER WOMAN (Warner Brothers Television, 1975) (ABC-TV movie) d Leonard Horn, s Lynda Carter, Lyle Waggoner.

840A. YOUNG GUNS
Billy the Kid and his cohorts get in trouble in the Old West.
YOUNG GUNS (20th Century-Fox, 1988) d Christopher Cain, s Emilio Estevez, Keifer Sutherland.
YOUNG GUNS II (Announced 1990)

YOUNG LADY CHATTERLEY
See LADY CHATTERLEY

841. YOUNG PIONEERS
Dakota homesteaders are featured in these television pictures.
YOUNG PIONEERS (ABC Circle Films, 1976) (ABC-TV movie) d Michael O'Herlihy, s Roger Kern, Linda Purl.
YOUNG PIONEERS' CHRISTMAS (ABC Circle Films, 1976) (ABC-TV movie) d Michael O'Herlihy, s Roger Kern, Linda Purl.

842. ZAPPED
A teenager acquires telekenetic powers, which he uses largely to unbutton the blouse of his girlfriend, in the initial outing of this series.
ZAPPED (Embassy, 1982) d Robert J. Rosenthal, s Scott Baio, Heather Thomas.
ZAPPED AGAIN (ITC, 1989) d Doug Campbell, s Todd Eric Andrews, Kelli Williams.

843. ZATOICHI
These are Oriental adventures featuring a blind swordsman.
ZATOICHI (Daiei, 1968) d Kimoyoshi Yasuda.
ZATOICHI MEETS YOJIMBO (Bijou, 1970) d Kihachi Okamoto, s Shintaro Katso, Toshiro Mifune.
ZATOICHI'S CANE SWORD (Daiei, 1971) d Kimoyoshi Yasuda.
ZATOICHI AT LARGE (Toho, 1973) d Kazuo Mori.

844. ZORRO
The California version of the SCARLET PIMPERNEL appeared in short stories written by Johnston McCulley beginning in 1919 in *All-Story Weekly*. Television versions aired 1957-59 and 60-61 (with Guy Williams); 1983 (as a situation comedy with Henry Darrow); and 1990- (with Duncan Regehr).

364 MOTION PICTURE SERIES & SEQUELS

THE MARK OF ZORRO (United Artists, 1920) d Fred Niblo, s Douglas Fairbanks, Marguerite de la Motte.
DON Q, SON OF ZORRO (United Artists, 1925) d Donald Crisp, s Douglas Fairbanks, Mary Astor.
THE BOLD CABALLERO (Republic, 1936) d Wells Root, s Robert Livingston, Heather Angel.
ZORRO RIDES AGAIN (Republic, 1937) (twelve-episode serial) d William Witney and John English, s John Carroll, Helen Christian.
ZORRO'S FIGHTING LEGION (Republic, 1939) (twelve chapters) d William Witney and John English, s Ronald Davidson, Franklyn Adreon.
THE MARK OF ZORRO (20th Century-Fox, 1940) d Rouben Mamoulian, s Tyrone Power.
ZORRO'S BLACK WHIP (Republic, 1944) (twelve chapters) d Spencer Gordon Bennet and Wallace Grissell, s Basil Dickey, Jesse Duffy.
SON OF ZORRO (Republic, 1947) (thirteen episodes) d Spencer Bennet and Fred C. Brannon, s George Turner, Peggy Stewart, Roy Barcroft.
GHOST OF ZORRO (Republic, 1949) (twelve chapters) d Fred C. Brannon, s Clayton Moore, Pamela Blake, Roy Barcroft.
ZORRO THE AVENGER (Walt Disney, 1960) d Charles Barton, s Guy Williams, Henry Calvin.
ZORRO (1961) d Duccio Tessari, s Alain Delon, Stanley Baker.
ZORRO AND THE THREE MUSKETEERS (Golden Era, 1962) d Marino Vacca, s Gordon Scott, Jose Greci.
ZORRO THE AVENGER (Norberto Solino, 1963) d Joaquin Luis Romero Marchent, s Frank Latimore, Mary Anderson.

Sean Connery was the first to play the role of Ian Fleming's dapper spy 007 on the big screen. Appearing with him in DR. NO is Ursula Andress.

MOTION PICTURE SERIES & SEQUELS 365

Something is puzzling George "Gabby" Hayes, perennial sidekick to dozens of B Western heroes including Roy Rogers.

SAMSON AND THE SLAVE QUEEN (American-International, 1964) [aka ZORRO AGAINST MACISTE] d Umberto Lenzi, s Pierre Brice.
ZORRO THE REBEL (Romana Film, 1966) d Pierro Pierotti, s Howard Ross, Dina De Santis.
ZORRO IN THE COURT OF SPAIN (1968) d Guido Zurli, s George Ardisson, Jack Stuart.
ZORRO, MARQUIS OF NAVARRA (Romana Film, 1971) d Jean Monty, s Nadior Moretti, Maria Luisa Longo.
THE MARK OF ZORRO (20th Century-Fox, 1974) (ABC-TV movie) d Don McDougall, s Frank Langella, Ricardo Montalban.
EROTIC ADVENTURES OF ZORRO (1973)
ZORRO (Titanus, 1975) d Duccio Tessari, s Alain Delon, Stanley Baker.
ZORRO, THE GAY BLADE (20th Century-Fox, 1981) d Peter Medak, s George Hamilton, Lauren Hutton.

845. ZULU
South African is the setting for the story of the British and the Zulus. The second picture gives the background of the first film, of the British mishandling which lead to a massacre of 1,200 soldiers in 1879.
ZULU (Embassy, 1964) d Cy Endfield, s Stanley Baker, Jack Hawkins, Ulla Jacobsson.
ZULU DAWN (Samarkand, 1979) d Douglas Hickox, s Burt Lancaster, Peter O'Toole.

REFERENCES

Adams, Les, and Buck Rainey, *Shoot 'Em Ups* (New Rochelle, New York: Arlington House, 1978)

Aros, Andrew A., *A Title Guide to the Talkies, 1964 Through 1974* (Metuchen, New Jersey: Scarecrow Press, 1977)

-- *A Title Guide to the Talkies, 1975 Through 1984* (Metuchen, New Jersey: Scarecrow Press, 1986)

Barbour, Alan G., *Days of Thrills and Adventure* (New York: Colliers, 1970)

Bogle, Donald, *Toms, Coons, Mulattoes, Mammies & Bucks: An Interpretive History of Blacks in American Films* (expanded edition) (New York: Continuum, 1989)

Castleman, Harry, and Walter J. Podrazik, *Harry and Wally's Favorite TV Shows: A Fact-Filled Opinionated Guide to The Best and Worst on TV* (New York: Prentice-Hall, 1989)

Canby, Vincent, "A Revolution Reshapes Movies" (*The New York Times*, 7 January 1990)

Catalog of Copyright Entries, Cumulative Series: 1904-1912 Identified from the Records of the United States Copyright Office (Washington, D.C.: Library of Congress, 1951); 1912-1939 (Washington, D.C.: Library of Congress, 1951); 1940-1949 (Washington, D.C.: Library of Congress, 1953); 1950-1959 (Washington, D.C.: Library of Congress, 1961); 1960-1971 (Washington, D.C.: Library of Congress, 1971).

Cline, William C., *In the Nick of Time* (Jefferson, North Carolina: McFarland, 1984)

Connelly, Robert, *The Motion Picture Guide: Silent Film 1910-1936* (Chicago, Illinois: Cinebooks, 1986)

Dimmitt, Richard Bertrand, *A Title Guide to the Talkies: A Comprehensive Listing of 16,000 Feature-Length Films From October, 1927, Until December, 1963* (Metuchen, New Jersey: Scarecrow Press, 1965) (two volumes)

Directory of Adult Films: Adam Film World Guide 1987 (Los Angeles, California: Knight Publishing, 1987)

Drew, Bernard A., "From Pulp to Celluloid," *Film Comment*, July-August 1978, 65-67.

--, *Lawmen in Scarlet: A Reference Guide to Royal Canadian Mounted Police Fiction and Films* (Metuchen, New Jersey: Scarecrow Press, 1990)

Dunning, John, *Tune in Yesterday: The Ultimate Encyclopedia of Old-Time Radio 1925-1976* (Englewood Cliffs, New Jersey: Prentice-Hall, 1976)

Ebert, Roger, 1990 Edition, *Roger Ebert's Movie Home Companion* (Kansas City, Missouri: Andrews, McMeel & Parker, 1989)

Enser, A.G.S., *Filmed Books and Plays: A List of Books and Plays from Which Films Have Been Made, 1928-86* (Brookfield, Vermont: Gower, 1987)

Essoe, Gabe, *Tarzan of the Movies: A Pictorial History of More Than Fifty Years of Edgar Rice Burroughs' Legendary Hero* (Secaucus, New Jersey: Citadel Press, 1968)

Everson, William K., *The Detective in Film: A Pictorial Treasury of the Screen Sleuth from 1903 to the Present* (Secaucus, New Jersey: Citadel, 1972)
Frank, Allan, *The Science Fiction and Fantasy Film Handbook* (Totowa, New Jersey: Barnes & Noble Books, 1982)
Gabree, John, *Gangsters from Little Caesar to the Godfather* (New York: Pyramid, 1973)
Gehring, Wes D., *Handbook of American Film Genres* (Westport, Connecticut: Greenwood Press, 1988)
Glut, Donald F., *The Dracula Book* (Metuchen, New Jersey.: Scarecrow, 1975)
--, *The Frankenstein Legend: A Tribute to Mary Shelley and Boris Karloff* (Metuchen, New Jersey: Scarecrow, 1973)
--, and Jim Harmon, *The Great Television Heroes* (Garden City, New York: Doubleday, 1975)
Halliwell, Leslie, *The Filmgoer's Companion*, fourth edition (New York: Avon, 1975)
--, *Halliwell's Film Guide*, sixth edition (New York; Charles Scribner's, 1989)
Hardy, Phil, editor, *The Encyclopedia of Horror Movies* (New York: Harper & Row, 1986)
Hayes, David, and Brent Walker, *The Films of the Bowery Boys: A Pictorial History of the Dead End Kids* (Secaucus, New Jersey: Citadel Press, 1984)
HBO's Guide to Movies on Videocassette and Cable TV 1990 (New York: Harper & Row, 1989)
Herx, Henry, and Tony Zaza, *The Family Guide to Movies on Video: The Moral and Entertainment Values of 5,000 Movies on TV and Videocassette* (New York: Crossroad, 1988)
Hilger, Michael, *The American Indian in Film* (Metuchen, New Jersey: Scarecrow Press, 1986)
Holland, Ted, *B Western Actors Encyclopedia: Facts, Photos and Filmographies for More than 250 Familiar Faces* (Jefferson, North Carolina: McFarland, 1989)
Kael, Pauline, *5001 Nights at the Movies: A Guide from A to Z* (New York: Henry Holt, 1985)
Kagan, Norman, *The War Film* (New York: Pyramid, 1974)
Kinnard, Roy, *Fifty Years of Serial Thrills* (Metuchen, New Jersey: Scarecrow, 1983)
Lahue, Kalton C., *Bound and Gagged: The Story of the Silent Serials* (New York: Castle, 1968)
--, *Mack Sennett's Keystone: The Man, The Myth, and the Comedies* (New York: A.S. Barnes, 1971)
--, *World of Laughter: The Motion Picture Comedy Short, 1910-1930* (Norman, Oklahoma: University of Oklahoma Press, 1966)
--, and Terry Brewer, *Kops and Custards: The Legend of Keystone Films* (Norman, Oklahoma: University of Oklahoma Press, 1968)
Langman, Larry, and Edgar Borg, *Encyclopedia of American War Films* (New York: Garland, 1989)

Lee, Raymond, *Not So Dumb: Animals in the Movies* (New York: A.S. Barnes, 1970)
Lenberg, Jeff, *The Encyclopedia of Animated Cartoon Series* (Revised) (New York; DaCapo Press, 1985)
Lieberman, Susan, and Frances Cable, *Memorable Film Characters: An Index to Roles and Performers, 1915-1983* (Westport, Connecticut: Greenwood Press, 1984)
Maltin, Leonard, *The Great Movie Comedians from Charlie Chaplin to Woody Allen* (New York: Crown, 1978)
--, *The Great Movie Shorts: Those Wonderful One- and Two-Reelers of the Thirties and Forties* (New York: Bonanza, 1972)
--, *1990 Edition, Leonard Maltin's TV Movies and Video Guide* (New York: New American Library, 1989)
-- and Richard W. Bann, *Our Gang: The Life and Times of the Little Rascals* (New York: Crown, 1977)
Marill, Alvin H., *Movies Made for Television: The Telefeature and the Mini-Series 1964-1984* (New York: Zoetrope, 1984)
Martin, Mick, Marsha Porter and Ed Remitz, *Video Movie Guide for Kids* (New York: Ballantine, 1987)
--, and Marsha Porter, *Video Movie Guide 1990* (New York: Ballantine, 1989)
Michael, Paul, editor, *The Great American Movie Book* (Englewood Cliffs, New Jersey: Prentice-Hall, 1980)
McCarty, John, *Splatter Movie Guide* (New York: St. Martin's Press, 1989)
Moss, Robert F., *Karloff and Company: The Horror Film* (New York: Pyramid, 1974)
Motion Pictures 1894-1912, Identified from the Records of the United States Copyright Office (Washington, D.C.: United States Copyright Office, 1953)
Nash, Jay Robert, and Stanley Ralph Ross, *The Motion Picture Guide* (Chicago, Illinois: Cinebooks, 1987) and annual supplements.
Nevins, Francis M., *The Films of Hopalong Cassidy* (Waynesville, North Carolina: World of Yesterday, 1988)
Newman, Kim, *Nightmare Movies: A Critical Guide to Contemporary Horror Film* (New York: Harmony, 1989)
New York Times Film Reviews, 1913-1986 (New York: Garland Publishing, continuing series)
Nivers, Kemp R., edited by Bebe Bergsten, *Motion Pictures from the Library Of Congress Paper Print Collection 1894-1912* (Berkeley, California: University of California Press, 1967)
Novak, Ralph and Peter Travers, editors, *People Magazine Guide To Movies on Video* (New York: Collier Books, 1987)
Nowlan, Robert A., and Gwendolyn Wright Nowlan, *Cinema Sequels and Remakes, 1903-1987* (Jefferson, North Carolina: McFarland, 1989)
Parish, James Robert, *The Great Movie Series* (New York: A.S. Barnes, 1971)
--, *Great Combat Pictures* (Metuchen, New Jersey: Scarecrow, forthcoming)

--, and Michael R. Pitts, *Great Detective Pictures* (Metuchen, New Jersey: Scarecrow)
--, and Michael R. Pitts, *Great Detective Pictures II* (Metuchen, New Jersey: Scarecrow, forthcoming)
--, and Michael R. Pitts, *The Great Gangster Pictures* (Netuchen, New Jersey: Scarecrow, 1976)
--, and Michael R. Pitts, *The Great Gangster Pictures II* (Metuchen, New Jersey: Scarecrow, 1987)
--, and Michael R. Pitts, *The Great Science Fiction Pictures* (Metuchen, New Jersey: Scarecrow, 1977)
--, and Michael R. Pitts, *The Great Spy Pictures* (Metuchen, New Jersey: Scarecrow, 1974)
--, and Michael R. Pitts, *The Great Spy Pictures II* (Metuchen, New Jersey: Scarecrow, 1986)
--, and Michael R. Pitts, *The Great Western Pictures* (Metuchen, New Jersey: Scarecrow, 1976)
--, and Michael R. Pitts, *The Great Western Pictures II* (Metuchen, New Jersey: Scarecrow, 1988)
Peary, Danny, *Guide for the Film Fanatic* (New York; Simon & Schuster, 1986)
Penzler, Otto, *The Private Lives of Private Eyes, Spies, Crimefighters, and Other Good Guys* (New York: Grosset & Dunlap, 1977)
Phantom of the Movies, *The Phantom's Ultimate Video Guide* (New York: Dell, 1989)
Pitts, Michael R., *Famous Movie Detectives* (Metuchen, New Jersey: Scarecrow)
--, *Famous Movie Detectives II* (Metuchen, New Jersey: Scarecrow, forthcoming)
--, *Western Movies: A TV and Video Guide to 4200 Genre Films* (Jefferson, North Carolina: McFarland, 1986)
Pringle, David, *Imaginary People: A Who's Who of Modern Fictional Characters* (London: Paladin Grafton Books, 1987)
Rainey, Buck, *Heroes of the Range: Yesterday's Saturday Matinee Movie Cowboy* (Metuchen, New Jersey: Scarecrow, 1987)
--, *Shoot-Em Ups II* (Metuchen, New Jersey: Scarecrow, forthcoming)
Ramsaye, Terry, *A Million and One Nights: A History of the Motion Picture Through 1925* (New York: Touchstone, 1986)
Rimmer, Robert H., *The X-Rated Videotape Guide* (revised and updated) (New York: Harmony, 1986)
Robertson, Patrick, *Guinness Film Facts & Feats* (New York: Sterling Publishing, 1985)
Scheuer, Steven H., *1990-1991 Movies on TV and Videocassette* (New York: Bantam, 1989)
Sennett, Ted, *Lunatics and Lovers: The Years of the Screwball Movie Comedy from "Dinner at Eight" to "The Miracle of Morgan's Creek"* (New Rochelle, New York: Arlington House, 1973)

Skorman, Richard, *Off-Hollywood Movies: A Film Lover's Guide* (New York: Harmony, 1989)
Steinbrunner, Chris, and Otto Penzler, editors, *Encyclopedia of Mystery & Detection* (New York: McGraw-Hill, 1971)
Stewart, John, *Filmarama Vol. 1: The Formidable Years 1893-1919* (Metuchen, New Jersey: Scarecrow, 1975)
--, *Filmarama Vol. 2: The Flaming Years 1920-1929* (Metuchen, New Jersey: Scarecrow, 1977)
Terrace, Vincent, *The Complete Encyclopedia of Television Programs 1947-1976* (two volumes) (New York: A.S. Barnes, 1976)
Thomas, Tony, *The West That Never Was: Hollywood's Vision of the Cowboys and Gunfighters* (New York: Citadel Press, 1989)
Turano, Jim, "Sequel Fever!" *Video Marketplace*, (Volume 3, Number 3) January/February 1990, 8-9.
Variety Cannes '89 (special issue) (May 1989)
Variety Film Reviews 1907-1980: A Sixteen Volume Set including an Index to Titles (New York: Garland, 1983)
Variety 31st International Film Annual, 4 May 1988
Vernalye, Jerry, editor, *500 Best British and Foreign Films to Buy, Rent or Videotape* (New York: William Morrow, 1988)
Warren, Jon R., *Warren's Movie Poster Price Guide* (New York: Harmony, 1986)
Weaver, John T., *Twenty Years of Silents 1908-1928* (Metuchen, New Jersey: Scarecrow, 1971)
Weiss, Ken, and Ed Goodgold, *To Be Continued...: A Complete Guide to Motion Picture Serials* (New York: Bonanza Books, 1972)
Wiener, Tom, *The Book of Video Lists 1990 Edition* (New York: Madison Books, 1989)
Willis, Donald C., *Horror and Science Fiction Films (1913-71)* (Metuchen, New Jersey: Scarecrow, 1972)
--, *Horror and Science Fiction Films (1972-81)* (Metuchen, New Jersey: Scarecrow, 1982)
--, *Horror and Science Fiction Films (1981-83)* (Metuchen, New Jersey: Scarecrow, 1984)
X-Rated Movie Handbook, 1990 Edition (Adam Film World Guide Vol. 4 No. 12) (Los Angeles, California: Knight Publishing, 1989)
Zinman, David, *Saturday Afternoon at the Bijou* (New Rochelle, New York: Arlington House, 1973)

Publicity stills courtesy Movie Star News.
Laserprinting courtesy James DelGrande Design.

TITLE INDEX

Films in the main section are indexed here by title, with the initial article (A, An, The) dropped except in the case of foreign titles. For series in which the same introductory words are used (such as *Ma and Pa Kettle Go to Town, Ma and Pa Kettle Back on the Farm*, etc.), a single entry is given (*Ma and Pa Kettle... [all] 469*).

Abbott and Costello... (all) 1
Abbott and Costello Meet Dr. Jekyll and Mr. Hyde 1, 207
Abbott and Costello Meet Frankenstein 1, 203, 259, 837
Abbott and Costello Meet the Invisible Man 1, 374
Abbott and Costello Meet the Keystone Kops 1, 412
Abbott and Costello Meet the Mummy 1, 527
Abilene Trail 818
Abominable Dr. Phibes 210
Absent-Minded Professor 2
Accidental Accidents 127
Accidental Death 220
Ace of Scotland Yard 80
Ache in Every Stake 760
Aching Youths 127
Acro-Batty 585
Across the Badlands 213
Across the Plains 460
Across the Rio Grande 389
Across the Sierras 823
Act of Murder 220
Act Your Age 517
Adios, Sabata 660
A-Ducking They Did Go 760
Adventure of Sherlock Holmes' Smarter Brother 677

Adventurer 129
Adventures of a Rookie 644
Adventures of Arsene Lupin 32
Adventures of Bill and Bob 67
Adventures of Hercules 337
Adventures of Huckleberry Finn 767
Adventures of Long John Silver 788
Adventures of Mark Twain 767
Adventures of Nick Carter 541
Adventures of Red Ryder 617
Adventures of Robin Hood 634
Adventures of Robinson Crusoe 635
Adventures of Rusty 658
Adventures of Ruth 659
Adventures of Sherlock Holmes... (all) 677
Adventures of Tarzan 742
Adventure of the Speckled Band 677
Adventures of the Wilderness Family 827
Adventurous Blonde 781
Aeronautics 585
Affairs of Annabel 27
Affairs of Cappy Ricks 116
Affairs of Dobie Gillis 196
Affairs of Jimmy Valentine 7
Affairs of Robin Hood 634
After Midnight 89
After the Thin Man 753
After Thirty 3
Against All Odds 269
Agatha Christie's "A Caribbean Mystery" 380
Agatha Christie's "Dead Man's Folly" 336
Agatha Christie's "Thirteen at Dinner" 336
A-Haunting We Will Go 434
Ain't It Aggravatin' 585
Air Fright 752
Air Hoppers 583
Airplane... (all) 4
Airport... (all) 5
Air Raid Wardens 434

Air Tight 91
Aladdin's Lantern 560
Alarm 412
Alaska Love 22
Alexander: The Other Side of Dawn 175
Alfalfa's... (all) 560
Alfie... (all) 6
Alias Billy the Kid 725
Alias Boston Blackie 89
Alias Jimmy Valentine (all) 7
Alias Smith & Jones 8
Alias the Wolf 461
Alibi 336
Alibi Baby 517
Alibi Bye Bye 141
Alibi Racket 166
Alien 9
Aliens 9
Alimony Aches 22
Alkali Bests Broncho Billy 97
Alkali Ike... (all) 10
All Aboard 323
All About Hash 560
All-American Blondes 22
All-American Kickback 22
All-American Toothache 752
Allan Quatermain and the Lost City of Gold 11
All at Sea 703
All Creatures Great and Small (all) 13
All Dressed Up 703
All Gummed Up 760
All in a Day 703
All Lit Up 703
Allez Oop 108, 579
All For Nothing 127
Alligator... (all) 14
All Night Long 325
All Over Town 554
All Parts 127
All Quiet on the Western Front 15
All Steamed Up 141
All Teed Up 127
All the World's a Stooge 760
All Things Bright and Beautiful 13
All Wet 127, 703
All Work and No Pay 22
Alone in New York 815
Along the Mohawk Trail 437

372 MOTION PICTURE SERIES & SEQUELS

Along the Navajo Trail 648
Along the Oregon Trail 511
Along the Sundown Trail 268
Alphabet Murders 336, 380
Alphonse and Gaston (all) 15A
Alum and Eve 751
Alvin Purple... (all) 16
Amazing Captain Nemo 793
Amazing Exploits of the Clutching Hand 160
Amazing Tails... (all) 17
Ambrose... (all) 18
Ambushers 490
American Boyfriends 532
American Graffitti 19
American Ninja... (all) 20
American Soldier in Love and War (all) 20A
American Werewolf in London 837
Am I Having Fun 22
Amityville Horror... (all) 21
Among Those Present 323
Among Vultures 553
Ancient Cures 585
Andy Clyde Gets Spring Chicken 22
Andy Hardy... (all) 23
Andy Goes Wild 22
Andy Plays Hooky 22
Anesthesia 585
Angel 24
Angelique 26
Angel of the Island 25
Angel of the Night 25
Angels' Alley 90
Angel's Back 25
Angels Die Hard 333
Angels in Disguise 90
Angel III: The Final Chapter 24
Angels Wash Their Faces 176
Angels With Dirty Faces 176
Anger of the Golem 304
Angora Love 434
Animal Crackers 488
Animals in Action 585
Ankles Away 22
Annabel Takes a Tour 27
Anne... (all) 28
Annie 452
Anniversary Trouble 560
Another Fine Mess 434

Another Part of the Forest 448
Another Thin Man 752
Another Wild Idea 127
Antique Shop 106
Ants in the Pantry 760
Anvil Chorus 703
Anybody's War 794
Any Old Port 434, 703
Any Which Way You Can 234
Apache Country 282
Apache Gold 553
Apache Kid 199
A-Plumbing We Will Go 760
Apple Dumpling Gang... (all) 31
Apple in His Eye 517
Appointment with Murder 240
April Fool 127
Aqua Antics 585
Aquatic Artistry 583
Aquatic Kids 585
Arabian Nights 127
Arbor Day 560
Are Brunettes Safe? 127
Are Crooks Dishonest 323
Are Husbands Human? 703
Are Waitresses Safe? 61
Argentine Nights 630
Arizona Bound 655
Arizona Cyclone 395
Arizona Frontier 749
Arizona Kid 648
Arizona Legion 285
Arizona Manhunt 656
Arizona Nights 102
Arizona Ranger 764
Arizona Stagecoach 614
Arizona Territory 818
Arizona Terror 199
Arizona Whirlwind 784
Arkansas Judge 812
Army Champions 585
Around the World 410
Arrest Bulldog Drummond 104
Arsene Lupin... (all) 32
Arthur... (all) 33
Art in the Raw 517
Artists and Models... (all) 34
Artists and Muddles 22
Ask Father 323
Ask Grandma 560

Asleep at the Switch 61
Asleep in the Fleet 751
Assignment Terror 158
Assistant Wives 127
Astray from the Steerage 73
At First Sight 127
Athletic Daze 579
Athletiquiz 585
Atoll K 434
Atom Man Vs. Superman 728
At Sea Ashore 752
Attack of the Killer Tomatoes 417
Attack of the Mayan Mummy 527
Attempt to Kill 220
At The Old Stage Door 323
Attention, Suckers 581
At the Circus 488
At the Ringside 703
At the Villa Rose 368
Audioscopiks 582
Aunt Peg... (all) 35
Auto Antics 560
Avenging Angel 24
Average Husband 22
Awful Goof 127
Awful Tooth 560

Babes and Boobs 430
Babes in the Goods 752
Babes in Toyland 434
Babbling Brook 106
Babes in Arms 37
Babes on Broadway 37
Bab's... (all) 36
Baby Blues 560
Baby Brother 560
Baby Clothes 560
Baby Days 517
Babyface (all) 39
Babylon... (all) 40
Baby Makes Two 292
Baby Sitters Jitters 760
Back at the Front 797
Backfire 220
Back from the Front 760
Back in the Saddle 280
Backside to the Future (all) 43
Back Stage 560
Backs to Nature 752
Back to Bataan 51
Back to Nature 401

Back to the Beach 53
Back to the Future (all) 44
Back to the Woods 323, 760
Back Trail 396
Bacon Grabbers 434
Bad Boy 127
Bad Girls (all) 45
Bad Housekeeping 517
Badman from Red Butte 395
Bad Man of Deadwood 648
Bad Men of Thunder Gap 748
Badminton 585
Bad News Bears... (all) 46
Bakery 430
Balloonatic 108
Bandage Bait 585
Bandit King of Texas 12
Bandit Makes Good 97
Bandit of Sherwood Forest 634
Bandits of Dark Canyon 12
Bandits of El Dorado 213
Bandits of the Badlands 725
Bandits of the West 12
Bangville Police 412
Bank 129
Bank Shot 202
Barbed Wire 282
Barber... (all) 48A
Barber's Daughter 22
Barbara Dare's... (all) 47
Barbarian Queen (all) 48
Barbaric Beast of Boggy Creek 85
Barbee-Cues 585
Bargain Day 560
Bargain of the Century 751
Barnum & Ringling Inc. 560
Barnyard 430
Bar-Rac's Night Out 585
Bar 20... (all) 351
Baseball Bill 49A
Bashful 323
Basketball Technique 583
Basket Case (all) 50
Bataan 51
Bath Between 141
Bathing Beauties and Big Boobs 430
Bath Tub Perils 412
Batman (all) 52
Batman Dracula 203
Battle for the Planet of the Apes 596

Battle of Ambrose and Walrus 18
Battle of the Century 434
Battling Butler 108
Battle Royal 61
Beach Blanket Bingo 53
Beach Club 73
Beach Party 53
Bear Facts 560
Bears and Bad Men 430
Bear Shooters 560
Beast and the Magic Sword 158
Beat it 323
Beau Geste (all) 54
Beau Hunks 434
Beau Ideal 54
Beau Sabreur 54
Beauty and the Bandit 140
Beauty and the Bus 752
Beaux and Errors 517
Be Big 434
Bed and Board
Bedlam of Beards 141
Bedlam in Paradise 760
Bed of Roses 703
Bedroom Eyes (all) 55
Bedtime for Bonzo 87
Bedtime Worries 560
Beer Barrel Polecats 760
Bee's Buzz 22
Bees in His Bonnet 323
Before Breakfast 323
Before the Public 703
Beginner's Luck 560
Behind Blue Eyes (all) 56
Behind That Curtain 128
Behind the Criminal 166
Behind the Eight-Ball 630
Behind the Green Door (all) 57
Behind the Headlines 585
Behind the Mask 672
Behind the Screen 129
Belle of Samoa 141
Belles of St. Trinian's 58
Belles on Their Toes 133
Belle Starr (all) 59
Bell Hop 430
Bells of Capistrano 280
Bells of Coronado 651
Bells of Rosarita 648
Bells of San Angelo 647
Bells of St. Mary's 301
Below the Border 655

Below Zero 434
Ben 831
Beneath the Law 141
Beneath the Planet of the Apes 596
Beneath Western Skies 400
Benjamin Franklin Jr. 560
Benji (all) 60
Benson Murder Case 589
Be Reasonable 73
Berth Marks 434
Best Man 73
Better Movies 560
Betty... (all) 61A
Between Showers 129
Between the Acts 430
Between Two Women 208
Beverly Hills Cop (all) 62
Beware of Blondie 83
Beware! The Blob 81
Beyond the Door (all) 63
Beyond the Pecos 642
Beyond the Poseidon Adventure 603
Beyond the Purple Hills 282
Beyond the Sacramento 823
Beyond the Valley of the Dolls 803
Be Your Age 127
Bicycle Flirt 73
Big Bad Mama (all) 64
Big Bang 661
Big Beef 517
Big Broadcast... (all) 65
Big Business 401, 434, 560
Big Ears 560
Big Flash 325
Big Game 703
Bigger and Better 90
Bigger and Better Blondes 127
Big Idea 323, 703
Big Kick 325
Big Noise 434
Big Palooka 22
Big Premiere 560
Big Red Riding Hood 127
Big Show 280
Big Sleep 588
Big Squawk 127
Big Squeel 22
Big Squirt 127
Big Store 488
Big Show 560
Big-Top Pee-Wee 571

374 MOTION PICTURE SERIES & SEQUELS

Big Town 560
Bike Bug 703
Bikini Beach 53
Bill 66
Billion Dollar Brain 326
Bill on His Own 66
Billy... (all) 72
Billy Blazes, Esq. 323
Billy Jack... (all) 75
Billy the Kid... (all) 74
Billy the Kid Returns 653
Billy the Kid Versus Dracula 203
Bionic Showdown 687
Bird in the Head 760
Birds of a Feather 426
Birthday Blues 560
Bishop Murder Case 589
Bitch... (all) 76
Black Bird 477
Black Caesar 77
Black Camel 128
Black Coffee 336
Blackenstein 259
Black Frankenstein 259
Black Harvest of Countess Dracula 158
Black Hills 219
Black Hills Ambush 12
Black Lash 431
Blackie's Redemption 89
Black Inferno 203
Black Magic 128
Black Market Rustlers 614
Black Nine 49A
Black Sherlock Holmes 677
Blacksmith 108
Black Stallion 78
Black Widow 577
Blacula 79
Blake of Scotland Yard (all) 80
Blake the Lawbreaker 671
Blarney Stone 105
Blasted Event 517
Blazing Across the Pecos 213
Blazing Frontier 74
Blazing Guns 784
Blazing Hills 282
Blazing the Western Trail 213
Blazing Trail 213
Blissful Blunder 22
Blitz Kiss 223
Blitz on the Fritz 325

Blob 81
Block and Tackle 579
Block Busters 214
Blocked Trail 756
Blockheads 434
Bloe 'Em Up 703
Blonde and Groom 325
Blonde Atom Bomb 22
Blonde Dynamite 90
Blonde for a Day 500
Blondes at Work 781
Blonde's Revenge 61
Blonde Stayed On 22
Blondie... (all) 83
Blood and Roses 120
Blood and Thunder 91
Blood is My Heritage 203
Blood from the Mummy's Tomb 527
Blood of Dracula 203
Blood of Dracula's Castle 203
Blood of Dr. Jekyll 207
Blood of Frankenstein 203
Blood of Fu Manchu 269
Blood of the Demon 203
Blood Sport 190
Blood Suckers 211
Bloody Scream of Dracula 203
Blotto 434
Blue Blazes 108
Blue Canadian Skies 282
Blue Dulac 661
Blue Montana Skies 280
Blue Murder at St. Trinian's 58
Blues Busters 90
Blue Steel 459
Blue Sunday 703
Blue, White and Perfect 500
Bluffer 22
Blunder Boys 760
Blunderful Time 22
Boast and Boldness 430
Boat 108
Bodies in Heat... (all) 84
Bogey Man 88
Boggy Creek II 85
Bohemian Girl 434
Boiling Point 351
Bold Caballero 844
Bold Frontiersman 12
Bomba... (all) 86
Bonanza Town 213
Bone Crushers 579

Bonnie Scotland 434
Bon Voyage 517
Bonzo Goes to College 87
Boobie Dupes 760
Boobs in Arms 760
Boobs in the Woods 22, 325
Boodle and Bandits 430
Boogeyman (all) 88
Boogie Woogie 633
Boom Goes the Groom 22
Booster 127
Boot Hill bandits 614
Boots and Saddles 280
Booty and the Beast 760
Border Badmen 74
Border Bandits 396
Border Buckaroos 748
Border City Rustlers 826
Border Feud 431
Border G-Man 284
Borderland 351
Border Patrol 351
Border Saddlemates 624
Border Treasure 764
Border Vigilantes 351
Bored of Education 560
Borrowed Trouble 351
Borrowing Trouble 401
Boss of Boomtown 642
Boss of Bullion City 395
Boss of Hangtown Mesa 395
Boss of Rawhide 748
Boston Blackie... (all) 89
Both Barrels Blazing 213
Boudoir Butler 22
Bouncing Babies 560
Bourbon Street Shadows 672
Bowery Battalion 90
Bowery Blitzkreig 214
Bowery Bombshell 90
Bowery Boys Meet the Monsters 90
Bowery Buckaroos 90
Bowery Champs 214
Bowery to Bagdad 90
Boxing Gloves 560
Bowling Tricks 585
Bow Wows 703
Boy, Oh, Boy 22
Boys Help Themselves to Foxy Grandpa's Cigars 257A
Boys of the City 214
Boys, Still Determined, Try It Again on Foxy

MOTION PICTURE SERIES & SEQUELS 375

Grandpa, with the Same Result 257A
Boys Think They Have One On Foxy Grandpa, But He Fools Them 257A
Boys to Board 560
Boys Town 92
Boys Try to Put One Over on Foxy Grandpa 257A
Boys Will Be Joys 560
Braddock: Missing in Action III 507
Bram Stoker's Count Dracula 203
Brand of Fear 389
Brand of the Devil 748
Brasher Doubloon 588
Brats 434
Brawn of the North 722
Brazilian Connection 661
Breakin'... (all) 93
Brenda Star... (all) 94
Bric-a-Brac 517
Bride and Gloom 323
Bride by Mistake 626
Brideless Groom 760
Bride of Frankenstein 259
Bride's Bereavement 489
Brides of Dracula 203
Brides of Fu Manchu 269
Bride's Relations 21
Bridge on the River Kwai 95
Bright Eyes 61
Brighton Mystery 551
Bring Home the Turkey 560
Bringing Up Father 388
Bring Me the Head of Dobie Gillis 196
Broadway Melody... (all) 96
Broke in China 61
Bromo and Juliet 127
Bronco Billy... (all) 97
Bronze Buckaroo 322
Brother Knows 517
Brother Rat... (all) 98
Brothers of the Saddle 764
Brute 163
Bubble Trouble 760
Bubbling Over 703
Bubbling Troubles 560
Buccaneers 560
Buckaroo From Powder River 213

Buckaroo Sheriff of Texas 656
Bucking the Tiger 61
Buck Privates... (all) 99
Buck Rogers... (all) 100
Buddy's... (all) 103
Bulldog Drummond... (all) 104
Bullets and Saddles 614
Bullets for Bandits 825
Bull Fighter 73
Bullfighters 434
Bulls and Bears 22
Bumping into Broadway 323
Bumptious... (all) 104A
Bum's Rush 703
Bum Voyage 752
Bundle of Bliss 22
Bungalow Boobs 127
Bungalowing 421
Bungle... (all) 104B
Bunny... (all) 105
Burglar to the Rescue 672
Buried Loot 166
Buried Treasure 560
Burns and Allen in Lambchops 106
Bury Me Not on the Lone Prairie 395
Bus Pests 585
Buster and His Dog... (all) 107
Buster Brown (all) 107
Busy Bodies 434, 760
Busy Day 18
Butch and Sundance: The Early Years 109
Butch Cassidy and the Sundance Kid 109
Butcher's Nightmare 61
Butter Fingers 73
Button My Back 73
Buyer Beware 166
Buzzy... (all) 110
By Heck 73
By the Light of the Silvery Moon 573
By the Sad Sea Waves 323
By the Sea 129

Cabiri 471
Cactus Makes Perfect 760
Caddyshack (all) 111
California Firebrand 512

California Gold Rush 617
California or Bust 703
Calamity Anne... (all) 112
Call A Cop 91
Call a Taxi 703
Call Her Sausage 743
Calling All Curs 760
Calling All Doctors 127
Calling All Kids 560
Calling All Pa's 585
Call a Messenger 453
Call for Mr. Cave Man 703
Calling Bulldog Drummond 104
Calling Dr. Death 365
Calling Dr. Gillespie 208
Calling Dr. Kildare 208
Calling Hubby's Bluff 73
Calling Paul Temple 569
Calling Philo Vance 589
Calling Wild Bill Elliott 824
Call of the Canyon 280
Call of the Coocoos 434
Calla of the Klondike 515
Call of the Prairie 351
Call the Mesquiteers 756
Call the Witness 703
Camera Caught 585
Cameraman 108
Camera Sleuth 585
Came the Brawn 560
Camping Out 517
Campus Crushes 22
Canary Murder Case 589
Candidate for Murder 220
Candid Camermaniacs 585
Candy Goes to Hollywood 113
Canned Fishing 560
Cannibal Attack 405
Cannon 114
Cannonball 22
Cannon Ball Express 73
Cannonball Run (all) 115
Canyon Raiders 819
Cappy Ricks Comes Back 116
Cappy Ricks Returns 116
Captain America (all) 117
Captain Blood... (all) 118
Captain Kidd's Kids 323
Captain Nemo and the Underwater City 793
Captain Pirate 118

376 MOTION PICTURE SERIES & SEQUELS

Captain Sinbad 685
Captain Spanky's Show Boat 560
Captain Tugboat Annie 792
Captive Girl 405
Captive Wild Woman 119
Capture of Grizzly Adams 312
Caravan Trail 219
Career of Crime (all) 119A
Caretaker's Daughter 127
Carolina Blues 410
Carolina Moon 280
Carpetbaggers 121
Carry Harry 325
Carry On... (all) 122
Carson City Cyclone 199
Carson City Kid 648
Carson City Raiders 12
Carter Case 520
Carter Case: The Craig Kennedy Serial 160
Caryl of the Mountains 629
Case of Royal Murder 677
Case of the Black Cat 575
Case of the Curious Bride 575
Case of the Fantastical Casebook 677
Case of the Howling Dog 575
Case of the Lucky Legs 575
Case of the Mounting Fortune 677
Case of the Stuttering Bishop 575
Case of the Velvet Claws 575
Casey... (all) 122A
Cash and Carry 476, 760
Cash Customers 703
Cash Stashers 585
Casino Murder Case 589
Casino Royale 378
Cassidy of Bar 20 351
Castaways on Gilligan's Island 293
Castle in the Desert 128
Castle of Fu Manchu 269
Catalina Rowboat Race 696
Catch as Catch Can 751
Cat College 585
Cat, Dog & Co. 560
Cat People 123
Cat's Meow 325
Cat's Paw 323
Cattle Stampede 74

Caught From Behind (all) 124
Caught in a Cabaret 129
Caught in the Act 22
Caught in the End 61
Caught in the Rain 129
Caught Plastered 839
Cemetery Girls 203
Century Turns 330
Chain Letter Dimes 581
Chalk Up 579
Challenge 104
Challenge for Robin Hood 634
Challenge of Rin Tin Tin 629
Challenge of the Range 213
Challenge to Lassie 432
Champeen 560
Champion 129
Chandu... (all) 126
Change Partners 220
Chappaqua 203
Charley, My Boy 127
Charlie Chan... (all) 128
Charlie McCarthy, Detective 130
Chases of Pimple Street 127
Chasing Husbands 127
Cheaper by the Dozen 133
Cheaters at Play 461
Check Your Guns 219
Cheech & Chong's... (all) 134
Cheerful Liar 61
Chemist 108
Cherokee Flash 725
Cherokee Uprising 818
Cheyenne Kid 460
Cheyenne Roundup 395
Cheyenne Takes Over 431
Cheyenne Wildcat 617
Chick Carter, Detective 541
Chicken Feed 560
Chickens Comes Home 434
Chicken Thief 615
Child of Divorce 813
Children of the Damned 806
Child's Play (all) 130B
Chimp 434
Chinatown 136
Chinese Cat 128
Chinese Connection (all) 131
Chinese Ring 128
Chinese Parrot 128
Chinese Web 709
Chip of the Flying U 132, 395

Choo-Choo 560
Chop Suey & Co. 323
Christmas Lilies of the Field 444
C.H.U.D. (all) 137
Chump at Oxford 434
Chumps 22
Chumps and Chances 430
Chump Takes a Bump 127
Cinderella Swings It 666
Cinders of Love 412
Cipher Bureau 138
Circle of Children 139
Circus 129
Circus Cyclone 61
Circus Fever 560
Circus Hoodoo 325
Circus Show-Up 672
Circus Today 73
Cisco Kid... (all) 140
City Lights 129
City Slicker 323
Clancy at the Bat 22
Clancy Street Boys 214
Clarence the Cop... (all) 140A
Clark and McCullough... (all) 141
Clash of the Wolves 629
Class of '44 724
Class of Nuke 'Em High 142
Claudia 143
Claudia and David 143
Cleopatra Jones... (all) 144
Clean Sweep 517
Clever Dummy 61
Clipped Wings 90
Clock Wise 517
Close Call for Boston Blackie 89
Close Call for Ellery Queen 225
Cloudhopper 430
Clown Princes 560
Club Exotica... (all) 145
Clue of the New Pin 220
Clue of the Second Goblet 671
Clue of the Silver Key 220
Clue of the Twisted Candle 220
Clutching Hand 160
Coast of Skeletons 663
Cobbler 560
Cockeyed Cavaliers 839

MOTION PICTURE SERIES & SEQUELS 377

Cocoanuts 488
Cocoon... (all) 146
Code of the Cactus 443
Code of the Mounted 547
Code of the Outlaw 756
Code of the Prairie 725
Code of the Saddle 396
Code of the Silver Sage 12
Coffins on Wheels 166
Cohen... (all) 148
Cohens and Kellys... (all) 149
Cold Comrades 351
Cold Turkey 325
College 108
College Holiday 106
College Humor 106
College Scandal 150
College Swing 106
College Vamp 22
Colorado 648
Colorado Pioneers 617
Colorado Ranger 675
Colorado Serenade 219
Colorado Sundown 624
Colorado Sunset 280
Color of Money 358
Color Out of Space 169
Color Scales 578
Come Across 166
Come Back, Charleston Blue 147
Come Back, Miss Pipps 560
Come Clean 434
Come On Cowboys 756
Come Out Fighting 214
Coming of Angels.. (all) 152
Comin' Round the Mountain 1, 280
Commencement 560
Commotion on the Ocean 760
Commuting 421
Conan... (all) 153
Concorde Airport '79 5
Confessions from a Holiday Camp 154
Confessions of a Window Cleaner 154
Confessions of a Pop Performer 154
Confessions of Boston Blackie 89
Congo Maisie 476
Conquest of Cheyenne 617
Conquest of the Planet of the Apes 596

Constable 22
Contest Crazy 517
Convict 13 108
Cooks and Crooks 517
Cop au Vin 155
Cop Hater 222
Cops 108
Corner Pocket 703
Corny Casanovas 760
Corporation and the Ranch Girl 613A
Cotton Comes to Harlem 147
Counsel on de Fence 325
Count 129
Count Dracula 203
Counter Jumper 430
Countess Dracula... (all) 203
Countess Sweedie 731
Count of Monte Cristo 157
Country Gentlemen 554
Count Takes the Count 127
Count the Clues 456
Count the Votes 323
County Hospital 434
Count Yorga, Vampire 159
Count Your Change 323
Courage Mountain: The Further Adventures of Heidi 331
Courage of Lassie 432
Courage of the North 514
Courageous Dr. Christian 205
Courtin' Trouble 389
Courtship of Andy Hardy 23
Courtship of Miles Sandwich 703
Courtship of the Newt 633
Cousin Wilbur 560
Covered Trailer 339
Covered Wagon Days 756
Covered Wagon Raid 12
Cowboy and the Prize Fighter 617
Cowboy and the Senorita 654
Cowboy Cavalier 389
Cowboy Commandos 614
Cowboy Counselor 350
Cowboy Blues 411
Cowboy From Sundown 749
Cowboys from Texas 756
Cowboy Serenade 280
Cowcatcher's Daughter 22
Cracked Iceman 127
Cracked Nuts 839
Cracked Wedding Bells 703

Crack Your Heels 323
Cradle Robbers 560
Crash Goes the Hash 760
Crashing Las Vegas 90
Crashing the Movies 585
Crashing Thru' 620, 818
Crazy Fat Ethel II 161
Crazy Feet 127
Crazy House 554
Crazy Like A Fox 127
Crazy Over Horses 90
Creators of Foxy Grandpa 257A
Creature from the Black Lagoon 162
Creature Walks Among Us 162
Creeping Unknown 609
Creeps 760
Creepshow (all) 164
Crew Racing 583
Crime Control 633
Crime Doctor... (all) 165
Crime of Dr. Mabuse 209
Crime on Their Hands 760
Crime School 176
Criminal is Born 166
Critters... (all) 167
Crocodile Dundee (all) 168
Crooked Alley 89
Crooked River 675
Crossed Trails 396
Cry of the Werewolf 837
Cuban Rhythm 585
Cuckoo Cavaliers 760
Cuckoo on a Choo Choo 760
Cuckoos 839
Culinary Carving 585
Cupid's Day Off 61
Cure 129
Cured in the Excitement 73
Curious Contests 585
Curse... (all) 169
Curse of Dracula 203
Curse of Frankenstein 259
Curse of the Cat People 123
Curse of the Devil 158
Curse of the Fly 255
Curse of the Golem 303
Curse of the Mummy's Tomb 527
Curse of the Pink Panther 592
Curse of the Werewolf 837
Cut the Cards 703
Cyclone Fury 213

378 MOTION PICTURE SERIES & SEQUELS

Cyclone Kid 199

D.A... (all) 170
Daddy Boy 61
Dad for a Day 560
Dakota Kid 656
Daleks: Invasion Earth 198
Dallas Cowboy Cheerleaders (all) 171
Dalton's Women 431
Damien -- Omen II 556
Damsel in Distress 106
Dance With Me, Henry 1
Dancing Masters 434
Dancing Romeo 560
Danger Ahead 620
Dangerous Money 128
Dangerous Playground 351
Danger Zone (all) 172
Daredevil 61
Dare-Deviltry 583
Daring Caballero 140
Dark Alibi 128
Dark and Gruesome 356
Dark Command 648
Dark Delusions 208
Darker Than Amber 787
Dark Magic 633
Dark Shadows 166
Dartmouth Days 581
Dash of Courage 412
Date with the Falcon 240
Daughter of Shanghai 383
Daughter of the Dragon 269
Daughters of Joshua Cabe (all) 173
Davy Crockett... (all) 174
Dawn of the Dead 543
Dawn: Portrait of a Teenage Runaway 175
Dawn Riders 459
Day at the Races 488
Daydreams 108
Day for Thanks on Waltons Mountain 811
Day of Rest 633
Day of the Dead 543
Day of the Panther 565
Day's Life 129
Days of Buffalo Bill 725
Days of Jesse James 648
Days of Old 703
Days of Old Cheyenne 199
Dead Don't Dream 351

Dead End 176
Dead End Kids on Dress Parade 176
Deadlier Than the Male 104
Deadly Affair 695
Deadly Spawn (all) 177
Dead Man's Chest 220
Dead Man's Eyes 365
Dead Man's Gold 431
Dead Man's Gulch 199
Dead Man's Trail 398
Dead Men Tell 128
Dead or Alive 748
Death Drums Along the River 663
Death Goes North 629
Death Nurse 161
Death Valley Manhunt 824
Dead People 621
Dead Pool 194
Deafula 203
Dear Old Pal 703
Death on the Nile 336
Deathstalker... (all) 179
Death Trap 220
Death Valley Gunfighter 12
Death Valley Outlaws 199
Death Valley Rangers 784
Death Wish... (all) 180
Dear Brat 178
Dearly Departed 703
Dear Ruth 178
Dear Wife 178
Debbie... (all) 181
Decathlon Champion 585
Deerslayer 437
Deep in the Heart of Texas 395
Deep Sea Liar 61
Deep Throat (all) 182
Defective Detectives 325
Delinquent Bridegroom 61
Delta Force (all) 183
Demetrius and the Gladiators 632
Demons (all) 184
Denver Kid 12
Derby Day 560
Desert Bandit 199
Desert Death 166
Desert Horseman 213
Desert Passage 764
Desert Regatta 579
Desert Trail 459
Desert Vigilante 213

Desperado 184
Desperadoes of Dodge City 12
Desperadoes Outpost 12
Desperado Trail 553
Desperate Chance for Ellery Queen 225
Desperate Trails 395
Destination Saturn 100
Destroy All Monsters 300
Detective 242
Detectives Wanted 141
Devil Goddess 405
Devil in Miss Jones (all) 187
Devil Riders 74
Devil's Angels 333
Devil's Cargo 240
Devil's Mask 362
Devil's Playground 351
Devil's Trail 825
Dew Drop Inn 430
Dexterity 585
Diabolical Dr. Mabuse 209
Diamond Demon 585
Diamond from the Sky 187A
Diamond Jim 188
Diamonds Are Forever 378
Dick Barton... (all) 189
Dick Tracy... (all) 191
Did'Ja Know 585
Die Hard (all) 192
Die, Monster, Die 169
Dig That Gold 517
Dig That Uranium 90
Dig U 703
Dinner Hour 703
Diplomaniacs 839
Diplomats 141
Dippy Dentist 703
Dirty Dozen.... (all) 193
Dirty Harry 194
Dirty Work 434
Disciple of Dracula 203
Disorder in the Court 760
Ditto 108
Dive In 579
Divorce Dodger 73
Divot Diggers 560
Diziana 839
Dizzy Detectives 760
Dizzy Doctors 760
Dizzy Pilots 760
Django... (all) 195
Docks of New Orleans 128
Docks of New York 214
Doctor, Feel My Pulse 805

MOTION PICTURE SERIES & SEQUELS 379

Doctoring a Leak 61
Doctor Jack 323
Doctor Jekyll and Sister Hyde 207
Doctor Jekyll and the Werewolf 158
Doctor... (all) 197
Doctor Jekyll and Miss Osbourne 207
Doctor's Orders 91
Doctor Who and the Daleks 198
Do Detectives Think 434
Does Dracula Really Suck 203
Dog Days 560
Dog Daze 560
Dog Doctor 22
Doggone Mixup 325
Dog Heaven 560
Dog House 585
Dog Shy 127
Dogs is Dogs 560
Dog's Life 129
Dogs 'n Ducks 585
Dog of the Regiment 629
Dogs of War 560
Doing Time 703
Doin' Their Bit 560
Dollar Dizzy 127
Do Me a Favor 703
Dome Doctor 430
Domineering Male 585
Don Camillo Monseigneur 200
Done in Oil 752
Donkey Baseball 581
Don Q, Son of Zorro 844
Don't Bite Your Dentist 22
Don't Fence Me In 648
Don't Forget 127
Don't Get Jealous 74
Don't Lie 560
Don't Rock the Boat 703
Don't Shove 323
Don't Throw That Knife 760
Don't Weaken 703
Doomed Caravan 351
Doomed to Die 526
Do or Diet 517
Dopey Dicks 760
Dora's Dunkin' Donuts 22
Dorothy and the Scarecrow 835
Do Someone A Favor 585
Double 220

Double-Barreled Detective Story 677
Double Diving 585
Double Identity 758
Double Trouble 703
Double Whoopee 434
Dough and Dynamite 129
Doughboy 703
Dough Boys 108
Down and Out 703
Down Dakota Way 651
Downfall 220
Down in Arkansaw 812
Down Laredo Way 624
Down Mexico Way 280
Down on the Farm 61, 401
Down Texas Way 655
Do Your Duty 703
Dracula... (all) 203
Dracula's Desire 552
Dracula Versus Frankenstein 158, 259
Drafted in the Depot 517
Dragnet (all) 204
Dragon Murder Case 589
Dr. and Mrs. Jekyll 207
Dr. Black and Mr. White 207
Dr. Black, Mr. Hyde 207
Dr. Christian Meets the Women 205
Dressed to Kill 500, 677
Dr. Gillespie... (all) 208
Dr. Goldfoot... (all) 206
Dr. Hekyll and Mr. Hype 207
Drifters 74
Drifting Along 396
Drifting Westward 460
Driftin' Kid 766
Driftin' River 219\
Drink Hearty 703
Dr. Jekyll 207
Dr. Jekyll Jr. (207)
Dr. Jekyll and Mr. Blood 207
Dr. Jekyll and Mr. Hyde (all) 207
Dr. Jekyll and the Wolfman 158
Dr. Jekyll's Dungeon of Death 207
Dr. Josser 404
Dr. Kildare... (all) 208
Dr. Mabuse... (all) 209
Dr. No 378
Drowning Pool 440
Dr. Phibes Rises Again 210

Dr. Terror's Gallery of Horrors 203, 211
Dr. Terror's House of Horrors 211
Drug Busters: Snakeeater II 698A
Druggist's Dilemma 141
Drum 480
Drums of Fu Manchu 269
Drunk Driving 166
Duality of Man 207
Duck Hunter 73
Ducking a Discord 61
Duck Soup 434, 488, 517
Dude... (all) 211A
Dude Bandit 350
Duel Personalities 560
Dugan of the Badlands 69
Dull Care 430
Dumb Bell 703
Dumb's the Word 517
Dummies 430
Dummy Ache 517
Dunces and Danger 430
Dunked in the Deep 760
Durango Kid 213
Dutiful But Dumb 760
Dutiful Dub 323
Dynamite Canyon 766
Dynamite Pass 764

Eagle's Brood 351
Earl of Puddlestone 339
Early Sports Quiz 585
Early to Bed 434
Ears of Experience 517
Eastern Westerner 323
East Lynne With Variations 61
East Side Kids 214
Easy Street 129
Echo Murders 671
Ecstasy Girls (all) 216
Eddie and the Cruisers... (all) 217
Edgar and the Goliath 517
Edgar Hamlet 517
Edison, Marconi & Co. 560
Edison the Man 754
Educating Father 401
E-Flat Man 108
Egg and I 469
Eight-Ball Andy 22
813 32

Eight is Enough... (all) 221
El Dorado Pass 213
Eleanor and Franklin... (all) 224
Eleanor, First Lady of the World 224
Electric House 108
Election Day 560
Election Daze 560
Ellery Queen... (all) 225
Elmo... (all) 226
El Paso Stampede 12
Elsa Maxwell... (all) 227
Elusive Pimpernell 665
Emmanuelle... (all) 228
Empire of Ash (all) 229
Empire Strikes Back 713
Enemy Agents Meet Ellery Queen 225
Enemy of the Law 748
Enforcer 194
Ensign Pulver 508
Enter Arsene Lupin 32
Enter the Dragon 230
Enter the Ninja 231
Equestrian Acrobatics 585
Equestrian Quiz 585
Ernest... (all) 232
Erotic Adventures of Candy 113
Erotic Adventures of Heidi 331
Erotic Adventures of Zorro 844
Escape from Bondage 815
Escape from the Planet of the Apes 596
Escape to Witch Mountain 233
Even as I.O.U. 760
Evening Alone 633
Everybody's Baby 401
Every Home Should Have One 203
Every Man for Himself 560
Everything's Ducky 141
Every Saturday Night 401
Every Which Way But Loose 234
Every Woman Has a Fantasy (all) 235
Evil Dead (all) 236
Evil of Frankenstein 259
Evil Under the Sun 336
Exorcist... (all) 237

Exploits of Elaine 160
Exploring England with Will Rogers 834
Exterminator (all) 238
Eye of the Eagle (all) 239
Eyes of Texas 647
Eyes of the Night 212

Face in the Fog 89
Face of a Stranger 220
Face of Fu Manchu 269
Face on the Ballroom Floor 129
Fainting Lover 22
Fair and Muddy 560
Fala... (all) 585
Falcon... (all) 240
Fallen Arches 127
Fall Guy 166, 430, 585
False Alarms 760
False Colors 351
False Faces 461
False Paradise 351
False Roomers 141, 517
Family Affair 23
Family Entrance 127
Family Group 127
Family Troubles 560
Fancy Answers 585
Fangs of the Arctic 515
Fangs of the Wild 629
Fantastic Disappearing Man 203
Fantasy Island 241
Farewell, My Lovely 588
Far Frontier 647
Farm 169
Farmer For A Day 22
Farm Hands 560
Fast and Furious 391
Fast and Loose 391
Fast Company 391, 560
Fast Freight 560
Fast on the Draw 675
Fast Work 127
Fatal Hour 517
Fatal Mallet 129
Fate's Fathead 127
Father Brown 242
Father Makes Good 335
Father of the Bride 243
Father's Little Dividend 243
Father's Wild Game 335
Father Takes the Air 335

Fatty... (all) 244
Fatty and Mabel Adrift 244, 470
Fatty and Mabel at the San Diego Exposition 244, 470
Fatty and Mabel's Married Life 244, 470
Fatty and Mabel Viewing the World's Fair at San Francisco 244, 470
Fatty Joins the Force 244, 412
Fat Wives for Thin 22
F.D.R. -- The Last year 224
Fear in Fun Park 661
Feathered Pests 517
Feathered Serpent 128
Feather Your Nest 517
Feed 'Em and Weep 560
Feeling Rosy 22
Feet First 323
Feet of Mud 325
Fellow Citizens 703
Fellow Romans 703
Femme... (all) 245
Fence Riders 818
Feudin' Fools 90
Few Dollars for Django 195
Fickle Fatty's Fall 244
Fiddlers Three 755, 760
Fiddlesticks 325
Fifi Blows her Top 760
Fifteen Minutes 703
Fifty Million Frenchmen 554
Fifty Million Husbands 127
Fightin' Fish 581
Fightin' Fools 560
Fighting Bill Carson 74
Fighting Bill Fargo 395
Fighting Deputy 261
Fighting Fluid 127
Fighting Fools 90
Fighting Frontiersman 213
Fighting Mad 620
Fighting Parson 325, 350
Fighting Pest 127
Fighting Pioneers 624
Fighting Ranger 396
Fighting Redhead 617
Fighting Renegade 443
Fighting Texan 547
Fighting Trooper 547
Fighting Trouble 90
Fighting Valley 748
Fighting Vigilantes 431

MOTION PICTURE SERIES & SEQUELS 381

Fight Night 73
File 113 510
Film Antics 585
Film Johnnie 129
Final Chapter -- Walking tall 809
Final Conflict 556
Finder's Keepers 36
Find the Girl 703
Fine Feathers 581
Finishing Touch 434
Fire 703
Firebrands of Arizona 725
Fire Fighters 560
Fireman 129
Fireman, Save My Child 323
Fireman, Save My Choo Choo 22
Fireside Brewer 73
Firestorm (all) 247
First Aid 585
First Blood 612
First Hundred Years 325
First in War 127
First Round-Up 560
First Seven Years 560
Fisherman's Paradise 578
Fish Feathers 517
Fish Hooky 560
Fishing Feats 585
Fishing for Fun 585
Fish Tales 585
Fishy Tales 560
Fistful of Dollars 484
Fisticuffs 585
Fists of Fury (all) 248
Fits in a Fiddle 141
Fit to be Tied 106
Five Little Peppers... (all) 249
Five Million Years to Earth 609
Five to One 220
Fixer Upper 434
Fixin' Fool 585
Fixin' Tricks 585
Flag Lieutenant 250
Flagpole Jitters 760
Flame of the West 396
Flaming Bullets 748
Flaming Frontier 553
Flash Gordon... (all) 252
Flashing Guns 396
Flat Broke 703
Flat Foot Stooges 760

Flat Two 220
Flesh Gordon... (all) 252A
Fletch... (all) 253
Flickering Youth 325
Flicker Memories 585
Fling in the Ring 760
Flipper... (all) 254
Flirt 323
Flirting in the Park 82
Flirting with Marriage 49A
Flirty Four-Flushers 73
Flivvering 421
Floor Below 703
Floorwalker 129
Fluttering Hearts 127
Fly (all) 255
Fly-Away Baby 781
Fly Cop 430
Flying Deuces 434
Flying Down to Zero 141
Flying Elephants 434
Flying Hunters 581
Flying Saucer Daffy 760
Flying Spikes 579
Flying U Ranch 132
Flying Wild 214
Fly My Kite 560
Follow the Arrow 585
Follow the Crowd 323
Follow the Leader 214
Food of the Gods 256
Fool About Women 22
Fool Coverage 517
Foolish Husbands 73
Foolproof 166
Fool's Gold 351
Football Footwork 579
Football Romeo 560
Football Teamwork 583
Football Thrills... (all) 585
Footlight Glamour 83
For a Few Dollars More 484
Forbidden Passage 166
Forbidden Trails 655
Force 10 From Navarone 313
For Crimin' Out Loud 760
Forgotten Babies 560
Forgotten Man 633
Forgotten Sweeties 127
For Heaven's Sake 323
For Love of Mabel 470
For Pete's Sake 560
For Ten Thousand Bucks 61
For the Common Defense 166
For the Love of Benji 60

For the Love of Ludwig 22
For the Love of Rusty 658
Fort Savage Raiders 213
Fortunes of Captain Blood 118
48 HRS. (all) 256A
Forty-Five Minutes from Hollywood 434
40 Naughty Girls 342
Forty Thieves 351
For Your Eyes Only 378
Four Daughters 257
400 Blows 30
Four Mothers 257
Four Musketeers 757
Four Parts 127
Four-Star Border 127
Fourth Alarm 560
Fourth Square 220
Four Wives 257
Foxy Grandpa... (all) 257A
Fra Diavolo 434
Fraidy Cat 127
Framing Youth 560
Francis... (all) 258
Frankenstein 158
Frankenstein... (all) 259
Frankenstein's Bloody Terror 158
Frankenstein Meets Dracula 203
Frankenstein Meets the Wolf Man 837
Frauds and Frenzies 430
Freckles... (all) 260
Free and Easy 108
Free, Blonde and 21 352
Free Eats 560
Free Wheeling 560
French Connection (all) 262
Fresh as a Freshman 296
Freshman 263
Fresh Paint 703
Fresh Painter 22, 292
Friday the 13th... (all) 264, 265
Friend Indeed 585
Friendly Neighbors 812
Fright Night (all) 266
Fright Night 760
Frightened Flirts 61
Frisco Tornado 12
Frog 267
From Bad to Worse 127
From Hand to Mouth 323

From Nurse to Worse 760
From Rags to Britches 73
From Russia With Love 378
From Soup to Nuts 434
Frontier Agent 396
Frontier Feud 396
Frontier Fugitives 748
Frontier Gunlaw 213
Frontier Marshal 12
Frontier Outlaws 74
Frontier Outpost 213
Frontier Phantom 431
Frontier Pony Express 650
Frontier Revenge 431
Frontiersman 351
Frontier Town 749
Frozen Assets 22
Frozen Ghost 365
Frozen North 108
Frozen River 629
Fuelin' Around 760
Fugitive from Sonora 199
Fugitive of the Plains 74
Fugitive Valley 614
Full O'Pep 703
Fully Insured 703
Funeral in Berlin 326
Funny Girl 270
Funny Lady 270
Furnace Trouble 633
Further Adventures of Sherlock Holmes... (all) 677
Further Adventures of the Flag Lieutenant 250
Further Adventures of the Wilderness Family 827
Further Exploits of Sexton Blake 671
Further Tales from the Crypt 738
Further Up the Creek 799
Fury of Hercules 337
Fury of the Congo 405
Fury of the Wolfman 158, 837
Future Force (all) 271
Futureworld 814
Fuzz 222
Fuzzy Settles Down 74

Gall and Golf 430
Galloping Devil 132
Galloping Dynamite 547
Galloping Thunder 213
Game for Three Losers 220
Game of Death (all) 273
Gamera... (all) 274
Gangs of Sonora 756
Gangster's Den 74
Gangsters of the Frontier 748
Garden Murder Case 589
Gas House Kids... (all) 275
Gasoline Wedding 323
Gasoloons 517
Gate (all) 276
Gathering (all) 277
Gator 279
'Gator Bait... (all) 278
Gaucho Serenade 280
Gauchos of El Dorado 756
Gay Amigo 140
Gay Caballero 140
Gay Cavalier 140
Gay Falcon 240
Gay Nighties 141
Gay Ranchero 647
Gem of a Jam 760
Gemini Twins 120
Gene Autry and the Mounties 282
General 108
General Nuisance 108
General Spanky 560
Gentleman From Texas 396
Gentleman Joe Palooka 393
Gentleman of Nerve 129
Gentlemen Marry Brunettes 283
Gentlemen Prefer Blondes 283
Gentlemen With Guns 73
Gents in a Jam 760
Gents Without cents 760
George White's Scandals... (all) 286
Gert and Daisy... (all) 287
Get Busy 703
Get Out and Get Under 323
Get-Rich-Quick Wallingford 288
Gettin' Clamor 585
Getting Acquainted 129, 412
Getting His Goat 703
Ghidrah, the Three-Headed Monster 300
Ghostbusters (all) 289
Ghost Catchers 554

Ghost Chasers 90
Ghost City 69
Ghost Guns 396
Ghost in the Invisible Bikini 53
Ghost of Frankenstein 259
Ghost of Hidden Valley 74
Ghost of Zorro 844
Ghost Parade 22
Ghosts on the Loose 214
Ghost Talks 760
Ghost Town Gold 756
Ghost Town Law 655
Ghost Town Renegades 431
Ghoulies (all) 290
Giants Vs. Yanks 560
Giddap 73
Giddy Age 22
Gidget... (all) 291
Gift For Heidi 331
Gigantis, the Fire Monster 300
Giggle Water 517
Gildersleeve... (all) 308
Gilding the Lily 585
Ginger... (all) 294
Ginger's Sex Asylum 669
Girl Crazy 22, 839
Girl Friday 661
Girl from Mexico 498
Girl from San Lorenzo 140
Girl Grief 127
Girl Hunters 504
Girl in Overalls 476
Girl in the Limousine 430
Girl in the Park 242
Girl Shock 127
Girl Shy 323
Girl, the Gold Watch & Dynamite 295
Girl, the Gold Watch & Everything 295
Girl Trouble 102
Git Along Little Dogies 280
Give Till It Hurts 166
Give Us Wings 453
Giving the Bride Away 703
G.I. Wanna Go Home 760
Glad Rags to Riches 38
Global Quiz 585
Glorious Fourth 560
Glove Affair 296
Glove Slingers 296
Glove Taps 560

MOTION PICTURE SERIES & SEQUELS 383

Gnaw: Food of the Gods Part 2 (256)
Go As You Please 703
Goat 108
Go Chase Yourself 22
Godfather (all) 297
Godmother (all) 298
Gods Must Be Crazy (all) 299
Godzilla... (all) 300
Go Get 'Em Hutch 359
Go-Getter 116
Goin' Fishin' 560
Going Bye Bye 434
Going! Going! Gone! 323
Going My Way 301
Going to Press 560
Gold Digger of Weepah 73
Gold Dust Gertie 554
Golden Eye 128
Golden Idol 86
Golden Stallion 651
Golden Trail 749
Golden Voyage of Sinbad 685
Goldfinger 378
Gold Ghost 108
Goldie and the Boxer.... (all) 302
Gold Is Where You Lose It 22
Gold Mine in the Sky 280
Gold Rush 129
Gold Rush Maisie 476
Goldtown Ghost Riders 280
Goldwyn Follies 630
Golem... (all) 304
Golf 430
Golf Chump 517
Golfers 22
Golf Mistakes 585
Golf Nut 73
Goliath and the Island of Vampires 471
Goliath and the Vampires 471
Gone to the Country 703
Good Bad Boys 560
Good Housekeeping 517
Good, the Bad, the Ugly 484
Goodbye Emmanuelle 228
Goodbye Legs 22
Good Cheer 560
Good Morning, Vietnam 303A
Goodness, A Ghost 325
Goof on the Roof 760

Goofs and Saddles 760
Goofy Movies (all) 580
Gor 304
Gorilla 630
Go Sea Monster 300
Go West 108, 488
Gown Shop 430
Grab the Ghost 703
Gracie Allen Murder Case 589
Gracie At Bat 22
Grand Bounce 585
Grand Canyon 648
Grand Hooter 127
Grandma's Boy 323
Grandma's Girl 22
Grand Ole Opry 812
Grandpa Goes to Town 339
Grand Slam Opera 108
Graveyard Shift 305
Grease (all) 306
Great Escape... (all) 307
Great Gildersleeve 308
Great Glovers 296
Great Gobs 127
Great Guns 434
Great Hospital Mystery 549
Great Office Mystery 671
Great O'Malley 555
Great Stagecoach Robbery 617
Great St. Trinian's Train Robbery 58
Great Train Robbery 97
Green Cat 703
Greene Murder Case 589
Green Grass of Wyoming 533
Green Hornet... (all) 309
Greetings 310
Gremlins (all) 311
Greystoke: The Legend of Tarzan, Lord of the Apes 742
Grid Rules 585
Grin and Bear It 517
Grips, Grunts and Groans 760
Grocery Clerk 430
Groovie Movie 585
Growing Pains 560
Guess What Happened to Count Dracula 203
Guest Pests 585
Gumball Rally 115
Gunfire 625
Gun in His Hand 166

Gun Law 284
Gun Law Justice 389
Gunman 819
Gunman from Bodie 655
Gunmen of Abilene 22
Gunning for Justice 396
Gunning for Vengeance 213
Gun Play 764
Gun Runner 389
Guns and Greasers 430
Guns and Guitars 280
Guns a Poppin' 760
Gunslingers 818
Gunsmoke 396
Gunsmoke... (all) 312A
Gunsmoke Mesa 748
Gunsmoke Ranch 756
Gun Smugglers 764
Guns of Navarone 313
Guns of the Law 748
Guns of the Magnificent Seven 475
Gun Talk 396
Gussle... (all) 314
Gymnasium 73
Gymnastic Rhythm 585
Gymnastics 583
Gypped in the Penthouse 760

Habeas Corpus 434
Hale and Hearty 703
Half-Baked Relations 22
Half Breed 553
Half Holiday 22
Half Shot at Sunrise 839
Half-Shot Shooters 760
Half-Wits Holiday 760
Halloween... (all) 315
Halloween that Almost Wasn't 203
Ham... (all) 317
Hammer the Toff 765
Handlebars 581
Hands Across the Border 654
Hands Across the Rockies 823
Hansom Cabman 325
Happiness is a Warm Clue 128
Happy Tho Married 517
Happy Hooker... (all) 319
Happy Warriors 581
Hardbodies (all) 320
Hard Boiled 127

Hard Boiled Mahoney 90
Hard Hombre 350
Hard Knocks 127
Hard Luck 108
Hard Ride 333
Hardys Ride High 23
Harem 61
Harem's Night 61
Harlem... (all) 322
Harlem Globetrotters 321
Harlem Globetrotters on Gilligan's Island 293, 321
Harnessed Rhythm 583
Harper 440
Harrad... (all) 324
Hasty Marraige 127
Hats Off 434
Haunted Honeymoon 463
Haunted House 108
Haunted Mine 396
Haunted Ranch 614
Haunted Spoks 323
Haunted trails 818
Have Rocket, Will Travel 760
Have You Ever Wondered 585
Having a Wonderful Crime 394
Having Babies (all) 327
Hawaii 328
Hawaiians 328
Hawaii Vice... (all) 329
Hawk of Powder River 219
Hawk of Wild River 213
Hayfoot, Strawfoot 73
Hayseed Romance 108
Head Guy 325
Headin' for the Rio Grande 750
Heading for Trouble 517
Heading West 213
Headwaiter 430
Healthy, Wealthy and Dumb 760
Heap Big Chief 323
Hear 'Em Rave 323
Heartburn 517
Heart of Arizona 351
Heart of the Golden West 648
Heart of the Rio Grande 280
Heart of the Rockies 649, 756
Heart of the West 351

Hearts are Thumps 560
Heather And Yon 22
Heavenly Days 246
Heavenly Daze 760
Heavenly Twins... (all) 329A
Heavens! My Husband 22
Heckler 127
He Cooked His Goose 760
Hec Ramsey 330
He Did and He Didn't 61
He Done His Duty 22
Heebee Jeebees 560
Heidi... (all) 331
Held for a Ransom 677
Heldorado 648
He Leads, Others Follow 323
Helen Keller -- The Miracle Continues 505
Helicopter Spies 483
Hellbound: Hellraiser II 332
Hello Baby 127
Hello Mabel 470
Hello, Mary Lou: Prom Night II 606
Hello, Prosperity 22
Hello, Television 22
Hellraiser 332
Hell's Angels... (all) 333
Hell's Creatures 158
Hell's Kitchen 176
Hell Up In Harlem 77
Hellzapoppin 554
He Looked Crooked 61
Helping Grandma 560
Helping Hands 560
Helpmates 434
Help Wanted 166
Henry Aldrich... (all) 334
Henry and Dizzy 334
Henry the Rainmaker 335
Herbie... (all) 466
Her Boyfriend 430
Hercules... (all) 337
Here Comes Cookie 106
Here Comes Mr. Zerk 325
Here Come the Coeds 1
Here Come the Huggetts 355
Here Come the Girls 323
Here Come the Marines 90
Here's Flash Casey 251
Here We Go Again 246
Heroes at Leisure 585
Heroes of the Hills 756
Heroes of the Saddle 756
Hers to Hold 759

He Was Only Feudin' 22
Hey Nanny Nanny 141
Hey There 323
Hick 430
Hidden Danger 396
Hidden Eye 212
Hidden Gold 351
Hidden Valley Outlaws 824
Hide and Seek, Detectives 61
Hide and Shriek 560
Higgins Family 339
High and Dizzy 323
High and Low 222
High Beer Pressure 517
High C's 127
Higher than a Kite 760
High Flyers 839
High Gear 91
Highlander (all) 340
High Noon (all) 341
High Riders 333
High Rollers 703
High Sign 108
High Society 90, 560
High Window 588
Hiking Through Holland with Will Rogers 834
Hillbilly Blitzkreig 49
Hillbilly Goat 517
Hills Have Eyes (all) 343
Hills of Home 432
Hills of Utah 282
Hills of Wyoming 351
Hill Tillies 752
Hi, Mom! 310
Hindoos and Hazards 430
Hi'- Neighbor! 560
Hips Hips Hooray 839
Hired and Fired 61, 141
His Best Girl 703
His Blowout 61
His Bogus Boast 61
His Bridal Fright 127
His Bridal Sweet 325
His Brother's Ghost 74
His Ex Marks the Spot 108
His Favorite Passtime 129
His Fighting Blood 547
His First Flame 325
His Home Sweet Home 430
His Majesty, the Scarecrow of Oz 835
His Marriage Mixup 325
His Marriage Wow 325

MOTION PICTURE SERIES & SEQUELS 385

His Musical Career 129
His New Job 129
His New Mama 325
His New Profession 129
His New Steno 73
His Only Father 323
His Prehistoric Past 129
His Royal Shyness 22, 323
His Silent Racket 127
His Tale Is Told 22
Historical Oddities 585
History of White People in America (all) 344
His Trysting Place 129
His Unlucky Night 73
His Weak Moment 22
His Wooden Wedding 127
Hit and Run Driver 166
Hitch Hiker 325
Hit Him Again 323
Hit Parade... (all) 345
Hit The Ice 1
Hit the Road 453
Hit the Saddle 756
Hittin' the Trail 750
Hi-Ya, Chum 630
Hoboken to Hollywood 73
Hocus-Pocus 703, 760
Hogan... (all) 346
Hog Wild 434
Hoi Polloi 760
Hokus and Focus 141
Hold 'Em Jail 839
Hold That Baby 90
Hold That Ghost 1
Hold That Hypnotist 90
Hold That Line 90
Hold That Lion 760
Hold Your Temper 517
Holiday Camp 355
Hollywood Boulevard (all) 347
Hollywood Daredevils 585
Hollywood Hero 61
Hollywood High (all) 348
Hollywood Kid 61
Hollywood Party 434
Hollywood Review of 1929 434
Hollywood Scout 585
Hollywood Star 22
Holy Terror 560
Home Canning 517
Homecoming -- A Christmas Story 811

Home Early 633
Home in Oklahoma 648
Home in Wyoming 280
Home Made Movies 61
Home Maid 585
Home Movies 633
Home on the Prairie 280
Home on the Rage 22
Home on the Range 511
Homesteaders 617
Home Stretch 703
Homicide for Three 577
Honey, I Shrunk the Kids 348A
Honeymoon Hardships 73
Honky Donkey 560
Honolulu 106
Hoofs and Goofs 760
Hook and Ladder 560
Hooked and Rooked 22
Hook, Line and Sinker 703, 839
Hooks and Jabs 325
Hoosegow 434
Hop-a-long Cassidy 351
Hopalong Cassidy... (all) 351
Hoppy Serves a Writ 351
Hoppy's Holiday 351
Horror of Dracula 203
Horror of Frankenstein 259
Horse Feathers 488
Horsemen of the Sierras 213
Horses Collars 760
Horseshoes 430
Horsing Around 760
Hostile Country 675
Host to a Ghost 22, 517
Hotel Anchovy 630
Hotel for Women 352
Hot Foot 517
Hot Ice 760
Hot Lead 764
Hot Money 752
Hot Off the Pres 703
Hot on Ice 585
Hot Patrika 22
Hot Rock 202
Hot Scots 760
Hot Shots 90
Hot Stuff 760
Hotter Than Hot 325
Hot Water 323, 401
Hound of the Baskervilles 677
Hour for Lunch 633

House... (all) 353
House of Dracula 203, 259, 837
House of Dracula's Daughter 203
House of Fear 677
House of Frankenstein 203, 259, 837
House of Fright 207
House of Horrors 163
House of Mystery 672
House of the Arrow 368
House on Bear Mountain 203
House Without a Key 128
How Come? 585
How Dry I Am 703
How High is Up? 760
Howling... (all) 354
How Lt. Pimple Captured the Kaiser 591A
How Max Went Around the World 490A
How Rastus... (all) 615
How Spry I Am 22
How to be a Detective 633
How to Behave 633
How to Break 90 at Croquet 633
How to Clean House 517
How to Eat 633
How to Figure Income Tax 633
How to Hold Your Husband 585
How to Raise a Baby 633
How to Read 633
How to Sleep 633
How to Start the Day 633
How to Steal the World 483
How to Stuff a Wild Bikini 53
How to Sub-Let 633
How to Take a Vacation 633
How to Train a Dog 633
How to Vote 633
How to Watch Football 633
Hubby's Latest Alibi 73
Hubby's Quiet Little Game 73
Hubby's Weekend 73
Huckleberry Finn 767
Huggetts Abroad 355
Hugs and Mugs 760
Hula La La 760
Human Targets 629

Humbus and Husbands 430
Hunger Pains 82
Huns and Hyphens 430
Hunting for Germans in Berlin with Will Rogers 834
Hunted Men 383
Hurling 585
Hurricane Hutch 359
Husbands Beware 760
Hustler 358, 703
Hypnotized 794

I Am Curious... (all) 360
I, A Woman... (all) 361
I Can Hardly Wait 760
Ice Aces 585
Ice Cold Cocos 73
Iceman's Ball 141
Idaho 653
Idiots Deluxe 760
Idle Class 129
Idle Roomers 760
I Do 323
I Don't Remember 325
If a Body Meets a Body 760
I'll Be Suing You 752
I'll Build It Myself 517
Illegal Traffic 383
I'll Fix That 517
I'll Never Heil Again 760
I'll Take Vanilla 127
I Love a Mystery 362
I Love Children, But 585
I Love My Husband, But 585
I Love My Mother-in-Law 585
I Love My Wife 585
I'm a Civilian 633
I'm A Father 22
Imagine My Embarrassment 127
I'm a Monkey's Uncle 760
Immigrant 129
I'm On My Way 323
I, Monster 207
Important Business 633
In a Pig's Eye 141
Inbad the Sailor 73
In Case You're Curious 585
Incident at Midnight 220
Income Tax Sappy 760
In Conference 22
Incredible Hulk... (all) 363

Indian Agent 764
Indiana Jones... (all) 364
Indian Signs 517
Indian Territory 282
Indian Tomb 762
In Fast Company 90
Inferior Decorator 517
Inflation 582
Influence on Bronco Billy 97
International Crime 672
In the Sweet Pie and Pie 760
Invisible Avenger 672
In Holland 141
In Hollywood with Potash and Perlmutter 604
In-Laws Are Out 517
In Love at 40 517
Innocent Husbands 127
Innocents 366
In Old Amarillo 652
In Old Arizona 140
In Old Caliente 648
In Old Cheyenne 648
In Old Colorado 351
In Old Mexico 351
In Old Missouri 812
In Old Monterey 280
Insatiable (all) 367
In Society 1
Inspector Clouseau 592
Inspector Hornleigh... (all) 369
Inspector Lavardin 155
Inspector Maigret 370
Insulting the Sultan 703
Interference of Bronco Billy 97
International House 106
International Velvet 537
Interns 371
Interns Can't Take Money 208
Intimate Realities (all) 373
In the Clutches of a Gang 412
In the Devil's Doghouse 141
In the Dog House 22
In the Frame 190
In the Heat of the Night 807
In the Line of Duty (all) 372
In the Money 90
In the Movies 703
In the Navy 1
In the Park 129
Invisible Agent 374
Invisible Man... (all) 374

Invisible Woman 374
In Walked Charley 127
Ipcress file 326
Iron Eagle (all) 375
Iron Mask 757
Iron Mitt 61
Iron Mountain Trail 624
Iron Nag 73
Iroquois Trail 437
Is Everybody Happy? 127
I Shot Jesse James 386
Is Marriage the Bunk? 127
Isn't Life Terrible 127
It 303
It Ain't Hay 1
It Always Happens 22
It Could Happen to You 585
It Happened All Night 517
It Happened One Day 127
I, The Jury 504
It Lives Again 376
It's a Bear 560
It's a Boy 73, 703
It's a Dog's Life 585
It's a Gift 703
It's a Great Life 83
It's a Hard Life 703
It's Alive... (all) 376
It's a Wild Life 323
It's The Cat's 22
It's Your Move 517
It Would Serve 'Em Right 585
I Was a Teenage Frankenstein 259
I Was a Teenage Vampire 203
I Was a Teenage Werewolf 837

Jack and the Beanstalk 1
Jack Frost 703
Jack 'n Jill (all) 377
Jackpot 166
Jacqueline Susann's 'Valley of the Dolls 1981' 803
Jade Mask 128
Jail Bait 108
Jail Bird 703
Jail Busters 90
Jalopy 90
Jane Bond... (all) 379
Jason... (all) 381
Jaws... (all) 382
Jaws of Steel 629

Jazzed Honeymoon 323
Jealous Jolts 61
Jeepers Creepers 812
Jeffries Jr. 127
Jekyll and Hyde Together
    Again 207
Jerk 385
Jerk Too 385
Jesse James... (all) 386
Jesse James at Bay 648
Jesse James Jr. 199
Jesse James Meets
    Frankenstein's
    Daughter 259
Jewel of the Nile 643
Jiggs and Maggie... (all) 388
Jimmy the Kid 202
Jinx Money 90
Jitney Elopement 129
Jitterbugs 434
Jitters the Butler 141
Joan Medford is Missing 163
Joe Named Palooka 393
Joe Palooka... (all) 393
Johnny Wadd 399
Join the Circus 703
Jolly Jilter 61
Jones and His New Neighbors 522
Jones and the Lady Book Agent 522
Joneses Have Amateur Theatricals 522
Jones Family... (all) 401
Jonker Diamond 584
Josser... (all) 404
Journey Back to Oz 835
Joy Rider 703
Joyriding 318
Joy Scouts 560
Jubilo Jr. 560
Judge Hardy... (all) 23
Jump Jump Jump 22
Jump Your Job 703
Junction City 213
Jungle Captive 119
Jungle Gents 90
Jungle Jim... (all) 405
Jungle Juveniles (all) 585
Jungle Man-Easters 405
Jungle Manhunt 405
Jungle Moon Men 405
Jungle Wolf 406
Jungle Woman 119
Junior G-Men... (all) 407

MOTION PICTURE SERIES & SEQUELS 387

Jury Goes Round and Round 805
Just A Bear 22
Just a Minute 127
Just Before Dawn 165
Just Dropped In 323
Just For a Kid 61
Justice of the West 456
Just Neighbors 323
Just Off Broadway 500
Just Suppose 585
Just What I Needed 585
Just William's Luck 832

Kansas City Massacre 496
Kansas Cyclone 199
Kansas Raiders 386
Kansas Terrors 756
Karate Kid (all) 409
Karate Killers 483
Katzenjammer Kids... (all) 409A
Keep 'Em Flying 1
Keep 'Em Sailing 166
Keep 'Em Slugging 453
Keeping in Shape 633
Keep Young 585
Kennedy's Castle 517
Kennedy the Great 517
Kennel Murder Case 589
Kenny Rogers as The Gambler... (all) 272
Kensington Mystery 551
Kentucky Kernels 839
Kentucky Moonshine 630
Kettles... (all) 469
Kicked Out 323
Kicking the Germ out of Germany 323
Kickin' the Crown ARound 141
Kickoff 91
Kid 129
Kid Auto Races at Venice 129
Kid Brother 323
Kid Comes Back 415
Kiddie Cure 560
Kid Dynamite 214
Kid from Amarillo 213
Kid from Borneo 560
Kid from Broken Gun 213
Kid Galahad 415
Kid in Afrida 38
Kid in Hollywood 38

Kid Rides Again 74
Kid's Last Fight 38
Kid's Last Ride 614
Kid Speed 430
Killer Ape 405
Killer Dog 585
Killer Leopard 86
Kill And Kill Again 418
Kill or be Killed 418
Kill the Nerve 703
King 325
King Kong... (all) 419
King Kong Vs. The Thing 300
King of Alcatraz 383
King of Dodge City 825
King of the Bandits 140
King of the Bullwhip 431
King of the Cowboys 653
King of the Mounties 420
King of the Royal Mounted 420
King Robot 552
King Solomon's Mines (all) 11
Kiss and Tell 156, 269
Kiss For Corliss 156
Kiss Me Deadly 504
Kiss Me Quick 203
Kitchen Cynic 517
Knee Action 22
Knight Duty 325
Knight of the Plains 261
Knights Out 141
Knockout 91
Know Your Money 166
Knutsy Knights 760
Kojak... (all) 422
Kung Fu 424
Kung Fu: The Movie 424
Kung Fu Warlords (all) 425

La Cage Aux Folles (all) 426
L.A. Crackdown (all) 427
Lad an' a Lamp 560
Ladies Last 91
Lady Chatterly's Lover 428
Lady Dracula 203
Lady Frankenstein 259
Lady in Cement 768
Lady in the Iron Mask 757
Lady in the Lake 588
Lady in the Morgue 71
Lady Robin Hood 634
La Fiesta de Santa Barbara 584

388 MOTION PICTURE SERIES & SEQUELS

Lamb 323
Landlording It 585
Landlubber 61
Land of Hunted Men 614
Land of Oz 835
Land of the Lawless 396
Land of the Outlaws 396
Land of the Valley 396
Land of Wanted Men 69
Landrush 213
Land Time Forgot 429
Laramie 213
Laramie Mountains 213
Laramie Trail 400
Larceny in Her Heart 500
La Savate 585
Lassie... (all) 432
Last Adventures of Sherlock Holmes... (all) 677
Last Days of Boot Hill 213
Last Days of Patton 568
Last Express 212
Last Frontier Uprising 511
Last Horseman 657
Last Installment 166
Last Musketeer 624
Last of the Lone Wolf 461
Last of the Mohicans 437
Last of the Pony Express 280
Last of the Redmen 437
Last of the Renegades 553
Last Picture Show 433
Last Remake of Beau Geste 54
Last Warning 71
Late Lodgers 703
Latest Triumph of Sherlock Holmes 677
Laughing Gas 129
Laughing Gravy 434
Laurel and Hardy Murder Case 434
Law and Order 74, 395, 703
Law Comes to Gunsight 396
Lawless 456
Lawless Code 389
Lawless Cowboys 819
Lawless Empire 213
Lawless Frontier 459
Lawless Valley 285
Lawmen 396
Law of the Badlands 764
Law of the Canyon 213
Law of the Golden West 512
Law of the Lash 431
Law of the North 69

Law of the Pampas 351
Law of the Range 395
Law of the Ranger 747
Law of the Saddle 457
Law of the West 396
Law of the Wild 629
Law of the Wolf 629
Law Rides Again 784
Lawyer 434
Lazy Days 560
Leading Lizzie Astray 18
Leading Man 61
Leadville Gunslinger 12
League of Frightened Men 538
Leaping Love 127
Leather Burners 351
Leatherface: The Texas Chainsaw Massacre 3 746
Leather Necker 325
Leatherstocking 437
Leave 'Em Laughing 434
Leave It to Blondie 83
Leave It to Henry 335
Legend of Boggy Creek 85
Legend of Grizzly Adams 312
Legend of Machine Gun Kelly 496
Legend of Nigger Charley 438
Legend of the Lone Ranger 456
Legend of the Seven Golden Vampires 203
Lemon Meringue 517
Lesson in Golf 579
Lesson No. 1 633
Let 'Er Go 73
Lethal Weapon (all) 439
Let's Cogitate 585
Let's Dance 106, 584
Let's Do It Again 800
Let's Do Things 751
Let's Get Tough 214
Let's Go 323
Let's Go Navy 90
Let's Talk Turkey 585
Liberty 434
Licensed to Kill 441
Licensed to Love and Kill 545
License to Kill 378
Life and Times of Grizzly Adams 312

Life at the Top 645
Life Begins at College 630
Life Begins for Andy Hardy 23
Life Hesitates at 40 127
Life With Blondie 83
Life With Henry 334
Life Without Soul 259
Life With the Lyons 442
Lighter That Failed 127
Lighthouse by the Sea 629
Lightning Bill Carson 443
Lightning Carson Rides Again 443
Lightning Guns 213
Lightning Love 430
Lightning Raiders 74
Lightning Warrior 629
Light Showers 703
Lights of Old Santa Fe 648
Like a Wolf on the Fold 764A
Lilies of the Field 444
Lillian Russell 188
Limousine Love 127
Linda Lovelace... (all) 445
Lions on the Loose 585
Lion's Roar 73
Lion's Whiskers 73
Listen, Judge 760
List of Adrian Messenger 29
Little Annie Rooney 446
Little Billy... (all) 447
Little Daddy 560
Little Foxes 448
Little Giant 1
Little Girls Blue (all) 449
Little House on the Prairie... (all) 450
Little Joe the Wrangler 395
Little Men 454
Little Miss Pinkerton 560
Little Mother 560
Little Orphan Annie 451
Little Orphan Dusty (all) 452
Little Papa 560
Little Ranger 560
Little Sinner 560
Little Tough Guys 453
Little Women 454
Little World of Don Camillo 200
Live and Learn 703
Live and Let Die 378

Live Ghost 434
Live Wires 90
Living Daylights 378
Lizzies of the Field 73
Local bad Man 350
Locker 69 220
Locks and Bonds 517
Loco Boy Makes Good 760
Lodge Night 22, 560
London Bobby 703
Lone Defender 629
Lone Hand Texan 213
Lone Ranger... (all) 456
Lone Rider... (all) 457
Lonesome Luke... (all) 458
Lonesome Trailer 223
Lone Star Moonlight 411
Lone Star Raiders 756
Lone Star Trail 395
Lone Star Vigilantes 825
Lone Texas Ranger 617
Lone Wolf... (all) 461
Long Chase 8
Longest Day 464
Long Fliv the King 127
Long Goodbye 588
Long John Silver 788
Long Rifle and the Tomahawk 437
Looking for Danger 90
Looking For Sally 127
Looking for Trouble 703
Looking Glass War 695
Look Out Below 323
Look Pleasant Please 323
Look What's Happened to Rosemary's Baby 646
Look Who's Laughing 130, 246
Loose Ends (all) 462
Loose in London 90
Loose Loot 760
Loose Relations 22
Looser Than Loose 127
Lord Edgeware Dies 336
Lord of the Jungle 86
Lose No Time 703
Lost -- A Cook 61
Lost and Found 61
Lost Canyon 351
Lost in Alaska 1
Lost in Harlem 1
Lost in Limehouse 489
Lost Trail 396
Lost Tribe 405

Lovable Trouble 22
Love and Doughnuts 61
Love and Hisses 141
Love at First Bite 203, 760
Love At Twenty 30
Love Boat (all) 465
Love Bug 466, 560
Love Business 560
Love Comes to Nooneville 22
Love 'Em and Weep
Love Fever 91
Love Finds Andy Hardy 23
Love Happy 488
Love, Honor and Obey 73
Love in Bloom 106
Love Laughs at Andy Hardy 23
Love, Loot and Crash 412
Love Master 722
Love My Dog 560
Love Nest 108
Love Nest on Wheels 108
Love on a Budget 401
Love on a Ladder 517
Love on the Run 30
Love Pains 91
Loves and Times of Scaramouche 664
Love's A-Poppin 22

Love's Detour 127
Love's Languid Lure 61
Love's Outcast 61
Love Story 467
Love Thief 412
Lovey: A Circle of Children Part II 139
Love Your Landlord 517
Lt. Daring... (all) 467A
Lt. Pimple on Secret Service 591A
Lt. Robin Crusoe, U.S.N. 635
Luckiest Guy in the World 166
Luck of the Foolish 325
Lucky Cisco Kid 140
Lucky Corner 560
Lucky Losers 90
Lucky Stars 325
Lucky Stiff 394
Lucky Texan 459
Luke... (all) 458
Lumberjack 351
Luncheon at Twelve 127
Lunkhead 22
Lust for a Vampire 120
Lust in Space (all) 468
Lust of Dracula 203
Lyons in Paris 442

Lynda Carter brings the comic book heroine WONDER WOMAN to life in a tele-movie and in a weekly television series.

Ma and Pa 73
Ma and Pa Kettle... (all) 469
Mabel... (all) 470
Mabel and Fatty's Wash Day 244, 470
Mabel, Fatty and the Law 244, 470
Mabel's and Fatty's Simple Life 244, 470
Mabel's Busy Day 129, 470
Mabel's Strange Predicament 129, 470
Maciste... (all) 471
Macon County Line 472
Mad About Men 506
Mad About Moonshine 517
Madame Frankenstein 259
Made in USA 566
Mad Lust of a Hot Vampire 203
Mad Max... (all) 473
Mad Mission (all) 474
Mad Monster Party 203
Mad Wednesday 263
Magic Cloak of Oz 835
Magic of Lassie 432
Magnificent Seven... (all) 475
Magnum Force 194
Maid in Hollywood 752
Maid Made Mad 22
Maids a la Mode 751
Maid to Order 517
Maigret... (all) 370
Mail and Female 560
Mail Train 369
Main Chance 220
Maintain the Right 585
Maisie... (all) 476
Major League 476A
Make it Snappy 703
Malice in the Palace 760
Making of O'Malley 555
Malpas Mystery 220
Maltese Falcon 477
Mama Dracula 203
Mama Loves Papa 91
Mama Misbehave 127
Mama's Little Pirate 560
Man Against the Mob... (all) 477A
Man and a Woman... (all) 478
Man Around the House 585
Man at the Carlton 220
Man Bites Love Bug 127
Man Called Horse 479

Mandarin Mystery 225
Man Detained 220
Man Friday 635
Mandigo 480
Mandrake... (all) 481
Man from Cheyenne 648
Man from Hell's River 629
Man from Montana 395
Man from Music Mountain 280, 651
Man from Oklahoma 648
Man from Rainbow Valley 511
Man from Snowy River 482
Man from the Black Hills 398
Man from Thunder River 824
Man from Tumbleweeds 823
Man from Utah 459
Manhattan Merry-Go-Round 280
Manhattan Monkey Business 127
Man Hunter 629
Maniac 483A
Maniac Cop II 483A
Man in the Iron Mask 757
Man is News 684
Man on the Eiffel Tower 370
Man's Angle 633
Man's Greatest Friend 585
Man's Land 350
Man Who Came from Ummo 158
Man Who Was Nobody 220
Man Who Watched the Trains Go By 370
Man Who Wouldn't Die 500
Man With One Red Shoe 740
Man With the Golden Gun 378
Man With the Twisted Lip 677
Man With Two Heads 207
Many Happy Returns 106
Many Sappy Returns 127
Many Scrappy Returns 127
Marathon 323
Marauders 351
Marcus-Nelson Murders 422
Marcus Welby, MD... (all) 485
Marilyn Chambers... (all) 486
Marinated Mariner 22

Marine Circus 585
Marines in the Making 585
Marked -- For Murder 748
Marked Trails 784
Mark of the Devil (all) 487
Mark of the Gorilla 405
Mark of the Lash 431
Mark of the Whistler 821
Mark of the Wolfman 158
Mark of Zorro 844
Marlowe 588
Marriage Circus 61
Marriage Humor 325
Marriage of Convenience 220
Married Life 61
Marshal of Amarillo 12
Marshal of Cedar Rock 12
Marshal of Cripple Creek 617
Marshal of Heldorado 675
Marshal of Laredo 617
Marshal of Mesa City 285
Marshal of Reno 617
Marvelous Maciste 471
Mary, Queen of Tots 560
Masked Mamas 73
Masked Mirth 61
Masked Raiders 764
Masked Rider 395
Mask of Fu Manchu 269
Masks of Death 677
Mason of the Mounted 69
Masquerader 129
Master Minds 90
Match Play 22
Meddlers and Moonshine 430
Matri-Phony 760
Matt Helm 490
Max... (all) 490A
McCloud: Who Killed Miss USA? 491
McHale's Navy... (all) 493
Mealtime 585
Me and My Pal 434
Meatballs (all) 494
Meatmen 141
Medicine Men 141
Men in Black 760
Meet Boston Blackie 89
Meet Dr. Christian 205
Meet Mr. Callaghan 692
Meet Sexton Blake 671
Meet the Girls 495
Meet the Missus 339
Melodies of Old and New 560

MOTION PICTURE SERIES & SEQUELS

Melody For Three 205
Melody of the Plains 261
Melody Trail 280
Melon-Drama 141
Melvin Purvis: G-Man 496
Memory Tricks 585
Men in Fright 560
Men of Boys Town 92
Men of Sherwood Forest 634
Men O'War 434
Mental Poise 633
Menu 581
Merchant of Menace 517
Merry Chase 331A
Merry Mavericks 760
Merry Men of Sherwood 634
Merry Mixup 760
Mexicali Rose 280
Mexican Hayride 1
Mexican Spitfire... (all) 498
Miami Spice (all) 499
Michael Shayne, Private Detective 500
Mickey... (all) 501
Mickey Spillane's... (all) 504
Micro-Phonies 760
Microscopic Mysteries 581
Midnight Cabaret 430
Midnight Express (all) 501A
Midnight Patrol 434
Midsummer Mush 127
Mighty Lak a Goat 560
Mighty Like a Moose 127
Mike and Jake... (all) 503
Mike Fright 560
Milky Way 323
Millerson Case 165
Millionaire Cat 141
Million Year Kid 214
Mind Needer 127
Mind of Mr. Reeder 387
Mind Over Mouse 517
Miner Affair 22
Miniver Story 524
Miracle Money 166
Miracle Worker 505
Miranda 506
Mirror Crack'd 380
Misadventures of Merlin Jones 497
Miss Annie Rooney 446
Missed Fortune 760
Misses Stooge 752
Missing in Action... (all) 507
Missing Lady 672

Missing Millions 89
Missing Rembrandt 677
Missourians 512
Missouri Outlaw 199
Miss Robin Hood 634
Mister Roberts 508
Mister Smarty 22
Mister V 665
Mitt Me Tonight 296
Mixed Magic 108
Moan & Groan Inc. 560
Mob Town 453
Modeling for Money 585
Modern Times 129
Modesty Blaise 509
Money Squawks 22
Money to Burn 339, 703
Money To Loan 166
Monkey Business 488, 560, 760
Monkey Business in Africa 22
Monkey Shines 331A
Monkey's Uncle 497
Mon Oncle 421
Monsieur Hulot's Holiday 521
Monsieur Lecoq, Detective 510
Monster of Fate 303
Monster of Frankenstein 259
Monster Rumble 203
Monsters from the Unknown Planet 300
Monster Zerio 300
Montana Belle 59
Montana Incident 819
Montana Kid 69
Monte Cristo 157
Monty Python... (all) 513
Mooching Through Georgia 108
Moonlight on the Range 261
Moonraker 378
Moon Over Montana 390
Moonshiner's Daughter 489
Mopey Dope 325
More American Graffitti 19
More Than Magic 456
More Wild Wild West 830
Morning After 703
Morning, Judge 517
Mosconi Story 585
Mother-in-Law's Day 517
Mother Riley... (all) 552

Mother's Day on Waltons Mountain 811
Motorboat Mamas 73
Motorcycle Cossacks 581
Motorcycle Mania 579
Motoring Mamas 73
Motor Maniacs 517
Mountain Family Robinson 827
Mountain Moonlight 812
Mountain Rhythm 280, 812
Mouse on the Moon 516
Mouse that Roared 516
Move On 323
Movie Crazy 323
Movie Maniacs 760
Movie Night 127
Movie Pests 585
Moving 421
Mr. Belvedere... (all) 518
Mr. Boggs... (all) 519
Mr. Bride 127
Mr. Clyde Goes to Broadway 22
Mr. District Attorney 520
Mr. Hex 90
Mr. Hulot's Holiday 521
Mr. Jack... (all) 521A
Mr. Jones... (all) 522
Mr. Moto... (all) 523
Mr. Muggs Rides Again 214
Mr. Muggs Steps Out 214
Mrs. O'Malley and Mr. Malone 342
Mr. Reeder in Room 13
Mr. Robinson Crusoe 635
Mrs. Jones... (all) 522
Mrs. Miniver 524
Mrs. O'Malley and Mr. Malone 394
Mrs. Sundance... (all) 525
Mr. Wise Guy 214
Mr. Wong... (all) 526
Muddy Romance 412
Mugger 222
Muggsy... (all) 526A
Mug Town 453
Mule Train 282
Mummy... (all) 527
Mummy's Boys 839
Mummy's Dummies 760
Mum's the Word 127
Munster, Go Home 528
Munsters' Revenge 528
Muppet Movie 529

Muppets Take Manhattan 529
Murder Ahoy 380
Murder at a Gallop 380
Murder at Site Three 671
Murder by an Aristocrat 549
Murder by Death 677
Murder by Decree 677
Murderer's Row 490
Murder Goes to College 530
Murder in Northumberland 677
Murder in Peyton Place 586
Murder is My Business 500
Murder Me, Murder You 504
Murder Most Foul 380
Murder My Sweet 586
Murder of Dr. Harrigan 549
Murder on a Bridle Path 342
Murder on a Honeymoon 342
Murder on the Blackboard 342
Murder on the Orient Express 336
Murder on the Yukon 620
Murders in the Rue Morgue 125
Murder Over New York 128
Murder She Said 380
Murder With Mirrors 380
Muscle Beach Party 53
Muscle Bound 73
Muscle Up a Little Closer 760
Mush and Milk 560
Musical Marvel 61
Music Box 434
Music Fiends 141
Music Made Simple 633
Musiquiz 585
Mustang Pete's Love Affair 10
Musty Musketeers 760
Mutiny in the County 517
Mutiny on the Body 697
Mutts and Movies 430
Mutts to You 760
My American Cousin 532
My Favorite Spy 410
My Friend Flicka 533
My Friend Irma... (all) 534
My Friend Jekyll 207
My Goodness 73
My Gun is Quick 504
My Little Feller 22
My Pal Dr. Jekyll 207

My Pal Trigger 648
My Son the Vampire 552
Mysterious Desperado 764
Mysterious Dr. Fu Manchu 269
Mysterious Intruder 821
Mysterious Island... (all) 793
Mysterious Mr. Moto 523
Mysterious Mystery 560
Mysterious Rider 74
Mystery at Villa Rose 368
Mystery House 549
Mystery Man 351, 703
Mystery of Chalk Hill 330
Mystery of Marie Roget 125
Mystery of Mr. Wong 526
Mystery of the Golden Eye 128
Mystery of the Silent Death 671
My Tomato 633
My Uncle 521
My Wife's Relations 108
My Wife's Relatives 339

Nag in the Bag 697
Name the Day 703
Nancy Drew... (all) 535
National Lampoon's... Vacation (all) 536
National Nuts 61
National Velvet 537
Nature in the Wrong 127
Naughty Nineties 1
Navajo Trail 396
Navajo Trail Raiders 12
Navigator 108
Nearly a Maid 703
Nearly Rich 703
'Neath Arizona Skies 459
'Neath Brooklyn Bridge 214
Neighborhood House 127
Neighbor Pests 585
Neighbors 108
Nero Wolfe 538
Nevada City 648
Nevada Raiders 819
Nevada Smith 121
Never a Dull Moment 630
Never Back Losers 220
Neverending Story (all) 539
Never Mention Murder 220
Never the Dames Shall Meet 127

Never Say Never Again 378
Never Touched Me 323
Never Weaken 323
New Adventures of Get-Rich-Quick Wallingford 288
New Adventures of Heidi 331
New Adventures of Pippi Longstocking 594
New Adventures of Snow White 702
New Adventures of Tarzan 742
New Audioscopiks 582
New Daughters of Joshua Cabe 173
New Exploits of Elaine 160
New Frontier 756
New Halfback 22
New Interns 371
New Janitor 129
Newlyweds' House Guest 540
New Original Wonder Woman 840
New Pupil 560
News Hounds 90
Next Aisle Over 323
Nick Carter... (all) 541
Nickel Nurser 127
Night and a Blonde 356
Night at the Movies 633
Night at the Opera 488
Nightcomers 366
Night Cry 629
Night Games 434
Night in Casablanca 488
Night in the Snow 129
Nightmare on Elm Street... (all) 542
Nightmare Sisters 706
Night 'N' Gales 560
Night of Mystery 589
Night of the Howling Beast 158
Night of the Living Dead 455, 543
Night Out 129
Night Owls 434
Night Raiders 819
Night Riders 756
Nightshirt Bandit 127
Nights of Dracula 203
Nights of the Werewolf 158

Night Stage to Galveston 282
Night Stalker 544
Night Strangler 544
Night Time in Nevada 647
Ninja III: The Domination 231
Nip and Tuck 73
Nipups 581
Nitwits 839
No Census, No Feeling 760
No Children 703
Nocturna 203
No Dough, Boys 760
No Father to Guide Him 127
No Greater Love 357
No Holds Barred 90
Noise of Bombs 412
Noisy Naggers and Nosey Neighbors 430
Noisy Neighbors 517
Noisy Noises 560
No More Relatives 517
No Mother to Guide Him 61
No News is Good News 633
No No Lady 22
No. 1 of the Secret Service 545
No Retreat, No Surrender (all) 546
Non-Stop Kid 323
Noose Hangs High 1
Northern Frontier 547
Northern Mystery 551
Northern Patrol 515
North from the Lone Star 823
North of the Great Divide 648
North of the Rio Grande 351
North of the Rockies 825
Northwest Territory 515
Nosferatu... (all) 548
No Stop-Over 703
Not Above Suspicion 456
Not Guilty 22
Nothing But Nerves 633
Nothing But Pleasure 108
Nothing But Trouble 323, 434
Not on My Account 517
Notorious Lone Wolf 461
Notorious Sophie Lang 705
No Wedding Bells 430
Now I'll Tell You One 127
Now It Can Be Sold 22
Now or Never 323

Now We'll Tell One 127
Now You See It 585
Number Please 323
Number Six 220
Nursemaid Who Disappeared 29
Nurse to You 127
Nutty But Nice 760

Oath of Vengeance 74
Octopussy 378
Odor in the Court 141
Of Cash and Hash 760
Official Officers 560
Off the Trolley 323
Off to Buffalo 127
Off to the Races 401
Oh, Daddy 73
Oh, God... (all) 550
Oh, Heavenly Dog 60
Oh, Mabel Behave 470
Oh, My Operation 106
Oh, Oh, Cleopatra 489, 839
Oh, Sailor Behave 554
Oh, Say, Can You Sue 22
Oh, Susannah 280
Oh, What a Man 430
Oils Well that Ends Well 760
Oily to Bed, Oily to Rise 760
Okay, Toots 127
Oklahoma Badlands 12
Oklahoma Blues 389
Oklahoma Frontier 395
Oklahoma Jim 69
Oklahoma Justice 398
Oklahoma Renegades 756
Old Barn 22
Old Barn Dance 280
Old Bull 751
Old Coral 280
Old Dracula 203
Old-Fashioned Movie 215
Old Frontier 512
Old Gray Hoss 560
Old Gypsy Custom 22
Old Homestead 812
Old Maid... (all) 550A
Old Mother Riley... (all) 552
Old Oklahoma Plains 624
Old Overland Trail 624
Old Raid Mule 22
Old Sawbones 22
Old Sea Dog 703

Old Shatterhand 553
Old Spanish Custom 108
Old Surehand 553
Old Texas Trail 642
Old Wallop 560
Old Warhorse 703
Old West 282
Oliver's Story 467
Olympic Events 579
Olympic Games 560
Olympic Ski Champions 585
Omen 556
On Again, Off Again 839
Once Over 703
Once Over, Light 106
Once Upon a Prime Time 203
One A.M. 129
One Dangerous Night 461
One Good Turn 434
One Horse Farmers 752
One Hundred Percent Service 106
One in a Million 630
One Mama Man 127
One Mask Too Many 456
One More Time 203, 661
One Mysterious Night 89
One Night in the Tropics 1
One of Our Spies is Missing 483
One of the Family 127
One of the Smiths 127
One Police Plaza 557
One-Run Elmer 108
One Spooky Night 22, 73
One Spy Too Many 473
One Terrible Day 560
1-2-3 Go! 560
One Week 108
One Wild Ride 560
On Her Majesty's Secret Service 378
On Ice 325
On Location 703
On Moonlight Bay 573
On Patrol 73
On the Avenue 630
On the Fire 323
On the Great White Trail 620
On Their Own 401
On the Jump 323
On the Lazy Line 807
On the Loose 751
On the Old Spanish Trail 647
On the Run 220

On the Wrong Trek 127
On Top of Old Smokey 280
Open Another Bottle 703
Opened by Mistake 752
Opening Day 633
Orchids and Ermine 501
Order in Court 703
Oregon Trail 395, 725
Oregon Trail Scouts 617
Organization 807
Original Old Mother Riley 552
Orlak, the Hell of Frankenstein 259
Other Side of the Mountain (all) 559
Our Gang... (all) 560
Our Hospitality 108
Our Relations 434
Our Wife 434
Out California Way 511
Outcasts of Black Mesa 203
Outcasts of the Trail 512
Outdoor Pajamas 127
Outer Space Jitters 760
Outfit 566
Out for Fun 585
Outlaw Brand 389
Outlaw Country 431
Outlaw -- Josie Wales 403
Outlaw Ladies (all) 561
Outlaw of Gor 304
Outlaw of the Plains 74
Outlaw Roundup 748
Outlaws is Coming 760
Outlaws of Border Pass 457
Outlaws of Pineridge 199
Outlaws of Sonora 756
Outlaws of Stampede Pass 396
Outlaws of Texas 818
Outlaws of the Cherokee Trail 756
Outlaws of the Desert 351
Outlaws of the Rockies 203
Outlaws Paradise 443
Outlaw Trail 784
Out West 760
Out West with the Hardys 23
Out West with the Peppers 249
Overland Mail 824
Overland Riders 74
Overland Stage Raiders 756
Overland Telegraph 764

Overland Trails 396
Over the Bounding Main 834
Over the Fence 323
Over-the-Hill Gang... (all) 562
Over the Santa Fe Trail 411
Over There 325
Over Thereabouts 73
Own Your Own Home 703
Oz 835
Ozark Romance 323

Pack Train 280
Pack Up Your Troubles 434, 630
Pain in the Pullman 760
Painted Desert 284
Painted Hills 432
Pair of Kings 430
Pajama Party 53, 751
Paleface 108, 563
Palooka 393
Palooka from Paducah 108
Pals and Gals 760
Pals of the Golden West 652
Pals of the Pecos 756
Pals of the Saddle 756
Pals of the Silver Sage 749
Panama Patrol 138
Pancho Villa... (all) 564
Pan Handlers 752
Panic is On 127
Paradise Canyon 459
Pardon Me 703
Pardon Mon Affaaire... (all) 567
Pardon My Backfire 760
Pardon My Berth Marks 108
Pardon My Clutch 760
Pardon My Nightshirt 22
Pardon My Sarong 1
Pardon My Scotch 760
Pardon My Wrench 22, 282
Pardon Our Nerve 495
Pardon Us 434
Parenthood 565A
Parole Fixer 383
Paris Express 370
Paris Playboys 90
Park Your Car 703
Parlor, Bedroom and Bath 108
Parlor, Bedroom and Wrath 517
Partner 220

Partners Again 604
Partners in Crime 220, 530
Partners of the Plains 351
Partners of the Sunset 389
Partners of the Trail 396
Part Two, Walking Tall 809
Party Fever 560
Passing the Buck 430
Passionate Plumber 108
Passport to Suez 461
Patchwork Girl of Oz 835
Pathfinder... (all) 437
Patient in Room 18 549
Patrolling the Ether 166
Patton 568
Paul Temple... (all) 569
Pawnbroker's Heart 61
Pawnshop 129
Pawns of Satan 203
Pay as You Exit 560
Pay Day 129
Pay Your Dues 323
P.C. Josser 404
Peaches and Plumbers 73
Peach O'Reno 839
Pearl... (all) 569A
Pearl of Death 163, 667
Pearls and Devil-Fish 578
Peck's Bad Boy... (all) 570
Pecos River 203
Pedestrian Safety 585
Peeping Pete A Bandit 412
Pee-Wee's Big Adventure 571
Penguin Pool Murder 342
Penitentiary (all) 572
Penny... (all) 585
Penny-in-the-Slot 703
Penrod... (all) 573
People that Time Forgot 429
People Vs. Dr. Kildare 208
Peppery Salt 22
Perfect Clown 430
Perfect Day 434
Perfect Lady 127
Perfect Setup 166
Perils of Pauline 574
Perry Mason... (all) 575
Personal Touch (all) 576
Persons in Hiding 383
Pest Control 585
Pest from the West 108
Pest Man Wins 760
Pete Smith's Scrapbook 585
Pet Peeves 585
Petticoat Politics 339

Petting Preferred 325
Peyton Place... (all) 586
Phantasm 587
Phantom of Chinatown 526
Phantom of the Plains 617
Phantom of the Rue Morgue 125
Phantom Patrol 547
Phantom Pinto 110
Phantom Plainsman 756
Phantom Raiders 541
Phantoms Inc. 166
Phantom Stallion 624
Phantom Thief 89
Phantom Valley 203
Philo Vance... (all) 589
Phone Sex Girls (all) 590
Phony Express 760
Physical (all) 591
Piano Mooner 325
Pichianni troupe 581
Pickaninnies and Watermelon 615
Pick a Star 434
Pickled Peaches 325
Pickled Peppers 82
Picture Pirates 61
Pie a la Maid 127
Piece of the Action 800
Pie Covered Wagon 38
Pies and Guys 760
Pigskin 579
Pigskin Champions 585
Pigskin Palooka 560
Pigskin Skill 585
Pillow of Death 365
Pimpernel Smith 665
Pimple... (all) 591A
Pinched 323
Pinch in Time 356
Pinch Singer 560
Pink Pajamas 73
Pink Panther... (all) 592
Pinocchio... (all) 593
Pinto Bandit 748
Pioneer Days 459
Pioneer Justice 431
Pioneer Marshal 512
Pioneers 437, 749
Pioneers of the Frontier 823
Pioneers of the West 756
Pipe the Whiskers 323
Pip from Pittsburgh 127
Pippi... (all) 594
Piranha... (all) 595

Pirates on Horseback 351
Piscatorial Pleasures 578
Pistol Harvest 760
Pistol Packin' Nitwits 325
Pistols for Breakfast 323
Pitfalls of a Big City 61
Plagues and Puppy Love 430
Plain and Fancy Girls 127
Plain Clothes 325
Planet of the Apes 596
Plan for Destruction 166
Plans and Pajamas 430
Playback 220
Playhouse 108
Playing by Ear 585
Playing Hookey 560
Playing the Ponies 760
Playmates 410
Playtime 521
Pleasant Journey 560
Please Answer 585
Pleasure Hunt (all) 597
Plot Thickens 342
Pluck and Plotters 430
Plumber 61, 412
Poetry of Nature 585
Point Blank 566
Poisoned Ivory 517
Poker at Eight 127
Police 129
Police Academy... (all) 599
Pollytix in Washington 38
Polo 583
Pop Goes the Easel 760
Poltergeist (all) 600
Pony Post 295
Pooch 560
Poor Fish 127
Poor White Trash (all) 601
Porky's... (all) 602
Portrait of a Dead Girl 491
Poseidon Adventure 603
Position Wanted 127
Postman 585
Potash and Permutter 604
Poultry a la Mode 61
Pound Foolish 166
Powder and Smoke 127
Powder River Rustlers 12
Powdersmoke Range 756
Power of the Whistler 821
Practical Jokers 560. 585
Prairie 437
Prairie Badmen 74
Prairie Express 396

Prairie Gunsmoke 825
Prairie Moon 280
Prairie Pals 268
Prairie Pioneers 756
Prairie Raiders 213
Prairie Roundup 213
Prairie Rustlers 74
Prairie Schooners 823
Pranks of Buster Brown 107
Prescription: Murder 151
Pretty Peaches (all) 605
Pride of Pikeville 61
Pride of the Bowery 214
Pride of the Plains 400
Pride of the West 351
Prince, King of Dogs 581
Prince of the Plains 512
Prince of Thieves 634
Priscilla... (all) 605A
Private Eyes 90
Private Life of Oliver the Eighth 434
Private Life of Sherlock Holmes 667
Private Snuffy Smith 49
Prize Maid 540
Problem Child 565A
Prodigal Bridegroom 61
Professor Beware 323
Pro Football 581
Prom Night... (all) 606
Property Man 129
Prunes and Politics 517
Psycho (all) 607
Public Cowboy No. 1 280
Public Enemy... (all) 608
Public Ghost No. 1 127
Publicity Pays 127
Public Pays 166
Pulling a Bone 106
Punch Drunks 760
Punch the Clock 703
Punchy Cowpunchers 760
Puppetmaster (all) 608A
Pups is Pups 560
Pure Hell at St. Trinian's 58
Purity Squad 166
Purple Death from Outer Space 252
Purple Vigilantes 756
Pursuit to Algiers 667
Putting Pants on Philip 434
Pygmy Island 405

396 MOTION PICTURE SERIES & SEQUELS

Quack Doctor 73
Quatermass... (all) 609
Queen of the Mob 383
Queen of the Pirates 610
Quicker'n a Wink 585
Quick on the Trigger 213
Quiet Forth 517
Quiet, Please 517
Quiet Street 560
Quiz Biz 585
Quiz Whiz 760

Racing Canines 583
Racket Cheers 22
Racketeers of the Range 285
Radio Bugs 560
Radio Detective 160
Radio Hams 585
Radio Kisses 22
Radio Murder Mystery 667
Radio Rampage 517
Raffles... (all) 611
Ragged Girl of Oz 835
Ragtime Cowboy Joe 395
Raiders of Red Gap 457
Raiders of the Border 396
Raiders of the Lost Ark 364
Raiders of the Range 756
Raiders of the San Joaquin 395
Raiders of the South 396
Raiders of the Tomahawk 213
Raiders of the West 268
Railroadin' 560
Rainbow Over the Range 749
Rainbow Over the Rockies 390
Rainbow Riders 102
Rainbow Trail 627
Rainbow Valley 459
Rainmakers 839
Rainy Days 560
Raise the Rent 703
Rajah 323
Rambo... (all) 612
Rambone... (all) 613
Rampage at Apache Wells 553
Ranch Girl's... (all) 613A
Rancho Grande 280
Randy Rides Alone 459
Range Beyond the Blue 219
Range Busters 614
Range Defenders 756

Range Land 396, 818
Ranger and the Lady 648
Ranger Courage 747
Range Renegades 389
Ranger of the Cherokee 512
Rangers Ride 389
Rangers Step In 747
Rangers Take Over 748
Range War 351
Ransom for a Dead Man 151
Rascals and Robbers -- The Secret Adventures of Tom Sawyer and Huck Finn 767
Rasp 29
Raspberry Romance 61
Rastus... (all) 615
Rat (616)
Rattling Romeo 127
Rawhide Mail 102
Rawhide Rangers 395
Readin' and Writin' 560
Ready Willing But Unable 223
Real American Hero 809
Real McCoy 127
Re-Animator (all) 616A
Reckless Ranger 747
Recreation 129
Red Blood of Courage 547
Red Dragon 128
Red Hot Hottentots 703
Redman and the Renegades 437
Red Noses 751
Red River Range 756
Red River Renegades 725
Red River Shore 624
Red River Valley 280, 648
Red Scare 672
Red Sonja 150
Red Spider 557
Red Stallion... (all) 618
Reducing 585
Reeling Down the Rhine with Will Rogers 834
Reel Virginian 61
Remedy for Riches 205
Remember When? 325
Renegade 74
Renegade Trail 351
Renegade Ranger 284
Renegades of Sonora 12
Renegades of the Rio Grande 642

Renegades of the Sage 213
Renfrew ... (all) 620
Rent Collector 430
Rescue from Gilligan's Island 293
Respect the Law 166
Restless Knights 760
Return Fire: Jungle Wolf II 406
Return from the Past 211
Return from the River Kwai 95
Return from Witch Mountain 233
Return of a Man Called Horse 479
Return of Boston Blackie 89
Return of Bulldog Drummond 104
Return of Chandu 126
Return of Count Yorga 159
Return of Desperado 185
Return of Don Camillo 200
Return of Dracula 203
Return of Dr. Fu Manchu 269
Return of Frank Cannon 114
Return of Frank James 386
Return of Jimmy Valentine 7
Return of Johnny Wadd 399
Return of Josey Wales 403
Return of Marcus Welby M.D. 485
Return of Monte Cristo 157
Return of Mr. Moto 523
Return of Raffles 611
Return of Rin Tin Tin 629
Return of Sabata 660
Return of Sam McCloud 491
Return of Sherlock Holmes 667
Return of Sophie Lang 705
Return of Swamp Thing 729
Return of the Cisco Kid 140
Return of the Dragon 230
Return of the Durango Kid 213
Return of the Fly 255
Return of the Frog 267
Return of the Hulk 363
Return of the Jedi 713
Return of the Killer Tomatoes 417
Return of the Lash 431
Return of the Living Dead 455, (all) 621

MOTION PICTURE SERIES & SEQUELS 397

Return of the Man from
 U.N.C.L.E. 483
Return of the Musketeers 757
Return of the Pink Panther
 592
Return of the Rangers 748
Return of the Rat 616
Return of the Riddle Rider
 627A
Return of the Scarlet
 Pimpernell 665
Return of the Seven 475
Return of the Shaggy Dog 674
Return of the Six-Million
 Dollar Man 687
Return of the Streetfighter
 719
Return of the Tall Blond
 Man with One Black
 Shoe 740
Return of the Vampire 837
Return of the Whistler 821
Return of the Wolfman 158,
 203
Return of the World's
 Greatest Detective
 667
Return of Walpurgis 158
Return of Wild Bill 823
Return to Boggy Creek 85
Return to Fantasy Island 241
Return to Macon County 472
Return to Oz 835
Return to Peyton Place 586
Return to Sender 220
Return to Snowy River Part
 II 482
Return to Treasure Island 788
Reunion in Rhythm 560
Revenge of Dracula 203
Revenge of Frankenstein 259
Revenge of Tarzan 742
Revenge of the Boogeyman 88
Revenge of the Creature 162
Revenge of the Living Dead
 621
Revenge of the Nerds... (all)
 622
Revenge of the Ninja 231
Revenge of the Pink Panther
 592
Revenge of the Screaming
 Dead 621
Revenge of the Stepford
 Wives 716

Reward of Bronco Billy 97
Rhythm and Weep 760
Rhythm of the Rio Grande
 749
Rhythms of the Saddle 280
Ribald Tales of Robin Hood
 634
Richest Girl in the World
 626
Ricochet 220
Riddle Rider 627A
Ride 'Em Cowboy 1
Ride 'Em Cowgirl 201
Ride On, Vaquero 140
Ride, Ranger, Ride 280
Rider from Tucson 764
Ride, Ryder, Ride 617
Riders in the Sky 282
Riders of Destiny 459
Riders of Pasco Basin 395
Riders of the Black Hills 756
Riders of the Dawn 390
Riders of the Deadline 351
Riders of the Dusk 818
Riders of the Lone Star 213
Riders of the Northwest
 Mounted 657
Riders of the Purple Sage 627
Riders of the Range 764
Riders of the Rio Grande 756
Riders of the Rockies 750
Riders of the Santa Fe 642
Riders of the Timberline 351
Riders of the West 655
Riders of the Whistling
 Skull 756
Ride Tenderfoot Ride 280
Ridin' Down the Canyon 648
Ridin' Down the Trail 389
Ridin' Gents 102
Riding the California Trail
 140
Ridin' on a Rainbow 280
Ridin' the Cherokee Trail 749
Ridin' the Outlaw Trail 213
Ridin' the Sunset Trail 766
Riff Raff Girls 628
Rififi... (all) 628
Ring and the Belle 22
Ringside Maisie 476
Ring Up the Curtain 323
Rink 129
Rinty of the Desert 629
Rio Grande Patrol 764
Rio Grande Ranger 747

Rio Rita 1, 839
Rip Sew and Stitch 760
Risks and Roughnecks 430
Rivals 220
Rival Sherlock Holmes 667
River's End 758
Road Agent 764
Road Back 15
Road to... (all) 631
Road to Eternity 357
Road Warrior 473
Roaming Cowboy 261
Roaming Romeo 325
Roamin' Holiday 560
Roaming the Emerald Isle
 with Will Rogers
 834
Roaring Frontiers 825
Roaring Rangers 213
Roaring Sixguns 547
Roaring Westward 389
Roarin' Lead 756
Robe 632
Robin and Marion 634
Robin and the Seven Hoods
 634
Robin Hood... (all) 634
Robin Hoodnik 634
Robin Hood of Monterey 140
Robin Hood of Texas 281
Robin Hood of the Pecos 648
Robinson Crusoe... (all) 635
Robocop (all) 636
Robofox (all) 637
Robot Wrecks 560
Rock-a-by-Baby 703
Rockin' Through the Rockies
 760
Rock 'N' Roll High School...
 (all) 638
Rock, Pretty Baby 639
Rocky (all) 640
Rocky Horror Picture Show
 641
Rocky Mountain Rangers 756
Rodeo King and the Senorita
 623
Rogues of Sherwood Forest
 634
Rogue Song 434
Rolling Down the Great
 Divide 268
Rollin' Home to Texas 749
Rollin' Plains 750
Roll On, Texas Moon 648

Roll, Thunder, Roll 617
Romance of Digestion 633
Romance of Elaine 160
Romance of Tarzan 742
Romance of the Potato 585
Romance of the Rio Grande 140
Romance of the West 218
Romance on the Range 648
Romancing the Stone 643
Romans and Rascals 430
Romeo and Juliet 61
Rookies in Burma 644
Room at the Top 645
Rooms and Rumors 430
Room Service 488
Rooster Cogburn 791
Rootin' Tootin' Rhythm 280
Roping Her Romeo 61
Roping Wild Bears 581
Rosemary's Baby 646
Rough House Rhythm 517
Rough on Rents 517
Rough Riders of Cheyenne 725
Rough Riders' Roundup 650
Rough Riding 585
Rough Ridin' Rhythm 547
Rough Seas 127
Rough Toughs and Rooftops 430
Rough, Tough West 213
Rounders 129
Roundup 261
Round Up Time in Texas 280
Rover's Big Chance 560
Rovin' Tumbleweeds 280
Royal Razz 127
Ruby Love 127
Rugby 581
Rule 'Em and Weep 489
Rummies and Razors 430
Rumpus in the Harem 760
Run 'Em Ragged 703
Runt Page 38
Rushin' Ballet 560
Rush Orders 703
Rustlers 764
Rustler's Hideout 74
Rustlers of Devil's Canyon 617
Rustlers of the Badlands 213
Rustlers on Horseback 12
Rustlers' Valley 351
Rusty... (all) 658

Rusty Romeos 760
Ruth... (all) 659

Sabata 660
Saddle Aces 625
Saddle Legion 764
Saddlemates 756
Saddle Mountain Roundup 614
Saddle Pals 281
Saddles and Sagebrush 657
Saddle Serenade 390
Safari Drums 86
Safe at Home 585
Safety First Ambrose 18
Safety in Numbers 401
Safety Last 323
Safety Sleuth 585
Saga of Death Valley 648f
Sagebrush Trail 459
Sagebrush Troubador 280
Saginaw Trail 280
Sailor-Made Man 323
Sailors Beware 434
Sailors Three 755
Saint... (all) 661
Salone Vs. Shenendoah 61
Salt and Pepper 662
Salt Lake Raiders 12
Salute the Toff 767
Sammy in Siberia 323
Sammy's Scandalous Schemes 423
Sammy Vs. Cupid 423
Samson and the Slave Queen 844
San Antone Ambush 512
San Antonio Kid 617
Sanders of the River 663
Sandy... (all) 42
Santa Fe Marshal 351
Santa Fe Saddlemates 725
Santa Fe Scouts 756
Santa Fe Stampede 756
Santa Fe Uprising 617
Sappy Birthday 22
Sappy Bullfighters 760
Sappy Pappy 22
Saps at Sea 434
Sap Takes a Wrap 127
Satanic Rites of Dracula 203
Satan Met a Lady 477
Satan's Cradle 140
Saturday Afternoon 325

Saturday Morning 560
Saturday's Lesson 560
Saucy Madeline 61
Savage Frontier 12
Savage Mutiny 405
Savage Seven 333
Saved by the Belle 760
Save Your Money 703
Saving Mabel's Dad 470
Sawmill 430
Scamps and Scandals 430
Scarab Murder Case 589
Scaramouche 664
Scarecrow 108
Scarlet Clue 128
Scarlet Pimpernel 665
Scars of Dracula 203
Scar Tissue 330
Scattergood Baines... (all) 666
Scheming Schemers 760
School Begins 560
School Days 430
School's Out 560
Scientifiquiz 585
Scotch 22
Scotched in Scotland 760
Scram 434
Scrambled Brains 760
Scrap Happy 585
Scratch as Scratch Can 141
Scratch Scratch Scratch 22
Scream, Blacula, Scream 79
Scum of the Earth 601
Sea Dog's Tale 73
Sea For Yourself 585
Sealed Lips 672
Seal Skins 751
Sea Raiders 453
Search 456
Search for Danger 240
Sea Squawk 325
Second Childhood 560
Second Coming 621
Second Hundred Years 434
Secret Agent X-9 667
Secret of Dr. Kildare 208
Secret of Dr. Mabuse 209
Secrets of the Lone Wolf 461
Secrets of the Underground 520
Secrets of the Wasteland 351
Secret of the Whistler 821
Seeing Hands 585
Seeing Nellie Home 127
Seeing the World 560

MOTION PICTURE SERIES & SEQUELS 399

Seein' Things 560
See My Lawyer 554
See Your Doctor 633
Self-Defense 585
Self-Made Maids 760
Sensational Janine (all) 668
Sequel to the Diamond from the Sky 187A
Sesame Street Presents Follow That Bird 529
Set 'Em Up 585
Set-Up 220
Seven Brothers Meet Dracula 203
Seven Chances 108
Seven-Per-Cent Solution 677
Seven Samurai 475
Seventh Column 585
Seventh Voyage of Sinbad 685
Sex Asylum... (all) 669
Sex Life of the Poly 633
Sex Lives of the Rich and Famous (all) 670
Sexton Blake... (all) 671
Sexton Pimple 591A
Shadow... (all) 672
Shadow of Dracula 203
Shadow of the Thin Man 753
Shadow of the Werewolf 158
Shadow Over Chinatown 128
Shadows in the Night 165
Shadows of Death 74
Shadows of the West 818
Shadows of Tombstone 624
Shadows on the Range 396
Shadows on the Sage 756
Shadow Valley 219
Shaft... (all) 673
Shaggy D.A. 674
Shaggy Dog 674
Shake 'Em Up 703
Shampoo the Magician 356
Shanghai Chest 128
Shanghai Cobra 128
Shanghaied 128
Shanghaied Lovers 325
Share-Out 220
Share the Wealth 22
Sharks and Swordfish 578
Shatterhand 553
She 676
She Gets Her Man 476
Sheik 678
Shells and Shivers 430

She Loved Him Plenty 61
She Loves Me Not 323
Shepherd of the Ozarks 812
Sheriff... (all) 676A
Sheriff Nell... (all) 676B
Sheriff Nell's Tussle 61, 676B
Sheriff of Cimarron 725
Sheriff of Las Vegas 617
Sheriff of Medicine Bow 396
Sheriff of Redwood Valley 617
Sheriff of Sage Valley 74
Sheriff of Tombstone 648
Sheriff of Wichita 12
Sherlock Holmes... (all) 677
Sherlock Jr. 108
Sherman Said It 127
She's Oil Mine 108
She's So Fine (all) 679
She-Wolf of London 837
Shivering Shakespeare 560
Shivering Sherlocks 760
Shivering Spooks 560
Shiver My Timbers 560
Shivers 325
Shock 63
Shock Treatment 641
Shootin' Injuns 560
Shoot on Sight 703
Shopping With Wifie 22
Short Circuit (all) 680
Shot in the Dark 592
Shot in the Fracas 61
Shot in the Front 760
Should Husbands Be Watched 127
Should Husbands Work? 339
Should Married Men Go Home? 434
Should Sleepwalkers Marry? 73
Show 430
Show Business 751
Showdown 351
Show Girl... (all) 681
Shriek of Araby 61
Shrimp 325
Shrimps for a Day 560
Sic 'Em Towser 323
Sidewalks of New York 108
Sierra Sue 280
Sign of Four 677
Silencers 490
Silent Call 722

Silent Conflict 351
Silent Night, Deadly Night... (all) 682
Silent Passenger 463
Silk (all) 683
Silken Threads 671
Silly Billies 839
Silver Blaze 677
Silver Bullet 395
Silver Canyon 282
Silver City Bonanza 623
Silver City Raiders 657
Silver on the Sage 351
Silver Raiders 818
Silver Range 396
Silver Spurs 653
Silver Trail 629
Silver Trails 389
Simple Life 430
Simple Lifers 764A
Simple Sap 430
Sinbad... (all) 685
Sing a Song of Six Pants 760
Sing, Baby, Sing 630
Singing Cowgirl 201
Singing Hill 280
Singing Musketeer 757
Singing on the Trail 411
Singing Vagabond 280
Sing, Sister, Sing 752
Sinister Journey 351
Sinister Man 220
Sink or Swim 703
Sin of Harold Diddlebock 263
Sins of the Wealthy (all) 686
Sioux City Sue 281
Si Senor 323
Sitter Downers 760
Sitting Pretty 518
Sittin' Pretty 127
Six Gun Gospel 396
Six-Gun Law 213
Six Gun Serenade 390
Six-Gun Trail 443
Six Million Dollar Man 687
Six of a Kind 106
Ski Birds 585
Skids and Scalawags 430
Skinner... (all) 688
Skinners in Silk 73
Skinny... (all) 689
Skinny the Moocher 127
Skip the Maloo 127
Skirt Shy 325
Ski Skill 585

400 MOTION PICTURE SERIES & SEQUELS

Skull and Crown 629
Sky Bandits 620
Sky Boy 325
Sky Dragon 128
Sky Murder 541
Sky Science 585
Sky Scraper 325
Sky Skiers 585
Slap Happy Sleuths 760
Slaughter.. (all) 690
Slave of the Vampire 203
Slayground 566
Sleepaway Camp... (all) 691
Sleepers West 500
Sleeping Cardinal 677
Sleepless Tuesday 517
Sleuth 430
Sleuths 61
Slightly at Sea 517
Slightly Static 752
Slipper Slickers 703
Slippery Pearls 839
Slippery Silks 760
Slipping Wives 434
Slips and Slackers 430
Slumber Party Massacre (all) 693
Small Talk 560
Small Town Idol 61, 73
Small Town Princess 73
Smart Alecks 214
Smart Blonde 781
Smile Please 325
Smile Wins 560
Smiley... (all) 693
Smith's... (all) 696
Smokey and the Bandit (all) 698
Smoky Canyon 213
Smugglers 90
Snakeeater 698A
Snake Eyes (all) 699
Snake Fist... (all) 700
Snake River Desperadoes 213
Snakeville... (all) 701
Snappy Sneezer 127
Sneak Easily 751
Sneezing Beezers 73
Snitch in Time 760
Snooper Service 325
Snow Birds 579
Snow Dog 515
Snow Was Black 370
Snow White... (all) 702

Snow White and the Three Stooges 760
Snuffy Smith: Yardbird 49
Snug in a Jug 141
Soak the Old 166
Soapsuds and Sapheads 430
Social Sea Lions 585
Social Terrors 517
Sockabye Baby 760
Sock Me to Sleep 517
Socks Appeal 296
Soft Money 323
Software Murders 661
Sold at Auction 703
Soldier Man 325
Soldier's Prayer 357
Solid Concrete 430
Solo for Sparrow 220
So Long, Mr. Chumps 760
Sombrero Kid 199
Some Baby 703
Some Girls Do 104
Some Liars 61
Some More of Samoa 760
Something Simple 127
Somewhere in Camp 704
Somewhere in Civvies 704
Somewhere in England 704
Somewhere in Politics 704
Somewhere in Turkey 323
Somewhere on Leave 704
Song of Arizona 648
Song of God's Country 512
Song of Old Wyoming 218
Songs and Bullets 261
Songs of the Buckaroo 750
Song of the Drifter 389
Song of the Range 389
Song of the Sierras 390
Song of the Thin Man 753
Song of the Trail 547
Song of the Wasteland 390
Son of a Badman 431
Son of Belle Starr 59
Son of Billy the Kid 431
Son of Blob 81
Son of Captain Blood 118
Son of Davy Crockett 823
Son of Dracula 203
Son of Dr. Jekyll 207
Son of Flubber 2
Son of Frankenstein 259
Son of Godzilla 300
Son of Kong 419
Son of Lassie 432

Son of Monte Cristo 157
Son of Paleface 563
Son of Roaring Dawn 395
Son of Robin Hood 634
Son of Sheik 678
Son of Sinbad 685
Son of Tarzan 742
Son of Zorro 844
Sonora Stagecoach 784
Sons of the Desert 434
Sons of the Pioneers 648
Sophie Lang Goes West 705
Sorority Babes in the Slimeball Bowl-o-Rama 706
Sorority Sisters 706
So This is Africa 839
Soul of a Heel 22
Soul of Nigger Charley 438
Sounder (all) 707
Soup and Fish 752
Southern Exposure 127
South of Caliente 652
South of Death Valley 213
South of Monterey 140
South of Rio 512
South of Santa Fe 648
South of the Border 280
South of the Boudoir 127
South of the Chisholm Trail 213
South of the Rio Grande 140
South Pacivic trail 624
South Seasickness 517
Southward Ho 648
So You... (all) 392
So You're... (all) 392
So You Won't Squawk 108
Space Ship Sappy 760
Spanish Cape Mystery 225
Spanking Age 560
Spanky 560
Speak Easily 108
Speckled Band 677
Speed 22
Speed in the Gay '90s 22
Speed to Spare 702
Speedy 323
Spellbinder 633
Spider... (all) 708
Spiderman 709
Spider Woman... (all) 710
Spies and Spills 430
Spite Marriage 108
Splash 579

MOTION PICTURE SERIES & SEQUELS

Spoilers of the Plains 649
Spook Busters 90
Spook Chasers 90
Spook Louder 760
Spooks 760
Spooks and Spasms 430
Spook Speaks 108
Spook Spoofing 560
Spooks Run Wild 214
Spook to Me 22
Spook Town 748
Spooky Hooky 560
Sporting Nuts 581
Sports and Splashes 430
Sportsman 430
Sportsman's Memories 585
Sports Oddities 585
Sports on Ice 585
Sports Quiz 585
Sports Sticklers 585
Sports Trix 585
Spot Cash 703
Spots Before Your Eyes 585
Spring Fever 323
Springtime in Texas 390
Springtime in the Rockies 280
Springtime in the Sierras 647
Sprucin' Up 560
Spuds 430
Spy Chasers 90
Spy in the Green Hat 483
Spy Who Came in From The Cold 695
Spy Who Loved Me 378
Spy With My Face 483
Squareheads 760
Squibs... (all) 711
Stagecoach Buckaroo 395
Stagecoach Driver 819
Stagecoach Express 199
Stagecoach Kid 764
Stagecoach Outlaws 74
Stagecoach to Denver 617
Stagecoach War 351
Stage Door Canteen 410
Stage Fright 560
Stage Hand 325
Stage Struck 703
Stage to Blue River 819
Stage to Mesa City 431
Star Boarder 61, 129, 430
Stardust of the Sage 280
Starlight Over Texas 750
Star Packer 459
Stars and Bars 412

Stars Over Texas 219
Star Trek... (all) 712
Start Something 703
Star Virgin 203
Star Wars 713
Star Worms (all) 714
Steamboat Bill Jr. 108
Stepfather (all) 715
Stepford Children 716
Stepford Wives 716
Step Forward 61
Step Lively, Jeeves 384
Stepping Out 127
Steptoe and Son... (all) 717
Stewed, Fried and Boiled 633
Stick to Your Guns 351
Sting (all) 718
Sting of Stings 127
Stolen Booking 61
Stolen Goods 127
Stolen Heirlooms 671
Stolen Kisses 30
Stone Age 703
Stone Age Romeos 760
Stop! Look! and Listen 430
Stop! Luke! and Listen! 458
Storm Over Wyoming 764
Story of Dr. Carver 585
Story of Robin Hood 634
Stout Hearts and Willing Hands 489
Straight, Place and Show 630
Straight Shooter 443
Strange Case of Dr. Kekyll and Mr. Hyde 207
Strange Confession 365
Strange Gamble 351
Strange Innertube 743
Stranger from Pecos 396
Stranger from Ponco City 213
Stranger from Santa Fe 396
Strangers in the House 370
Strangler's Web 220
Strawberry Roan 282
Streetfighter's Last Revenge 719
Streets of Ghost Town 213
Street Warriors (all) 720
Strictly Modern 703
Strictly Unreliable 751
Strike of the Panther 565
Strike One! 49A
Strikes and Spares 581
Stripes and Strumbles 430

Stripped to Kill (all) 721
Stuck in the Sticks 22
Studio Stampede 61
Studio Stoops 760
Studio Visit 585
Study in Scarlet 677
Study in Terror 677
Stuffie 585
Stuntman 430
St. Xwhere (all) 723
Subhumanoid Meltdown 142
Sucker List 166
Sudden Impact 194
Sue My Lawyer 325
Summer of '42 724
Sundown in Santa Fe 12
Sun Down Limited 560
Sunset in Wyoming 280
Sun Valley Cyclone 617
Sugar Daddies 434
Sugar Plum Papa 22
Suitor 430
Summer Love 639
Sun Comes Up 432
Sunday Calm 560
Sunk by the Census 517
Sunk in the Sink 22
Sunkissed Sweeties 22
Sunnyside 129
Sunset in El Dorado 648
Sunset in the Desert 648
Sunset Serenade 648
Sunset Trail 351
Super Cue Man 585
Superfly... (all) 726
Supergirl 728
Supergirls... (all) 727
Super-Hopper-Dyne 73
Superman... (all) 728
Super Snooper 22
Sure Cures 585
Surfboard Rhythm 585
Surf Heroes 585
Surprised Parties 560
Swamp Thing 729
Swat the Crook 323
Sweater Girl 150
Sweedie... (all) 731
Sweet and Hot 760
Sweeney (all) 732
Sweet Daddy 127
Sweet Memories 585
Sweet Spirits of the Nighter 223
Swing Fever 410

Swing High 579
Swing Shift Maisie 476
Swing Your Partners 323
Swing Your Swingers 22
Swiss Miss 434
Switch Hitters (all) 733
Sword of Sherwood Forest 634

Tabasco Kid 127
Table Tennis 583
Table Toppers 585
Taboo (all) 734
Taboo American Style... (all) 735
Tailspin Tommy... (all) 736
'Taint Legal 517
Take a Chance 323
Take a Cue 585
Take Me Back to Oklahoma 749
Take Your Medicine 22
Taking Care of Baby 581
Takin' It All Off 737
Takin' It Off 737
Tale of a Dog 560
Tale of Gold 456
Tales from the Crypt 738
Tales of Blood and Terror 203
Tales of Robin Hood 634
Talk Dirty to Me (all) 739
Tall Blond Man with One Black Shoe 740
Taming of the Snood 108
Taming Target 61
Tammy... (all) 741
Tango Tangles 129
Target 764
Tars and Stripes 108
Tarzan... (all) 742
Tarz & Jane & Boy & Cheeta 742
Tarzoon, Shame of the Jungle 742
Tassels in the Air 760
Taste of Blood 203
Taste the Blood of Dracula 203
Taxi Troubles 22
Teacher's Beau 560
Teacher's Pest 127
Teacher's Pet 560
Teaching the Teacher 703
Teenage Fantasies (all) 744

Teenage Frankenstein 203
Teen Wolf... (all) 745
Teeth of the Tiger 32
Television Turmoil 517
Tell 'Em Nothing 127
Telling Whoppers 560
Tell Them Johnny Wadd is Here 399
Temptation Harbor 370
Tender Dracula 203
Ten Dollars or Ten Days 61
Ten Minute Egg 127
Ten Nights in a Barroom... (all) 745A
Tennis Tactics 585
Tenting Tonight on the Old Campground 395
Ten Years Old 560
Termites of 1938 760
Terror by Night 677
Terror of Dracula 548
Terror of the Mummy 527
Terrors on Horseback 74
Terror Trail 213
Test 629
Testament of Dr. Mabuse 209
Texans Never Cry 282
Texas Chainsaw Massacre (all) 746
Texas City 398
Texas Dynamo 213
Texas Kid 396
Texas Lawmen
Texas Manhunt 268
Texas Masquerade 351
Texas Panhandle 213
Texas Pioneers 69
Texas Terror 459
Texas to Bataan 614
Texas Trail 351
Texas Trouble Shooters 614
Texasville 433
Texas Wildcats 443
Tex Rides with the Boy Scouts 750
Thanks Again 517
Thank You, Jeeves 384
Thank You, Mr. Jeeves 384
Thank You, Mr. Moto 523
That Gang of Mine 214
That Inferior Feeling 633
That's Him 323
That's His Story 585
That's My Wife 434

That's Right, You're Wrong 410
That's What You Think 585
Their First Mistake 434
Them Thar Hills 434
Their Purple Moment 434
There Ain't No Santa Claus 127
There Goes Kelly 798
There He Goes 325
There's Always A Woman 68
There's That Woman Again 68
They Call Me Mr. Tibbs 807
They Call Me Trinity 789
They Go Boom 434
They Made Me a Criminal 176
They Meet Again 205
They Might Be Giants 677
They're Always Caught 166
They Stooge to Conga 760
Thick and Thin 703
Thicker Than Water 434
Things We Can Do Without 585
Think Fast, Mr. Moto 523
Think First 166
Think It Over 166
Thin Man... (all) 753
Thin Twins 127
Third-Dimensional Murder 582
Third Round 104
Thirteen Lead Soldiers 104
13th Hour 821
This is a Living 585
This Man in Paris 684
Those Good Old Days 585
Those Love Pangs 129
Thousand Eyes of Dr. Mabuse 209
Three Ages 108
Three Arabian Nuts 760
Three Chumps Ahead 752
Three Cockeyed Sailors 755
Three Dark Horses 760
Three Dumb Clucks 760
Three Foolish Weeks 61
Three Hams on Rye 760
365 Days 703
Three in the Saddle 748
Three Little Beers 760
Three Little Pigskins 760
Three Little Pirates 760

Three Little Sew and Sews 760
Three Little Twerps 760
Three Loan Wolves 760
Three Men from Texas 351
Three Men in a Tub 560
Three Men in White 208
Three Mesquiteers 756
Three Missing Links 760
Three Musketeers 630, 757
Three on a Limb 108
Three on a Rope 585
Three on a Ticket 500
Three on the Trail 351
Three Pests in a Mess 760
Three Sappy People 760
Three Smart Boys 560
Three Smart Girls... (all) 759
Three Smart Guys 560
Three Smart Saps 760
Three Stooges... (all) 760
Three Texas Steers 756
Three Troubledoers 760
Thrill For Thelma 166
Throttle Pushers 579
Through Switzerland and Bavaria with Will Rogers 834
Through the Dark 89
Thru Thin and Ticket 489
Thunder at the Border 553
Thunderball 378
Thunderhead, Son of FLicka 533
Thundering Caravans 12
Thundering Fleas 560
Thundering Gunslingers 74
Thundering Tenors 127
Thundering Trail 431
Thundering Trails 756
Thunder Mountain 764
Thunder River Feud 614
Thunder Warrior (all) 761
Tied for Life 325
Tiger of Eschnapur 762
Tiger of the Seven Seas 610
Tillie... (all) 763
Timber Stampede 285
Timber Terrors 514
Timber Toppers 579
Timber War 547
Time for Dying 386
Time of Their Lives 1
Time Out for Lessons 560
Time Out for Trouble 127

Time to Kill 500
Time to Remember 220
Timid Young Man 108
Tin Man 752
Tiny Troubles 560
Tioga Kid 219
Tip 323
Tip Off Girls 383
Tips on Trips 585
Tired Business Men 560
Tired Feet 325
Tireman, Spare My Tires 325
Tire Trouble 560
Tish... (all) 764A
Tit for Tat 434
Titled Tenderfoot 826
To Have and To Hold 220
To Heir Is Human 325
To Love a Vampire 120
Tom Edison -- The Boy Who Lit Up the World 754
Tom Sawyer... (all) 767
Tonto Basin Outlaws 614
Tonto Kid 625
Tony Rome 768
Too Busy to Work 401
Toodles... (all) 768A
Too Many Husbands 22
Too Many Mamas 127
Too Many Suspects 225
Too Many Winners 500
Too Many Women 91
Tooth Will Out 760
Top Flat 752
Topnotchers 215
Topper... (all) 769
Tora-San Goes to Vienna 780
Torchy... (all) 781
Tornado in the Saddle 657
Tornado Range 219
Torrid 782
Torrid House 782
Torrid Without a Cause 782
Torture Money 166
To Trap a Spy 483
Tough as They Come 453
Tough Luck 703
Tough Luck and Tin Lizzies 430
Tough Winter 560, 703
Towed in a Hole 434
Toxic Avenger... (all) 783
Track and Field 585
Tracked by the Police 629

Trackers 456
Traffic 521
Trail Beyond 459
Trail Blazers 756
Trail Dust 351
Trailer Tragedy 517
Trail Guide 764
Trailing Danger 396
Trailing Double Trouble 614
Trail of Robin Hood 649
Trail of Terror 748
Trail of the Pink Panther 592
Trail of the Rustlers 213
Trail of the Silver Spurs 614
Trail of the Yukon 515
Trail Riders 614
Trail's End 396
Trails of the Wild 547
Trail to Laredo 213
Trail to Mexico 390
Trail to San Antone 281
Trained Hoofs 584
Tramp 129
Tramp Tramp Tramp 22
Tramp Trouble 517
Trancers (all) 785
Transaction (all) 786
Trap 128
Trapped 672
Trapped by Boston Blackie 89
Traps and Tangles 430
Trap Them and Kill Them 228
Travis McGee... (all) 787
Treachery of Bronco Billy's Pal 97
Treasure Blues 752
Treasure Island 788
Treasure of Silver Lake 553
Treasurer's Report 633
Treasures from Trash 585
Trial of Billy Jack 75
Trial of the Incredible Hulk 363
Trick Golf 581
Tricky Dicks 760
Trigger Finger 396
Trigger Jr. 651
Trigger Man 396
Trigger Smith 460
Trigger Trail 642
Trigger Trio 756
Trimmed in Furs 325
Trimmed in Gold 73
Trinity is Still My Name 789
Triple Crossing 760

Triple Trouble 90, 129
Trip to Paris 401
Triumph of Robin Hood 634
Triumph of Sherlock Holmes 677
Triumph of the Rat 616
Triumphs of a Man Called Horse 479
Trotting Through Turkey 703
Trouble Brewing 430
Trouble Finds Andy Clyde 22
Trouble in Sundown 285
Trouble Makers 90
Trouble or Nothing 517
Trouble With Angels 790
Trouble With Husbands 633
Trout Fishing 578
True Confessions of Tori Welles 782
True Grit... (all) 791
Truth 456
Tucson Raiders 617
Tugboat Annie... (all) 792
Tumbleweed Trail 219, 268
Tumbling Tumbleweed 280
Tuxedo Junction 812
Twenty Minutes of Love 129
20th Century Oz 835
20,000 Leagues Under the Sea 793
23 Paces to Baker Street 29
£20,000 Kiss 220
Twice Shy 190
Twice Two 434
Twilight in the Sierras 651
Twilight on the Rio Grande 281
Twilight on the Trail 351
Twins of Dracula 120
Twins of Evil 120
Twin Triplets 752
Two April Fools 22
Two Faces of Dr. Jekyll 207
Two-Fisted Justice 614
Two-Fisted Stranger 213
Two for the Money 517
Two-Gun Gussie 323
Two-Gun Sheriff 199
Two Jakes 136
Two Jills and a Jeep 22
Two Lips and Juleps 489
Two Local Yokels 22
Two Scrambled 323
Two Tars 434
2001: A Space Odyssey 795

2010 795
Two Too Young 560
Two Tough Tenderfeet 61

Unaccustomed as We Are 434
Uncivil Warbirds 760
Uncivil Warriors 760
Uncle Josh... (all) 795A
Uncle Tom's Uncle 560
Uncle Tom Without the Cabin 61
Under Arizona Skies 396
Under California Stars 647
Under Colorado Skies 511
Undercover Girl 476
Undercover Maisie 476
Undercover Man 351
Under Fiesta Stars 280
Under Mexicali Stars 623
Understudy: The Graveyard Shift II 303
Under Texas Skies 756
Under the Tonto Rim 764
Under Western Stars 653
Uneasy Terms 692
Uneasy Three 127
Unexpected Father 42
Unexpected Guest 351
Unexpected Riches 560
Unknown 362
Unknown Ranger 747
Unlucky Dog 517
Unnatural Act (all) 796
Up from the Beach 464
Up Front 797
Up Goes Maisie 476
Up in Daisy's Penthouse 760
Up in Smoke 90, 134
Up in the Air 798
Uppercut O'Brien 22
Upper Hand 628
Up the Creek 799
Uptown Saturday Night 800
Us 127
Utah 648
Utah Trail 750
Utah Wagon Train 623

V... (all) 802
Vacation Loves 22
Vagabond 129
Vagabond Loafers 760
Valiant Hombre 140

Valley of Fear 396, 677
Valley of Fire 282
Valley of Hunted Men 756
Valley of Silent Men 757
Valley of Terror 547
Valley of the Dolls 803
Valley of the Headhunters 405
Valley of Vengeance 74
Vampira 203
Vampire 203, 804
Vampire Ambrose 18
Vampire Lovers 120
Vampire Over London 552
Vampire of Dr. Dracula 158
Vampire's Coffin 804
Vampires Vs. Hercules 337
Vamp Till Ready 127
Vampyr 120
Vanishing Outpost 431
Vanishing Westerner 512
Vault of Horror 738
Vengeance of Fu Manchu 269
Vengeance of Rannah 629
Vengeance of She 676
Vengeance of the Mummy 527
Vengeance of the West 825
Vengeance Vow 456
Verdict 220
Very Missing Person 342
Victory Quiz 585
Victory Vittles 585
View to a Kill 378
Vigilante Hideout 12
Vigilantes of Boomtown 617
Vigilantes of Dodge City 617
Vigilantes Ride 657
Village of the Damned 806
Village of the Giants 256
Vindicator 259
Violent is the Word for Curly 760
Vital Victuals 581
Viuva Cisco Kid 140
Vocalizing 517
Voice of the Whistler 821
Voodoo Tiger 405
Vote for Huggett 355

Wagon Team 282
Wagon Tracks West 824
Wagon Wheels Westward 617

MOTION PICTURE SERIES & SEQUELS 405

Waiting for Baby 633
Waldo's Last Stand 560
Walking Tall 809
Walking the Baby 106
Walkout 703
Wall Street Blues 73, 517
Wall Street Cowboy 648
Waltons 811
Waltzing Around 141
Waltz Me Around 703
Wanderers of the West 766
Wandering Waistlines 73
Wandering Willies 73
Wanted: A Master 585
Wanted Dead or Alive 819
Wanted -- $5,000 323
Wanted: One Egg 585
Wanted: The Sundance
    Woman 525
War Babies 38
War Feathers 560
War Mama 751
Washee Ironee 560
Watchers (all) 811A
Watchman 22
Watch Out 325
Water Bugs 585
Water Sports 583
Water Trix 585
Water Wisdom 585
Watts Monster 207
Watusi 11
Way of All Pants 127
Way Out West 434
Weary Willie... (all) 811B
Weather Wizards 585
We Can Dream, Can't We?
    585
Wedding Bells 585
Wedding on Waltons
    Mountain 811
Wedding Worries 560
Wednesday's Child 813
Wee Wee, Monsieur 760
We Faw Down 434
Weird Woman 365
Welcome Danger 323
Well, I'll Be... 430
We're Not Dressing 106
Werewolf 837
Werewolf and the Yeti 158
Werewolf in a Girl's
    Dormitory 837
Werewolf of London 837

Werewolf of Washington
    837
Werewolf's Shadow 158
Werewolf Versus the
    Vampire Women
    158
Werewolves on Wheels 837
We Shall See 220
Western Cyclone 74
Western Heritage 764
Western Jamboree 280
Western Kimono 10
Western Renegades 397
Westland Case 71
West of Cimarron 756
West of Dodge City 213
West of El Dorado 397
West of Pinto Basin 614
West of Sonora 213
West of Texas 748
West of the Brazos 675
West of the Divide 459
West of the Law 655
West of the Rio Grande 396
West of Zanzibar 816
West Point of the South 584
West to Glory 219
Westward Bound 784
Westward Ho 756
Westward Ho-Hum 517
Westward Trail 219
Westworld 814
We Want Our Mummy 760
We Will All Meet in
    Paradise 567
Wham Bam Slam 760
What About Daddy? 585
What a Bozo 127
What a Whopper 703
Whatever Happened to Dobie
    Gillis? 196
What D'ya Know 585
What Fur 517
What I Want Next 585
What Makes Lizzy Dizzy?
    325
What! No Beer? 108
What, No Cigarettes? 517
What! No Men? 223
What Price Gloria 38
What Price Goofy 127
What Price Safety 166
What Price Taxi 743
What's the Matador? 760
What's Your IQ... (all) 585

What Women Did For Me
    127
When A Man's A Prince 61
When Ambrose Dared
    Walrus 18
When Love Is Blind 61
When Papa Died 61
When Summer Comes 73
When the Wind Blows 560,
    703
Where Am I? 703
Where Angels Go -- Trouble
    Follows 790
Where No Vultures Fly 815
Where's My Wandering Boy
    Tonight? 61
Where's the Fire? 703
Where the Boys Are... (all)
    817
Where the Buffalo Roam 750
Where the Bullets Fly 441
Where the North Begins 629
While America Sleeps 166
While London Sleeps 629
While the Patient Slept 549
Whippet Racing 579
Whirling Around France
    with Will Rogers
    834
Whirl o' the West 703
Whirls and Girls 22
Whirlwind 280
Whirlwind Raiders 213
Whispering Skull 748
Whispering Smith... (all) 820
Whispering Whiskers 73
Whispering Whoopee 127
Whistler 821
Whistles and Windows 430
Whistling in Brooklyn 810
Whistling Bullets 547
Whistling in Dixie 809
Whistling Hills 398
Whistling in the Dark 810
White Cockatoo 549
White Lightning 279
Who Done It? 1, 760
Who Killed Max? 490A
Whoops I'm an Indian 760
Whose Little Wife Are You?
    61
Who's Hugh? 356
Who Was Maddox? 220
Why Ben Bolted 61
Why Bring That Up? 794

406 MOTION PICTURE SERIES & SEQUELS

Why Bronco Billy Left Bear Country 97
Why, Daddy? 633
Why Foxy Grandpa Escaped a Ducking 257A
Why Girls Love Sailors 434
Why Go Home? 703
Why Husbands Go Mad 127
Why Is It? 585
Why Marry? 703
Why Men Work 127
Why Pick On Me? 323
Why Worry? 323
Wicked City 61
Wicked Sensations (all) 822
Wide Open Spaces 489
Wide Open Town 351
Wife Decoy 356
Wife's Life 585
Wife to Spare 22
Wiggle Your Ears 560
Wild and Wolly 579
Wild Angels 333
Wild Babies 91
Wildcat of Tucson 823
Wildcat Trooper 547
Wild Country 219
Wilderness Family Part 2 827
Wilderness Mail 547
Wild Frontier 12
Wild Geese (all) 828
Wild Goose Chaser 61
Wild Horse 350
Wild Horse Ambush 656
Wild Horse Canyon 460
Wild Horse Cyclone 74
Wild Horse Mesa 764
Wild Horse Range 460
Wild Horse Rodeo 756
Wild Horse Rustlers 457
Wild Horses 585
Wild Horse Stampede 784
Wild Posses 560
Wild Things (all) 829
Wild West 219
Wild Wild West Revisited 830
Wilful Ambrose 18
Willard 831
William Comes to Town 832
Willie... (all) 833
Will Power 517
Winnetou... (all) 553
Winning of the West 280

Wished on Mabel 470
Wistful Widow of Wagon Gap 1
Witch's Curse 471
With Hercules to the Center of the Earth 337
With Love and Hisses 434
Without a Clue 677
Without Apparent Motive 220
With Will Rogers... (all) 834
Witness 633
Wiz 835
Wizard of Oz 835
Wizards of the Lost Kingdom (all) 836
Wolf Hunters 515
Wolf in Thief's Clothing 22
Wolf Man 837
Wolfman of Count Dracula 158
Woman 129
Woman Haters 760
Woman in Green 677
Women are Trouble 251
Women in Hiding 166
Women's Penitentiary (all) 838
Wonderful Land of Oz 835
Wonder Woman 840
Work 129
World of Abbott and Costello 1
Worries and Wobbles 430
Worst Crime of All 203
Wrangler's Roost 614
Wrecking Crew 490
Wreckity Wreck 743
Wrong Again 434
Wrong Direction 517
Wrong Miss Wright 127
Wrong Number 661
Wrong Son 585
Wrong Way Butch 585
Wrong Way Out 166
Wyoming Bandit 12
Wyoming Hurricane 657
Wyoming Outlaw 756

Yale Vs. Harvard 560
Yankee Doodle Andy 22
Yankee Doodle In Berlin 61
Years to Come 703
Ye Olde Minstrels 560

Yes, We Have No Bonanza 760
Yodelin' Kid from Pine Ridge 280
Yojimbo 484
Yokel 703
Yoke's on Me 760
You Can't Do That To Me 476
You Drive Me Crazy 517
You'll Find Out 410
You Natzy Spy 760
York Mystery 551
You Can't Win 585
Young At Heart 257
Young Bill Hickok 648
Young Buffalo Bill 648
Young Dr. Kildare 208
Young Frankenstein 259
Young Guns (all) 840A
Young Ironsides 127
Young Lady Chatterly 428
Young Mr. Jazz 323
Young Oldfield 127
Young Pioneers... (all) 841
Young Sherlock Holmes 677
Young Sherlocks 560
Young Tom Edison 754
You Only Live Twice 378
You're Darn Tootin' 434
You're Next 703
You're Not So Tough 453
You're Only Young Once 23
You're Telling Me 91
Your Own Back Yard 560
You Said a Hatful 127
Your Technocracy and Mine 633
You the People 166
You Were Never Uglier 22
Yukon Flight 620
Yukon Gold 515
Yukon Jake 61
Yukon Manhunt 515
Yukon Vengeance 515

Zany Adventures of Robin Hood 634
Zapped... (all) 842
Zatoichi... (all) 843
Zontan -- Hound of Dracula 203
Zorro... (all) 844
Zulu... (all) 845

ADDENDA (Not indexed)

9. ALIEN
ALIENS III (in development, 1990) d Renny Harlin.

14. ALLIGATOR
ALLIGATOR II: THE RETURN (Manley Productions, announced 1990) d Jon Hess, s Joseph Bologna, Dee Wallace Stone.

16A. AMANDA BY NIGHT
In these X-rated films, a police detective helps the heroine solve crimes.
AMANDA BY NIGHT (Caballero, 1980) s Veronica Hart.
AMANDA BY NIGHT II (Caballero, 1987) d Jack Remy, s Veronica Hart.

21. AMITYVILLE HORROR
THE AMITYVILLE CURSE (Image, announced 1990) d Tom Berry, s Kim Coates.

31A. ARMY BRAT
On a dare, The Brat joins the military, in the first of these X-rated pictures.
ARMY BRAT (Vivid, 1987) d Paul Thomas, s Jamie Summers, Tom Byron.
STILL THE BRAT (Vivid, 1988) d Paul Thomas, s Nikki Randall, Aja.
THE WILD BRAT (Vivid, 1988) d Paul Thomas, s Jamie Summers, Megan Leigh.
ARMY BRAT II (Vivid, 1989) d Paul Thomas, s Julianne James, Tracey Adams.

50. BASKET CASE
BASKET CASE 2 (Glickenhause Entertainment, 1990) d Frank Henenlotter, s Kevin Van Hentearyck, Annie Ross, Kathryn Meisle.

62. BEVERLY HILLS COP
BEVERLY HILLS COP III (in development, 1990)

68A. BILL AND TED'S EXCELLENT ADVENTURE
Goof-off teens travel back into history.
BILL AND TED'S EXCELLENT ADVENTURE (1989) d Stephen Herek, s Keanu Reeves, Alex Winter.
BILL AND TED'S EXCELLENT ADVENTURE II (announced 1990) s Keanu Reeves, Alex Winter.

83A. BLUE LAGOON
Shipwrecked youths fall in love.
BLUE LAGOON (GFD/Individual, 1949) d Frank Launders, s Jean Simmons, Donald Houston.
BLUE LAGOON (Columbia, 1980) d Randal Kleiser, s Brooke Shields, Christopher Atkins.
BLUE LAGOON 2: THE SECOND GENERATION (in works, 1990)

109A. BUTTS MOTEL
These X-rated pictures are take-offs on PSYCHO and its horrific Bates Motel.

408 MOTION PICTURE SERIES & SEQUELS

BUTTS MOTEL (Executive, 1989) d Scotty Fox, s Carol Cummings.
BUTTS MOTEL II (Executive, 1989) d Scotty Fox, s Trinity Loren.
BUTTS MOTEL III: DOUBLE OCCUPANCY (Executive, 1989) d Bobby Hollander, s Debi Diamond.

113A. CANDY STRIPERS
These are X-rated pictures with a hospital setting.
CANDY STRIPERS (Arrow, 1978) s Amber Hunt.
CANDY STRIPERS II (Arrow, 1985) s Colleen Brennan.
CANDY STRIPERS III (Arrow, 1986) s Siobhan Hunter.

124. CAUGHT FROM BEHIND
CAUGHT FROM BEHIND VII (Hollywood, 1987) s Lisa DeLeeuw.
CAUGHT FROM BEHIND VIII (Hollywood, 1988) s Barbie Dahl.

183. DELTA FORCE
DELTA FORCE 2: THE COLUMBIAN CONNECTION (Cannon, 1990)

192A. DIRTY DANCING
Dancing and romance in the Catskills.
DIRTY DANCING (1987) d Emile Ardolini, s Jennifer Grey, Patrick Swayze.
DIRTY DANCING II (announced 1990) s Jennifer Grey, Patrick Swayze.

236. EVIL DEAD
EVIL DEAD III (DeLaurentiis, announced 1990) d Sam Raimi.

247. FIRESTORM
FIRESTORM III (Command, 1989) d Cecil Howard, s Sharon Kane, Ali Moore.

262. FRENCH CONNECTION, THE
POPEYE DOYLE (TV movie 1986) d Peter Levin, s Ed O'Neill, Mathew Laurence.

271A. F/X
A movie special effects whiz is hired by the Justice Department to stage a fake mob assassination.
F/X (Orion, 1986) d Robert Mandel, s Bryan Brown, Brian Dennehy, Diane Venora.
F/X 2 (Orion, announced 1990) d Richard Franklin, s Bryan Brown, Brian Dennehy.

303A. GOOD MORNING, VIETNAM
GOOD MORNING, CHICAGO (in works, 1990)

311. GREMLINS
GREMLINS 2: MONOLITH (announced 1990) d Joe Dante, s Zach Galligan, Phoebe Cates.

329. HAWAII VICE
HAWAII VICE IV (CDI, 1989) d Norm Pera, s Kascha, Lynn LeMay.

MOTION PICTURE SERIES & SEQUELS 409

HAWAII VICE V (CDI 1989) d N. Normai, s Kascha, Lynn LeMay.

377A. JAGGED EDGE
A publisher accused of murdering his wife falls in love with his attorney.
JAGGED EDGE (Columbia, 1985) d Richard Marquand, s Jeff Bridges, Glenn
    Close, Peter Coyote.
JAGGED EDGE II (announced 1990) s Glenn Close.

382A. JEAN DE FLORETTE
The first picture is a story of greed and passion as a man valiantly battles nature and a greedy neighbor. It is based on Marcel Pagnol's novel. In the sequel, the daughter seeks revenge on the neighbor who destroyed her father.
JEAN DE FLORETTE (1986) d Claude Berri, s Yves Montand, Gerard Depardieu,
    Daniel Auteil.
MANON OF THE SPRING (1987) d Claude Berri, s Yves Montand, Daniel
    Auteil, Emmanuelle Beart.

418A. KINGDOM OF THE SPIDERS
Tarantulas are on the rampage in this chiller.
KINGDOM OF THE SPIDERS (Arachnid/Dimension, 1977) d John Cardos, s
    William Shatner, Tiffany Boling.
KINGDOM OF THE SPIDERS II (21st Century Film, announced 1990) d William
    Shatner, s William Shatner.

439. LETHAL WEAPON
LETHAL WEAPON III (in development) d Richard Donner, s Mel Gibson, Danny
    Glover.

422. KOJAK
KOJAK: NONE SO BLIND (TV-movie, 1990) s Telly Savalas, Rip Torn.

461A. LOOK WHO'S TALKING
At last, we can hear a baby's wiseacre thoughts (voice of Bruce Willis).
LOOK WHO'S TALKING (1990) s John Travolta, Kirstie Alley.
LOOK WHO'S TALKING II (in works)

462. LOOSE ENDS
LOOSE ENDS VI: THE DARK SIDE (4-Play, 1989) d Bruce Seven, s Bionca,
    Megan Leigh.

464A. LOVE AT FIRST BITE
Dracula is played for laughs.
LOVE AT FIRST BITE (1979) d Stan Dragoti, s George Hamilton, Susan St.
    James.
LOVE AT SECOND BITE: DRACULA COMES TO HOLLYWOOD (in works)

483AA. MANIAC
A scalping murderer is on the rampage.
MANIAC (Columbia/Hammer, 1980) d William Lustwig, s Joe Spinelli, Caroline
    Munro.

MANIAC II (Manley Productions, announced 1990)

483B. MANNEQUIN
An ancient spirit takes over a fashion store mannequin.
MANNEQUIN (MGM, 1987) d Michael Gottlieb, s Andrew McCarthy, Kim Cattrall.
MANNEQUIN ON THE MOVE

488A. MARY POPPINS
A bewitched nanny transforms an English household. Based on P.L. Travers book.
MARY POPPINS (Disney, 1964) d Robert Stevenson, s Julie Andrews, Dick Van Dyke.
MARY POPPINS 2 (Disney, in works)

534A. MYSTIC PIZZA
Three young women working at a Mystic, Connecticut, pizza shop have adventures in love.
MYSTIC PIZZA (1988) d Donald Petrie, s Julia Roberts, Annabeth Gish, Lili Taylor.
MYSTIC PIZZA 2 (in works)

534B. NAKED GUN, THE
Deadpan cop Frank Drebin originally appeared in the television comedy show *Police Squad*.
THE NAKED GUN: FROM THE FILES OF POLICE SQUAD (1988) d David Zucker, s Leslie Nielsen.
THE NAKED GUN II: THE SMELL OF FEAR (announced 1990) s Leslie Nielsen.

541A. NICOLE STANTON STORY, THE
These are X-rated pictures.
THE NICOLE STANTON STORY: THE RISE (Caballero, 1989) d Henri Pachard, s Eva Allen, John Leslie.
THE NICOLE STANTON STORY: TO THE TOP (Caballero, 1989) d Henri Pachard, s Eva Allen, John Leslie.

542. NIGHTMARE ON ELM STREET, A
A NIGHTMARE ON ELM STREET VI (announced 1991)

548A. NOT QUITE HUMAN
A scientist creates a boy android and sends him to school. The plots are derived from the children's book series by Seth McEvoy.
NOT QUITE HUMAN (Cable TV movie, 1987) d Steven Stern, s Alan Thicke, Jay Underwood, Robyn Lively, Joseph Bologna.
NOT QUITE HUMAN II (Cable TV movie, 1989) s Alan Thicke, Jay Underwood.

575. PERRY MASON
PERRY MASON: THE CASE OF DESPERATE DECEPTION (TV movie 1990) s Raymond Burr, Yvette Mimieux.

576. PERSONAL TOUCH
PERSONAL TOUCH IV (Arrow, 1989) d Bobby Hollander, s Jade East, Shane Hunter, Trinity Loren.

604A. PREDATOR
Soldiers of fortune are assigned to a South American rescue mission, in the first entry.
PREDATOR (1987) d John McTiernan, s Arnold Schwarzenegger, Carl Weathers.
PREDATOR II: BODY COUNT (announced) s Danny Glover.

607. PSYCHO
PSYCHO IV (in works) s Anthony Perkins.

612. RAMBO
RAMBO IV (in works) d Sylvester Stallone, s Sylvester Stallone.

663A. SATURDAY NIGHT FEVER
A Brooklyn youth finds success on the disco dance floor.
SATURDAY NIGHT FEVER (Paramount, 1977) d John Badham, s John Travolta.
STAYING ALIVE (Paramount, 1983) d Sylvester Stallone, s John Travolta.

663B. SCANNERS
Mindreaders can explode the brains of others.
SCANNERS (Filmplan International, 1981) d David Cronenberg, s Jennifer O'Neill.
SCANNERS II: THE NEW ORDER (Image, announced 1990) d Christian Duguay, s David Hewlett, Yvon Ponton.

680. SHORT CIRCUIT
SHORT CIRCUIT III (in works)

685A. SINNERS
These are X-rated films.
SINNERS (Command, 1988) d Cecil Howard, s Laurie Smith, Paul Thomas.
SINNERS II (Command, 1989) d Cecil Howard, s Laurie Smith, Kimberly Carson.

693. SLUMBER PARTY MASSACRE
SLUMBER PARTY MASSACRE III (Concorde, announced 1990) (aka NIGHT LIGHT) s Maria Ford.

726. SUPERFLY
THE RETURN OF SUPERFLY (INI/Film Venture, announced 1990) d Sig Shore, s Nathan Purdee.

733. SWITCH HITTERS
SWITCH HITTERS IV (Intropics, 1989) d Ginny Padox, s Jeanna Lynn, Butch Taylor.

745A. TERROR WITHIN, THE
After the apocalypse, a monster attacks an underground medical center.
THE TERROR WITHIN (1988) d Tierry Notz, s Andrea Stevens.
THE TERROR WITHIN PART II: THE FIGHT FOR THE MOJAVE LAB
 (Concorde, announced 1990)

755A. THREE MEN AND A BABY
A trio of bachelors come into custody of a baby.
THREE MEN AND A BABY (1985) d Coline Serreau, s Roland Giraud
THREE MEN AND A BABY (Touchstone, 1987) d Leonard Nimoy, s Tom
 Selleck, Steve Guttenberg, Ted Danson.
THREE MEN AND A LITTLE LADY (Touchstone, announced) s Tom Selleck,
 Steve Guttenberg, Ted Danson.

792A. TWENTY-SOMETHING
A young reporter wants to climb the corporate ladder, in the first of these X-rated
 pictures.
TWENTY-SOMETHING (Vivid, 1988) d Paul Thoam, s Alicia Monet.
TWENTY-SOMETHING II (Vivid, 1988) d Paul Thomas, s Alicia Monet.
TWENTY-SOMETHING III: EXECUTIVE SUITE (Vivid, 1989) d Paul Thomas,
 s Tori Welles.

795A. TWO WOMEN
An Italian woman and her daughter are raped by soldiers during World War II.
Based on the novel by Alberto Moravia.
TWO WOMEN (1961) d Vittorio De Sica, s Sophia Loren.
TWO WOMEN II (Manley Productions, announced 1990) s Sophia Loren.

821A. WHO FRAMED ROGER RABBIT?
A human gumshoe is hired to clear a 'toon hare of murder. There was also an
animated Roger short, TUMMY TROUBLE, released with HONEY, I SHRUNK
THE KIDS in 1989.
WHO FRAMED ROGER RABBIT? (Disney, 1988) d Robert Zemeckis, s Bob
 Hoskins, Christopher Lloyd.
WHO FRAMED ROGER RABBIT II (in works)

839A. WITCHCRAFT
"After 300 years in the womb of Hell -- the Son of Satan is born."
WITCHCRAFT (Academy Entertainment, 1988) d Robert Spera, s Anat Topol-
 Barzlial.
WITCHCRAFT PART II: The Temptress (Academy Entertainment, 1990)

840A. YOUNG GUNS
YOUNG GUNS II: HELLBENT FOR LEATHER (announced 1990) s Emilio
 Estevez, Kiefer Sutherland, Lou Diamond Phillips.

845. ZORRO
ZORRO: THE LEGEND BEGINS (Family Channel, 1990) (TV-movie) s Duncan
 Regehr.

For Product Safety Concerns and Information please contact our EU representative GPSR@taylorandfrancis.com
Taylor & Francis Verlag GmbH, Kaufingerstraße 24, 80331 München, Germany

www.ingramcontent.com/pod-product-compliance
Lightning Source LLC
Chambersburg PA
CBHW052138300426
44115CB00011B/1434